DATE DUE

THE ROSENBERG FILE

The
ROSENBERG FILE
A SEARCH FOR THE TRUTH

*Ronald Radosh and
Joyce Milton*

HOLT, RINEHART AND WINSTON
New York

Published by Holt, Rinehart and Winston,
383 Madison Avenue, New York, New York 10017.

Published simultaneously in Canada by Holt, Rinehart and
Winston of Canada, Limited.

Library of Congress Cataloging in Publication Data
Radosh, Ronald, 1937-
The Rosenberg file.
Bibliography: p.
Includes index.
1. Rosenberg, Julius, 1918–1953.   2. Rosenberg,
Ethel, 1916–1953.   3. Trials (Espionage)—New York
(N.Y.)   4. Trials (Conspiracy)—New York (N.Y.)
I. Milton, Joyce.   II. Title.
KF224.R6R32   1983   345.73'0231   82-15569
347.305231

ISBN: 0-03-049036-7

Designer: Ellen Lo Giudice
Printed in the United States of America
3   5   7   9   10   8   6   4   2

ISBN 0-03-049036-7

Who was telling the truth—the Rosenbergs or Greenglass? Who was telling the truth—Sobell or Elitcher? It will be a long time, if ever, before we know for certain. We may wake up one morning to learn that the Rosenbergs were guilty. We may wake up to learn that they were innocent. But I doubt whether we will ever find there was a deliberate frameup. Fanaticism had the same momentum on both sides.

—I. F. Stone
I. F. Stone's Weekly
July 2, 1956

CONTENTS

AUTHORS' NOTES

Almost thirty years ago, as a young high school student, I stood amidst thousands of other New Yorkers who had gathered on East Seventeenth Street off Union Square, in what was to be a deathwatch vigil for Ethel and Julius Rosenberg. I remember vividly hearing the novelist Howard Fast take the microphone and announce to the crowd that there was no more hope of reprieve: the executioner had already performed the first of his wretched tasks. Julius Rosenberg was dead. Tears and sobs seized the crowd. We had stood there, silently, from late afternoon until that moment thinking that against all odds our presence might somehow persuade President Eisenhower to grant executive clemency.

The futile campaign to save the Rosenbergs from death was the beginning of my political education as well as my entree into the world of the American Left. I had read about the Sacco-Vanzetti case and heard it discussed by my elders. For my generation, it seemed, the execution of the Rosenbergs on charges that they had given the secret of the atomic bomb to the Russians was yet another lesson in the failure of American capitalist justice, proof that radicals in America were doomed to persecution and even death for being true to their ideals. It never crossed my mind during those years that the Rosenbergs might be something other than martyred innocents. I certainly knew they were not guilty of what J. Edgar Hoover called "the crime of the century." It simply became an article of faith, an axiom, that Julius and Ethel Rosenberg were the victims of a government-sponsored conspiracy.

As an adult, although I no longer subscribed to the pro-Soviet views of my adolescence, I continued to hold to my earnest belief in the Rosenbergs' total innocence, always thinking that in the future new evidence might emerge to prove the complicity of the government in a frame-up. When the Rosenbergs' two sons, Michael and Robert Meeropol, finally sued the U.S. government for all FBI files pertaining to the case, I assumed that the release of this material would lead to the final vindication the Meeropols and their supporters had been predicting.

. Indeed, I joined them as a member of the executive committee of the newly formed National Committee to Re-Open the Rosenberg Case. And in June 1974 I sat in a front-row seat at Carnegie Hall to celebrate their decision to start their final and decisive campaign to set the record straight. I believed the American people were ready for a new assessment of a highly politicized case born of the very decade that launched the career of Richard Nixon.

It was about this time that an old friend and political associate, James Weinstein, now editor of the independent socialist newspaper *In These Times*, told me a story—recounted later in this book— which suggested that perhaps Julius Rosenberg had been in some form of espionage after all. I realized with a jolt that there might be more to the case than I had always assumed. I told Weinstein's story to a close friend of Michael Meeropol; he informed me that there was nothing to it. Yet, try as I might, I could not push the tale out of my mind. And when the Committee to Re-Open the Rosenberg Case began to issue press releases based on only selected documents exhumed from the FBI files—documents they claimed proved the theory of a governmental frame-up—my suspicions as a trained historian were aroused. I knew that one or a few documents, taken out of context, prove little. By now I was painfully aware that the legal battle to win release of the files was not leading to the expected comprehensive and objective review of the new material's significance.

Such a reexamination, I reasoned, was critically important, and not just to the faithful few who had continued to work and hope for the Rosenbergs' vindication. Some twenty-five years after their trial, the Rosenbergs still haunted the national conscience. Two young parents had been put to death despite their continued protestations of innocence. Their *Death House Letters* had been published around the world and turned the executions into an international cause célèbre. In the era of Watergate, and in the wake of shocking revelations about J. Edgar Hoover's use of the FBI to persecute individuals whose politics offended him, it was easier than ever for many Americans to believe that the Rosenbergs were hapless victims of Cold War hysteria, singled out because of their political views, and perhaps also because of their Jewishness—and for no other reason.

Only after I had decided that a completely new look at the case was called for did I begin to appreciate the magnitude of the task. The amount of new material to be examined was vast. To begin with, it would be necessary to comb through more than 200,000 pages of documents released under the Freedom of Information Act—including not just the FBI investigation files on the case but also so-called referral files from such other agencies as the CIA and the Department of the Navy, which were made available to the public for the first time in 1980.

In addition, scores of individuals close to the case, many of whom had never before spoken for the record, agreed to be interviewed by me and my then collaborator, free-lance journalist Sol Stern. Even David Greenglass, Ethel Rosenberg's brother, and his wife, Ruth, consented for the first time since the trial to talk about the circumstances that led to their becoming the chief government witnesses against their own relatives.

The late O. John Rogge, attorney for the Greenglasses as well as for another key prosecution witness, Max Elitcher, not only kindly consented to help bring us together with the Greenglasses but opened his files on the case to us. Fyke Farmer, the Nashville, Tennessee, lawyer who played a central role in the last-minute battle to save the Rosenbergs from the electric chair, also provided us with copies of his files. We found an invaluable source in the unpublished memoirs of Irwin Edelman, whose persistence did much to win a last-minute stay of execution granted by Justice William O. Douglas. Other useful documents not drawn on by previous investigators of the case were found in the Justice Department archives of the Foley Square Courthouse in New York City and in the files of the Philadelphia law firm that represented Harry Gold, another government witness and one of the most controversial figures in the case.

From the beginning, it was apparent to me that not everyone was enthusiastic at the prospect of reopening the Rosenberg case for such a thorough review. It was even suggested to me that the very undertaking was a betrayal of the cause. Perhaps the most extreme statement of this point of view emerged during a phone conversation with an individual who had been among the principal figures in the case. When I requested a meeting, I was asked what more there could possibly be to write about since so much had already been said. I responded with a litany of the unanswered questions that still troubled me, only to be asked, quite curtly, "Are you interested in the historical truth?" I replied that as a historian, this was one of my principal concerns. The person I was speaking to retorted: "At this time and juncture we're living in, do you think this is helpful? How will the historical truth hurt the establishment?" He then went on to explain that he was a radical, not a liberal, and that in the present era it was best that the historical truth should not come out.

One uncomfortable aspect of the historical truth that we had to deal with from the beginning was the realization that the Communist Party, U.S.A. had indeed served as a recruiting ground for spies. After the Bolshevization of the Party in the late 1920s, the political strategy of the Party was determined according to the dictates of Soviet policy rather than by the special needs of the American working class. Of course, loyal party members justified this in their own minds by refusing to admit there was any contradiction between the two interests. And from there it was only a short step for some of the more zealous to exchange Party activism for a particularly exciting form of "secret work"—espionage. Many of these amateur spies did little more than play at espionage; their targets were industrial rather than military and their methods were sometimes more legal than not. Later, during World War II, this amateur spying escalated, becoming more ambitious in its pursuit of military secrets; the perpetrators justified their actions on the grounds that their efforts were going to help a misunderstood and gallant ally in the struggle against Hitler. Several former ranking members of the Party suggested to us early on that Julius Rosenberg's background fit the general pattern of those recruited for this type of secret work.

A few individuals we spoke to went further, echoing that earlier warning that there were two forms of truth where the Rosenberg case was concerned: the historical truth and the Party's truth. There was a peculiar form of doublethink which allowed some of our informants to proclaim the Rosenbergs' innocence in public while conceding privately that they had been involved in espionage after all—but an espionage that was justifiable on ideological grounds. One well-known left-wing lawyer, for example, opened an interview with me by stating bluntly: "I'm not one of those who thinks the Rosenbergs weren't engaged in espionage." Then he went on to threaten to sue if this statement were ever attributed to him and to lecture me on the necessity of presenting the Rosenbergs solely as victims of Cold War hysteria.

Another venerable and well-established Communist party lawyer, whose career goes back to the late 1920s, began our conversation by slamming his fist on his desk and bellowing: "Of course they were guilty. But you can't quote me. My public position is that the Rosenbergs were innocent." And he elaborated: "What's wrong with what they did? If I were in their place, I would have done the same thing. What was so bad about helping Stalin get the A-bomb? It was the responsibility of a good Communist to do whatever he could to help the Red Army gain victory." Then, like his colleague, he reiterated, "Don't think I'm so dumb that I don't believe the Rosenbergs weren't engaged in espionage."

By this time, I too believed that the Rosenbergs were far from being total innocents. The preliminary results of my research were revealed in a 1979 article in *The New Republic*, which I coauthored with Sol Stern. The article concluded that Julius Rosenberg had been the central figure—in the parlance of espionage novels, the ringmaster—in a spy network whose activities were far more extensive than had ever been previously revealed, either at the time of his trial or in any of the earlier books on the case. The piece was also highly critical of the government, and in particular of its treatment of Ethel Rosenberg.

The *TNR* article received a great deal of media attention, drawing fierce attacks both from defenders of the U.S. government's actions and from supporters of the Rosenbergs. Among the latter was the Rosenbergs' younger son, Robert Meeropol, who charged that Sol Stern and I were trying to smear the entire American Left and "resurrect the whole constellation of ideas" that led to his parents' death. To my distress, many of my friends and acquaintances shared this view. People I had known for years stopped talking to me. Others suggested that I had become by this one act an "enemy of the people," a traitor to the heritage of the Left. The most common refrain I heard was, "Why did you do it? Why this piece now?" or, in yet another version, "You shouldn't have written that article."

These exchanges led me to reexamine my motives for undertaking a full-length review of the case. As a man of the democratic Left, I certainly had no interest in serving the cause of domestic reaction or in justifying the actions of the new Cold Warriors. But historical truth also had its claims—even if some of that truth was unpleasant. To deny this would be to concede that the Left stands for falsehood—for the perpetuation of a myth regardless of the facts of the matter and, ultimately, for the right to define truth as whatever myth or constellation of myths serves the interest of a particular political position.

Although hundreds of thousands of words have been written about the Rosenberg case, most of them have only fueled the speculation about what really happened. Newly available evidence—much of it released by the government only after a bitter legal battle waged by the Rosenbergs' children—makes it possible to answer some crucial questions for the first time, questions about the Rosenbergs, about the much criticized legal strategy of their lawyer, Emanuel Bloch, and about the actions of such key officials as the prosecutor, Irving H. Saypol, his young assistant, Roy Cohn, and the trial magistrate, Judge Irving Kaufman. I felt that it was necessary to review all this evidence as objectively as possible—and that the task not be left to those whose emotional stake in the case is so great that they cannot bear to see where the evidence points.

Thirty years ago, I. F. Stone concluded that it was impossible to sort out the question of guilt or innocence in the Rosenberg case because "we just don't know enough yet." Someday, Stone predicted, it might be possible to separate the case from the context of the "Cold War frenzies" and reopen it to the light in a spirit of "calm consideration." It is in just that spirit that I and my new collaborator, Joyce Milton, have undertaken this book. Our conclusions will not please everyone. That we know. But the commitment to historical truth has to stand above the desires of the various contenders. And from this commitment, once made, there can be no turning back.

RONALD RADOSH

Like Ronald Radosh, I too originally held the conviction that Julius and Ethel Rosenberg were innocent victims of a government frame-up. My own interest in the case began in the mid-1960s when I was a student at Swarthmore College. Several of my close friends there were the children of individuals who had lost jobs and suffered social and professional ostracism as the result of their refusal to cooperate with congressional Red-hunting committees. I had heard their bitter reminiscences of how baseless allegations, and in some cases the simple decision to take a principled stand on the Fifth Amendment, had cut short promising careers and disrupted family life. On the face of it, it seemed all too likely that the charges against the Rosenbergs had been just another, more extreme product of Cold War hysteria. Already disposed to believe in a frame-up, I read Miriam and Walter Schneir's *Invitation to an Inquest* and found their arguments convincing. And my beliefs were further strengthened when I learned through mutual acquaintances that one of my fellow Swarthmoreans was Julius and Ethel Rosenberg's older son. Michael Meeropol, though he had not yet spoken publicly about his parents' case, was sincerely convinced of their innocence.

Several years later, when the Meeropol brothers announced their determination to reopen their parents' case, I looked forward to dramatic revelations. But much to my disappointment, the successful suit for the release of government documents on the case failed to produce the spate of devastating counterattacks that I had expected. Instead, there were hints that the FBI files contained new damaging allegations against the Rosenbergs—allegations that drove their defenders to still more tortuous attempts at rebuttal. By the time Ron Radosh and Sol Stern published their 1979 *New Republic* piece, my confidence in my long-held beliefs was shaken, but I still could not reconcile the new evidence with my feeling that so many individuals I had discussed the subject with—individuals who all seemed to have more direct knowledge of the circumstances than I—firmly believed that the Rosenbergs were innocent victims.

In the spring of 1981, I met Ronald Radosh. He was then looking for a collaborator to help him analyze and write a book based on the mass of documentary evidence he had accumulated. Working with Ron seemed to me to be a unique opportunity to satisfy my own curiosity and to participate in investigating an important chapter in American history.

JOYCE MILTON

PROLOGUE

It was the campaign to exonerate Tom Mooney that first awakened Julius Rosenberg's interest in politics. In 1933, when Rosenberg was a senior at Seward Park High School on New York's Lower East Side, he was returning from a Sunday job selling penny candy when he stopped to listen to a soapbox orator. The man was delivering an impassioned speech on the plight of Mooney, a former West Coast labor leader then serving the sixteenth year of a life sentence for his part in a bombing that had killed ten people. Rosenberg listened as the speaker told how Mooney had been framed on perjured testimony, enduring two years on death row before his sentence was commuted to life. That night, after finishing his homework, Rosenberg read several pamphlets he had been given by the speaker. The next day, he volunteered to collect signatures for the petition drive to free Mooney.

Whatever special significance the Mooney case was to have for Julius Rosenberg's development—and it would take on increasing personal meaning over the years—it was only one of many causes that captured his youthful imagination. In the fall of 1934, Rosenberg, still only sixteen years old, entered the City College of New York. There he became part of a generation of students highly politicized by the economic turmoil of the Depression at home and the rising tide of fascism abroad. During his freshman year at CCNY,

Rosenberg saw the whole student body rise to protest the university president's decision to welcome a delegation of Italian Fascist students. He campaigned for justice for the Scottsboro boys, and in 1936 he was among the organizers of CCNY's branch of the American Student Union, a national organization that combined enthusiastic support for the policies of the New Deal with endorsement of the Loyalist side in the Spanish Civil War.

After graduating with a major in electrical engineering in February 1939, Rosenberg remained politically active, giving much of his spare time to the support of the Federation of Architects, Engineers, Chemists and Technicians (FAECT), one of the few unions of its day devoted to representing white-collar professionals. Soon, however, he also began to take on other responsibilities. During the summer after his graduation, he married Ethel Greenglass, a young woman who had been briefly active in labor organizing. And after working at several free-lance engineering jobs for local firms, he found a permanent position as a civilian engineer with the Army Signal Corps, a job that he held continuously until the spring of 1945, when he was summarily dismissed on charges of having concealed his membership in the Communist Party. Then, after working briefly for the Emerson Radio Corporation, he set up his own machine shop in partnership with his brother-in-law Bernard Greenglass and a neighbor, Isidor Goldstein. A second Greenglass brother-in-law, David, joined the partnership after his release from the U.S. Army in 1946.

By the summer of 1950, Julius and Ethel Rosenberg were to all appearances a quite unremarkable young married couple. They were the parents of two sons—Michael, born in 1943, and Robert, born in 1947—and they lived in a three-room apartment in a modern high-rise development located in the same neighborhood where they had both been born and reared. Neither Julius nor Ethel had been politically active for some years. Nor is there any indication that the Rosenbergs' names had come to the attention of any government investigative body since Julius's dismissal by the Signal Corps five years earlier. The Rosenbergs could be said to be unusual only to the extent that business troubles and Ethel's bouts of ill health had kept them from enjoying the prosperity that came to so many of their peers after the war.

But the Rosenbergs' lives were changed forever on the night of June 15, 1950, when David Greenglass, Ethel's brother, named Julius

Rosenberg as the man who had recruited him to spy for the Soviet Union. Julius Rosenberg was arrested one month later on a charge of conspiracy to commit espionage, and Ethel was arraigned on the same charge on August 11. At their trial the following March, David Greenglass, backed up by his wife, Ruth, claimed that Julius had begun spying for the Russians while still employed by the Signal Corps and by 1945 had been in a position to deliver atomic secrets provided by Greenglass directly to Soviet agents. After the war, moreover, he had been a master spy controlling a network that included contacts in upstate New York and Ohio. The Greenglasses also claimed that Ethel Rosenberg had known and approved of her husband's activities, and that on one occasion she had assisted her husband by typing David's handwritten notes containing a description of the atomic bomb.

The Rosenbergs' response to these accusations was to call them a malicious invention: the Greenglasses knew that they could win leniency for their own crimes, whatever they may have been, by pointing their fingers at supposedly more important traitors. Julius and Ethel were vulnerable because of their past political associations, and it was all too easy for David and Ruth to name their in-laws, settling their grudge over the failure of the family business in the bargain. The Rosenbergs continued to proclaim their innocence, both during their trial and throughout more than two years spent on death row awaiting execution, with a tenacity that impressed many who had originally believed them guilty.

The contrast between the fanatical, veteran spies described by the Greenglasses and the victimized law-abiding couple that the Rosenbergs claimed to be could not have been more striking. But, wherever the truth lay, something more than a family feud run out of control had to be involved. If the Rosenbergs were framed, this could hardly have been accomplished without the knowing participation of key figures in the Federal Bureau of Investigation and on the federal prosecutor's staff. On the other hand, if the Greenglasses' charges were true, then one must ask how the Rosenberg spy network could have operated undetected for more than five years. And why, even after David Greenglass's confession, was the government able to bring charges against only one other alleged member of the ring—a thirty-three-year-old electrical engineer named Morton Sobell?

The judge who sentenced Julius and Ethel Rosenberg to death

called their crime "worse than murder," charging them with the responsibility for the Korean conflict and for the millions who might yet die in a Soviet atomic attack. The Rosenbergs' position, expressed in scores of letters written from their cells in Sing Sing penitentiary, was that they were innocent victims of capitalist justice in the tradition of Tom Mooney, Sacco and Vanzetti, and the Scottsboro boys. The reality that lay behind these two rhetorical extremes is the hidden Rosenberg case.

1

Klaus Fuchs Confesses

In traditional warfare, espionage is a sideshow played out against the larger drama of troop movements, campaign strategy, and battles. But in a Cold War, espionage takes center stage and the unmasked spy or traitor becomes the surrogate for the enemy soldiers who never venture within range of the front lines.

By 1949 the Cold War mentality had secured its grip on America. The United States emerged from World War II as the strongest power on earth; yet America seemed unable to translate that strength into the security it craved. Americans perceived that they were being threatened anew by the spread of communism in Eastern Europe and Asia and, especially, by the Soviets' acquisition of the atomic bomb. Americans had power; yet, as the astute British observer Godfrey Hodgson put it, "the world refused to be molded by it." It was this immensely frustrating discovery that gave McCarthyism its opportunity.

Senator Joseph McCarthy was crude, a classic demagogue. But in his uncouth way he expressed an assumption that was shared by millions of Americans: The United States was failing to attain its foreign-policy goals not because of the natural limitations on the exercise of power, but because of internal treason. Long before

McCarthy, President Truman and his Democrats had warned against the threat of communism and stressed the dangers of internal subversion. McCarthy merely carried this warning a step further by imputing all of America's "failures"—beginning with Yalta and Potsdam—to the efforts of Communists working their schemes from desks in our own State Department.

The momentum of unfolding events gave McCarthy his opportunity. The Czech coup in March 1948 had been the final demonstration that Stalin's intentions toward Eastern Europe were hardly benign. In the spring of 1949, Chiang Kai-shek's government fell to the Chinese Red Army—leaving Americans, unprepared for this development, to wonder just who was responsible for the "loss" of China. On August 28, the Russians exploded their first atomic bomb, shattering America's confidence in its own nuclear supremacy. And if 1949 was a year of disillusionment, 1950 promised to be the time for assigning blame. On January 21, a jury in a New York federal court convicted former New Dealer Alger Hiss of perjury for denying under oath that he had passed secret State Department documents to a Communist agent named Whittaker Chambers. Twelve days later came the arrest in England of former Manhattan Project physicist Klaus Fuchs, who confessed to having been a Soviet spy since the early 1940s. It was just one week after that, on February 9, 1950, that Joe McCarthy, hitherto an obscure junior senator from Wisconsin, startled a women's club audience in Wheeling, West Virginia, by brandishing a piece of paper on which, supposedly, were the names of 205 Communist agents still employed at State.

Although McCarthy certainly did not originate the notion that all of America's problems could be laid to the machinations of Communist conspirators inside the government, it was he who expressed it most bluntly: "The reason why we find ourselves in a position of impotency," he told his worried compatriots, "is not because our only powerful potential enemy has sent men to invade our shores but, rather, because of the traitorous actions of those who have been treated so well by this nation."

Distressed by McCarthy's call for a wholesale anti-Communist witch-hunt, liberals hastened to attack his wild accusations. Though divided on the issue of Hiss's guilt, the liberals held in contempt the idea that any single reversal, from Mao Tse-tung's victory in China to the Soviet nuclear success, could be laid at the door of a few underground Communists. Unfortunately for those who hoped to restore a semblance of reason to the debate over America's foreign-policy failures, yet another spy saga—related to the Fuchs case but with implications touching closer to home—was about to unfold: After years of frustrating failures, U.S. intelligence authorities were closing in on the trail of a network of engineers and scientists who had been passing data on defense projects to the Soviet Union at least since 1944, if not earlier.

The first clue to the existence of this spy ring surfaced early in World War II with the discovery on a Finnish battlefield of a tattered, partially burned KGB code book. Compared to the machine-scrambled codes of the Germans, the KGB system was relatively primitive, being based on 999 five-digit numbers, each of which corresponded to a single word, letter, or key phrase. Unfortunately for our cryptanalysts, there were complications. For one thing, the recovered code book itself was incomplete. For another, it was meant to be used in conjunction with a series of special note pads, each page of which contained a different series of additives—five-digit numbers that, when added to the original series of ciphers, produced endless variations on the basic system. Soviet operatives throughout the world had been issued such note pads, with instructions to use each page only once and then immediately destroy it.

The first real break in the KGB codes did not come until 1944, when agents of the Federal Bureau of Investigation began sifting through a mound of documents that had been stolen during a burglary of the New York offices of the Soviet Government Purchasing Commission, a known front for KGB industrial espionage operations. To the delight of the FBI, the Commission's office had for some reason been issued a duplicate set of the one-time-only note pads. Of course, pages that had actually been used had been disposed of in accordance with orders; however, Purchasing Commission employees had carelessly filed away copies of some messages—in both their enciphered and nonenciphered forms.

American cryptanalysts laboriously began comparing these routine, nonsensitive documents with hundreds of intercepted communications sent by the Soviet Consulate to the KGB during the same year, 1944. They were looking for messages that might have used the same set of additives. It was a painstaking process, but one that eventually enabled the experts to reconstruct the entire 999 entries of the original code book.

In the spring of 1948, one of the first significant messages to be deciphered through this project came into the hands of FBI counter-intelligence officer Robert Lamphere. The message, written in 1944 by a Soviet agent serving undercover on his consulate's staff, was clearly a report on the recruiting efforts of an American spy. The spy himself was not identified, but two of his potential recruits were: Max Elitcher, an employee of the Navy Ordnance Department, and Joel Barr, an engineer who worked on airborne radar systems for the Western Electric Company. An FBI investigation of Elitcher showed that he was almost certainly a Communist, but otherwise turned up nothing substantial. Joel Barr's case seemed more promising, especially after an FBI employee called Barr's mother (without identifying himself) and learned that her son was then traveling in Finland near the Soviet border. Lamphere turned Barr's case over to the CIA, where it languished throughout 1949. Either the CIA did not consider the Bureau's tip sufficiently important to deserve priority or it was convinced, as an Agency report later claimed, that "speed [must be] sacrificed for the sake of discretion."

Momentarily stymied, Lamphere continued to hope for another break that would lead him to the energetic American agent who had tried to bring Barr and Elitcher into the KGB fold. "We were trying to find out the identity of who was running the network as far back as 'forty-eight," Lamphere reminisced during a recent interview. "I was looking for the guy who was trying to recruit Elitcher, and I hadn't any idea who he was."

After a few months, however, Lamphere's own attention was diverted from the Elitcher-Barr case by another, seemingly unrelated document unscrambled from the consulate files. The new document turned out to be nothing less than a verbatim report from the German-born British atomic scientist Klaus Fuchs on the progress of the Manhattan Project. Ever since 1946, when British physicist Alan Nunn May had confessed to using his position on the National Research Council of Canada to gather information for the Soviets, there had been rumors that the wartime effort to build the first atomic bomb had been riddled with Soviet spies. Most such charges were clearly politically motivated, such as the attack on physicist Edward U. Condon, who happened to be a vocal advocate of civilian control of atomic energy. The Fuchs report, deciphered in the summer of 1949, was the first hard evidence that Soviet intelligence had actually penetrated inside Los Alamos. But even it did not prove conclusively that the spy was Fuchs himself. Indeed, this seemed unthinkable at first. It was entirely possible that Fuchs's report had fallen into the hands of a Soviet agent by some more devious route.

Throughout the fall, Lamphere discussed the problem with H. A. R. ("Kim") Philby, Washington liaison of MI-6, the British counterintelligence unit. Philby was one of two British security officials privy to regular reports on the progress of the cryptanalysts' assault on the KGB code. As Lamphere now ruefully recalls, Philby took an alert and active interest in the American efforts, frequently dropping in to chat about the code breakers' latest successes. It may well have been Philby who, in October, told Lamphere about a chance development that might provide the perfect opening for a further interrogation of the respected Dr. Fuchs. It seems that Fuchs's aged father, who was still living in Germany, had been offered a teaching post at Leipzig University in the eastern zone. Dr. Fuchs had reported this offer to British security himself, thus almost inviting a reexamination of his security status.

Of course, Kim Philby also happened to be a Soviet double agent. So even before the British had a chance to follow through with the investigation of Fuchs, word of their intentions went out to Soviet intelligence operatives. Thus, also in October, a Soviet operative sought out Klaus Fuchs's American courier and warned that it might soon be necessary for the courier to flee the country.

In the meantime, American and British investigators, unaware that the Russians already knew of their interest in Fuchs, were looking for additional scraps of information that would either confirm or rebut their suspicions. A check on Fuchs's background quickly confirmed that he had been a member of the German Communist Party during the early 1930s—information known to the British Home Office for years, but never considered serious enough to merit further investigation. Fuchs's name and address had even turned up among the papers of one of the members of the Canadian spy ring unmasked in 1946, though under circumstances that had seemed quite innocent at the time. But the piece of evidence that clinched the security investigators' interest was a chance reference in another decoded Soviet document to a British atomic spy whose sister was then attending an American university. Fuchs, whose sister Kristel had been a student at Swarthmore College during the time covered by the document, fit the bill.

The job of confronting Fuchs with the evidence against him was assigned by the British to James Skardon, the near-legendary spy-catcher who had taken the confessions of such wartime traitors as William Joyce ("Lord Hawhaw")—and whose efforts to unmask Philby were yet to come. Skardon was convinced of Fuchs's guilt and he very much wanted a full confession, which would establish once and for all the extent of Soviet atomic espionage activities during the war and restore American confidence in the integrity of the British security system. At all costs, he wanted to avoid a repetition of the case of Alan Nunn May, who had gone through his trial unrepentant, accepting a ten-year sentence rather than give away the names of his confederates.

It was December 21, 1949, before Skardon was finally ready to go down to Fuchs's laboratory at the Harwell Atomic Research Establishment for the first time, ostensibly to discuss with Fuchs the problem of his father's East German teaching appointment. Skardon was prepared for a long and arduous ordeal, but to his surprise he discovered that Klaus Fuchs was ripe for confession. Fuchs, it turned out, had been greatly disappointed by the Soviet Union's postwar policy in Eastern Europe. He had tried rather fitfully to break off his relationship with the Soviet intelligence and, no doubt correctly, he interpreted the job offer made to his father as an attempt by the Soviets to get the old man under their control, where he could be used as a guarantee of his son's continued cooperation.

While Fuchs was not quite ready to tell Skardon everything, he seemed relieved to be able to talk about his past, including his youthful membership in the Party. Klaus Fuchs had been born in Germany in 1911, the son of a Lutheran pastor who converted to Quakerism and became active in the Social Democratic Party shortly after World War I. As a boy, Fuchs had been greatly influenced by his father's stern idealism and his continual emphasis on each individual's need to follow the dictates of his "inner light." The pacifist part of the father's teachings did not make quite the same impression, however, and while still a student Fuchs became convinced that the Social Democratic Party lacked the backbone to stand up to the Nazis. The young Fuchs became a Communist and in January 1933 he took part in street fighting against the Brown Shirts in his home city of Kiel. When the Gestapo later began rounding up Communist youths, Fuchs managed to escape via France to England, where a sympathetic Quaker family took him in and arranged for him to receive a scholarship to study physics at Bristol University. Fuchs worked hard, taking a doctorate in 1937, moving on to do advanced studies at Edinburgh University under another émigré scientist, Professor Max Born.

Fuchs's career was just beginning to take off in 1940 when all German nationals residing in England were ordered placed in internment camps. On short notice, the young physicist found himself shipped off to Quebec, Canada, where he and other anti-Fascist refugees were thrown in with Germans who happened to be open Nazi sympathizers. In the stress of the times, neither the camp administrators nor the local Quebecois were much inclined to make distinctions between pro- and anti-Nazi Germans. Fuchs spent several agonizing months behind barbed wire, wearing a prisoner-of-war uniform. Thanks to the intervention of Professor Born and other colleagues, he was rescued from this humiliating experience and, by the beginning of 1941, he was back at Edinburgh University. Later that spring, he was asked by Professor Rudolf Peierls to come to work in Birmingham on a war-related project known as the "Tube Alloys" program. Fuchs had already accepted the offer and was working away at the mathematical calculations given him by Peierls before it dawned on him that Tube Alloys was a cover name for British atomic-bomb research.

Only after he listened to Fuchs's lengthy reminiscences did Skardon play his hand. Would Fuchs care to comment, he wondered, on the existence of "precise information" that showed he had been in contact with a Soviet agent while working as a Manhattan Project scientist in New York? Skardon's charge was at least part bluff since his information, however "precise," was insufficient to convict Fuchs in a court of law. If Fuchs had simply stood his ground, it is quite unlikely he would ever have been convicted of anything. But Klaus Fuchs was burdened with a guilty conscience and, it seems, by a naïve overestimation of his own importance to British science. In further conversations, Skardon gradually came to realize that Fuchs did not fully realize the seriousness of the charges against him. The physicist seemed to be under the impression that if he owned up to his past crimes, all would be forgiven. He might even be able to remain in his post as head of the theoretical division of Harwell. Skardon encouraged this naïveté to the fullest.

But when Fuchs finally succumbed to Skardon's reassurances on January 24, even the experienced spy hunter was shocked by the nature and extent of his revelations. Fuchs outlined an espionage career that had begun shortly after his recruitment to Tube Alloys and ended in early 1949. In a statement dictated shortly after his initial confession, Fuchs said:

> At first I thought that all I would do would be to inform the Russian authorities that work on the atomic bomb was going on. I concentrated ... mainly on the product of my own work, but in particular at Los Alamos, I did what I consider the worst I have done, namely to give information about the principle of the design of the plutonium bomb.

Even after making this admission, far more sweeping than anything Skardon had expected, Fuchs still seemed unable to appreciate that there was anything criminal in what he had done. His primary concern was whether he would still be permitted to represent Britain at a forthcoming Anglo-American conference on the declassification of atomic research data!

Fuchs put nothing in writing on January 24, and he was not actually placed under arrest until February 2; by then, he had voluntarily traveled up from Harwell to London three times to dictate his confessions in ever greater detail. British security, of course, was keeping a close watch in case their quarry should try to escape, but Fuchs appeared to have no interest in flight. Nor, it seems, did Soviet intelligence make any effort to rescue the man who had once been such a valuable agent. Fuchs would not have been receptive to help from this quarter in any case, and it appears that the Soviets had already written him off, secure in the knowledge that it would take British and American intelligence months to track down any of the leads Fuchs had to offer.

By the time Fuchs came to trial on March 1, his conviction was a mere formality. The prosecution called only one witness, James Skardon, and the entire proceedings were over in one hour and twenty-seven minutes. Fuchs was convicted of four counts of espionage—none specifically tied to his tenure at Los Alamos out of deference to the Americans, who felt that too much public discussion of this information could only interfere with their search for Fuchs's American contact. As for the sentence, it surprised only Fuchs, whose former overconfidence had by now given way to the belief that he was headed for the gallows. Fortunately for him, British law made a distinction between passing military secrets to wartime enemies and espionage that was directed toward aiding friendly countries. Fuchs, guilty only of the latter, was given a fourteen-year sentence.

Fourteen years was the maximum sentence allowable, but some of the more vocal anti-Communist politicians in America denounced it as a travesty. Senator Brien McMahon and other hawkish members of the Joint Congressional Committee on Atomic Energy even wondered whether the United States ought to try to extradite Fuchs from England for a trial on capital charges under American law. Still more Americans were shocked by the admission of British Attorney General Sir Hartley Shawcross, under questioning by the defense, that the Home Office had been in possession all along of information about Fuchs's Communist past. How could the British have been so blind as to give top security clearance to a convinced Communist? And how could they have then sent that same individual off to work on the Manhattan Project without so much as warning the Americans of his past association? To many, Shawcross's admission was one more proof that Britain was too lax in matters of Communist infiltration to make a wholly reliable ally. It was also said to confirm the wisdom of the Truman policy of extensive loyalty investigations for government employees.

In reality it is unlikely that American security officials would have been any more capable than their British counterparts of singling out Klaus Fuchs from the many candidates for wartime atomic research who shared very similar backgrounds. Loyalty investigations were always better suited to identifying nonconformists and dissenters, who were many, than actual spies, who were few.

The fact was that back in 1941, when Fuchs was investigated for his clearance, the overworked British investigators had been looking for Nazi spies, not Communist ones. What's more, the only evidence of Fuchs's communism that the investigators had before them was a 1934 Gestapo report that had been forwarded by the German consulate to the Bristol police shortly after Fuchs took up residence in that city. In England of 1941, the Gestapo was hardly a respected source. British security was in possession of hundreds of unverifiable and frequently untrue Gestapo-inspired charges against refugees who were guilty of nothing except a history of anti-Nazi activity. In Fuchs's favor, he was highly recommended by Professor Born and others. And Rudolf Peierls particularly wanted him on the Tube Alloys project. So many of the country's first-rank physicists had already gone into other aspects of war-related research that the security service could hardly afford to eliminate one of Peierls's prime candidates because he might once, long ago, have been attracted to communism. Fuchs, moreover, had done nothing since his arrival in England eight years before to attract the slightest untoward attention.

So Klaus Fuchs was routinely granted clearance to go to work as a member of the Peierls team. In 1943, as part of an Anglo-American agreement to work cooperatively on the problem of the fission bomb, Fuchs was transferred to Columbia University in New York City. There he continued to look for a feasible method of producing weapons-grade uranium through the so-called gaseous diffusion method.

Before he left England, Fuchs discussed his new assignment with his Soviet control and was given instructions for meeting an American national who would henceforth act as his special courier. The instructions left no room for a slipup based on mistaken identities. As Fuchs later explained to FBI agents Hugh Clegg and Robert Lamphere, the plan was that at a specified time and place he was to "meet an individual who would be wearing gloves and would have an additional pair of gloves in his hands, while I would have a ball in my own hand."

Between December 1943 and August 1944, Fuchs met at least four more times with this same courier, whom he knew only as "Raymond": once at night under a ramp leading to the Queensborough Bridge, once on an Upper West Side street corner, once near a movie theater on the Grand Concourse in the Bronx, and once at a subway entrance near the Museum of Natural History. Most of these encounters lasted only a minute or two, but the last and longest of the assignations ended with the two men strolling through Central Park for nearly half an hour.

Then, quite unexpectedly, Fuchs failed to keep an appointment to meet Raymond at the Brooklyn Museum. Fuchs also disappeared from his lab at Columbia at about the same time, and when weeks passed with no word from their erstwhile valuable source, Raymond's controllers dispatched him to the home of Kristel Heineman, Fuchs's sister, who was living with her American husband in Cambridge, Massachusetts. Raymond introduced himself to the Heinemans as an old friend who had somehow lost touch with Klaus. Mrs. Heineman was not encouraging. She knew only that her brother had been transferred to an installation somewhere in the Southwest. Perhaps he would be coming to Massachusetts for a visit in some months, and if he showed up in Cambridge she would let him know that his friend had asked about him.

Fuchs, meanwhile, had made a deliberate decision not to inform his Soviet control about his new assignment to the theoretical division of the main Manhattan District installation at Los Alamos, New Mexico. Impressed by the tight security precautions surrounding his transfer and by the sense of esprit de corps shared by his new colleagues in the desert compound, he had determined that it would be best to sever his connections with the Soviets, at least for the time being.

For most of the Manhattan Project scientists, assignment to Los Alamos meant enforced separation from their real work and from the comforts of home—sacrifices made bearable only by the sense of shared mission. But Klaus Fuchs seemed to thrive on his new regime. Always physically frail, he responded almost miraculously to the desert climate and was able to enjoy horseback riding and other forms of outdoor exercise for the first time. Even the semimilitary discipline and the claustrophobic social life, which some of his co-workers found nearly intolerable, suited the bachelor physicist well. He was less lonely than he had been in any other period of his adult life. Busy with his work and enjoying the company of some of the most stimulating minds in his field, Fuchs had little time to think about his dealings with Raymond; for a time, even his emotional commitment to aiding the cause of the Soviet Union receded to the back of his mind.

Certainly, Fuchs's new colleagues had no reason to suspect that there was anything out of the ordinary in his past. The ascetic, chain-smoking émigré physicist fit almost too neatly into the role of the single-minded theoretician, too devoted to his work even to bother with marriage. In the laboratory, Fuchs showed a respect for detail and procedure that made him a logical choice when there was a report to be written up or new data to be summarized. He was also known to be a stickler for regulations, impatient with colleagues who could not bring themselves to take seriously the more petty requirements of the security code imposed by their army hosts.

In his private life, Fuchs was just absentminded enough to

arouse the maternal instincts of his colleagues' wives. Throughout his career there was always at least one married woman friend who took it upon herself to look after poor Klaus by running errands, inviting him for long stays with the family, and even on occasion choosing his clothes for him. In return, Fuchs was a considerate and undemanding friend, the sort who could always be counted on to show up with a small but thoughtful gift for his hostess and fit in unobtrusively when an extra man was needed for dinner. Nor did Dr. Fuchs disgrace himself at parties. He was an excellent dancer as well as a phenomenal drinker, able to down shots of whiskey all evening without showing so much as a crack in his self-control. All these qualities made Fuchs an especially welcome addition to the constricted social scene at Los Alamos. Everyone liked him and enjoyed his company even though no one actually knew him very well.

By the spring of 1945, however, Klaus Fuchs became aware that at least some of his Los Alamos colleagues had begun to have second thoughts about the goal of their work. During the early years of the Manhattan Project, it had been widely assumed that the Allies were engaged in a desperate race to produce an atomic weapon before the Nazis did. Leo Szilard, another refugee from nazism, had proposed the bomb project to the British and then to the Americans only because he was convinced that such top German nuclear physicists as Werner Heisenberg were already at work on a Nazi bomb. Fear that the Nazis were well ahead in the competition remained very much alive throughout the war. In 1942, for example, rumor circulated among Manhattan Project scientists at the University of Chicago that the Germans had perfected a method of bombarding civilian populations with radioactive dust.

Then, in November 1944, an advance American intelligence unit in Europe discovered a cache of documents that strongly suggested there had never been a concerted effort on the part of the Germans to produce a nuclear weapon. The reasons for Germany's failure—if it can be called that—were complex. The German nuclear physicists had never gotten themselves mobilized to move the bomb project ahead, either out of a reluctance to serve Hitler, as Werner Heisenberg would later claim, or as a result of their stiff-necked resistance to sharing control of "their" discovery with mere engineers and military types. More importantly, the Nazi leadership had never made the atomic bomb a top priority, largely because of Hitler's optimistic belief that victory would be won long before such a weapon could ever be perfected.

The American intelligence team's report on the nonexistence of the German bomb was supposedly top secret. But since its technical content had to be read and evaluated by more than one high-level physicist, word of the report's contents eventually filtered down through the ranks of Manhattan Project scientific personnel. For some, it triggered a crisis of conscience. It had already become obvious to many that they had been naïve in believing that the bomb would be used on civilian populations only as a last resort. The superweapon belonged to the military, and, from the military point of view, weapons existed only to be used. As Leo Szilard wrote of this period, "In 1945, we ceased worrying about what the Germans might do to us and we began worrying about what the United States might do to other countries."

One of the worries that preoccupied the more politically aware scientists was the looming prospect of a postwar arms race. Only quick action to bring control of atomic energy policy into the hands of civilians and to set up some international mechanism for sharing atomic "secrets" could avert a ruinous competition for nuclear supremacy. It was obvious to the scientists, if not to their military masters, that an American monopoly of atomic energy could last a few years at most. Perhaps, some suggested, we could best use our temporary advantage by giving our atomic "secrets" away, in exchange for a series of international treaties dictated largely on our terms.

Such discussions were most intense at the Manhattan District outpost at the University of Chicago, but they also went on at Los Alamos. Later some of his colleagues would recall that Klaus Fuchs had been present during a number of these conversations without revealing any decided opinions one way or the other. No one had thought Fuchs's silence remarkable. Klaus was known to be something of a pedant, indifferent to the larger implications of his work.

Fuchs could afford to keep quiet since he was about to take the disposition of the atomic "secrets" into his own hands. In February 1945, he went back east for a ten-day holiday with Kristel and her husband. Kristel, innocently trying to do her brother a favor, had informed Raymond of Fuchs's plans, and before the vacation was up the Soviet courier arrived on the Heinemans' doorstep.

For whatever reasons, Fuchs decided that the time had come to slip back into his double role. At a meeting in Boston before his return to Los Alamos, Fuchs outlined for Raymond some recent developments on the Manhattan Project, including the race to perfect an implosion-type lens for use in a plutonium fission bomb. As a theoretician, Fuchs had little direct knowledge of day-to-day work on the lens; however, he promised to learn all he could upon his return to New Mexico. In June he kept his promise, rendezvousing with Raymond near the Castillo Bridge in Santa Fe to turn over more information on the bomb's design and to give advance notice of the forthcoming test in the desert near Alamogordo later that month.

In September, though the war was now over, he slipped away from Los Alamos on the excuse that he was going to Santa Fe to buy liquor for a party. There he met Raymond and handed over the most complete set of notes he had volunteered so far, including his eyewitness report of the Alamogordo test and calculations on the actual dimensions of the bomb.

After Fuchs was exposed in 1950, many of his former Los Alamos colleagues found it incredible that he could have lived and worked with them in close quarters for more than a year and a half without betraying himself. It was commonly supposed that Fuchs was a consummate actor, his entire persona a cleverly devised pose. As Hans Bethe, Fuchs's immediate superior during the war, recalled in an interview with the *Washington Star* days after the announcement of the confession: "We were very friendly together, but I didn't know anything of his real opinions. . . . If he was a spy, he played his role perfectly." Fuchs himself had a different explanation. He had suffered, he said, from a kind of "controlled schizophrenia" that made it possible for him to divide his conscience into separate compartments. He had been devoted to his work and even felt a certain loyalty to his British and American co-workers; the fact that he was simultaneously betraying them to Raymond had not consciously worried him at the time.

Fuchs's use of the term "controlled schizophrenia" was seized on by the British prosecutor Sir Christmas Humphreys, who described Fuchs as a "Jekyll and Hyde" dual personality with a mind that was possibly "unique . . . a new precedent in the field of psychiatry." This explanation was comforting in that it went far to excuse the failure of British and American security services to detect Fuchs's activities for so long. But the prisoner himself was bewildered and perhaps slightly amused by the suggestion that he had been in any way unique. As he made clear in his discussions with James Skardon, Fuchs had been consistently impressed with his contacts' ability to ask pointed and informed questions about the progress of his work. He had always taken it for granted that he was not the Russians' only source within the Manhattan Project. There had been others.

2

The Search for Raymond

When the announcement of Klaus Fuchs's confession exploded into the headlines on February 2, 1950, the FBI was left in an embarrassing and rather awkward position. American intelligence agencies had been directly responsible for providing the information that led to Fuchs's exposure, yet there was very little opportunity to savor the taste of victory. Although British security authorities generously acknowledged the assistance of the Americans and refrained from releasing portions of Fuchs's confession that dealt with his activities at Los Alamos, it was no secret that the British physicist had been spying for the Soviets while he held key positions within the Manhattan Project between 1943 and 1946.

How had Fuchs managed to slip through the net of the American security investigators? Who had been his partners in betraying the secret of the atom bomb? And why had the FBI, which claimed (not quite accurately) to have a spotless record in unmasking Nazi spies and saboteurs during the war, been so remiss in uncovering the Soviet plot to steal atomic data?

The very secrecy surrounding the details of Fuchs's crime fueled the controversy, as did the widespread though quite unfounded speculation that Fuchs had also given the Soviets details of the projected

"Super" or hydrogen bomb. J. Edgar Hoover was under pressure even from such usually reliable allies as Representative Richard Nixon of California, who called for a "full-scale congressional investigation" of atomic espionage.

Hoover realized that if the FBI did not soon find and arrest the man known as Raymond, it was in danger of looking ridiculous. The problem was that not even Fuchs knew Raymond's real name. All the Bureau had to go on was Fuchs's vague description of an American, almost certainly Jewish and most likely a chemist by profession. Physically, Raymond was said to be around forty and about five feet ten inches tall with a "broad" build and round face. If Fuchs had any more specific information that might be of use, the FBI could not find out; to Hoover's fury, the British were refusing to allow his agents access to their prize catch.

The FBI did have descriptions given by two additional witnesses, Kristel and Robert Heineman. According to Kristel Heineman, Raymond was about forty-five, 180 pounds, five feet eight and one-half inches tall, and stocky. Her husband, whose memory was to prove the most accurate, remembered Fuchs's courier as about thirty years old (as of 1945), five feet eight inches tall, with a round, full face, a stocky build, and dark, prematurely thinning hair.

One or another of the three descriptions the FBI had been given would have applied to more than a few million men. Fortunately, the FBI did not have to rely on looks alone. Research into the Bureau's own files quickly produced the name of a likely candidate for Raymond: Joseph Arnold Robbins, described in FBI files as a left-wing chemical engineer who had graduated from CCNY in 1941. The British agreed to show Fuchs photos forwarded from Washington, and on March 10, 1950, Fuchs identified snapshots of Robbins with "very fair certainty." The Bureau now mistakenly believed that it had the right man. Agents undertook surveillance of Robbins in his Brooklyn neighborhood and plans were made to bring Robert Heineman from Cambridge to observe their quarry secretly.

Just when the FBI was preparing to approach Robbins for questioning, the results of a routine check into his background proved conclusively that he had been on the East Coast throughout the summer of 1945 and could not possibly have been the man who met Fuchs in New Mexico in either June or September.

It was only after giving up on Robbins that the FBI began to focus on two other likely suspects, Abraham Brothman and Harry Gold. Both men had been named before a federal grand jury in 1947 by Elizabeth Terrill Bentley, the so-called Red Spy Queen who had become a turncoat after the death of her lover and espionage superior, Jacob Golos. Bentley had claimed then that Brothman's Queens County engineering firm served as a clearinghouse for Soviet industrial espionage, and she had named Brothman's sometime employee Harry Gold as the man who succeeded her as liaison between Brothman and the Soviets. Although the grand jury had failed to indict either man, choosing to believe their claims that they had known Golos only as a legitimate business promoter, the FBI felt in retrospect that Gold and Brothman's scientific training and alleged involvement in Golos's operation made the two men worth checking out.

From the beginning, the FBI considered Harry Gold the more likely candidate for Raymond. It was he whom Bentley had alleged worked as a courier, and, what was more, Brothman's appearance did not remotely correspond to any of the physical characteristics recalled by Fuchs in his testimony about Raymond. On May 9, Hoover ordered an all-out effort to locate Harry Gold.

The search led first to Brothman's engineering firm, where Gold was last known to have been employed. Brothman, however, told the FBI that Gold had not worked for him since before the grand jury investigation. Next the manhunt focused on Philadelphia, Gold's hometown. By May 15, Special Agents T. Scott Miller, Jr., and Richard E. Brennan of the Philadelphia Bureau office had discovered that Gold was still living with his father and brothers in that city and working as a chemist at the Heart Station Laboratory of the Philadelphia General Hospital.

That same day, Brennan and Miller dropped in on Gold at his job. On seeing Gold, the agents claimed in their report on the visit, they were immediately struck by his physical resemblance to the Bureau's last suspect, Joseph Arnold Robbins. Gold, however, seemed unfazed by the FBI's renewed interest in him. He willingly answered questions about his background for some five hours. Miller and Brennan concluded that Gold believed Abe Brothman was the real target of their investigation. This was an impression that the agents, in whatever fashion, apparently did their best to foster. "It was advisable," their report noted later, that Gold "should continue to think this way."

In fact, the agents' pretense of an interest in Brothman had not fooled Harry Gold for one minute. Although he had managed to appear calm and composed, inwardly he was terrified. He had been expecting just such a visit ever since the previous October, when a Soviet agent had contacted him to warn of the possibility of Klaus Fuchs's impending arrest. Gold had been in sporadic touch with the Soviets ever since, traveling to New York for bimonthly assignations, and he had even been given instructions for contacting them in case of just such an emergency as Miller and Brennan's visit portended. Gold later wrote:

> Curiously enough, when Special Agents Miller and Brennan walked into the Heart Station Laboratory that afternoon, even before they showed me their identification, I knew who they were. And when they said they would like to speak to me about Brothman—"and other matters," that last phrase was the one which disturbed me. . . . And questions such as, "Were you ever west of the Mississippi" were, to put it mildly, disturbing.

Gold, however, was apparently in no psychological state to consider escape, with or without Soviet help. From the day the agents arrived at his lab, he regarded their investigation with a kind of fatalism, hoping that it would fail but doing little or nothing to deflect the curiosity of his interrogators. Within the week, Gold's resistance would collapse completely and he would offer the FBI a voluntary confession.

"The beginning was a relatively innocent one," Harry Gold was to tell his lawyers in June 1950, explaining how he had blundered into a career in espionage. For the man who had become the most productive Soviet agent in the United States to claim innocence, even "relative" innocence, may seem ingenuous, but Gold might have been speaking not just for himself but for an entire group of Americans who were drawn into the business of spying through their admiration for the Soviet social experiment. A pudgy, stoop-shouldered chemist, Gold had little in common with the spies of fiction, whether the dashing special agents of the James Bond thrillers or the dedicated professionals of the world of John le Carré. He had begun as an industrial spy, collecting secrets that belonged not to any government, but to capitalist businessmen. When he later turned to military espionage, he did so in the belief that he was helping an ally by redressing the shortsighted policies of American bureaucrats. In his own mind, Gold was able to rationalize that he was making a significant, if slightly unorthodox, contribution to the Allied war effort. Even after he had pleaded guilty and contritely accepted a thirty-year prison sentence, Gold rankled at the language of the indictment, which charged him "with intent to harm and injure the United States." This "horribly wrong statement," Gold explained, was a total distortion of his motives. Doing injury to his adopted country had been the last thing on his mind.

Harry Gold was born in Berne, Switzerland, in 1912, the son of Russian Jews who emigrated to the United States before Gold was two years old. Gold's parents chose to bypass the teeming slums of the Lower East Side, settling instead in a tough South Philadelphia neighborhood. Their decision took its toll on young Harry. One of Gold's most vivid school memories was of being beaten up by older boys who preyed on those children daring enough to try to frequent the public library. It was also impossible to avoid fights with "the Neckers," boys who lived in the marshy, semirural section called The Neck. The poor families of The Neck resented their newly arrived immigrant neighbors for their ability to command skilled jobs, and the children vented their frustration with anti-Semitic slurs and what Gold described as "brick-throwing, window-smashing forays." The situation would have been bad enough in any case, but Harry Gold was a shy, awkward child with few friends and no natural allies. As he grew older, he came to see himself as a solitary victim of social injustice.

In 1915, Sam Gold was hired by the Victor Talking Machine Company, the forerunner of RCA. The family's fortunes appeared to be on the rise. As a skilled cabinetmaker, Sam Gold was a valued and productive worker in the shop of a small company. But his contentment ended abruptly in 1920 when Victor shifted to mass-production techniques and hired a large number of unskilled Italian immigrants. "These men were crudely anti-Semitic," Harry Gold wrote, "and made Pop, one of the few Jewish workers, the object of their 'humour.' They stole his chisels, put glue on his tools and good clothes, and in general made life intolerable for him."

Although Harry Gold only learned the full story of his father's difficulties years later from his mother, much of what was going on could not be hidden from the sensitive young boy. As Gold recalled it:

> Beginning about 1926, my father came under an Irish foreman at RCA, a man who was more bitterly intolerant than anyone Pop had yet encountered. He told Pop, "You Jew son-of-a-bitch, I'm going to make you quit," and so put him on a specifically speeded up production line, where my father was the only one handsanding cabinets. Then Sam Gold would come home at night with the skin partially rubbed off. . . . Mom would bathe the wounded members and would put ointment on them, and Pop would go back to work the next morning. But he never quit.

In the meantime, Gold's mother had become fascinated by Debsian socialism, and the entire family became regular readers of the *Jewish Daily Forward*. While still in high school, Harry Gold was an admirer of Norman Thomas. Socialism offered the hope of justice and a vision of a free and egalitarian society. Communism, by contrast, was a poorly understood and not very appealing ideology. When a friend confided that he had become a Communist, Gold had only "a feeling of revulsion."

Gold graduated from high school near the top of his class and went to work as a laboratory assistant for the Pennsylvania Sugar Company. By working seven days a week, he was able to scrape together enough money to enter the University of Pennsylvania in September 1930. Unfortunately, his meager savings ran out before he could take his degree, and by March 1932 he had returned to his former job. The struggle to pay for his education had only deepened his commitment to Norman Thomas and the American Socialists. But, like many Socialists, Gold found that his antipathy for the Communist Party, U.S.A. did not extend to the Soviet Union. In the early years of the Depression, the Soviet "experiment" offered a beacon of hope to many who were looking for an alternative to the apparent bankruptcy of the capitalist economic system. The beacon shone all the brighter in December 1932 when, ten days before Christmas, Gold was laid off from his job.

"Then it was," Gold remembered, "that Ferdinand (Fred) Heller, a research chemist in the main lab, suggested that I should take my family to the Birobidjan area of Soviet Russia." The idea of emigrating to the Soviet Union, possibly in the company of his fellow Socialist Heller, was intriguing but ultimately not very practical. Before long, however, Heller came up with a more useful suggestion. A friend and classmate of his named Tom Black was leaving a position at the Holbrook Manufacturing Company in Jersey City for a better offer. Perhaps Black could arrange for Gold to take over his old job.

A week later, Heller received a telegram from Black saying that if Gold wanted the job he should come to Jersey City immediately. Taking a worn cardboard suitcase and six dollars he had borrowed from another friend, Gold caught a Greyhound bus and arrived late at night at Black's apartment.

Black made him feel at ease immediately with a "huge friendly grin . . . and the bear-like grip of his hand." The two men stayed up talking until 6:00 A.M., with Black briefing Gold on the background information on soap chemistry that he would need for his new work. In the course of the conversation, Black also warned Gold of the need to hide his Jewishness, since the man who would be his superintendent was violently anti-Semitic. Gold's natural dismay at this news gave Black the opportunity to launch into a discussion of politics. "Tom told me very frankly that he was a Communist Party member, and that Heller had purposely sent me to [him]" because, as a Socialist, "I was a likely recruit to the more militant organization." Black was to lecture his new acquaintance nonstop for nearly five hours, telling him that "capitalism was doomed here in the United States, that the only country to which the working man owed allegiance was the Soviet Union, and that the only reasonable way of life was Communism."

Gold listened to it all, patiently and without protest. After all, he needed the job. The thirty dollars' salary Holbrook paid each week would be enough to keep his entire family off relief. By budgeting seven dollars weekly for his own food and rent, and four dollars for the weekend round-trip train fare to Philadelphia, Gold would be able to turn over nineteen dollars to his parents and brother. Under the circumstances, Gold agreed to accompany Black to Communist Party meetings.

If we can believe his statement of two decades later, Gold was not impressed with the Party members he encountered:

There I met such assorted characters as: Joe Mackenzie the seaman, a young man with gaps in his teeth (due to his penchant, when drunk, for slugging it out with Jersey City's uniformly out-size police); an earnest old Pole who was an ex-anarchist; and a volatile Greek barber who once in petulance at a meeting which had drearily degenerated into a discussion of Marxian dialectics, declared, "the hell with this stuff—give me five good men and I'll take Journal Square by storm!" These were at least sincere, but there were others, people who frankly were in it only for the purpose of gratifying some ulterior motives: a whole host of despicable bohemians who prattled of free love; others who obviously were lazy bums, and would never work under any economic system, depression or no depression; and, finally, a certain type . . . (endless, boring talkers,) and to whom no one but this weird conglomeration of individuals would listen, if even they did. Nothing was accomplished at these meetings . . . and, in spite of Tom's enthusiasm, the whole dreary crew seemed to be a very futile threat to even the admittedly unsteady economy of the United States in early 1933.

Gold genuinely liked and respected Tom Black, however, and when Black suggested that he pay a visit to a Party school that operated near Union Square in New York City, Gold agreed. He returned home with an armload of Marxist books and pamphlets, which he took to read and discuss with his mentor.

In September, Gold was suddenly offered a chance to return to the Pennsylvania Sugar Company. The pay would be the same as at his present job, but he would be given the chance to set up and direct his own lab and would no longer have to commute from Jersey City to Philadelphia every weekend to see his family. In addition, he would finally "be freed of Tom's endless importuning to join the Communist Party."

Upon returning to his family and his new employment, Gold also enrolled in courses in chemical engineering in the Drexel Institute of Technology's evening division. Although his new routine kept him busy, Gold found that he was still seeing a good deal of Tom Black. Black came down from Jersey City frequently to visit, charming Gold's parents while continuing to urge his friend to take up a commitment to communism. Then, in mid-1934, Black suddenly had a change of heart. The Communist Party members, particularly in Philadelphia, were a "shabby and shoddy lot," he told Gold, run through with "informers and opportunists" who were all too ready to engage rank-and-file workers in useless clashes with the police. This

was more or less what Gold had thought all along, and he felt gratified that Tom Black was at last beginning to see things as they were.

After announcing his disaffection from the Party, the normally
ebullient Tom Black was quiet for some months. Early in 1935, however, he showed up at the Gold family apartment in Philadelphia
trumpeting a new enthusiasm. Black told Gold that he had recently
met a representative of AMTORG, the organization responsible for
all Soviet trade with the United States, and been offered a direct and
effective way to help the Soviet experiment, one that bypassed all
those dreary and counterproductive Party meetings. AMTORG, it
seems, was in great need of industrial formulas—for paper sizers, fill-
er materials, vitamin D concentrate from fish oils, synthetic deter-
gents, and so on.

Harry Gold admitted that he saw nothing wrong in principle
with passing such information to the Soviets since it would only be a
way of helping a Socialist economy catch up with the more industri-
alized capitalist nations. This was all the encouragement Black needed to produce a more specific list of what was wanted, including data
on industrial solvents used for lacquers and varnishes—ethyl acetate,
ethyl chloride, amyl acetate; specialized chemicals for blending mo-
tor fuels. All of these were being worked on by the Pennsylvania Sugar Company's subsidiaries. Would Gold agree to make them available to AMTORG?

At first, Gold asked for time to think that proposition over, but
"actually I had already formed my judgement . . . in fact, I was even
to a certain extent eager to." In the first place, the arrangement
would enable him to discharge his debt and get Tom Black "off my
neck" at last. More important, he felt that he was finally being offered a chance to use his education and professional status in a way
that would contribute something positive to the world. Why
shouldn't the Soviet people, survivors of czarist oppression and a violent revolutionary struggle, be given a chance to enjoy a measure of
the better things in life?

Finally, Harry Gold had convinced himself that by aiding the
Soviets he would be contributing to the eradication of anti-Semitism.
From the beginning of their friendship, Tom Black had constantly
harped on the "fact" that the Soviet Union was the only country in
the world where anti-Semitism was a crime against the state—whereas, in America, anti-Jewish hatemongering "could get a man elected

to public office." In the Christian West, Black had argued, anti-Semitism might be suppressed but it could never be eliminated. Only scientific socialism could defeat it forever, and only the Soviet Union would stand up against the growing, worldwide menace of fascism. In Gold's words: "To me, Nazism and Fascism and anti-Semitism were identical. . . . Anything that was against anti-Semitism I was for, and so the chance to help strengthen the Soviet Union appeared as such a wonderful opportunity."

Unlike some others, who would agree to work for AMTORG without quite realizing that what they were doing violated the law, Gold understood from the first that he would be committing illegal acts. While Tom Black talked only of "obtaining" information, Gold was well aware that this was really a euphemism for stealing.

At first, Gold's conscience was troubled by the prospect of deceiving Dr. Gustav Reich, the director of research at Pennsylvania Sugar. Reich had always treated him with kindness and had given him an opportunity to direct his own lab. For some seven months, Gold did little—putting off Tom Black with the story that he had not found any good way of copying the documents that were in Reich's office. Finally, Black told his friend that if he could just manage to get the documents to New York, AMTORG would arrange to have them copied at its own expense. It was soon after this that Black introduced Gold to his first Soviet operative—the man known variously as Paul Smith or Paul Peterson. Gold surrendered the formula for processing phosphoric acid from waste bone-black and sulphuric acid. He was gratified to receive "high praise" for this from Paul, even though he could not quite understand why it should be considered so valuable.

In the months and years that followed, Harry Gold found the rewards of his new role outweighed the burden of guilt he felt for betraying his boss, his colleagues, and his family. Like Klaus Fuchs, Gold was a man who had developed few close emotional ties, and so the continual lies required by his new role, which might have ruined the personal relationships of a more social man, became for him a rather amusing game. In the meantime, his contacts with "Paul" and a succession of Soviet controls filled a vacuum, injecting an element of drama into his otherwise drab life and allowing him to feel that he was indeed doing something "positive" to fight injustice.

Once the resources of the Pennsylvania Sugar Company had

been exhausted, Gold accepted an assignment to act as contact man for other potential informers, some of them none too eager to cooperate. By this point, he regarded the need to pressure these informants, occasionally to the point of outright blackmail, as just one of the petty annoyances of his unpaid avocation:

> The planning of a meeting with a Soviet agent; the careful preparation for obtaining data from Penn Sugar, the writing of technical reports and the filching of blueprints for copying (and then returning them); the meetings with Paul Smith or Ruga or Fred or Semenov, in New York or Cincinnati or . . . Buffalo; or going to a rendezvous with Al Slack in Tennessee or Klaus Fuchs in Cambridge or Santa Fe—and the difficulties I had in raising money for all these trips . . . the cajoling of Brothman to do work and the outright blackmailing of Ben Smilg for the same purpose; and the many lies I had to tell at home, and to my friends, to explain my whereabouts during these absences from home (Mom was certain that I was carrying on a series of clandestine love affairs and nothing could have been farther from the truth); the hours of waiting on street corners, waiting dubiously and fearfully in strange towns where I had no business to be, and the uneasy killing of time in cheap movies . . . all these became so very deeply ingrained in me. It was a drudgery and I hated it.

Gold's strategy for dealing with such tensions and inconveniences was similar to that of Fuchs, who had admitted to developing a dual personality. Gold said:

> When on a mission, I just completely subordinated myself to the task at hand, whether it was delivering data I had myself obtained, or a report I had written or whether it concerned getting information from a person such as Klaus Fuchs or Al Slack or Abe Brothman. Once I had started out on a trip, I totally forgot home and family and work and friends and just became a single-minded automaton, set to do a job. . . . Probably this attitude was partly unconscious, but it was certainly present and, above all, it was most effective. And when the task was completed and I returned home, the same process again took place, but this time in reverse. I would return to work and would become completely absorbed in it . . . and I would cast away and bury all thought and all memory of everything that had happened on the trip.

Gold's dual life was not entirely drab, however. Sam Semenov, who became Gold's Soviet control in 1942, had suggested that Gold tell his new contacts that he was a family man—apparently on the grounds that this would make him seem more sympathetic and trustworthy. Before long, Gold was carrying out this suggestion in a manner that no doubt would have shocked and appalled Semenov, concocting vivid stories about an imaginary wife, Sarah, who had married him after breaking off with an underworld boyfriend known as "Nigger Nate"; Sarah's slovenly mother; and twin children named David and Eppie. Gold's contacts, especially Abe Brothman, whom he came to know rather well, were treated to a running narrative of his personal difficulties—one of the twins was stricken with polio; Sarah and Gold quarreled and decided to separate; Gold's soldier brother was killed in New Guinea—all of them quite imaginary.

In retrospect, Gold was quite aware of the neurotic impulses behind this fantasized personal history. He even confessed that his fantasies reflected difficulties with his mother, who remained the only woman in his life. For example, a quarrel they had over Gold's plan to move to New York at one point was transformed by him into stories about his quarrels with his imaginary wife. But pathetic as it may have been, Gold's fantasy family never actually got him into trouble. Gold knew very well that the stories he had concocted were lies, and in this sense, he always stayed in control of his fantasy life. Indeed, his anecdotes were so consistent that they completely fooled those who heard them, including some who were in close contact with Gold over a period of years.

An aspect of Gold's mental compartmentalization that was to prove far more dangerous to him was the growing tendency of Harry Gold the private citizen to deal carelessly and even sloppily with the evidence left over from his forays into the life of Harry Gold, espionage courier. On returning from a journey, he simply stuffed armfuls of unsubmitted blueprints, drafts of reports, note cards, street maps, and the like into a spare closet in the cellar of his Philadelphia home. Year after year, incriminating documents were allowed to pile up, while Gold sought relief from the tension of his double life in extended bouts of heavy drinking.

For years on end, Gold had neither the time nor the motivation to reexamine the political beliefs that had set him on his chosen path. When he expressed passing doubts about the rightness of the Soviet invasion of Finland, he accepted the assurance of his superior that the move had been necessary to unseat the pro-Fascist Junker Baron Mannerheim and to protect Russia's "future welfare." News of the Nazi-Soviet pact was harder to swallow—particularly in view of Molotov's widely reported comment that "fascism [is] a matter of taste." On this occasion, at least, Gold felt compelled to protest directly to his Soviet controller. "Semenov laughed uproariously," Gold recalled, "when I told him that this was entirely too much. . . . 'Look, you fool, don't tell me that you [too] have been taken in by the frantic blathering of the press [Semenov replied]. See here, what the Soviet Union needs more than anything else in the world is time, precious time. . . . When the hour comes, you'll see, we'll sweep over Germany and Hitler like nothing ever imagined before, and the Nazis will be obliterated once and for all.' "

Gold's willingness to accept both the political excuses and the drudgery imposed on him is no doubt a credit to the skill of his chiefs in exploiting his loneliness and his desperate need for a sense of fulfillment. The most skillful of all was Semon Markovich Semenov, known as "Sam," who impressed Gold tremendously with his suave manners and taste for the good things in life. Though Russian-born, Sam spoke impeccable, American-accented English and could converse knowledgeably about English literature as well as chemical engineering.

Semenov played on Gold's need for respect and stature by treating him as a co-worker in the noble, if often dreary, field of espionage. When Gold complained about the boring trips he was being asked to undertake, Semenov countered by talking about his own homesickness for Russia, which could be assuaged only by attending ice hockey games in Madison Square Garden. "He would tell me how much joy he had gotten out of skating in Russia, and how he regretted that he was too busy to take advantage of the few opportunities here."

And when Gold had difficulty with Abe Brothman, who was stalling on an earlier promise to hand over some much-desired information, Semenov exuded sympathy. "Look at you, you not only look like a ghost, you are one—you're positively dead on your feet and exhausted. What must your mother think!" Then Semenov offered to take Gold to a bar for drinks and a good meal, bought him a parlor-car seat on the train back to Philadelphia, and shoved a handful of expensive cigars into his jacket pocket. "Someday," he told Gold in parting, he hoped that Gold could give up "this lousy business" and return to a normal life. Gold, who at this point had served the Soviets for more than eight years without even receiving payment for his expenses, was overwhelmed by Sam's concern and generosity.

Eventually, of course, Gold did get his reward—though not in the form of money. Late in 1943, Semenov told him that he was being given a new and more important assignment. He was to break off his old contacts immediately, because from now on he would be working only with "a group of American scientists in New York" and, in particular, with "a man recently come to this country from England." According to Gold, this was none other than Klaus Fuchs. Gold's contacts with Fuchs were limited to a few brief meetings over a period of two years—so brief, in fact, that Fuchs would hardly be able to remember what Gold looked like. Yet to Gold, Fuchs was memorable. A distinguished scientist who had experienced and fought fascism firsthand, Fuchs's example seemed to vindicate Gold's actions.

After an eight-year apprenticeship, Gold had finally entered the big leagues of espionage. The only disappointment was that this apex of his career was so short-lived. Having turned over the results of his September 1945 trip to Santa Fe to Anatoli Yakovlev, who had replaced Semenov in 1944, Gold heard nothing more from the Soviets for more than a year. And when Yakovlev did contact him again in December 1946, Gold's innocent mention that he had violated one of the basic rules of espionage by accepting a job with his former contact Abe Brothman enraged Yakovlev and marked the end of any useful career that Gold might have had left.

Throughout his twelve years of work for the Soviets, Harry Gold had never faced any serious threat of exposure. His first close call came in 1947; then, just as Yakovlev had predicted, it was his relationship with Abe Brothman that nearly proved his undoing.

In the course of the admissions she made to the FBI in 1945, Elizabeth Bentley had described ten meetings with Brothman that took place in 1940. Acting as courier, she picked up blueprints from Brothman and handed them over to her boss, Jacob Golos. Bentley had always found Brothman a difficult person to deal with and she was relieved when Golos told her that he was disappointed with the quality of information Brothman had been providing and had "vowed to turn him over to someone else." Bentley insisted to the FBI that she never did learn the identity of the man who was taking over for her.

In 1947, when the FBI first got around to asking him about

Bentley's accusation, Brothman freely admitted turning over blueprints to Bentley, but he insisted that the transactions had been completely legal and aboveboard. Sometime during 1938 or 1939, Brothman recalled, a friend who had contact with the Soviet government had suggested that Brothman try to obtain a contract to sell it some of the industrial equipment he had designed. Accordingly, Brothman got together the plans for "shafts, vats and other equipment necessary in the operation of a plant manufacturing chemicals" and gave them to Golos and Bentley, who had been introduced to him only as Golos's secretary, "Helen." Brothman stressed that he had never given Golos blueprints of a restricted, secret, or classified nature, and that all of the materials he did hand over were his own personal property. "It was common practice in the engineering field to turn over blueprints to various individuals in an effort to obtain contracts," Brothman insisted. As far as he was concerned, Jacob Golos had never been anything more than a business contact.

Since he had already told the FBI that his dealings with Golos were nothing more than a legitimate business deal, Brothman may have felt that he could hardly refuse to tell the FBI the name of the person he dealt with after 1940. At any rate, he felt pressured enough to add yet another name to the Bureau's list of suspects, that of Harry Gold, then in his own employ. "Sometime in 1940," he said, "Helen stopped coming to [my] office and another individual named Harry Gold came . . . and said he represented Golos."

Shortly after this 1947 visit from the Bureau, Brothman called in his then employee Harry Gold. "The FBI were here . . . they know everything," Gold remembers him shouting. "They know you were a courier—They have a photograph of you and me in a restaurant! Look, we don't have much time. . . . You have got to tell the same story I told of how we met. . . . Someone has ratted! It must be that bitch Helen!"

In actuality, Gold had been reporting to the Soviet agent "Sam" Semenov during this period and had never even met Jacob Golos. In order to corroborate Brothman's story, however, he agreed to invent a tale that would place Brothman's dealings with Golos in an innocent light. Thus, when questioned by the FBI shortly after their interview with Brothman, Gold identified a photograph of Golos as the man he had once known as "Jacob Gollis or Gollish." Gold claimed that he had been introduced to Golos during a 1941 meeting of the

American Chemical Society by Carter Hoodless, an executive of the Penn Sugar Company. Golos had presented himself as a legitimate business promoter and hired Gold on a consulting basis to evaluate a set of proposals drawn up by Brothman. Gold also said that he had worked free-lance for Golos on and off for two years until both he and Brothman concluded that Golos was a "fly-by-night" operator. Finally, Gold took a job working directly for Abe Brothman at the latter's laboratory in Queens, New York.

This was essentially the version of their relationship that Gold and Brothman testified to when they were called before the federal grand jury in New York in 1947. Three years later, however, Gold repudiated this story. According to his 1950 statements to the FBI, the meeting at the American Chemical Society convocation had never taken place. Carter Hoodless, for that matter, had no connection with Golos. The name of the Penn Sugar representative had been inserted into the account only because Hoodless was deceased and could not contradict the story.

According to Harry Gold, he and Abe Brothman had met late one night in 1947 at Brothman's lab to iron out the stories they would tell in their forthcoming grand-jury appearances. The meeting started out with Brothman apologizing for having given Gold's name to the FBI in the first place, a betrayal he rationalized on the grounds that suspicion would probably have fallen on Gold sooner or later in any case. But when the two men began to compare alibis and discuss the kinds of questions they might be asked before the grand jury, Brothman's gratitude turned to horror. Although he had known that Gold was an espionage courier, he apparently had not realized that Gold reported directly to Soviet intelligence officers rather than to a supposedly legitimate businessman such as Golos. Nor had he ever suspected, as he now learned for the first time, that Gold's anecdotes about his personal life were nothing more than an elaborate cover story. There was no wife Sarah, no twin children, and no brother dead on a New Guinea battlefield.

The more Brothman learned about Gold, the more he began to realize that he had inadvertently led the FBI to the one man who could destroy him. In a panic, he began to wonder whether it wouldn't be best to confess everything before he was exposed by the unraveling of Gold's lies. Over the years, Brothman had given Gold some technical data on industrial processes that might be deemed of national security importance, notably formulas for a batch-continuous process for Buna-S synthetic rubber. However, much of this data, including the Buna-S information, had eventually been made available to the Soviet Union through Lend-Lease. Under the circumstances, it seemed unlikely that he could be indicted for wartime espionage.

Harry Gold was horrified by Brothman's talk of confession. Convinced that the explanation they had already given the FBI would stand up under the grand jury's scrutiny Gold enlisted Brothman's business partner, Miriam Moskowitz, to convince Brothman to stand fast.

Surprisingly enough, Gold turned out to be correct, at least for the time being. The grand jury found no basis for indicting either man. But Harry Gold's friendship with Abe Brothman was finished, as was his usefulness as a Soviet courier. Gold retired from his tumultuous but exciting double life to the routine existence of a hospital laboratory chemist. Ironically, once he had the leisure to look back on his adventures, he had to admit he no longer believed the Soviet Union was a utopia. Nor did he still consider it a defender of Judaism: Soviet Birobidzhan, proclaimed for years as an enclave of Jewish settlement, had never been anything more than "a mammoth concentration camp for those Jews who persisted in clinging to their beliefs." Sealing Gold's disillusionment, the death of his mother earlier that same year had left him filled with remorse for the many small deceptions he had practiced on her over the years.

In 1948, Gold fell in love with a woman he had met through his job in the hospital lab. The normal family life he had longed for seemed within his grasp for the first time, and he proposed marriage in August 1949. But the relationship was ended because of a problem Gold delicately referred to as his "lack of ardor"—and which he blamed on his obsessive fear that his past would be exposed. After this episode Gold resigned himself to the fact he was unlikely ever to marry or have a family of his own, aside from his father and unmarried brother who still shared the family home in Philadelphia with him. Nor would he ever regain the sense of commitment and pride he had felt when he believed he was doing his small part to bring about the destruction of fascism.

On that day in early February 1950 when Gold picked up his morning newspaper and learned about Klaus Fuchs's confession, he knew that what little peace of mind he had left was about to be shattered. Although he had never spoken to anyone about his role as Raymond, he decided now to confide in his old friend Tom Black, calling him late one night to say that he had "urgent personal business" to discuss. Black agreed to meet Gold in Philadelphia's Broad Street station. As the two men paced the neighboring streets, Gold asked Black to promise that if anything happened to him, "Pop and Yus" (his father and brother) would be taken care of. Finally, Gold got to the point. "The FBI is looking for Klaus Fuchs's American contact," he told the startled Black, "and I am that man."

There was nothing for Gold to do now but hope that if and when the FBI showed up he would be able to fool them as he had done once before. Gold confessed his secret role to Black in February. It took until May for the two FBI agents to beat the trail to Gold. At first, he held up rather well. There was still nothing definite against Gold, and the agents did not push too hard. But on May 16, 1950, two FBI agents from the New York office talked to Miriam Moskowitz, who happened to mention that when he worked for Abe Brothman in 1946, Gold had often talked about his twin children and a brother who had been killed in the Pacific. That rang a bell. The FBI realized that Kristel Heineman, when asked to identify her brother's anonymous visitor, had noted that Raymond also spoke to her about his twin children. When agents Miller and Brennan brought up the subject of a "redheaded wife and two children" with Gold the next day, he knew that he was deeply implicated but "did the best [he] could to steer the conversation away from this deadly reef" and continued his strategy of trying to overwhelm the investigators with cooperation. During a nine-hour interview on May 17, he willingly wrote out pages of his handwriting and printing, allowed the agents to take motion pictures of him, and invited them to make a search of his own house. The only condition Gold imposed was that the search take place on the following Monday, May 22, a day when his father and brother would be away from home.

As the day of the search approached, Gold's nervousness mounted. He knew that there were enough incriminating documents squirreled away in his cellar closet to convict him, but his dread of dealing with the situation was so great that he procrastinated all weekend. As he recalled it:

> Yes, I was almost in the clear, but, instead of going home
> and frenziedly cleaning out all of that incriminating evidence,

which I knew was there (though even I had no idea as to the extent of the material), I went back to the medical school . . . I actually did not begin my search for damaging bits of evidence until 5 A.M. on Monday—because I felt that any such undue activity on my part would only alarm Pop and Yus. . . . But when I started to look, in the depressing grayness of the early morning, I was horrified: Good Lord! Here was a letter from Slack, dated February 1945; a stub of a plane ticket from Albuquerque to Kansas City; a rough draft of a report of a visit to Cambridge, Massachusetts; a street map of Dayton, Ohio; a card containing instructions from Sam relating to a procedure for approaching Ben Smilg. All this was there and more—I tore it all up and flushed it down the toilet. Yes, I had taken care of everything.

Or so he thought. When Brennan and Miller arrived on the 22nd, they started combing through Gold's belongings with a thoroughness he found appalling. One by one, they riffled through the pages of his chemical references and math and physics textbooks and started in on his school and lab notes and personal library. "Then it began," wrote Gold:

> First a copy of Paul de Kruif's "Microbe Hunters" in a pocket edition turned up: and in the lower right hand corner of the inside cover was a tiny tag, "Sibley Curr and Lindsay."
> "What is this?" said Dick. "Oh, I don't know," I replied. "I must have picked it up on a used book counter somewhere." . . .
> But I did know; the tag bore the name of a Rochester department store and I had purchased the book during a visit to see Al Slack.
> Then Scott found a Pennsylvania Train Schedule: Washington–Philadelphia–New York–Boston–Montreal; and it was dated 1945. "How about this?" "Goodness knows, I probably got it when I went to New York to see Brothman." . . . actually I had used this on one of my trips to see Mrs. Heineman. . . .

Gold thought that while these might be somewhat incriminating he was still in the clear:

> Then came the stunning blow. From in back of my bulky copy of Walker, Lewis and McAdams "Principles of Chemical Engineering" Dick pulled a sickeningly familiar tan-colored street

map of Santa Fe. Oh, God! This I had overlooked. I knew that it
existed, but in my hasty scrutiny that morning could not find it
and assumed that at some previous time it must have been destroyed.

. . . "Give me a minute," I said, as I sank down on the chair
which Miller had just vacated. I accepted a cigarette and then,
after a few moments, said the fatal words: "Yes, I am the man to
whom Klaus Fuchs gave the information on atomic energy."

Possession of a street map of Santa Fe was hardly enough to
convict a man of espionage, but Gold was now convinced that the
FBI knew everything it needed to know. Perhaps he would have been
less quick to collapse if he had realized that Klaus Fuchs still had not
identified him as Raymond.

Ironically, news of Harry Gold's confession created consternation at Bureau headquarters. It had come too soon. Rumors that a
big break in the hunt for Raymond was imminent had been building
up in the press for days, and now that Gold had actually signed a
confession, it would be impossible to delay arresting him. Yet J. Edgar Hoover had very much wanted to accompany the arrest with an
announcement that Klaus Fuchs had positively identified Gold as
Raymond. This sequence of identification and arrest was not really
necessary to secure Gold's conviction, but it would make a more dramatic story and put an extra gloss on the FBI's success.

Unfortunately for Hoover, Klaus Fuchs did not share his sense
of urgency. On May 20, FBI agents Hugh Clegg and Robert Lamphere, who had been interrogating Fuchs at Wormwood Scrubbs
prison since British security finally gave its permission in mid-May,
secured some old still photos of Harry Gold. After examining them,
Fuchs complained that the pictures were so blurry he could tell nothing one way or the other. Fuchs had, however, given Clegg and Lamphere a new physical description of Raymond, which encouraged
them to think that the FBI was on the right track in suspecting Gold.
Fuchs now said that Raymond was about five feet eight inches tall,
weighed 175 pounds, and had dark hair and a broad face. He also
recalled that Raymond had spoken of having a wife and children and
living in the Philadelphia area.

On May 22, Clegg and Lamphere tried again. This time they
showed Fuchs some poor-quality motion pictures that had been tak-

en of Gold with his permission on the 17th. Fuchs viewed the films three times and agreed that the man shown was "very like" Raymond, but in the end he refused to make a definite identification, objecting that something about the man's mannerisms struck him as not quite right. Clegg and Lamphere suspected that Fuchs was not so much genuinely uncertain as reluctant to cause the downfall of one of his former confederates. They began to wonder whether they would ever be able to get an unequivocal statement.

It was later that same day, after 10:00 A.M. Philadelphia time, that Harry Gold confessed. There was as yet no confirmation from Fuchs, and consummate bureaucrat that he was, Hoover decided to fudge. Gold was not formally arraigned until the next day (significantly, perhaps, considering the speed with which the Bureau could arrange arraignments when it desired), and so the story of Raymond's capture did not appear until the morning of the 24th. Typical of the coverage of the arrest was a *New York Times* headline trumpeting "PHILADELPHIAN SEIZED AS SPY ON THE BASIS OF DATA FROM FUCHS." The accompanying article, datelined from Washington on May 23, reported that "Gold had been arrested on espionage charges based on information supplied by Dr. Fuchs."

This was no mere misunderstanding. In a widely publicized article that appeared in the *Reader's Digest* in May 1951, Hoover refined the official version of Raymond's capture, claiming that the Bureau had sifted through the records of some 1,200 subjects before finally narrowing the search to Gold. The article also claimed that "quite by coincidence, less than an hour after [Gold's] confession, a cable was received at FBI headquarters in Washington, saying that Dr. Fuchs, after seeing secretly taken movies, had identified Harry Gold as his American partner." Hoover's account of the Raymond manhunt may have been clever public relations—but, in hindsight, more critical readers suspected that several elements in his story, particularly Fuchs's fortuitously timed identification, were a bit too neat.

An examination of internal FBI memoranda shows that these suspicions are justified, at least in part. The May 22 cable from London did exist—but it did not confirm what Hoover claimed.

What really happened was this: FBI investigations chief A. H. Belmont learned of Harry Gold's confession at 11:25 A.M. on the morning of May 22, less than one hour after Gold made his critical admission to agents Miller and Brennan. The timing of Gold's confession coincided with Fuchs's statement, made in London, that motion pictures he had been shown of Gold on May 22 appeared "very likely" to be that of Gold, although he was quite equivocal. The FBI received this information by cable on May 22 at precisely 11:08 A.M. But this ambivalent identification by Fuchs was not sufficient for their needs.

It is for this reason that Belmont's first reaction was to order that new still photos and motion pictures of the suspect be shot that very afternoon and forwarded to England by air courier. In the meantime, Clegg and Lamphere were ordered by cable to prolong their interview with Fuchs "as long as possible without interruption." The reason for this urgency was that Belmont very much wanted to have Fuchs's confirmation before going public about Gold. But the strategy did not work. Fuchs did not even see the new photos and movies until the morning of May 24, London time. By this time, of course, Gold had already signed his full confession. Fortunately for the FBI, which was already committed to Gold as their man, Fuchs readily agreed that the individual in the new, sharper pictures was Raymond. "That is him," he told Clegg and Lamphere, "my American contact."

Curious about this discrepancy between the account of Fuchs's identification cooked up by the Bureau for public consumption and the evidence in the Bureau's own files, we spoke with ex-FBI agent Robert Lamphere a second time, in January 1982. Lamphere began our conversation by repeating the Hoover version that Fuchs's positive identification and Gold's confession had occurred just minutes apart. When we informed him that this was not the sequence revealed in the files, Lamphere expressed incredulity and then insisted that he didn't "remember that timing thing. The whole pressure of the world was on my shoulders to get that thing wrapped up." Nevertheless, Lamphere was adamant that Fuchs had not been informed that Harry Gold had already confessed. For that matter, he denied that either he or Clegg knew about it.

Although Lamphere appeared to be honestly trying to recall the details of an event that had occurred three decades before, the documentary evidence suggests his memory was playing tricks on him. The May 22 cable from London—the cable that Lamphere remembered—had only established Fuchs's imprecise identification of Gold as a man "very like" Raymond. Moreover, it is difficult to believe that Bureau headquarters would have kept their agents in London uninformed about Gold's confession. Klaus Fuchs had been reluctant all along to play the role of an informer, and one can only wonder whether his sudden ability to "recognize" Raymond did not have something to do with the knowledge that Gold had already confessed, thus removing the onus of responsibility from himself.

Hoover's press aides were guilty of misleading the public about the facts of Gold's capture. However, this does not justify the more sweeping charges of some Rosenberg-case critics who have claimed that Gold was not Raymond and that Fuchs *never* identified him as such. It is one thing to suggest that Klaus Fuchs was reluctant to help the FBI track down a man who had once been his ally and quite another to suggest that the convicted spy knowingly identified the wrong man and then sat back in silence while Gold went on to wrongfully accuse other innocent parties. Everything that is known about Fuchs suggests that he adhered meticulously to his own standard of honor, such as it was. Moreover, the information that Fuchs gave Clegg and Lamphere prior to May 22 about his dealings with Raymond squares all too well with the story Gold poured out in his first statement to agents Miller and Brennan. The corollary charge that Harry Gold was gradually primed by his FBI interrogators with facts that had come from Fuchs is equally unsupportable. Gold was ripe for confession and once he started talking, he gave the essential outline of his career as Raymond in a single signed and witnessed statement.

When Harry Gold broke down in the presence of Scott Miller and Richard Brennan, he clung to the hope that he would be able to confess his role as Raymond without implicating the other espionage contacts he had dealt with over the years. As he later told his court-appointed lawyers, he had not wanted to "turn 'rat' and 'squealer.' " But Gold, who was described by Brennan and Miller as being "in a highly emotional state," was no match for his interrogators. He had not been in custody for twenty-four hours before he unintentionally provided that first link in the chain that would eventually lead the Bureau to two more suspects: David and Ruth Greenglass.

Certainly the FBI had no intention of allowing Gold to get away with anything less than a full account of his activities. Immediately upon learning that Gold had agreed to talk, A. H. Belmont in Washington cabled instructions to the Philadelphia office on how to handle their prize catch. Gold was to be "exhaustively interviewed for all information in his possession," in particular for "descriptions of his contacts in the espionage field." In doing this the agents were to question Gold closely about his travels, aliases used, "hotels where he stopped, etc. . . . to permit us to establish verification of his story through investigation." Belmont, naturally, expressed a special interest in learning about "other persons engaged in espionage at Los Alamos or at any other locations."

Gold could not withstand this intensive grilling for long. The seven-page statement that he dictated on May 22 named no contacts apart from Fuchs. In the course of enumerating his meetings with Fuchs, however, Gold mentioned that on two occasions—in June and September 1945—he had passed through Albuquerque, New Mexico, on his way to assignations in Santa Fe. Gold said that during the course of the September journey, he had stayed overnight at the Albuquerque Hilton. And of the June trip he said:

> I travelled to Albuquerque on this first meeting via train to Chicago then by train to Albuquerque, and finally by bus to Santa Fe. My meeting with Dr. Fuchs was on Saturday afternoon. Then I returned from Santa Fe to Albuquerque by bus that same day. As I recall, I slept in the hallway of a rooming house where those who were unable to obtain local hotel accommodations were bedded.

This passage in Gold's statement may have raised the same questions in the minds of his interrogators that later occurred to those who wished to challenge Gold's story. To reach Santa Fe from Chicago, it is not necessary to travel via Albuquerque. Why had Gold planned his itinerary in this way?

Gold did have a specific reason for arranging his travel plans to take him to Albuquerque, but not until June 1, 1950, did he reveal what it had been. By this time, Gold had realized that it would be impossible for him to draw the line at talking about Fuchs. A Bureau memorandum prepared by agent C. E. Hennrich reveals that on that day, Gold announced he was prepared to name three individuals besides Fuchs who were implicated in espionage.

The first person Gold spoke about was Alfred Dean Slack—or

Al Slack, as he called him—a man he had described in earlier interrogations only as Martin from Rochester. Gold told the agents that he had contacted Slack seven times at various places including Rochester, New York; Kingsport, Tennessee; and Oak Ridge, Tennessee. Slack, he said, had given him information on explosives and photographic processes.

The third man Gold mentioned was his old friend Thomas Black. Gold identified Black as the person who had recruited him to espionage work by introducing him in 1936 to the Soviet agent Gold knew as Paul Smith.

Gold could not remember the name of the second man. According to agent Hennrich's memo, he described him in this way:

> ... A soldier, non-commissioned, married, no children (name not recalled.) Gold stated that he contacted this individual at Albuquerque, New Mexico on the trip to Santa Fe, when he met Fuchs in September of 1945, when he, Gold, stayed at the Hilton Hotel. He picked up information from this soldier described by Gold as "general information on installation." He states that if supplied with a map of Albuquerque, New Mexico, he can show where this soldier lived. He paid the soldier $500 for the information obtained.

During the same interrogation Gold added that he had sought out the soldier on Saturday night, found no one at home, and returned on Sunday morning. He said that he had used "the name Frank Kessler in his meeting with the soldier," whom he believed to be a native of the Bronx or Brooklyn. Gold also recalled that the soldier had told him that he would be returning to New York soon on furlough. In parting, the soldier had given him "the address of his mother-in-law or father-in-law in New York City for a possible future meeting."

This was precisely the kind of information the agents had been told to concentrate on, and they wasted no time in following up the lead. Questioned again the next day, Gold still could not remember the soldier's name, but he was able to fill in many more details about the meeting. These are recorded in two documents—a signed statement made by Gold to agents Richard E. Brennan and T. Scott Miller, Jr., dated June 2, and an FBI memo from assistant FBI director D. M. ("Mickey") Ladd to Hoover.

Gold's statement begins by recalling how he had met his Soviet contact "John" (Anatoli Yakovlev) in New York "to discuss plans for my departure for New Mexico." In the course of this meeting John had given Gold the name and address of the Albuquerque soldier along with an envelope containing $500, to be handed over in exchange for the expected information only if the soldier were to "indicate a need for funds."

> Of his visit to the soldier, Gold said: I cannot remember this man's name, but I believe he lived on the second or third floor of a house, the exact address of which I cannot remember. It was, however, somewhere north of East Central Ave., one or two blocks north and somewhere between N. High Street and N. Pine Street.

Also, Gold now corrected himself on one key point: his meeting with the soldier had taken place during the course of his June 1945 stopover in Albuquerque and *not* the one in September. He also expressed some doubt as to whether he had used either the name Frank Kessler or Frank Martin. But he did stress that "I used some form of recognition, involving the first name of a man, and stating that he had sent me. This individual recognized the password."

Gold told agents Brennan and Miller that when he had visited the soldier's apartment on Sunday afternoon he had been given an envelope with three to five pages of written information and "possibly one sketch." He recalled that the data dealt with a description of Los Alamos and "some bit of structural equipment of a machine," and that the soldier himself was a draftsman, machinist, electrician, or worker in a physics laboratory. Once again, Gold recalled that the GI had suggested meeting in New York during his upcoming furlough and mentioned his father-in-law in the Bronx whose name "may have been Philip."

Asked for a physical description of the GI, Gold remembered him as being not more than twenty-five years old, five feet seven inches, sturdily built, with dark brown or black curly hair, a snub nose and a wide mouth (a description that fits David Greenglass quite well). And, most important, Gold recalled meeting the soldier's wife and that "her name may have been Ruth, although I am not sure."

In his summarizing memo to Hoover, deputy director Ladd concluded that Gold had now provided them with "a fairly detailed description" of the unidentified GI, adding that Gold had indicated that the subject had a Bronx or Brooklyn accent, was probably Jewish, and had been recently married at the time of the 1945 meeting. Ladd also expressed the opinion that Gold would be able to identify the subject's Albuquerque residence from maps or motion pictures.

But Ladd was wrong about one thing. His memo ends by citing agent Scott Miller's judgment that "Theodore Hall, subject of an espionage case, who was at one time at Los Alamos, might be identical with this individual."

This statement is highly significant because it indicates that the agents who interviewed Harry Gold in Philadelphia on June 2, 1950, had never heard of David Greenglass. The Greenglass name was to enter the case later that same day, but only because it happened to come to the attention of FBI personnel in New Mexico who had been assigned to check Los Alamos records in search of individuals who might fit the description given by Harry Gold.

Actually, the FBI's quick identification of David Greenglass as a "logical suspect" in the Harry Gold case was something of a fluke. It occurred only because Greenglass had been among a group of veterans questioned in January 1950 in connection with a routine investigation spurred by the belated discovery that Manhattan Project workers had made a practice of pilfering small amounts of uranium for souvenirs. When the agents noticed Greenglass's name on a list of those who had been interviewed in this connection, and discovered that he had a wife named Ruth and had lived at 209 North High Street, it occurred to them that they might have stumbled across the very man they were looking for.

One day later, on June 3, Harry Gold was shown two photographs of David Greenglass—a 1940 graduation picture and a new surveillance photo, snapped without Greenglass's knowledge. To the agents' disappointment, Gold could say only that the graduation photo "resembled" the man he had met in Albuquerque. As a Bureau teletype explains, "based upon the fact that Gold had no knowledge of unsub [unidentified subject] prior to his contact with him and had but two brief associations with him on June third [1945] ... Gold had been cautious and hesitant in making positive identification."

By the end of their June 3 session the Philadelphia Bureau felt that Gold had been "milked dry." They urged that Greenglass, who was then in New York, be picked up for questioning immediately. Gold had suggested that the "unsub" had at least one other contact who had never been identified, and thus might be a link to a larger operation. However, the FBI still had a very weak case at this point, as they themselves admitted. "Even considering the most profitable outcome of outstanding leads," the agents explained, "the case is not strong legally from a point of proof of espionage or conspiracy because of lack of corroboration."

In spite of pleas from the Philadelphia office, David Greenglass was not questioned immediately. But within the week Gold did give the agents the more positive identification they were looking for. As Ladd had proposed, the Bureau had taken moving pictures of David Greenglass's former house at 209 North High Street. The appearance of the building had changed considerably between 1945 and 1950; in the course of remodeling, the front porch Harry Gold remembered had been removed and a new living room built on. When he was shown the movies for the first time, Gold had found the house unrecognizable. By June 7, however, he had picked it out as "that most clearly resembling the house he visited in June of 1945."

A week later, on June 15, 1950, Gold was shown some photos of Greenglass that had been taken five years earlier. Gold immediately identified these 1945 snapshots. He signed the back of each photo, and made the statement that "This is the man I contacted in Albuquerque, New Mexico in June, 1945, on instructions from my Soviet espionage superior, 'JOHN.' The man in the picture gave me information relative to his work at Los Alamos, New Mexico, which information I later gave to 'JOHN.' "

On that same day, the FBI called in David Greenglass for questioning. Apart from Gold's word, there was still no hard evidence against Greenglass, and the Bureau could only hope that they would be able to glean some corroborating information. They succeeded beyond their wildest dreams. In his very first interview, Greenglass admitted that, as a machinist stationed at the Los Alamos atom-bomb facility during the war, he had passed information to Gold. In addition, he implicated his twenty-six-year-old wife, Ruth, and his brother-in-law, Julius Rosenberg.

3

"Either Convert Our Friends or Drop Them"

In October 1949, shortly after word of Klaus Fuchs's imminent arrest went out to the KGB's American network, David Greenglass was warned by his brother-in-law Julius Rosenberg that he might soon have to flee the country. When the time came, their Russian "friends" would take care of all the necessary arrangements, Julius promised. David could take his wife and children with him, and there would be a good job waiting for him somewhere in the Soviet bloc.

Greenglass at first thought that Julius was being melodramatic. It was four years since he had cooperated in the theft of information about the construction of the atomic bomb, and he could hardly believe that anyone was going to make a big deal out of that now. After all, everything he had done had been for the good of the war effort.

In 1949 Greenglass was still struggling to pick up the threads of the civilian life that had been interrupted by his service in the army. Except for those years in the service, he had lived all his life in the same Lower East Side neighborhood, and he had no desire to settle anywhere else. The prospect of taking his wife and children behind the Iron Curtain, of saying good-bye forever to America, was simply overwhelming. The first thought that popped into his head was: "If I go, I'll never read 'Li'l Abner' again."

David Greenglass's refusal to take his brother-in-law's warning seriously was entirely in character. Only twenty-seven, Greenglass was a brash young man who acted first and considered the consequences of his actions later—if at all. He came from a milieu where the Communist Party's view of world affairs was accepted as dogma and he had had almost no liberal education, having gone straight from junior high to a specialized aviation high school and from there to Brooklyn Polytechnic Institute. In the judgment of one of his supervisors at Los Alamos, he was a "loudmouth," always spouting half-baked political ideas, but his skill as a machinist made up for his sometimes irritating personality. In his personal life, Greenglass was inclined to form fierce loyalties—to his wife, his children, and, for a time, to communism. However, his relations with his brother-in-law Julius had been strained for some time, partly because he felt that Julius put ideology ahead of the interests of his family and business. Thirty years later, a gray-haired prosperous-looking suburbanite, David Greenglass is able to look back on his younger self with considerable detachment: "I was young, stupid, and immature, but I was a good Communist."

The youngest in a family of four children, David—or "Doovey" as he was called at home—grew up on Sheriff Street on New York's Lower East Side in an unheated tenement flat furnished with little more than the smell of his mother's baking and, in later years, the stacks of political tracts that his sister, Ethel, brought home by the armful. His father, Barnet Greenglass, was a gentle, soft-spoken man who spent most of his time in his sewing-machine repair shop, which was located on the ground floor below the family apartment. Home was dominated by the clash of personalities between David's mother, Tessie, and his sister, Ethel, who was seven years his elder. Tessie Greenglass had two interests in life: religion, which she had plenty of, and financial security, which she could only hope to live to see her children achieve. Her only daughter, Ethel, who was bright enough to see the limitations of her mother's way of thinking at an early age, rebelled by becoming enamored of the theater. Doovey was usually the only audience present during their frequent arguments, and the two women competed for his approval.

Ethel Greenglass, born in 1915, was a formidable older sister. Plain, slightly dumpy, and not conspicuously talented either as an actress or a singer, she nevertheless exuded determination that made others respect her. As a schoolgirl, she never had time for friends or hanging around the neighborhood. There was always homework to be done, books to be read, or a school play, in which she was invariably the leading lady. She skipped several grades and, at fifteen, graduated from Seward Park High School into a shattered economy in which a job advertisement in the newspaper could attract enough desperate applicants to start a riot. Undaunted, Ethel had a job within a month of receiving her diploma, going to work as a clerk in the office of a shipping company. And she kept that job for four years—until she was fired for organizing 150 women co-workers in a strike that culminated in the women lying down in the middle of Thirty-sixth Street to block the way of the company's delivery trucks. After losing her job, she promptly did two things: filed a complaint with the National Labor Relations Board, which she won, and found a better job that paid twice the salary.

Nor was Ethel one to waste her spare time. In the evenings, she starred in a neighborhood amateur theatrical group, took singing lessons, and became the youngest member of a respected amateur chorus, the Schola Cantorum, which gave concerts in Carnegie Hall. She also made the rounds of the vaudeville amateur nights, always singing the same song, "Ciribiribin." Since she had a pleasant if badly trained voice and a woeful expression that won the sympathy of the audience, she usually came out a prizewinner. Some weeks she made more money singing than she did at her job at the shipping company, and she even did a turn on national radio as a contestant on the Major Bowes Amateur Hour. Ethel, in short, was a go-getter; but nothing she did earned her a word of praise from Tessie Greenglass, who berated her for not having a beau and covered her ears as if in pain when Ethel practiced her singing.

Just about the time that her rendition of "Ciribiribin" was beginning to run out of potential audiences, Ethel did a New Year's Eve benefit for the International Seamen's Union. There, while waiting to go on stage, she met the one and only love of her life, Julius Rosenberg.

Like Ethel Greenglass, Julius Rosenberg was a product of the Lower East Side. His father, Harry, an immigrant from Poland, had gone to work as a garment industry sample maker. His mother, Sophie, also an immigrant, had been too busy caring for her five children ever to learn to read and write English. Julius himself had attended the Downtown Talmud Torah, the same religious school where Ethel had been a pupil, and had graduated from Seward Park High School. But unlike Ethel's family, which seemed permanently mired in poverty and bad luck, the Rosenbergs were upwardly mobile. Since 1929 they had lived in the Lavanberg Homes, a housing project that boasted central steam heat, still a luxury for dwellers in the surrounding tenement blocks. Julius had never been under pressure to quit school and go to work like so many of his Seward Park classmates; Harry Rosenberg was proud of his son's studious bent and hoped that Julius would eventually become a rabbi. As a boy, Julius had shown signs that he would follow his father's wishes. He was a quiet, serious youth, promising enough in his Hebrew studies to make a lasting impression on several of his teachers at Talmud Torah. But by his senior year in high school, he had found a passion: politics.

By the time he graduated from high school at age sixteen, Julius had decided against rabbinical studies and in favor of entering the City College of New York, where he chose to major in electrical engineering. Engineering was scientific and practical, a logical choice for a student who felt most at home with hard facts. It also happened to be a major much favored by more politically aware students since it would entitle them to membership in the Federation of Architects, Engineers, Chemists and Technicians (FAECT), a militant union for white-collar professionals with a pro-Communist leadership.

Julius soon became firmly established as part of a small group of engineering and science students who made up the active core of the Steinmetz Club, the campus branch of the Young Communist League, or YCL. "Julie" was by no means the group's intellectual star or even its natural leader. He was not a brilliant student like his friend William Mutterperl (who later changed his name to William Perl). Nor did he have the charm and self-confidence of Joel Barr, another member of the in-crowd. But in the endless political arguments that went on over tepid cups of coffee in the alcoves of the CCNY main building, he was noticed. Fellow students who chanced to disagree with him found him a doctrinaire and inflexible opponent; however, his friends admired his ability to verbally demolish the occasional Trotskyist troublemaker bold enough to venture into their alcove. Julie was to be affectionately remembered as a stalwart who never missed a leafleting session, a demonstration, or a meeting.

By the time he began dating Ethel Greenglass, Julius was spending so much time on political activities that his graduation was in jeopardy. When they began to get serious, Ethel insisted that he drop his friends for the time being and spend his evenings studying at her family's Sheriff Street apartment. Ethel was hardly unusual in wanting to make sure that her future husband did not throw away his chances for a college degree, but her success in getting Julius to stick to the books aroused the resentment of some of his YCL friends, who groused that Julie was allowing himself to be bossed around by an older woman. (Ethel was twenty-one to Julius's eighteen.) Ethel, whose strong will was apparent to everyone who met her, was assumed to be the dominant personality of the couple—an impression that would later work to her disadvantage.

Julius's own family was not at all enthusiastic about the direction he had chosen, and he and Ethel spent more and more of their free hours in her kitchen, studying and talking. As a result, David Greenglass, just fourteen in 1936, came to regard Julius almost as an older brother. Julius encouraged David's interest in science with gifts of books and a chemistry set and, of course, he talked to the teenager about politics, encouraging him to join the Young Communist League. David eventually joined up, at first mostly for the chance to play in the YCL handball league.

Julius graduated from CCNY in 1939, a semester behind the rest of his class, and he and Ethel were married that same summer. The couple moved into one room of a tiny apartment in the Williamsburg section of Brooklyn, where they shared kitchen facilities with their cotenants, the Marcus Pogarskys. After struggling along for some months doing free-lance work, Julius was hired as a civilian employee of the U.S. Army Signal Corps in the fall of 1940. In 1942, he was promoted to the position of engineer inspector. The job required him to travel throughout New York and New Jersey inspecting electronics parts produced by private industry under contract to the Signal Corps. But, in compensation for the travel, the higher salary enabled the Rosenbergs to move into their first real home, a three-room apartment in the new Knickerbocker Village housing project on the Lower East Side.

With Ethel's marriage to Julius, David Greenglass, just seventeen, had become the last child left at home. David finished high school and enrolled in Brooklyn Polytechnic Institute, but his idea of becoming a scientist soon took second place to the need to earn money. He dropped out of Polytechnic after one semester and soon began dreaming of saving enough to get a place of his own and marry his sweetheart, a neighborhood girl named Ruth Printz. By the fall of 1942, David and Ruth realized that if they did not marry soon the war might force them to postpone their plans indefinitely. An older Greenglass brother, Bernie, was already in the service, and David expected that he would be drafted at any time. The wedding took place at the end of November, and David and Ruth moved to a cold-water flat on Stanton Street, just blocks away from their childhood homes.

At the beginning of 1943 both the Rosenbergs and the Greenglasses were passionate believers in communism. David and Ruth, just twenty and eighteen years old respectively, were still members of the Young Communist League. Julius and Ethel, meanwhile, had graduated to full membership in the Communist Party and Julius, always a dedicated activist, had become chairman of Branch 16B of the Party's Industrial Division. The group regularly held its meetings in his and Ethel's new apartment.

It was the era of the second Popular Front, when Party members were being urged to do everything in their power to support the war effort. Communist leader Earl Browder stressed that Party membership was thoroughly compatible with American patriotism, and the wartime alliance between the United States and the Soviet Union lent credibility to his assertions. Hollywood movies like *Song of Russia* and *Mission to Moscow*, reflecting a utopian view of the Soviet Union, were being made with the official blessing of the U.S. government, and such conservative figures as Winston Churchill and General Douglas MacArthur heaped praise on our heroic Russian allies. President Roosevelt had even accepted an honorary membership in FAECT.

When David Greenglass was inducted into the army in April, he felt that his coming stint in the service would be a contribution not just to his country, but to the ultimate triumph of socialism. He even looked forward to military service as an opportunity to recruit his fellow GI's to the Communist cause.

With so many of the Party's other activities in labor organizing and civil rights curtailed for the duration of the war, service in the armed forces remained one of the few ways that dedicated Party members could feel they were making a significant contribution. But the army was not an option for Julius Rosenberg. Long subject to bothersome allergies and respiratory infections, Rosenberg probably could not have passed the army physical even if he had tried to enlist. In any case, his civil-service job with the Signal Corps carried an automatic exemption; as a graduate engineer he was too valuable to be spared.

Although Julius Rosenberg remained at his Signal Corps job, 1943 did mark a major change in his life. Sometime late in that year, he and Ethel quietly dropped out of the Party activities that had been so important to them since they were teenagers. And the following February, when Branch 16B was dissolved as part of a routine Party reorganization, they alone of the old members failed to take up their new assignment to a neighborhood Party club.

It is easy to imagine a perfectly innocent explanation for the Rosenbergs' decision to leave the Party. Ethel had given birth to her first child in the spring of 1943, and Julius had a demanding government job, which would be threatened if his Communist affiliation came to light. They would certainly not be the first young marrieds to discover that their growing professional and family responsibilities left them with neither the time nor the taste for political activism.

However, Ruth Greenglass would later charge that her in-laws had dropped out for quite different motives. Ruth would claim that sometime in 1943 Julius confided to her that he had begun to feel he was "slated for" something better than routine Party work. Julius had decided, said Ruth, that "he would rather do something active than be active in the Party itself." He told her that he had begun, on his own initiative, to try to make contact with someone who could help him enter a new line of activity. David Greenglass would charge even more pointedly that earlier that year, before he left for the army, Julius had begun to talk to him, always in abstract terms, about the subject of espionage.

Which explanation of the Rosenbergs' defection from the Party is the correct one?

It is true that the Rosenbergs' political affiliations had caused trouble for Julius with the Signal Corps and would do so again. In the spring of 1941, not long after Julius went to work for the Corps, a routine loyalty check had uncovered the fact that Ethel had signed a Communist Party nominating petition in 1939 and that the couple the Rosenbergs lived with in Brooklyn were active Communists. Faced with this information, Rosenberg, according to hearing records, made a spirited defense, pointing out quite rightly that his wife's and his friends' actions should not be held against him: "Even if [Ethel] did sign a petition, I don't see how that would affect me. After all, she is a different person and has rights." Rosenberg managed to avoid having to swear under oath that he was not a Party member, though it is obvious in retrospect that some of his statements to the hearing officers fell short of complete candor. "I am quite sure she [Ethel] is no Communist," Rosenberg said. "We never discuss politics, but I am quite sure her views are similar to my own."

Not long after, at a follow-up hearing held on March 8, 1941, Rosenberg admitted that his wife had signed the nominating petition, but only as a favor to a stranger who came to her door collecting signatures. Julius also argued that dismissal would be especially unfair since out of loyalty to the Signal Corps he had recently turned down an offer of a better job—as a junior aeronautical engineer working for the National Advisory Committee for Aeronautics at Langley Field, Virginia. Explained Rosenberg:

> I talked it over with my wife and . . . I decided that I did not want to appear to be running out under fire. Besides, I feel under obligation to the Department. It takes two solid months of training for a Radio Inspector to do any work at all. Besides they have been very good there to me. My health has been a little bad lately. I have had a lot of boils due to a lack of iron in my system. I have to take special injections every day and they have kept me on work in the city and not sent me away on any work.

The hearing officers apparently agreed that there was no reason to lose a perfectly qualified engineer just because his wife had once signed a petition. Rosenberg retained his job and the matter was dropped.

The Rosenbergs had no further warning of problems with Julius's government employment until the beginning of 1945 or, at the earliest, the end of 1944. Sometime previous to this, the FBI had forwarded to U.S. Army Intelligence a photostatic copy of a Communist Party membership card showing that one Julius Rosenberg had been inducted into the Party on December 12, 1939. The Army did not feel there was sufficient evidence to show that the holder of the card was the same Julius Rosenberg who was a Signal Corps employee. But in the fall of 1944, the FBI supplied a second photostat—this time reflecting Rosenberg's transfer to the East Side Party Club, a transfer which in fact he had never taken up. The second card confirmed Rosenberg's address, and so Army Intelligence ordered a loyalty investigation. On the basis of a report completed in February 1945, Rosenberg was dismissed.

The dismissal became something of a cause célèbre because a Signal Corps intelligence officer, Captain John W. Henderson, was sympathetic enough to show Rosenberg a summary of the file prepared by security investigators. The summary did not reveal that the Army actually had documentary evidence of Rosenberg's CP membership, but it did list, as a strike against him, his membership in FAECT. Rosenberg reported this to his union, which fired off indignant protests to the War Department. Captain Henderson received a reprimand, and the Army took the position that the comments about FAECT had been confidential background information and were unrelated to the eventual cause of the firing.

The timing of these two incidents with the Signal Corps shows that they could not have been the specific cause of the Rosenbergs' decision to drop out of the Party in the winter of 1943–44. Nor is there any hint that the Rosenbergs had been worried at that time about the impact of their political activities or that they had become disaffected from their former activism. But, as several former well-placed Party members have confirmed, the Rosenbergs' disappearance from Party functions fit the pattern followed by those who were tapped for some form of secret work. Our most cautious source was Max Gordon, a reporter and senior editor of the *Daily Worker* during the 1940s and 1950s. Gordon told us that he had no specific knowledge of whether the Rosenbergs had ever been engaged in espionage but that their abrupt departure from the Party ranks was consistent with this interpretation. "By and large, anyone who became a spy for the Soviet Union was completely separated from the Party," Gordon told us. "In the main, they [the Soviets] recruited their spies not from Party people, but they may have recruited some from Party people, too. A guy who was a dedicated guy . . . might have offered his services, and if he was involved in electronics, he might have felt he was useful in that regard." When asked if he thought that this was what happened in the case of Julius Rosenberg, Gordon could only say, "That's possible. I wouldn't toss it out."

A far more decided opinion was offered by John Gates, who was editor-in-chief of the *Daily Worker* at the time and later became one of the first wave of Communist leaders to be tried and sentenced under the Smith Act. "Julius Rosenberg was very active in City College . . . and one fine day he disappeared. We knew there was only one explanation . . . in our movement at the time. It could have been for only one reason, since he certainly hadn't changed his political views." And that reason, Gates made clear, was espionage.

In support of his statement, Gates recalled that when the Rosenbergs left the Party their subscription to the *Daily Worker* was also canceled, not in the regular manner by the subscription department but by a direct order from the Party's Central Committee. Gates's memory was confirmed for us by Junius Scales, an ex-Communist who had been chairman of the North Carolina Communist Party. When a Party member was recruited for espionage, Gates told us, "one of the surefire things was that their subs to the *Worker* and the *Daily Worker* were canceled." And Scales recalled hearing from a colleague at the time that the Rosenbergs quit the Party that "the task [of canceling their subscriptions] was handled at the very highest level at the time. It wasn't done routinely." Because he had been told this, Scales was not surprised when Julius and Ethel Rosenberg were later arrested on spy charges. "I had no doubt about the involvement of the Rosenbergs," he assured us.

The recollections of these former Party functionaries provide circumstantial corroboration for the Greenglasses' version of events. More direct evidence is found in a series of letters exchanged by David and Ruth Greenglass during the period between his induction into the army in April 1943 and the fall of 1944. These letters were seized by the FBI during the course of a search of the Greenglass apartment in June 1950; they were never used in court and their very existence remained unsuspected until they were released by the government along with other Rosenberg case documents in 1975.*

The Greenglass correspondence directly contradicts Julius Rosenberg's later assertion under oath that he knew nothing about the atomic-bomb project or his brother-in-law's role until after the Hiroshima explosion at the earliest—and that he had no firm memory of

---

*This valuable source, unavailable to previous researchers on the case, has been examined by the authors in two versions—a typed transcript prepared by FBI stenographers and a set of photocopies of the handwritten originals.

discussing it until after the war ended. At the same time, the letters also undercut the Greenglasses' later portrayal of themselves as having been naïve and malleable youngsters who were caught off guard when a trusted older relative suddenly invited them to join an espionage conspiracy. The story that unfolds is quite a different one—of a fervently Communist GI, eager at first to proselytize for the Party among his peers, and later just as eager to take part in a "project" that sounds very much like espionage.

The Greenglass correspondence begins on April 28, 1943, shortly after David's induction. From the very first, David's declarations of love for Ruth inevitably merged with expressions of his political enthusiasm:

> Although I'd love to have you in my arms I am content without so long as there is a vital battle to be fought with a cruel, ruthless foe. Victory shall be ours and the future is socialism's.

On May 1, while enrolled in army machinist's school in Aberdeen, Maryland, David wrote, striving to impress Ruth with the superior intelligence of the new friends he was making. Intelligent they may have been, but the reality was that Greenglass had little interest in friendships that might expose him to new ideas and experiences. He was still choosing his friends only from among those who shared his political beliefs and read little that did not explicitly hew to the Party line:

> While at Fort Dix I met four comrades and boy they were tops in their respective lines. One of them had 150 I.Q. out of a possible 153. We made quite a group ... but I never had a chance to finish an argument. ... By the way darling I read and enjoyed your letters and also the clippings from PM you had put in. I'd like to see some clippings from the Daily Worker too. Something like Mike Gold or Sender Garlin or the "Veteran Commander." I really miss them.

Ruth, in a letter dated the very next day, May 2, strove to keep up her husband's spirits by describing the annual May Day rally in Union Square. (May Day also happened to be Ruth's birthday, a coincidence that Julius always teased her about.)

Well darling here it is Sunday and I went to the rally. Well sweetheart all I can say is that I am sorry I missed so many other May Days when I had the opportunity to march side by side with you. The spirit of the people was magnificent. . . . I'm going to buy tomorrow's Worker and send you the writeup on it. I almost forgot to tell you this. On the subway on the way to the stadium five girls came on the platform singing and harmonizing beautifully. The melodies struck a chord in my mind and suddenly I remembered the film we saw of the Russian folk dances and music. Remember at the Stanley Theater and again at the Irving Place. These girls were singing Russian folk songs and everyone on the platform crowded around to hear. . . . Perhaps the voices of 75,000 working men and women that were brought together today, perhaps their voices demanding an early invasion of Europe will be heard and then my dear we will be together to build—under socialism—our future. . . .

As David's army superiors later confirmed in their interviews with FBI investigators, his constant proselytizing sometimes led to friction between him and his superior officers. One such incident may have inspired the advice Ruth passed along on May 26:

Dearest, remember what Julie told you, as a Communist it's up to you to set an example to the other soldiers and you can't do that if an officer has a grudge against you.

Whatever the problem may have been on this particular occasion, it must not have had serious consequences. A few days later, David was in a cheerful frame of mind, filled with hope for the ultimate victory of Marxism:

Although we are materialists we base our materialism on humanity and humanity is love. It is the most powerful force in the world. It is causing us to win where we are outnumbered. The victory shall be ours. The freedom shall be greater because of our great feeling that only democratic and freedom-loving peoples can foster. Darling, we who understand can bring understanding to others because we are in love and have our Marxist outlook.

On July 14, Ruth replied with the first of several letters keeping David informed about organizational changes that were just then reshaping the Communist movement:

> I saw Ida tonight and she gave me a report of what happened at the branch president's meeting. There is a new program afoot now. The YCL will disband and we'll form some sort of youth, anti-fascist, win-the-war club on a national scale. I think this was suggested principally because many people shy away from our club because of "Communist" in our club name. It seems they're afraid of political entanglement and its antagonism is very old and set. Therefore the plan is to form the type of group I mentioned and try to draw all youth into it to make them aware of what we're fighting for. The Communists from the Party will still try to recruit into the Party but there will be no YCL. . . . Darling, do you remember one Florence . . .? Well the other day she walked into our office and she says she has known me for the longest time. She told me that she knows you. She claims she was once sent from Club Monroe to recruit you. Do you know her? Also, did you belong to Monroe or only Colin Kelly, and how long have you been a member of the League. That's just a by the way I'd like to know.

David, having been promoted from private to corporal and again to T/5 (Technician Fifth Class), was still hoping to convert his entire unit to communism:

> Darling, during lunch I had two discussions on political questions with some fellows. I used the utmost patience and care in the choice of words so that I could get my point across and still not be suspected of Communism. Well, I believe that I did get something across to them and I will continue to work on them further. I'll raise the red flag yet so don't worry about the future.

Although there was an obvious element of naïveté in David's talk of raising the red flag over his unit, he was not as out of touch with reality as the comment might suggest. In 1943 and 1944, the Communist Party had more members than at any other point in its history and was gaining new recruits at the rate of several thousand a week, thanks largely to Earl Browder's policy of vigorous support for the war effort and for the reelection of Roosevelt.

Ruth, too, felt that she had a mission to politicize her friends. Although she later told the FBI that she had attended meetings of her Young Communist League club only "spasmodically" and become its president for a time only because of her relationship to Ethel, Ruth was finding it difficult to get along with friends who did not share her devotion to the cause. On September 19, she wrote:

> Phyllis finished dressing first so she and Herbie came to Diana's house to wait for her. I don't quite remember how it happened but before I knew it the conversation took a sudden turn and we were all discussing current events. It didn't take much time for me to notice that they were all anti-Soviet. They started shooting questions at me until I asked why I was being cross-examined. Phyllis piped up, "as president of the YCL you should know the answer." I have no idea how she found out about it but there was such scathing sarcasm in her voice that I picked up my head in surprise. . . . They think I have a private wire to get information daily from Joe Stalin himself. I saw that I wasn't able to cope with these characters so I changed the subject. . . .

Three months later, Ruth was still smarting about various political disagreements she had been having with old friends from the neighborhood. David wrote back offering comfort and advice:

> Darling, you are right it is our twisted phsycollogy [*sic*] that is due in the greater part to our "social structure," namely, capitalism with its economic hold on everyone, teaching them to grasp what they can and giving them no real future to look to. Dearest, at present we are fighting a war to give people a chance at least. I hope that we can do away with the rotten structure as quickly as possible. . . . Dearest, you are no snob, what you say is true and there are only two ways to look at it. Either convert our friends or drop them. And I don't believe in giving up easily, do you.

Again, in January 1944, David wrote Ruth bringing her up to date on his recent reading:

> I am reading another book called "What Makes Sammy Run" by SCHULMAN [*sic*] and so far it is pretty good. Darling,

is the Random House Publishers the Party press? You see that is
the publisher of this book. . . .

David obviously did not realize that Budd Schulberg's famous
novel was published by a major New York publisher. Anything "progressive," he assumed, had to emanate from the Party. And later in
this same letter, David reiterated an earlier request for a subscription
to the New York *Post*, a major afternoon daily known at the time for
its liberal, prolabor stance. Apparently Ruth had to be reassured that
the *Post* was suitable reading material:

> Sweetheart, that comrade in the shop doesn't realize that
> we have sort of a united front with all anti-fascist groups and
> therefore the Post comes under that heading. I like certain col-
> umns in it and I'd rather read it than the Herald Tribune or
> Sun. . . . So darling, a subscription to the Post is what I want in
> view of the fact that a Worker would just about put me in the
> guard house.

In a letter mailed on the same date, Ruth wrote of her vision of
the future:

> Still I hope that our children will be brought up in a social-
> ist world and our money will be useless, I look forward to that
> day when necessities and luxuries are to be had by all and sun-
> dry just so long as he justifies living by work. . . . I am reading
> "Battle Hymn of China" and I am certainly enjoying it, it's a
> powerful book. Darling a lot of the things you told me about
> China (things that never appear in the press) when you were try-
> ing to convert me I'm reading in this book.

A week later, on January 10, Ruth sent David more news of the
organizational changes taking place within the Communist movement. In keeping with his belief that Communists ought to mute
their revolutionary rhetoric and work to bring about Soviet-American friendship in the postwar era, Browder had decided that the
Communist Party was to be reconstituted as the Communist Political
Association. Ruth attended the rally where this impending change
was announced in public for the first time:

> I went to the meeting at the Garden tonight and somehow I
> missed Ethel. I don't know. I'm going to call her tomorrow and

find out. The meeting was very good as you can imagine. Browder, Amter, Elizabeth Gurley Flynn, Clayton Powell and some others spoke.

Have you heard that the Communist Party may dissolve? As Browder put it tonight, when the war is over the people won't be ready to accept socialism and all its reforms and to offer it to them may alienate it more than ever.... The central committees of the parties have proposed that the Party dissolve and a committee of political education be formed. However, this is only a proposal and will probably not be acted on before May of this year. Still it is a thought and deserves every consideration.

Many younger Communists and YCLers, particularly those who had been attracted to the Party because of its support for civil rights and the labor movement, favored the creation of the Communist Political Association, which promised greater flexibility and a structure more in tune with American political realities. Though his understanding of the issues involved was clearly minimal at this point, David Greenglass felt inclined to side with Browder's opponents, the tough hard-line Stalinists led by William Z. Foster:

> Dearest, I felt terribly let down when I read in the papers out here that the C.P. was going to dissolve. Of course, they made no mention of the why and wherefore of this move. But no matter what, I think it is a bad move. You see, dear, it is a symbol of strength and political understanding to me and to thousands of other former YCLers in the service. And its dissolution would seem to us as the taking away of support to our political beliefs. It would put us in the position of a thinking Socialist and not a doing one because of the lack of organization to carry out our program. Maybe I have my facts wrong and the move is right, but how can I tell without actually knowing what is going on. Darling, please send me that speech and whatever literature the New Committee of Political Education puts out. Darling, this is vital in the boosting of my morale. Please don't delay in sending me the Browder speech. Send all literature pertaining to the speech. Find out from Ethel what she and Julie think about it. Ask her to get the literature. Darling, I love you and no matter what happens in America politically. In the end it will be Europe and a large part of Asia that will turn Socialist and the American end of the world will of necessity follow in the same course. So, dear, we still look forward to a Socialist America and we shall have that world in our time.

Two more letters, dated January 18 and 25, show that David, now stationed at Fort Ord in California, was still attempting to win recruits from among his fellow noncoms:

> I wanted to answer you at once but I got involved in a discussion of socialism, communism and capitalism. Boy I really got into a rip-roaring argument. Of course, when the dust of discussion settled I had convinced many of my listeners in at least the morale [sic] right of our cause. You see, dear, it is not because I am so wonderful, but because our philosophy is so logical and correct that no argument can stand against it. I am sure that if we educated people to our point of view we would have a socialist America pretty quickly. You see, dear, all we have to do is to put out more literature than the capitalist press can lie about or distort. . . .

> Of late I have been having the most wonderful discussions on our native-American fascists, and I have been convincing the fellows right along. I'll have my company raise the Red Flag yet.

Ruth, meanwhile, was considering an invitation to become a full-fledged member of the Party. On February 13 she told David:

> It seems that the Party is having a recruiting drive and I've been "invited" to join. It's part of a plan, dear. . . . I told Libie that I'd join, but not until I get back from California. However, she said it was important that I join now because there was a drive going on, but I didn't feel that way. When I join, I want to become active—not just to enroll, pay dues and then leave and send my dues in. I don't want to be that kind of a member.

Revealing her willingness to join and take an active role in the Party, Ruth showed that she was far from the passive and unreflective person she would remember herself as being, when, twenty-five years later, she said of her YCL membership, "I was born into it. I was not ideological."

Indeed, with each passing day, the commitment of the Greenglasses to the Soviet Union grew stronger. In a letter written to Ruth on June 29, 1944, David explained:

Darling, I have been reading a lot of books on the Soviet Union. Dear, I can see how farsighted and intelligent those leaders are. They are really geniuses, everyone of them. I have been revising what I think and how I think politically. Having found out all the truth about the Soviets, both good and bad, I have come to a stronger and more resolute faith and belief in the principles of Socialism and Communism. I believe that every time the Soviet Government used force they did so with pain in their hearts and the belief that what they were doing was to produce good for the greatest number. The tremendous sacrifices of blood, sweat, and tears of the Soviet peoples is a feat that surpasses all sacrifices of the past. More power to the Soviet Union and a fruitful and abundant life for their peoples.

At the time, David was stationed in Jackson, Mississippi, as a machinist in a heavy vehicles ordnance unit that was preparing to go overseas. Just before the unit was to ship out, David was separated from it and informed that he would be staying stateside. He was convinced that the action was a retaliation for his political views:

Dear, don't worry about the fact that I was taken out of my old outfit. It was a matter of politics. The First Sergeant didn't like me and, besides that, some of my politics must have reached his ears. This theory was upheld by the fact that another fellow from my former battalion, of like political opinion, was also "chosen" for this outfit. So you can see, dear, one of the higher-ups got rid of me.

Far from being "gotten rid of," David had been chosen to work on the top-secret Manhattan Project. He was first sent to Oak Ridge, Tennessee, a secret installation with ten times the personnel of Los Alamos.

David still did not know the nature of the project he was to be working on. But Ruth apparently did. On July 31, Ruth wrote:

Julie was in the house and he told me what you must be working on. Sweets, I can't discuss with you (and certainly no one else either) but when I see you I'll tell you what I think it is and you needn't commit yourself.

A few days later, David was in transit to Los Alamos. He wrote from Kansas City to warn Ruth not to mention his secret assignment to anyone—or almost anyone:

> Dear, I have been very reticent in my writing about what I am doing or going to do because it is a classified top secrecy project and as such I can't say anything. In fact, I am not even supposed to say this much. Darling, in this type of work at my place of residence there is censorship of mail going out and all off the post calls. So dear, you know why I didn't want you to say anything on the telephone. That is why I write C now dear instead of comrade. P.S. .... Not a word to anybody about anything except maybe Julie.

In October, a letter postmarked from Santa Fe contained a rather cryptic reference:

> I want to speak to that person I told you about. Well, the outcome of that was that I should see him about Thursday or Friday and he would let me know then. I have every confidence dear so don't worry. I'll let you know definitely one way or the other.

The FBI's file of transcribed letters ends with this message. However, one more letter that was never transcribed was found by us in the file of handwritten originals. Dated November 4, 1944, it shows David writing to Ruth to say:

> I am worried about whether you understand what my telegram is about? I really shouldn't because I know that you are intelligent and will understand. I was happy to hear that you spent a pleasant day with the Rosenbergs. My darling, I most certainly will be glad to be part of the community project that Julius and his friends have in mind. Count me in dear or should I say it has my vote. If it has yours, count us in.

When we showed this letter to the Greenglasses in 1979, and quoted from a few of the others, they were somewhat taken aback. They claimed to have completely forgotten about the letters' existence. David Greenglass agreed that they showed that he had been trying to alert Julius Rosenberg about the nature of his work on the atomic bomb as early as the summer of 1944. As for the "friends" mentioned in the last letter, David told us that this was a euphemism for the Russians. Although it would seem that he had hardly been reluctant to breach Los Alamos security by letting Julius know the nature of his secret work, David insisted that he nevertheless felt that he had been "sucked into" the conspiracy by his brother-in-law through a softening up process that had begun nearly two years earlier with supposedly theoretical talk about the Soviet Union's need for scientific data. "I had been conditioned a long time before," he told us. "Then when I got to Oak Ridge, I said, 'Gee.' "

Not long after this last letter was written, Ruth began making plans to visit David in New Mexico. David had been able to put together five days' leave and he and Ruth decided that it would be a good opportunity for them to spend their second wedding anniversary together. Just before she left New York in mid-November 1944, Ruth had dinner with the Rosenbergs at their apartment.

In Ruth's court testimony describing the evening's conversation, Julius was tremendously excited about David's assignment to Los Alamos. He did his best to explain the significance of the atomic bomb to the uncomprehending Ruth, stressing that it was "the biggest thing yet, that it was top secret, and that he felt that it was information that should be shared." Would Ruth talk to David in Albuquerque and find out whether he was willing to cooperate?

According to Ruth, she immediately protested that she didn't "like the idea." Then Ethel, who so far had said little, quietly suggested that this was something Davey would want to do. Why didn't Ruth deliver the message and let him decide? At any rate, Ruth was not so reluctant as to refuse Julius's offer of money to help pay for her train trip.

In Albuquerque, Ruth registered at the Hotel Franciscan. David soon joined her. It was only toward the end of the visit that she brought up Julius's request. She and David talked the matter over while strolling along Route 66, beyond the edge of town. David Greenglass later told us that his feelings during this conversation were a jumble of fear and anticipation, like the feeling one has before plunging into a cold lake. He and Ruth agree that it was then, and only then, that they made their final decision to go along with Julius's plan. Back at the hotel, David told Ruth in as much detail as he could remember about the layout and operations of the Los Alamos installation, adding for good measure the names of some prominent scientists he knew to be working on the project. Ruth carried this information back to New York.

Ruth would later testify that, a few days after her return home, Julius Rosenberg came alone to her Stanton Street apartment to find out what Ruth had learned. Different versions of this visit—given by Ruth, Julius, and a witness, Ruth's sister, Dorothy Abel—would play a significant role in the Rosenbergs' trial.

The next stage of the conspiracy, again according to Ruth Greenglass, began in January 1945 when David received a furlough and returned to New York for a brief visit. Soon after his arrival, Julius once again dropped in at the Stanton Street apartment and quizzed David on his knowledge of Los Alamos operations. After Julius's departure, David sat down and prepared some handwritten notes, including several sketches of a high-explosive lens mold that he was familiar with in his capacity as a model-maker for George Kistiakowsky's laboratory. David's sketches may have been technically imperfect—and in any case they concerned a design for a flat-type lens mold that was only one of a series of working models. Nevertheless, they had great potential espionage value. At minimum, they were an indication that Los Alamos scientists were committed to perfecting a high-explosive lens—an arrangement of shaped charges used to create an implosion shock wave. This in turn suggested that the Manhattan Project had abandoned an earlier gun-type bomb design in favor of the plutonium-fired implosion device.

Several days after Julius's visit, David and Ruth went to the Rosenbergs' apartment for dinner. When they arrived, they encountered another guest, Ann Sidorovich of Cleveland, Ohio. Ann and her husband, Michael, were friends of the Rosenbergs, and Michael was also known to David Greenglass, having briefly been a classmate of his at Brooklyn Polytech. Ann departed after about an hour. It was only then, according to David and Ruth, that Julius announced that in the future Ann would be acting as a courier, carrying material from the Greenglasses in New Mexico back to New York. Over dinner, Julius suggested several plans for meetings between Ruth and Ann. His initial suggestion—that the two women rendezvous in a Denver movie theater—was rejected as too complicated. It was finally agreed that they could just as easily meet outside a Safeway supermarket on Albuquerque's Central Avenue.

Later, after the table had been cleared, Julius asked Ruth to step into the kitchen so that he could give her a recognition signal, to be used in case another courier had to take Ann's place. Julius took a Jell-O box from the kitchen cabinet, removed the contents, and cut the side panel of the box into two irregularly shaped pieces. One he kept. The other he gave to Ruth, who took it into the living room to show her husband. David would later testify that he remarked on what a clever idea the Jell-O box was and Julius, obviously pleased, replied, "The simplest things are the cleverest."

The Greenglasses' version of what went on at this family dinner party was to be hotly contested by both the Rosenbergs and Ann Sidorovich. Sidorovich later gave sworn testimony before a grand jury denying that she had ever discussed becoming a courier with the Rosenbergs and saying that she had no memory of having been present on the evening in question. It is worth noting, however, that in August 1950 Ann Sidorovich conceded to FBI investigators that she and her husband had been in New York City on a one-week vacation during January 1945—something David and Ruth would hardly have known, much less remembered accurately five years later, unless they had met her as they said they did. Of course, not even the Greenglasses claimed that Mrs. Sidorovich had been present when Julius named her as a courier. This could be taken as evidence that the Greenglasses were clever enough to concoct a story that Sidorovich would be unable to refute; or it could simply mean that Julius was following sound espionage practice in shielding his courier.

According to David Greenglass, one final incident occurred during the latter part of his two-week furlough. It began one weekday evening with a phone call from Julius saying that he was with someone he wanted David to meet. David borrowed his father-in-law's car and drove to the appointed place on First Avenue near Forty-second Street. After a few minutes, Julius emerged from a nearby bar, looked over the car, and then returned with a stranger who was wearing a hat that made his face difficult to see. The stranger got into the backseat of the car with Rosenberg and told David to drive around the block. As David drove, the man plied him with questions about the lens mold design. But David had no new information to add to what he had already written up for Julius.

It was several weeks after this alleged incident that Julius learned that he was being let go by the Signal Corps. He was not to be out of work long, for he was hired almost immediately by the Emerson Radio Corporation, where he was put to work as an engineer on some of the same military contract projects he had once inspected. In other respects, the circumstances of the firing had quite an impact. Harry Rosenberg refused to see or speak with his son for nearly a year, not relenting until he was fatally ill with the kidney infection that killed him in 1946.

In the second half of February, Ruth Greenglass moved to Albuquerque, where she found a secretarial job and rented an inexpensive apartment. David began commuting the forty miles from Los Alamos to be with her on weekends. Ruth suffered a miscarriage in April and shortly thereafter she claims to have received a letter from Ethel, expressing sympathy and indicating that "a member of the family" would be coming to visit them on the third or fourth Saturday in May. Ruth interpreted this as notice of Ann Sidorovich's plans and on both Saturdays she went to the Safeway store on Central Avenue at the time previously agreed upon. But Ann Sidorovich never appeared.

A week later, however, on the Sunday morning of June 3, 1945, a man the Greenglasses later identified as Harry Gold showed up at their apartment. Gold produced Julius's half of the Jell-O box side. David Greenglass told his visitor that he did not have any written material prepared, since he had not wanted to take the chance of keeping such papers lying around the house. After asking Gold to return that afternoon, he quickly wrote out six or seven pages of information, chiefly about the high-explosive lens molds. He also prepared several draftsman's sketches to illustrate his notes. When Gold returned at about four o'clock, David gave him the material and received a sealed envelope in exchange. In the envelope was $500.

Harry Gold had mentioned that he would return the following September. However, Gold's failure to materialize in the early days of that month hardly mattered, since David and Ruth returned to New York for a visit that same month. On this September 1945 trip, David would later claim, he gave Julius Rosenberg the last installment of the data he had gleaned from his job at Los Alamos, including a general description of the design of the plutonium or implosion-type bomb.

David Greenglass was due to be discharged from the army at the end of February 1946. Julius urged him to stay on at Los Alamos as a civilian employee, but he rejected the idea. He missed New York, and he hated the idea of being separated from Ruth all week long, seeing her only during his weekend commutes to their cramped apartment in Albuquerque. Instead, he and Julius agreed to activate their plan of going into business together.

Shortly after David's return home, David became the fourth partner in the G & R Engineering Company, which Rosenberg had founded with David's brother Bernard and a Knickerbocker Village neighbor, Isidore Goldstein, who was included primarily because he was able to put up some desperately needed capital. The business started in Barnet Greenglass's sewing-machine shop on Sheriff Street but soon moved to a shabby storefront on East Third Street, where David was to set up and supervise a small machine shop while Bernard and Julius concentrated on rounding up business.

After a few months it became evident that the lucrative contracts Julius had told David to expect—from contacts he had made during his time in the Signal Corps as well as from AMTORG—were never going to materialize. The partners, concluding that their problem was insufficient capital, rounded up another investor—a matzoh manufacturer and small-time business speculator named David Schein. With Schein's money, they were able to move the shop, renamed Pitt Machine Products, Inc., into a larger and more appropriate space on East Houston Street. Business, however, remained slow. There was only a handful of clients, mostly small manufacturers who had met Julius through the Party.

Julius Rosenberg later blamed the failure of the machine shop on David's slipshod work. It is difficult to disprove such an assertion, though it does seem unlikely that Greenglass would have lasted in the Los Alamos machine shop, and even been promoted to foreman, had he been incompetent. David, in turn, attributed the shop's bad straits to Julius's indifference to everything but his "secret work." Now that he had returned to civilian life, David's priorities had begun to change; he wanted nothing more than to earn a good living and start a family. Julius, David claimed, made numerous attempts to rekindle his in-law's waning enthusiasm for spying.

First of all, David later told the FBI, Julius had confided that he was keeping two apartments, one somewhere in Greenwich Village and another at Avenue B near Twelfth Street on the Lower East

Side; both were used for microfilming documents. The Avenue B apartment was untenanted, and David and Ruth were welcome to live there rent-free. It was a tempting offer in view of the housing shortage in postwar New York, but David refused. He was beginning to feel that his life was already too much under Julius's control.

And when David decided to further his interrupted education by taking courses at Pratt Institute in Brooklyn, Julius came up with an attractive alternative offer. Why shouldn't David aim higher? He could study nuclear physics at MIT under the GI bill, and Julius would see to it that there was enough money to cover David's personal expenses for as long as he was in school. Of course, David would also be in an excellent position to pass on the odd bits of classified information from time to time. At this stage of his life, David could hardly see himself as a nuclear physicist. He dismissed the notion as another of his brother-in-law's fantasies.

On July 17, 1950, David told the FBI that Julius had gradually allowed himself to talk more freely about the nature of his "secret work," apparently in an attempt to impress the younger man with the importance of the spy ring's activities. It began, David said, with Julius confiding that he had made his first move into espionage while working as a Signal Corps inspector. He had known at the time that the Soviet radio and electronics industry was foundering (David assumed that this was a reference to radar) and had tried to help by picking up copies of tube manuals. During his brief stint at Emerson Radio in 1945 after he left the Signal Corps, Julius is said to have bragged later, he had managed to steal a proximity fuse—a fire-control device used in connection with the Norden bombsight. Although the fuses were closely guarded in theory, it had been quite easy for him to slip one into the briefcase he used for carrying his lunch. From this small beginning, Rosenberg claimed, he had built a network that grew to include contacts with "scientists and engineers in Cleveland, Ohio and upstate New York ... [including] Syracuse, Rochester, Buffalo and Schenectady."

Normally, David claimed, these scientists used a technician or some other "insignificant person" to carry data to New York, where it was left in a prearranged spot in a movie theater. Julius would pick up the material and either hand it directly to a Soviet agent or take it to one of his secret apartments for photocopying.

Beginning sometime in 1947, David also recalled in his statement, Julius began to talk of more and more grandiose successes. He claimed that one of his operatives had managed to steal information about a "thinking machine" that could send out interceptor guided missiles to knock enemy missiles out of the air. And he also spoke mysteriously about a "sky platform," to be located in space at a point where gravity ceases to exist. To David, this sounded like science fiction.

On another occasion, which David placed in 1948, he was working at the milling machine in the shop when he overheard Julius casually telling Bernard Greenglass that it would soon be possible to build an atomic-powered airplane—the mathematics of the thing had already been worked out. David's experience at Los Alamos had left him with an awareness of radiation hazards that was still lacking among the general public, and he took the first opportunity to ask Julius privately whether radiation from an on-board reactor wouldn't harm the pilot. Julius assured him that this problem had been solved; a shield would protect the pilot from exposure. He added, David recalled, that he had learned about the plane from "one of his boys."

By late 1948, it was becoming obvious that the machine-shop business was not going to survive. Bernard Greenglass, seeing how things were shaping up, had already dropped out of the partnership, and David was becoming increasingly frustrated. He had a newborn child to support, and Julius's complete indifference to making money was maddening. Nor was Greenglass any longer the gung-ho Communist he had been during his army days. Although he still considered himself a Socialist at heart, his infatuation with Stalin and Stalinist Russia had soured.

In a recent interview, David Greenglass recalled that sometime in late 1948 or early 1949, he was walking down Third Avenue in Manhattan with Julius when the latter began to meditate on the risks they had taken to help the Soviet Union. "We've got to be like soldiers," David recalled Julius saying. "It doesn't matter if Stalin is sending his troops to be killed. What difference does it make as long as the victory is ours? Except that I won't be around for the final victory, and neither will you." David Greenglass no longer thought of himself as one of Stalin's soldiers. David told us that his unspoken reaction had been, "Who wants to stand up for Stalin? What about Tito? What about Berlin?"

The already shaky relationship between the Rosenbergs and the

Greenglasses deteriorated further in the autumn of 1949. It had now been some months since David was able to draw a regular salary from the machine shop, and he had decided that he would have to leave the business and take a paying job. The Greenglasses were now so hard up that they began borrowing small sums of money from Julius—loans that eventually amounted to nearly a thousand dollars. David felt that he and Ruth were entitled to the money since they had never received any return on the savings they invested in the partnership back in 1946. But the chief cause of the strain, according to David, was Julius's warning in October that it might soon be necessary for the Greenglasses to leave the country permanently. The prospect of spending the rest of his life somewhere in the Soviet bloc no longer held any allure for David; but, above all, he was annoyed by the warning, because it seemed to be yet another instance of Julius's penchant for melodrama. He saw no point in telling Julius how he really felt. It was easier to keep quiet and hope that the alarm would pass.

By Christmas, David was broke and he went around to the machine shop to discuss pulling out of the business entirely. Julius invited David into the shop's tiny office to talk in private. There he confided to David that he was already trying to borrow $5,000 from a cousin in order to buy out their silent partner, David Schein. Greenglass ventured that he still had a certificate representing twenty-five of the business's outstanding shares and Julius might want to buy these as well.

The reply to this suggestion was a good deal more than Greenglass had bargained for. Rosenberg mused that of course David ought to be thinking about signing over the shares since he, Greenglass, was "hot" and would have to leave for Paris soon in any case. The best way to handle it would be for David to turn over the certificate immediately in exchange for a promissory note for $1,000.

David was shaken. What did Julius mean by saying he was "hot," he demanded. Julius tried to calm the younger man, suggesting that they continue the discussion away from the office. Steering David outside, he offered to buy him a cup of coffee at a nearby shop on Avenue C. There, sharing a quiet booth in the nearly deserted coffee shop, Julius explained that "something is happening" that would eventually make it necessary for Greenglass to flee to Paris. The whole operation might have to go underground and he was planning to dispose of the microfilming apartment soon.

"Do you mean the Twelfth Street apartment?" David remembered asking.

"No," Julius replied. "I mean the Greenwich Village apartment." The Twelfth Street and Avenue B place, he added, had already been given up.

Rosenberg went on to advise that the Greenglasses obtain U.S. passports and visas for France as soon as possible. On his passport application, David should say that his reason for traveling was the need to dispose of some property he owned in France. When the time came to leave, there would be money to pay ship passage for the Greenglass family; once in Paris, they would be met by a member of the espionage ring.

David left the coffee shop thoroughly confused. He still could not believe that it would really become necessary for him to run away, and he decided that in any case he did not want to worry Ruth, who was four months pregnant with their second child. However, he had to have something to tell her about the outcome of the discussion about getting out of the Pitt partnership. When he brought up the idea of signing over the stock certificate in return for a promissory note, Ruth was dubious. At first, she wanted to hold out for $2,000, which she felt was nearer the true value of the shares. David pointed out that, under the circumstances, they might be lucky to get the thousand. Eventually Ruth agreed that David should go ahead and have the certificate notarized but not turn it over to Julius for a while in the hopes that the Rosenbergs would first come up with some cash.

That New Year's Eve, the Greenglasses attended a party at the home of some old friends on Forsyth Street. Listening to the group reminisce about high school, David began to get depressed. He wondered whether Julius's warning was serious and whether this might be the last New Year's he and Ruth would ever spend with their old crowd.

The year 1950 began with a bad omen for David Greenglass, but he refused to recognize it for what it was.

During the last weekend in January, while David was out of the house, two FBI agents came around to his Rivington Street apartment looking for him. Both Ruth and he were worried, and wondered whether they should refuse to talk to the agents altogether, but when David called Julius with the news he was advised that he might as well speak to the agents and find out as much as possible without volunteering any information in return.

When the FBI men returned that afternoon, David found to his relief that they were trying to track down a number of uranium hemispheres that were missing from the Theta Shop at Los Alamos where he had worked during the war. The hollow hemispheres, each slightly larger than a walnut, were not considered to have enough uranium to be worth the cost of recovery. Workers at the Theta Shop had commonly used them for ashtrays; some took them as souvenirs.

Although one of the uranium hemispheres was sitting in a drawer in the Greenglass apartment at that very moment, David denied any knowledge of the missing material. After asking a few routine questions, the agents departed. Julius, informed of the outcome of the meeting, agreed that there was nothing to worry about for now. David concluded that if the government had nothing more against him than a vague suspicion about the stolen uranium—which, indeed, it did not at that time—then he was going to come through the whole business without difficulty. Julius had merely been exaggerating again. That evening, David walked down to the East River Drive and pitched the uranium into the water.

Six days later, on February 2, 1950, Klaus Fuchs was arrested in England. Julius came down to Rivington Street to warn David that the man Fuchs had given atomic secrets to was the same man David had passed information to in Albuquerque. If he were arrested, Greenglass would surely be the next to come under suspicion.

Since David had still not told Ruth of Julius's October warning about having to flee the country, he and Julius left the house in order to talk more freely. The two men strolled for nearly forty-five minutes in nearby Hamilton Fish Park while Julius explained that the Russians always tried to stay six months ahead of the FBI. Normally, there would have been plenty of time for Greenglass to think about getting out, but Fuchs had been under suspicion for some time before the first interrogations mentioned in the press accounts of his arrest. Once his courier was located, things might move quickly.

Under the circumstances, David pointed out, the smart thing would be to get in touch with the courier and have *him* stay out of sight for a while. Julius muttered something to the effect that Ethel had suggested the same thing. Everyone in the network was hoping that the courier would stay out of sight. But they couldn't count on it. That was why it was important for the Greenglasses to leave soon.

David Greenglass was still unconvinced. If the Russians were so clever, working "six months ahead," he ought to be safe. At any rate, he still did not see his actions as on a par with those Fuchs was charged with. Rather than precipitate an argument, Greenglass did not refuse point-blank. He let Julius think he was considering the possibility of leaving, but that there were obstacles. First, there were enormous debts that he and Ruth had run up over the last few years. They couldn't possibly consider leaving until those were paid off.

Julius became impatient. People who were leaving the country to escape arrest didn't go around paying off their debts ahead of time. Forget about the money, he urged; just take Ruth and the baby and get out. Greenglass promised to think the matter over, but as he left the park he decided that he still did not want to bother Ruth about a step that might never be necessary. It was all so unreal.

Shortly after that conversation, something happened that made discussing the problem with Ruth out of the question. Early on the morning of February 14, while standing in front of the open gas heater that was used to warm their tiny apartment, Ruth stepped too close to the grating and her nightgown went up in flames. David slapped the fire out with his hands, but by the time the fire was extinguished Ruth had suffered serious burns over a large part of her body. Rushed to Gouverneur Hospital, Ruth lay in critical condition for several days, kept alive by blood transfusions and delirious with fever. She was six months pregnant and had already suffered one miscarriage back in 1945. The fear of losing this baby was almost harder to bear than the physical pain.

Ruth did not lose her baby, but she remained hospitalized for two months. David, who had recently found a job machining models for a large company, had to arrange to work the night shift while Ruth's sister, Dorothy Abel, took care of their infant son. During the days he took care of little Stephen, visited Ruth at the hospital, and tried to catch an hour or so of sleep whenever he could. Another man might have considered leaving on the theory that Ruth and the children would be able to join him later, but David could not bear the thought of voluntarily leaving Ruth behind. Even when he was in the army, they had always tried to be together every minute they possibly could. It was easier to believe that the danger from the FBI was a phantom of Julius's imagination.

Ruth Greenglass was released from the hospital in early April and in mid-May she gave birth to a healthy daughter. She and the child came home from the hospital on the morning of May 24, 1950. Later that day, before David left for the afternoon shift at his new job, Julius Rosenberg showed up at the apartment brandishing a copy of the *Herald Tribune* and pointing to the front-page photograph of Harry Gold, who had just been arrested in Philadelphia. This, he practically screeched, was the same man who had come to see them in Albuquerque. Didn't they recognize him? Didn't they realize that now they could not possibly refuse to get away? Take the children, take the clothes, and go, Julius urged.

This was the first Ruth had heard about the whole business and, in truth, she did not recognize the photo of Gold, who had lost some hair and gained a good deal of weight since that brief meeting in Albuquerque five years before. David, however, knew that Julius was telling the truth when he insisted that Gold *was* the man. Sensing that it would be pointless to argue further, he listened unprotestingly while Julius outlined the new arrangements that had been made on their behalf.

Since David and Ruth had never done anything about obtaining passports, the new plan called for them and the children to take a train to Mexico, which they could enter without passports using routinely issued Mexican tourist cards. Once in Mexico City they were to rent an apartment and write a letter to the Soviet Embassy in that city, mentioning something about the United Nations in the body of the letter. Three days after the letter was mailed, David was to go to the Plaza de la "something or other" (David never did remember the full Spanish name) at 5:00 P.M. and stand near the statue of Christopher Columbus, holding his thumb in a Mexico City street guide. Soon a man would approach and ask, "Have you ever seen such a statue before?" Greenglass should reply, "No. I have lived in Oklahoma all my life." The man would then answer something to the effect that there were much nicer statues in Paris. At that point the stranger would hand over American passports made out for Greenglass and his family as well as expense money and instructions for traveling to either Berne, Switzerland, or Stockholm, Sweden.

Once the Greenglasses were safely in Europe, the process would be repeated all over again—in the case of Sweden, for example, the directions called for standing near a statue of Linnaeus—and this time they would receive documents to enable them to enter Czechoslovakia. As soon as they were behind the Iron Curtain, all that David had to do was to write to the Soviet ambassador in Prague stating, "I am here."

In the course of this explanation, Rosenberg produced a white envelope stuffed with $1,000 in ten- and twenty-dollar bills and suggested that if David and Ruth were foolish enough to insist on paying off their debts before they left, they ought to start immediately and be discreet. David said he would do so, but that the thousand would hardly cover it. It wasn't just a matter of foolish principle, he reminded Julius; the people he owed were his friends and were almost all as hard pressed as he was.

Julius said that David's scruples were all very well, but that he ought to be thinking about getting a lawyer just in case. He, Julius, already had one; what's more, he and Ethel were planning to leave the country too, as soon as the rest of the ring were safely under way. When David asked how much time he and Ruth had to get organized, Julius said that they should plan to be gone by June 11 or 12 at the very latest.

After Julius left their apartment, Ruth and David discussed for the first time the very real prospect of arrest. Ruth, though more of a realist than her husband, agreed that leaving home to spend the rest of their lives in the Soviet Union was a drastic step. She also distrusted Julius and wondered whether his elaborate escape plans were as foolproof as he seemed to think. As she recalled in a recent interview, her first reaction was that Julius "must have been reading too much science fiction." In the end, the Greenglasses decided that they would not leave the country at all but allow Julius to think that they had. Instead they would find some out-of-the-way corner of the Catskills, rent a small cabin, and stay there until the Rosenbergs themselves had fled. David felt that if by some chance the FBI did begin an extensive search for him he could leave his family in the mountains while he dropped out of sight for a few months. As they whispered together over the sleeping form of their newborn child, David and Ruth promised each other that they would put their plan into effect by June 12 at the very latest.

Nothing more was heard from Julius Rosenberg until five days later, May 28, when he appeared at the door early in the morning and rousted David from a sound sleep for another stroll through the park. This time Julius had brought a thick wad of small bills, $4,000 in all, and he promised David that there would be another $2,000 from him in a few days and still more once the Greenglasses were in touch with their Mexican contact.

Julius was by now so nervous that he did not even want to be seen in his brother-in-law's company. When David spotted some old friends, Mr. and Mrs. Herman Einsohn, approaching on the other side of Delancey Street, Julius urged that they hurry on by. David ignored him and crossed the street to say hello to the Einsohns—they owed him $40, which he was eager to collect—and Julius went on ahead to a quiet spot on the edge of the East River. When David caught up, the two men sat quietly for a while, each no doubt wondering whether the other was really going to carry through on his vow to leave. The next time they saw each other, the brothers-in-law would both be under arrest.

Sometime during the second week of June, it became all too obvious to the Greenglasses that they were being watched. For several days, a van belonging to an "Acme Construction Company" with a First Avenue address had been parked prominently outside their building; when Ruth checked the address, she discovered that no such company existed. Nevertheless, neither of them could bring themselves to face the urgency of their situation. The chief cause of their procrastination—or at least the only wholly rational cause—was Ruth's poor health. The burns on her legs had become reinfected, and her doctor warned that she might soon have to be hospitalized.

Finally, on June 10, David decided that he had better do something about his plan of finding a Catskills hideaway for Ruth and the children. Early that morning, he headed for the Fiftieth Street bus station and caught a bus to Phoenicia, New York. But when he disembarked in the tiny Catskills town, David discovered that a car driven by two plainclothesmen had been behind him all the way. There was no point in scouting for a hideout with the Bureau watching his every move, so he dejectedly took the next bus back home.

Julius's June 12 deadline came and went. Ruth was ordered into the hospital and David, working nights and caring for the children during the day, tried to convince himself that if the FBI seriously intended to bring him in for questioning, they would have already done so.

Then, on the afternoon of June 15, four FBI agents appeared at the door of the Greenglass apartment. Harry Gold had finally identified Greenglass's photograph that morning in Philadelphia, and after

David's abortive trip to the Catskills, the FBI did not want to take any more risks that he might successfully slip out of town.

Rather to the agents' surprise, David appeared quite unruffled by their presence, engaging in small talk and even giving permission for an immediate search of his apartment. The agents spent nearly five hours going through the Greenglasses' personal possessions but did not attempt any serious interrogation until early evening when Ruth's sister, Dorothy Abel, arrived to pick up the children, who had been in David's care all afternoon. Then David agreed to go along to the FBI office in the Foley Square Federal Building for more questioning.

In the FBI's twenty-ninth-floor offices in the Federal Building, the discussion at first continued in the same relaxed mood. But, unknown to Greenglass, about two dozen snapshots seized by the FBI during the search of his apartment were at that moment being rushed to Philadelphia, where Harry Gold was waiting to examine them. Shortly after nine o'clock, Special Agent Cornelius called from the Philadelphia office to say that Gold had seen the pictures of Ruth and David and immediately confirmed his identification. The FBI's search for the suspect who was previously known only as "Unknown American #5" was over.

When Greenglass was confronted with the information that Harry Gold had already identified him, his pose of cocky self-assurance deserted him. Informed that Gold said he had taken $500 in exchange for secret data, Greenglass broke down and admitted the truth of the charge, but insisted that he "did not furnish the information for the money but for the cause."

Once he had admitted recognizing Gold's photograph, David could think only of how this would affect Ruth. She had been through so much in the past months that he did not think she could survive the trauma of arrest and prison. Sometime after midnight, when he finally broke down and agreed to put his name to a confession, all he asked in return was that Ruth be "kept out of it." If she were not, he threatened, he would commit suicide.

Greenglass's interrogators, meanwhile, were delighted with their success in getting a signed confession and in persuading their prisoner to agree to spend the night in an unused office in FBI headquarters. According to the FBI's report on that night's proceedings, Greenglass never exercised his right to demand a phone call, although during the last hour of the questioning he did began casting hints about an "attorney and mentioned the name of O. John Rogge."

The statement that Greenglass signed before finally going to sleep that night was brief, but it was sufficiently damning of Ruth and Julius as well as himself. The confession states that Julius's invitation to engage in espionage had been carried by Ruth when she came to New Mexico in November 1944. David also admitted that he had accepted $500 from Harry Gold. However, he claimed that he could not remember whether the piece of "torn card" he gave to Harry Gold had come from Ruth or directly from Julius Rosenberg—this, apparently, in an attempt to minimize Ruth's role.

At 8:30 the next morning, Ruth Greenglass received a call in her hospital room from Louis Abel, her sister's husband. Louis told her that David was in FBI custody and that he had asked that O. John Rogge be hired as his legal representative. Fortunately for the Greenglasses, they had been cautious enough to remove the $4,000 from its hiding place in the chimney of their apartment on the day before Ruth entered the hospital. All of the money, except for $100 the Greenglasses had spent, was now safely stashed inside a hammock in the Abels' living room. Ruth instructed Louis to offer the money to Rogge as a retainer.

David's choice of Rogge was an interesting one. A former U.S. assistant attorney general, Rogge had gone on to stake out a career in the New York State branch of the American Labor Party; in 1948 he'd been a candidate on the slate of Henry Wallace's new Progressive Party. He was one of the country's most prominent radical lawyers, a celebrity of the far left. But those who followed Rogge's career closely were aware that his political allegiances were in flux. Increasingly disillusioned with Stalinism and with Stalin's American defenders, Rogge might have welcomed an opportunity to expose the role of American Communists in Soviet espionage activities. Thus Rogge's appearance as David Greenglass's counsel, while it seemed to the general public an obvious instance of one Red defending another, was interpreted by more sophisticated observers as an indication that Greenglass might eventually turn up as a prosecution witness against his former confederates.

To understand how perplexing and ultimately shocking Rogge's change of heart was to his former allies, one has only to recall that it was Rogge himself who had provided the impetus that led the top

American Communist leaders to decide to take the Party underground. On November 7, 1947, the year after he was ousted from his Justice Department post, Rogge charged that the Department was planning "a dramatic round-up of dozens of Communist leaders and alleged fellow-travellers"—a Cold War replay of the notorious Palmer Raids of 1919—which he predicted would take place in little more than a week.

Although the mass arrests failed to occur on schedule, Rogge's charges were interpreted by top Communists as solid evidence from one in a position to know that the American Communist Party was not going to be allowed to function legally for long. It also provided powerful ammunition for the hard-line Fosterite faction of the Party whose leader, William Z. Foster, contended that the Truman administration was committed to an agenda of war and fascism and that the era of coexistence predicted by his rival, Earl Browder, was an impossibility.

As a lawyer in private practice, Rogge went on to become the Vice-President of the left-wing National Lawyers Guild in 1949 and, more significantly, a top supporter of the Civil Rights Congress, the legal-political arm of the Communist Party that was devoted to the cause of racial equality. In the latter capacity, he became one of three CRC lawyers assigned to the case of the Trenton Six, one of the most widely publicized Party causes of the postwar era, an attempt to overturn death sentences meted out to six black youths who had been convicted of the murder of a furniture store owner.

Rogge was also prominently associated with a number of political causes that placed him firmly in the pro-Communist—as opposed to merely the democratic left—camp. For example, he had joined with W. E. B. Du Bois to form the Peace Information Center; he was also an American delegate to the Communist bloc World Peace Congress—initiator of the famous Stockholm Peace Petition, a rather innocuous condemnation of atomic bombs.

Yet, by 1950, Rogge's faith in pro-Communist causes seemed to have been abruptly shaken. The catalyst, apparently, was Stalin's decision to expel Yugoslavia from the family of Communist nations and to condemn Tito as an agent of American imperialism. In March 1950, Rogge agreed to serve as first legal counsel for Tito's Yugoslavia in the United States, and he registered with the Department of Justice under the terms of the Foreign Agents Registration Act.

Simply to side with Tito in his dispute with Stalin was enough to damage one's credentials in pro-Communist circles at the time. But Rogge, as Tito's actual American counsel, was beyond the pale, and he soon found himself roundly denounced by his erstwhile friends. In November 1950, still officially Vice-Chairman of the Permanent Committee of the World Peace Congress, Rogge used his position to deliver a scathing denunciation of Soviet foreign policy at an important Congress meeting—an act of some courage since the session was held in Warsaw. Not surprisingly, Rogge's speech caused an uproar. One fellow American delegate, Charles P. Howard (the keynoter of the 1948 Wallace convention), condemned Rogge as "not only a lawyer for Tito but . . . the advocate for the slaveholder Jefferson . . . and of King George III."

From that point on, Rogge's honeymoon with the pro-Communist Left was officially over. Eventually, when the U.S. government sought unsuccessfully to prosecute Du Bois for his foreign-policy views, he was even to testify against the noted black leader—an action that would prompt Du Bois to nickname his former ally, "Rogge the rat."

How much did David Greenglass know about Rogge's political odyssey when he chose him for his attorney? When we spoke to David Greenglass, he recalled that he had thought of Rogge because he remembered the lawyer had appeared as counsel to Philip Jaffe, former editor of *Amerasia*, who had been accused by the Tydings Committee of using his magazine's extensive research files as a cover for an espionage operation. Jaffe, who has described himself as a "close fellow-traveler" of the Party up to 1945 and an ardent admirer of Earl Browder, became an outspoken critic of the Party after Browder's fall. If Greenglass had more than a passing familiarity with the *Amerasia* incident, he would have known this. And in terms of political affinities, Rogge was certainly a logical choice: Rogge was close enough to the Left to understand and sympathize with the motives that had led Greenglass into espionage in the first place; on the other hand, he had openly repudiated Stalinism and the American Communist Party. Greenglass, whose own political loyalties were drifting as events in Europe more clearly revealed Stalin's true face, was also aware of Rogge's open support of Tito. Thus he felt that Rogge could be relied upon to represent his interests and not those of the American Communists.

Greenglass may have been clear about who he wanted as his attorney, but he had not thought through the other realities of his situation. His confused state of mind on the morning after his confession was all too evident to Herbert Fabricant, a partner of O. John Rogge's, who interviewed Greenglass that morning shortly before his arraignment. Greenglass told Fabricant that he had purposely made "confusing" statements to the FBI in order to keep Ruth out of the picture. Given that Greenglass had explicitly named Ruth as Julius's messenger, Fabricant found it hard to comprehend David's apparent confidence that he had successfully shielded his wife. As Fabricant wrote in his memo on the conversation, "I fail to see how his mind operated. . . ."

Nor did Greenglass appear to grasp the repercussions of his naming of Rosenberg. Asked whether he intended to cooperate with the government and testify against his brother-in-law, his answer was emphatic: "Hell, no!" He even asked Fabricant to see that Julius was informed of what had happened so far. If Greenglass had been in the process of fabricating accusations against Rosenberg, he would hardly have wanted his victim to be kept up to date on the situation. One might even speculate that Greenglass was clinging to the idea that if Rosenberg were told, he might yet escape—saving himself and perhaps, in the bargain, removing from the picture an important part of the case against the Greenglasses.

Ruth Greenglass, meanwhile, had already received a visit from the FBI. Speaking from her hospital bed, Ruth told the agents that no one resembling Harry Gold had ever visited her and her husband in Albuquerque. No one, she said, had ever visited them other than a few neighborhood acquaintances. Told that her husband had already confessed to giving data to Gold, Ruth said quite firmly that she would believe that when she heard it from his own mouth. End of conversation.

That same afternoon, Ruth heard from Herbert Fabricant that David had indeed signed a statement for the FBI, but now intended to plead innocent. Ruth assured Fabricant that she had no intention of cooperating with the government either and that from now on David would stand firm.

Rogge and Fabricant felt it was a little late for David and Ruth to be assuming a defiant stance, since David had already signed a confession. Three days later, Rogge and his other law partner, Robert Gordon, went to see Ruth, who had just been released from the hospital. In a 1978 interview, Rogge recalled his shock and dismay at the conditions he found. The Rivington Street flat was even shabbier than he had expected, a dismal walk-up with no central heating or hot water and with primitive kitchen facilities. Ruth, a petite woman to begin with, had lost a good deal of weight since her accident and looked positively skeletal as she struggled to heat her baby's formula with one hand and cope with her two-year-old toddler with the other. Ruth was distraught over the possibility that she would be arrested and separated from her children, particularly the baby, which she had scarcely been with since it was born.

The prospect of David's extradition to New Mexico was also dismaying. Ruth reminded Rogge that New Mexico residents had resented the influx of servicemen during the War, particularly those who brought along wives to compete with local residents for civilian jobs and scarce housing. She was apprehensive that a Jewish ex-GI accused of spying for a Communist country would not stand a chance with a conservative New Mexico jury. Rogge, too, felt that extradition to New Mexico would be a disaster. Yet he could not encourage Ruth's attempt to use the argument that her husband was emotionally unstable. Rogge, moreover, saw no way of satisfying Ruth's faint hope that David's confession might be thrown out by the court. That was a possibility he considered most unlikely.

Rogge's conversation with Ruth was interrupted in mid-course by the arrival of several Greenglass relatives—Louis Abel, Bernard Greenglass, the eldest Greenglass brother, Sam, and another family member, Issy Feit. Rogge laid out for the group David's options as he saw them, stressing the possibility that the Greenglasses could plead guilty and become government witnesses—in his view the only chance for them both to escape heavy sentences. In trying to win Ruth over, Rogge mentioned several cases in which clients of his, having pleaded guilty, had gotten off with as little as three to five years for serious crimes. In his own mind, Rogge was making no promises that David would fare as well, but the hope that her husband might have to serve only three years had been firmly planted in Ruth's mind. For the first time, she promised to at least present the case for cooperation to David when she was well enough to visit him in prison. The meeting ended, according to Robert Gordon's description, with "a long discussion of J.R."

The following week, two days before a scheduled hearing on David's extradition to New Mexico, Rogge met with U.S. Attorney Irving H. Saypol and suggested that his client's eventual cooperation "could not be ruled out." Rogge also assured Saypol that he had no intention of turning the case into a political crusade; there was, as far as he could see, "no issue of civil rights involved." This assurance was necessary since there was already a ground swell of support in favor of defending Greenglass as a victim of political harassment and anti-Semitism. Some Lower East Side neighbors had been circulating a petition calling for David's release on bond, and even the anti-Communist *Jewish Daily Forward* had made inquiries about starting a defense fund. As it happened, Saypol was more than willing to stall extradition on the basis of Rogge's hints; he had no desire to hand over to the New Mexico prosecutors a major case that he felt rightfully belonged in his jurisdiction. On June 26, the prosecutors asked that procedures to transfer Greenglass to New Mexico be temporarily adjourned.

In the meantime, Rogge called the Washington office of the FBI in an attempt to arrange an interview with J. Edgar Hoover. He needed to know just where Greenglass fitted in the unfolding Fuchs-Gold case. Hoover, it developed, was out of town, but his assistant director, Ladd, agreed to schedule an appointment for the 26th.

The timing of the conference could hardly have been worse for David. Hostilities broke out in Korea on June 25, and the first shots of the faraway conflict were interpreted by many Americans to be the opening salvo of World War III. The Korean situation would eventually lead to increased clamor for the death sentence for captured "atom spies." American boys were to be sent overseas to fight and die, the reasoning went, and here were dangerous traitors sitting warm and secure in our prisons, at taxpayers' expense. Columnist Westbrook Pegler would even go so far as to advocate making "membership in Communist organizations or covert subsidies" of those organizations a capital offense. If Rogge had been hoping to arrange some sort of deal in exchange for David's guilty plea, events were working against him.

Unknown to Rogge, there was another factor that doomed his effort to get some hint of the FBI's plans in the Greenglass case. Rogge's break with the pro-Stalinist CP was well known on the Left. He was considered a turncoat at the very least, and later there would even be speculation that he had been set up as Greenglass's counsel while serving as a covert agent of the FBI. An examination of FBI interoffice memos on Rogge's attempt to arrange a conference show, on the contrary, that the FBI had either not kept abreast of Rogge's change of views or failed to see the distinction between a supporter of Stalin and a supporter of Tito. Hoover considered Rogge just another Red and therefore, by definition, untrustworthy. Informed of Rogge's upcoming appointment with Ladd, Hoover penned a warning to his assistant to "be extremely circumspect in any conversations with Rogge." Ladd followed this advice to a fault. He kept his appointment, but only to inform Rogge that the case was now out of the Bureau's hands and that he had better consult with the Department of Justice directly.

Returning from his wild goose chase in Washington, Rogge went to see David Greenglass in jail and learned, to his relief, that the conference with Ruth had worked. After twelve days of resistance, Greenglass had now decided that cooperation would be the best course after all.

In a recent interview, David Greenglass told us emphatically that his change of heart had nothing to do with either direct pressure from the government or any promises held out by Rogge. There was no deal offered. He had simply concluded that cooperation offered the only hope for him and his family. It had come down to a basic calculus of loyalties:

> It was all in my mind. They didn't put pressure on me. I said I gotta make a choice. This [indicating Ruth who sat beside him] gotta stay with me. They [the Rosenbergs] gotta take care of themselves. In my mind, all they had to do was have a conversation, the same as I had a conversation.

David Greenglass's "conversation" with the government did not begin immediately. That afternoon, Rogge informed the FBI (still very much involved despite Ladd's protestations to the contrary) that he had been authorized by his client to promise full cooperation. But he would not let the FBI actually talk to David until the matter of the New Mexico extradition had been settled. In the meantime, Rogge had done nothing about David Greenglass's instruction to Fabricant that Julius Rosenberg be informed of his confession. Rogge was doing his best to see that the Rosenbergs knew nothing and he asked the FBI to make sure that their own actions did not provide the tip-off.

4

"Your Guy and My Guy Are Relatives"

The FBI saw Julius Rosenberg as just the next in a row of falling dominoes. If he confessed, as Harry Gold and David Greenglass had confessed before him, he could lead them to another round of arrests in the biggest spy hunt ever. David Greenglass's first statement had given few details about Rosenberg's role. The Bureau had no way of knowing whether Greenglass's brother-in-law was a key figure in the conspiracy or a relatively minor one who might lead them to the true organizers. J. Edgar Hoover, buoyed by his agents' success so far, put pressure on the New York field office to waste no time in finding out. The very first cable informing FBI headquarters of the results of the Greenglass interrogation bears a penciled note from Hoover, exhorting: "We Must Move Promptly."

But the Rosenberg domino did not tip over. When FBI agents showed up at his apartment shortly after eight o'clock on the morning of June 16, 1950, Julius Rosenberg reacted with considerable poise. After calmly finishing his morning shave, he politely but firmly refused the agents permission to search his home without a warrant but agreed to accompany them to Foley Square for questioning.

Initially, FBI agents William Norton and John Harrington told Rosenberg only that David Greenglass had been picked up for questioning in connection with charges arising out of his work at Los Alamos years before. Rosenberg took the news calmly—perhaps too calmly to avoid arousing the suspicions of the FBI agents. Rosenberg spoke as if he were under the impression that David had been picked up in connection with the stolen-uranium investigation. The agents said nothing to suggest otherwise until he had claimed to have learned about David's wartime work at Los Alamos only after Hiroshima.

At that point, agent Harrington abruptly changed course. "What would you say if we told you your brother-in-law said you asked him to supply information to the Russians?" he asked.

"Bring him here," Julius replied. "I'll call him a liar to his face."

It happened that David Greenglass was napping on a cot in a room down the corridor at that very moment. But the agents were not ready for a confrontation. When Rosenberg demanded permission to call his lawyer, Norton and Harrington stalled as long as they could, offering cigarettes and sandwiches and assuring Rosenberg— quite misleadingly, of course—that there was no need for him to have legal advice since he was not under suspicion. Finally, at about three in the afternoon, after Ethel had called the FBI trying to find out why her husband was being detained so long, Rosenberg was handed the phone. Immediately he dialed the office of FAECT counsel Victor Rabinowitz. Rabinowitz was out on business but his law partner came to the phone. "Ask the FBI if you are under arrest," he snapped as soon as he learned what the situation was.

"Am I under arrest?" Julius asked Norton.

"No," came the reply.

Julius relayed the message to the lawyer, who advised: "Then pick yourself up and come down to our office."

Bowing in mock politeness, Julius departed. Not until he reached the street and saw a newspaper did he realize that Greenglass had actually been arraigned that day and was being held on $100,000 bond.

From Foley Square, Julius Rosenberg went straight to the office of Victor Rabinowitz. Rosenberg wanted the FAECT counsel to represent him, but Rabinowitz had recently been involved with the defense of the accused spy Judith Coplon and he felt that to become identified with another espionage case so soon would do nothing to advance either his own career or the chances of his would-be client.

He gave Rosenberg the name of another lawyer, Emanuel Hirsch Bloch.

That same evening, Rosenberg managed to reach Bloch, who was entertaining guests at his apartment on lower Fifth Avenue. Bloch agreed to slip away from his company long enough to meet Rosenberg near the IND subway entrance on Sixth Avenue and Eighth Street. The two men walked around the block and then repaired to an Eighth Street coffee shop, where Rosenberg described his experience with the FBI.

Manny Bloch was a short, stocky man whose deep-set eyes, ringed with puffy bags, gave him a perpetually doleful expression and made him look older than his forty-nine years. Bloch apparently had no premonition that he was taking on a case that would consume the remaining years of his life. On the contrary, he later recalled sizing up Julius Rosenberg as "a sweet intellectual sort of fellow" whose difficulties amounted to no more than "just another routine" Fifth Amendment case. He told Julius that he "was in the same boat with hundreds of others" and advised him of his constitutional right against self-incrimination.

Bloch's failure to foresee the celebrity that would eventually attach to the Rosenberg case is hardly surprising. Nevertheless, his account of his first impression of the case seems disingenuous. David Greenglass had already been named as an "atom spy" in the press. And if this was not enough to tip off Bloch that Julius's problems were more than routine, there was the fact that Rabinowitz had already decided he did not want to become involved.

Rabinowitz had certainly not sent Rosenberg to a novice. Although Manny Bloch liked to portray himself in court as an obscure people's lawyer, he had actually won quite a reputation in some of the most visible political cases of the previous decade. A member of the National Lawyers Guild and the Civil Rights Congress, Bloch had been part of the defense team for Willie McGee and was still serving as one of the three CRC attorneys assigned to the case of the Trenton Six, then before the appeals courts. Bloch was also well known for his recent representation of Steve Nelson, a leader of the Communist Party in Pittsburgh. Nelson, a former close friend of J. Robert Oppenheimer and his wife, Kitty, had been called before HUAC and questioned about charges that, in 1943, he had received classified atomic secrets from scientists working at the Berkeley Radiation Laboratory. Although Bloch had advised his client to remain silent on constitutional grounds, Nelson interspersed his Fifth Amendment answers with denunciations of the Committee, drawing some thirty-eight contempt-of-Congress citations as well as national media attention for himself and his attorney.

Bloch's reputation as a crusader for left-wing causes may not have been the only reason his name occurred to Victor Rabinowitz. It happens that Bloch also had a long association with O. John Rogge, who had already been named in newspaper accounts as David Greenglass's attorney. Bloch and Rogge had worked together on the Trenton Six defense and were still counsel of record for the case. They had their law offices in the same building at 401 Broadway, and Bloch had regular access to the Rogge firm's law library. At the moment, the most any lawyer could do for Julius Rosenberg was to keep apprised of David Greenglass's situation and, if possible, to prevent what eventually happened—David's decision to turn government witness. As the result of Rogge's recent political defection, his relations with many of the lawyers he had worked with in the past were not good. If anyone could be expected to keep the lines of communication open and figure out how Rogge intended to handle the Greenglass matter, it was Manny Bloch.

In the meantime, Julius Rosenberg continued to follow his normal day-to-day routine while the FBI maintained what it called a "discreet surveillance." Agents Norton and Harrington, now permanently assigned to Rosenberg's case, were not at all happy with the situation. Until and unless David Greenglass expanded on the accusations made in his statement of the night of June 15–16, they could not justify arresting Rosenberg—not, at least, on any charge that would justify a high enough bail to keep him in jail. Encouraged by David Greenglass's quick capitulation, the Bureau had taken a chance in questioning Rosenberg so soon. The gamble had not paid off and now Norton, Harrington, and their superiors in the New York office were faced with the tricky assignment of making sure their quarry did not slip away before they had the basis for an arrest.

A memorandum prepared by New York Bureau supervisor Al Tuohy reflects the frustration and frayed nerves that afflicted his agents as the days went by without a clear signal from O. John Rogge agreeing to further interrogation of the Greenglasses. Tuohy described the Knickerbocker Village housing project as a surveillance man's nightmare. The project covered an entire city block and consisted of numerous separate buildings whose basements were connected by a network of underground passageways. All this was located in the middle of a "pushcart" neighborhood where longtime residents and small businesspeople knew each other by sight and FBI agents were all too conspicuous. Tuohy concluded that there was no way to keep a minute-to-minute watch on the suspect's movements without blanketing the entire neighborhood with agents or posting a watch outside his apartment door. Both of these strategies were rejected as inconsistent with the Bureau's hope that, kept on a loose rein, Rosenberg might lead them to a meeting with his Soviet control.

In spite of Tuohy's reluctance to go beyond "discreet" surveillance, Julius Rosenberg knew very well that he was being watched, at least some of the time. Why then did he not seize the opportunity afforded by the Bureau's "discreet" methods and make his escape? One explanation would be that Rosenberg had no reason to flee; he was innocent. But there are other possibilities quite consistent with his guilt.

Soviet intelligence had been willing to protect its American agents to the extent of arranging an escape route. However, it would hardly risk a currently productive operative by instructing him to make contact with someone who was already under suspicion. David Greenglass's quick capitulation had upset the timetable. Even if Rosenberg had doubted his brother-in-law's ability to hold up indefinitely under pressure, he would hardly have anticipated that Greenglass would break down and name his own relatives after only a few hours of questioning. And assuming that the Rosenberg spy network was as extensive as Greenglass claimed, then Julius would have needed time—perhaps weeks—to find ways to warn his far-flung contacts without leading his FBI tail directly to their doorsteps.

There was another factor that made flight most unlikely once FBI surveillance was under way. Rosenberg was a devoted family man who would hardly have considered absconding without taking his wife and children along. It might have been possible for him to get away alone, but it is difficult to imagine how he and Ethel, with two young boys in tow, could have slipped through the FBI's net.

Finally, Rosenberg may have been hoping that if he did nothing out of the ordinary for some time, the FBI would eventually give up its watch on him. He could not be sure that Norton and Harrington were not bluffing when they claimed Greenglass had already named him. Indeed, if the agents were telling the truth, why was he not already under arrest? The real explanation—that Greenglass was still wavering on the matter of cooperation—was by no means the only possibility to be considered.

Newspaper accounts of David Greenglass's arraignment and his first hearing on the question of extradition to New Mexico had stressed the prisoner's defiant behavior and the obvious antagonism between U.S. Attorney Irving Saypol and O. John Rogge. It was not until July 12, when Greenglass's second extradition hearing ended in a government request for a postponement, that the press began to speculate that Greenglass's counsel was leaning toward a guilty plea. This speculation was capped by a story in the New York *Journal-American* on Thursday, July 13, that said Saypol and Rogge had left the courtroom "practically arm in arm."

According to Ruth, it was during this same week that Ethel made an attempt to sound her out about David's intentions. Ethel arrived at Tessie Greenglass's apartment, where Ruth was visiting, her arms laden with fresh baked goods, and offered to take Ruth's toddler, Stephen, out for a picnic. Ruth later claimed in court that Ethel had taken her aside, out of Tessie's hearing, and told her that Julius's lawyer had asked that she find out what David was planning to do. She asked hopefully whether Ruth really thought it would be "a dirty shame for David to take the blame and sit for two." Ruth Greenglass also told us in a recent interview that by this point she was actually afraid that Ethel intended to kidnap her son and hold him hostage in exchange for David's silence.

Although we have only Ruth's word for it that Ethel's visit was anything but a perfectly innocent attempt to comfort her sister-in-law and find out what was going on, it is interesting that the entire Greenglass family had sided with Ruth and David. The Greenglass relatives knew quite well that David was being urged by his lawyers to cooperate with the government—several of them had attended a conference in Rogge's office during which David's options were again discussed—yet not one of them saw fit to drop a hint to Julius and Ethel.

Tessie Greenglass, it is true, had always favored her youngest son over her strong-willed and unconventional daughter. But Bernard Greenglass, one of the older brothers, had been close enough to

Julius Rosenberg to enter into the machine-shop partnership with him and David. Could the bitterness over the business's failure have run so deep as to turn Bernard into the Rosenbergs' enemy? In a later conference attended by both Herbert Fabricant and Manny Bloch, Bernard would dismiss the family-feud theory as ridiculous. He admitted that both he and David had quarreled with Julius over business—such disagreements were inevitable, Bernard claimed, given Julius's determination to "be King Tut or nothing"—but he denied that the rest of the family was nursing a grudge against the Rosenbergs. For reasons that can only be surmised, the Greenglasses simply believed that Ruth and David were the injured parties.

In any event, Ruth's cold reception to Ethel's overtures, combined with the *Journal-American* story, would have given the Rosenbergs ample reason to suspect something was afoot. FBI supervisor Tuohy was nervous enough about the *Journal-American* piece alone to conclude that if Rosenberg had any idea of running he would do so during the coming weekend. At his wit's end, Tuohy teletyped FBI investigations chief A. H. Belmont in Washington for advice. Belmont's reply was not comforting. "Later that evening," Tuohy wrote,

> Inspector Belmont called. He inquired as to when we had last seen Rosenberg. I told him five minutes ago we had placed him in his apartment at Rivington Street [*sic*]; that he was extremely hot. Mr. Belmont advised that the Bureau had already presented information previously to the [Justice] Department, and that they had not authorized on Rosenberg. The Bureau was attempting to contact the Department to give them additional information, but it did not appear we would have an answer on prosecution over the weekend. The department does not exactly know what it wants to do about Ruth Greenglass.
>
> Mr. Belmont wanted to know if we knew of any reason why ROSENBERG should attempt to skip this weekend any more than he would have last weekend. . . . Mr. Belmont stated that because of the lateness of the day and the impending weekend, plus the fact that we had not gone into the GREENGLASSES' interviews as thoroughly as we would like, the Bureau was inclined not to press for an arrest of Rosenberg at this time. I told him we felt the same way, but told him our problem of attempting to keep track of ROSENBERG in the event he decided to

take a powder. . . . [He said] we should try to be reasonably sure of his whereabouts until the GREENGLASSES' stories crystallized and signed statements are taken covering the essential facts of Rosenberg's activities. We should be certain not to burn up ROSENBERG on the surveillance, but be reasonably sure we know where he is.

On Saturday morning, Ethel Rosenberg paid another visit to her mother and, apparently quite by chance, ran into Ruth, who was there with her new baby. Acting on orders from Rogge, Ruth assured Ethel that she and David were planning to "fight this case." This, of course, was a lie. She and David had been interviewed by the FBI the previous day and David had agreed to submit to another interrogation that coming Monday. Ruth's Friday statement had confirmed and expanded upon the main point in David's original confession: that is, that in November 1944, Julius Rosenberg, in Ethel's presence, had asked Ruth to talk her husband into spying and that Harry Gold had identified himself by means of the recognition password arranged by Rosenberg. David's Monday statement would cover Julius's payments of money to finance the Greenglasses' flight as well as the allegations about the broader scope of the Rosenberg network: the two lower Manhattan apartments used for microfilming, the offers to fund David's education at MIT, the "sky platform," and so on.

On the basis of these new statements, the FBI felt it now had enough information to proceed against Rosenberg. Monday afternoon, after David Greenglass had been returned to his cell, officials at FBI headquarters showed a teletype transcript of Greenglass's latest statements to James McInerney of the Justice Department. McInerney agreed that there was now enough evidence for a charge of conspiracy to commit espionage. As soon as Richard Whelan, assistant special agent in charge of the New York office, learned of McInerney's decision, he dispatched agent William Norton to swear out a complaint before federal judge John F. X. McGohey.

J. Edgar Hoover, following the unfolding drama almost minute by minute from his office in Washington, was livid over the New York Bureau's insistence on delaying the arrest long enough to secure a proper warrant. The director suspected that U.S. Attorney Saypol, tipped off by the Justice Department, would want to inform the press of Rosenberg's impending arrest so that the story would be covered for the next morning's papers. If everything failed to go exactly as planned, a leak to the press might alert Rosenberg and give him a chance to elude capture at the last moment. In a scrawled note on the bottom of a memo to D. M. Ladd, Hoover complained acidly that "the solicitude of the Dept. & strict observance of technicalities in favor of openly avowed conspirators is shocking."

Notwithstanding Hoover's impatience, Whelan refused to act without a warrant. However, Washington's displeasure obviously put pressure on the New York agents to demonstrate their ardor and efficiency. McGohey's warrant was received at 6:55 P.M.; less than an hour later, Norton and Harrington arrived at Knickerbocker Village, joining a surveillance team already in the area. When Rosenberg answered the door, he was immediately clapped into handcuffs in full view of his terrified young sons. Then, while he was hustled out of the apartment and down in the elevator to a waiting car, a backup team swarmed through the one-bedroom flat, confiscating papers, books, and jewelry—the last as part of a search for a gold watch David Greenglass had alleged was given to Julius by the Russians. In the ensuing confusion, Ethel Rosenberg somehow had the presence of mind to demand that the agents produce their warrant and allow her to call her attorney—an assertion of her constitutional rights that an FBI report on the arrest would dismiss as a "typical Communist remonstrance."

Ethel, according to this same account, "was told to keep quiet and get in the bedroom with the children, which she did." Julius, meanwhile, was taken directly to Foley Square for arraignment. There a phalanx of reporters and photographers awaited his arrival. Somehow the press had been tipped off after all, despite the U.S. attorney's promise to the contrary made to Hoover.

Held in prison on $100,000 bail, Rosenberg continued to maintain his innocence. Despite frequent speculation in the newspapers that he or Greenglass or both were facing the death penalty, there is no indication that Rosenberg and his lawyer ever so much as discussed the possibility of pleading guilty. Bloch, it would seem, still thought there was a possibility that something might be worked out with Rogge. The late O. John Rogge told us that, shortly after Rosenberg's arrest, Manny Bloch had dropped into his office with a proposal. "Your guy and my guy are relatives," Rogge recalled

Bloch saying. "If they refuse to testify against each other, the government will have no case." This was not, strictly speaking, an accurate description of the situation, since Harry Gold could still have testified against the Greenglasses. But, in any event, it was too late for Rogge to entertain such an arrangement even if he had wanted to.

Ethel, meanwhile, invited the press into her apartment on the morning after the arrest to give her own reaction to the charges. Posing in front of her kitchen sink with dish towel in hand, Ethel looked very much like a typical housewife totally bewildered by the FBI's interest in her husband. "Neither my husband nor I have ever been Communists," she told reporters, "and we don't know any Communists. The whole thing is ridiculous."

As an obvious candidate for a grand jury subpoena, Ethel might have been well advised to keep a low profile and avoid making statements that could easily be proven false. However heartening her behavior may have been to Julius, it could only tempt the prosecutors into thinking she might be goaded into making similar denials under oath.

Up to the very day of Julius's arrest, the FBI's interest in Ethel Rosenberg had been nil. Julius alone was the target of their investigation. The statements made by the Greenglasses on July 14, and subsequently, did give some hint that Ethel might be indictable; David and Ruth had placed Ethel in the room during several key conversations and there was also the matter of the ambiguously worded letter that Ruth claimed Ethel had written to her in New Mexico shortly after Ruth suffered a miscarriage. But the evidence against Ethel rested entirely on the Greenglasses' uncorroborated word and placed her in an accessory role at best. During the second half of July an intensive investigation of Julius Rosenberg's activities began to produce evidence that confirmed the existence of the spy ring David Greenglass had described. This investigation branched off in several directions, but still none of the new leads focused attention on Ethel.

From the very first, the government's interest in Ethel was based less on her own alleged complicity than on the possibility that the threat of prosecuting her could be used to pressure her husband into a full confession. A Bureau memo reporting to D. M. Ladd and Hoover on the arrest of Julius and the search of his apartment makes this point explicitly. "The indications are definite," said Belmont, "that [Rosenberg] possesses the identity of a number of individuals who have been engaged in Soviet espionage." Therefore, Belmont recommended, the agents in New York should "consider every possible means to make him talk, including . . . a careful study of the involvement of Ethel Rosenberg in order that charges be placed against her, if possible." Hoover approved, adding his handwritten comment in the margin: "Yes by all means. If the criminal division [of the Justice Department] procrastinates too long let me know and I will see the A.G."

Hoover waited only two days before making good on his promise, dashing off a note to Attorney General J. Howard McGrath. "There is no question," Hoover wrote, but that "if Julius Rosenberg would furnish details of his extensive espionage activities it would be possible to proceed against other individuals . . . *proceeding against his wife might serve as a lever in this matter* [emphasis added]."

Although it was the FBI that first suggested arresting Ethel, their enthusiasm for this course was soon exceeded by that of U.S. Attorney Saypol. By the first of August, Saypol was so impatient to bring Ethel into custody that he did not even want to wait for her appearance before the grand jury, slated for August 8. Saypol's eagerness shocked Richard Whelan, assistant special agent in charge of the New York FBI office. The cautious Whelan obviously did not consider that there was sufficient evidence against Ethel and he complained to his superior, Belmont, that to ask for a warrant now, when Ethel was already under a grand-jury subpoena, might make it appear that the government was attempting to compel her to turn against her husband. Belmont was inclined to agree. Though conceding privately that the Bureau had little ground for objecting since it was they who had needled Saypol to move against Ethel in the first place, he agreed to call Assistant Attorney General McInerney and persuade him that Saypol was moving too fast.

That same day, August 1, Belmont fired off a private memo to D. M. Ladd, warning him that Saypol might be trying to turn Ethel's arrest into a personal coup. This was distressing to the Bureau, which wanted to control the tempo of the still very much active investigation into Rosenberg's affairs and to get all the credit in the press as well. "Knowing Saypol's proclivities for publicity," Belmont claimed, "it is apparent that what he has in mind is marching Ethel right down before the [U.S. commissioner] and having a complaint and warrant executed. . . .This should be kept in mind . . . in connection with a possible press release."

The charge that Saypol wanted to manage Ethel's arrest in a

way that would generate maximum news coverage for the U.S. Attorney's office was no doubt accurate. But there was another reason why Saypol did not want to wait until the grand jury had taken its course. The grand jurors had so far shown no interest in bringing charges against Mrs. Rosenberg. On the contrary, their attention had been focused on Ruth Greenglass. Ruth, by her own admission, had played a far more active role in the conspiracy, and the grand jurors saw her as a logical target for indictment. Their attitude did not change until Assistant U.S. Attorney Myles Lane informed them that action against Mrs. Greenglass would interfere with the government's ability to prosecute the case successfully. Eventually, Ruth was named as an unindicted coconspirator.

The grand jurors' interest in Ethel does not appear to have increased significantly even after her first appearance before them on the 8th. Wearing a powder-blue and white polka-dot dress and a modest straw hat, Ethel looked pale but quite composed. She can hardly have fit the grand jurors' image of an atom spy. Under questioning by Myles Lane, Ethel admitted that she had once signed a Communist Party nominating petition—hardly a crime, though it almost seemed one in the virulently anti-Communist summer of 1950. Then she retreated to the ground of the Fifth Amendment, refusing to answer any questions dealing with the specific charges, including the query, "Have you every met Harry Gold?"—a question she could almost certainly have honestly answered in the negative.

Ethel left the hearing room convinced that she had acquitted herself well, and Manny Bloch agreed. Although she had resorted to the Fifth Amendment more often than may have been necessary, her caution was justified. More than one witness has been trapped by overconfidence in trying to pick and choose the questions that might lead to self-incrimination. And while Lane's questions had been framed to deal only with Ethel's own activities, so that technically she was not asked to testify against her own husband, it was possible that the grand jurors would still see her as a loyal wife, more interested in shielding Julius Rosenberg than herself.

Irving Saypol may have foreseen the same possibility, since Ethel's testimony made him all the more determined to arrest her immediately rather than wait until the grand jury had taken its course. Ethel was issued a second summons to return to the grand-jury room on August 11. On that occasion she was run through a list of questions almost identical to those she had been asked three days earlier. It would be hard to say who was more puzzled by this repeat performance, Ethel or the grand jurors.

If Saypol had really wanted to compel Ethel to answer Lane's questions, he could have tried to obtain a court order forcing her to testify, by holding over her head the threat of a contempt citation. But the real purpose of bringing Ethel back to the grand jury a second time appears to have been to stage her arrest under the most dramatic circumstances possible—in the hope, perhaps, that she would break down and make damaging statements in the course of the arraignment.

After finishing with the grand jury, Ethel was allowed to leave the courthouse. While walking across Foley Square to catch the subway, she was accosted by two FBI agents who steered her back inside and up to the Bureau's offices on the twenty-ninth floor. The process of obtaining a warrant was set in motion than and there, while Ethel waited in an adjoining room; her arraignment before the U.S. commissioner followed momentarily and bail was set at $100,000—the same high figure that had been imposed in her husband's case.

Ethel's arrest was so unexpected that Manny Bloch had left his office for the afternoon and could not be reached. His father, Alexander Bloch, arrived at the courthouse just in time to represent Ethel at her arraignment and to protest unsuccessfully against the prohibitive bail. The elder Mr. Bloch, a man in his seventies whose legal experience was primarily as a representative of the furriers' union, remained Ethel's counsel of record throughout her trial. His background made him an unusual choice for a defendant in an espionage case. In fact, his chief qualification, aside from his willingness to accept an impecunious and highly unpopular client, was that he was prepared to work closely with his son in presenting a unified defense. Ethel appears never to have questioned the wisdom of this arrangement.

The bitterest blow of all was the U.S. commissioner's refusal to delay Ethel's imprisonment long enough to allow her to make some arrangement for the care of her sons, who had been left with a neighbor for the afternoon. That evening, the boys were picked up by Tessie Greenglass, who none too happily took them into her home. A less satisfactory custody situation could hardly be imagined. Nor did it last long. Tessie Greenglass protested that the children, now seven and three years old, were too undisciplined and that in any case she could not afford the expense of feeding them. Before long they were removed to the Hebrew Children's Home in the Bronx.

Arrest left Ethel devastated. The cool and almost contemptuous demeanor that she was to display in all her courtroom appearances was only one side of her character. Matrons in charge of the ninth floor of the Women's House of Detention in Greenwich Village, where Ethel was housed, reported that she suffered frequent migraine headaches and could be heard sobbing herself to sleep at night. Her need for contact with her husband was almost obsessive, and when she was taken along with the other women to exercise on the prison's roof, she spent the entire exercise period pressed against the wire fence, looking toward the nearby men's facility in the hope that she might catch a fleeting glimpse of Julius. It is little wonder that the FBI and the prosecutors thought Ethel might break down completely, forcing Julius Rosenberg to confess in order to end her ordeal.

Ethel was undoubtedly being used as a pawn to push Julius into confessing. This does not mean that anyone in the Justice Department believed they were persecuting an innocent woman. Both the FBI and the prosecutors found the Greenglasses' accusations against Ethel credible. Indeed, based on the entire range of evidence, it would be hard to imagine that Ethel did not know and approve of her husband's activities. Perhaps she was even his full partner, as would later be charged. On the other hand, based on the limited evidence available, one might hypothesize that Ethel had never been entirely comfortable with Julius's chosen course. She had taken to her bed suffering from a nervous collapse after Julius lost his Signal Corps job and had sought psychiatric counseling, ostensibly because she found it difficult to cope with her high-strung elder son. Living with a man who saw himself as a "soldier of Stalin" could not have been easy.

An interesting perspective on Ethel's state of mind during this period after her arrest emerges from the reminiscences of some of Ethel's fellow House of Detention inmates who were interviewed by journalist Virginia Gardner for her book *The Rosenberg Story*. One woman who befriended Ethel in prison recalls being by turns infuriated and admiring of a quality she described as Ethel's "idealism." Although Gardner is intent on interpreting this remark as evidence that Ethel was a veritable saint, it seems, judging by the full context of the woman's quoted statements, that she is really describing Ethel's inability to take a practical approach to human relationships—or to accept that there is a difference between the way things ought to be and the way they are in reality. According to this woman, Ethel idolized her husband and believed in general that those who had once won her trust could do no wrong. This attitude made her an easy mark for inmate cons, and might have made it difficult for her to survive in jail if her naïveté had not also aroused the protective instincts of some of the more street-wise inmates.

Ironically, the arrest and jailing of Ethel may, in the long run, have strengthened her determination to maintain her silence whatever the cost. The prisoners' code against informing was usually more honored in the breach than in the observance and the ability of this woman, who had at first seemed soft and middle class by the standards of most of the other prisoners, to withstand the pressure to confess made her something of a heroine.

Weeks and then months went by. Ethel appeared to be adjusting to life in the Women's House of Detention and Julius showed no sign that the threatened prosecution of his wife would make him amenable to cooperation with the government. The theory behind Ethel's arrest had not panned out, but the government was now committed to prosecuting her as a partner in the conspiracy. And in the meantime, the FBI's investigation had produced some tantalizing evidence of a wider spy ring, though still without adding anything to the rather shaky case against Ethel Rosenberg.

5

The Other Spy Ring

On or about June 16, 1950, the day David Greenglass's arrest was announced to the press, Joel Barr disappeared from his rented apartment at the Villa Régine in the Paris suburb of Neuilly. He left behind his clothes, his books, and a recently purchased motorcycle that had been his pride and joy. He was never seen or heard from again.

That same day in New York, thirty-three-year-old Morton Sobell, like Barr a former CCNY acquaintance of Julius Rosenberg's, went to his boss at the Reeves Instrument Company and asked for a leave of absence, pleading exhaustion and overwork. Although Sobell was working on the final stages of a critical project, he was granted the time off. Six days later he flew to Mexico with his wife, Helen, their young son, and his twelve-year-old stepdaughter. Once in Mexico, Sobell began to act like a man in the grip of panic. He sent letters to his father and sister-in-law through a New York friend, William Danziger, and he began to use a variety of thinly disguised aliases, including M. Sowell, Marvin Sand, and Morton Solt. After July 18, when Julius Rosenberg's arrest was made public, Sobell cashed in his family's return air tickets and began making the round of shipping offices in Vera Cruz and Tampico, trying to book passage to Europe for himself and his family.

On July 27, Joel Barr's best friend, Al Sarant, drove to New York City for a rendezvous with Carol Dayton, an Ithaca, New

York, neighbor with whom he had been having an affair for some time. The pair drove cross-country in Sarant's car and on August 9 crossed the border into Hermosillo, Mexico, using forged tourist cards made out to Mr. and Mrs. Bruce Dayton. Then, like Joel Barr, they disappeared without a trace.

Also, on Sunday, July 23, 1950, six days after Julius Rosenberg's arrest, William Perl, a noted aeronautical engineer who had been a classmate of Julius Rosenberg's and a friend of Barr's and Sarant's, was at home in his Cleveland apartment when he received a visit from a woman he recognized as Vivian Glassman of New York. Miss Glassman sat down on Perl's couch and began writing out a message in longhand on a pad of $8\frac{1}{2}$-$\times$-11 ruled paper. The message mentioned the names of Joel Barr and Julius Rosenberg, and it offered Perl $2,000 along with instructions to flee the country via Mexico. Perl told his visitor that she "did not know what she was talking about" and angrily asked her to leave. As soon as she had gone, he flushed the message down the toilet.

Were these four incidents part of the dissolution of a spy ring? Or were they, as defenders of the Rosenbergs have long maintained, unrelated and perfectly innocent occurrences? The story of the "other" spy ring has long been one of the most enigmatic aspects of the Rosenberg case. Even today, there are many unanswered questions, but it is possible for the first time to understand why the FBI felt sure that it had stumbled onto an extensive conspiracy, involving much more than David Greenglass's admitted theft of A-bomb secrets.

David Greenglass had been able to give the FBI only two names to support his claim that Julius Rosenberg was a Soviet spymaster. One was Ann Sidorovich and the other was Joel Barr. The latter's name initially appears in the course of Greenglass's first lengthy statement to the Bureau on July 17. Recalling his discussions with Julius about the possibility of fleeing to Mexico, Greenglass remembered that he had wondered out loud whether the FBI would allow someone who was under suspicion to cross the border. Julius in turn had assured him that he was giving too much credit to the FBI, telling him: "Oh, they let other people out who are more important than you are . . . they let Barr out, Joel Barr, and he was a member of our espionage ring."

Joel Barr was also one of the two American citizens who had been mentioned in the KGB secret messages deciphered in 1948.

There is no reason, however, to suppose that up to this point the Bureau suspected any connection between Barr and Greenglass. After it was discovered that Barr was living abroad, the FBI's investigation of Barr had been placed on inactive status, while Robert Lamphere, the agent responsible for coordinating the case with the CIA, had himself been preoccupied for months with developments in the Fuchs-Gold case. It was only after Barr's name cropped up so casually in David Greenglass's statement that the FBI moved to discover Barr's current whereabouts.

By July 25, 1950, the FBI had somehow learned Barr's latest address in Paris, and on that date Hoover sent an "URGENT" cable to the U.S. Embassy asking the legal attaché to locate and interview the subject. The attaché went out to Neuilly only to learn he was too late. The landlady of the Villa Régine could tell him only that no one had seen Barr since June 15 or 16. It was all very puzzling, she added, since the young man had neither paid his last month's rent bill nor left instructions about what she should do with his personal belongings.

In the meantime, FBI agents interrogating Greenglass found he knew even less about Joel Barr than had already been discovered in the course of their own investigation two years previously. Greenglass knew Barr by sight and recalled having met him on several occasions at the Rosenbergs' apartment in the company of Barr's fiancée, Vivian Glassman, who was also a close friend of Ethel Rosenberg's. Greenglass, however, did not claim to have any direct knowledge of Barr's involvement in the spy ring. He could relate only that Rosenberg had told him it would be possible for him to flee the country, since a more important person, Joel Barr, had already done so and was working for the Russians somewhere in Europe. When the agents queried Ruth about Barr, she said he had gone to Europe under the pretext of studying music, and she thought he was now in Finland.

Ruth Greenglass's version of why Joel Barr had gone abroad later received at least partial confirmation from Julius Rosenberg, who testified at his trial that Barr had gone to Europe to study music. Barr was indeed a talented amateur pianist, but it was another aspect of his background that interested the FBI. He was also a graduate electrical engineer who had worked extensively on defense-related projects, including state-of-the-art radar systems.

Born in 1916, Joel Barr had majored in engineering at City College of New York, graduating in 1938. In 1940 he was hired by the Signal Corps laboratory in Fort Monmouth, New Jersey, where his co-workers included Alfred Sarant, soon to become his closest friend, and Vivian Glassman, later his fiancée. A confident, sociable young man, Barr made friends easily and was recognized by his co-workers as a natural leader with an outstanding mind. Barr's promising career at Fort Monmouth was nonetheless cut short after two years when the army learned he had once signed a Communist Party nominating petition. Barr was dismissed.

Experienced electrical engineers were in short supply during the war, and Barr did not stay unemployed long. His next job was with the Western Electric Company, an important defense contractor. On his application form, Barr did not mention the reason for his dismissal from the Signal Corps. His new employers assigned him to classified work on the APQ-13 radar system, designed to be used by B-29s for low-altitude bombing.

The development of airborne radar systems was one of the most sensitive and high-pressured areas of weapons research. At the beginning of the war, air-corps bombardiers were still locating their targets visually, and bombing at night or in overcast weather was frequently out of the question. Only the application of the most up-to-the-minute microwave radar technology made it possible to build radar sets that were compact enough to use on planes and ships, able to resist jamming by the enemy, and still accurate enough to distinguish between two closely placed targets. The first airborne radar systems were tested in 1941 and did not go into production until 1942, the year Barr came to Western Electric.

Barr's assignment, specifically, was to work on the Mod 13 computer—not a digital computer in the modern sense of the word, but a calculator that used electronic relays to set up a self-correcting timing system for bombardments. The mathematical theory for such "computers," which were also used for directing antiaircraft fire, had been worked out by John von Neumann and Julian Bigelow and was one of the first sophisticated applications of the electronic feedback principle and a first step toward the postwar computer revolution.* As an electrical engineer, Barr was responsible for debugging the

---

*In the opinion of Vannevar Bush of the wartime Office of Scientific Research and Development, who asked von Neumann and Bigelow to study the problem in the first place, there were two major challenges facing American science during the war: the development of the atomic bomb and the perfection of automatic tracking devices.

Mod 13, a task for which he was allowed complete freedom of movement throughout the plant.

As Ted Taylor, Barr's superior at Western Electric, told the FBI in 1951, the APQ-13 project had been officially classified as secret though not top secret, and anyone who understood the general principles of that particular system could be expected to have a good knowledge of its closely related sister radar systems as well. Engineers in Barr's position were not just permitted but expected to work at home on their own, and Barr "could have carried briefcases out of the plant at any time without question." In the three years that he remained at Western Electric, Barr was allowed responsibility above that of other men on his job level because he was the sort of person who seemed to have a grasp of the entire operation and therefore, in Taylor's words, "was leaned on very heavily by the officials of Western Electric while he worked there."

Barr resigned from Western Electric in September 1945 and spent the next year studying for his master's degree in engineering at Columbia University. In October 1946, he went to work for the Sperry Gyroscope Company, where he was assigned to special Air Force projects involving long-range radar systems. Eric J. Isbister, head of a division in Sperry's department of radio engineering and Barr's immediate boss, told the FBI that he had considered Barr a "brilliant" engineer and that Barr had dealt with Air Force contracts rated "top secret at Sperry . . . considered secret of the highest classification." (However, in response to an inquiry by the Senate Subcommittee on Internal Security made years later, in 1957, Sperry Gyroscope's personnel department denied that Barr had ever worked on classified projects.)

In October 1947, Barr was dismissed from Sperry, having been denied government clearance to handle classified documents. Several months later, he began making plans to go abroad. In a written statement submitted with his passport application, Barr stated that he intended to study toward a doctorate in engineering at the Royal Technical Institute in Stockholm and at Delft University in the Netherlands. Barr talked over these plans with his brothers as well, and one of them agreed to buy his car to help him raise cash for the trip.

Barr's impending trip to Europe apparently led to a rift with his fiancée, Vivian Glassman. According to Glassman's 1950 statements to the FBI, when Barr first began talking about going abroad she had planned to go with him, expecting that they would be married before leaving New York. At first Barr seemed agreeable, even changing his steamship reservations so that he and Glassman would be able to sail together. But as the January 21, 1948, departure date grew nearer, Glassman found that she could not pin Barr down to any specific wedding plans. Barr's reluctance to commit himself to marriage became the source of what Glassman described to the FBI as growing "personal differences." And in the end, the engagement was broken, and Barr sailed for Europe alone.

Although Joel Barr's career had been cut short when he was fired from Sperry, he had so far not been connected in any way to espionage. The first hint of such involvement did not come until later in 1948, after Barr had already left the country, when his name surfaced in the text of a KGB message. The text of this message has never been released; however, an intriguing reference in a summary report on Barr prepared by the FBI in late 1948 notes that during 1944 Barr is "believed to have acted as an intermediary between persons who were working on wartime nuclear fission research and for MGB agents."

In the course of trying to track down Barr in the fall of 1948, an agent in the New York office of the FBI called the home of Barr's mother pretending to be an acquaintance who had lost touch with her son. He was told that Barr was currently in Finland. This information caused some concern that Barr might be planning to defect to the Soviet bloc. However, Barr soon moved on to Sweden, where he registered at Stockholm's Royal Technical Institute. A report summarizing Barr's movements in Europe notes that:

> [A] confidential source further advised that in 1948 Barr arrived in France and then proceded [sic] to fly by plane to Holland where he enrolled at the University of Delft and remained there until March 1948. On March 31, 1948, he travelled to Finland where he spent six months touring the country supporting himself by playing the piano. He then arrived in Sweden from Abo, Finland on August 25, 1948 and thereupon enrolled ... in Stockholm. According to this confidential source, he devoted little attention to his studies, attending classes only on occasion and narrowly avoiding expulsion. ... Barr claimed to be supported partly by funds sent to him by a brother who resided in

New York. Following the completion of the course of instruction . . . at the Royal Technical Institute Barr had indicated to
some of his associates that he intended to return to the United
States in the near future.

This report ends with a notation that Barr's case would be taken
up again by the Bureau after his arrival back in the United States.
But Joel Barr never did return home.

Julius Rosenberg was arrested on July 17, the same day that David Greenglass first told his interrogators about Joel Barr. Still unaware of Barr's disappearance on the very day Greenglass's arrest
was announced in the press, the Bureau began to investigate the possible links between Barr and Julius Rosenberg. One of the first people
its agents talked to was Alfred Sarant, Barr's close friend, an electrical engineer who had worked at Fort Monmouth and at Western
Electric, and who was also a friend of Rosenberg's. According to a
"highly confidential" informant, Barr, Sarant, and Rosenberg had all
belonged to the same Communist Party unit—Branch 16B of the Industrial Division. All three men had dropped out of the Party
abruptly and at the same time, shortly after this unit was dissolved in
1944.

On the afternoon of July 19, 1950, Special Agents John D. Mahoney and Peter Maxson of the Albany Bureau office called at Sarant's home in Ithaca, New York. They discovered that Sarant,
though wary and nervous, was willing to respond to their questions
about his friendship with Rosenberg.

At first, Al Sarant insisted to the agents that he barely knew Rosenberg. As best he could remember, he had not met Rosenberg until
1941 or 1942 when Joel Barr, his co-worker at Fort Monmouth, had
asked him to donate blood for Rosenberg's ailing father. Sarant went
with Barr to the blood bank and there he was introduced to Julius
Rosenberg. Pressed for details of his subsequent friendship with Rosenberg, Sarant was vague. No doubt he had seen Julius at union
meetings and restaurants and once he had been in the Rosenbergs'
apartment. However, he insisted that he and his wife had had no contact with Julius and Ethel after 1946, when the Sarants had left New
York City for Ithaca.

When agent Mahoney asked pointedly whether Rosenberg had
ever propositioned him for espionage work, Sarant's memory im-

proved dramatically. Once, Sarant confided, when he and Julius were walking alone together, he had had the distinct feeling that he was being "sounded out." "But," he told the agents with some satisfaction, "I did not bite."

Mahoney and Maxson left the Sarant home that afternoon with mixed feelings. They did not believe that Sarant's belated memory of having been "sounded out" was the whole truth and their superior, agent Wall, later relayed the opinion to Washington that Sarant "appeared to be a Communist through and through." Wall also suggested that Sarant's wife, who was out of town on the day of the interview, might have gone to New York to check out the situation with other Rosenberg friends. On the other hand, the thirty-two-year-old Sarant appeared to be a naturally high-strung individual who might give the impression of nervousness even if he had nothing to hide. And Sarant had been willing to cooperate, however guardedly. He had even signed a waiver giving permission for two FBI agents to search his home.

This waiver was more than the FBI had any reason to hope for, since they had no grounds for a court-issued search warrant. On learning of the existence of the waiver, A. H. Belmont in Washington urged Albany that the search be carried out as soon as possible, "before Sarant changes his mind," and that interviews with the subject be continued "for as long as he will stand for it."

Sarant continued to "stand for it" for another week. In the course of several lengthy interviews, he admitted to having known that Joel Barr was a Communist Party member. Otherwise, the talks yielded little but a series of emphatic denials—especially to any suggestion that Rosenberg and he had seen each other since 1946.

The search of the Sarant home conducted that same week turned up nothing to prove he was lying about his relationship with Rosenberg. The searchers did discover a Bates pop-up address file that listed the Rosenbergs' address—a find that the Albany office considered suspicious, although in fact it proved nothing, since the Rosenbergs' address had not changed since 1943. On the other hand, several seemingly innocuous items did expose contradictions in Sarant's story about his relationship with Joel Barr and Vivian Glassman.

First of all, the search of Sarant's home turned up a set of vacation snapshots showing Sarant and Barr with Glassman. These photographs would hardly have been worthy of interest except that Sarant, in his initial interview with the FBI, had denied more than a superficial acquaintance with Joel Barr's fiancée, telling the agents that he could not even remember her last name. Upon being confronted with the pictures, however, Sarant admitted that they had gone on a two-week canoeing trip during the summer of 1944. Another set of pictures, Sarant admitted, dated from a second canoe trip, taken by Sarant and his wife, Louise, with Barr and Glassman.

Sarant had obviously been trying to avoid identifying Glassman. But was this just the normal impulse of a man who did not want to set the FBI on the track of an innocent friend, or did Sarant have some other reason? Ironically, Sarant himself provided a further clue to his motives on July 22, when he admitted to FBI investigators that he had received a money order from Glassman in payment for one month's rent on a New York apartment she had sublet from him.

This apartment—number 6I at 65 Morton Street in Greenwich Village—was quickly becoming one of the focal points of the FBI's investigation. The Bureau suspected it of being the secret Greenwich Village apartment described by David Greenglass in his statements of July 17 and 19—the site of much of Rosenberg's undercover microfilming activity. Sarant, however, described the Morton Street flat as a typical bachelor apartment, which he had shared originally with his friend, Joel Barr. Later, after Sarant married and decided to settle in Ithaca, he had kept the lease in his name, subletting it to various friends as a favor.

Certainly, it has never been uncommon to hold onto the lease of an inexpensive apartment in housing-scarce New York. And, in many respects, the picture that emerges of the Morton Street apartment during Sarant and Barr's tenancy, even in the FBI's own interviews with acquaintances who visited there, hardly makes it sound like a center for clandestine activities. Joel Barr, the more outgoing and socially adept of the roommates, kept a large collection of classical records and frequently invited friends in for evening "musicales." Sarant, for his part, was more interested in developing a close relationship with one woman, and for much of 1944 he was deeply engrossed in a love affair with Gladys Meyer, a young woman who lived across the hall. When the romance broke up, Sarant was disconsolate and called on a number of mutual friends to consult about the "Gladys Meyer problem," asking them to act as intermediaries in winning back her affections. By early 1945, however, Sarant had found a new love, Louise ("Puss") Ross. Sarant and Ross were married in the summer of 1945. They remained at Morton Street (Barr having apparently moved back to his parents' apartment) until September 1946, when they decided to move to Ithaca, where Louise's father was a prominent lawyer. When the Sarants left town, Joel Barr asked to sublease the apartment. And after Barr's departure for Europe, according to Sarant, the apartment had been inhabited by a CCNY acquaintance of Barr's, an aeronautical engineer named William Perl.

At least partial confirmation of this picture of Sarant's life during the period just prior to his marriage is provided by Gladys Meyer, the woman he had been dating. Thirty-five years later, Meyer spoke fondly of Sarant and the private lover's existence she and he had once shared. Meyer told us that by 1945 Sarant had dropped all political activities and that "for at least part of the time that I knew him he was not in the Party," even though "we both knew where our loyalties lay. There was no question about that." Meyer denied knowing of any clandestine activities connected with the Morton Street flat; however, she surprised us with the cryptic comment that she would not be surprised if Sarant had been leading a few dual lives.

The FBI's suspicions about the Morton Street flat at first centered on its difficulties in pinning down just who had lived there during the years after the Sarants moved to Ithaca. When questioned about this, Sarant seemed unusually vague. He told the agents that some of the time he had received payment from his subtenants by money order, but that for much of the period he had received lump-sum payments in cash covering several months' rent at a time—an arrangement that seemed odd considering the supposed limited financial resources of the tenants. Also, there was the matter of the Vivian Glassman money order. A confidential source, presumably inside the Ithaca Post Office, had confirmed to the FBI that this money order was sent to Sarant in August 1949. It was not clear why Glassman had been paying rent to Sarant in 1949, since this was long after Barr's departure for Europe and she herself was living in another apartment at the time.

There may have been logical explanations for all this, but as Bureau investigators dug deeper, they found more questions than answers. During the same week that agents from the Albany office were talking to Sarant in Ithaca, FBI investigators in New York sought out the 65 Morton Street building superintendent, Floyd Elwyn. He told them that he had been inside the apartment shortly after Al Sarant moved out in 1946 and had considered its furnishings odd indeed. According to Elwyn, the flat had contained nothing but three single cots, some work benches, electrical tools, and a reflector-type flood lamp suspended from a wall bracket over the kitchen table.

Confronted with this description, Sarant denied that the apartment had ever been without ordinary furniture, but he told agent Mahoney that he and Barr had been avid amateur photographers and had purchased a good deal of equipment, including flood lamps, floor lamps, and a developing tank. Sarant also said that at the time they roomed together Barr had owned a Leica camera, while he made do with a less expensive "Bee Bee" model. But all this equipment had been used only to take amateur photos, mainly portraits of girls. Later, however, he conceded that they may have used their set-up on occasions "to take document photos of sheet music."

If this set-up seemed rather elaborate for a pair of hobbyists, it was comparatively less expensive than another venture Barr and Sarant undertook together in 1945. FBI agents in New York learned that, beginning that summer, approximately at the time when Sarant married Louise Ross, he and Joel Barr had rented a storefront at 227 West Eleventh Street, several blocks from the Morton Street apartment building. In the window there had been a sign in black-and-gold lettering identifying the shop as "Sarant Laboratories, Inc." The business had indeed been legally incorporated and the partners had had letterhead stationery and calling cards made up by relatives of Joel Barr's who were in the printing business. Yet, according to another man who had rented space in the building during the same period, Sarant Laboratories did little or no business and the tenants were seldom seen.

To the FBI, Sarant Laboratories had all the hallmarks of a front. But when Sarant was first asked about the Eleventh Street premises on July 22, he described it as a "combination hobby and work shop." Questioned about the printed stationery and painted sign, Sarant became unusually agitated and insisted that these had been Joel Barr's ideas. Personally, he had never understood why such frills were necessary since the shop had never been intended as a business operation. He also added that Sarant Laboratories had never filed tax returns since it had never earned any profits and emphatically denied that he or Barr had ever solicited any government contracts.

But the FBI already knew that Sarant was lying. Among a box of personal papers found during the search of the Sarants' home was a letter that was obviously in response to an earlier solicitation of funds and information for a defense-related contract. Dated June 27, 1945, the letter was Sarant's reply to an inquiry from the Navy Bureau of Ships asking for clarification on a proposal for a "suggested method of voice transmission over a beam of light."

In his reply, Sarant explained that he and his partner had made "a number of fundamental experiments" that proved the practicability of their system but that they lacked the necessary lab and model-making equipment for further tests. Noting that navy scientists had objected that frequency shifts of light-transmitted signals would produce unacceptable noise, Sarant replied that it would be possible to eliminate this problem with the use of "our unique drives" and "fine gratings."

"With Navy sponsorship, we will be able to proceed at once with the development of this model," the letter went on, expressing in closing the desire that "we . . . as citizens and graduate engineers" might be able to "devote our energy to the successful completion of this project, which we are sure will give our country a valuable war weapon." The letter, signed by Sarant, bore the notation that it had been typed by "VG"—who may or may not have been Vivian Glassman.

The FBI wanted to know more about the purpose of Sarant Laboratories, but as of July 22, it was not yet ready to push Sarant too hard. At this point, it was still assumed that Joel Barr was in Paris and might be found at any time. Sarant had already established a pattern of blaming awkward circumstances on Barr, and the FBI may well have hoped that he would have more to say when Barr was taken into custody. Sarant is described in an FBI report covering this week as tense and extremely "surveillance conscious"—understandably, since the presence of FBI agents watching his home at all hours had been obvious enough to attract the attention of his neighbors. But, at the same time, Sarant seems to have impressed his interrogators as a man who was most unlikely to resort to desperate tactics to evade further interrogation. He was, after all, a married man with two young sons, four and two years old. He had a pleasant home that he had built himself, and was apparently very proud of, and an independent contracting and painting business that could hardly survive without his constant attentions.

Under the circumstances, the FBI office in Albany was not unduly worried when Sarant informed it on July 25 that he was planning to spend a week's vacation with relatives on Long Island. Albany duly notified New York to pick up surveillance of Sarant there on the off chance that he would try to contact some members of the Rosenberg group.

Sarant made no attempt to see any acquaintances of the Rosenbergs in New York City. Instead, he went there with Carol Dayton, a young married woman who was a next-door neighbor of his in Ithaca. Sarant and Dayton then drove together to the home of Sarant's relatives on Long Island.

Mrs. Electra Jayson, the only member of the Sarant family who was willing to discuss this episode, remembers that when her brother showed up with Carol Dayton, he begged her to help him shake the FBI. Sarant confided that he was under investigation in connection with the Rosenberg case and that it didn't matter whether he was guilty or innocent: either way, his problems were sure to bring terrible shame on the whole family unless he managed to escape. When asked where he was planning to escape to, Sarant answered mysteriously, "It's better if you don't know."

At that point, Mrs. Jayson decided that the best course was to help her brother out of his jam without asking any more awkward questions. On the evening of August 4, she took Sarant and Dayton to Roosevelt Raceway, where she and her husband maintained a stable of trotting horses. Taking advantage of the crowds and confusion, she was able to sneak the pair out through the paddock and into the car while the FBI surveillance man remained behind, waiting for them all to leave by the public exits.

While Mrs. Jayson and her husband were left behind to bear the brunt of the FBI's displeasure at having been so easily fooled, Al Sarant and Carol Dayton made a cross-country dash to the home of some of Dayton's relatives in Tucson, Arizona. On August 9, five days after leaving New York, they crossed into Mexico, and, on August 12, a couple using Mexican tourist cards issued to Mr. and Mrs. Weldon Bruce Dayton flew from Guadalajara to Mexico City. From there, they simply dropped out of sight.

In the meantime, the search for Joel Barr was also coming to a dead end. The Bureau had learned from the U.S. Embassy in Paris of Barr's disappearance. Its last remaining hope of getting information about Barr's destination lay in Samuel Perl, an American student traveling in Europe who was believed to be one of the last people to speak with Barr before he left Paris. The lead to Perl had come from his older brother, Barr's friend William Perl, who said that some time in early 1950 he had asked Sam to look up Barr. William Perl, a respected aeronautical engineer, had been going through a routine security check in connection with an appointment to a position with the Atomic Energy Commission and, he told the FBI, the AEC loyalty investigators had raised questions about his ties to such "alleged Communists" as Joel Barr and Alfred Sarant. (This was possibly because Perl had once lived at the Sarant apartment on Morton Street.) Perl said that he had asked his brother, Sam, to speak with Barr and find out whether there was anything in Barr's past that might cause further difficulties with the AEC.

On July 29, U.S. consular officials in Spain finally managed to locate Sam Perl and ask him what he knew of Joel Barr's whereabouts. Sam Perl said that although the news that his brother was having security problems had come as a complete surprise, he had sought out Barr as requested. Barr had assured him that he had never been an active Communist and that he had been fired from his jobs at Fort Monmouth and in private industry solely as the result of mistaken information that caused him to "be blacklisted as a Communist." Sam Perl added that he had last seen Barr on June 2, and that Barr had mentioned then that he was going to leave Paris soon but refused to say where he was going.

A supporting report in the FBI files, identified only as coming from a "confidential informant," gives a more intriguing version of Perl's June 2 conversation with Joel Barr. According to this report, Barr's last words to Perl were uncannily reminiscent of what Al Sarant told his sister—i.e., that "it would be better if he [Sam Perl] did not know his intended destination."

In a recent interview, Samuel Perl confirmed the rather mysterious flavor of Joel Barr's last words to him. "He said he's going to leave and I asked him, 'Where are you going?'" Perl recalled. "He said he wouldn't tell me. He said 'Don't worry. I just won't be around.'" Interestingly enough, Perl denied that his brother, William, now deceased, had ever asked him to get in touch with Joel

Barr. As he remembered it, Barr had approached him at the Student Site Club in Paris.

As far as the FBI was concerned the double disappearance of Al Sarant and Joel Barr was tantamount to an admission of guilt. In retrospect, of course, another possibility must be considered. The prospect of being tied to a case of atomic espionage, of being pressured to testify against old friends, and, at the very least, of being publicly branded as a Communist, might have been enough to prompt innocent men to drop out of sight. This is exactly the theory put forth by Walter and Miriam Schneir in *Invitation to an Inquest.*

Personal motives may also have played a part in Al Sarant's decision to leave Ithaca. Neither the Sarant nor the Dayton marriage had been going well for some time. The high-pressure personality of Al Sarant caused trouble with his wife, Louise, whose approach to housekeeping and life in general was described to friends as "relaxed." Carol Dayton, for her part, apparently was bored with her life as a faculty wife. During the stressful days following the appearance of the FBI at the Sarant home, Carol Dayton had broken down and confessed to her husband the true extent of her relationship with Sarant. She did not, however, ask Dayton for a divorce. Insisting that she needed time "to think things over," she told her husband that she planned to go to Boston to stay with friends for a few days.

In the opinion of the Schneirs, Sarant must have decided to seize the chance to escape both a bad mess with the FBI and a bad marriage. He persuaded Carol Dayton to skip Boston and meet him in New York. From there they relied on family connections to help them get out of the country.

A letter written by Carol Dayton from Tucson just before she disappeared gives some clue to her confused state of mind at the time. Addressed to her good friend Judith Bregman, whom she was supposedly going to visit in Boston, it began on an apologetic note:

Dear Judy—

You probably know by now that I'm supposed to be in Boston looking for a house for us. That I am not is the result of many strange circumstances. In any case, it will look better to certain people in Ithaca if this letter to Bruce (enclosed) comes with a Boston postmark. So will you send it there for me, please?

And you would be a most wonderful help if you could manage to turn up a house or apartment. Have you heard of anything? Weiskopf is going on a sabbatic [*sic*]—that's a possibility. I had a paper with names to contact but now I can't locate it. Oh woe.

Bruce's parents are visiting Ithaca. I hope he has finished his thesis—in which case he would have more visiting time. My kids are there, and boy, do I miss them!

Thanks, Judy, and please find us a house!

Bye now!
Carol

By the time Judith Bregman received these messages, however, she knew that her friend Carol Dayton had disappeared under mysterious circumstances. She forwarded the enclosure to Bruce Dayton as asked, but not before she had read it and reported its contents to the FBI. In this letter, according to FBI records, Carol Dayton told her husband that she did not dare communicate with him directly but assured him that she planned to be in Boston by the time they were scheduled to move. Bregman could not recall the letter word for word, but she said that one phrase that had impressed itself on her memory was Carol Dayton's protest that she was "held by circumstances beyond her control." Bregman also recalled that there had been instructions for Bruce Dayton to destroy the letter after reading it.

Carol Dayton was known to her friends as a warm, gregarious woman and a devoted mother. She left behind her two small children, the youngest still an infant. Did she really intend to desert them forever? Bruce Dayton didn't think so. After reading his wife's last letter to him, he refused to discuss her disappearance with the FBI, saying only that he expected his wife to return some day and did not want to do anything that might jeopardize his chances of effecting a reconciliation.

From the tone of Carol Dayton's last letters it seems likely that she had agreed to help her lover flee the country, without ever suspecting that she was making a commitment that would deprive her permanently of her children. She may have learned only belatedly that Sarant really was involved in espionage and intended to use Mexico as an escape route behind the Iron Curtain. At some point she either decided to go with Sarant or was told that she had no choice. Fear of arrest and of involvement in a scandal that could destroy the happiness of her children might have been powerful motives for following her lover into exile.

In the immediate aftermath of Sarant's disappearance, it might have been possible to believe that panic and passion had combined to drive him away from Ithaca. However, it is more difficult to understand why an innocent man and his companion should have remained in hiding for thirty years. Al Sarant was never charged with a crime, and after the Rosenbergs' trial and execution, he would no longer have had reason to fear being called as a reluctant witness against them. Louise Sarant, who in any case had been left with all his property and the custody of their two young sons, obtained a divorce on grounds of desertion and would no longer have been an obstacle to his relationship with Carol Dayton.

The suggestion of one former friend of theirs that Sarant and Dayton must have been killed in a car crash is quite unlikely. There would certainly have been an attempt to identify the bodies of a North American couple who died in a crash on the Mexican roads, and since the Mexican government was actively looking for the bearers of tourist cards issued to Mr. and Mrs. Dayton, the accident would have most probably come to their attention. Similarly, a fatal accident involving victims carrying other forged papers would be likely to attract police notice. By far the most probable explanation for the failure of the Mexican police to find Sarant and Dayton is that the couple had contacts who helped them establish a false identity and get out of the country promptly. Without assistance, it would have been extremely difficult for an American couple who possessed neither U.S. passports nor a large sum of money to escape detection for long.

If theories about Sarant have been offered, Joel Barr's disappearance has never been plausibly explained by those who would deny the existence of an espionage ring. In fact, nothing is really known of Barr after he disappeared in 1950. In 1957 the U.S. Department of Justice told a *Look* magazine reporter that Joel Barr was "living behind the Iron Curtain." Most likely he was. But if the Justice Department had facts to back up this claim, they were never revealed to the public. FBI documents released under the Freedom of Information Act reveal that sporadic attempts to learn about Barr's whereabouts from U.S. intelligence contacts inside the Soviet Union continued into the early 1970s. As of 1974, when the Barr file ends, there were still no leads.

As for the relatives that Sarant, Dayton, and Barr left behind, the years have not softened their reluctance to discuss the case. The former Louise Sarant, contacted by phone at her home in upper New York State, said only, "I have no intention of discussing it." Then she hung up. Joel Barr's brother, Bernard Barr, at first agreed to an interview and then changed his mind, saying it would serve no useful purpose. All he would say on the phone was that his brother had been "swallowed up" in Europe and that no one in his family had ever had any news of him again. Carol Dayton's ex-husband, Weldon Bruce Dayton, teaches physics at a college in California. Asked to comment on the fate of his wife, all he would say was: "I have never heard anything from either my wife or from Alfred Sarant. Never, period. Nobody knows anything about them."

While FBI agents in Ithaca were still questioning Al Sarant, the Cleveland office of the Bureau was puzzling over a bizarre incident involving William Perl, one of the country's leading experts in the design of supersonic aircraft. Perl came to the attention of the FBI initially because he had once sublet the 65 Morton Street apartment in Greenwich Village from Al Sarant and was known to have been a good friend of Joel Barr's. In a routine interview on July 20, 1950, Perl gave a rather vague account of the sublet arrangement that contradicted Al Sarant on several points. In the same interview, he vehemently denied knowing the Rosenbergs. He appeared to be, at best, a peripheral figure in the evolving picture of Julius Rosenberg's activities.

Then, on July 24, Perl phoned Special Agent R. J. Abbaticchio at the Cleveland office to say that he wanted to talk about something that was troubling him. On the previous afternoon (Sunday, July 23), Perl said, he had answered a knock on his door to find Vivian Glassman, an acquaintance from New York. Indicating by gestures that she did not want to speak freely because Perl's apartment might be bugged, Glassman wrote out a message in longhand—a message that, in effect, offered Perl $2,000 along with instructions to leave the country immediately.

In a written statement Perl gave on July 26 to three other FBI agents, he supplied further details of Glassman's communication:

> she had been instructed by a stranger, one whom she did not
> know, to speak to an aeronautical engineer in Cleveland and to

give this engineer money and instructions on how to leave the country. She wrote down something about a ship incident concerning herself and Barr . . . I got the impression that she had been instructed to use this incident as a means of identifying herself to me. Somewhere along the line she also wrote that she knew Julius Rosenberg. I recall that she wrote the name Mexico down in connection with her instructions to leave the country. I remember her writing down the word friend in connection with the aeronautical engineer that she was trying to get in touch with in Cleveland. It was my understanding that she took me to be that aeronautical engineer. I am actually an aeronautical research scientist at this time. . . .

According to Perl, he had angrily told Glassman that "she did not know what she was talking about" and that he hoped "she had nothing on her conscience." After questioning her to learn how she had obtained his current address (from a former landlady—Perl had moved quite recently), he "invited" his visitor to leave at once. Shaken and upset, he immediately tore the papers she left behind into small pieces and flushed them down the toilet.

Perl claimed to know Vivian Glassman only slightly despite the fact she had been the fiancée of his friend Joel Barr and was the sister of his own girlfriend, Eleanor Glassman, at whose New York apartment he had lived for two weeks only a few months earlier. On the whole, his implication that she had somehow sought out the wrong man did not seem very likely, but what really mystified the Bureau was that Perl had brought the whole potentially incriminating incident to their attention *after* destroying the physical evidence that supported his version of what had happened. Even allowing for the shock and panic Perl must have felt at the time, this was foolish behavior on the part of a highly intelligent man who already had reason to know that he might be investigated in connection with the case.

From Perl's point of view, of course, his actions were perfectly logical. He had no desire to give the FBI evidence that might provide them with an excuse to arrest Vivian Glassman. On the other hand, he could not afford to take the chance that the FBI did not already know the details of her mission.

The first prominent scientist to be mentioned in the case since the arrest of Klaus Fuchs, William Perl had been for some time a very frightened man. After graduating from CCNY in 1939, his career had moved quickly and steadily forward. From 1940 on, he had worked for the National Advisory Committee for Aeronautics, first at Langley Field in Virginia and later at the Lewis Flight Propulsion Laboratory in Cleveland. In 1946, as soon as the war was over and he could be released from projects of immediate importance, NACA had sent Perl to Columbia University for doctoral studies in physics. There he also served as technical assistant to Dr. Theodore von Karman, who was then chairman of the Air Force Scientific Advisory Board. In June 1948, Perl returned to Cleveland, where he supervised a group of fifteen researchers studying jet-propulsion mechanisms and design problems related to supersonic flight. He also continued working on his doctoral dissertation, which was based on classified data supplied by NACA. Tall and broad-shouldered, with dark good looks and a quiet, sensitive manner, Perl was known around NACA as something of a lone wolf who had dated a number of female employees but had no close friends or confidants. Not that anyone thought he would have much to confide in any case—the dedication that had made Perl a leader in the field of aeronautics at the age of thirty-two had left little time for other interests.

But though he seldom mentioned them to his colleagues in Cleveland, Perl did have a circle of old friends in New York, friends such as Julius Rosenberg, Joel Barr, and Morton Sobell. They had all been among the active members of CCNY's Steinmetz Club. Sobell, in particular, had been one of Perl's closest college friends, and the two continued to correspond even though they were seldom in New York at the same time during the years following their graduations.

In the spring of 1946, William Perl had spent some time in California doing research at Cal Tech. He and his wife, the former Henrietta Savidge, whom he had married in New York in 1944, stayed with a friend of hers in San Rafael. The impromptu living arrangements put a strain on Perl's marriage, and when summer came and the project at Cal Tech wound up, he and Hetti decided to separate. She stayed in California for the time being and he went on to New York to begin his studies at Columbia. A few months later, Joel Barr suggested that Perl move into Sarant's former apartment on Morton Street since he was no longer using the place.

By this time, the Morton Street premises could be considered habitable only by someone like Perl whose mind was on other things. The living room was furnished only with a desk and packing boxes full of the previous tenants' belongings. The kitchen was so grimy that Perl seldom attempted to eat there, taking his meals at the near-by Blue Mill restaurant. Nevertheless, Perl stayed on at Morton Street until shortly before he finished up at Columbia in June 1948, and Hetti, who had come on to New York and effected at least a par-tial reconciliation, lived there as well for some weeks. Perl used the Morton Street address on his voter registration application and con-firmed it when he voted on two occasions, once in 1947 and once in 1948.

When Perl moved back to Cleveland, the apartment was passed on to a series of other friends and acquaintances of Perl's, remaining in Al Sarant's name until the end of January 1950. At that time, its current inhabitants were told on short notice that they would have to vacate because Sarant had decided to give up the lease. Sarant told the FBI that he had kept the lease until 1950 as a favor to Perl and his friends, and that Perl had forwarded the rent to him by mail through January, when he sent word that his friends no longer need-ed the apartment. Perl denied this, saying that he had never paid rent to Sarant at all until sometime in 1948, and then only for a few months. Later he changed his story and said he had paid rent by money order to Sarant as late as 1949.

In any event, William Perl's worries began in November 1949 after he was asked to fill out two routine security questionnaires, one for NACA and one for the Atomic Energy Commission. Presumably worried that his connection with two former Communists, Barr and Sarant, would raise questions, Perl omitted mentioning the Morton Street address on a list of his residences over the past ten years. Also, for reasons that can only be guessed at, he told the first of a series of lies about his marriage, stating that he and Hetti Savidge had been divorced in Las Vegas in 1944.*

Somehow or other, the NACA loyalty board found out about Perl's friendship with Joel Barr anyway and asked him about it. Perl was frantic. Confiding to Hetti that he was sure the security investi-gations were already in the hands of the FBI, Perl began looking

---

*In July 1950, Perl told the FBI that his marriage to Henrietta Savidge had been common-law, and that the couple had considered themselves divorced by mutual consent in 1944. However, in August 1950, Perl filed for divorce in New York, stating in his application that he and Sa-vidge were married on September 1, 1944, in New York City. The divorce was granted, but Perl and Savidge remarried in a religious ceremony in 1951.

around for a university teaching position. After applying to work at the University of Chicago under Enrico Fermi and at Western Reserve, he finally arranged a position in the physics department at Columbia. He was scheduled to begin his appointment in September 1950.

Perl's suspicion that he had been the subject of an FBI investigation as early as the previous April was apparently quite unfounded. It is possible that FBI investigators had talked to his ex-wife in connection with the NACA loyalty probe; however, the Cleveland FBI office's report on Perl made in July shows that he was unknown to their agents before that time. Perl's hints to them that he knew the FBI had been watching him for months evoked bewilderment.

The Cleveland office's files indicate moreover that the only reason Perl was contacted in the week after Julius Rosenberg's arrest was that Alfred Sarant had mentioned him as one of the subtenants of 65 Morton Street; the Bureau viewed him as a possible source of information about Sarant but not as an active suspect. After their initial interview with him, the Cleveland office decided that surveillance of Perl was unwarranted. In fact, their interest in him might have lapsed altogether except that Perl seemed determined to keep their curiosity alive through his own behavior.

Telling the FBI about Vivian Glassman's appearance at his apartment was only the first step. Two days later, a visibly shaky Perl showed up at the Cleveland Bureau office once again, carrying a typed affidavit that reported two more "suspicious" incidents, both of which had occurred on Tuesday, July 25. First of all, said Perl, he had received two strange postcards in the morning mail. One was from his younger brother Sam (whose conversation with Joel Barr in Paris Perl had already reported in his initial talk with the FBI). The card was mailed from the south of France, where Sam was currently traveling; its message ended with the phrase "Good food, good wine, good living!" The second card, from the University of Tennessee library, had borne only the typed words "Good Food" above a printed form message "to the effect that the above material was not available."

The only logical explanation for Perl coming forward about these postcards was that he assumed the Bureau was conducting a mail cover and he wanted to go on record as being as mystified by them as anyone else. Since the actual postcards were never produced, it is also just barely conceivable that Perl invented them, hoping to divert attention from the Glassman incident. A third possibility—that the card from the University of Tennessee was planted by the FBI to scare Perl into talking—is even more unlikely: such a plant would have been aimed at getting Perl to give information about either Rosenberg or Sarant, neither of whom was connected with the University of Tennessee. In any event, the subtle implications of the coinciding messages, the very stuff that spy fiction is made of, do not seem to have fired the imagination of the Cleveland Bureau. Perl's story about the postcards was filed away and never referred to again.

The second incident mentioned in Perl's affidavit showed even more clearly how close to the edge of panic he had come. Later on that same Tuesday, Perl returned to his apartment to find a copy of the Marxist journal *Science and Society* resting on top of his living-room bookcase. He was sure that he had never placed the magazine there himself. Perl complained that the magazine and the postcards were part of an FBI plot "to manufacture evidence against me." Interestingly enough, Perl acknowledged that the particular copy of *Science and Society* had been in his bookcase all along, left there, he said, by a previous tenant of the furnished apartment. What he was reporting was its inexplicable move from the shelf to the top of the bookcase. Since this report was made on July 28, two days after FBI agents had come to his home, at his request, to discuss the visit of Vivian Glassman, it would seem that Perl thought they might have noticed the magazine lying around and decided that he had better "explain" its presence.

The chief result of Perl's attempts to outsmart the FBI was that on August 3, agents of the New York Bureau descended on Vivian Glassman, who must have been quite startled to learn that Perl had told the Bureau all about their recent encounter. Under the circumstances, Glassman behaved with considerably more self-possession than either Perl or Sarant had shown. Readily conceding that she had once been engaged to Joel Barr, Glassman also said that she had met the Rosenbergs while canvassing their neighborhood for the American Labor Party and had become friendly with Ethel Rosenberg in particular. She then confirmed the essential details of Perl's story, denying only that her message had ever referred to the name Rosenberg in any way.

On the evening of July 21, Glassman said, she had been chatting on the phone with her current boyfriend, Ernest Pataki, when a stranger knocked on her door. Something about the stranger's manner made her uncomfortable, and she consulted with Pataki before deciding to let him in. He advised her to go ahead, but to leave the phone off the hook just in case there was a problem.

As soon as the stranger came into her living room, Glassman recalled, he had asked her whether she knew someone named John. She said she didn't. The man then mentioned Joel Barr, identifying himself as "the man who had helped Barr go to Europe." Though still confused, Glassman decided that anyone who was a friend of Barr's must be trustworthy. It was then that the stranger had asked her to go to Cleveland to speak with a certain aeronautical engineer whom Glassman recognized as William Perl, a man her sister Eleanor was "very fond of." After receiving explicit instructions as to what she should tell Perl, she had been given $2,000 in small bills wrapped between pieces of black cardboard and held together with a rubber band.

In spite of the fact that she had no idea why such an errand might be necessary or who was asking her to undertake it, Glassman said, she immediately made plane reservations for Cleveland under the assumed name of Mrs. S. Goldberg. The next morning she went to her sister Eleanor's apartment while Eleanor was at work, let herself in with a duplicate key, and found a letter which bore a return address for William Perl. Then she went directly to La Guardia Airport, caught the 12:35 P.M. flight for Cleveland, and registered at the Regent Hotel, once again using the name S. Goldberg.

It was the next day before she managed to locate Perl, who had recently moved, and when she did deliver her message he immediately told her that she was "crazy to get involved with such people." Glassman was now stuck with the $2,000, which she did not dare touch even though she had paid her own way to Cleveland, not a minor factor on a social worker's salary. She kept the money intact in her apartment until the next Thursday night, when the same stranger showed up again to learn the results of her trip.

Once she had told her story to the FBI, Glassman began to dictate a written statement, then changed her mind, saying that she would like to consult a lawyer before signing anything. From that day on, she never said another word for the record about her role in the case.

Summoned to appear before the grand jury on August 11, Glass-man was seated in the waiting room across from Ethel Rosenberg. The two sat facing each other for over an hour without ever betray-ing the smallest sign of recognition. Later that morning Glassman conferred with prosecutors Irving Saypol and Myles Lane and told them she had been advised by her lawyers of her right against self-incrimination and did not intend to answer any questions without a grant of immunity.

Saypol and Lane balked. Ethel Rosenberg's arrest was imminent and they felt that the shock would frighten Glassman into talking without a deal. Glassman was handed another summons for the next Monday. Once again she refused to answer any questions. There were still more summonses—for August 15, 19, 24, 28, and Septem-ber 6. Glassman was told that unless she agreed to testify, she would be jailed for contempt. She was placed under FBI surveillance, and a neighbor was enlisted to make notes on any comings and goings from her apartment that the agents might miss seeing. When she walked in the park with her father and her boyfriend, an anonymous-looking but not inconspicuous man watched the proceedings from a nearby parked car. Agents interviewed her boyfriend and went through her friends' trash. Nothing budged her.

Finally, in September, Glassman agreed through her lawyer to view some photos of men who were considered candidates to be the stranger who had sent her on her wild goose chase to Cleveland. Glassman had earlier declined to identify snapshots of Barr, Sarant, Anatoli Yakovlev, and Michael Sidorovich as being the man who contacted her. Now she looked at pictures of Weldon Bruce Dayton, William Danziger, Max Elitcher, Semon Semonov, and Morton So-bell, and some other old acquaintances of the Rosenbergs. None of these, she said, was the man in question. As the array of pictures sug-gests, the FBI had not the slightest idea of who the "stranger" might have been and was flailing around aimlessly, hoping to get lucky. Later, when they thought they had learned through other evidence who the man might have been, Glassman declined even to look over any more photos. She had committed no crime, she told the prosecu-tors, and she would have nothing else to say—ever.

Today Vivian Glassman lives in New York under her married name. She still refuses to comment, saying only that "reporters can say whatever they want" and that the record speaks for itself.

William Perl did not do so well for himself with the grand jury. Having previously admitted too much, he now erred on the side of too many denials. In sworn testimony on August 18, 1950, Perl denied ever knowing either Julius Rosenberg or Morton Sobell. No doubt Perl felt that taking the Fifth Amendment as Glassman had would destroy his career; however, the course he chose was even more reckless. Perl's long-standing friendships with both men were well known to too many people, and the FBI already had more evidence than it needed—from records showing that the three men had taken the same courses together at CCNY in the late 1930s to correspondence in Perl's own hand that discussed his friendship with Sobell.

The FBI was convinced by now that Perl had been involved in espionage but had decided that he either could not or did not want to flee. They felt sure that Vivian Glassman knew very well that her errand had something to do with the Rosenbergs—and possibly knew a good deal more. As yet, they could prove none of it. They did have one option: they could indict William Perl for perjury.

6

Max Elitcher: The Ride to Catherine Slip

Joel Barr, Al Sarant, and William Perl were not the only individuals who had come under suspicion in the wake of Julius Rosenberg's arrest. During the weeks the FBI had Rosenberg under surveillance, it had been compiling a list of his former CCNY acquaintances who had gone on to work in war-related research. One name that stood out as a particularly promising lead was that of Max Elitcher—the Navy Ordnance Department employee who had been mentioned in the KGB secret message transmitted in 1944 but not decoded by the Americans until 1948.

Max Elitcher was one of a small group of friends who had gone to work for the Navy Bureau of Ordnance in Washington after taking engineering degrees at CCNY. Elitcher had first come to the attention of Naval Intelligence loyalty investigators in January 1941, when he and another CCNY alumnus, Morton Sobell, were observed using Sobell's car to ferry passengers to an anticonscription rally sponsored by the American Peace Mobilization Committee. This particular investigation lapsed without ever establishing definitely that either man was a Communist Party member; and, in any case, Sobell left government employment that same year to take graduate courses at the University of Michigan. From Michigan, Sobell returned to the navy, then went on to work at the General Electric laboratories in Schenectady, New York, and at the Reeves Instrument Company in New York City, where he was assigned to work on secret air force and navy contracts. But he and Max Elitcher remained friends and, in 1948, when Elitcher became aware that he was being watched by the FBI, he mistakenly suspected that the Bureau's interest in him was again connected with his relationship to Sobell.

Elitcher had some reason to be nervous, since he had falsely sworn on a loyalty affidavit that he was not a Party member, and he decided that it would be prudent to leave government employment while he could still do so voluntarily. With assistance from Sobell, he was able to obtain a job at Reeves Instrument in his specialty of fire-control radar (which has to do with the automatic aiming and firing of naval artillery) and he and his wife, Helene, settled down in Queens, New York, in a house whose backyard connected with the Sobells' property.

In the summer of 1950, when the FBI first learned that there might be a connection between Max Elitcher and Julius Rosenberg, Elitcher was once again a very frightened man. His friend Morton Sobell had not appeared at work since June 16, the day David Greenglass's arrest was announced in the newspapers, and Elitcher himself had not seen Sobell since June 22, when at Sobell's request he had picked up his friend's paycheck and a suit of clothes left at a dry cleaner near the office and had delivered them to Sobell's house. The next day, the Sobells were gone.

All the next week, Max Elitcher and his wife watched the deliveries from the dairy piling up on their neighbors' doorstep. The fact that the Sobells' Ford was still in its garage also suggested that the family was not away on any ordinary vacation. A few days later, when Elitcher saw Helen Sobell's younger sister, Edith Levitov, in the backyard, and she told him rather mysteriously that Sobell had "gone away to a farm" for a few days, he concluded that Sobell would not be returning any time soon and that his flight had something to do with their mutual acquaintance Julius Rosenberg.

When two FBI agents showed up at Reeves on July 20, three days after Rosenberg's arrest, Elitcher's worst fears were confirmed. Elitcher had no directly traceable current connection with Rosenberg, so the very speed with which the Bureau had turned up his name raised the possibility that Rosenberg had already confessed and implicated him. If this were so—and with Sobell already gone—there seemed little point in remaining silent and giving the appearance that he was more deeply involved in Rosenberg's affairs than he actually was. After a few minutes of hesitation, Elitcher agreed to drop by the FBI's Foley Square offices and tell what he knew.

That afternoon, Max Elitcher sat down with FBI agents Vincent Cahill and James O'Brien and began to relate the story of a visit he had received from Rosenberg in the summer of 1944. According to Elitcher, Rosenberg, whom he had seen only once since their graduation from CCNY five years earlier, had suddenly called him up and mentioned that he was in Washington in connection with Signal Corps business and would like to drop by for a visit. Though rather surprised, Elitcher had suggested that Rosenberg come over that afternoon. But when Rosenberg arrived, it was evident that he had something more than a social call in mind. After making small talk for a few minutes, he had asked Helene Elitcher if she would mind leaving the room so that he could discuss some business with her husband.

Rosenberg, said Elitcher, then began to speak earnestly about "the great role Russia was playing in the war and the great sacrifice she was making. [He said] some persons were contributing to the Russian war effort by giving information concerning secret material and developments to the Russians, which they would not ordinarily receive. He asked me if I would contribute in this way."

Between that first visit and the spring of 1948, there had been "six to eight" more conversations on the same theme between Elitcher and Rosenberg. Each time he had put Julius off, never actually handing over any data but never flatly refusing the overtures either. Rosenberg, meanwhile, had striven valiantly to overcome Elitcher's reluctance, and in their last discussion in the spring of 1948, he had promised that his spy network now had a contact in Washington who could relieve Elitcher of the risks of carrying stolen materials to New York in person. During this meeting, Elitcher later recalled, Rosenberg gave the impression that his plans were more grandiose than ever, and he regaled his skeptical acquaintance with a description of a new briefcase he had obtained that, if tampered with, would immediately expose any microfilm stored inside "so that there would be no way of finding out what was on the films."

Rosenberg also made an effort to cultivate the Elitchers socially.

During one of their vacations in New York, Max and Helene had been invited to have dinner with Julius Rosenberg, Joel Barr, and others at a Greenwich Village restaurant. The group then spent the rest of the evening enjoying the cool breezes on the patio of Barr's parents' penthouse apartment on the Upper West Side of Manhattan. On another occasion, they had been invited to a party at Al Sarant's Morton Street flat. And once, during a period when Ethel Rosenberg and her children were out of town for the summer, Julius had invited Max and Helene to spend the night at the Rosenberg apartment after Helene complained that her in-laws' guest bedroom was infested with bedbugs. That evening, Elitcher recalled, he had asked Julius how he had happened to become involved in espionage and Julius had answered that he had long wanted to do something "more than ordinary" to benefit Russia but that it had taken him some time to make the right contacts.

Although Elitcher had no way of knowing it, the story he told the FBI about Rosenberg's approach to him in the summer of 1944 confirmed exactly the information the Bureau had received independently from the decoded KGB transmission. Less plausible, perhaps, was Elitcher's contention that he had discussed the possibility of turning spy with Rosenberg as many as eight times without ever committing himself one way or the other. Questioned repeatedly about this, Elitcher could only say that he had found Rosenberg's importuning immensely flattering. Ever since leaving high school, he added, he had felt that he was not living up to the high hopes that his parents had held for his career, and Julius's insistence that his work with the navy was important enough to be of interest to the Soviet Union had been a terrific ego builder.

Sensing that Cahill and O'Brien were not completely satisfied with his story, Elitcher invited them to drive back to his home and interview his wife. Upon arriving home with Cahill and O'Brien in tow, Elitcher learned that Helene had already spoken to two other FBI men earlier that day. She had given a statement about her social contacts with Rosenberg that confirmed her husband's version of events—right down to Julius's request during his first visit to her house that she leave the room so he and Max could speak privately.

Up to the time the FBI left his house on the night of July 20, Max Elitcher had still not so much as mentioned the name of Morton Sobell. Exactly what happened to change this situation is unclear.

However, the FBI certainly knew of the two men's long association as revealed in Elitcher's security files, and Elitcher must have realized that his co-worker and neighbor's unexplained absence would be bound to cause suspicion sooner or later. At any rate, with or without prompting, Elitcher gave a second statement to the FBI the very next day; in it, he admitted that Julius Rosenberg's trump card in trying to recruit him back in 1944 had been the assurance that their mutual friend Sobell was already cooperating in passing information. Elitcher also confessed that it was Sobell who had arranged several of his later meetings with Rosenberg in New York and that on one occasion Sobell had mentioned that Rosenberg "wants to talk to you about the same thing he talked to you about before." Sobell, he added, was still in touch with Julius Rosenberg and had mentioned an appointment to meet him downtown as recently as six months ago.

All this was suspicious sounding, but so vague that it hardly added up to usable evidence. Nor was there much solid information in the various investigative files on Sobell that began in 1941 and stretched on through two exhaustive security reviews by Air Force and Navy intelligence in connection with Sobell's work on secret military contracts at Reeves. In retrospect, the thick files of raw investigative reports that had been compiled on Sobell over the years reveal more about the prejudices of the investigators and their informants than they do about Sobell. Navy investigators had gone to great trouble, for example, to establish that during his college years Sobell had once worked as a handyman at a Communist camp near Wingdale, New York, where, according to the camp's outraged neighbors, the guests included "chinks, niggers, Italians, and all nationalities—all up for a good time." In the same vein, a man who had once lived near the Washington apartment that Sobell and Elitcher had shared during their bachelor days told the FBI he considered both men "Communistic" because they entertained blacks in their apartment and spoke in favor of racial equality. Over the years, Sobell's files had swelled with additional complaints from supervisors and co-workers who noted that he was extremely "argumentative" and prone to preach politics on the job. But even the government loyalty investigators admitted that such grousing did not amount to much and Sobell's security clearance to work on top-secret projects had been affirmed as recently as the fall of 1949.

If Morton Sobell had been on hand to deny Elitcher's charges, it seems entirely possible that he would eventually have walked away from the situation a free man. But Sobell was nowhere to be found. At first the FBI's efforts to locate their missing suspect centered on Baltimore. A mail cover placed on Julius Rosenberg's apartment before his arrest had turned up a cryptically worded postcard from that city, and the Baltimore office of the Bureau was asked to be on guard against the possibility that Sobell and his family might try to slip on board a Soviet ship that happened to be docked there at the time.

Then, on July 24, the Washington office of the FBI learned from David Levitov, Helen Sobell's brother, that their mother had received a letter from the Sobells saying that the family was comfortably settled and had a maid. The letter, according to Levitov, had been enclosed in two envelopes and mailed from New York City on the 16th—apparently by a third party.

When Al Sarant and Carol Dayton fled to Mexico that same week, the FBI began to suspect that the Sobells' new home might also be located somewhere south of the border. And, sure enough, a check of airline records conducted early in August revealed that Morton and Helen Sobell, their infant son, Mark, and Helen Sobell's daughter by a previous marriage, Sydney, had all departed from La Guardia Airport on June 22, bound for Mexico City. Two airline stewardesses who had worked that flight also identified Sobell from a photograph; they remembered him because they had been struck by his resemblance to Oscar Levant.

It also developed that while the entire family had purchased round-trip tickets, all of the return tickets except Sydney's had been cashed in in Mexico City on July 22.*

In New York, meanwhile, agents Cahill and O'Brien were having a difficult time with their new star witness. J. Edgar Hoover was pressuring them for the identities of the other members of the secret Navy Department Party cell to which Elitcher admitted having belonged up until he left Washington in 1948. And Hoover was also eager for more information about several other Rosenberg acquaintances from CCNY who had gone to work for the navy along with Elitcher and Sobell—at least one of whom had gone on to a highly sensitive position in research related to submarine develop-

---

*Sydney normally lived part of the year with her father, Clarence Gurewitz, in Washington and the Sobells may have wanted to leave open the option of letting her return there.

ment. But Elitcher, though he had readily provided an outline of his relations with Rosenberg and Sobell, balked at questions that would lead to revealing the names of his former political associates.

Elitcher's position was that the activities of the secret Party cells of government employees must not be equated with military espionage. He was willing to talk about the latter but had no intention of turning political informer. His quite accurate assessment of the relationship between espionage and ordinary Party activity, as reiterated in a 1952 statement to agent Cahill, was that "to his knowledge he had never heard of members of the government groups of the Communist Party being contacted for espionage work, although . . . the secret cell organizations would be the logical place to draw recruits." Moreover, in Cahill's paraphrase of the statement, Elitcher insisted that "the Communist Party did not become involved in his dealings with Rosenberg" nor had Rosenberg ever mentioned the Party except to say that "at one time" (and presumably no longer) it would have been possible for him to arrange "through Party channels" to have a new recruit drop his official Communist affiliations.

While Elitcher and the Bureau wrangled over his reluctance to implicate political acquaintances, the process of building a case against Sobell ground to a halt. This lack of progress made the U.S. Attorney's office in New York fairly frantic; on August 3, Assistant U.S. Attorney Myles Lane complained to James McInerney, head of the Criminal Division of the Justice Department, that he was in the process of preparing a complaint against Sobell and found that Elitcher's testimony was "not sufficiently explicit as to the dates of certain overt acts." In fact, Elitcher had so far mentioned the date of only one conversation involving himself, Rosenberg, and Sobell—the one in May 1948 when he had finally refused to have any part of Julius's plan. McInerney sympathetically suggested that Lane go ahead and make up dates for the other four meetings alluded to in Elitcher's testimony and then ask the United States Commissioner to seal the complaint!

Two days later, Edward Scheidt, Special Agent in charge of the New York office of the FBI, wrote to Washington stressing that Elitcher might refuse to give any more information at all if pressed too hard about his political associations. Scheidt mentioned that the Elitchers had retained as their lawyer none other than O. John Rogge, who had advised them to cooperate, and that it made sense to interrogate Elitcher fully on the espionage charges as soon as possible. As for the political information, it was sure to come out later as Elitcher became more irrevocably committed to his role as a government witness. And indeed, Scheidt was correct—although Elitcher did not finally succumb to the pressure to name his navy cell colleagues until 1952, when he was unemployed and in need of a government letter of recommendation to reassure nervous potential employers.

By mid-August 1950, when Elitcher did agree to begin further interrogations on Sobell and his other CCNY connections, Sobell himself was haunting the ports of Tampico and Vera Cruz in Mexico, desperately trying to book freighter passage out of the country for himself and his family—a plan complicated by the fact that neither he nor his wife and children had valid passports, having entered Mexico on routinely issued tourist cards. Shipping-company literature that was found in Sobell's possession later showed that he had investigated at least a score of possible destinations all over Europe and South America, with Eastern Europe and Cuba figuring most often in his inquiries. By August 16, having failed to find an outbound ship that could accommodate him, Sobell returned exhausted to the apartment on Calle Octova de Cordoba in Mexico City where he had left his wife and family. He was enjoying a late supper when three Spanish-speaking men burst through the door waving pistols and belligerently accusing him of being "Johnny Jones," wanted for robbing a bank in Acapulco. When Sobell protested, he was roughed up, hauled kicking and screaming down four flights of stairs, and shoved into the backseat of a waiting car. The armed men then returned to the apartment, grabbed up as many of the family's belongings as they could, and forced Helen Sobell and her children into a second car.

As the two cars sped northward, they were soon joined by at least eight other vehicles, forming a caravan that drove nonstop all the way to the Texas border some eight hundred miles to the north. A little more than twenty-four hours after the men first broke into his living room, Sobell found himself at the International Bridge on the border between Nuevo Laredo, Mexico, and Laredo, Texas, being transferred into the waiting arms of the FBI. He was arrested on the basis of the warrant sworn out twelve days earlier in New York charging him with "five overt acts" of "having conspired with Julius Rosenberg and others" to violate the espionage statute.

If the charges against Sobell were so vague as to sow confusion among his attorneys right through the last day of his trial, the intentions of the prosecutors were both obvious and chilling. In a brief statement announcing Sobell's arraignment in Manhattan federal court, U.S. Attorney Saypol declared that Sobell was accused of having "many dealings with Rosenberg in the conspiracy to supply Russia with atomic secrets." The phrase signaled Saypol's intention to prove that Sobell, along with Rosenberg and Greenglass, was part of a single conspiracy—though on second reading it is clear that Saypol had not said in so many words that Sobell personally was involved in atomic espionage. This subtlety, as might be expected, escaped the attention of the press. The next morning, the New York *Daily News* announced Sobell's arrest under a banner headline that proclaimed: "FLEEING RADAR EXPERT NABBED AS ATOM SPY," while the *Herald Tribune* described Sobell as the latest "Soviet atomic spy suspect."

Saypol's readiness to link Sobell with an *atomic* conspiracy may have been intended in part to frighten the accused into a confession. Sobell's hasty flight (undertaken, it seems, without waiting for instructions on how to make contact with an agent who could direct him to safety) combined with his needless use of transparent aliases on his travels within Mexico indicated weakness to the prosecution. But if Sobell could be rash and indiscreet, he was also a man with a very high opinion of his own intelligence and he did not appreciate being bluffed. Helen Sobell, who had made her own way back from Texas after being abruptly released at the border, was now in New York, urging her husband to keep up his courage and remain silent. And Sobell, on his part, looked forward to matching wits at his trial with a prosecuting attorney for whom he had nothing but contempt.

Although the big payoff that Saypol was hoping for—Sobell's confession—failed to materialize, Max Elitcher did finally provide enough additional details about his former friend's activities to make a presentable conspiracy case. During a series of twelve interviews that began on August 5 and culminated on October 20, Elitcher came up with a telling anecdote that was to become the most dramatic testimony against Sobell during the trial. It placed him not just on the scene during discussions of espionage but at the center of the actual exchange of secret data.

Elitcher's story involved a house-hunting trip to New York that he and Helene had made in 1948, just before he left Navy Ordnance to work at Reeves. They had been planning, said Elitcher, to stay at the home of the Sobells in Queens, but while they drove through Baltimore Helene had noticed that their car was being followed and became alarmed. When they reached New York and the same car was still right behind them, Elitcher decided that it would be better not to go directly to Sobell's house and headed instead for his mother's apartment on Lexington Avenue in Manhattan. After making small talk for several hours, the Elitchers returned to their car and, satisfied that their tail was no longer in sight, decided it was safe to go on to Queens.*

Upon arriving at the Sobell house, Elitcher took his friend aside and confessed his suspicion that he was being tailed. At first, he recalled, Morton was furious that his guests had taken the chance of coming to Flushing at all, but once he had gotten over his initial pique he "did not seem to know what to do . . . and for the time being nothing was done." No more was said about the problem. After dinner, however, Sobell confided privately to Elitcher that he had some material for Julius that he considered "too good to throw away" but too dangerous to keep around the house under the circumstances. Pleading that he was too tired to drive into the city alone, Sobell persuaded Elitcher to accompany him while he delivered the goods.

At the car, Elitcher saw Sobell take a small 35-mm film can out of his jacket pocket and place it in the glove compartment. Then, following Sobell's instructions, he took the wheel and proceeded into Manhattan and down the East River Drive to a deserted waterfront street named Catherine Slip. Elitcher waited in the parked car while Sobell walked off to deliver the film—presumably to the Rosenberg apartment in Knickerbocker Village two blocks away.

Elitcher, still preoccupied with his own fears, was eager to hear what Rosenberg had to say about his experience of being tailed earlier that day. "What did Julie think about it?" he remembers asking as soon as Sobell returned to the car.

"Julie says there's nothing to worry about," Sobell had replied, adding that Rosenberg thought Elitcher must be suffering from an overactive imagination since his connection with the whole business was so slight that it was "very unlikely" he would be under surveillance.

This story of the midnight ride to Catherine Slip, which Max

---

*Helene Elitcher's evident awareness that it would be unwise to lead their pursuer to Sobell may explain why Elitcher waited so long to volunteer this story.

Elitcher was later to repeat so tellingly on the witness stand, has been roundly attacked by defenders of Sobell and the Rosenbergs, who point out that there is no evidence beyond Elitcher's word to prove it ever happened. As one critic notes, Sobell would have been rather foolish to have risked delivering incriminating film in the company of a houseguest who had just warned him that he believed he was being followed by government agents.

Perhaps there was an element of foolhardiness in Sobell's behavior—not, incidentally, inconsistent with his later conduct—but as Elitcher was convinced that he had lost his pursuers in Manhattan, Sobell may well have reasoned that he was safe, at least for the time being. In fact, Sobell and Elitcher were not followed to Catherine Slip, although a team of FBI agents had actually tailed Elitcher all the way to Sobell's doorstep.

An examination of the FBI files on Max Elitcher shows that, for a period of several months during mid-1948, he was indeed being followed by FBI agents investigating him as a result of the KGB code break. A mail cover had been placed on Elitcher's home and there was even some consideration of installing electronic surveillance—though apparently this plan was abandoned. And in a 1949 FBI memorandum summarizing the results of the surveillance of Elitcher, there appears the following passage, which offers at least partial confirmation that Elitcher was telling the truth:

> On July 30, 1948, the physical surveillance of the Elitcher car was taken over by SA's William J. McCarthy, John J. Ward and Daniel F. Garle at 4:10 P.M. The Elitcher car was surveilled immediately to 1571 Lexington Avenue where Elitcher's family resides. From the time the car left the express highway on the west side of New York until it arrived at Elitcher's family residence, both Helene and Max gave definite indications of checking for surveillance. They remained there [at 1571 Lexington] until the middle of the evening and then proceeded to the home of Morton Sobell . . . where they apparently spent the night inasmuch as Elitcher's 1941 tudor [sic: two-door] Chevrolet sedan . . . was still observed parked in front of the Sobell home August 3, 1948.

The memorandum goes on to explain how it came to be that the Bureau, after following Elitcher all the way from Washington, gave up just when it might have been about to learn something of great interest:

> It should be stated that on the trip from Manhattan to the Sobells' home, it was confirmed without a doubt that the Elitchers' were "tail conscious" and, therefore, the surveillance was discontinued.

Special Agent Cahill, who was conducting the Elitcher interrogations, was of course aware of the existence of the 1948 report at least as early as October 1950, so there is always the possibility that it was mentioned to Elitcher to jog his memory or even to induce him to make up the story entirely. From reading Cahill's report comparing the two accounts, however, this seems unlikely. In telling this story for the first time, Elitcher had placed the incident in September of 1948 rather than in July, and Cahill's report reflects a genuine concern over the discrepancy in dates, a concern that would surely have been beside the point if Elitcher's version of the incident had not been offered independently.

Of course, the verification that the Elitchers really had been followed to Sobell's home on the night of the mission to Catherine Slip was never to be offered in court. To introduce this evidence into the public record would have raised too many sensitive and embarrassing questions. The story of the KGB codes was still classified and would not have been told at the trial even if it had been necessary to gain a conviction, which it was not. And no matter what reason the Bureau offered for following Elitcher back in 1948, it would have been awkward to have to admit that the Bureau had flubbed a chance to crack the Rosenberg spy ring a full year and a half before the British obtained a confession from Klaus Fuchs.

7

Gordon Dean of the AEC

Only when the threat of prosecuting Ethel as a coconspirator failed to produce any change in Julius Rosenberg's attitude did the government consider a further escalation in its "lever" strategy—demanding the death penalty for Julius himself. The execution of an individual convicted of conspiracy as opposed to the more serious charge of treason was unprecedented in U.S. history. The Justice Department planned to ask for it now only because the prosecutors had come to believe their own rhetorical claim that the existence of "atom spies" posed a grave threat to the national security.

As the prosecutors worked to prepare their case, however, they began to realize that their entire strategy might be snagged on a procedural Catch-22. In order to convince a judge—not to mention that vital court, public opinion—that Rosenberg's crime was serious enough to warrant execution, it would be necessary to prove that he and Greenglass had access to vital atomic secrets. But to demonstrate this in an open courtroom involved the risk that still more important data would be divulged. The worry was not so much what David Greenglass himself might say on the witness stand; though no one could be absolutely sure, it was assumed that essentially everything he knew about the bomb was already in the hands of the Soviets.

There was a serious possibility, however, that expert witnesses called to verify the importance of Greenglass's information would be unable to make their points without revealing additional data that was still secret.

The power to remove this snag by declassifying the data necessary for a successful prosecution rested with the Atomic Energy Commission and its chairman, Gordon Dean. A recent Truman appointee, Dean was a former Justice Department attorney and practicing lawyer who knew little about atomic energy but much about the ways of political survival. Quite early on, Dean recognized that the Rosenberg case was going to be the hottest issue he would face during his tenure as AEC chairman. On the one hand, he wanted to cooperate with the Justice Department to bring about a solid conviction. On the other, as a man who understood the dangers of running afoul of anti-Communist crusaders in Washington, he was sensitive to the possibility that by being too accommodating in releasing classified materials he might be exposing himself and his staff to subsequent charges of being "soft" on national security.

Dean had to walk a fine line and he knew it. In addition to asking his chief security officer, John A. Waters, to report on the implications of the technical data included in Greenglass's pretrial statements, he arranged for Greenglass to be interrogated in a six-hour session. Greenglass was asked to go over his statement phrase by phrase and show in detail how he had learned each item of information about the bomb. The questions, though asked by Myles Lane, were carefully prepared by Dr. James G. Beckerley, the chief of the AEC's Division of Classification.

The reports of Beckerley and Waters did little to make Gordon Dean's job easier. Beckerley came away from his meeting with Greenglass convinced that the former Los Alamos machinist was basically telling the truth and that despite certain technical errors in the data he had given the Russians—or, rather, in the data as he remembered it five years later—Greenglass's reports touched on a number of areas that were still top secret.

Waters, who agreed, suggested that it might be useful to break down the information set forth in Greenglass's statements into four basic categories:

1. General background about the layout and organization of the Los Alamos facility, including the lists of "potential recruits," which

named a number of top scientists whose involvement with the Manhattan Project had been a wartime secret.

2. Descriptions and sketches of lens molds used in implosion experiments, which Greenglass said he had given to Julius in January 1945 and to Gold later that same year.

3. Greenglass's general description of the so-called naval-type bomb, which had been used at Nagasaki.

4. A description and sketch relating to a certain "levitation" experiment designed to calculate a reduction in the amount of plutonium or uranium necessary to detonate a bomb.

Interestingly enough, given the emphasis on the lens-mold sketches in most post-trial discussions of the case, Waters told the AEC commissioners that this item, along with the general description of Los Alamos, was the least sensitive area of Greenglass's information and might be discussed at the trial without fear of compromising ongoing research. Point 3, the general description of the Nagasaki bomb, was trickier, since the United States still did not want to release specific details of the weapon's design. But by far the most sensitive area was the levitation information, since it involved disclosures about a type of experimental setup still used in 1951 in improving nuclear weapons designs.

In an appearance before the five AEC commissioners on February 7, 1951, Waters said that no discussion of point 4 should be permitted at the upcoming trial. It ought to be possible, however, to allow testimony on point 3, provided that the prosecutors agreed to question the AEC's expert witnesses in such a way that it would not be necessary for them to reveal design details not actually mentioned by Greenglass. If this were done, Waters added, the simplest course would be not to release any documents ahead of time but simply to wait and see what actually came out at the trial. Allowing de facto declassification in this way had certain risks, but Waters felt these were more than compensated for by the potential value of making a strong case against Rosenberg. In any event, the AEC could send an observer to the trial who would be empowered to intervene if the experts' testimony wandered into unapproved areas. The Commission would also warn all of its employees not to speculate publicly after the fact on any of the courtroom testimony.

Waters recommended and Dean agreed that, before committing itself to this policy, the AEC should get some political backing from

Capitol Hill. A meeting with the Joint Committee on Atomic Energy was scheduled for February 8, and Myles Lane, Irving Saypol's chief assistant and the attorney who had followed the unfolding of the Rosenberg case most closely up to that time, came down from New York to outline the plans of the prosecution.

In a memorandum he prepared for Saypol after the meeting, Lane noted that he had gone "over the evidence which we have obtained from Greenglass" and he emphasized why it was critical that it be presented at the trial. They could not get a conviction for conspiracy if all they could present to the jury was that Greenglass gave out some names and a description of the Los Alamos plant. Stressing the widespread espionage activities of Julius Rosenberg, Lane also emphasized that it was conceivable Rosenberg might have knowledge of other individuals who were still working in the AEC setup. Then Lane got to the heart of the case: "I pointed out that if we were to be in a position to elicit any information from Rosenberg respecting any other espionage leads he might have . . . it would be necessary for us to obtain a conviction against him."

Even before this meeting took place, Dean had already picked up the notion—no doubt from some source in the Justice Department—that the issue of Greenglass's testimony was related to getting the death penalty for Rosenberg. As he wrote in his official diary on February 6: "Greenglass has been talking, and they hope to get the fellow Rosenberg, the big one. The problem is how much can Greenglass be allowed to say? How important is it to get the death sentence by having Greenglass tell everything . . . ?"

Sure enough, when Myles Lane met with Dean and various AEC employees on the morning of February 8 to prepare for the congressional committee meeting that afternoon, the most important question on Dean's mind was whether AEC cooperation would lead to the death penalty for Rosenberg. Lane, rather taken aback, refused to commit himself. But Dean wanted an answer before the meeting went any further.

Finally, Lane left the conference room and made a quick phone call to Raymond Whearty at the Justice Department where, as he later wrote in a memo to Saypol, "I left word . . . respecting the Commission's desires." Ten or fifteen minutes later, Whearty returned the call to say that he had checked with James McInerney, who had checked with Deputy Attorney General Peyton Ford, who had given them the green light. If Julius Rosenberg was convicted, the Justice Department intended to ask for his execution.

Immediately after this conference ended, all present adjourned to the Senate side of the Capitol Building for a special closed session of the Joint Committee on Atomic Energy where Lane, in a succinct and forceful presentation, outlined to the congressmen why the Justice Department considered Julius Rosenberg "the keystone to a lot of other potential espionage agents."

In his briefing of the Committee, Lane made special mention of David Greenglass's charge that Rosenberg had stolen data on a proposed "sky platform," assuring the Congressmen that this was a highly secret project and "not just something out of Jules Verne." "I cite that," he concluded, "to show you how far these people have gone ... and it is my personal conviction, and this morning I checked with the Department, and they agreed—that the only thing that will break this man Rosenberg is the prospect of a death penalty or getting the chair, plus that if we can convict his wife, too, and give her a stiff sentence of 25 or 30 years, that combination may serve to make this fellow disgorge and give us the information on those other individuals. I can't guarantee that."

Senator Brien McMahon, the Committee chairman, then mused about Rosenberg: "He is pretty tough, isn't he?"

Replied Lane: "It is about the only thing you can use as a lever on these people."

"In other words," McMahon summed up, "what you are saying is that you think what you want to do is have Greenglass divulge some new secret information on the chance that the death penalty would result to Rosenberg."

Lane: "Yes."

Gordon Dean then rushed to assure the congressmen that the risk involved would be small, since it was assumed that all the really vital information involved had reached the Russians years ago— through Fuchs and Gold, if not by way of Rosenberg. However, one committee member, Representative W. Sterling Cole of New York, was still puzzling over the logic of Lane's argument. "Why," asked Cole, "is this evidence any more essential to get a conviction to support the death penalty than to get a conviction?"

Said Lane: "Mr. Congressman, I think you know that it is not too difficult to get a conviction in some conspiracy cases. You have to prove the agreement by an overt act. But to get a death penalty, I seriously doubt from my own experience, that any judge would impose a death penalty merely because a man testified there was an agreement and they passed out information respecting the number of people that were working there [at Los Alamos] or the names of the scientists who were working there. Another thing, I assume this case will go all the way to the Supreme Court, because the death penalty is involved and I think we should have as strong a case as we can. . . ."

Lane's concern for building an airtight case did not seem to apply to Ethel Rosenberg, however. In response to questions about whether David Greenglass was actually committed to testifying against his own sister, Lane admitted that "the case is not too strong against Mrs. Rosenberg. But for the purpose of acting as a deterrent, I think it is very important that she be convicted too, and given a strong sentence." In other words, Ethel's conviction was desirable to strike fear into other amateur spies, active or potential.

Impressed by Lane's argument about the need for a deterrent, the Committee agreed to Dean's plans for declassification. Senator Bourke Hickenlooper apparently expressed the consensus of the Committee when he spoke in support of Dean using his "calculated judgment" on the matter. He concluded: "I hope that the Commission and the Department of Justice can work out as satisfactory a method as is possible with as great assurance as possible to introduce fully sufficient evidence to hook this fellow with the most severe penalty you can give."

As a result of Lane's visit to Washington, the AEC agreed to declassify most of the material covered by David Greenglass's statements. However, there were certain restrictions. The commissioners did not want the information on the levitation experiments used, and they also planned to reclassify other material covered in the technical testimony. No one seriously believed that material once brought out in open court could ever really be classified retroactively in any meaningful sense, but reclassification was justified by the AEC on the grounds that it would discourage working nuclear scientists from speculating publicly on the significance of the data.

Myles Lane no doubt believed that he worked out the best compromise possible. The caution of the AEC may have had less to do with security considerations per se than with the fear that outspoken congressional critics like McMahon would use charges of laxness as a weapon to destroy the AEC's program for civilian control of atomic energy. Nevertheless, as Lane would explain in his memo to his boss, Saypol, the AEC's cooperation was vital. "It might be difficult to obtain a conviction for conspiracy," Lane wrote, "if the only evidence we were in a position to present would be the fact that Greenglass gave out a few names and a description of the Los Alamos plant."

Saypol, however, was livid over the results of Lane's Washington trip. He felt that there were still too many strings attached to the AEC's declassification decision. Suppression of part of the technical evidence—for example, information that Greenglass had given the Russians data on levitation experiments—might provide an opening for the Rosenberg-Sobell defense attorneys to claim that their clients had been denied their constitutional right to be presented with the evidence against them.

Saypol was also upset about the tenor of the conversation at the meeting on Capitol Hill. There had been too much loose talk: an admission that the prosecutors considered their case against Ethel Rosenberg weak as well as discussion of the death penalty as a tactic to "break" Julius Rosenberg. This concern is reflected in a letter Saypol wrote to Peyton Ford, complaining that premature discussion of the death penalty "might be deemed prejudicial and a subject of condemnation by the courts. Accordingly, while I shall continue to prosecute the case on the premise that it is the most serious of offenses and that the defendants are subject to capital punishment if convicted, nevertheless, I shall make no advance commitment in that regard." Whether Saypol was genuinely aghast at the content of the discussion or merely at the indiscretion of saying such things in front of politicians is difficult to say.

As for Lane, his role in the upcoming Rosenberg prosecution suddenly diminished to the point of near invisibility, and Saypol began relying more and more heavily on two junior assistants—James B. Kilsheimer and Roy Cohn. Down in Washington, Gordon Dean did not learn about this shift in responsibility until March 2, 1951, four days before the opening of the trial; when he did, he regarded the change as a betrayal. The AEC's commitment to honor the arrangements worked out with Lane was based entirely on the informal understanding that Lane would personally conduct the examination of Greenglass and the two technical witnesses that the AEC was providing to back up his story. Dean had felt confident that Lane, a man who "understood our problems," would abide by the agreement to limit his direct questions in such a way that classified information the AEC still considered sensitive—particularly on the subject of levitation—could not be brought out by defense counsel on cross-examination. Now, at the eleventh hour, Dean learned from William Denson and C. Arthur Rolander, Jr., the AEC's liaison men in New York, that Saypol's eager young assistants, particularly Cohn, wanted no restrictions on their freedom to question the expert witnesses.

On March 7, when the process of selecting a jury to try the Rosenbergs was already under way in U.S. Federal Court in Manhattan, Dean called Peyton Ford to demand that the AEC be provided in advance with a list of the questions that the prosecution planned to ask John Derry and Walter Koski, the AEC's expert witnesses. Summarizing what he told Ford, Dean wrote in his diary:

> We are quite disturbed. . . . The two fellows assigned by Saypol to handle this case are pretty young fellows. . . . Ford said he understood that this fellow Cohen [*sic*] is a very bright fellow—one of the smartest to come down the pike in a long time; he had an outstanding mind. GD [Dean refers to himself in the third person throughout his diary] said he was sure of that. GD just doesn't think he appreciates the danger of opening this thing up completely.

By now Dean's carefully worked out plan was beginning to fray on all sides. The next day, March 8, he received a phone call from Hickenlooper. Hickenlooper had heard about the problem that had arisen with Saypol and was extremely upset. As he now reminded Dean, it was Hickenlooper who had asked by far the most searching questions during the Committee's February 8 meeting with Lane.

In particular, Hickenlooper had suggested then that if the Rosenberg and Sobell lawyers were smart, they would subpoena a number of leading atomic scientists to testify for the defense; Hickenlooper had mentioned J. Robert Oppenheimer especially. If the scientists were asked direct questions involving classified technical data, the senator wondered, would they be within their rights to refuse to answer? Hickenlooper foresaw that such a strategy would raise a constitutional issue and might at the very least create grounds for the defense to claim on appeal that it had been prevented from presenting its case. Even the normally unflappable Myles Lane had admitted, when asked this question on February 8, that he had no idea of what would happen if the defense took this tack. Now Hickenlooper warned Dean that his "fears [had been] revived," and Dean, taking the cue, promised that if necessary he would go up to New York personally and see that matters did not get out of hand.

That same day, Dean also learned the outcome of his conversation with Peyton Ford, and the answer he got was far from reassuring. James McInerney called from the Justice Department to say that the questions the prosecution planned to ask John Derry would be forwarded to Dean over the weekend, but that it was too late to do anything about Koski's testimony since it was scheduled for the next day. The best he could suggest was that the questions Saypol planned to ask Koski might be cleared through Denson and Rolander, the AEC liaisons who were attending the trial.

At the end of a discouraging day, Dean wrote again to Peyton Ford, expressing his concern about "the inherent danger involved in the cross-examination" and reminding him that the Joint Committee had expressed its "extreme interest" in the handling of the problem. Obviously digging in for battle, Dean added a brand new demand that "drawings, sketches, or documents introduced as evidence at the trial not be made available to the public as far as possible."

Upon arriving in his office the next morning, Dean learned that Irving Saypol had no intention whatsoever of honoring the promise that McInerney had made the day before. Insisting on his independence, he refused to release any questions in advance to Dean or to anyone else. The only good news was that the trial was slower than expected in getting under way and Koski's appearance on the witness stand had been put off until the following Monday. The time had now come for Dean to play his final card. Picking up the telephone, he managed to get through to Attorney General Howard McGrath himself and got him to agree to a 10:00 A.M. Saturday conference at the McGrath home. Once Dean and his top aides were actually inside McGrath's living room, they hoped to persuade him to exert some heavy pressure and bring Saypol back into line.

J. Edgar Hoover, meanwhile, was closely monitoring the growing rift between Dean and the U.S. Attorney's office. After a March 2 meeting between Saypol and his assistants and the AEC liaison men in New York, one of the AEC employees had confided his uneasiness over Lane's diminished role in the prosecution to Richard Whelan of the FBI. Whelan in turn promptly reported this to A. H. Belmont in Washington, and Belmont relayed the gossip to Hoover, emphasizing the unnamed AEC employee's judgment that Cohn and Kilsheimer "displayed a lack of maturity," and that Saypol himself was ill prepared. Hoover's reply for the time being was a curt note informing his underlings that "I don't see how this is any of our business."

But if Hoover declined to get involved for the moment, his own memos would soon reflect similar criticisms of the prosecutor's staff. Like Saypol, who was primarily concerned with getting a conviction, and the AEC, which wanted to come out of the trial without facing criticism of its effectiveness in protecting classified material, Hoover had his own priorities. He was hoping that the prosecution would bring out the wider outlines of the Rosenberg ring's activities—an approach that would assure that the FBI received maximum credit for its investigative efforts and also lay the groundwork for further spy trials.

While Saypol and his assistants, Gordon Dean, and Hoover's staff were all jockeying for position on the eve of the big trial, Harry Gold—the man who had made it all possible—was snugly ensconced in the so-called singer's heaven on the eleventh floor of the New York City jail known as the Tombs.

Since his confession in May 1950, Gold had proved to be as loyal to the government attorneys as he had once been to his Soviet masters. He had undergone more than sixty hours of questioning by the FBI, served as a key witness in two trials, and was now a prospective star witness in the Rosenberg-Sobell case because he would be able to link the thefts of atomic data to an actual Soviet agent, Anatoli Yakovlev. In return for his services, Harry Gold would receive a thirty-year sentence, an arrangement which suggests that neither he nor his lawyers had done any bargaining to speak of. By all accounts, Gold did not find the prospect of a long incarceration unpleasant. Freedom and the choices that went with it had always been a burden he was ready to give up at the first opportunity. And, if rumors of the treatment accorded "songbirds" on the eleventh floor are to be believed, Gold was beginning his prison career in considerable comfort. There was even a daily ration of cigars.

Although Gold had capitulated readily to the government's demands that he testify against his former associates in espionage, he was not one of those apostate Communists who took pleasure in exposing his erstwhile allies. Nor was it his fault that his brief tenure as Klaus Fuchs's mysterious courier Raymond seemed to have left him with a kind of Midas touch in reverse: everyone Gold had touched in his long career was now turned as if by magic into an "atom spy."

The first victim of the "atom spy" syndrome was Alfred Dean Slack, who was arrested at his Syracuse, New York, home on June 15, 1950—the same day that the FBI picked up David Greenglass. Information given to the press at the time of Slack's arrest had included mention that Slack had worked briefly for the Manhattan Project at Oak Ridge, Tennessee, and this gave rise to expectations Slack would be charged with atomic espionage. In reality, the charges had nothing to do with Oak Ridge. Slack was an industrial chemist who had furnished information to Gold over a period of years, from 1940 to 1944. During the first part of this period, he had been working for Eastman Kodak in Rochester, New York, and had turned over rather routine information dealing with the recovery of silver from scrap film and the manufacturing of Kodachrome. Later, Slack went to work for the Holston Ordnance Works in Kingsport, Tennessee, and from this job he was able to steal data and materials, including a sample of the explosive known as RDX and a report on its manufacturing process.

Confronted with blueprints and notes recovered from Harry Gold's "Fibber McGee's closet," and with a card bearing Gold's address that was found during a search of Slack's own home, Slack readily confessed that he was guilty of the charges leveled by Gold. He also admitted that, unlike most amateur spies who had cooperated for ideological reasons, he had happily accepted payment of $200 per report. Perhaps Slack had felt he was duping the Russians all along, since most of the information he passed on was readily and legally available in published sources. Even the RDX data, the most important coup of his espionage career, was merely a report on a particular manufacturing process and not a basic formula for RDX itself, which had been internationally known for years. Unfortunately for Slack, handing over the RDX data during wartime made him chargeable under the espionage statute.

As it had turned out that the charges against Slack had nothing whatsoever to do with the Manhattan Project, his trial in September

1950 caused barely a ripple of attention in the press. The presiding judge, however, was not about to let a confessed Soviet spy off lightly. At the end of the four-day proceedings, Slack was sentenced to fifteen years, five more than the prosecutors had recommended.

The next of Gold's old allies to be prosecuted on the basis of his statements were Abraham Brothman and his business partner, Miriam Moskowitz, whose arrests came on July 29, 1950, two weeks after Slack was picked up.

Brothman, known as "The Penguin," had been described by Elizabeth Terrill Bentley back in 1945 as one of the stalwarts of the industrial espionage ring run by Jacob Golos. But once again, Brothman had nothing to do with atomic espionage. Even more than Slack, Brothman had functioned throughout his career on the murky fringes of legality. Most of the data he had given to Gold (Brothman claimed all of it) was from published papers or from his own work. And, in his case, the government conceded that it had no grounds for an espionage charge. As Hoover wrote on July 31, 1950, just two days after Brothman's arrest:

> In an espionage case against Brothman, it would, of course, be necessary to establish as one of the elements of the offense, that he [Brothman] agreed to furnish *information relating to the national defense* [emphasis in the original]. It does not appear from our analysis . . . that there is evidence on this point.

And indeed when Brothman was finally brought to trial in November, the charge was not espionage but obstruction of justice. The charge stemmed from the false story he and Gold had concocted back in 1947 to counter Bentley's testimony about Brothman being "turned over" to a new espionage courier—who was, of course, Gold himself. Miriam Moskowitz, who had supported the false story, was accused of the lesser crime of conspiring to obstruct justice.

In many respects, the Brothman-Moskowitz trial served as a tune-up for the more important Rosenberg-Sobell trial to come. It marked the first courtroom appearance of the "Red Spy Queen," Elizabeth Bentley, who had been talking to the FBI, a New York grand jury, and various congressional committees since her defection from communism in 1945. It was also the first time that Harry Gold would have to face cross-examination at the hands of a hostile defense attorney. The judge was Irving R. Kaufman, soon to preside over the trial of the Rosenbergs, and the prosecutors were Irving Saypol and his assistant Roy Cohn.

Testifying against his old friends with what one *New York Times* reporter described as "an air of complete dejection," Harry Gold appeared to be trying to mitigate his betrayal of former friends by carefully outlining the distinction between the industrial spy ring to which Brothman had belonged and the atomic spy operation run by Yakovlev.

As Gold himself explained it, the Soviets had relied on industrial espionage during the 1930s and early 1940s because American companies either would not sell technical data to them or sold only incomplete and outdated information. Also, quite frankly, it was cheaper to steal the data than to purchase it. A case in point was the batch-continuous process for producing Buna-S synthetic rubber, a process Brothman himself had helped develop. The Russians were very happy indeed to have this in 1941, several years before it became available to them legally through the Lend-Lease program. (One reason these activities had gone unchecked despite the often lax secrecy measures was that the American government had not perceived Soviet industrial espionage as a real threat. Those spies who were caught received lenient treatment, or, more often, were never indicted.)

In a tough cross-examination, defense attorney William Kleinman forced Gold to recapitulate the entire story of his fantasy wife and twin children, getting Gold to admit that he had kept up the story even after he and Brothman became personal friends because he had become "so tangled up in a web of lies that it was easier to continue . . . than to try and straighten the whole hideous mess out. . . . It is a wonder steam didn't come out of my ears at times."

Gold also recounted the tale of how he had once overcome Brothman's reluctance to continue his activities by arranging for him to meet an important "Soviet official" who had supposedly made a special trip to New York to meet Brothman and thank him for his good work. Under a pledge of strict secrecy, Brothman was led to a New York hotel room and introduced to the "dignitary"—actually Sam Semenov—who somehow managed to keep a straight face while telling Brothman that his value to Russia was greater than "two or three brigades" of ordinary men. As Gold told it, Brothman had been so completely taken in that the next day he had called the meeting "a thrill that he could never forget."

Under the circumstances, it is difficult to avoid feeling a rush of sympathy for Abe Brothman. Whatever his motives for getting involved with Jacob Golos, he was kept in line for years through a combination of flattery, trickery, and implied threats. Even the very grand-jury episode for which he and Moskowitz were being tried was something they had been talked into by Gold against their better judgment. For this, they received the maximum sentence permitted under the law from Judge Kaufman, who congratulated the prosecution for its "ingenuity" in finding a statute under which the defendants could be tried at all.

Abe Brothman, whose seven-year sentence was eventually reduced to two years, would almost certainly never have spent a day in jail were it not for his bad luck in dealing with an atom spy. Nevertheless, the fact remains that, after hearing Gold and Brothman's contradictory stories about what had transpired during the grand-jury hearings in 1947, the jury had chosen to believe Gold. Harry Gold was, in fact, a very impressive witness, all the more so because, unlike those professional ex-Communists Whittaker Chambers and Elizabeth Bentley, he neither indulged in public breast-beating nor painted dire pictures of an international conspiracy with tentacles reaching into every corner of American life.

Not until after the Rosenbergs' execution would critics think to advance the notion—later espoused by John Wexley and Walter and Miriam Schneir—that Gold's admissions about his fantasy family were evidence that he was a psychopathic personality who had created his entire spy career out of his own imagination. Recently released FBI files do show, however, that the government was well prepared to provide other witnesses who could support Gold's story in the event that he had proved less than impressive on the witness stand.

The most important of these potential witnesses was Thomas Black, the man who had originally recruited Gold. Black was prepared to testify that he had visited Brothman's lab on at least six occasions beginning in 1942 and heard numerous discussions of information Brothman was providing to the Russians. Black was ready to reveal that, at one point during the war, Gold had told him that Brothman was "a very valuable contact that he wanted to turn over to me if he were drafted into the army."

Black, who was first interviewed by the FBI in June 1950, shortly after Gold's initial confession, was also prepared to describe how sometime in 1933 or 1934 he and another man, Fred Heller, had gone to the New York office of AMTORG, the Soviet trading company, to inquire about emigrating to the Soviet Union and found themselves recruited for industrial-espionage work instead. Later Black had brought Gold into the project by introducing him to the Soviet agent known as Paul Smith or Paul Peterson.

Tom Black knew very well how innocent it had all seemed back in 1935, when he had asked Harry Gold to contribute commercial data to help a nation that he saw as poor, deserving, and struggling to make a success of the greatest social experiment ever attempted. And perhaps if Gold's lawyer, former Republican National Chairman John D. M. Hamilton, had seen fit to call Black to testify at Gold's trial in December 1950, Hamilton might have had an easier time in his attempt to explain to the judge the difference between industrial espionage and the theft of national defense secrets.

The view of Russia shared by Tom Black and Harry Gold during the 1930s was never as universal as they seemed to believe. But certainly it had wide credence—enough to attract many individuals to industrial espionage who would never have considered such activities under other circumstances. And some of these individuals, including Harry Gold, eventually became so deeply involved that they formed a willing, and virtually captive, recruiting pool for the Soviet military espionage network. By 1950, however, the idealistic motives that had led Gold and others into the mire of espionage no longer counted as a mitigating factor in the eyes of their fellow Americans. Quite the reverse: a spy who admitted to working for money would almost have received more understanding than one who acknowledged Communist sympathies. The judges who presided over the trials of the so-called atom spies felt compelled to demonstrate their anticommunism by imposing sentences even stiffer than those considered appropriate by the prosecuting attorneys and the FBI. What happened to Slack, Moskowitz, and Brothman happened also to their accuser, Harry Gold, at his sentencing in December 1950: Judge James McGranery tacked on an extra five years to the twenty-five-year sentence the U.S. attorney had demanded.

When Harry Gold was transferred to the Tombs' eleventh floor after entering his guilty plea in a Philadelphia courtroom on July 20, 1950, he was joining another very important prisoner—David Greenglass. The transfer of Greenglass from the Federal House of Detention, where he had been housed since his arrest a month earlier, was arranged by the U.S. Attorney on July 19, in order to prevent pretrial contact between Greenglass and his brother-in-law, Julius Rosenberg, who was now a prisoner there. Reporting the change to Hoover, an FBI memorandum notes that as a cooperative witness, Greenglass was the obvious candidate for the preferential treatment accorded "songbirds" at the Tombs. Moreover, he had to be moved anyway since he had already been involved in several squabbles with other inmates who, in the words of FBI Special Agent Whelan, "apparently don't like spies."

For defenders of the Rosenbergs, the government's decision to house its two chief witnesses where they could be in daily contact with each other has long seemed tantamount to proof of a conspiracy to frame Julius and Ethel. "What possible reason was there for Gold and Greenglass to be lodged in the same prison," asks John Wexley, "unless it was for the express purpose of their collaboration?" Going on to answer his own rhetorical question, Wexley envisions Harry Gold, his briefcase bulging with notes and papers, patiently tutoring the slow-witted David Greenglass on atomic-bomb construction while Roy Cohn, playing the role of schoolmaster, appears periodically to administer "test quizzes" to his prize witnesses.

In reality, the relationship between Gold and Greenglass was far less cozy than this scenario would have it. During the early months of their incarceration, the two men did meet together for regular chess games, but by December they had developed an active dislike of each other. Gold, relieved of the psychological burden that had weighed on him for so long, was almost glad to be in prison. He devoted himself enthusiastically to a program of reading and self-education and had little sympathy for Greenglass, who was too despondent over his situation to appreciate the opportunities for self-improvement that life in jail afforded.

Nor was there any need for the kind of wholesale manufacture of testimony Wexley envisions. The versions of their June 1945 meeting that Gold and Greenglass had given the FBI independently agreed in their important essentials. There were, however, certain minor differences in the two men's stories—differences that hardly cast doubt on the truthfulness of either confession but that might have a significant impact on Gold's value as a courtroom witness against Julius Rosenberg.

Both David Greenglass and his wife distinctly remembered that Gold had introduced himself as "Dave from Pittsburgh." Gold, on the other hand, had no memory of using this particular name. In his June 1, 1950, statement to the FBI, Gold said that he might have introduced himself as Frank Kessler or Frank Martin—both aliases he had used frequently over the years. Also, Gold had said that it was standard practice for him to identify himself further by bringing "greetings" from someone, although he could not recall what name he had used in this particular instance.

A more fundamental question from the prosecutor's point of view was whether the name of Julius Rosenberg had ever come up during the meeting. David and Ruth insisted that it had. Ruth, they recalled, had mentioned that they would be returning to New York when David's furlough came through in the fall, and she had suggested that Gold might want to contact them there by calling her brother-in-law Julius. Harry Gold, significantly enough, had told the FBI a very similar story—except that he had been unable to recall the name Ruth had used. At first he thought that the name might be "Philip" and that this Philip was David's father-in-law.

It is hardly surprising that Gold's memory would be less than clear on this point. The question of "Philip" was a minor detail of a meeting that had occurred five years before—one of the scores of such meetings that Gold had participated in over the years, and by no means as important from his point of view as his contacts with Fuchs. Moreover, Gold never had any intention of following up on Ruth's suggestion. Gold dealt only with his control, Anatoli Yakovlev, and Ruth was being very indiscreet in giving the name of her own contact to a courier she had met but once.

Gold's memory on this point showed no signs of improvement until July 10, 1950. By this time, of course, the FBI was already closing in on Julius Rosenberg. Gold now said of the incident:

> During a conversation I had with Mrs. GREENGLASS on the occasion of my first meeting, that is the morning meeting . . . Mrs. Greenglass told me that when they returned to New York . . . which was to take place in about December of 1945, that I could contact them by getting in touch with a relative. . . . I believe the man questioned [sic: in question] was supposed to be Mrs. GREENGLASS's father, that is, the father-in-law of DA-

VID GREENGLASS and I had previously stated that I believe his name to be PHILIP and that he lived in the Bronx, New York. Since that time I have come to the belief that the more likely possibility may have been that this man was either an uncle of a relative of Mrs. GREENGLASS, and that his name may have been JULIUS . . . there is also the possibility that the location in New York may have been the Bronx [*sic*]. Mrs. GREENGLASS also told me that just prior to her leaving New York, in April of 1945, she had talked with JULIUS and had explained this arrangement to him.

The name Julius had now appeared in one of Gold's statements for the first time. One can't help suspecting that it did not spontaneously spring into Gold's consciousness but had been suggested to him as a "likely possibility." On the other hand, this would not mean that Gold was telling a deliberate lie. He had never been certain about the name Philip. Perhaps "Julius" did sound right to him.

After the arrest of Rosenberg in mid-July, the prosecutors became more eager to tidy up the remaining discrepancies between the Gold and Greenglass accounts. The record of an August 1 interrogation conducted by Myles Lane shows Lane offering tidbits of information to Gold, "just to refresh your memory." Lane asked, for example, "if there was any possibility that you might have introduced yourself as Dave?"

"It strikes a very familiar chord in my memory," Gold replied, adding that he now felt "Dave" was a "distinct possibility."

But when it came to the name of the person he had supposedly brought "greetings" from, Gold was still intent on grappling with his own poor memory. By this time, he had decided that the name was probably Ben. This name, which had no particular associations for Gold, had been given him by Anatoli Yakovlev before he left New York and he thought he had used it, as instructed, on his arrival at the Greenglass apartment:

I said I brought greetings from Ben in Brooklyn, and I produced the irregular shaped piece of cardboard. Greenglass said, "Oh, yes, come in"—smiled. . . . He went to his wallet and produced the matching piece of cardboard. I then asked him whether he had any information for me and he said that he did, but that he would not have it prepared until the afternoon.

Just as defenders of the Rosenbergs have long suspected, the FBI and the prosecutors did eventually decide to bring Gold and Greenglass together in an effort to iron out the differences between their stories. On December 28, 1950, FBI agent J. C. Walsh conducted a simultaneous interview of the two men in the hope that he could obtain "their concentrated effort in recalling" certain details. Walsh's report on this joint interview shows how Gold and Greenglass were encouraged to come up with testimony that would mesh neatly and convincingly.

One point that still bothered Walsh concerned the name Gold had used to identify himself. Although Gold had seemed inclined to settle on "Dave" during his August interview with Myles Lane, he had now reverted to thinking he had used the alias Frank Kessler. Only now, in Greenglass's presence, did Gold recall something that made him think that "Dave" or "David" was correct after all. As agent Walsh reported:

> GREENGLASS stated that GOLD introduced himself to him and his wife as DAVID; GREENGLASS is quite certain about this item and he added that both he and his wife have since recalled that this was the name used by GOLD. GOLD asserted that he could not recall definitely what name he used and to this point believed that he used the name of Kessler. However, in the course of this joint interview with GREENGLASS, GOLD recalls that the name he did use at the time of his first [i.e., morning] meeting with GREENGLASS was commented on as being similar or the same as GREENGLASS's name or some other relative's name; therefore GOLD now believes that GREENGLASS's recollection is correct and that he did use the name of "DAVE."

Walsh's report also contains a very revealing exchange on the subject of the elusive "Ben." As reflected in this memo, Greenglass had never claimed to remember being given "greetings" from anyone. It was Gold's insistence now that he had delivered "greetings from Ben" that struck Greenglass as wrong and led him to suggest another possibility.

> Concerning the reported salutation "Greetings from Ben," GREENGLASS says that he had no recollection of such a statement by GOLD, pointing out further that the name BEN would

mean nothing to him. GREENGLASS proposed that possibly GOLD had said "greetings from Julius" which would of course make sense to GREENGLASS. GOLD's spontaneous comment to this was that possibly GREENGLASS was right and that he had mentioned the name of JULIUS rather than BEN. GOLD, however, is not at all clear on this point. He asserted that on every occasion of his meeting with a new contact he always "brought greetings" from someone in accordance with prior instructions, therefore, it is his contention that [*sic*] did bring greetings to GREENGLASS on this occasion.

For those who still hope to vindicate the Rosenbergs, this passage is *the* smoking gun in the case. In the words of one writer associated with the reborn Rosenberg defense committee, Walsh's report is the final proof "that Gold and Greenglass together with agents of the government created false testimony to suit the needs of the prosecution."

Other commentators have been more cautious. Historian Athan Theoharis, for example, asks whether the documents show "a case of FBI officials coaching a vulnerable and cooperative witness" or simply a "case of overkill, an attempt to minimize the [anticipated] defense efforts to discredit the government's star witness."

As these varying interpretations suggest, it is not easy to draw the line between the legitimate interrogation of a potential witness and the planting of the seed of perjury. In this instance, the subsequent statements of participants in this joint interview do not definitively clear up the confusion.

Harry Gold, in a 1965 communication to his lawyers, insisted that he had put forth the name Ben originally merely as one example of the kind of names he had frequently used in connection with such "greetings." He wrote:

> Granted that this is about as far away from evidence as you can get, yet I feel very sure of the ground when I say that my subsequent use of the name Julius represents an independent remembrance, not an unwitting corroboration. The FBI log on this matter may help here.

On the other hand, the recollections of former FBI agent Richard Brennan, who was present at the joint interview, will do little to reassure the skeptical. In an interview with filmmaker Alvin Goldstein, Brennan insisted that the December 28 meeting with Green-glass was held for the legitimate purpose of helping Gold reconstruct in his own mind certain aspects of an incident years in the past. Feed-ing a name to a witness, Brennan insisted, "was not wrong as such" and, in any case, the FBI "didn't plant that idea in Gold's mind . . . it was given to him as a suggestion." And Brennan then added that when Gold was first asked whether the form of the greeting might have been "Julie sent me" or "Julius sent me," he immediately "brightened up with a great light." The cynical might wonder wheth-er the light that switched on in Gold's brain was the revival of an authentic memory or merely the realization that these were the phrases that the FBI was waiting to hear. And one may wonder whether the distinction between a "plant" and a "suggestion"—so clear in Brennan's mind—was fully appreciated by Gold.

In any event, Harry Gold left the December 28 conference with-out ever expressing any certainty that he had used the phrase "Julius sent me" or "I come from Julius." Gold continued to express doubts about the correctness of the name Julius in this context right up to March 5, 1951—the day before the Rosenberg-Sobell trial began. Then, finally, agent Walsh was able to report, no doubt much to his relief, "that after considerable reflection [Gold] is quite certain that on the occasion of the first meeting he had with GREENGLASS he brought greetings from JULIUS, and that such was done under the direction of YAKOVLEV."

An even more significant change in testimony occurred just ten days before the Rosenbergs were to go on trial, when Ruth and David Greenglass offered a completely new story about the extent of Ethel's involvement.

Until then, the case against Ethel had been built almost entirely on two incidents mentioned by Ruth. First, Ruth claimed that Ethel had been present in November 1944 when Julius brought up the sub-ject of Ruth's asking her husband to participate in a "mutual ex-change of information." When Ruth expressed reluctance, she said, Ethel had chimed in, urging her to carry the message and let David decide for himself. Second, Ruth told the FBI that, after entertaining the Greenglasses at dinner during David's January 1945 furlough, Ethel had stood in her kitchen and watched Julius cut up the Jell-O package that was to be used as a recognition signal.

David Greenglass, meanwhile, had contributed next to nothing to the case against his sister. Though he did place Ethel around the table at that same dinner when Julius had filled him in on the Russians' knowledge of the atomic bomb, he also stated that neither of the women took part in the conversation and that most of what was being discussed appeared to have gone "over their heads."

It had now been nearly six months since Ethel's arrest, six months in which the FBI had every opportunity to build a case against her, but if the Bureau had managed to uncover any additional evidence of Ethel's active involvement in the spy ring, this is certainly not reflected in the FBI files released so far. On the contrary, the raw investigative files of the FBI are filled with allegations about Julius Rosenberg—allegations that invariably show him conducting his operations from secret apartments, at the offices of his machine-shop business, and in assignations at movie theaters, on street corners, and in lonely spots on Long Island beaches or in Westchester County parks. The only variations from this pattern, apparently, were the two occasions mentioned by Ruth Greenglass. With the exception of Vivian Glassman (who was also Joel Barr's fiancée), the individuals suspected by the FBI of having been part of the spy ring were basically friends of Julius's, not Ethel's. And even in his boasting to David Greenglass, Julius refers to the accomplishments of "my boys"—never "our boys."

In light of the meager evidence linking Ethel to the conspiracy, it is little wonder that Myles Lane was pessimistic about the government's prospects for getting a conviction when he outlined the prosecution strategy to the AEC. But then, in late February, the Greenglasses suddenly recalled an incident that placed Ethel at the very center of Julius's activities, serving as her husband's dutiful typist and aide.

What prompted this fortuitously timed revelation is a mystery. The FBI files released so far indicate that Ruth Greenglass was reinterviewed on February 23 and 24, 1951, and that she volunteered "additional information" on Ethel. Two days later, David Greenglass was also reinterviewed. According to the summary cable sent to Hoover, he "furnished in substance the same information as related by Ruth Greenglass." Oddly, the FBI files contain only summaries of these crucial February 1951 sessions; earlier interrogations were recorded and transcribed verbatim.

Both the Greenglasses now claimed that, in September 1945, David had passed along his handwritten notes and sketches of the plutonium bomb right in the Rosenbergs' living room. According to the FBI cablegram, Ruth then reported that "Julius took the info into the bathroom and read it and when he came out he called Ethel and told her she had to type this info immediately. [Ruth] said Ethel then sat down at the typewriter which she had placed on a bridge table in the living room and proceeded to type the info which David had given to Julius."

In addition, Ruth now said that at the January 1945 dinner party mentioned previously she had happened to ask Ethel why she was looking so tired, and Ethel had replied that she had been "up late" the night before typing the material Dave had just given Julie. "She [Ethel] told Ruth that she always typed Julius's material . . . and that occasionally she had to stay up late at night to do this."

Why had the Greenglasses waited so long to talk about these particular incidents? One obvious possibility is the desire to shield Ethel. This is the explanation given by James B. Kilsheimer, who attended the February interrogation sessions in his capacity as a junior assistant U.S. attorney. Interviewed recently in his office in New York, where he is now in private practice, Kilsheimer recalled that at first "David had a reluctance to talk about his sister." But the emergence of their new story, he insisted, "wasn't sudden. It was a gradual breakdown. Each time I went to talk to him there would be additional information."

This picture of David Greenglass "gradually" disgorging new information is not, however, reflected in the FBI files. The story of the typing was not "additional" information: it was a flat-out contradiction of the account David Greenglass had previously given of how he had delivered the sketch and notes on the atomic bomb to Julius Rosenberg.

Here is how Greenglass described the September 1945 transaction in his signed statement dated July 17, 1950:

> Almost as soon as I got to New York City Julius Rosenberg got in touch with me and I met him on the street somewhere in the city. At that time I furnished Julius Rosenberg with an unsealed envelope containing the information I had been able to gather concerning the atomic bomb, as well as a couple of sketches of the molds which make up the bomb.

Shortly before Ethel's arrest, in an August 4, 1950, interrogation by Myles Lane, David had been repeatedly questioned about his sister's role but reiterated that "when we were alone [Julius] brought the subject up" and at that time "I gave him a complete description of what I knew."

Lane then asked: "Was Ethel present on any of these occasions [when David gave Julius information]?"

> DAVID GREENGLASS: Never.
> LANE: Did Ethel ever talk to you about it?
> GREENGLASS: Never spoke to me and that's a fact. Aside from trying to protect my sister, believe me that's a fact.

Nearly thirty years later, during a two-and-a-half-hour interview with the Greenglasses, nearly forty minutes were spent trying to clear up the contradictions between this statement and the Greenglasses' later version of Ethel's involvement. Both David and Ruth declared that they still stood by their final story, which placed Ethel as the typist of stolen atomic secrets, and they emphatically denied that they had ever been subject to any improper pressure from either the FBI or the prosecutors. As discussion of the typing incident proceeded, however, the Greenglasses' memories on this point were so vague that the interviewers came away with more doubts than ever.

Perhaps the most surprising moment of the interview was the Greenglasses' reaction when it was mentioned that their evidence, and their evidence alone, had led to Ethel's arrest. Both David and Ruth reacted to this statement with shock and disbelief. They had always assumed, they said, that Ethel had been implicated by others, Max Elitcher in particular.

Nor did Ruth and David admit to recalling that the typing incident was not mentioned in their interrogations until February. "You mean that was the first mention of it?" Ruth asked in astonishment. Then she added: "I don't remember when I told them [the FBI] a particular thing. . . . At a certain point the agents became friends. They can elicit whatever they want from you."

Ruth then conceded that she never had the details of the September 1945 typing scene fixed in her mind. She just assumed "that we probably went over there and did it at that time, frankly because that would have been the way it would have been done." Asked if she could remember the incident today, Ruth said, "No. . . . I remember

David bringing something and giving it in his [Julius's] house, but as to whether it was this time [September 1945], I can't remember."

David, too, was hazy about the circumstances of the September 1945 transfer of data—this despite the fact that he still had vivid recall of other conversations between himself and Julius Rosenberg, giving his interviewers accounts that tallied with and occasionally expanded upon statements he had made to the FBI decades earlier. Reluctantly, David did make a stab at describing the particulars of the delivery:

> This is many years later. This is not five years later but forty [*sic*] years later that we are talking about almost. OK. What happened I think is this: I remember him coming over and giving him the sketch and later on he said, "It's got to be typed and you better come over." The idea was for me to stand there correcting. That's how it came about. That's why we went over, but I already gave him the sketch.

This version contradicts David's trial testimony that he brought the sketch with him when he and Ruth went to the Rosenbergs' for dinner.

One thing that emerged quite clearly during several conversations with the Greenglasses was that they considered the details of the typing episode irrelevant since they were convinced, then as now, of Ethel's deep involvement in her husband's activities.

This became most evident when one of the interviewers mentioned a Justice Department memorandum prepared in June 1953 that showed that one of the questions Department lawyers wanted to ask Rosenberg was: "Was your wife cognizant of your activities?"

> DAVID: That's just overwhelming. She was cognizant. They knew she was cognizant.
> INTERVIEWER: How did they know?
> DAVID: Because she was involved with that.
> INTERVIEWER: Because she was around?
> DAVID: No, because she used to say, "You know how busy Julius is. We're both involved." She'd come right out and say things like that.

Added Ruth: "I was with the agent [an unnamed FBI agent] until the night before the death. All night. And he kept saying to me that there was an open line to Washington and he always led me to believe that she [Ethel] was very deeply involved. I had no idea. . . ."

A few minutes later, Ruth returned to this subject. "I know she had to know," she reiterated. "I know there are husbands and wives where they never know what they are doing. But this was not the case with them."

The Greenglasses were close to both Julius and Ethel and in all probability their opinion of Ethel's complicity is correct. For obvious reasons, it was standard procedure for Soviet agents to recruit husbands and wives together. Everything we know of Ethel's attitudes and character, moreover, suggests that she would have supported and actively participated in Julius's activities. Although it is true that Ethel was preoccupied with raising a family from 1943 on, and frequently suffered from poor health, Ruth Greenglass is most likely correct in her insistence that Ethel hardly fit the stereotype of the passive housewife oblivious to the details of her husband's comings and goings.

When it comes to assessing the hard evidence, however, the case for Ethel's involvement becomes more difficult to document. While it is impossible to prove that the typing episode did *not* take place, one may equally well question prosecutor Irving Saypol's assertions at the trial, which had Ethel striking the keys of her typewriter "blow by blow against her own country, in the interests of the Soviets."

In retrospect, even the reason advanced for having David's notes typed by Ethel makes little sense. From the day of David's arrest, both he and his wife had consistently claimed that David's information was turned over to Harry Gold and to Rosenberg in handwritten form. Judging by the interrogation reports for which full transcripts have been released, Myles Lane was never satisfied with this explanation. Thus on August 2, 1950, questioning Ruth in the presence of FBI agents Harrington and Norton, Lane attempted to maneuver Ruth into an admission that *she* had transcribed some of the material her husband gave to Harry Gold in June 1945.

Q: Between 10 o'clock in the morning when Gold first appeared until 4 o'clock in the afternoon, Dave no doubt did some work on the typewriter?
A: We had no typewriter.
Q: Who typed the material?
A: It was handwritten.

Q: It wasn't typed, and he wrote it down during that interval? Do you remember how many sheets it took?

A: No.

Q: Did you work on any of it, or did he have you write any of it up?

A: I don't recall—it wasn't legible—Dave's handwriting isn't always legible.*

One can only wonder whether at some later date either Ruth or David was asked the same question—"Who typed the material?"—in terms that suggested that it was known that *someone* had typed the data. If so, it is entirely possible that one or the other, in denying that it was Ruth, hedged the statement with a phrase to the effect that "it must have been Ethel." If so, then the other could well have felt pressure to confirm the statement by dredging up details of the alleged occasion.

Although admittedly hypothetical, this reconstruction is given some support by statements made by both the Greenglasses when asked by their interviewers to recall how Ethel's name first came to be mentioned in connection with a meeting that September. Thus Ruth, in trying to remember how the subject of the typing came up, finally said: "It was almost as if we threw that in to involve her and I began to think of why that occurred. And I realized that I had no typewriter and that the information David had brought home [from Los Alamos] had been handwritten. . . ."

David, too, insisted that his determination to "keep the ladies out of it" had gradually given way under repeated questions about Ethel: "Well, I recall at one point—it's in my mind—that one of the FBI men said to me, 'You came to Julius's apartment and you discussed all this stuff. Where was Ethel?' So at that point I said, 'Yeah, she must have been around.' Because obviously she was."

And later, in a sort of summary statement volunteered at the end of the interview, David Greenglass remarked: "If it was a choice between her [indicating Ruth] and my sister, I'd take her any day—that was the choice I thought I had. It was all in my mind. Nobody put pressure on me."

---

*As it happens, FBI files contain scores of pages in David Greenglass's handwriting, including his wartime letters, all of them very easy to read, even in poor-quality photocopies.

Examination of the transcript of the Greenglasses' February 1951 interrogations—if such documents exist—might resolve some lingering doubts about the evolution of what turned out to be the key piece of evidence against Ethel Rosenberg. In the meantime, one can only conclude that the evidence of Ethel's active participation is less than totally convincing.

Finally, the residue of doubt that Ethel served as her husband's typist is reinforced by a curious tidbit that was supplied to the FBI by a secret informer in July 1951, several months after the Rosenbergs' trial but while their appeal was still pending in the higher court. According to this informant, Julius had told him "that he [Julius] had typed on various occasions for many hours in the Morton Street apartment" and that "in order to alleviate some of the noise created by typing, he placed rubber caps under the typewriter table legs and would let the water run in the bathroom."

Although statements by this same informer incriminatory of Julius Rosenberg were later used by the FBI as "secret evidence" in support of his guilt, this particular item—describing a procedure so at variance with the casual "bridge table in the living room" approach to typing described at the trial, was not deemed significant enough to merit mention in the Bureau's summary report.

8

The Trial Begins

The charge against Julius and Ethel Rosenberg and Morton Sobell was conspiracy to commit espionage. But from the moment their trial convened on the gray and dreary morning of March 6, 1951, the shadow of a still more serious accusation—treason—loomed over the courtoom.

The Rosenberg-Sobell case attracted extraordinary interest—not because the defendants had any substantial public support, but because everyone was curious to see the three previously obscure individuals who had been netted as the result of what was undoubtedly the best publicized spy hunt of all times. The case also had all the elements that make for high courtroom drama: defendants who staunchly maintained their innocence, the possibility of appearances by celebrated atomic scientists and the notorious "Red Spy Queen" Elizabeth Bentley, and the public airing of a family feud, already familiar in outline to readers of the *Jewish Daily Forward*, which had published a series of articles on the Greenglasses.

If all this were not enough to attract attention, there was also the fact that the case was being prosecuted by U.S. Attorney Irving Saypol, whose reputation as the nemesis of "Red" defendants had made him the favorite of right-wing journalists and aroused the professional jealousy of J. Edgar Hoover. A bulldoglike figure with a firm set of jaw and slicked-back graying hair, Saypol looked the part of the hard-nosed prosecutor. No orator, however, he spoke in a monotone that was barely audible to reporters in the press box, and his addiction to bad jokes would at one point during the trial cause the judge to beg him to "restrain your desire to be another Milton Berle."

Saypol's reputation rested almost entirely on his prosecution of suspected Communists, including Alger Hiss and the eleven Smith Act defendants. His most recent triumph had been the perjury conviction of William Remington, a Commerce Department employee accused of having lied under oath in denying Elizabeth Bentley's claim that he had furnished her with classified documents from the War Production Board. This record, topped off by his role as prosecutor of the Rosenbergs, would result in Saypol being hailed by *Time* magazine as "the nation's Number One legal hunter of top Communists."

It was no secret to the opposing counsel that Saypol regarded them, not to mention the defendants, as little better than agents of the devil. At the very outset of the trial, in one of his few personal asides to his opposite numbers at the defense table, Saypol warned Manny Bloch menacingly that "if your clients don't confess they are doomed." From that point on, the prosecutor barely observed the formalities of courtroom manners. His opponents were rarely accorded a courteous word and certainly never conceded a request, however small.

Saypol's hostility threw Manny Bloch into a panic from which he never entirely recovered. Bloch had taken the Rosenbergs' case knowing that they intended to claim their innocence to the last and that their chances of escaping conviction were almost nil. It was one thing, however, to contemplate the abstract possibility of a legal defeat and another to confront a hostile prosecutor who was determined to push for the death penalty. In an attempt to regain the psychological advantage over his adversary, Bloch was to vacillate between game efforts at verbal sparring and fawning compliments so obviously insincere that they are embarrassing to read in the cold print of the record. Neither approach ever caused so much as a crack in Saypol's armor of self-righteousness.

On the first day of the trial, which was to be devoted to the formalities of jury selection, the hall outside Foley Square's courtroom number 107 was already filled with a crush of curious trial buffs, reporters, and semiofficial observers, more than had ever been seen there during the earlier trials of Alger Hiss, Judith Coplon, or William Remington. Most of the spectators had come in the hope and expectation of seeing the atom spies convicted, but there was also a tiny coterie of Rosenberg sympathizers, mostly women, who made occasional attempts to gain the ear of the members of the jury pool as they passed in the corridor. In spite of the crowding, the atmosphere inside the courtroom was anything but circuslike. As the reporter for *The New York Times* noted, even during the tedious business of examining potential jurors, "an indefinable tenseness pervaded the courtroom. . . . The silence was extraordinary."

Despite the sensitive political aspects of the case, the jury was impaneled in just a day and a half. This was largely because the presiding judge, Irving R. Kaufman, in accordance with common practice in federal trials, conducted the voir dire himself. In addition to being asked about personal contacts with the FBI, members of HUAC, lawyers and principals in the case, the City College of New York, and organizations either friendly to or opposed to communism, the jury pool was read the entire list of organizations on the attorney general's list—beginning with the Abraham Lincoln Brigade and on down through the United Committee for South Slavic Americans, the Walt Whitman School of Social Science, and the Washington Book Shop Association. One man, a journalist, who admitted familiarity with left-wing publications such as *In Fact*, was eventually excused by the Court. None of the prospective jurors admitted any "bias" against HUAC or the loyalty-oath program. Nor did any "oppose the use of atomic weapons in war . . . [or] feel that developments and information concerning atomic energy should be revealed to Russia or any Russian satellite country." Some did object to capital punishment, and were excused on that ground.

Formalities out of the way, the U.S. attorney and chief prosecutor launched into his opening statement with a matter-of-fact explanation of the conspiracy law. He had not spoken for five minutes, however, when he became the first to give voice to what many present assumed was the real issue. "The evidence will show," Saypol promised, "that the loyalty and the allegiance of the Rosenbergs and Sobell were not to our country, but that it [*sic*] was to Communism, Communism in this country and throughout the world."

Emanuel Bloch was instantly on his feet, objecting that Saypol's remarks about communism were "irrelevant" because "Communism is not on trial here"—a sentiment he had already addressed to the jury during the impaneling and one that was soon to emerge as the major theme of his defense. Its futility was evident from the outset when Judge Kaufman ruled that testimony about the defendants' belief in communism would be allowed in order to establish their motivation.

But for the defendants, there was still worse to come as Saypol warmed to his subject. Accusing the Rosenbergs of persuading David Greenglass "to play the treacherous role of a modern Benedict Arnold," Saypol went on to promise that "the evidence will show that these defendants joined with their co-conspirators in a deliberate, carefully planned conspiracy to deliver to the Soviet Union the information and the weapons the Soviet Union could use to destroy us." And again: "The evidence of the treasonable acts of these three defendants you will find overwhelming ... [they] have committed the most serious crime which can be committed against the people of this country."

After such a speech it is hardly surprising that editorial writers and newspaper columnists all over the country seemed confused about the actual charge against the Rosenbergs or that so many took the occasion to urge the death penalty for treason. Saypol had no qualms about equating conspiracy to commit espionage with treason in his address to the jury. Nevertheless, it is most unlikely that the defendants could ever have been convicted of treason. Because of the seriousness of that crime, the standards of proof in a treason trial are quite strict. For one thing, the government would have had to produce two separate witnesses to each and every overt act cited in the charge. Moreover, the fact that the Soviet Union had not been at war with the United States at the time the theft of atomic secrets was alleged to have taken place might have made it all but impossible to prove treasonable intent.

The standards required for a conspiracy conviction, on the other hand, are so minimal that conspiracy law has been called either "the last resort of the people" or the "prosecutor's friend," depending on the writer's point of view. Not only is hearsay testimony admissible, but once the existence of a conspiracy has been established each conspirator may be held liable for the acts of all the others, whether or not he had specific knowledge of them. Most important, it would not even be necessary to prove that the conspirators had actually succeeded in their plans, only that they had conspired together toward a given end.

Under the circumstances, it was relatively easy to get a conviction for conspiracy. But, as Myles Lane had pointed out during his presentation to the Joint Committee on Atomic Energy, the prosecutors hoped for more than a simple guilty verdict; their plan from the outset had been to establish a case strong enough to justify stiff sentences—and, if possible, a death sentence for Julius Rosenberg. Crucial to this hope was the government's ability to show that the recruitment of Greenglass was not an isolated incident, but part of an ongoing espionage operation directed by the Rosenbergs. Indications are that the original working outline for the trial, prepared by Myles Lane, had called for a fairly painstaking effort on the government's part to establish the larger outlines of the Rosenberg spy ring. And the list of prospective witnesses read out during the voir dire had included a number of individuals who might be questioned about these connections—Vivian Glassman, the Sidoroviches, Louise Sarant, Joel Barr's brother Arthur, and, of course, William Perl. Even if some of these witnesses proved uncooperative, their appearances could be used to inform judge and jury of the suspicious disappearances that had followed Rosenberg's arrest. Also listed as potential witnesses were key FBI agents in the case who could establish, among other things, that Rosenberg and Sobell's employment histories included work on classified military contracts.

But this strategy would never be carried through. Roy Cohn, the junior assistant whom Saypol had come to rely on increasingly in the weeks before the trial opened, had prepared a second, streamlined trial outline, and this was the one Saypol chose to use. The wisdom of this change in approach is difficult to evaluate in hindsight. Perhaps it was justified by the possibility that a long, complex trial would have served no purpose except to tire the jury and muddy the basic issues. On the other hand, there is no question that among the factors helping to make a shorter trial possible were the last-minute changes in the testimony of several key witnesses. Now that Harry Gold was ready to say that he carried "greetings from Julius," and David and Ruth had recalled Ethel's typing, there was surely less need to present supporting evidence to convince the jury of the Rosenbergs' guilt. The last-minute changes in testimony thus made the prosecution's task easier—perhaps, suspiciously so—but they would also result in the presentation of a case that would be vulnerable to later attacks by those who sought to show that the Rosenbergs had been framed. Certainly the new prosecution strategy made it less clear just where the third defendant, Morton Sobell, fit into the case.

Virtually the entire case presented against Sobell rested on the story of the trial's first witness, Max Elitcher. A tall, slightly stoop-shouldered man, Elitcher wore a wan expression and spoke in a barely audible voice that betrayed his lack of enthusiasm for the task ahead. In response to Saypol's first question, Elitcher began his story in 1939, when his high school pal Sobell had invited him to join the Young Communist League. This line of questioning elicited frantic objections from Sobell's lawyer Edward Kuntz, who complained that the conspiracy alleged in the case did not even go back to 1939 and that, furthermore, previous court decisions had indicated that membership in the YCL could not be equated with membership in the Party. Judge Kaufman responded by urging Saypol to move along and establish a connection to the matter at hand.

Saypol obliged by leading Elitcher into a detailed recital of his contacts with Rosenberg—beginning with Rosenberg's 1944 visit to Elitcher's Washington apartment and the evening the next summer when the Elitchers had slept over at Rosenberg's apartment because Helene Elitcher had refused to stay at Max's parents' house one more night. On that occasion, Elitcher said, Ethel and the children had been away, staying at a summer cabin somewhere in New Jersey, and Julius had confided, out of Helene's hearing, that he had been under great tension because of troubles with the Signal Corps. For weeks, Julius told Max, he had worried that the Army had evidence connecting him to espionage, only to learn that the whole matter involved nothing more than an accusation that he was a Party member.

Elitcher's testimony also connected Rosenberg to Sobell. He told of a business trip to Schenectady in early 1946 when he had stayed overnight at Sobell's house. Sobell had asked him for classified pamphlets describing a new antisubmarine weapon being developed by the Navy Bureau of Ordnance. In late 1947, Elitcher said, he and Sobell had had lunch at the Sugar Bowl restaurant in New York City. Sobell had questioned him about problems he had been having with his wife, expressing nervousness that Helene Elitcher might know too much about "this espionage business." Elitcher also told of how both Sobell and Rosenberg had later tried unsuccessfully to talk him out of leaving the Bureau of Ordnance to work at Reeves. Julius, he said, had taken him to dinner at Manny Wolf's restaurant on Third Avenue and offered to help him get a job with Bell Laboratories in New Jersey or subsidize further technical courses for Elitcher if he would agree to go back to school instead of moving to Reeves, where Sobell already worked. Said Elitcher:

> In the course of this conversation I also asked him about how he had started in this venture and he told me that he had a long time ago decided that this was what he wanted to do and he made it a point to get close to people, people in the Communist Party—he didn't specify any person or their positions—and he kept getting close from one person to another, until he was able to approach someone, Russian . . . who would listen to his proposition.

On this dramatic note, court was adjourned for lunch. But Saypol had saved Elitcher's most damaging story—that of his and Sobell's furtive drive to Catherine Slip—for the afternoon session. Elitcher told the tale much as he had originally recounted it to the FBI, but he included one colorful detail that he had not mentioned until his final interrogation on October 23 of the previous year. After Sobell returned to the car without the film can, he said, while relating his fears that he had been followed to New York by the FBI, Elitcher asked if Julius might have been known to the confessed spy Elizabeth Bentley. Sobell replied, not too reassuringly, that Julius had once talked to Bentley on the phone but "he was pretty sure she didn't know who he was and therefore everything was all right." This mention of Bentley was the most sensational revelation of the trial to date. It was also a considerable blow to the defense since it indicated that the inclusion of Bentley's name on the pretrial list of potential prosecution witnesses had been no empty bluff.

It was no secret that everyone on the defense side regarded Max Elitcher as a Judas. On strict orders from the FBI and their lawyer, O. John Rogge, the Elitchers had managed to keep the secret of their intent to cooperate with the government until some weeks after Morton Sobell's arrest. Helen Sobell was particularly outraged that the Elitchers had come around when she was selling her house and furniture to pay her husband's defense fees and selected her daughter's piano, bookcases, and some lawn furniture, all of which they took in exchange for their half interest in the washing machine the two families owned jointly. Helen later said that while she had thought that the Elitchers were driving a hard bargain, she had, at the time, considered the gesture to be basically a friendly one.

The Elitchers' deception had worked better than one might expect. Although the Sobells felt more deeply betrayed than ever when they learned that their former friend was actually going to appear as a government witness, they still could not quite believe that he had been cooperating with the FBI from the beginning. The suspicion that Elitcher must have initially resisted talking to the FBI—and may well have made false and misleading statements to investigators before he finally broke down—colored the defense attorney's approach to him. If evidence could be brought out to show that Elitcher had changed his original story under pressure, then the defense would gain an immediate advantage.

In questioning Elitcher, Emanuel Bloch and Edward Kuntz hammered away at the circumstances of the witness's initial meetings with the FBI, looking for contradictions between what Elitcher remembered telling the Bureau originally and his devastatingly detailed courtroom testimony. Though the exercise was largely futile, Kuntz did manage to draw out an admission that Elitcher had not recalled the conversation with Sobell about Bentley until after he heard Bentley's name mentioned by one of the FBI agents who was interrogating him. And Bloch got Elitcher to admit repeatedly that he had been "scared to death" for years and had cooperated with the FBI largely out of fear that he might be prosecuted for perjury for denying his Communist Party membership on his navy security questionnaire. But Elitcher's admission of weakness probably did little to make the jury doubt his story. Who wouldn't have been frightened to find himself involved, however peripherally, in a major espionage case?

Although the cross-examination of Elitcher did not succeed in destroying his credibility, the defense did create enough doubts about the consistency of his story to convince Judge Kaufman that there were grounds for ordering the FBI to produce the records of the witness's pretrial statements to the FBI and to the grand jury.

The irony of this victory was that, alone among all the major prosecution witnesses who had decided to cooperate with the FBI from the very outset, Elitcher gave pretrial statements that were strikingly consistent with his testimony in court. True, he had originally omitted mention of several important incidents, particularly those involving Sobell. But there were no outright contradictions—nothing to compare, say, with the typing story of the Greenglasses or Harry Gold's confusion over the password he had used in Albuquerque.

On the Monday following Elitcher's dismissal from the stand, Judge Kaufman ordered an hour-and-a-half lunch recess so that the defense team might have the opportunity to examine the Elitcher documents the government had provided. Sobell's lawyers, Edward Kuntz and Harold Phillips, protested unavailingly that they would prefer to have at least overnight to go through the material. In the end, the lunch break was long enough to convince them that there were no buried gems that could be mined to the advantage of the defense.

Although the order to produce Elitcher's pretrial statements had amounted to little more than a minor annoyance, it set a worrisome precedent. Irving Saypol, undoubtedly aware that his handling of the case had been the subject of continual petty criticisms from Hoover, used the occasion to get in a dig of his own. In a March 9 telephone conversation with Ray Whearty of the Justice Department, Saypol complained: "We are moving along all right," but "we have got our little problems, the usual questions on whether or not FBI statements should be made available because of inconsistencies. I am going to write a letter to the effect that the Bureau should not [in future] take signed statements. They don't mean a thing."

Saypol's real problem, of course, was not with what was in the FBI statements—he had based his case on them—but what was *not* in them, namely the story of Ethel's typing of secret documents and Harry Gold's memory of using the name Julius. The possibility that these "inconsistencies" might be revealed in court was not at all a welcome one.

Elitcher, meanwhile, wanted nothing more than to have his ordeal brought to a close. Summoned to appear in court that Monday morning in case the defense wished to recall him, Elitcher arrived a frightened man. As Irving Saypol informed the judge and the opposing attorneys in a bench conference out of the jury's hearing, Elitcher had received an anonymous note warning him to "watch out for the time bomb." Not even Saypol believed that the note represented a serious threat on the witness's life. He told Kaufman that he was mentioning the event as a "precautionary measure" and that the matter had been referred to the New York Police Department but not to the FBI.

Elitcher would not be the only principal in the case to become the target of hate mail; even Judge Kaufman himself would eventually receive anonymous threats. But the incident, coming as it did so early in the trial, was a serious embarrassment to Manny Bloch. Obviously shocked and surprised by this attempt to tamper with a witness, Bloch was thrown further on the defensive. As he pointed out to the judge, the defendants had all been imprisoned for months and could hardly be personally responsible for sending the letter to Elitcher. Nevertheless, the threat did nothing to enhance the picture Bloch was trying to present of his clients as innocent people, more bewildered than angry at their present plight. The jury, naturally, knew nothing about the letter and would not be influenced; but Bloch could not be sure that the same could be said for Judge Kaufman, who would have the ultimate power to pass sentence in the event of conviction.

After all this, the defense lawyers found nothing in Elitcher's statements that would make it worth their while to summon him back to the stand. Although it was true that Elitcher had not mentioned the Catherine Slip incident until some weeks after his first statement to the Bureau, the story did not contradict anything he had said earlier, so reopening the issue would most likely only result in a rehashing of his already damaging testimony, impressing it still further on the minds of the jury.

Elitcher's role in the trial was now over, but the enmity of the Sobells and their friends certainly did not abate with time. Helen Sobell was later to charge publicly that Max Elitcher had perjured himself for money, and that Elitcher had purchased a new car, and his wife, Helene, a fur coat, with payment received from the government. Although the accusation that Elitcher had received money from the government cannot be positively disproven, it does not fit well with Elitcher's own admission on the stand that he was "scared to death" of being prosecuted—either for perjury in swearing falsely on a government questionnaire or as a member of the conspiracy itself. The record of the pretrial statements shows that the Elitchers had cooperated from the first, primarily out of fear that Julius Rosenberg had already named them. The government had their signed statements. There was hardly any need to offer a bribe.

Nor does this picture of Max and Helene flaunting the luxuries they had purchased with their thirty talents of silver accord with the picture of Elitcher's situation that emerges from his later dealings with his lawyer, O. John Rogge. When it became known that Elitcher was the subject of an FBI investigation and would be appearing as a witness at the atom-spy conspiracy trial, the Reeves Instrument Company demanded his resignation. Unemployed, and for all practical purposes unemployable in his specialty of military fire-control systems, Elitcher pleaded with Rogge to intercede with the government for a character reference that would clear him of all suspicion of espionage.

Whether the government actually came through with assistance in finding a new job is unclear. However, Elitcher, who had once been appalled at the very suggestion that he name his former party associates to FBI interrogators, was to make two more appearances as a cooperative government witness: first, at the perjury trial of William Perl in 1953, and a few months later, before a closed session of the House Un-American Activities Committee, where he supplied a list of the members of the Party cell he had belonged to in Washington. FBI agent Scheidt's prediction that once Elitcher had been induced to talk about espionage he would be unable to resist the pressure to become a political informer as well had turned out to be correct.

9

David Greenglass

David Greenglass, who followed Max Elitcher on the witness stand, did not look like a man who was testifying under duress. The heavy-set, wavy-haired twenty-nine-year-old spoke in a steady voice, easily audible in the back rows of the spectators' seats. Under questioning by Roy Cohn, Greenglass reviewed his career as an army machinist, which culminated in an assignment as assistant foreman in the lab serving George Kistiakowski's high-explosives unit at Los Alamos. Then the questioning backtracked to the mid-1930s, when David, still a teenager, first recalled hearing his older sister and her boyfriend, Julius Rosenberg, praising the virtues of the Socialist system.

When David talked about his sister and brother-in-law his facial features frequently rearranged themselves into a broad grin. The involuntary smile, which he would be unable to control even when Manny Bloch called attention to it, was probably evidence of nervousness. But some courtroom observers interpreted it as gloating. Whatever one's reading, no one could doubt that he felt a deep resentment of the Rosenbergs, deeper perhaps than he was consciously aware. But what was the cause? Was this a case of a vindictive relative carrying a family feud to bizarre and horrible lengths, as Emanuel Bloch had intimated in his opening statement? Or did Greenglass blame Julius and Ethel for having been all too willing to sacrifice his life, as well as their own, to the cause they so fervently believed in?

While the jury, the press, and the spectators were primarily interested in fathoming Greenglass's motives, the prosecutors and the AEC liaisons were far more concerned about the content of his forthcoming testimony. The AEC hoped that certain categories of information Greenglass had admitted to giving to the Russians—such as a sketch for a spherical lens mold design and a description of a series of plutonium reduction experiments—would not come up in court. Still more irksome was the AEC's stipulation for the handling of its expert witnesses, particularly Walter Koski, the expert on high-explosive lenses. It was the AEC's idea to limit Koski's testimony to a general discussion of lens molds, with no mention of the spherical lens-mold sketch in particular and no broader testimony on A-bomb design in general—a subject reserved for a subsequent witness. The plan was to protect Koski from searching cross-examination that might broach on these areas by getting him on and off the witness stand before Greenglass had a chance to characterize the kinds of technical information he had stolen. Of course, there was nothing to prevent the defense from recalling Koski after Greenglass's testimony was finished, but this was considered unlikely.

Not ten minutes before he took the stand, David Greenglass received stern instructions from Roy Cohn. Cohn explained that his initial questions would lead up to the first occasion of Greenglass's giving written data to Rosenberg in January 1945. But when Cohn asked *what* had been given to Rosenberg, Greenglass was to mention only that he had supplied the names of certain atomic physicists who were working incognito at Los Alamos. The rest, Cohn explained, would all come out in due course.

Controlling the pace of the testimony in this way may have seemed simple enough to the AEC liaisons, but Cohn's instructions made little impact on the nervous witness. And by the time the questioning reached a discussion of the events of January 1945, Greenglass had completely forgotten what he was supposed to mention first. Thus when Cohn asked Greenglass what information Julius had wanted, the witness started to mention lens molds.

Cohn backtracked, looking for the answer he wanted: "What else?"

"And he told me to write it up, to write up anything I knew about the atomic bomb."

Cohn tried again. "What else?"

"He gave me a description of the bomb."

Prosecutor and witness danced back and forth for three more questions before Greenglass finally realized what Cohn was fishing for and began ticking off the list of scientists' names he had given Rosenberg. Cohn then announced with relief that the testimony seemed to have reached a good stopping place.

It was still early for adjournment, but after a brief off-the-record conference with Cohn, Judge Kaufman granted his request to wrap it up for the day, much as it hurt his "Scotch soul" to waste good courtroom time.

Shortly after five o'clock that afternoon, the prosecutor's staff and the AEC liaisons met for a strategy session. Cohn, judging by the transcript of the meeting, was in high dudgeon. He obviously believed that he had been asked to do the impossible, and he did not feel like taking the blame for Greenglass's memory lapse.

"We said, no matter how the question is asked, don't give that answer. Just leave that out for the time being," Cohn sputtered. And "he went ahead and said he told him about the bomb. He gave that answer. . . ."

The AEC's William Denson was unsympathetic. "You kept asking, 'What else?' 'What else?'"

"Sure I asked, because he left out the whole thing!" Cohn protested.

So far, Irving Saypol had had little to say, letting the voluble and excited Cohn ramble on about his "crystal clear" refusal to take responsibility for the day's snafu. But Saypol, too, was irritated. The FBI and the AEC had laid out his case for him in "black and white," he complained, but the flow of testimony in the courtroom just couldn't be that neatly controlled. Saypol was particularly annoyed by the AEC's request that he not permit any mention of Greenglass's delivery to Julius of information on plutonium reduction experiments. This was the very data the AEC had characterized as "the most sensitive technical information disclosed by Greenglass." How was he supposed to make his case if he was not supposed to bring up the "most sensitive" data?

DENSON: We proceeded on the assumption [that] you could prove that case and obtain whatever penalties are considered appropriate without introducing that element.

SAYPOL: There is not a man alive that can tell you what the import would be of withholding that ... if we withheld that from his direct testimony and it is brought out under cross-examination, then [it] may destroy him as a witness.

When Denson still refused to budge from his position that the experiments should not be mentioned except as a last resort, Saypol blew up. "How am I ever to justify that? What kind of a boob ... ? You want me to be the martyr in this case?"

Denson replied mildly that he did not believe the defense would attempt to bring out testimony about the reduction experiments.

Myles Lane agreed. His feeling was that Bloch would not want to delve too deeply into the details of what Greenglass was alleged to have stolen. "I think," mused Lane, "they would only be harming themselves."

Lane and Denson's optimism was not widely shared. Despite their disagreements, both Gordon Dean and Irving Saypol expected the defense to challenge the technical testimony aggressively. Neither had a clear idea of how this would be done, but the feeling was that Emanuel Bloch would somehow force the government to pay a price for the Rosenbergs' conviction by getting its witnesses to disgorge as much classified information as possible.

Nor did the results of David Greenglass's first day on the stand do anything to increase Gordon Dean's confidence in Saypol and Cohn's ability to deal with the expected challenge. It was during the weekend following this incident that Dean went to Attorney General McGrath's home and persuaded him to put pressure on Saypol to hew closely to the AEC's list of suggested questions.

Monday, March 12, began with Greenglass resuming the stand to take his actions up through Harry Gold's arrival at his home in Albuquerque in June 1945. During the course of his testimony, Greenglass also presented two sketches of lens molds: one representing a crude drawing he had given Rosenberg in January 1945 and another somewhat more detailed representation of the so-called flat-type lens mold he had passed to Gold that June. As soon as both of these were in evidence, the prosecution asked permission to interrupt Greenglass's testimony to bring on their expert witness, Koski.

Following the strategy he had agreed on with the AEC liaisons and undertaking the examination of Koski himself, Saypol began with the least sensitive area of the Greenglass material: the lens mold. Koski, a physical chemist, first explained the difference between an *explosion*, in which shock waves travel outward, and an *implosion*, in which "the waves are converging and the energy is concentrating itself." The implosion lens in question had nothing to do with optical lenses but was basically a device for shaping charges of explosives so that they would produce a converging detonation wave.

> SAYPOL: Well, once again, so that we as laymen might understand, I take it our common conception of a lens is a piece of glass used to focus light, is that right?
> KOSKI: Yes, that is right.
> SAYPOL: What is the distinction between a glass lens and the one you were working on?
> KOSKI: Well, a glass lens essentially focuses light. An explosive lens focuses a detonation wave or a high pressure force coming in.

During late 1944 and the first half of 1945, Koski said, he had been working on a design for a particular "flat type" lens mold. The usual procedure was for him to deliver sketches of the mold to the Los Alamos Theta Shop, which would then produce prototypes he could test experimentally. David Greenglass had been a Theta Shop foreman at the time, and Koski now agreed with Saypol that the sketch labeled Exhibit 2 was a "substantially accurate replica" of one of the designs he had given Theta Shop during that period. Koski also vouched for two more sketches, Exhibits 6 and 7, which were freehand representations of lens-mold sketches.

Finally, Koski went on record as saying that the designs used in the sketches had been "new and original" in 1945 and could not possibly have been taken from published books or articles.

> SAYPOL: And up to that point and continuing right up until this trial has the information relating to the lens mold and the lens and the experimentation to which you have testified continued to be secret information?
> KOSKI: It still is.
> SAYPOL: Except as divulged at this trial?
> KOSKI: Correct.

Saypol now asked Judge Kaufman's permission to introduce a statement into the record that the subject matter of Koski's testimony had been declassified for the purposes of the trial "and that subsequent to the trial it is to be reclassified." Saypol's statement faithfully reflected the position of the AEC, but it was obviously open to ridicule from the defense lawyers. If the material were really still secret as of 1951, why was the government allowing it to be revealed in open court? And what could conceivably be the point of "reclassifying" information that had already been paraded before a room full of reporters and spectators? As the trial transcript shows, Judge Kaufman invited Emanuel Bloch to present his objections:

> THE COURT: Counsel [for the defense] doesn't take issue with that statement?
> BLOCH: No, not at all. I read about it in the newspapers before Mr. Saypol stated it.

Whether he knew it or not, Emanuel Bloch had more or less conceded that the implosion-lens sketches were important enough to merit classified status—not just in 1945, when Greenglass obtained them, but in 1951 as well. By the time he actually began cross-examining Koski, the battle was already half lost, and the few doubts he was able to raise then did not put a dent in Koski's composure. Koski was forced to concede that Greenglass was only an "ordinary machinist" and that the sketches in question did not specify either the absolute or relative dimensions of the lens mold. Nevertheless, the prosecution more than made up for lost ground during its redirect examination when Koski was allowed to testify, despite Bloch's heated protest that the witness was a scientific expert and not a political or military analyst, that the data in the sketch would have been of great help to a foreign power:

> SAYPOL: Would I be exaggerating if I were to say colloquially that one expert, interested in finding out what was going on at Los Alamos, could get enough from those exhibits in evidence which you have before you to reveal what was going on at Los Alamos?
> KOSKI: One could.

And again, minutes later:

> SAYPOL: Distinguishing between relative dimensions and design, it is [*sic*] not the fact that design of the component was the primary fact of importance of these sketches?
> KOSKI: It was.

Koski left the stand without having to face any of the potentially awkward questions the prosecution had anticipated. He had not been asked for further details about the dimensions of the lens mold or the process of its development and testing. He had not been asked to substantiate his statements about the value of the sketches to a "foreign power" by describing the state of Soviet atomic research. Most important, no one had asked why the Soviets would have needed data from an "ordinary machinist" when they already were receiving technical reports from Dr. Koski's colleague Klaus Fuchs.

Koski's departure from the stand was the signal for everyone at the prosecution table, U.S. attorneys and AEC representatives alike, to breathe a sigh of relief. But this small victory was nothing compared to the surprising events the afternoon's testimony would bring. Lunch break that day was longer than usual because the Rosenberg and Sobell attorneys were being given the opportunity to study the Elitcher pretrial statements. When they found no reason to recall Elitcher, however, a fresh and rested-looking David Greenglass was returned to the stand. There he began to recount, with barely concealed pride, how he had managed to obtain for his brother-in-law a "pretty good description" of the atomic bomb that was dropped on Nagasaki.

According to Greenglass, when Julius had briefed him on his mission in January 1945—at the same dinner party where Ruth Greenglass was given half a Jello-O box top as a recognition symbol—he had described the basic design of the bomb that was later used on Hiroshima. As Greenglass recalled it:

> He [Julius] said there was fissionable material at one end of a cube and at the other end of the cube there was a sliding member that was also of fissionable material and when they brought these two together under great pressure that would be—a nuclear reaction would take place.

Upon returning to Los Alamos after his furlough, Greenglass said, he had learned that the bomb Julius described was already technically obsolete. (In fact, the bomb dropped on Hiroshima was the one and only weapon of this design ever built.) By keeping his eyes open and getting into conversations with "a number of people involved in different parts of the project," Greenglass testified, he had eventually been able to form a fairly good overall concept of the newer implosion-type weapon. When he returned to New York for a second furlough in September 1945, he had told Julius of the new developments afoot at Los Alamos. Julius had immediately given him $200 and said he wanted the information "immediately, as soon as I could possibly get it written up."

By two o'clock that same afternoon, Greenglass said, he had written up about twelve pages of descriptive material and drawn several sketches, which he and Ruth then took over to the Rosenberg apartment. One of those sketches, a cross-section drawing of the Nagasaki bomb, had been duplicated by Greenglass the previous weekend; and Roy Cohn now asked the court's permission to introduce it as Exhibit 8.

Emanuel Bloch leaped to his feet—not, as everyone expected, to challenge the validity of a machinist's "pretty good description," but to demand that the sketch immediately be impounded "so that it remains secret from the Court, the jury and counsel."

Irving Saypol was so flabbergasted by this move that he could not refrain from chiding his opponent. "That is a very strange request coming from the defendants," he mused aloud.

> BLOCH: Not a strange request coming from me at the present.
> SAYPOL: . . . If I had said it or my colleague, Mr. Cohn had said it, there might have been some criticism.
> THE COURT: As a matter of fact, there might have been some question on appeal. I welcome the suggestion from the defense because it removes the question completely.

Bloch was still not finished. As Roy Cohn began questioning Greenglass about the contents of the twelve pages of descriptive material that had accompanied the sketch, Bloch interrupted, requesting permission to approach the bench. He wanted to speak, he said, about a problem that had been weighing on his conscience.

BLOCH: . . . I was not at all sure in my own mind whether or not even at this late date, this information might not be used to the advantage of a foreign power. Remember, I am talking personally. . . . I am perfectly satisfied that this also be kept secret.

THE COURT: Do you want it to be done *in camera* without the spectators being present?

Bloch indicated that he did. Once again Irving Saypol was incredulous. "We obviously have been proceeding on the assumption . . . that under the law we are required to apprise the defendant of the nature of the case. . . ." But after having Bloch repeat that he had no objection to the move, Judge Kaufman ordered the spectators and press out of the courtroom.

With a few words, Manny Bloch had managed to do more than the prosecution could ever hope to do to convince the jury that what it was about to hear really was "the secret of the atom bomb." Why else would it be necessary to exclude the press and the public from hearing the testimony?

Bloch's request left Morton Sobell's lawyers momentarily stunned into silence. By the time they found their voices and lodged a protest, it was too late. By a previously agreed-upon rule, each defense lawyer was empowered to speak for all unless there was an immediate clarification from his colleagues.

While Sobell's counsel was still squirming over the exclusion of the press, Bloch grew even more expansive and volunteered a further concession. Rather than force the government to establish that Greenglass's data had included secret information related to the national defense, he said, he was prepared to stipulate that it did and move on to other matters. Explained Bloch: "I would like to stipulate as an American citizen and as a person who owes his allegiance to this country. I would like to stipulate it first to save the expense; I understand it would save quite an expense to the government to bring all these people here."

The suggestion that it would be unpatriotic to require the state to set forth the full evidence against defendants charged with a capital crime certainly sounds out of character for a defense lawyer, particularly one who had devoted his career to representing the politically unpopular causes championed by the National Lawyers Guild and the Civil Rights Congress. As for Bloch's concern to save the government expense, it is simply incredible.

This latest offer was the final straw for Sobell's attorney Harold Phillips. He adamantly refused to join in any such stipulation, "For the reason that I do not feel that an attorney in a criminal case should make concessions which will save the People from the necessity of proving things, which in the course of the proof we may be able to refute."

In the end, however, it was the press that had the last word on the matter. While the court was enjoying a short recess, the reporters who had been relegated to the corridor sent a delegation in to the judge's chambers to report that they were, in Kaufman's mild phrase, "rather agitated" over the barring order. Back in court, Kaufman announced that, on reflection, he felt he would have to ask Saypol to confer with representatives of the Atomic Energy Commission to determine whether the exclusion of reporters was really necessary.

But Saypol was not the one who had objected to the press in the first place. He did not have to confer with the AEC. He was prepared to agree right away. It was Manny Bloch who still continued to protest the decision to let the press back in, complaining that "otherwise I believe the purpose would be defeated. . . ."

Bloch's continuing pleas that the press be enjoined to secrecy were overruled by Judge Kaufman, who readmitted reporters with the comment that they would only be "enjoined to good taste"—apparently a veiled injunction to self-censorship. Nevertheless, the reporters present did their best to give an informative summary of Greenglass's oral description of his sketch, and on the whole their reports were quite balanced. As much of the press pointed out, the "Greenglass bomb" was accurate enough to have revealed the basic approach being employed at Los Alamos without being either completely accurate or comprehensive. As Howard Blakeslee of the Associated Press summed it up, the Greenglass description combined the "dangerous secret" of implosion with some improvised supporting material that was "partly Rube Goldberg stuff."

But while Bloch had lost his battle to exclude reporters, his original motion for impounding still stood. Exhibit 8 and Greenglass's accompanying description—two lengthy paragraphs in printed form—were excluded from the public transcript of the trial. This material did not appear in later published versions of the transcripts and was not even seen by the various higher court judges who reviewed the case. The effects of this move by Bloch were bizarre, to say the least. Regardless of the stated purposes, one might argue that the AEC's desire to "reclassify" technical data brought out during the trial was designed in part to preserve the mystique of atomic secrecy and inhibit public evaluation of the significance of the Rosenbergs' crime to our national security. But the AEC's plan, whatever its goal, had been totally unworkable. Once the testimony was on the public record, a "reclassification" stamp would be merely symbolic. Emanuel Bloch, on the other hand, had succeeded in doing what the AEC would have loved to bring about but did not dare to propose. The impounded testimony was now truly protected from public scrutiny, and it was to remain so until 1966, when it was finally released in response to a petition by attorneys Marshall Perlin and William Kunstler.

In defense of Bloch's unorthodox tactic, he had little or no hope of mounting an effective challenge to the government's presentation of the technical evidence, no matter what course he took. Not only did he lack advance knowledge of the specific data Greenglass would testify to stealing, but he and the other defense lawyers appear to have had only the vaguest understanding of the scientific background of the atomic bomb's development. Gloria Agrin, the young lawyer who helped Bloch and his father prepare the Rosenbergs' defense, told journalist Ted Morgan in 1975 that she sat through David Greenglass's testimony under the impression that the lens mold he was talking about had something to do with cameras and photography. "We learned about implosion at the same time as the jury," Agrin confessed. "We had no background in physics or science." And speaking of the physicists who were later to provide affidavits on behalf of the Rosenbergs and Sobell, Agrin gave way to bitterness, pointing out that not one of these experts had made himself available during the trial: "At the time . . . where were all these lovely scientists?"

Bloch later said that his call for impounding the technical evidence had been a move made out of desperation motivated more by fear than by logic. He had felt the need, he said, for a "grandstand play," one designed to impress the jury and, more importantly, the judge, with his and his clients' patriotic concern for protecting the national security. If so, then Bloch showed a poor understanding of psychology.

The kindest interpretation of Bloch's admission that he felt the need for a patriotic gesture at this juncture in the trial is that he believed his clients' case was already lost and was looking for a chance to win the sympathy of the judge and avert the death penalty he saw in store, at least for Julius Rosenberg. Technically, his stance was not logically inconsistent with continuing to profess his clients' innocence: the Rosenbergs did not claim that Greenglass had never been a spy, only that they had never been involved with his activities. Nevertheless, it was not Bloch's job to bolster the credibility of the chief prosecution witness in the eyes of the jury. By any accepted standards of lawyerly behavior, his move was so extraordinary as to border on malpractice.

A less generous assessment of Bloch's motivations would be that he was privately convinced of his clients' guilt and wanted to spare the Communist Party the embarrassment of having the details exposed in the press. At the same time, Bloch may have reasoned, he would also be serving the interests of the Rosenbergs: keeping the details of the stolen data out of the newspapers would make it easier to present them as victims of political persecution in the court of public opinion. Bloch's statement that readmitting the press would "defeat the purpose" of his motion lends support to this interpretation. He had already made his patriotic speech. There was nothing to be gained from continuing to argue for the exclusion of the press *against* the express wishes of the judge.

Whatever Bloch's reasons, the prosecutors were jubilant over his move. Not only did they believe he had hurt his clients in the eyes of the jury, but the looming conflict over how much classified information would be permitted to emerge in expert testimony had suddenly been defused. This sense of relief was shared by Gordon Dean, who wrote in his diary the next day:

> Hollis [one of the AEC observers at the trial] called to say that we have a little good news. . . . Koski was a brilliant witness. They [the defense] only asked him three questions on cross-examination. The feeling among our fellows up there is very different now. The boys seemed to "light up" over night.

The only fear was that the government had escaped momentary embarrassment at the cost of future trouble. Both Gordon Dean and his informant Hollis agreed that Bloch's ploy in calling for the impounding was an error that might later cause the case to run aground in the appellate courts. Calling Bloch's move "very foolish," Dean worried that a new and uncontrollable element had now been introduced into the case. There was now "some grounds for a 'reversible error' even without the defendants' consent."

Retaking the stand after Koski's dismissal, Greenglass began immediately with his version of the typing incident in September 1945—which, he now said, had concluded with Julius burning the handwritten notes in a frying pan. From there, Greenglass went on to describe how Julius had boasted of his espionage contacts, how he had encouraged his brother-in-law to study nuclear engineering and other subjects that might put him in a position to spy further for the Russians, and how, eventually, he had urged the Greenglasses to flee to Mexico.

When Roy Cohn was finally finished with his direct examination, the witness was turned over to Emanuel Bloch, who spent the better part of a day and a half probing for cracks in Greenglass's façade of confidence. Given David's reputation for being something of a hothead, Bloch no doubt felt that if he kept up the pressure long enough, the witness might blurt out something that would destroy his credibility in the eyes of the jury. But given that Bloch had allowed Greenglass to testify virtually unchallenged on such complex matters as high-explosive lens molds, this belated effort was bound to be something of an anticlimax. Asked about his educational background, Greenglass cheerfully admitted that he had never studied calculus, nuclear physics, or other advanced scientific subjects. And he conceded that he had a poor academic record overall, admitting unabashedly that he had done poorly during his semester at Brooklyn Polytech because "I was quite young at the time, and I liked to play around more than I liked to go to school, so I cut classes the whole term."

Encouraged by this admission, Bloch pressed on, asking: "Do you know what an isotope is?"

Unfortunately for Bloch, Greenglass did know, and he reeled off the definition without a pause: "An isotope is an element having the same atomic structure, but a different atomic weight."

Further attempts by Bloch to find cracks in Greenglass's story seemed equally scattershot and pointless. The witness conceded, for example, that he did not recall the specific flavor indicated on the Jell-O box that was used as a signal by him and Gold. (The facsimile presented in court was from a box of "imitation raspberry"—apparently Roy Cohn's selection.) Bloch then pressed on with questions about the paper wrapper that had contained the $4,000 allegedly delivered by Julius and got Greenglass to admit that he did not really know that the paper was brown, only that it was a shade "everyone accepts" as brown. Greenglass, it developed, was color blind. But it is difficult to imagine how this admission, wrung from him so painstakingly by Bloch, did anything to help the defense's case. If anything, it gave Greenglass an excuse for not remembering the specific appearance of the Jell-O box.

The whole episode was typical of the dead ends that kept confronting Emanuel Bloch every time he attempted to mount a concerted attack on some aspect of the prosecution's story. No witness was more vulnerable to attacks on his character than David Greenglass. The fact that he had not yet been sentenced for his admitted role in the conspiracy—and that his wife, though named as a coconspirator, had never been indicted—gave him an obvious motive for saying what the government wanted to hear. On top of that, his statement under oath that he still loved his sister Ethel even though he was testifying against her on a capital charge can hardly have failed to make the jurors wince with embarrassment. Still, it was one thing to say that Greenglass was sacrificing his sister to save his own neck but quite another to suggest that his entire confession had been fabricated to frame her.

In the long run, Bloch's effort to convince the jury that David Greenglass was a weak, easily manipulated character was of doubtful value. For if Greenglass was a puppet, then who had been pulling the strings, if not Julius Rosenberg? The defense might possibly have gained more ground if Bloch had forced Greenglass to admit that back in 1944 and 1945 he had held strong political convictions of his own, convictions that might have given him a motive to turn spy for his own ends, rather than as a sort of family favor to an importuning relative. Yet when David himself ventured into this delicate area by admitting that he had considered his actions justified "on the basis of the philosophy I believed in" at that time, Bloch did not seem inclined to elicit any specific information about the nature of that philosophy. Instead he continued to search for new ways to make

Greenglass look the fool, getting him to talk not about his motives, but about his doubts.

It was a line of attack that frequently went awry, as when Bloch asked why, if Greenglass had reservations about stealing Los Alamos secrets, he had not refused to go along with Julius's plan. Greenglass's reply was unhesitating:

> I had a kind of hero worship there and I did not want my hero to fail. . . . That is exactly why I did not stop the thing after I had the doubts.
> BLOCH: You say you had a hero worship?
> GREENGLASS: That is right.
> BLOCH: Who was your hero?
> GREENGLASS: Julius Rosenberg.

10

Ruth Greenglass

The appearance of Ruth Greenglass midway through the seventh day of the trial created a considerable stir in the courtroom. Ruth's red lipstick, fashionable if inexpensive clothing, and modish hairdo—upswept waves in front and a rolled bun at the nape of her neck—would hardly have made her conspicuous in a typical Manhattan crowd. But the more jaded reporters in the press box, always alert for a chance to inject a whiff of glamour and sex into their copy, felt justified in describing her as a "buxom brunette." Insofar as they created the impression that Ruth was a femme fatale, the reporters' stories were certainly exaggerated; nevertheless, they accurately conveyed the essence of the spectators' reaction to Ruth. This self-possessed, carefully dressed young woman did not seem to belong to the same milieu as the Rosenbergs and, before she had even opened her mouth to speak, her presence on the witness stand introduced an element of conflict into the unfolding story.

Ruth was certainly prepared to live up to expectations. Unlike her husband, who had remained under the spell of his "hero worship" for Julius for some time after his discharge, Ruth had long ago changed her opinion of the Rosenbergs. She was no longer the enthusiastic Young Communist she had been at age nineteen when she had agreed to carry Julius's message to her husband in New Mexico. Indeed, her idealism had dissipated quite rapidly after the war as she began to realize that Julius was totally unconcerned with making a financial success of G & R Engineering. She knew very well that her husband was not ambitious or highly motivated, but he was perfectly capable of making a good living if he chose to settle down, and it galled her that Julius had no qualms about sacrificing David's future to his precious cause. The final straw for her had come when Julius forced her husband to give up the technical courses he had registered for because they kept him away from the shop two afternoons a week, even though he was willing to drop his own work to carry out a mission for the Russians whenever the need arose. Ethel, David, and to some extent even their brother Bernard Greenglass, the shop's third partner, all seemed to have adjusted to Julius's way of behaving as if no one's concerns mattered in comparison with his own. As an outsider to the family, Ruth had quickly come to resent this attitude, and to resent it with the special fury that came from the realization that David's and her own involvement in Julius's schemes had given him a lasting power over their lives. Nor, by this time, did she have any residue of sympathy for Ethel, who had shown that she intended to side with Julius no matter what—even if it meant placing David's life in jeopardy.

Questioned by Saypol's twenty-nine-year-old assistant, James B. Kilsheimer, who had been present when the story of Ethel's typing first came out weeks before, Ruth confidently backed up the essential points of her husband's story, adding for good measure accounts of two private conversations. On the subject of the typing, Ruth mentioned a time several days after David had given Julius the first installment of his notes on Los Alamos in January 1945. In recounting the story of a dinnertime visit she and her husband had made to the Rosenbergs' apartment several days after David turned over the material, Ruth recalled that she had commented on how tired Ethel looked:

> ... and I asked her what she had been doing. She said she had been typing; and I asked her if she had found David's notes hard to distinguish. She said no, she was used to his handwriting. Then she said that Julie, too, was tired; that he was very busy; he ran around a good deal; that all his time and energies were used in this thing; that it was the most important thing in the world to

him; that he had to make a good impression; that it sometimes cost him as much as $50 to $75 an evening to entertain his friends.

There was something rather odd, perhaps, about Ruth placing this conversation in January, since David claimed only to have given Julius several sketches with accompanying descriptive labels and a list of a handful of scientists' names—hardly enough to tire out a skilled typist. However, if Ruth's memory was faulty on this point, Ethel's lawyer never saw fit to challenge her.

A second and more damaging incident mentioned by Ruth occurred shortly after this dinner party and before she joined her husband in New Mexico in February 1945. Ruth was at home in her Stanton Street apartment when Julius showed up unexpectedly. Saying that he had something private to discuss, Julius had asked Ruth's sixteen-year-old sister, who happened to be visiting at the time, to take a magazine and go into the bathroom. Then, when they were alone, Julius had given her instructions to meet his courier in front of the Albuquerque Safeway store during the last week in April or the first week in May.

These instructions were never carried out because on April 18, Ruth suffered a miscarriage and, with David away at Los Alamos for much of the week, she had been forced to move in temporarily with a friend who could look after her while she recovered. Not daring to write anything specific about the courier, Ruth had informed Ethel of the situation by letter. According to Ruth, her sister-in-law had written in reply that "she was sympathetic about my illness and that a member of the family would come out to visit me on the third or fourth Saturday in May." Ruth had interpreted this message to mean that she should be in front of the Safeway store at the previously agreed upon time on those days. But although she waited for more than an hour on both occasions, no one showed up. Instead, Harry Gold had come directly to the Greenglass apartment—one week later, on the first Saturday in June.

Ruth Greenglass's memory for detail and her precise way of expressing herself made her an invaluable witness and a difficult one for the defense to challenge. On cross-examination, Ethel's lawyer Alexander Bloch gamely tried to turn Ruth's strength into a weakness, asking her to repeat her answers to the same questions several times over in an effort to demonstrate that Ruth was merely parroting back a set of previously memorized replies. To an extent, Bloch's approach was effective. On several points, Ruth repeated long answers virtually word for word, and there was a certain polish to her testimony that suggested that it was a carefully rehearsed performance.

But the elder Bloch failed to capitalize on this demonstration by finding and exploiting a flaw in Ruth's smoothly delivered story. This was partly because Ruth, even if she had practically memorized parts of her testimony, was not without resources of her own. Anyone reading back over the statements she gave the FBI after her decision to cooperate would have to be struck by the concreteness of her account. In contrast to David, who was sometimes vague about such things, Ruth was the sort of person who remembered to mention names of hotels, addresses, snatches of conversation, and so on. It was she who had, from the very first, recalled that the recognition signal that David described as a piece of "cut or torn cardboard" was actually half of a Jell-O box panel.

Before allowing Ruth to leave the stand, Manny Bloch took over from his father and made one final attempt to shake her story about the money that Julius had given the Greenglasses to aid their flight to Mexico. David and Ruth claimed to have received a total of $5,000. The first $1,000 had gone partly to pay old debts, with the rest set aside to finance their flight to the Catskills if necessary. The second payment of $4,000 the Greenglasses had given intact to Louis Abel, Ruth's brother-in-law, and all but $100 of this sum was eventually turned over to O. John Rogge in payment of the Greenglasses' legal fees. There was only the Greenglasses' word for it that the first $1,000 had ever passed through their hands. But the existence of the $4,000 was indisputable. And $4,000 was a large sum in 1950, particularly for a young couple who had been without a steady income for more than a year during the period David was working for the failing machine-shop business.

The defense's attempt to deal with the money issue was a muddle. In cross-examining Ruth, Manny Bloch did his best to plant the suggestion in the jurors' minds that the $5,000 represented a legitimate payment of Rosenberg's business debt to the Greenglasses. After a complicated series of questions designed to provoke Ruth into admitting that she was nursing grievances against Julius over money,

Bloch asked about the financial arrangements that were made in 1948, at the time that the machine-shop business "went bad":

> BLOCH: . . . Did you tell Julius Rosenberg that you thought your husband wasn't getting enough salary?
> RUTH: I can't answer it just that way Mr. Bloch. Julius Rosenberg told me in 1947 that he didn't care whether the business was a success or not, and I was very enraged. I said that David and Bernie [Greenglass] had put all their earnings into that business. To them it meant something; they were earning a living, and he said he didn't care because he could get $10,000 or $15,000 as a front for any business for his activities. That was in 1947.

Whether Ruth was telling the truth about this conversation is impossible to say. But perhaps Julius Rosenberg did boast to her at one time about having access to front money when he needed it. At any rate, Ruth's description of the machine-shop business as a front threw Manny Bloch into a state of confusion. He did his best to recover, asking Ruth why a legitimate businessman, David Schein, would have put money into a front operation. But Ruth was unfazed. Schein's honest intentions did not make any difference to the real situation.

Bloch's discomfiture was so obvious that Irving Saypol could no longer repress his amusement.

> SAYPOL: I think Mr. Bloch is getting unduly exercised.
> BLOCH: I am not exercised; believe me, I am cool, or at least I hope I am.

But Bloch's further attempts to shake Ruth's story were even less rewarding. Pressed further about the $1,000 that Rosenberg admitted owing for payment for David's interest in the business, Ruth continued to deny that this had anything to do with the sums of money she and her husband received for their flight to Mexico. The money for Mexico had involved much larger sums. In fact, she blurted out, Rosenberg had at one time promised to give them $6,000 in flight money—$1,000 more than he eventually brought them.

> RUTH: . . . This was not coming from the business Mr. Bloch.

BLOCH: What was not coming from the business?
RUTH: $6,000, that he promised me.
BLOCH: Yes, but I didn't ask you that.
RUTH: Well, it wasn't paid for the investment.
JUDGE KAUFMAN: Who was it coming from?
RUTH: From the Russians, for us to leave the country.

Ruth got the best of her verbal sparring with Manny Bloch, but a skeptical juror might still have wondered whether there wasn't something to Bloch's charges. Perhaps the money had nothing to do with financing an escape to Mexico. Perhaps it represented the payment of a legitimate business debt.

To believe this, however, one had to know more than what the money had been intended for. One had to know where it had come from. Everyone agreed that the machine-shop business had been virtually moribund by the spring of 1950. And individuals in the Rosenbergs' circumstances would hardly have $5,000 in cash lying around. Julius would have had to borrow the money, or at least withdraw it from a bank. And if the Rosenbergs could show that they had done any such thing they had every reason to try to prove it.

But when Julius Rosenberg took the stand later in the trial he would make no attempt to claim that there was a connection between the money and the payment of his business debt to the Greenglasses. His position was that he had never given David any large sum of money. So Bloch's attempt to draw a connection between the $5,000 and the business was a red herring.

The only remaining possibility was that the money had come into the Greenglasses' possession from some source other than the Rosenbergs. But no one has ever been able to demonstrate what that source might have been. Long after the trial, some defenders of the Rosenbergs would suggest that the money had been stashed away by David during his army years—and that it represented earnings from the black market or possibly even espionage activities undertaken independently of the Rosenbergs. If so, it is difficult to understand why the money went unspent for years, while David and Ruth lived in poverty, in an apartment that did not even have central heating. Such restraint is difficult to reconcile with the same theorists' contention that David was a feckless, not overly bright young man and Ruth a grasping harridan constantly nagging her husband for money.

11

The Arrest of William Perl

Damaging as Ruth Greenglass's testimony was, an event taking place outside the courtroom dealt a far worse blow to the Rosenbergs' hopes for an acquittal. On the morning of March 15, the same day that Bloch was scheduled to begin his cross-examination of Ruth, *The New York Times* announced the arrest of William Perl.

Although Perl was formally charged with perjury for having lied to the grand jury six months earlier, no one who glanced at the *Times*'s front page that morning could have failed to see the connection between Perl's indictment and the trial already in progress. Under a front-page headline that proclaimed, "COLUMBIA TEACHER ARRESTED, LINKED TO 2 ON TRIAL AS SPIES," the *Times* noted that "Perl had been listed by the government as a potential witness in the current atomic espionage trial." Saypol had gone on to tell the press that Perl's "intended role" would be to corroborate certain statements made by a key government witness. Presumably he was referring to Ruth Greenglass, who had told the FBI about Ethel Rosenberg's friendship with Vivian Glassman.

The timing of Perl's arrest threw the Rosenberg defense into turmoil. Morton Sobell, in his autobiography, *On Doing Time*, writes that he first learned of Perl's arrest when he was brought into court that morning and found the Rosenbergs and their lawyers in the midst of an agitated discussion. There is no way to know just what Julius Rosenberg, who had heard all about how Perl had led the FBI to Vivian Glassman, told his lawyers to prepare them for meeting this threat. Most likely it was just enough to leave Manny Bloch feeling more hemmed in than ever. Though Bloch was to maintain to the day of his death that he believed in the Rosenbergs' innocence, he would have had to be terribly naïve not to have realized by this point that he and his father had to tread carefully in their cross-examinations lest they turn up matters better left buried. His clients had so far given him next to nothing that he could use in building a defense, even vetoing a plan to call character witnesses on their behalf on the grounds that they did not want to ask their friends to jeopardize their reputations and jobs by appearing in such a controversial case. Now, midway through the trial, he was faced with the threat that the prosecution might produce one of these friends, a nationally prominent scientist, to testify in support of Greenglass.

No one on the defense side could afford to assume that this threat was a hollow one—though, as it turned out, this was the case. William Perl had not confessed to anything and would never appear on the witness stand.

Aside from the prospect of Perl's actually appearing on the stand, his arrest raised the very real possibility that the jury would be affected by the surrounding publicity. The Rosenberg-Sobell jury was never sequestered and, even though the jurors were under strict orders from the judge to avoid reading newspapers, it is difficult to believe that each and every one of them had remained ignorant of an event so prominently featured in the morning papers and on radio news. In exchange for another headline-making coup, Irving Saypol had presented the defense with a golden opportunity to win a motion for a mistrial.

In discussing this incident in his book *The Judgment of Julius and Ethel Rosenberg*, John Wexley describes the timing of Perl's arrest as an example of collusion and "calculated fraud" on the part of Saypol, Hoover, and Judge Kaufman. The reality is both more complex and more interesting:

From the first day of the trial, FBI agents in New York and Washington had been seething over what they considered to be the prosecution's mishandling of the case. FBI memos on the trial are filled with complaints about Saypol's lack of preparation and Cohn's inexperience. Naturally, there was another side to the ongoing sniping between the Bureau and the U.S. Attorney's office that is not reflected in Bureau files. The U.S. Attorney's office had at least as good reasons for mistrusting the competence of the FBI, whose inept and illegal investigative tactics had caused it considerable trouble in the recent past, as when the conviction of the alleged spy Judith Coplon was overturned on appeal, in part because of revelations of illegal FBI wiretaps. In any case, regardless of the merits of the argument, relations between the two agencies were hardly cozy and disagreements over the handling of William Perl's case almost precipitated a complete breakdown.

Ever since Perl's appearance before the Rosenberg grand jury in the summer of 1950, Hoover had been eager to see Perl indicted—for perjury, if not for espionage. Hoover was convinced that Perl, and perhaps Ann and Michael Sidorovich as well, would break down and confess under pressure. But Irving Saypol, for reasons of his own, had done nothing to pursue the matter. Perhaps he wanted to wait until after the Rosenberg-Sobell trial, or perhaps he preferred to bide his time in case it became possible to prosecute for espionage. In the very week before the Rosenberg-Sobell trial opened, Hoover went over Saypol's head and appealed directly to the Attorney General's office. Assistant Attorney General James McInerney then passed along to Saypol word of Hoover's opinion that perjury arrests would be of "invaluable assistance," not just to the trial at hand, but in the FBI's continuing investigations of Soviet espionage activities.

Saypol was still unconvinced of the wisdom of moving against either Perl or the Sidoroviches while the trial was actually in progress. Saypol knew very well that, while Hoover had nothing to lose from this move, the prosecution would be putting itself in a very bad light—particularly if the expected confessions failed to materialize.

But the FBI was hard to resist; and Saypol's young assistant Roy Cohn, at least, felt confident that Perl could be pressured into a confession. If so, why shouldn't he and the U.S. Attorney's office have the credit for succeeding where the FBI had failed?

On March 4, 1951, just two days before the trial began, Cohn called Perl into his office for a conference. During this meeting— and again a day later in the presence of Perl's attorney, Raymond L. Wise—Cohn warned Perl that the government wanted the full story of his role in the Rosenberg espionage network. Exactly whose authority Cohn was acting on is unclear, but the motive behind the conference was obvious: if Perl had agreed to cooperate at once, it would have been a tremendous coup for Cohn and Saypol and an embarrassment for their detractors in the Federal Bureau of Investigation.

When the news of what Cohn had done reached Bureau headquarters in Washington, it caused a minor furor. In his report summarizing the incident to his superiors, A. H. Belmont criticized Cohn severely for his "possibly questionable ethical tactics" and recommended that the FBI "take no part" in the forthcoming arrest of Perl and dissociate itself from the whole matter by refusing even to issue a press release. Detracting somewhat from the force of Belmont's righteous indignation, the memo goes on to state the real cause for his anger, which was that in warning Perl of his forthcoming arrest Cohn had "negated the psychological effect" of surprise and given Perl a chance to consult with an attorney beforehand. Noting that Perl had by now arranged to pay Wise a $5,000 retainer, Belmont concluded that "the possibility of [Perl's] making any statement without further consultation with his attorney is now remote."

Although the original rationale for arresting Perl no longer held up, both sides were now committed to the plan. Saypol had informed McInerney on March 9 that he would accede to Hoover's request, and on March 13, while Roy Cohn was busy in court examining David Greenglass, Saypol went to the grand jury—still in session on the floor below—and asked it to hand up a perjury indictment against Perl. In Washington, meanwhile, Hoover and his aides D. M. ("Mickey") Ladd and L. B. Nichols overruled Belmont's recommendation that the Bureau dissociate itself from Saypol's actions, noting, in Nichols's words, that "since Perl's case does grow out of the Fuchs-Gold case, it seems to me like the Bureau should receive the credit."

Just as Belmont had predicted, William Perl was advised by his attorney of his right to remain silent. In the aftermath of the arrest, Saypol was left without the surprise witness he had originally been promised but with the problem of parrying the defense attorneys' objections to the prejudicial publicity.

The first defense attorney to lodge a complaint was feisty Edward Kuntz, one of Sobell's lawyers, who rushed up to complain to

Judge Kaufman that "I have never before tried a case in the newspapers in my life." Realizing, as Kuntz had momentarily forgotten, that the defense could lose its right to appeal if it took it upon itself to reveal Perl's arrest to the jury, Saypol leaped into the fray, goading Kuntz by professing his willingness to have the whole matter hashed out "in open court." Judge Kaufman's admonitions to Kuntz to "keep your voice down" were not, as Wexley charges, so much an attempt to "hush up the defense" as a way of warning Kuntz against falling victim to Saypol's taunts.

In the wake of this short but sharp exchange between Kuntz and Saypol, who were bitter enemies out of court as well as in, Kaufman suggested that the matter of the newspaper stories be taken up again that afternoon when everyone had taken time to calm down. But oddly enough, when the afternoon conference was held, Kuntz failed to make a formal motion for a mistrial or even for the questioning of the jury to see if any of them had in fact read Saypol's statements about Perl.

The failure of any of the defense attorneys to make a formal objection over this incident is striking. Saypol's statement to the press was certainly inflammatory—a 1952 Court of Appeals decision would characterize it as "wholly reprehensible"—but the defense's decision not to pursue its protest would all but destroy its ability to use the statement as later grounds for appeal. Manny Bloch and the rest of the defense team had certainly not been hesitant to make objections and even motions for mistrial over relatively minor points, so it would be interesting to know what was said during the *in camera* conference with Kaufman to cause them to acquiesce on this particular issue. One can only wonder whether Saypol mollified the opposition lawyers by promising that Perl would not be called to testify at the trial. In reality this was hardly a concession, since Perl had shown no indication of admitting any involvement with Rosenberg or Sobell, but of course the defense could not have known this. Whatever Saypol may have said off the record, the defense made a serious blunder in accepting his assurances—not to mention that as a result of Kuntz's outburst the jurors now knew, if they were not aware of it before, that something dramatic relating to the case had been printed in that morning's papers.

In the meantime, the government lawyers proceeded to reinforce the impact of Ruth's testimony by producing two supporting witnesses: her sister, Dorothy Printz Abel, and Dorothy's husband, Louis. Dorothy Abel confirmed Ruth's recollection of Julius's visit to the Stanton Street apartment in 1945. And Louis Abel agreed that he had held $4,000 for the Greenglasses just previous to David's arrest. The money, still in its original brown paper wrapper, had been hidden inside a hassock in the Abels' living room.

12

Harry Gold

The next witness, Harry Gold, did not claim that he had ever known Julius or Ethel Rosenberg by name. He had even expressed doubts, up to the very day before the trial began, about whether he had ever used the first name Julius in connection with his greetings to David and Ruth Greenglass. But Gold did believe that he recognized Julius Rosenberg from newspaper photos that appeared after Rosenberg's arrest in mid-July 1950. On August 1, shortly after Gold was transferred to the Tombs following his own trial in Philadelphia, he told assistant prosecutor Myles Lane that Rosenberg "closely resembled" a contact he had seen only once, during an abortive rendezvous near a Queens subway station in February 1950, just months prior to his own arrest.

As Gold explained it to Lane, he had been out of touch with the Soviets for some years when, much to his surprise, a Russian agent he did not recognize showed up at his Philadelphia home one Saturday bearing half of a torn slip of paper—a prearranged signal that Gold had set up with his former control, Yakovlev. The date was "late October or early November" 1949, and Gold was warned that he might have to flee the country in the near future. During the course of his visit, the Russian gave elaborate instructions for making contact in case of an emergency: Gold was to place a precisely word-ed help-wanted advertisement in the classified columns of *The New*

York Times. In addition, Gold was to keep in regular touch by appearing at an appointed place at 10:00 A.M. on the first Sunday of alternate months. Gold was to be smoking a pipe and his contact would be smoking a cigar. If there was no message for Gold at that particular time, then the contact would merely take note of his appearance and leave.

Gold recalled that he particularly remembered the assignation that took place on the first Sunday in February 1950. Klaus Fuchs had been arrested the preceding Thursday, and Gold was feeling panicky. As ordered, he had showed up at the agreed-upon meeting place—a small park near the Ninetieth Street Elmhurst station of the Flushing subway line in Queens. When ten o'clock came, he glanced nervously across the street and saw a man wearing a dark suit and a light-colored brown raincoat and smoking a cigar. "In passing me," Gold told Lane, "he peered somewhat closely at my face." Gold had assumed that this man was his contact, but either the man with the cigar was not sure of Gold or there was no message at that time. Disappointed, Gold returned to Philadelphia.

After telling Myles Lane and FBI agents Norton and Harrington this story, Gold identified two photos of Rosenberg as "very much like" the cigar-smoking man he had seen that day. For reasons that are not entirely clear, the prosecution decided not to ask Gold to tell about this incident as part of his direct testimony at the trial; perhaps they considered Gold's identification too vague to be convincing, or perhaps they were saving it to introduce on redirect examination if necessary. Gold badgered junior Assistant U.S. Attorney John Foley to procure his pipe from his brother and father so that he could confront Julius with it in court. It was, he told Foley, a very distinctive oversized pipe, "carved by John Middleton . . . a curved pipe with a large brown bowl."

The prosecutors, understandably, did not think much of Gold's idea. A defendant who had remained silent under enormous pressure for eight months was hardly likely to give himself away over a trifle like a carved pipe. In any case, the attorneys already knew that according to David Greenglass, Rosenberg had recognized Gold's photo when it appeared in the *Herald Tribune* after his arrest in May 1950. Thus Rosenberg was hardly likely to be surprised to learn that Gold was the same Russian agent he had seen the preceding February.

So, in the event, Harry Gold appeared in court without his John Middleton pipe, and there was no gasp of recognition from Julius Rosenberg. But if Gold was disappointed by the lack of drama surrounding his appearance, he was probably the only one present who felt that way.

At first glance, Harry Gold did not look the part of the mysterious Raymond whose saga had become public knowledge through Hoover's much discussed *Reader's Digest* article. Never an impressive-looking figure, Gold seemed to have shrunk both spiritually and physically since his arrest the previous year. His slightly seedy appearance and subservient manner suggested a small-time hood or a functionary in some marginally respectable business. But when Gold opened his mouth to speak, his precise, almost professorial diction left little doubt of his intelligence and lent an air of authority to his description of elaborately choreographed secret meetings and cross-country courier runs. Moreover, Gold began his testimony by acknowledging that he had already received a thirty-year sentence for espionage and was currently facing no other charges. In contrast to David Greenglass and Max Elitcher, he had nothing to gain by cooperation with the government. A man with a colorful past but no future, Gold had reached the point where he could discuss his career with an emotional detachment that made a tremendous impression on jury and spectators alike.

Oddly enough, Gold's aura of expertise got an immediate boost from the defense lawyers, who objected vehemently to the witness's introductory description of himself as having been involved in "espionage work for the Soviet Union." Objecting to this self-characterization as "damaging evidence" that was both "conclusory" and "incompetent, irrelevant, and immaterial," Manny Bloch demanded that Gold give "some proof" to substantiate his claim. Judge Kaufman, normally not overly sympathetic to the defense counsel's problems, recognized this as an unwitting invitation to allow the prosecution to produce otherwise inadmissible testimony about Gold's career previous to the opening date of the conspiracy—testimony that would in the long run only bolster Gold's image as a knowledgeable master spy. When Kaufman's warnings went unheeded, this is exactly what happened. No doubt secretly delighted, Myles Lane acceded to the defense request for substantiation by letting Gold detail the standard operating procedure he had used throughout his more than twelve years as a courier. Gold explained that, in meeting new informants, there had always been a double set of recognition signals: first, a code phrase "usually used in the form of a greeting," and second, a sign involving some "object or piece of paper." All this, of course, echoed David Greenglass's description of what had occurred in Albuquerque in 1945 and made the seemingly quirky use of a Jell-O box by Julius Rosenberg suddenly more understandable.

This established, Harry Gold went on to explain how he had received his orders to visit Greenglass from Anatoli Yakovlev in the Volks Bar on Third Avenue and Forty-second Street in Manhattan. Yakovlev, who had seemed uncharacteristically tense, sat with Gold in a rear booth, nursing his drink and complaining that he was under pressure to learn more details about the lens that Klaus Fuchs had called "a new device to trigger the atom bomb." Then Yakovlev abruptly announced that Gold was to go to Sante Fe to meet Fuchs on the first Saturday in June, stopping in Albuquerque on the way back for a rendezvous with a new contact.

"I protested," Gold told the courtroom, explaining that he considered the journey to Santa Fe risky enough without the added complications of a side trip. Yakovlev, however, had no patience with Gold's argument. "I have been guiding you idiots through every step," he snapped. "You don't realize how important the mission to Albuquerque is."

Good soldier that he was, Harry Gold felt he had no choice but to give in. At this point, he testified:

> Yakovlev then gave me a piece of paper; it was onionskin paper, and on it was typed the following: First, the name "Greenglass," just "Greenglass." Then a number [on] "High Street"; all that I can recall about the number is . . . it was a low number and . . . the second figure was "0" and the last figure was either 5, 7, or 9; then underneath was "Albuquerque, New Mexico." The last thing that was on the paper was "Recognition signal. I come from Julius."

Gold's statement that he had received the phrase "I come from Julius" was devastating. His further testimony about his actual visit to the Greenglasses' High Street apartment stressed that "Julius" had been mentioned twice more after Gold delivered his initial greeting. Apparently quite surprised when Gold showed up at his home so early on Sunday morning, Greenglass had assured his caller that he would have the requested information ready by that afternoon. In the meantime, he volunteered to give Gold the names of some Los Alamos scientists who, in his opinion, would make "excellent recruits."

"I cut him very short indeed," Gold testified, adding that he had scolded Greenglass for his lack of caution, warning him that propositioning co-workers for espionage work would be a sure way to "bring the FBI down on our heads." Greenglass defended himself, saying that he had never been so foolish as to approach anyone directly, but had merely been making a "mental note" of likely possibilities. Besides, he protested, "Julius" had asked him to be on the lookout for promising recruits.

The name "Julius" was mentioned once more, Gold testified, this time by Ruth Greenglass, who had been present during much of the conversation. Ruth, he recalled, had mentioned that she had spoken to "Julius" before she left New York City for Albuquerque.

With nothing to do until the promised information was ready, a weary and apprehensive Gold went back to downtown Albuquerque and checked into the Hilton Hotel for a few hours' rest. He returned to the Greenglass apartment that afternoon, staying just long enough to pick up an envelope containing the notes and to be given a phone number, presumably that of Greenglass's "brother-in-law Julius," through whom Greenglass could be contacted when he returned to New York on his next furlough.

Gold left Albuquerque that same evening. On the train, he told the jury, he had looked over the Greenglass material and found that it consisted of "three or four handwritten pages plus a couple of sketches" that appeared to be of "a device of some kind." All of this, along with the data he had received from Fuchs, was turned over to Yakovlev on June 5, during a nighttime meeting on Metropolitan Avenue in Brooklyn. He heard nothing more about the trip until two weeks later when, in the course of a further meeting with Yakovlev, he was told that all the information had been passed on to the Soviet Union and that the data from Greenglass "was extremely excellent and very valuable."

Given this evaluation, Gold said, he had volunteered to renew his contact with Greenglass when he returned to New Mexico in September to see Fuchs, but Yakovlev had dismissed the idea as "inadvisable." On another occasion, Gold had suggested calling "Julius" during the time Greenglass was scheduled to be in New York for his Christmas furlough. This time, he was informed in no uncertain terms that such a decision was none of his business.

By Christmas of 1945, external events were already bringing Gold's work in atomic espionage to a close. Klaus Fuchs had warned him that September that cooperation between British and American scientists was no longer as "free and easy" as it had once been and that he might soon be returning to England. Yakovlev, too, was increasingly worried about the possibility of discovery and in January 1946 he warned Gold to be especially careful:

> He said that a very important person who had upon him information about the atom bomb had come to New York at the end of 1945 and that he, Yakovlev, had tried to get in touch with that person over a period of time, a period of a few days, but that the man had been trailed by Intelligence men continually. . . .

After one more meeting in the Earl Theater in the Bronx in February, Gold did not hear from the Soviets again until that December, when two tickets to a New York boxing match arrived in his mail. The tickets were a prearranged signal for Gold to appear at a meeting on a specified number of days after the match. But unfortunately, they had been mailed to the wrong address—6328 Kindred Street in Philadelphia instead of 6823 Kindred Street—so that by the time Gold received them he had missed his meeting.

Gold was by now working for his former contact Abraham Brothman in Queens, and on the day after Christmas Yakovlev reached him there by telephone and summoned him to a meeting at "the theater"—which Gold knew to be a reference to the Earl Theater.* There, however, he found not Yakovlev, but a stranger who walked with "a catlike stride, almost on the balls of his feet." The stranger showed him a torn piece of paper, bearing half of the phrase

---

*Since Yakovlev had called Gold at Brothman's to set up this meeting, he may already have known where Gold was working and merely wanted to hear it from Gold's own lips. On the other hand, Gold's testimony does not specify how Yakovlev got his work telephone number, so it is possible that the Soviet agent did not realize beforehand that he was calling Brothman's place of business.

"directions to Paul Street," which Gold himself had ripped apart in Yakovlev's presence the previous January. Only when he had satisfied himself that Gold was not being followed, had the stranger directed him to the bar on Third Avenue and Forty-second Street where Yakovlev was waiting.

Yakovlev, it seems, wanted to talk to Gold about the possibility of his going to Paris for two weeks to meet with a certain physicist. Would there be any problem for Gold in taking the necessary time off from work? Gold said there would not be, adding that the pressure of work at Brothman's was easing up a bit. "And then," related Gold,

> Yakovlev almost went through the roof of the saloon. He said, "You fool." He said, "You spoiled eleven years of work." He told me that I didn't realize what I had done, and he told me that I should have remembered that sometime in the summer of '45 he had told me that Brothman was under suspicion of having been engaged in espionage and that I should have remembered it.

With that, Yakovlev threw down a wad of money to pay for his drinks and stormed out of the bar. Gold followed, vainly trying to explain himself. "I walked along with him for a while, and he kept mumbling that I had created terrible damage and that he didn't know whether it could be repaired or not. Yakovlev then told me that he would not see me in the United States again, and he left me."

This was the end of Gold's relationship with Anatoli Yakovlev, and it brought his 1951 courtroom testimony to a close as well. After reading a Department of State document that confirmed that Yakovlev had left the country by ship in December 1946, Myles Lane declared that he had no more questions; court was adjourned until 10:30 the next morning, March 16.

Gold's testimony had indeed been damaging. For the first time, someone had spelled out the connection between this rather unlikely group of defendants and an actual Soviet agent. Court reconvened the next morning in an atmosphere charged with suspense. The press and better-informed spectators, who knew that Gold had been given a hard time by defense attorneys in his appearance at the Brothman-Moskowitz trial the previous year, waited breathlessly to see what

Manny Bloch would be able to do to undermine Gold's story. But, to everyone's surprise, there was to be no confrontation. Instead, Bloch confined himself to a terse declaration that "the defendants Rosenberg have no cross-examination of this witness." Gold's entire account would be allowed to stand.

Bloch's decision to let Harry Gold's testimony go unchallenged—one of the strangest of a series of seemingly inexplicable defense tactics—was only partly explained by Bloch's contention during his summation that Gold had not connected his client directly to Soviet espionage. "I didn't ask him one question because there is no doubt in my mind that he impressed you as well as he impressed everybody that he was telling the absolute truth. And what did he say? . . . Did Gold tell you that he ever met Rosenberg? . . . Strange isn't it? Gold, one of the top conspirators, never saw Rosenberg, never met him, never had any contact with him."

But of course Gold had connected Yakovlev and Rosenberg, no matter how loudly and how insistently Bloch might claim otherwise. Not only had Gold introduced the phrase "I come from Julius"— words that would be sure to weigh heavily in the jury's memory when it came time for their deliberations—but he had explicitly said that "Julius" was David's brother-in-law, hardly an identification that left room for doubt.

As Louis Nizer has pointed out, in his best-selling book on the case, *The Implosion Conspiracy*, any trial lawyer would have had to realize that there was a tremendous gamble inherent in asking the jury to believe the bulk of a witness's testimony and, at the same time, reject just those words that specifically implicated the defendant. Nizer suggests several strategies an enterprising cross-examiner might have employed against Harry Gold. For one, Gold's admission at the Brothman trial that he had lied regularly and repeatedly in the course of creating his espionage cover could surely have been used to undermine his credibility. Further, Bloch might well have returned to Gold's contention that he had invariably used false names in work. Why, then, had there been an exception made in the case of one name and one name only, that of Julius?

Given what we now know about the process by which Gold finally agreed to the phrase "I come from Julius," these arguments take on added force. Always a deferential and sometimes unguardedly candid witness, Gold would most likely have cheerfully admitted under pressure that he had originally recalled using the greeting "I come from Ben." Even a partial admission from Gold that he had not given the name Julius to the FBI during his original confession would probably have been enough to enable the defense to obtain copies of Gold's pretrial statements, as they had already done in the case of Elitcher. Setting aside the question of which version of Gold's "greeting" happened to be the true one, there is no question that the defense could have scored heavily by bringing the conflict to light.

Although the defense side had already struck out once in its attempt to find significant contradictions (in Max Elitcher's statements to the FBI), that alone cannot explain Bloch's failure to try again. Louis Nizer speculates that there can have been only one such reason, namely fear—fear that Gold, if pressed, might "blurt out something which, whether true or false, might sink the Rosenbergs."

Louis Nizer had no idea of what that "something" might have been. But if Rosenberg actually was aware of the fact that Harry Gold might be able to point the finger at him in court, then it is possible that Emanuel Bloch's fear was not so vague after all. Bloch had an entire evening and night after listening to Gold tell his story on direct examination, plenty of time in which to consult with his client over strategy. Had Julius Rosenberg said something, explicit or otherwise, to betray relief that Gold had not named him directly as the man he had once been asked to meet near a Queens subway station?

If so, it would go a long way to explain Bloch's later insistence that Harry Gold had not involved his client. Bloch knew that Gold's testimony might have been even more damaging than it actually was.

13

The Prosecution Wraps Up Its Case

The ninth day of the trial was taken up with the appearances of two reluctant witnesses: the Rosenberg family physician, Dr. George Bernhardt, and Morton Sobell's friend William Danziger.

Dr. Bernhardt opened the proceedings by testifying that, sometime in late May 1950, Julius Rosenberg had called his office to ask what kinds of inoculations were necessary for someone planning a trip to Mexico.

"I hesitated a little," Bernhardt recalled, "and he laughed and said, 'Don't get scared, it is not for me; it's for a friend of mine.' " Bernhardt did not explain why Julius's inquiry about Mexico should have been an occasion for alarm.

The doctor then told Rosenberg that normally smallpox and typhoid inoculations were necessary, except in the case of veterans, who needed only booster shots. At that point, Rosenberg had replied, "Yes, he is a veteran."

Bernhardt's testimony was really only a partial confirmation of David Greenglass's charge that Rosenberg had been trying to secure travel documents for him and Ruth. As Manny Bloch was to emphasize on cross-examination, the doctor did not claim that Rosenberg had actually requested him to forge vaccination certificates for this unnamed friend.

Nevertheless, the fact that Bernhardt had agreed to appear as a prosecution witness at all stunned Julius and Ethel Rosenberg. Dr. Bernie, as he was known to the Rosenberg children, was not just the family doctor but a friend, who sometimes allowed Julius to drop into his Knickerbocker Village apartment for allergy shots instead of seeing him at his office. He was also a Party sympathizer, if not actually a member, which made his testimony doubly stinging.

The Rosenbergs were simply unable to believe that a personal friend and political ally would turn against them. And their doubts were expressed for them by Bloch, who approached the bench before Bernhardt had a chance to speak and asked privately whether it was true, as he had heard, that the conversation Bernhardt was about to describe had been intercepted by an FBI wiretap. Irving Saypol dismissed this charge as "arid nonsense" [sic]— and probably quite truthfully since the FBI had no interest in Rosenberg as of May 1950, when the call took place. What seems more likely is that some FBI agent may have hinted at the existence of the wiretap evidence as a ruse to make Bernhardt cooperate.

Following Dr. Bernhardt on the witness stand was William Danziger, the friend who had forwarded mail from Morton Sobell in Mexico to Sobell's sister-in-law, Edith Levitov, and to his uncle Max Pasternak. Danziger had known Sobell since they were classmates at New York City's Stuyvesant High School. He had attended City College, where he was part of the Steinmetz Club clique that had included Julius Rosenberg. After graduation from CCNY in 1938, Danziger went on to work for the Navy Bureau of Ordnance, sharing a bachelor apartment for a time with Sobell. He stayed with the navy until March 1950, when he moved back to New York to take a job in private industry as a designer of electrical products.

Danziger had first been visited by FBI investigators not long after Julius Rosenberg's arrest and the Bureau's first interrogations of Max Elitcher. He had told them then that he had been in Sobell's house the night before Sobell and his family disappeared. According to Danziger, he had merely dropped by casually to borrow an electric drill that he needed for some repair work on his new place in the Bronx. When he arrived, he found the Sobells in the process of packing, apparently for an ordinary vacation. Sobell had mentioned that he and the family were going to Mexico City for a while.

It was not until after Sobell's arrest that Danziger admitted that he had also received at his business address several letters from Sobell containing enclosures that he was instructed to mail on to Sobell's relatives. Still, Danziger insisted that the personal notes to him had been routine. He had no idea why Sobell had wanted him to forward mail for him, or why Sobell had used the aliases Morton Sowell and Morton Levitov on the return addresses of the envelopes addressed to him.

Repeating his story on the witness stand, Danziger went on to admit that he had also visited Julius Rosenberg's machine shop twice after Sobell's departure for Mexico. Danziger said that he had been out of contact with Rosenberg for years, but that shortly after he moved back to New York Sobell had reminded him that their old friend was now in business for himself. Danziger's new job sometimes involved contracting out machine-shop work. Perhaps he could do Julie a favor and send some business his way. On two occasions, once in late June and once in early July 1950, Danziger had dropped in to talk to Rosenberg about the possibility of a contract, but Julius had finally told him that the shop was too busy to take on any new work.

Danziger had certainly woven an improbable chain of coincidences. Not only had he happened to drop in on Sobell on the very eve of the family's departure, but he had chanced to renew his old acquaintance with Rosenberg shortly thereafter—at a time when it was well known that Rosenberg's brother-in-law was under arrest for espionage. Yet Julius, who one would think would be grateful for a gesture of support and a chance to bring some business into his moribund shop, had told him that he was "rather tied up and that he couldn't accept any work for some months."

The FBI and the prosecutors were well aware of the weakness of Danziger's story, but only their threat to accuse him of being an accomplice to Sobell's flight had persuaded Danziger to testify at all. A report, admittedly unverifiable, that the FBI received from an informer at about the time of the trial gives a more plausible explanation for Danziger's visits to Rosenberg. He had received a plea for help from Sobell and had gone to Rosenberg to find out whether he could help their mutual friend get in contact with a Soviet agent in Mexico. Rosenberg had replied regretfully that Sobell should have waited for instructions before leaving the country. Now there was nothing he could do.

Even as far as it went, Danziger's testimony was damaging. He had shown that Sobell was using a mail drop to communicate with his family, hardly the action of a man on a normal vacation. And he established another link between Rosenberg and Sobell—a tenuous one, to be sure, though the jury might well choose to read more into the situation than Danziger had actually admitted. Yet the lawyers for the defendants had no questions. Danziger was dismissed.

After hearing these two witnesses, Saypol entered into evidence photostatic copies of Harry Gold's Albuquerque Hilton Hotel registration card and a bank ledger showing that Ruth Greenglass had deposited $400 in the Albuquerque National Trust and Savings Bank on the morning after Gold's visit. These exhibits went unchallenged at the time, though later they would be the center of a nagging controversy. Then, to the surprise and shock of the opposing counsel, Saypol announced that he had decided to dispense with calling certain witnesses whose testimony would be merely "cumulative" and would need four or five more days at the most to wrap up the government's case.

It had already been determined that there would be no court session the next Monday so that Saypol could attend his daughter's wedding. And when the trial did resume on Tuesday morning, March 20, Saypol's parade of witnesses moved even more quickly than he had estimated. The day began with an appearance by Candler Cobb, director of New York City's Selective Service Board. To the mystification of Sobell's lawyers, Saypol had Cobb introduce into evidence Sobell's Selective Service file. Even Judge Kaufman expressed skepticism over the relevance of Cobb's appearance, but he allowed Saypol to proceed. Cobb identified Morton Sobell's notarized signature on several documents in the file and, for the moment, it seemed that Cobb had been called for no other purpose than to give melodramatic proof that the defendant had always used the name Sobell, as opposed to Sowell or any other alias.

An additional purpose for Candler's appearance did not become evident until later in the day, when the government summoned Manuel Giner de Los Rios, an interior decorator who had lived next door to the Sobells in Mexico City. Speaking through an interpreter, Giner de Los Rios (who did know some English, though he did not feel fluent enough to use it in court) recalled that Sobell had asked him about ways to leave Mexico without proper papers. Explained

Giner de Los Rios: ". . . he said he was afraid to return to the Army, the U.S. Army, since he has already seen a war, has experienced a war."

Sobell had never served in the army, much less had firsthand experience of the war, as was evident from his draft record. One might justifiably wonder whether Giner de Los Rios, whose understanding of English was halting at best, was simply confused about what Sobell had told him of his reasons for coming to Mexico. However, his testimony too went unchallenged by Sobell's lawyers.

Sobell's use of aliases in Mexico was attested to by four more witnesses who had been brought to New York at the government's expense: Minerva Bravo Espinosa, an optical-store clerk, testified that Sobell had called himself M. Sand when he purchased a pair of eyeglasses from her in Vera Cruz. Two hotel clerks, José Broccado Vendrell and Dora Bautista, said that Sobell had used the names Morris Sand and Marvin Salt, respectively, when registering in hotels in Vera Cruz and Tampico. And Glenn Dennis, a traffic supervisor for the Mexican airline C.M.A., added that Sobell had flown from Tampico to Mexico City using the alias Morton Solt.

Once again, lawyers Kuntz and Phillips made no attempt to challenge the witnesses' recollections about Sobell's use of various aliases. But they did object when Roy Cohn introduced an immigration service record showing that Sobell had been "deported" from Mexico. At Harold Phillips's insistence, James S. Huggins, the immigration-service guard who had signed the card, was flown up from Texas to testify in person.

When Huggins appeared the next morning, he would add a curious footnote to the story of Sobell's flight. Although the record of Sobell's reentry into the United States bore the official notation "deported from Mexico," Huggins swore that he had had no conversation with the Mexican officials who had brought the prisoner to the border. No one had told him that Sobell had in fact been deported; this was merely a fact which he had "observed."

Meanwhile, interspersed with the various witnesses to Sobell's movements in Mexico, the government had wound up its presentation of the technical evidence. Since Manny Bloch had been prepared to concede the authenticity of the Greenglass sketches at the time that he called for their impounding, the testimony of additional government experts was rather a perfunctory exercise. The prosecution called only two more experts: Colonel John Lansdale, Jr., and John Derry. Lansdale, formerly chief security officer at Los Alamos, spoke in general terms about the tight security precautions that had prevailed there during the war, establishing that even the identity of some of the leading physicists, such as Niels Bohr, had been classified information. The authentication of Exhibit 8, Greenglass's sketch of the implosion-type bomb, was left to John Derry, an engineer who now worked for the AEC and who had served as liaison officer to General Leslie Groves, the senior officer in charge of the Manhattan Project. Derry, shown a copy of the sketch by Saypol, pronounced it "substantially accurate."

Manny Bloch by now seemed well aware of the adverse psychological impact of his attempted grandstand play in calling for the impounding of Exhibit 8 and he did his best to regain some lost ground by getting John Derry to admit that this sketch was by no means a "complete" or "detailed" representation of the Nagasaki bomb. But Judge Kaufman intervened:

> I don't think it was offered on the theory that it represented a complete—is that true, or am I mistaken?
>
> SAYPOL: Indeed not. As I said when I had the witness Koski on the stand, the import of this whole thing is that there was enough supplied to act on—
>
> KAUFMAN: That was my understanding of the question.
>
> SAYPOL: You remember, your Honor, I used the colloquialism tip off. That is exactly—

Interestingly, while Irving Saypol was allowed to interject his observation that the sketch had been enough to "tip off" the Soviets, Bloch was not permitted to question Derry on whether the sketch could have been done by "a machinist without any degree in engineering"—phraseology that was disallowed on the grounds that Bloch was indulging in "a bit of summation."

As the prosecution moved briskly through all these minor witnesses, it had gradually begun to dawn on the defense attorneys that the government was rapidly bringing its case to a close. Only a fraction of the more than one hundred witnesses listed in the prosecution's official roster had been heard from. There had been no sign of Michael and Ann Sidorovich, William Perl, Vivian Glassman, Louise

Sarant, or Joel Barr's brother Arthur, all of whom had been named as potential government witnesses. Nor had the jury heard from John Harrington and William Norton, or from Rex Shroder, the FBI agent in charge of the Sobell investigation. Instead, the tenth day of the trial closed with another minor figure, Lan Adomian, an employee of the AMTORG trading company, who identified a photo of the absent coconspirator Anatoli Yakovlev. As Adomian left the stand, Irving Saypol rose to say that he had run out of witnesses for the afternoon and expected to be wrapping up his case entirely sometime the next morning.

This announcement caused consternation at the defense table. Out of the hearing of the jury, Manny Bloch protested that Saypol had estimated the previous Friday that the government's case would take up the entire week. Moreover, Bloch and his father had not had access to the Rosenbergs over the weekend. Thus there had been only limited opportunity "for the purposes of going over the Government's witnesses' testimony which we think is fatal. . . ."

Bloch's Freudian slip—he obviously meant "vital"—was too much for Saypol to let pass. With obvious relish he interrupted to caution, "You do not want to go so far."

Judge Kaufman, hardly more sympathetic, pointed out that he had already gone beyond what was required in asking Saypol to give some advance notice of his intentions.

Bloch countered, "The reason I put it on the record is to have you give us a reasonable time. I think you have almost done it, but almost."

Finally, in response to a specific request from Bloch, Kaufman promised that the defense would be called upon no earlier than two o'clock the next afternoon.

14

Elizabeth Bentley: The Norfolk Connection

Over the objections of the FBI and his own assistant Roy Cohn, Irving Saypol had decided not to complicate his case by attempting to establish Julius Rosenberg's role as the coordinator of a wider spy network. He could not, however, resist the temptation to produce at least one ex-Communist "celebrity": namely, Elizabeth Terrill Bentley, the forty-four-year-old Vassar graduate who had been dubbed the "Red Spy Queen" by the tabloid press.

By the time she appeared at the Rosenberg-Sobell trial, Bentley was already well launched on the third phase of an ideological odyssey that had begun when she fell briefly under the spell of Italian fascism while doing graduate studies at the University of Florence. Her enthusiasm for Mussolini did not survive long after her return to the United States in 1934, however; back in New York, she joined the American League Against War and Fascism and, soon after, the Communist Party. For the next several years, Bentley was, in her own words, an "average run-of-the-mill Communist" whose activities, besides attending meetings and demonstrations, consisted of nothing more daring than trying to "infiltrate" the student newspaper at Columbia University Teacher's College, where she was then working toward a master's degree.

Then, in 1938, Bentley's linguistic ability resulted in her being hired as a secretary at the Italian Library of Information in New York. It did not take Bentley long to realize that her office was actually an arm of the Italian government's propaganda ministry, and, as a good Communist, she promptly volunteered to turn over whatever information she could glean on the job to the Party. At first no one seemed especially interested in listening to what Bentley had to offer, but when she persisted, she was eventually placed in contact with Jacob Golos, at the time the chief of Soviet espionage operations in the United States.

Jacob Golos was at first appalled by his new operative's amateurish enthusiasm for listening at closed doors and going through her bosses' trash. She had little notion of how to develop a believable cover for herself, and, just as Golos predicted, it was not long before the Italians discovered Bentley's true political orientation and fired her. But Bentley's personal devotion to Golos made her invaluable to him in other ways; and soon she had become both his lover and his confidential assistant, advancing from a purely behind-the-scenes role as a secretary and research assistant to act as a courier between Golos and a number of his contacts, including a group of government employees in Washington headed by economist Nathan Gregory Silvermaster.

Then, in late 1943, Golos died suddenly of a heart attack. With her lover gone, Bentley found it more and more difficult to sustain her romantic illusions about the role she was playing. The Soviet operatives with whom she was now forced to deal directly offended her by their cold professionalism and ill-concealed distrust of the amateur operatives recruited by Golos. Bentley began to look for a way out, and one finally presented itself in 1945 when—following a brief romantic liaison with an American military officer who may or may not have been working undercover for the FBI—Bentley walked into the local FBI office in New Haven, Connecticut, and began to tell all she knew.

Once Bentley had decided to defect, she became as devoted to exposing her former espionage contacts as she had once been to protecting them. A federal grand jury convened in New York City in the spring of 1947 heard Bentley name more than eighty individuals who she contended were linked to Golos's spy network. Bentley's accusations aside, hard evidence was lacking, and the grand jury failed to vote a single indictment. This anticlimactic development did nothing to tarnish Bentley's reputation as a professional ex-Communist, however. A series of feature articles published in the New York *World-Telegram* made her name a household word, and Bentley went on from the grand jury to serve as the star witness at the HUAC hearing on Communist espionage in the summer of 1948.

Bentley's role as an espionage courier was most likely as she described it. But, just as certainly, her numerous public statements— before congressional committees, in interviews, and on the lecture circuit—mixed the facts with a good measure of gossip and self-dramatization. In her testimony before HUAC, for example, Bentley named several individuals as Communists, only to admit later that she had never met the people in question and was merely repeating hearsay she had picked up from some unremembered source years before.

When Bentley decided to publish an autobiography, her role as an aspiring author generated a bizarre conflict that is surely unique in the annals of American jurisprudence. In 1950 a second New York grand jury was convened to consider a perjury indictment against Commerce Department employee William Remington, who had denied under oath Bentley's claim that he had furnished her with classified government documents relating to his work for the War Production Board. Remington was indicted, and his trial was well under way before his lawyers learned that the foreman of the grand jury, who had been instrumental in bringing in the indictment, had earlier been hired by Bentley's publisher to ghostwrite her forthcoming book.

The prosecutor at William Remington's trial, Irving Saypol, knew all about the grand jury foreman's interest in Bentley's book, and had still not hesitated to proceed with his perjury case. Nor did he have any hesitation now about introducing Bentley as an expert witness who could draw a connection, however tentative, between Julius Rosenberg and Jacob Golos.

The political climate in 1951 being what it was, Elizabeth Bentley's testimony against Julius Rosenberg was generally accepted as a convincing, if rather theatrical, capstone to the prosecution's case. Since that time, however, no aspect of the trial has inspired more criticism. Even Louis Nizer, who believed the Rosenbergs guilty as charged, expressed skepticism about the credibility of a "professional

And Herbert L. Packer, whose study *Ex-*
y examined Bentley's role in the William
d out that even more than most such pro-
had a strong financial stake in her ability
startling revelations, years after she had
ory to the FBI. "Miss Bentley's financial
ended on her bringing her story before the
and dramatic way."
ze her own importance, Bentley presented
nd as an expert, not just on Soviet espio-
d organizations of the American Commu-
er Manny Bloch's strenuous objections, she
latly that the American CP, "being part of
ional, only served the interests of Moscow,
a or espionage or sabotage."

But Bentley ... ot been called to the stand merely to give background information on Soviet espionage operations. Her name had been mentioned earlier by Max Elitcher in connection with his conversation with Sobell at Catherine Slip, and Bentley was now prepared to offer testimony to show that Rosenberg might indeed have had reason to wonder whether Bentley knew who he was.

Bentley's testimony concerned the existence of a mysterious "Julius" whom she had dealt with in the course of her work for Golos. According to Bentley, she was with Golos in his car one day in the fall of 1942 when he stopped near Knickerbocker Village on the Lower East Side to meet a certain contact of his who was an engineer. Bentley waited in the car while Golos met this unnamed man on a street corner, disappearing with him into a candy store a few doors down the street. Minutes later, Golos returned to the car carrying an envelope.

Since this incident had occurred in 1942, long before the beginning date of the conspiracy as outlined in the indictment against Rosenberg, Bentley was not permitted to describe the unknown man's appearance. Kaufman did allow her to testify, however, that between this meeting and November 1943, she had received at least five or six phone calls "in the wee small hours" from a man who identified himself by saying, "This is Julius." The message in all of these conversations was the same: the caller asked Bentley to alert Golos that he needed to get in touch with him.

Echoing as it did Harry Gold's phrase, "I come from Julius," Bentley's story of the mysterious voice heard over the telephone had great emotional impact. But on closer examination, it could hardly be said to prove anything. Bentley, Gold, and other ex-members of the Communist underground had consistently emphasized the use of false names in their work. "Julius," then, could have been just another alias. As Malcolm Sharp concluded in his 1956 study of the Rosenberg-Sobell trial, "the use of the word 'Julius' in a telephone call indicates little or nothing about the source of the call. Some would even consider it evidence that the person making the call was not named Julius."

The argument that Manny Bloch was later to make about waiving cross-examination of Harry Gold—that Gold's testimony did not connect his clients directly with any wrongdoing—might have been applied much more forcefully to Bentley's story. Yet Bloch did not allow *her* to escape the ordeal of a blistering cross-examination. Perhaps Bloch sensed a vulnerability in Bentley that he had failed to detect in Gold. More likely, he simply could not resist having his innings against a woman so bitterly despised by the Left.

Bloch started in on Bentley by attacking her morals, forcing her to admit that she and Golos had conducted their relationship outside of what she insisted on calling the institution of "bourgeois marriage." "Would you characterize your relationship with Mr. Golos as you being the mistress of Mr. Golos?" he asked.

"I don't feel that I am called upon to characterize it," Bentley replied tartly. "That is up to you."

Then, with Saypol demanding that the cross-examination move on to more "appropriate" topics, Bloch homed in on the fact that Bentley was by now earning a considerable income from her notoriety. Pressed for details of her financial situation, the witness professed not to know exactly what her income was but admitted to having "several" bank accounts.

Bloch was unable to shake Bentley's story; however, he did succeed in raising certain doubts. What evidence was there that Bentley had not made up this story about a mysterious caller named Julius just so that she could connect herself to the Rosenberg case and thereby gain publicity for her forthcoming book? Had Bentley referred to "Julius" in the original manuscript of her autobiography? Bloch asked. She said that she had. And had she written her account before or after she had been summoned by the FBI to talk about the Rosenberg case? Here, Bentley expressed some confusion: "I haven't the least idea when that material was written, but that was put into the book most definitely. Whether it is still in or whether it has been cut out I don't know."

Bentley's uncertainty created an opening for Bloch to subpoena the various drafts of her manuscript. He had nothing to lose. The damage of hearing the name Julius from Bentley's lips had already been done, and if it turned out that the "Julius" story was *not* in the book, then the defense might justifiably suggest that the whole episode had been cooked up by Bentley long after the fact, possibly in collusion with the FBI or the prosecutors. But having come this far, Manny Bloch did not follow up on his advantage. Either he was not optimistic about his chances of discovering anything to his clients' advantage, or he was too exhausted and distracted to make the effort.

Another opportunity to test the veracity of Bentley's testimony did not arise until 1975, when the text of her 107-page "confession" was released under the Freedom of Information Act. Bentley had contended all along that she had told the FBI about the mysterious phone calls from "Julius" in the course of this 1945 statement. Along with many other students of the case, we regarded this claim with considerable skepticism and approached Bentley's confession fully expecting to discover that she had lied. But, much to our surprise, we found that during the fall of 1945, Bentley had talked at length about this "Julius" to Special Agents Harold V. Kennedy and Joseph M. Kelley. The implications of this discovery are so shattering that Bentley's remarks must be quoted in full:

> Another group of whose existence I became aware sometime in the early summer of 1942 was composed of several engineers who, when I first learned of them, were located in New York City. I recall that on one occasion while I was driving through the lower East Side of the City of New York with GOLOS to keep a dinner engagement, he stopped the car and told me he had to meet someone: I remained in the car and saw GOLOS meet an individual on the street corner. I managed to get only a fleeting glimpse of this individual and I recall that he was tall, thin, and wore horn rimmed eyeglasses. GOLOS told me that this person was one of a group of engineers, and that he had given this person my residence telephone number so that he

would be able to reach GOLOS whenever he desired. He did not elaborate on the activities of this person and his associates nor did he ever identify any of them except that this one man to whom he gave my telephone number was referred to as "JU-LIUS." However, I do not believe this was his true name. I received two or three telephone calls from JULIUS telling me he wanted to see GOLOS and relayed the messages to GOLOS. Sometime later, probably in 1943, JULIUS and the others in the group proceeded to Norfolk, Virginia, where they secured employment of some kind, and I recall that on one occasion GO-LOS traveled to Norfolk to see them. Approximately six months prior to the death of GOLOS, he told me that he was turning over JULIUS and that group to some other Russian whom he did not identify. My last contact with JULIUS came shortly before the death of GOLOS, after the latter had turned the group over to someone else. On this occasion JULIUS telephoned me very early in the morning and said he wanted to see GOLOS. GOLOS told me later that the reason JULIUS had desired to see him was that he had lost his Russian contact and wanted to enlist GOLOS' aid in getting reestablished. I have no further knowledge of the identity nor of the activities of this group, except that, so far as I know or have reason to believe, GOLOS was not receiving any mail from them at any time either while they were in New York or after they moved to Norfolk. During a conversation I had with JACK, however, some time in the fall of 1944, when he and I were discussing the desirable types of information to be sought, he remarked that, though he was interested primarily in political data, he was always glad to receive information, for instance, "like that group of engineers down in Norfolk might secure—if they should learn something about a submarine, I would be glad to get it."

Julius Rosenberg had never worked in Norfolk. Nevertheless, as of the time of the trial, the FBI and the prosecutors had good reason to think that Rosenberg was the "Julius" described in this passage. The investigation of Rosenberg that began after his arrest had led the Bureau to believe that the focus of Rosenberg's espionage activities through 1944 had been an attempt to penetrate the Navy Bureau of Ordnance. And the Norfolk Naval Shipyard at Portsmouth, Virginia, was the center of work on classified naval ordnance projects, including those connected with fire-control devices. Morton Sobell, though he worked in the Ordnance Department's Washington offices, had been involved with numerous projects actually carried out at Norfolk, and the Bureau knew that on one occasion, when he was already working for Reeves in New York, Sobell had gone to Norfolk and boarded a ship that housed fire-control devices and other materiel of a classified nature and received a briefing for which he technically did not have clearance.

Then, too, there was Alfred Sarant's 1945 correspondence with the Navy Bureau of Ships, which had come to light during the search of his home. Nor did it seem entirely coincidental that William Perl had also been living near Norfolk during this period. Perl, whose residence had been Hampton, Virginia, had worked at the National Advisory Committee for Aeronautics (NACA) research facility at Langley Army Air Base until 1944, when he transferred to NACA's Cleveland office.

Finally, even Bentley's casual reference to the hope that the Norfolk group might discover "something about a submarine" must have struck a familiar chord in the minds of FBI investigators. Among numerous former CCNY acquaintances of Rosenberg's who had worked for the Navy during the early 1940s was one individual who had been closely connected with the development of sonar. The FBI's investigation of this man turned up no evidence to suggest that he had ever been involved in espionage; however, someone in the Bureau appears to have had a hunch that this former Rosenberg acquaintance might have been, like Max Elitcher, a target of an unsuccessful recruiting attempt. This, plus the fact that the acquaintance was known to have broken with the Party and renounced his former radical political views some years before the trial, apparently accounts for the hope—never realized—that he might eventually be persuaded to serve as a prosecution witness at Rosenberg and Sobell's trial.

As early as August 1950, the FBI suspected that Bentley's Julius—whom they had previously looked for without success—was actually Julius Rosenberg. And Bentley, called in for an interrogation, provided a tentative identification, saying that the picture of Rosenberg she was shown "resembled the general build and appearance" of the man she had seen briefly in 1942. However, much to the distress of the Bureau and representatives of the U.S. Attorney's office, Bentley insisted that she could not make a positive identification. She continued to stand firm on this point throughout a second interrogation session held a month before the trial opened, reiterating that "she did not remember seeing Julius's face close enough to see if he had a mustache."

Bentley's refusal to identify Rosenberg conclusively would have been less worrisome to the prosecutors if the entire contents of her 1945 statement had been admissible as testimony in court. But much of what Bentley had said—that "Julius" was the contact for a group of engineers and that he was connected with the theft of Navy secrets—was secondhand information, and hence inadmissible.

As a result, Myles Lane and James B. Kilsheimer were forced to conclude that she would not be the case-clinching witness they had hoped for. Their evaluation of the situation as of a month before the trial, as summarized in an FBI memorandum written by Edward Scheidt, was that "the bulk of the information Miss Bentley had was hearsay inasmuch as it concerned conversations between her and Jacob Golos, who is deceased." Thus, "her testimony on direct examination would have to be limited to the occasion when she observed 'Julius' in the vicinity of the Essex Market in New York City in 1941 [sic] and also to the conversations which she had on the telephone with 'Julius' in 1943."

Roy Cohn was not willing to give up so easily. According to Scheidt, Cohn was suggesting that Bentley might be able to identify a recording of Rosenberg's voice as being that of the same man she had heard on the phone in 1943. FBI agents Harrington and Norton objected that the only way to obtain such a recording would be through placing a bug either in Julius's cell at the House of Detention or in the marshal's holding cell at the Foley Square Courthouse. In any case, they argued, Julius's voice would certainly have changed in the intervening eight years since Bentley had heard it over the phone. Harrington, Norton, and Kilsheimer all agreed that Cohn's plan would not work, but it was Myles Lane who finally vetoed it decisively, declaring that "he unequivocally would not countenance" such an improper action.

Just as Lane and Kilsheimer had anticipated, Bentley was not permitted to testify on the witness stand to what she had learned about Rosenberg indirectly from Jacob Golos. Nevertheless, Bentley's story of the phone calls dovetailed with earlier testimony by Max Elitcher. On the night of the film-can delivery at Catherine Slip,

Elitcher had testified, Sobell told him that Rosenberg had once talked to Bentley on the phone but was "pretty sure she didn't know who he was."

One final question about Bentley's 1945 statement remains to be explored: Why had the FBI failed to follow up on her lead at the time? One might expect that in any concerted investigation, Julius Rosenberg's name would sooner or later crop up among the suspects. After all, he had been dismissed from a sensitive government position earlier that same year on charges of having lied about his Communist Party membership. Rosenberg, an engineer, fit the general physical description given by Bentley and had enjoyed access to information about classified defense projects during the period covered by the statement. Moreover, there is some reason to think that in her off-the-record statements to the FBI, Bentley had said something to suggest a connection between "Julius" and the Knickerbocker Village housing complex. This seems likely because the one suspect that the Bureau did make an effort to identify with "Julius" was a former resident of the same housing project.

But the FBI had focused on the wrong man. Its prime suspect was Julius Korchein, better known as Jules—ironically, an officer of FAECT, the same union that Rosenberg belonged to. Korchein did not fit Bentley's description as well as Rosenberg did. He was an architect, not an engineer, and he had moved from the Knickerbocker Village neighborhood before the time Bentley claimed to have seen Golos meet "Julius" there. But the FBI felt sure that he was the man they were looking for because, as of 1946, Korchein had been involved in a business partnership with none other than Abraham Brothman. Brothman was already under suspicion as a result of Bentley's revelations, so it seemed logical that his partner would be the "Julius" with whom Bentley had been in telephone contact.

When surveillance of Korchein failed to support this theory, the FBI never bothered to extend its search further. Like Bentley herself, and like so many commentators on the Rosenberg-Sobell trial, they concluded that "Julius" must have been an alias after all.

In the aftermath of Bentley's Rosenberg trial testimony, the FBI had occasion to feel defensive about its failure to identify her "Julius" with Rosenberg. When journalist Oliver Pilat was researching his book on the atom-spy trials in late 1951, he asked his FBI sources how they could account for this failure. Pilat's query touched off a string of self-justifying internal memoranda. In one of these, we find Hoover aide L. B. Nichols explaining to Hoover's chief assistant, Associate Director Clyde Tolson, that "it does not appear that a survey of all the tenants of Knickerbocker Village was conducted in view of the meager information and belief that 'Julius' was a cover name." Embarrassing as the error may have been in hindsight, the FBI's assumption was a natural one. How could it have guessed that Julius, the proud amateur, had disdained to take the elementary precaution of using a false name?

If Elizabeth Bentley had wished to become party to a frame-up, she could quite easily have invented some incident that involved her meeting Julius Rosenberg face to face. She refused and stuck in detail to the story she first told the FBI in 1945. That she resisted this temptation does not necessarily prove that she never lied or exaggerated under other circumstances and at other trials and testimonial appearances. But the overwhelming evidence of the FBI files is that in her testimony at the Rosenberg-Sobell trial, at least, Elizabeth Bentley had told the truth.

15

Julius Rosenberg for the Defense

Eight months of imprisonment had done nothing to shake Julius Rosenberg's sense of his own rectitude. Even the government's vindictive treatment of Ethel, far from undermining Julius's resolve as the prosecutors hoped, worked in the long run to convince him that he had been right all along in his belief that American justice was being perverted by hypocritical politicians and power seekers. The only trouble with this way of looking at things was that Julius continued to interpret every new twist of events as just another stage in the clash of two monolithic belief systems. If his prosecutors were wrong, then it followed that he was the blameless victim of a political witch-hunt, kin morally and intellectually to the Hollywood actors and writers who were confronting the red-baiting tactics of HUAC investigators even as his own trial began.

It was natural, then, that Julius counted on taking the stand to declare his own innocence and deny any knowledge of Soviet espionage. The chance that at least one juror would choose to believe him and his wife instead of his accusers offered a slim hope of winning an acquittal. But this was only part of his motivation. No matter what happened during the trial itself, Julius wanted to speak for the historical record, which he confidently expected would vindicate him eventually. Just as he had done in his old YCL days, Julius was still taking the long view.

Julius's ideas of how his defense should be conducted had the full support of his lawyer. Nor was there ever any serious possibility that he and Ethel would not stand together on every important aspect of their case. Alexander Bloch, Ethel's lawyer of record, had little experience with criminal trials and invariably deferred to his son's judgment. When it came to preparing their clients to take the stand, however, the father-and-son defense team did disagree on the important matter of how their clients should respond to Saypol's inevitable questions about their past links to the Communist Party. Manny Bloch felt strongly that Julius and Ethel should refuse to answer any such questions on Fifth Amendment grounds. His father, caring less for the principle of the matter than for the psychological impact of such a tactic on the jurors, argued that citing the Fifth Amendment would destroy whatever impression of candor the Rosenbergs had managed to convey in the rest of their testimony. The jury was bound to believe that the Rosenbergs were Communists anyway, he argued, so why not admit it and take the opportunity to explain that their political opinions had not prevented them from being loyal and law-abiding Americans.

When the two counselors were unable to resolve their difference of opinion, they agreed to present the alternatives to the Rosenbergs themselves. On March 5, the day before the trial opened, the Blochs interviewed Julius and Ethel separately in jail to hash out their difference of opinion. According to Emanuel Bloch's own account of these interviews as given to John Wexley, both Rosenbergs strongly favored using the Fifth Amendment as a matter of principle and practicality. Both William Remington and Alger Hiss had denied any connection with the Party on the stand, and their refusal to take the privilege had done them no good, so why open the way for a barrage of hostile questions about their own political beliefs and, worse, the names and activities of old friends and associates?

Explained in this way, the Rosenbergs' ultimate decision not to answer questions about their Communist affiliations makes sense. But this course presented certain dangers. First, by testifying in their own defense, Julius and Ethel were no longer legally entitled to pick and choose which questions they wished to answer. Except for a very narrow range of questions still protected under the privilege, they were effectively giving up their rights against self-incrimination, and Saypol, if he chose, could ask the judge to direct them to answer his inquiries. It is unclear whether Manny Bloch ever explained this to his clients. Perhaps he did, and they decided that they would have little to lose in any case by sticking to their claim of privilege even if ordered to answer by Kaufman.

Although Alger Hiss had been convicted in his second trial despite his own testimony and the distinguished character witnesses who had come forward in his behalf, it was also true that his first trial had ended in a hung jury—an outcome more favorable than the Rosenbergs had any right to hope for if they could not manage to convince someone in the jury box that they had more integrity than their in-laws. Ruth Greenglass had already said in her testimony that Julius and Ethel had given up open political activities at the time they had become involved in espionage, a statement that must have stirred the jurors' memories of Whittaker Chambers's well-publicized description at the Hiss trial of his life underground. If the Rosenbergs really were innocent, to let Ruth's statement go by without even attempting to counter it was taking a big chance.

In fact, resorting to the Fifth Amendment privilege seems the "practical" course only in light of the Rosenbergs' fears that the prosecution had more evidence than it had yet brought forth about their motives for leaving the Party. The less Julius and Ethel were willing to say on the stand about this aspect of their past, the better their chances of heading off a line of cross-examination that would expose the existence of other portions of the spy network. The list of prosecution witnesses made public at the outset of the trial was studded with the names of people who might still show up as surprise rebuttal witnesses to contradict any account the Rosenbergs might give of their past political associations. Louise Sarant, Al Sarant's wife; Arthur Barr, Joel's brother; and several old YCL and party acquaintances had all been included on the roster, and who could be sure what they might or might not be persuaded to say?

When the moment finally arrived for Julius Rosenberg to tell his story in his own words, however, the strategy that he agreed on with Ethel and with Manny Bloch would no longer matter as much as the personal impression he made by his demeanor. In spite of what Judge Kaufman had said in his pretrial lecture to the jury about their job being as mechanical as "adding up a column of figures," these jurors, like any others, were at least as interested in sizing up the defendant as in weighing each of his words. For twelve days the jury, the spectators, and the press had watched the Rosenbergs sit silently at the defense table, noticing how Ethel visibly paled and looked away when her own brother made his accusations and how Julius stared straight ahead in apparent defiance.

Julius Rosenberg's first chance to speak on his own behalf could not have come at a worse time psychologically. The day had begun with the bombshell testimony of Elizabeth Bentley and then subsided into hours of tedium as Manny Bloch argued for a mistrial on the grounds that the issue of communism had been brought in in a manner that was "inflammatory" and had planted an "incurable prejudice" in the minds of the jury. It was late afternoon when Judge Kaufman summarily dismissed Bloch's motions and the way was cleared for Julius to take the stand. By that time, the weary jury was recalled to the courtroom, only to hear an hour or so of routine questions about Rosenberg's background and family finances.

Aside from the unfortunate timing, Bloch's logic in having Rosenberg give the history of his life as a Knickerbocker Village tenant was basically good. Julius described his modest three-room apartment, whose rent had risen from $45.75 to a princely $51.00 at the time of his arrest, and told how he and Ethel had furnished the place with secondhand furniture either passed on by friends or purchased from ads in the Knickerbocker Village *News*, a tenants' weekly. Later, he would add that his wife Ethel had spent a total of about $300 on clothes in ten years' time, $80 of that on an inexpensive fur coat that she had remodeled several times and was still making do with at the time of her arrest. All of these details added up to a picture starkly different from that drawn by the Greenglasses, who had testified about Rosenberg receiving an Omega watch from the Russians and spending "$50 to $75 dollars a night" entertaining espionage contacts in nightclubs. Whatever sums of money may have passed through Julius Rosenberg's hands from time to time in his role as a spymaster, he certainly fitted no one's notions of a high-rolling man-about-town.

Manny Bloch steered Julius carefully through a series of questions designed to elicit specific denials: a console table that had been kept in the Rosenbergs' living room and which the Greenglasses had described as a gift from the Russians specially outfitted for microfilming had actually been purchased by Julius at Macy's for "about

$21." Julius had never given Ruth $150 to help pay for her trip to New Mexico in November 1944, nor had he ever received information on the atom bomb from Greenglass in January 1945. During David's furlough, he had never introduced him to a man on First Avenue near Forty-second Street who had asked for details of the bomb. He had never introduced Ann Sidorovich, a former Knickerbocker Village neighbor, to the Greenglasses as an espionage courier. But when Judge Kaufman took it upon himself to question the witness directly about his political beliefs, Rosenberg became more voluble.

> KAUFMAN: Did you ever discuss with Ann Sidorovich the respective preferences of economic systems between Russia and the United States.
>
> ROSENBERG: Well, your Honor, if you will let me answer that in my own way I want to explain that question.
>
> KAUFMAN: Go ahead.
>
> ROSENBERG: First of all, I am not an expert on matters of different economic systems, but in my normal social intercourse with my friends we discussed matters like that. And I believe there are merits in both systems, I mean from what I have been able to read and ascertain.
>
> KAUFMAN: I am not talking about your belief today. I am talking about your belief at that time, in January of 1945.
>
> ROSENBERG: Well, that is what I am talking about. At that time, what I believed at that time I still believe today. In the first place, I heartily approve of our system of justice as performed in this country, Anglo-Saxon jurisprudence. I am in favor, heartily in favor of our Constitution and Bill of Rights and I owe my allegiance to my country at all times.

Sensing that his client was not doing badly for himself, Bloch pursued the line of questioning begun by Kaufman:

> BLOCH: Do you owe allegiance to any other country?
>
> ROSENBERG: I do not.
>
> BLOCH: Have you any divided allegiance?
>
> ROSENBERG: I do not.
>
> BLOCH: Would you fight for this country—
>
> ROSENBERG: Yes, I will.
>
> BLOCH: If it were engaged in a war with any other country?
>
> ROSENBERG: Yes, I will, and in discussing the merits of oth-

er forms of governments, I discussed that with my friends on the basis of the performance of what they accomplished and I felt that the Soviet government has improved the lot of the underdog there, has made a lot of progress in eliminating illiteracy, has done a lot of reconstruction work and built up a lot of resources, and at the same time I felt that they contributed a major share in destroying the Hitler beast who killed six million of my co-religionists, and I feel emotional about that thing.

Considering the depth of anti-Communist feeling in 1951, for a defendant in an espionage trial to lecture the court about the accomplishments of the Soviet government required an extraordinary combination of courage and naïveté. On balance, the speech probably did Julius more good than harm, however. After the evasiveness of previous witnesses and the nervous objections of the defense lawyers every time the word "communism" was mentioned in the courtroom, Julius Rosenberg had shown himself as a man of firm convictions, however unpalatable they might be to the jurors.

Unfortunately for the witness, both his own attorney and Judge Kaufman were each for his own purpose reluctant to let well enough alone. Manny Bloch, searching for a more specific disavowal of illegal intent, pressed on by asking whether Julius ever made "any comparisons, in the sense the Court has asked you, about whether you preferred one system over the other."

ROSENBERG: No, I did not. I would like to state that my personal opinions are that the people of every country should decide for themselves what kind of government they want. If the English want a King, it is their business. If the Russians want communism, it is their business. If the Americans want our form of government, it is our business. I feel that the majority of people should decide for themselves what kind of government they want.

Through his persistence, Bloch had practically invited Kaufman to continue where he had previously been interrupted, and the judge was not slow to follow up Julius's denials by asking whether he had ever belonged to "any group" that had discussed the system of government in Russia.

Now, after speaking up so forthrightly, Julius was suddenly hesitant. "Well, your Honor, are you referring to political groups—is that what you are referring to?"

> KAUFMAN: Any group.
> ROSENBERG: Well, your Honor, I feel at this time that I refuse to answer a question that might tend to incriminate me.

With this refusal, the first of many that would be made before Rosenberg finally left the stand, the pendulum of sympathy began to swing in the other direction, and jurors and spectators alike prepared themselves to listen more skeptically to the witness's own account of his dealings with his in-laws, the Greenglasses, and with his former friend Max Elitcher.

According to Julius, the incident of the Jell-O box had never happened. He had never used the phrase, "The simplest things are the cleverest." He had visited Max Elitcher in Washington, it was true, but only during a routine business trip to Washington when "loneliness" had moved him to look up a college acquaintance he had not seen in years. The dinner at Manny Wolf's restaurant testified to by Elitcher had never occurred. Nor had he ever tried to persuade Greenglass to study nuclear physics, an unlikely idea in any case, Julius added, since David was not qualified for such courses.

Rosenberg agreed that he had visited Ruth Greenglass in her Stanton Street apartment shortly before she left for New Mexico for the second time in 1945, but the circumstances were quite different from those Ruth had described. What *had* occurred was that Ruth had asked him to send her teenaged sister Dorothy into the bathroom so that she could confide how desperately worried she was about her husband.

> ROSENBERG: Ruthie told me something to this effect: "Julius, I am terribly worried. David has an idea to make some money and take some things from the Army"; and I told her, "Warn David not to do anything foolish. He will only get himself in trouble. I have read some accounts in the newspapers about some G.I.'s doing foolish things and taking parts and gasoline from the Army and their getting themselves in trouble," and I told her, "Don't tell—make sure to tell him that he doesn't do anything of the sort."

After this conversation with Ruth, Rosenberg said, he heard no more about David having any trouble with the army and when his brother-in-law left the service in 1946, he became the foreman and head machinist in the business that Julius had formed with Bernard Greenglass. David was a troublesome business partner in many ways, frequently borrowing small sums of money, which were later charged up to the Greenglasses' share of the machine-shop debt, and taking so much time away from the shop that Julius accused him of "shirking." Neither he nor Pitt Machine Products, Julius insisted, had anything to do with Russia or the Russians, and if anyone had ever mentioned anything about a "sky platform" in the shop, it must have been David himself. Julius elaborated on this:

> ... I don't remember the specific incident but at that time in the Popular Science magazines and in the newspapers there was some talk about the Germans had done some work of some kind of suspended lens in the sky to concentrate the rays of the sun at the earth, and that is what I believe was the discussion we might have had at that time. Greenglass used to read the Popular Mechanics and the Popular Science and he always talked about things like that at the shop.

When David left the family business in late 1949, he had demanded a $1,000 cash payment in exchange for his share of the machine-shop stock—money Julius did not have. In an attempt to get David to give him a stock assignment without getting cash up front, Julius had gone to the Greenglass apartment sometime in May 1950. Then, around the middle of the month, David had dropped into Julius's office at the machine shop with something on his mind. Assuming David wanted to discuss the stock assignment further, Julius had suggested that they go for a walk in nearby Hamilton Fish Park, and it was there that David dropped his bombshell.

> "Julie, you got to get me $2,000. I need it at once," David had demanded.
> I said, "Look Dave, you know the arrangements I made with you. I obligated myself to Dave Schein. I gave him a down payment of $1,000. I have no cash left. You can't get blood out of a stone. I just don't have the money. What do you want it for?"
> He said: "I need the money. Don't ask me questions."

Finally, when Julius insisted that he could not get his hands on $2,000 no matter what, David had asked him for another favor: "He said, 'Will you go to your doctor and ask him to make out a certificate for a smallpox vaccination.' "

Though he had no idea of what kind of trouble David might be in, Julius insisted, he had agreed to go to Dr. Bernhardt to ask for a forged vaccination certificate "for a friend." The doctor turned him down flat. After relaying this message to David, he did not see either of the Greenglasses again until the end of May when David called the shop and told him he had something "very urgent" to discuss. Julius went to the Greenglasses' apartment the next morning, and when he arrived he barely had time to glance at Ruth's new baby before David, still unwashed and unshaved, pulled on a shirt and suggested that they go for a walk in the direction of the East River Drive. On the way they ran into two friends of David's, Herman and Diana Einsohn.

By the time they reached the Drive, David was so agitated that he was perspiring uncontrollably. He repeated his demands for money, but Julius turned him down. The best advice he could give was that David should go home and take a cold shower. Then David became abusive and threatening: " 'Well, Julie, I just got to have the money and if you don't get me the money you are going to be sorry.' I said, 'Look here, Dave, what are you trying to do, threaten me or blackmail me?' "

In spite of David's threats, Julius testified, he had never given his brother-in-law the money he demanded, and certainly he had never given him $4,000, which was more cash than he had ever seen at one time in his life. Later, discussing the problem with Ethel, he had complained that David had it in for him because of their business differences, but Ethel had insisted that if David was in trouble of some kind they should try to help. Reluctantly, at Ethel's urging, Julius had dropped in at the Greenglass apartment several days later to see if everything was still all right. But when he arrived, "everybody was very cool to me and I didn't want to bring the subject up in Ruthie's presence. . . . I saw that Davey was calmer at this point and wasn't going to do anything rash so I picked myself up after a few minutes and left the apartment."

This was the last Julius had seen or heard of his brother-in-law until the day two FBI agents came to the Rosenberg apartment and asked Julius to go down to Foley Square for questioning.

There were several problems with Rosenberg's story, not the least of them stemming from the fact that a banal tale of business disagreements and idle conversation based on articles from *Popular Science* would inevitably sound lame in comparison to David and Ruth's version of the events. Julius was prepared to concede those circumstantial aspects of his in-laws' story that could be confirmed by other individuals, such as Dorothy Abel, Dr. Bernhardt, and the Einsohns, but was unable to offer any independent support for his own version of events. In theory at least, the defense might have called witnesses of their own, character witnesses for the Rosenbergs and witnesses who could support allegations about David's shiftless behavior in the machine shop or his interest in black-market dealings while in the army, even their friend Ann Sidorovich, who could repeat the denials she had already made under oath before the grand jury. The failure of the defense to produce such backup witnesses constituted no proof of guilt. Perfectly innocent defendants might have had difficulty in getting anyone to come forward to testify in support of accused atomic spies. Nevertheless, the absence of a single friendly witness was striking. The Rosenbergs, it was later said, had wanted to spare their many friends the persecution that would surely befall anyone who spoke on their behalf. In fact, no one seems to have been eager to volunteer. Julius Rosenberg's two sisters did not even appear in the spectators' section.

The tone of Saypol's cross-examination was established immediately when he began by asking Julius about his college friendships. Did he know "a man or a boy named William Perl or Mutterperl?"

Under the surface of this apparently innocuous question lay a minefield of complications. A negative answer could be easily disproven: Rosenberg's friendship with Perl was too well known. On the other hand, Perl was already under a perjury indictment for denying that he knew Julius. Faced with a difficult situation, the witness made the worst possible choice. He plunged ahead, hoping to seize the initiative: "Your Honor, I read in the newspapers about . . ."

Judge Kaufman sensed where Rosenberg was headed and tried to warn him off. "You had better not say anything that you think may hurt you," he cautioned.

But the warning made no impression. "Yes, sir, that is what I want to say," Julius insisted. "I read in the newspapers about a man being arrested for perjury . . ."

Now even Saypol tried to interrupt. Julius, however, was determined to finish. "My name was mentioned and I feel that I refuse to answer any questions that might tend to incriminate me."

"You see," responded the prosecutor with obvious satisfaction, "that is all I wanted to know."

Rosenberg had made a serious blunder on two counts. First, despite the failure of the defense lawyers to file a formal objection, there was still a possibility that Perl's arrest in midtrial might later be found prejudicial, particularly if it could be shown that one or more jurors were aware of it. But the defense could not have it both ways. Either they wanted the jurors to know about Perl or they did not. Julius could not take it on himself to inform them of Perl's situation now and then later claim that their knowledge had prejudiced his case.

More importantly, Rosenberg's naïve and argumentative response betrayed a weakness that Saypol was to exploit to the fullest. Even the most innocent of witnesses is well advised not to try to score debating points against his interrogator. But Julius simply could not resist.

Julius seemed to regard the Fifth Amendment as a kind of slingshot that he could use at will to fend off the hostile questions of the Goliath of governmental power, personified by Irving Saypol. But while he did not seem to be aware of it, there was a technical question about his right to claim the Fifth Amendment privilege in this way.

Judge Kaufman recognized the issue at once and was prepared to make a ruling, but Saypol was quick to interrupt: "Now, in the posture of the case as it is, the witness raises a question of incrimination, apparently of his own making," he observed. ". . . I should ask the Court not to make any positive direction except as I may request it."

Saypol's concession would later be characterized by Judge Kaufman as "gracious." In reality, it was coldly calculated. Julius would be allowed to claim the Fifth Amendment privilege at will, but only because the U.S. attorney had concluded that he could turn the Fifth Amendment refuge into a trap.

Saypol returned again to the subject of Rosenberg's City College days, asking whether there was any "club or anything like that" that Julius and his friends had all belonged to. Rosenberg knew by now that he had made some sort of error in resorting to the Fifth Amendment too quickly, so this time he stalled, pretending not to understand the question, until Manny Bloch prompted him with the objection that the question was "intruding now in that ground of political activity . . ."

But Saypol was relentless. What group did Julius have in mind that was making him so "reticent"? Was it a Boy Scout troop? A Hillel club? A civic club? "Is there a group that all of you were active in together, as to which you raise the question of your constitutional privilege, that you don't want to tell us about?"

Naturally, Manny Bloch objected to this line of attack. And Judge Kaufman agreed that it was not allowable, but while Saypol was searching for a wording that might pass muster, the witness once again barged ahead.

"Can I state something," Julius asked, interrupting the lawyers' colloquy. "I would like to state, on any answer I made to this question, I don't intend to waive any part of my right to self-incrimination [sic], and if Mr. Saypol is referring to the Young Communist League of the Communist Party, I will not answer any question on it."

It was almost too easy. And Bloch, who had been doing his best to keep any mention of the Communist Party from being allowed, must have felt the beginnings of despair.

Saypol had already asked in passing about Joel Barr and received the reply from Julius that "to the best of my knowledge, he is in Europe today." Now the prosecutor returned to the subject of the witness's friends and acquaintances:

Did Rosenberg know an Oscar Vago? Vago, a former business partner of Abraham Brothman's, had been arrested some months earlier and linked unfairly by the press with Julius Rosenberg and espionage. Julius admitted having met Vago in the Federal House of Detention but denied any previous association.

What about Vivian Glassman? Glassman, too, had been mentioned in the newspapers, the press having reported, in connection with William Perl's arrest, the story of her mysterious visit to Cleveland. And Julius, perhaps unnecessarily, had even referred to Glassman in his direct testimony as a social acquaintance of his. "Isn't it a fact," Saypol pressed now, "that you gave [Glassman] $2,000 to take out to somebody in Cleveland?"

Rosenberg vowed that he had done no such thing.

Next, Saypol moved on to Al Sarant. Rosenberg admitted that he had visited Sarant's home in Ithaca sometime during 1949 or early 1950, but he denied Saypol's suggestion that he might have been there as recently as May or June of the latter year. Asked if he knew Sarant's present whereabouts, he said a bit defensively, "Well, I saw the name of his wife on the witness list, and the address is given as Ithaca, so I figured he is still in Ithaca."

"Don't you know he is in Mexico?" Saypol riposted.

Manny Bloch, Edward Kuntz, and Harold Phillips jumped up in unison to move for a mistrial, arguing that irrelevant references to Mexico were being used to create a smokescreen of implications prejudicial to their clients.

The motion was denied and Saypol went on to tick off yet another name. "Do you know a girl or a lady by the name of Carol Dayton?"

Answered Rosenberg, "I do not recall that name."

The jury must have found all this bewildering. Several of these individuals had not been mentioned in court previously and would never be mentioned again. In retrospect, moreover, it is clear that Saypol had no real purpose in asking about them other than to elicit a series of vaguely incriminating denials. Glassman's trip to Cleveland had not occurred until after Julius Rosenberg's arrest, for example, so it was impossible that Rosenberg had personally been the one who gave her the $2,000 to take to Perl.

Other subjects that Saypol dwelt on at some length in his cross-examination seemed petty and pointless. Rosenberg was asked about a collection can seized in the search of his apartment that bore the motto, "Save a Spanish Republican Child. Volveremos. We Will Return." He insisted that the can had been sent to him, unasked for, by the International Workers Order, an organization under which he held an insurance policy.

He was questioned in detail about the console table that David Greenglass had said was used for secret microfilming of stolen documents. Where had the table stood in the Rosenberg apartment? What other tables had the Rosenbergs owned and where did they get them? Julius maintained that he had purchased the console table in question at Macy's for approximately $21. "Don't you know," Saypol countered incredulously, "that you couldn't buy a console table in Macy's, if they had it, in 1944 and 1945, for less than $85?"

Still another series of questions concerned the watch that Rosenberg had allegedly received as a gift from the Russians. The prosecution produced several watches that had been taken during the search of the Rosenbergs' apartment. One was an old pocket watch Julius had inherited from his father. None were valuable. Julius did concede that he had once owned a more expensive watch, an Omega. He maintained, however, that the Omega had been a birthday gift from his father. In any case, it had been lost years ago when his younger son accidentally dropped it from a train window while the family was returning from a vacation in upstate New York.

The prosecutor's claim that both Julius and Ethel had been given watches as a symbolic reward for their espionage services may have been correct. Julius's story that the Omega had come from his father was not entirely convincing, especially since he conceded that the most expensive present he had ever received from his parents aside from the watch was a $25 war bond. But since nothing remotely resembling the incriminating timepieces had turned up among the defendants' possessions, it was their word against their accusers'. Once the dispute had been outlined to the jury, it seemed futile to belabor the issue with detailed questions about how the watch had been lost. If the witness had been more sympathetic, Saypol's hectoring and frequently sarcastic cross-examination on this and other topics might well have backfired.

But the fact was that Julius did not make a sympathetic impression, and for reasons that went beyond his unpopular politics. An innocent man in his situation might be expected to show fear, anger, or confusion. Julius impressed the jurors as "stony." And when asked about the period after David Greenglass's arrest, when he was under FBI surveillance, he refused to admit he had been so much as worried. Why should he have been when he had done nothing wrong, he insisted. This was too much for Judge Kaufman: "The fact that you saw an FBI agent looking into your place of business—"

Rosenberg insisted that the incident had made no particular impression on him.

> It didn't enter my mind as to what his purpose was.
> KAUFMAN: Is that the best answer you can give?
> ROSENBERG: Yes.

Saypol's apparently meandering interrogation did manage to probe some weak spots in Julius's version of his falling out with the

Greenglasses. None of these involved important questions of fact, it is true, but they hurt the overall credibility of the defendant's story. At one point, Saypol went back to review Julius's account of his visit to Ruth Greenglass when he had found her with her younger sister, Dorothy Abel. According to Julius, it was Ruth who had asked Dorothy to go into the bathroom so that they could talk privately about her fear that David was about to do something "foolish." Julius had interpreted this to mean that his brother-in-law was contemplating stealing from the army. Why then, wondered Saypol aloud, had Julius invested all his savings in a business partnership with this same brother-in-law? Hadn't he at least been curious enough to question David?

> ROSENBERG: Well, Mr. Saypol, David Greenglass talked about a lot of things. He used to boast about things. I don't know if he really did a thing like that [stealing], or just talked about it.

Another aspect of Rosenberg's testimony that did not quite ring true was his assertion that in May 1950 it had been David who had approached him, demanding $2,000 and a medical certificate for unspecified reasons. Julius said he had asked Dr. Bernhardt about the possibility of obtaining a false smallpox vaccination certificate without ever having a clear idea of why David wanted it. Further, when he had mentioned David's demands to Ethel, she had said something to the effect that "Ruthie must be nagging him for money again." Yet Ruth had just given birth and was still seriously ill from the aftereffects of the burns she had received sometime earlier. Wasn't this a strange time to be accusing her of "nagging"? And what could Ruth's money fixation have had to do with David's request for a smallpox vaccination certificate? Only after considerable prodding did Rosenberg admit that he might have connected David's unusual request with David's previous admission to him that he had been questioned months earlier about uranium samples stolen from Los Alamos. Nevertheless, Julius insisted he had not really anticipated that David was thinking about fleeing the country. Once again, it seemed difficult to believe that Rosenberg had so little curiosity about his brother-in-law's affairs.

But the most telling moment of the cross-examination occurred when Saypol returned to Julius's account of his second conversation with David about money, the one that had occurred as the two men were walking near the East River Drive.

Rosenberg's use of the world "blackmail" in his direct testimony about the conversation had passed largely unnoticed. But when Saypol managed to elicit the same word once again in going over the ground on cross-examination, it caused something of a stir. Judge Kaufman, who had been warning the prosecutor that the subject was "very well exhausted" and urging him to "get along," suddenly perked up.

KAUFMAN: Blackmail you? Where did he try to blackmail you?

ROSENBERG: Well, he threatened me to get money. I considered it blackmailing me.

KAUFMAN: What did he say he would do if you didn't give it to him? You said he said you would be sorry.

ROSENBERG: Yes. I consider it blackmail when someone says that.

KAUFMAN: Did he say what he would do to you?

ROSENBERG: No, he didn't.

KAUFMAN: Did he say he would go to the authorities and tell them you were in a conspiracy to steal the atomic bomb secret?

ROSENBERG: No.

KAUFMAN: Do you think that is what he had in mind?

ROSENBERG: How could I know what he had in mind?

KAUFMAN: What do you mean by blackmail then?

ROSENBERG: Maybe he threatened to punch me in the nose or something like that.

This exchange would remain vividly alive in the minds of the jurors when they began their deliberations later that same week. Julius's attempt to explain his brother-in-law's vengeful attitude had not been very convincing to those who heard it firsthand. His mention of "blackmail," on the other hand, had struck several jury members as sounding all too sincere. They felt sure that it was an unintentional admission of guilt.

Saypol was still not quite finished with Julius Rosenberg. Just that morning at about 11:45, the prosecutor had learned that the FBI had turned up a new surprise witness. His drawn-out cross-examination, which had tried the patience of Judge Kaufman, had been intended to allow time for the witness to be brought secretly into the courtroom to see the Rosenbergs and confirm that he would be able to identify them on the stand. Only after Saypol was sure that the elements of his plan were in place was he prepared to wind up his questions by bringing up a subject no one had touched on before: the possibility that the Rosenbergs themselves had secured passport pictures in preparation for flight to a foreign country.

Saypol approached the subject apparently as an afterthought at the end of a long series of questions about Party membership. Julius quickly denied that he had ordered any passport photos of himself in the months of May or June 1950. But Saypol began to get more specific:

> Did you go to a photographer's shop at 99 Park Row and have any photographs taken of yourself?
> ROSENBERG: I have been in many photographers' shops and had photos taken.

Obviously nervous, Julius explained that he and his family frequently stopped in at photo shops on impulse when they were out for a walk. He could not recall whether this had happened in May or June 1950.

Saypol pressed Julius to try harder to remember. Hadn't he had a conversation with a certain photographer sometime during the months at issue? "See if you can't recall," Saypol pushed on. "Try hard. May or June 1950, at 99 Park Row."

"I don't recall telling the man anything."

"You mean, you might have told him something, but you don't recall it now?"

"I don't recall my saying anything at this time."

"What don't you recall? Tell us that."

"I don't know sir."

"Do you remember telling the man at 99 Park Row that you had to go to France to settle an estate?"

"I didn't tell him anything of the sort."

Eventually, Julius was forced to admit that he *might* have been in the photographer's shop in question, though only to pose for family snapshots, not "passport photos." He could not recall the incident specifically nor could he describe the pictures that might have been taken or what happened to them. Saypol did not need to point out how strange it was that Rosenberg's memory should be so vague about what must have been one of the last family outings he had enjoyed before his arrest.

16

Morton Sobell's Silence

No one was more surprised than Edward Kuntz when the government failed to establish a link between his client and the theft of atomic secrets. A veteran trial lawyer who had defended many left-wing clients in difficult cases, Kuntz had agreed to represent Morton Sobell out of a sense of duty not unmixed with anticipation at locking horns with Irving Saypol, who had recently attacked him publicly at a meeting of the New York Bar Association.

Once committed to defending Sobell, however, Kuntz found himself fighting under severe handicaps. Sobell was not even mentioned in the twelve overt acts of the conspiracy indictment under which he was being tried, and Kuntz's battle to force the government to unseal the bill of particulars prepared at the time of his client's arrest got nowhere. The prosecutors would reveal only that Sobell was charged with having five conversations with Julius Rosenberg growing out of a conspiracy that he had joined "on or about June 15, 1944." To reveal more, they argued, would be tantamount to giving the defense a "complete blueprint" of the evidence they intended to present in court.

Worse still, Edward Kuntz never did have complete confidence in his client. Morton Sobell writes in his autobiography, *On Doing*

Time, of his failure "to establish any rapport" with his lawyers, either Kuntz or Harold Phillips, the younger co-counsel, who joined the case at Kuntz's invitation. Sobell suggests, no doubt realistically, that Kuntz and Phillips were initially standoffish because they did not believe his protestations of innocence and suspected that he might change his plea at any time.

This initial distrust was magnified by Sobell's fantasies that his lawyers would somehow magically rescue him from the nightmare in which he found himself trapped. Though by no means the complete innocent he has always publicly claimed to be, Morton Sobell was a peripheral figure in Rosenberg's espionage ring. He must have been overwhelmed at finding himself publicly branded an "atom spy" and psychologically unprepared to adjust to the isolation and powerlessness of prison life.

To make matters worse, Sobell's chief lifeline to the outside world was his wife, Helen, whose fierce devotion was matched by her faith that her husband would conduct himself as a true hero of the Left, eschewing the role of informer at all costs. Seeking to spare Sobell unnecessary anxiety, Helen did not tell him that she and other members of his family had been called to testify before the grand jury after his arrest. Sobell thus had no appreciation of the efforts of his lawyers to quash Helen's subpoena on the grounds that she should not be compelled to give evidence against her husband. The maneuver was not completely successful, but it did result in an agreement that limited the government's latitude in questioning Helen, protecting her against the kind of damaging questions that were directed at Ethel Rosenberg. Nor, in demanding of Helen that she find him a lawyer more to his liking, did Sobell understand the reality of her situation and his. The family home had already been sold to pay Kuntz and Phillips a $5,000 retainer, and there were few lawyers eager to take the case even had more money been available.

In retrospect, Sobell's lawyers were far more energetic and capable than he ever gave them credit for. Nevertheless, as he sat in Judge Kaufman's courtroom listening to the Greenglasses and Harry Gold tell a story that was no doubt as new to him as to any of the spectators, Sobell had good reason to be nervous about the advice he was getting from his counsel.

First of all, Edward Kuntz had advised him even before the trial that it would be counterproductive to bring up in court the subject of his kidnapping from Mexico. Kuntz warned that even if it could be shown that Sobell had been illegally deported and brought into the United States improperly, the federal government's ability to try him would not be affected. He also felt strongly that accusing the FBI of improper behavior would only alienate the sympathies of the jury. Given the political climate of the times, Kuntz may have been right in thinking that the jurors would only consider the charge that the FBI had gone to extraordinary lengths to capture Sobell as just one more proof of his guilt. But by failing to offer an alternative to the government's story of the so-called deportation, Kuntz had sacrificed the one aspect of his client's situation that might have won for him the jury's sympathy.

Not only did Sobell fail to present his own account of his trip to Mexico, but at Kuntz's urging he waived his right to present any defense whatsoever. As Kuntz saw it, the only witness to tie Sobell to any wrongdoing was Max Elitcher, and Elitcher did not even claim to know what was in the film can that he had helped Sobell deliver to someone who lived near Catherine Slip. Relieved that the prosecution's case had not been as damaging as he no doubt secretly expected, Kuntz advised Sobell to let well enough alone and trust the jury to see how slight the evidence really was.

In hindsight, it is easy to see the fallacy of Kuntz's position. But one may equally ask whether testifying would in fact have done Sobell any good. Comparing Sobell's own account of his trip to Mexico with an outline of questions prepared by the U.S. Attorney's office for possible use in the cross-examination of Sobell during the trial— admittedly a hypothetical exercise—it becomes apparent that, whatever line of defense he chose to take, Sobell would not have escaped the prosecution's attacks unscathed.

For example, in his autobiography Sobell explains that both he and his wife had for some time been concerned about the climate of "anti-Communist mania" that was sweeping the country. Since they both had signed loyalty oaths upon taking jobs at Reeves Instrument in 1947, and since his wife had been "officially accused of Communist Party membership" years before (when she was employed by the U.S. Bureau of Standards), they both felt it was only a matter of time until they became the target of an FBI investigation. Sobell goes on:

> In addition to this realistic fear there were other apprehensions which pervaded the American Left in 1950, and which I shared. The belief was widespread that World War III was in the offing.

It seemed to us that America was veering toward fascism, a fascism that would be much the same as that of Nazi Germany. We
saw mass roundups, concentration camps, and death ovens à la
Hitler.

Though for obvious reasons Sobell might not have chosen to use
such strong language on the stand, there is nothing inherently unbe-
lievable in his story. Plenty of people in 1949 and 1950 were terrified
of becoming targets of anti-Communist witch-hunts for far less reason. Nor were the Sobells alone in considering an extended trip to
Mexico as a solution to their problems. In the summer of 1950, Mexico City was filled with expatriate Americans hoping to duck subpoe-
nas to appear before HUAC or other investigative bodies.

But assuming Sobell had decided to reveal all this on the witness
stand, he would still have had to explain why he chose to leave the
country at the precise time that he did. Writing in 1974, Sobell says
only that "The evening newspapers on Friday June 16, carried headlines about a former army sergeant who had been arrested for the
theft of the atom bomb. I saw it as more fuel for the rising tempera-
ture of the cold war."

The next evening, continues Sobell, while on a family outing to
Coney Island with his wife, his stepdaughter, and one of her cousins,
he raised the subject of leaving the country. "If we went perhaps it
would be merely a long vacation. We could go with an open mind,"
he recalls telling Helen.

In this account, Sobell never says one way or the other whether
he recognized David Greenglass's name and made the connection between the arrest of his longtime friend Julius Rosenberg. The implication is that he did not. But of course no prosecuting attorney
would have allowed him to evade the issue. And an admission that
his "extended vacation" had indeed been prompted by the news accounts of Greenglass's apprehension would hardly have worked in
his favor. On the contrary, it was exactly the concession the cross-
examiners hoped to extract.

A second and altogether more likely line of defense that Sobell
might have taken at the time of his trial would have been the contention that his trip to Mexico was an ordinary family vacation with no
political motivations whatsoever and unconnected to the fate of David Greenglass. This, indeed, was the explanation given by Helen So-

bell in numerous speeches she made on her husband's behalf after his conviction.

But here, too, there were pitfalls: Sobell says in *On Doing Time* that the Mexico journey was logically timed to coincide with his completion of an important and demanding project at Reeves. He waxes so emotional on this point that his explanation is worth quoting at some length:

> One peculiarity of my character is that I have always felt a compulsion to finish a job, whatever the consequences. When I was a child and brought my father his meal, at the store [Sobell's father was a pharmacist], in a valise, the Gentile children of the neighborhood would taunt me with epithets like "kike" or "Christ killer" and sometimes threaten me. On more than one occasion they pelted me with stones and I ran for my life, carefully holding the valise horizontally so as not to spill any of the soup in the pot. The thought of abandoning the valise or swinging it so that I might run faster never occurred to me. Even when I was hit and my ear gashed, I still hung on to the valise as if it were dearer than life itself.
>
> For the last two years at Reeves this side of my personality had dominated as I single-mindedly devoted myself to completing the plotting board project. . . .
>
> In June of 1950, however, there came a time when I felt that all my tasks had been completed. . . .

Autobiographers have a latitude to plead their own case that is not allowed to witnesses in court. Sobell's protests that he was never a quitter or a coward even as a child are all very well, but on the specific issue of his work at Reeves he would have been far more vulnerable than this recollection suggests.

The pretrial investigative report prepared by the U.S. Attorney's office shows that the state of Sobell's work at Reeves would have become a major issue if Sobell himself had brought the subject up on the stand. With just this turn of events in mind, FBI investigators had interviewed Sobell's immediate superior, Edward Garrett. Garrett was prepared to testify that a few days after Sobell last appeared at his job on June 16, he called Sobell at home about some problems that had arisen in connection with his project. Garrett first spoke with Helen Sobell, who said that she felt reluctant to call her husband to the phone because he was not feeling well. When he insisted that the questions were important, Sobell finally came to the telephone and promised he would be back on the job on the following Monday and everything could be straightened out then. There was no mention of a vacation, to Mexico or anywhere else.

The following Monday, when Sobell did not show up, Garrett went to his superior, Harry Belock, who told him that he had received a note from Sobell asking for sick leave. As summarized in the words of the investigator, Garrett said "that he told Belock he thought Sobell's taking time off was strange, inasmuch as the project on which Sobell had been working was not completed and his assistance was greatly needed."

The calling of Garrett as a rebuttal witness was just one of the pitfalls that lay in wait for Sobell had he elected to take the stand. In addition to a long list of questions about his use of William Danziger's address as a mail drop, his use of numerous aliases, and conflicting stories about the arrangements he had made for the care of his car and the payment of the mortgage on his house, the prosecutors wanted to ask Sobell about the meaning of a certain statement he had supposedly made to FBI agent Rex Shroder shortly after his arrest. Shroder said that when he had informed Sobell that the charge against him was conspiracy to commit espionage and that it carried the death penalty, Sobell had heatedly (and, as it turned out, incorrectly) disputed the statement, arguing that the death penalty applied only in a charge of "atomic espionage."

In hindsight once again, it is easy enough to argue away the significance of this story. Shroder could have been lying; even if true, the anecdote only proves that Sobell had been reading about atomic espionage in the newspapers and was badly frightened. But the impact such testimony would have had on the jury can only be imagined. However slight, the story was the link between Sobell and atomic secrets that the prosecution had so far failed to forge. Perhaps Edward Kuntz was not so wrong after all in warning Sobell to stay off the witness stand and present no rebuttal to the story of his flight to Mexico. By remaining silent on these issues the defense assured that it was on strong ground in maintaining there was no connection between Sobell's activities and the conspiracy among the Rosenbergs, the Greenglasses, and Gold. This argument, refined into the "two conspiracies" theory, was to prove the most potent weapon in the defense arsenal when Kuntz and Phillips began the appeals process.

17

Ethel Rosenberg in Court

It was Ethel Rosenberg's unhappy fate to be simultaneously a defendant on trial for her own life and the only person who could substantiate her husband's version of his relationship with David and Ruth Greenglass. As a young wife and mother caught between the accusations of her brother and loyalty to her husband, Ethel had a ready-made claim on the jury's sympathy if only she could find a way to take advantage of it. But while it might have been very much to her advantage to speak with apparent candor and at length, giving the jury a chance to identify emotionally with her situation, there was the ever present danger that she might inadvertently say something that would contradict the story already told by Julius.

Apparently in order to avoid giving the prosecution room to drive a wedge between the testimony of husband and wife, Ethel's examination by Alexander Bloch consisted of little more than her terse denials to the elder Bloch's lengthy paraphrases of the Greenglasses' testimony. Ethel did speak briefly about her own background and she was able to make the point that both she and her eldest son had been in bad health in late 1944 and for much of 1945, she in particular suffering from aggravation of a congenital spinal curvature and low blood pressure—conditions that presumably would have left her little energy for keeping house, much less running a spy ring. But aside from denying that she had ever typed espionage material of any kind and giving her own version of her two meetings with Ruth after Julius's arrest, Ethel could add little to what her husband had already said.

Ethel Rosenberg told the court that when she saw Ruth Greenglass for the last time on the weekend before Julius's arrest, she had offered her moral support only to be coldly rebuffed. Ethel also told of walking with Ruth from the house of her own mother, Tessie Greenglass, to a store nearby owned by Ruth's mother, where the two women sat for some ten minutes soaking up the sun and watching over Ruth's newborn infant, who was out for the first time in his baby carriage. Ethel had been unable to offer Ruth money toward her husband's legal fees, she admitted, but she had certainly never said anything about wanting David to keep silent. On the contrary, she had hoped all along that David would "tell the truth, whatever it was."

"Even if it implicated him?" asked Judge Kaufman.

"That is right," Ethel insisted.

"Then what did you mean [by saying you would] stand by him?"

"Well, I wouldn't love him any less."

Ethel's protestations of willingness to "stand by" her brother, in obvious contrast to David's behavior toward her, might have had more impact on the jury had she permitted herself to display any sign of emotion at being so betrayed. But she did not. Beneath her composure was a barely concealed contempt for the whole proceedings, which no doubt counted heavily against her when the jury came to weigh her testimony. The same sexist stereotypes that might have disposed the jury to feel sorry for a wronged woman dragged into a serious crime out of loyalty to her husband could easily be turned against a woman who failed to display the proper signs of victimization. Ethel's behavior on the witness stand and the reaction to it by spectators and the press was to be the beginning of the persistent theory that she and not Julius was the moving force behind their espionage efforts—a theory that would later find some powerful adherents in high places and eventually cost her her life.

Buttressing the impact of Ethel's behavior on the stand was the fact that the physical evidence, which took center stage at the trial—

the Jell-O box recognition signal, the gold watches the Rosenbergs supposedly had received from the Soviets, the much-discussed console table, which David Greenglass had not considered important enough to mention in any of his early statements to the FBI—all added up to a view of the Rosenberg spy ring as very much of a cottage industry. The whole truth would not necessarily have exonerated Ethel, and indeed under the conspiracy charge the whole truth scarcely mattered, since Ethel could be found guilty for the actions of her coconspirators. But the endless searching questions about these particular items took their toll, and on cross-examination Irving Saypol began with just these topics.

Asked whether she and her family had purchased passport pictures in May or June 1950, Ethel volunteered that she and her husband were "snapshot hounds" who frequently dropped into photographers' shops on impulse, partly to satisfy the "precocious" curiosity of their elder son who loved machines and gadgets of all kinds. But despite having had all night to search her memory after hearing Julius waffle on the same questions, Ethel could not say one way or the other whether the family had posed for any photos on the dates Saypol was asking about. She did, however, deny that there had ever been any pictures taken specifically for passports.

Saypol soon moved on to attack Ethel's version of her relationship with David and Ruth Greenglass. Here it quickly became apparent that Ethel was going to be at least as ready as her husband to seek refuge in the Fifth Amendment. A striking example of this occurred when Saypol asked: "A little while ago you said that you did everything to help Davey, do you remember that?"

"Yes."

"Did you help him to join the Communist Party?"

"I refuse to answer."

Since there was nothing to indicate that David had ever actually joined the Party, with or without help from his sister, Ethel's answer must have been a reflexive response to a line of examination about her politics rather than a specific attempt to evade the question.

Oddly enough, it was the questions that Ethel had chosen to answer freely that gave Saypol his opening to destroy her credibility. Under questioning by her own attorney as well as by Saypol, Ethel had made specific denials of many aspects of the Greenglasses' testimony. Now Saypol began reading back portions of the grand-jury record from the previous August—when Ethel had taken the Fifth on almost identical questions. Before the grand jury, Ethel had refused to say whether she had ever talked to Ruth about David's work at Los Alamos, or whether she had ever seen sketches drawn by David while he was working at Los Alamos, even whether she had ever discussed the case with Greenglass at any time prior to his arrest.

Why, Saypol wondered out loud, had Ethel thought that answering these questions might incriminate her in some way? And how was it that she was now able to make definite denials to almost identical questions?

Ethel was flabbergasted. At first she could think of no reply to this unexpected line of attack.

Judge Kaufman intervened, counseling her that "in your own interest, I think you ought to think about it and see if you can give us some reason."

And at last, after much indecision, Ethel managed to sputter that all she had known at the time was that her husband and brother were under arrest and there were rumors that the latter was trying to implicate her. She had been frightened. The explanation made sense. But the jury was probably more impressed by Saypol's point that Ethel had refused to answer such a wide spectrum of questions, including those relating to whether she knew Harry Gold or Anatoli Yakovlev, and by her repeated protestations. "I can't recall right now what my reasons were at that time for using that right," Ethel said at one point.

"Well, the right as you expressed it, was that it might incriminate you," Saypol shot back. "You said, 'It might incriminate me.' Those were your words, were they not?"

Emanuel Bloch was incensed at what was happening. Use of the Fifth Amendment was not supposed to create a presumption of guilt, yet how could this be avoided if a witness could later be forced to say why the privilege was claimed? Bloch complained that there was a distinction between the grand-jury room, where Ethel had been compelled to testify under subpoena and without counsel present, and the trial itself, where she was testifying voluntarily. No matter how many times the jurors were warned not to draw inferences from Ethel's present answers and her earlier refusal to answer, they could not necessarily be relied upon to understand all the complexities of her situation.

Some years later, in passing on the case of *Grunewald v. United States*, the Supreme Court would come to a similar conclusion. But in 1951 there was no clear rule regarding this use of Fifth Amendment testimony. Judge Kaufman noted that he had protected the defendants' use of the Fifth Amendment throughout their testimony, even though there were occasions when it might have been challenged. Ethel Rosenberg had chosen voluntarily to answer certain questions, and now Kaufman ruled that it was admissible for Saypol to point out that these answers were inconsistent with her previous statements under oath.

Manny Bloch did his best to rehabilitate Ethel, getting her to repeat that she considered herself innocent of the charges against her. She asserted:

> I didn't believe I was guilty then [at the time of the grand jury], I don't believe it today. As a matter of fact, I know I wasn't guilty then, and I know I am not guilty now.
>
> KAUFMAN: The point is, you answered these questions at the trial and refused to [earlier] on the ground that it would tend to incriminate you before the grand jury.
>
> ETHEL ROSENBERG: As I said before, I can't remember now what reasons I might or might not have had to use the grounds of self-incrimination then.

On this note, her confidence obviously shaken, Ethel retired from the stand. Her departure marked the end of the defense team's presentation. Manny Bloch announced that the defendants Rosenberg had no more witnesses to call, and Edward Kuntz indicated that Morton Sobell would not be taking the stand to testify in his own behalf.

The prosecution, however, still had a few surprises in store. Saypol informed the court that he intended to call several rebuttal witnesses, beginning with Evelyn Cox, the part-time maid who had been hired by the Rosenbergs in late 1944. Mrs. Cox testified that she remembered the by now notorious console table well. Cleaning and dusting it had been part of her job and she had never noticed any peculiarities that might have made the table suitable for secret microfilming. On the other hand, she disputed Ethel's testimony that the table had come from Macy's. She distinctly remembered that when she admired the table, Mrs. Rosenberg had said that it was "a gift to her husband from a friend." Some time after this conversation, Mrs. Cox noticed that the table had been stored away in a closet, a move she considered odd since it was far and away the nicest piece of furniture the Rosenbergs owned.

Mrs. Cox was followed by O. John Rogge's secretary, Helen Pagano. She confirmed having received $3,900 wrapped in brown paper from Ruth's brother-in-law Louis Abel, on the afternoon after David Greenglass's arrest. (Louis Abel had already removed $100 to give to Ruth.) The point of this testimony was purely to remind the jury of a subject they had not heard about now for some time since the defense conceded that the $4,000 existed, though it denied that the money had come from Julius Rosenberg.

Saypol's third rebuttal witness, Ben Schneider, was a surprise to the spectators (his name had not been on the official witness list) though hardly to the Rosenbergs, who must have realized that the prosecutor's intense interest in their dealings with commercial photographers was leading to something. Schneider, it turned out, ran a small photo studio at 99 Park Row, in the vicinity of the Foley Square courthouse, and he testified that on a Saturday around the middle of June 1950, Julius and Ethel Rosenberg had dropped into his shop and posed for three dozen passport-type photos, including poses of individual family members alone and together in various combinations. Schneider remembered the Rosenbergs particularly because the order was of an unusual size—it cost about nine dollars—and because the couple's two boys had been so unruly that he was afraid they would damage the equipment in the shop. He felt sure that the pictures were intended for use in passports because the man he identified as Julius Rosenberg had mentioned that the family was going abroad—to France, where they had inherited some property.

Ben Schneider admitted in his testimony that he had not been contacted by the FBI until about 11:30 A.M. the previous day, which accounted for the government's failure to list him as a prospective witness. Although he had seen photos of both Julius and Ethel in the newspapers on a number of occasions, he had not connected them with the customers he had served in his shop until he identified the photos shown him by the FBI the day before. Nor could he produce either negatives or business records to confirm his story.

The extraordinary luck of the FBI in locating the Rosenbergs' passport photographer on the penultimate day of the trial has long seemed one of the more suspicious elements in the government's conduct of the case. If the Bureau had reason to believe that Julius and his family had ordered passport photographs, they could have canvassed all the shops in the city several times over in the seven months between Julius's arrest and the beginning of the trial. Beyond that, it was an awfully strange coincidence that the photographer they did locate happened to run a business in the neighborhood of the courthouse, one frequented by federal employees on official and unofficial business. These suspicions quickened in 1952 when Oliver Pilat, a journalist close to Irving Saypol, revealed that Schneider had been brought into the courtroom by two FBI agents on the afternoon before his testimony during the time that Julius Rosenberg was on the witness stand and made a surreptitious identification of the defendants. "He wanted to be sure," wrote Pilat, "and when he took the look, he nodded."

The fortuitous discovery of Ben Schneider was too much of a break for the prosecution to be pure coincidence, but there is another explanation that fits the facts at least as well as the theory that he was part of a frame-up. Before the trial began, the FBI had not bothered to check out the possibility that the Rosenbergs had gone to a professional photographer for passport pictures, most probably because the existence of photographic developing equipment, though not a camera, in the Rosenberg apartment at the time of Julius's arrest led them to conclude that he could easily have taken such pictures himself. For some reason, Julius did not do this. Perhaps he had already removed his camera from the apartment for safekeeping. Or perhaps he simply felt that doing photographic work at home when the FBI was already watching and might move in at any time was riskier than going to an outside photographer at a time when he was reasonably sure that he was not being followed. In any event, the FBI would never have learned of Schneider's existence—except that someone had tipped them off.

Manny Bloch, in fact, had had enough experience with "surprise" witnesses of this sort to suspect that something of the sort had occurred, and his inability to figure out exactly where the information had come from was to haunt him until long after the Rosenbergs' sentencing. In the meantime, there was little he could do to overcome the devastating impact of Schneider's testimony, which was made all the more dramatic by the balding photographer's nondescript appearance and air of not quite understanding why his contribution should be of any particular interest to such an important proceeding.

And while Ben Schneider sat in the witness box, looking very much like the last person who had ever expected to play a role of such importance, the case of the century fizzled out with a final display of mutual irritation on the part of the judge and the attorneys for both sides. Manny Bloch, in a vain attempt to get Schneider to admit that he might have been too busy to remember any one customer or group of customers from so long ago, had asked, "Now there are some Saturdays when you do a rather rushing business?"

Saypol interrupted. "Did you say 'a Russian business' or 'rushing business'?"

> BLOCH: I didn't know that Mr. Saypol was a punster.
> KAUFMAN: You mean you haven't found it out after all of these weeks?
> BLOCH: I have been giving him the benefit of the doubt.
> KUNTZ: It seems to me, Judge Kaufman, in a case like this, that humor is out of place.
> SAYPOL: It is not intended as humor. I just want to be clear what his language was.
> KAUFMAN: Let's go on. Try to restrain your desire to be another Milton Berle.

After a few more minutes of questioning punctuated by such aimless bickering, both the prosecution and the defense announced that they had completed their presentations. Judge Kaufman sent the jury home for the night, warning them that they should show up at 9:30 the next morning, prepared for a long day.

18

The Summation and the Jury's Verdict

The art of summation theoretically consists of placing facts already presented to the jury in a framework that admits of only one conclusion: either guilt or innocence, depending on which side is taking its turn. Summations in the Rosenberg case, however, described to an unusual degree a case different from the one that the jury had actually witnessed.

Manny Bloch, as the chief defense lawyer, launched into his review by effusively thanking Judge Kaufman for his "utmost courtesy" and Saypol's staff for the "many, many courtesies" it had extended. Bloch's kind words for the judge and the prosecution went beyond the usual platitudes appropriate to the occasion and seemed especially odd in view of the fact that just minutes earlier, out of the jury's hearing, his father had moved for a mistrial on the grounds that Kaufman's frequent interruptions to interrogate witnesses personally had made it impossible for the defendants to receive a fair trial.

That out of the way, Manny Bloch went on to deliver a summation that could only have come from a lawyer who knew his opponents had the upper hand. Bloch pointed to the Greenglasses as the villains of the occasion. David Greenglass's action in testifying against his own sister was "repulsive" and a violation of "every code that civilization has ever lived by. He is the lowest of the lowest animals that I have ever seen."

Well, not quite the lowest, since Bloch reserved the full force of his wrath for Ruth, the jezebel "who came here all dolled up, arrogant, smart, cute, eager beaver, like a phonograph record. . . . Let me tell you something," Bloch fumed. "She is so cute that she managed to wriggle out of this. . . . Well, if she can fool the FBI, I do hope she won't be able to fool you."

The suggestion that Ruth, and David as well, had somehow managed to "fool" the FBI was as close as Bloch came to presenting a coherent scenario consistent with his clients' innocence. Harry Gold, he conceded, "told the truth." Nor was he willing to go so far as to charge that the supporting evidence was part of a government frame-up. "I am not attributing anything wrong to the FBI or the prosecutor's staff," Bloch insisted at one point, "let us get that straight right now." Yet this denial did not prevent him, moments later, from referring to the photographer Ben Schneider as the "phony Hollywood finisher" to the case or from condemning Saypol's questions about Al Sarant as "a peculiar method of trying to poison you."

Bloch's appeal was to emotion rather than to reason. All too aware that the Rosenbergs faced death sentences if convicted, he seemed reluctant to offend either the jurors or the judge by charging a government plot against his clients. But Edward Kuntz, summing up for Morton Sobell, displayed no such hesitation. Kuntz branded Max Elitcher a perjuror and laid the rest of the case against Sobell at the feet of Irving Saypol, who, he claimed, had gone to Mexico personally and "dug up poison" that made the Sobells' innocent trip there look like evidence of guilty flight. Kuntz did his best, but was able to advance no good reason for Sobell's use of aliases in Mexico, which was dismissed rather confusingly as a "brainstorm."

Alexander Bloch did not present an individual summation on behalf of Ethel. She had cast her lot with her husband, and neither of the Blochs saw fit to draw attention to the fact that the prosecution's case against her was far weaker than that against her husband. To put forth such an argument might have seemed to be a concession that there was some validity to the case against Julius.

The privilege of speaking last belonged to the prosecution. Irving Saypol could not resist beginning his summation with a shot at his antagonist Edward Kuntz, whom he accused of engaging in "a game they call kicking the prosecutor around." But when, at the insistence of Judge Kaufman, Saypol finally settled down to his prepared speech, he delivered a spirited rebuttal to the attacks on his chief witnesses, the Greenglasses and Max Elitcher. Saypol argued that few criminal convictions would be possible if it were necessary to rely on witnesses of unimpeachable reputation. If the Greenglasses were not wholly admirable characters, this was hardly the fault of the government; after all, it was the defendants who had chosen them "as their associates and partners in crime." More to the point, perhaps, was Saypol's reminder that the jury was not being asked to rely on the word of these witnesses alone. There was the testimony of Harry Gold, which even Manny Bloch had described as truthful. And, Saypol added, "you have the documentary evidence of Gold's registration card, the [Greenglass] bank account, the wrapping paper [in which the $3,900 had been delivered to Rogge], the testimony of Dr. Bernhardt, Dorothy Abel, Evelyn Cox, of Schneider, who took the passport photos."

The only really striking aspect of Saypol's speech was the depth of his evaluation of the crime at hand. Although repeating for the record that the defendants were not being tried for Communist activities per se, he charged that Communist ideology had brought the defendants to a "worship and devotion" of the Soviet Union and given them the motive to do the "terrible things" with which they had been charged:

> These defendants before you are party to an agreement to spy and steal from their own country, to serve the interests of a foreign power which today seeks to wipe us off the face of the earth. It would use the produce of these defendants, the information received through them, from these traitors, to destroy Americans and the people of the United Nations.
>
> These defendants stand before you in the face of overwhelming proof of this terrible disloyalty, proof which transcends any emotional consideration and must eliminate any consideration of sympathy.
>
> No defendants ever stood before the bar of American justice less deserving of sympathy than these three.

The intricately choreographed courtroom maneuvers that fascinate lawyers and trial buffs frequently make little impression on juries. This was particularly true in the case of the eleven men and one woman empowered to decide the fate of the Rosenbergs and Morton Sobell.

The panel selected to hear the Rosenberg-Sobell case was a homogeneous lot, made up of three auditors and two accountants, an estimator and an assistant sales manager, a caterer and a restaurateur, a retired civil servant, a Consolidated Edison electrician (the only black), and a housewife who did not work outside her home.

There was not a single Jew. This was not the result of a deliberate prosecution strategy, as was later charged. Potential jurors with identifiably Jewish names were excused by the lawyers for both sides, but still more had excused themselves because they could not condone capital punishment. Also, the voir dire had, as is usual, eliminated potential jurors who had strong opinions about nuclear policy or who read widely at all. This process had worked so well that at least three of the jurors, and probably more, had managed to remain entirely oblivious to the well-publicized atom-spy hunt of the previous year. As Charles Duda, youngest of the jurors at twenty-nine, later told journalist Ted Morgan, "I never heard of these people before. I never even knew they had been arrested. It came as a complete surprise."

Since the jury had not been sequestered, the panelists had relatively little chance to get acquainted during the trial. After Judge Kaufman finished his charge, the group retired with the U.S. marshals to an Italian restaurant off Foley Square for an early dinner and then returned to the jury room, prepared for a long and difficult deliberation. Foreman Vincent Lebonitte decided that the members of the panel needed more time to talk together; so he insisted that they review the case as a group before even attempting a vote. When the first poll was finally taken, however, the unanimity of the vote surprised everyone. All twelve jurors were leaning toward conviction for two of the defendants and only one person was against convicting Ethel Rosenberg.

The reaction to the vote was distress—not so much over the position of the lone dissenter but at the prospect of almost immediate agreement. Several of the jurors felt strongly that they did not want to render a verdict too quickly and thus risk giving the impression they had disposed of human lives without due deliberation. So for the next several hours, the jurors went back to raking over the highlights of the case.

At about 8:10 P.M. the foreman sent a request to the judge asking if they could return to the courtroom to hear the court reporter read back the testimony of Ruth Greenglass. Manny Bloch, anticipating that the jury might be debating his father's point about the supposedly rehearsed quality of Ruth's story, asked Kaufman to have the reporter read the cross-examination of Ruth as well. This request was denied in the presence of the jury, and Bloch would later cite the judge's refusal as prejudicial in one of his appeals.

At 9:42 the jury sent another request to the judge, asking to see all the exhibits placed in evidence during the trial. Except for those sketches that had been impounded, all were duly sent by messenger into the jury room.

While the nervous defendants and their counsel waited in a downstairs conference room, trying to puzzle out the significance of these requests, the jury had barely touched on the issue that was keeping them from total agreement. It was not until sometime after 10:00 P.M. that the majority addressed the doubts of the lone dissenter, James Gibbons. Gibbons, it developed, was convinced of Ethel Rosenberg's guilt. But he was a devout Roman Catholic and he anticipated that Judge Kaufman might very well sentence Ethel to death. His conscience rebelled at the prospect of taking part in a decision that could lead to the execution of a mother of two children.

Several of the jurors, including the one woman, argued hotly with Gibbons about his "squeamish" attitude, but to no avail. Finally he agreed that he would go along with a guilty verdict on all three counts if the jury were permitted to recommend leniency.

At 10:55 the foreman sent a query to the judge on this subject and Kaufman, with the permission of the defense lawyers, had the court reporter read back the portion of his charge that dealt with punishment. It said, in part:

> The desire to avoid the performance of an unpleasant task cannot influence your verdict.
> Now I want to say that if you want to make a recommendation, you can if you desire, but I believe it should be stated to the jury that the recommendation you are going to make or intend to make should not in any way affect your decision . . . and it is my prerogative to follow or disregard any recommendation that you may make on the matter of punishment.

This statement offered little comfort to Mr. Gibbons and only hardened the determination of several of the other jurors, who were not in favor of recommending leniency in any event. By midnight they were further from agreement than ever and foreman Lebonitte asked the marshals for permission to retire for the night.

Oddly, no provisions had been made for the jurors to be housed overnight. And when the marshals began making their last-minute calls, they had difficulty finding a hotel with twelve vacant single rooms on the same floor—a necessity if the court officials were to be present to supervise the jurors' comings and goings. After some delay, accommodations were finally found at the Knickerbocker Hotel in midtown and the exhausted jurors were bundled off; they were not to get to their rooms and to sleep until after two in the morning.

Roused the next morning at seven for an early breakfast at a nearby Schrafft's, the group was feeling rather less patient and cheerful than it had been the previous day. Everyone was now eager for Gibbons to set aside his qualms and let them finish their task. Although there was no real acrimony, not even any outright argument, several of the more convinced panelists took Gibbons aside one by one and tried to change his mind. Foreman Lebonitte recalls asking Gibbons whether his conscience would not also be heavy if Ethel were released only to continue her espionage role?

Gibbons's concern for Ethel's children was all very well, he recalls saying. "But what if she takes part in a conspiracy that dooms *your* children?"

It was this argument, Lebonitte believes, that finally broke Gibbons's resolve. At 11:00 A.M., just one hour after beginning their formal deliberations for the day, the jury announced it had come to complete agreement. All three defendants were found guilty as charged.

"I felt like Pontius Pilate washing his hands," James Gibbons told Ted Morgan in 1975. "If you know your Bible, you'll understand."

What of the other jurors who had not shared Gibbons's reservations?

When Ted Morgan interviewed five of the surviving Rosenberg-Sobell jurors in 1975, he found that not one had been in the least influenced by the subsequent controversy over the trial. Several mentioned that they had been impressed by the testimony of the maid, Evelyn Cox, and the photographer, Ben Schneider, since both these witnesses were assumed to be impartial. They also agreed that the Rosenbergs' frequent resort to the Fifth Amendment had made a bad impression while denying that they would have convicted simply because they believed the defendants to be Communists. No one appeared to have given much thought to the content of the technical evidence, though foreman Lebonitte recalled that it was only upon Bloch's request that the courtroom be cleared that he had "become impressed with the importance of it all."

Overwhelmingly, however, the jurors Morgan talked to agreed that they were convinced of the Rosenbergs' guilt because they believed David Greenglass. The defense's contention that no man who testified against his own sister could possibly be trustworthy did not, it turned out, find any takers on the jury. They saw the matter differently. No one had liked Greenglass, and one juror went so far as to describe his simpering, involuntary grin on the stand as repulsive. But by the same token no one could believe that even he would go so far as to make up testimony against his own sister. If anything, it seems that the very jurors who felt the most outrage at Greenglass's violation of family solidarity were the ones who also found him most believable.

It was James Gibbons who told Morgan, "I couldn't understand it then and I don't understand it now. Jealousy's not enough. You just do not testify against a relative unless there's something in it."

As for Judge Kaufman's conduct of the trial, most of the jurors Morgan talked to had nothing but praise. One man, however, did recall a possibly compromising incident. It seems that one day after court had been adjourned, the judge had introduced the jurors to Senator Charles Tobey, who was then conducting hearings for the Kefauver committee on organized crime in a hearing room on one of the upper floors of the courthouse. The hearings had been much in the news, as had the witnesses' frequent resort to the Fifth Amendment. Tobey complimented the judge in the jurors' presence, saying, "We could use people like you upstairs."

Finally, once the trial was over all the jurors seemed relieved to be able to put the case behind them. Twenty-five years after the fact, three panelists contacted by Morgan refused to comment on their roles. And even James Gibbons reluctantly had become reconciled to the unpleasant decision he had made and wanted no further part in any campaign on the Rosenbergs' behalf. Gibbons stuck to his resolve even when Julius Rosenberg's brother showed up on his doorstep some two years later, pleading with him to write a letter to the President asking for executive clemency. Gibbons recalls that as he listened to his visitor's request the thought kept racing through his mind: "Why me?" He had made his choice and did not want to do anything to give the impression that he had been coerced or was critical of his fellow jurors. "He wouldn't take his foot from the door," Gibbons recalled. "I had to kick it away."

19

The Sentencing

Just days after the jury returned its verdict, rumors of the existence of the covert government "lever" strategy began surfacing in the press. One of the first and most chilling indications of what lay in store for the convicted conspirators was a column by conservative commentator Howard Rushmore that disclosed that capital punishment was being "carefully considered," not just for Julius Rosenberg but for Ethel and Morton Sobell as well. "A few months in the death house might loosen the tongues of one or more of the three traitors," Rushmore speculated, and lead to further arrests.

Rushmore's prediction was soon echoed by such New York gossip columnists as Leonard Lyons and Hy Gardner, journalists normally more concerned with the private lives of Hollywood and theater personalities than with criminal prosecutions. Gardner, for example, included an item in his "Early Bird on Broadway" column revealing that "inside sources would have you believe that the three atom spies will get the death penalty so that they will crack and talk."

Although none of the columnists cited the source of this rumor, it was widely assumed that it represented the thinking of the U.S. Attorney's office. Irving Saypol was well known for what the FBI called "proclivities for publicity" and his young assistant Cohn moved in café society circles and was especially friendly with Leonard Lyons.

Roy Cohn has told us that he never believed there was any possibility that the Rosenbergs would change their minds about talking once their trial was actually under way and that he was unaware that any of his colleagues in the prosecutor's office had harbored such hopes. But documents obtained from the archives of the Foley Square courthouse show that the lever theory was indeed still very much alive as the day fixed for the Rosenbergs' sentencing approached. A private memorandum prepared by Assistant U.S. Attorney James B. Kilsheimer, for example, used this reasoning in calling for a triple death sentence: "Whether or not the death penalty is actually carried out, I do not think is the important consideration at this time," Kilsheimer wrote. "However, I do think it should be imposed in an attempt to induce these defendants to reveal the extent of their illegal activities."

In theory, any ulterior motives the prosecutors might have in asking for the death penalty were irrelevant. Once the jury had rendered its verdict, full responsibility for deciding the defendants' fates lay with federal judge Kaufman, who would hardly impose a sentence of unprecedented harshness unless he were fully prepared to see it carried out. The judge's independence seemed doubly assured in this instance since Irving Kaufman was to announce that he had taken special pains to insulate himself from outside influences.

When Julius and Ethel Rosenberg stood before him for sentencing on the morning of April 5, 1951, Kaufman announced that he was taking the unusual step of asking prosecutor Saypol *not* to submit any formal government sentencing recommendation. Kaufman went on to explain that he was forgoing the usual practice of soliciting a recommendation precisely because of "the seriousness of the case and the lack of precedence [*sic*]. . . . The responsibility is so great that I believe the Court alone should assume the responsibility."

Kaufman described the process of making his decision as a solitary struggle of conscience, spurred by his keen awareness of the heavy burden he had taken on himself. "What I am about to say is not easy," he cautioned. "I have deliberated for hours, days, nights. . . . Every nerve, every fibre of my body has been taxed."

One can well believe that pronouncing sentence on the Rosenbergs was the most difficult and unpleasant task of Judge Kaufman's career. However, there is also reason to believe that Kaufman's ordeal was neither as lonely nor, for that matter, as drawn out as his statement for the record took pains to portray. Documents from FBI and AEC files strongly suggest that Kaufman participated in highly improper *ex parte* communications with various individuals connected with the prosecution.

The first indication that Judge Kaufman may have communicated off the record with an official of the Justice Department comes in AEC chairman Gordon Dean's office diary for February 7, a full month before the trial convened. Faced with deciding just how much classified information should be released for the use of the prosecutors, Dean had conferred by phone with James McInerney, chief of Justice's criminal division, about the possibility that Julius Rosenberg might still break down and make a full confession. According to the diary, "McInerney said there is no indication [of a confession] at this point and he doesn't think there will be unless we get a death sentence. *He talked to the judge and he is prepared to impose one if the evidence warrants* [emphasis added]."

If McInerney actually had conferred with Kaufman and received a private assurance of the judge's intentions, as this diary entry indicates, then Kaufman had already irretrievably compromised his position. Dean himself, as a member of the bar and a former law professor at the University of Southern California, had to understand the implication of McInerney's remark, so it seems most unlikely that his diary entry was the result of a casual misunderstanding.

The allegation that someone in the Justice Department, either James McInerney or another official, had a private pipeline to Judge Kaufman's thoughts on the case is supported from quite another source. An FBI memorandum released under the Freedom of Information Act in 1975 shows the Bureau's Director of Security A. H. Belmont reporting to Hoover's aide D. M. Ladd that:

> While talking to Whearty of the [Justice] Department on the afternoon of March 16, he commented that with regard to the Rosenberg case if Rosenberg is convicted then he thought Judge Kaufman would impose the death penalty. I inquired as to why he thought Kaufman would impose the death penalty and he said, "I know he will if he doesn't change his mind."

Still other FBI documents indicate that, contrary to his explicit public statements, Judge Kaufman continued to solicit advice on sentencing from various sources after the jury had returned its verdict.

Thus, according to information supplied to D. M. Ladd by Roy Barloga, an FBI supervisor in New York, Barloga had heard from Roy Cohn as of April 2 that Kaufman had consulted with District Court Judge Edward Weinfeld and Circuit Court of Appeals Judge Jerome N. Frank and was leaning toward a death sentence for both the Rosenbergs and a lengthy prison sentence for Morton Sobell. Cohn had reportedly advised Kaufman that while he personally favored capital sentences for all three defendants, "if Mrs. Rosenberg were sentenced to a prison term there was a possibility that she would talk and that additional criminal prosecutions could be had on the basis of her evidence." Roy Cohn not only has denied that he ever discussed the subject with Judge Kaufman, he also has condemned all the evidence of *ex parte* communications between Kaufman and the prosecutors as "double and triple hearsay," adding that "since I am one of those quoted, I know that no such confidence was ever shared." One can hardly resist pointing out how ironic it is that Cohn, who apparently had no trouble believing FBI reports about the Rosenbergs, Sobell, and others, should suddenly dismiss them as "unsupported speculation" when they reflect on his own actions. More to the point, however, Cohn magnifies his own role in the disputed incidents with the unsolicited confidence that "I . . . was the only one who could theoretically have had such [*ex parte*] contact." Theoretically or otherwise, the sum of the allegations points elsewhere.

Specifically addressing the subject of Kaufman's reported discussions of the sentences *after* the jury's verdict was in, Cohn has emphatically defended the right of a trial judge to consult with any and all sources. However, he also states flatly that "in the Rosenberg case it never happened."

But it did happen. Even if Barloga's version of a Cohn-Kaufman conference is dismissed as "hearsay," there remains a firsthand and quite detailed account of yet another off-the-record consultation. This comes in the form of a 1975 letter from Irving Saypol to then FBI Director Clarence Kelley. Saypol's daughter Barbara had read an article by Professor Allen Weinstein in the *Smith Alumnae Quarterly* in which certain questions about the Rosenberg sentencing procedure were raised. She was distressed by the article's implications that her father had, after all, delivered a recommendation on sentencing to Kaufman. Saypol, it seems, was bothered more by the article's suggestion that he had originally opposed recommending execution but had been "overruled" by officials of the Truman administration. To set the record straight once and for all, Saypol provided Kelley with his own version of his secret consultations with Judge Kaufman on the eve of the sentencing.

On the morning of April 4, 1951, Saypol was summoned to Judge Kaufman's quarters and asked for his views on the sentences to be imposed the next day. According to Saypol, he unhesitatingly told Kaufman that he favored execution for both the Rosenbergs and a thirty-year sentence for Sobell—precisely the terms Kaufman eventually imposed. But Kaufman was not satisfied with Saypol's opinion alone. He wanted to know what Justice and, in particular, the FBI thought he should do. When Saypol confessed that he had not asked for an opinion from Washington, the Judge suggested that he go down to the capital that afternoon and discuss the matter. Saypol caught the next plane to Washington, arriving in time for an afternoon conference with Deputy Attorney General Peyton Ford and James McInerney. Much to his irritation, Saypol learned that neither Ford nor McInerney, nor J. Edgar Hoover, who was consulted by phone, was willing to support his recommendation.

Although Saypol did not specify the nature of the disagreement in his letter to Kelley, noting only that there were "differences all round," other FBI documents reveal that there was strong resistance at Justice to Saypol's plan to demand the execution of Ethel Rosenberg. The first indication of uneasiness in the upper echelons of the Justice Department comes in an April 2, 1951, memo from the desk of J. Edgar Hoover. The director's memo described for his top aides a conversation with the normally aloof and unflappable Peyton Ford, who had called that day to express his dismay over the rumor that Saypol would call for the death penalty for Mrs. Rosenberg. Ford had qualms about sending a woman to the electric chair and he was hoping that Hoover would share his distaste for the prospect. Wasn't it possible, he had asked the director, that Mrs. Rosenberg might be willing to cooperate with the government eventually if her life were spared?

Hoover told Ford that he could hold out no hope on that score. But for his own reasons, he shared Ford's belief that a prison sentence would be more appropriate. In contrast to the chivalrous Ford, Hoover's primary objection to sending Ethel to the electric chair was a practical one. Always concerned about public opinion, Hoover foresaw what others, in the flush of victory, seemed intent on ignoring: A death sentence for Ethel might be in tune with public opinion of the moment, but once passions had cooled the execution of a wife and mother with no previous criminal record might well come to be perceived as cruel and vindictive. In contrast to Joe McCarthy, whose career as the Senate's most prominent Communist hunter was soon to be cut short by his penchant for confrontation, Hoover understood that there were limits to the American citizenry's support for the FBI's war against subversion. Hoover warned Ford that Ethel's execution would inevitably generate "a psychological reaction [on the part] of the public" which would reflect badly on the FBI, Justice, and the entire government.

In addition, although Hoover viewed the argument that Ethel should be spared solely because of her sex as sentimentalism, he does seem to have been genuinely appalled at just how far his plan to use Ethel as a "lever" had gone. Immediately after talking to Ford, Hoover ordered his assistant D. M. ("Mickey") Ladd to prepare a memorandum on the FBI's recommendations for sentencing, paying special attention to the mitigating factors in Ethel's situation. When Ladd complied, Hoover personally annotated Ladd's memo, underlining those points that struck him as particularly telling and incorporating them verbatim into his own report to the attorney general.

Both Ladd and Hoover's reports show that the FBI continued to regard Ethel as an accomplice who could "be presumed to be acting under the influence of her husband." Further, in Ladd's words, "Our evidence against her at the trial shows her participation consisted only in assisting in the activation of David Greenglass." In the category of humane considerations, Hoover chose to stress not Ethel's sex per se but her situation as the mother of two small children. Incredibly, Hoover appears to have been the only government official to raise this objection to the prospect of a double execution that would leave two children orphaned. Perhaps Hoover was primarily worried about the wave of public sympathy that the children's plight might generate. Then again, Hoover may have found the prospect of Ethel's execution genuinely repugnant. The bachelor Hoover had been closer to no one than to his own mother, sharing her house and caring for her devotedly until she died after a long illness in 1938, and an idealized conception of motherhood appears to have been as much a part of his ideological makeup as his reflexive hatred for "subversives." Significantly, he was not to change his mind about Ethel's fate until much later, when secret FBI reports gave him an excuse for convincing himself that Ethel was not a good mother after all.

In contrast to his plea for mercy toward Ethel Rosenberg, Hoover had no qualms about recommending the death sentence for Morton Sobell. His report to the attorney general noted tersely that "although the evidence was not as great on Sobell as it was on some of the other defendants it was sufficient for the jury to convict him. He has not cooperated with the government and had undoubtedly furnished high classified information to the Russians *although we cannot prove it*" (emphasis added).

Hoover's thoughts on Ethel's sentence fortified the reservations already felt by Peyton Ford, and when Saypol returned from Washington on the evening of April 4, he was forced to report to Kaufman that there was serious opposition in the Justice Department to his recommendation. Kaufman found this news so disturbing that he insisted that Saypol call Ford back immediately. As Saypol recalled the incident in his letter to Kelley:

> It was at a public function that night that I phoned Mr. Ford in the presence of the judge who was attending the same event. Upon narrating to him [Kaufman] the Washington division [of opinion] I was then asked by the judge to refrain from making any recommendation for punishment the next day in the course of my closing sentence.

Soliciting sentencing recommendations from the prosecutor's office was accepted practice in federal court. What was questionable about Kaufman's approach was his decision to listen to Saypol's opinions in private while keeping the substance of the recommendations—and indeed their very existence—secret from the defendants and their counsel. Why did Kaufman choose this course, particularly in a case where the sentencing decision meant the difference between life and death? Assuming Saypol's version of events is accurate, it would seem that Kaufman decided against hearing sentencing recommendation in open court only after he learned that Justice and the FBI were in favor of a prison sentence for Ethel Rosenberg. The most likely explanation for his decision is that he feared that Washington's ideas would influence Saypol's statements in court. Having already decided to condemn Ethel Rosenberg to death, the judge did not wish to have it known that he was going beyond what the government thought advisable.

In spite of Kaufman's decision not to hear a specific sentencing recommendation from Saypol, there were still formalities to go through before he could reveal his decision. When the hearing opened on the morning of April 5, Morton Sobell's lawyer Harold Phillips began by asking the court's permission to present an affidavit from his client, detailing the circumstances of his kidnapping and illegal removal from Mexico. Never entirely happy with the decision to keep Sobell from taking the stand, Phillips was now making a frantic last-minute attempt to undo the damage by getting at least some of the story of the kidnapping into the record. Kaufman agreed to hear the affidavit read, but not unexpectedly ruled against Phillips's motion, noting that Sobell and his lawyers had elected not to present the evidence during the trial and could not change their minds now just because their gamble had failed to pay off.

In any case, Kaufman ruled, even if there were questions about the legality of Sobell's "deportation," these did not constitute a "fatal flaw" in the case. Irving Saypol chimed in his agreement, citing a precedent that had established that "the circumstances under which a defendant . . . is brought into the jurisdiction from a foreign place" were irrelevant to the government's right to try him in a federal court.

Like Phillips, Emanuel Bloch attempted to use the sentencing hearing as a forum to outline some mitigating circumstances that he had been constrained from mentioning during the trial (because they were irrelevant to his clients' contention that there had been no conspiracy whatsoever). Attacking Saypol for his attempt to make the Rosenbergs scapegoats for the Korean conflict and, for that matter, the entire Cold War, Bloch tried to argue that Julius and Ethel had possessed neither the motive nor the means to change the course of history to America's detriment. The Rosenbergs, after all, were accused of helping a nation that had been our ally at the time; had they been captured and tried in 1945, there would have been none of the "hysteria and hullabaloo" that surrounded their trial in 1951.

Bloch then went on to read excerpts from a *Yale Law Journal* article that held that the Soviet Union would have perfected atomic weapons in due course, with or without the help of spies—a point that seems self-evident now but that was hardly so in 1951, when some otherwise knowledgeable Americans still found it difficult to believe a nation as technologically "primitive" as Russia could have duplicated our secret weapon through its own efforts.

Finally, Bloch concluded his plea by stressing that even such notorious wartime traitors as Tokyo Rose and Axis Sally had received sentences of ten to fifteen years for the more serious crime of treason. On what grounds should the Rosenbergs, who had never actively sided with their nation's wartime enemies, deserve to be treated more harshly? "The worst that can be said of them," Bloch reminded the court, "is that, ideologically, during the years when they [*sic*] were allied with the Soviet Union they were extremely sympathetic to the Soviet Union."

These are precisely the arguments that continue to be raised in protest against the Rosenbergs' sentence to this day, and Irving Kaufman's reply to Bloch demonstrates that he understood and explicitly rejected every one of them. Reacting to Bloch's argument that the crime would not have seemed so heinous back in 1945 when the Soviet Union was our ally, Kaufman pointed out that the evidence showed the conspiracy had continued well into the postwar years. "The nature of Russian terrorism is now self-evident," he noted. "Idealism as a rationale dissolves."

Kaufman's further remarks show that he also accepted that there never had been any hope of an indefinite American monopoly over atomic weapons. Yet this realization did not alter in the least his estimation of the seriousness of the crime. The singular factor of the case in Kaufman's mind was clearly ideological; and his remarks were almost a textbook exposition of the Cold War crisis mentality:

> The issue of punishment in this case is presented in a unique framework of history. It is so difficult to make people realize that this country is engaged in a life and death struggle with a completely different system. This struggle is not only manifested externally between these two forces but this case indicates quite clearly that it also involved the employment by the enemy of secret as well as overt outspoken forces among our own people. All our great democratic institutions are, therefore, directly involved in this great conflict.

Once it is taken as axiomatic that any event is historically "unique," the time for rational analysis is past. The specific damage done by the Rosenbergs' espionage was immaterial since, by merely enlisting in the wrong side of the unprecedented ideological struggle, they had potentially provided the extra thrust that could tip the balance in favor of the forces of darkness. Describing the defendants' crime as "worse than murder," Kaufman charged that

> putting into the hands of the Russians the A-bomb years before our best scientists predicted Russia would perfect the bomb has already caused, in my opinion, the Communist aggression in Korea, with the resultant casualties exceeding 50,000 and who knows but what that millions more innocent people may pay the price of your treason. Indeed, by your betrayal, you undoubtedly have altered the course of history to the disadvantage of our country.

That absolutely no evidence had been presented linking the Rosenbergs' activities to Soviet policy in Korea or anywhere else was irrelevant, as was Kaufman's momentary forgetfulness about the precise crime at issue.

Harsh as the judge's words were, they were not really surprising, echoing as they did prosecutor Saypol's words of a few days earlier. Kaufman's final remarks were, however, enough to evoke the first real show of emotion that the defendants had permitted themselves so far. Julius Rosenberg, Kaufman stated, had been the "prime mover" in the conspiracy. Ethel, although she was a mature woman who was three years older than her husband, had "encouraged and assisted" Julius in the commitment of his crimes. Indeed, he argued, Ethel "was a full-fledged partner." Judge Kaufman noted that he had searched his conscience for reasons why he should show mercy and he had found none. Therefore, he was sentencing both Julius and Ethel Rosenberg to die in the electric chair sometime during the week beginning Monday, May 21, 1951.

Both the Rosenbergs had been prepared for the possibility of Julius's receiving the maximum sentence. But despite the rumors in the newspapers, Ethel's sentence came as a terrible shock. Visibly shaken and ashen-faced, the couple were escorted from the courtroom and locked in separate cells off a basement corridor of the courthouse. The guard assigned to watch them as they awaited return to their respective prisons reported that later that day, Ethel had tried to bolster her own and her husband's spirits by singing the aria "Un bel dì" from *Madame Butterfly* in a clear though tremulous voice. Julius, no musician, had responded with "The Battle Hymn of the Republic," a brave if rather grimly impersonal answer to Puccini's aria of love and longing.

Back in the courtroom, meanwhile, Judge Kaufman finished his task for the day by addressing himself to the third defendant, Morton Sobell. Noting that he was refusing to do the "popular" thing—presumably, sentencing Sobell to death—Kaufman imposed a prison term of thirty years, the maximum allowed under the law. In addition, he placed on the record his recommendation that Sobell serve his full term without possibility of parole.

From the spectators' seats behind the defense table, Helen Sobell let loose a scream of anguish. Even after hearing the fate of the Rosenbergs, she and her husband had clung to the hope that he would receive a light sentence in view of the fact he had not been connected with the atomic bomb. Neither had any notion of how close Sobell had come to a still worse fate.

While the stunned Sobell, his wife, and his attorneys were ushered out to join the Rosenbergs and Bloch for a lunchtime conference in a basement meeting room, Irving Kaufman returned to his chambers. That afternoon, he gave a brief statement to the reporters who had covered the trial, confiding that he was exhausted from lack of sleep over worrying about the responsibility he had just had to discharge. According to the next morning's *New York Times*, Kaufman also said that he had visited his synagogue several times during the preceding week "seeking spiritual guidance" in making his final decision.

That same afternoon, Kaufman placed a call to Edward Scheidt, the chief of the FBI's New York office, asking him to pass on to Hoover his thanks and highest compliments. Kaufman's message, as relayed on to Washington by Scheidt, was that "the FBI did a fabulous job on this case, an outstanding job, and that he could not find the proper adjectives for it. . . . he feels very secure 'knowing we have an FBI.' "

Only one coconspirator remained to be dealt with. David Greenglass had been named as a codefendant with the Rosenbergs, Sobell, and Anatoli Yakovlev in the indictment handed down the previous October. But eight days later—fulfilling an agreement between O. John Rogge and Myles Lane that had averted Greenglass's prosecution in New Mexico—Greenglass had entered a guilty plea before a federal judge in New York. Sentencing had been deferred until after the trial.

Contrary to the charges that would be leveled later by the Rosenbergs' champions, Greenglass's attorney, Rogge, had never had an explicit deal with Lane on the matter of sentencing. But he did assume that there was a gentleman's understanding that David Greenglass would get off light, with a sentence of no more than five years. As the attorney who had shepherded not just the Greenglasses, but also Max Elitcher and Louis and Dorothy Abel, into the government's fold, Rogge felt that this consideration was owed to him.

This understanding, whose existence was taken for granted by Rogge, is not reflected at all in the prosecutors' confidential communications with the Justice Department. On the contrary, Irving Saypol had planned all along to request a fifteen-year sentence for his star witness. Nevertheless, the reality of the situation had not come home to Rogge until he learned of the Rosenbergs' sentences on April 5. Although he and the Greenglasses had been well aware of the talk of capital sentences in the press, none of them had expected that Ethel would be sentenced to death along with Julius. From Rogge's point of view, Kaufman's harsh decision was a disaster; once two death sentences had been handed down in the case it was highly unlikely that the admitted coconspirator, Greenglass, would be allowed to walk away with a three- to five-year sentence.

Speaking on Greenglass's behalf at his sentencing hearing the next morning, April 6, Rogge delivered an impassioned plea that betrayed his mood of desperation. As Bloch had before him, Rogge attempted to make the point that American attitudes toward the Soviet Union had been quite different during the period when David was recruited to the conspiracy. Russia had not been seen then as an implacable enemy; on the contrary, as Rogge noted by way of illustration, the president of the borough of the Bronx had even declared an official "Red Army Day." Rogge further pointed to Greenglass's otherwise blameless record and his youth at the time of the offense (Greenglass had been twenty-two in 1944) and noted that, unlike the Rosenbergs, he had changed his view of the Soviet Union after the war. Finally, and quite presciently, Rogge pointed out that a light sentence would encourage others in Greenglass's position to "come forward" while a heavy one could only assure that further espionage prosecutions would become more difficult. Rogge suggested that a "pat on the back" in the form of a sentence of a year and a day would be appropriate, though in the end he called for a more realistic three-year sentence.

This was not at all what Judge Kaufman had in mind.

While praising Rogge for "his service to the profession and to the country," Kaufman went on to deny him the one consideration that would justify the advice he had given his clients, in their eyes and his own. David Greenglass received fifteen years—a term Kaufman characterized as "neither a light sentence nor a heavy sentence, but just a sentence." It was also precisely the sentence Irving Saypol had asked for.

The Greenglass hearing took place on a Friday. That weekend, Irving Kaufman left for a vacation in Florida. He was exhausted, but brimming with pride over his role in the trial. He believed that he had acquitted himself well.

Only forty years old, youthful for a federal judge, Kaufman had been a prodigy who graduated from Fordham College when he was only eighteen and finished law school at twenty, a year before he was legally eligible to take the bar exam. At Fordham, his undergraduate classmates had nicknamed him "Pope Kaufman," reportedly because he regularly outshone his Catholic classmates in the school's required religious courses. The authoritarian demeanor that may also have contributed to this nickname remained very much a feature of Kaufman's character in later years. Journalist Oliver Pilat, in an effusively fawning profile, was to praise the "iron discipline" of the judge's personal habits; less admiring acquaintances, who unanimously refuse to be quoted by name, have characterized him as a "Napoleon" on the bench. Certainly it was no secret that Kaufman had ambitions to ascend to the Supreme Court of the United States, and even his detractors concede that he had the intellectual capacity for the job.

Although Kaufman's belief in the defendants' guilt had been evident throughout the trial, his prepared statements, and notably his charge to the jury, had been meticulously correct. There is every reason to suppose that his remarks in pronouncing sentence had been thought out with the same care and with an eye to how they might enhance his stature as a jurist ten, twenty, or even more years in the future. Not long before, at the Brothman-Moskowitz trial, Kaufman had described the judicial sentencing power as "almost Godlike." In refusing to entertain formal prosecution recommendations in the Rosenberg-Sobell case, he had chosen to accentuate the "godlike" aspect of his role. Unpleasant as the task of sending two individuals to their deaths may have been—particularly for a federal judge who is not often faced with capital cases—Kaufman expected his view of the historical importance of the Rosenbergs' crime to be vindicated over time. The case would be a milestone in his career.

The first hint that it might not turn out that way came less than two weeks after the trial when the *Jewish Day*, a New York weekly, ran an editorial questioning whether Kaufman's sentencing had not been motivated by a fear of being criticized for showing leniency toward fellow Jews. The suggestion that Kaufman might be suffering from a "Jewish complex" was later picked up by a number of Jewish as well as Christian spokesmen who were concerned that the judge's remarks blaming the Rosenbergs for the deaths of American soldiers in Korea were providing fodder for anti-Semitic propaganda. When it later became known that Kaufman's wife's maiden name was Rosenberg (no relation, of course, to the defendants), there was even speculation that the judge had felt a deep psychological animosity toward the couple whose actions had thrown into question the patriotism of "respectable" Jews such as himself and his family.

There may well be some truth to the accusation that Kaufman's attitude toward the Rosenbergs was charged by a current of reverse anti-Semitism. A remark made by Vincent Lebonitte, foreman of the all-Gentile jury, gives some hint of that. Lebonitte, an admirer of the way Kaufman conducted the trial, said too candidly: "I felt good that this was strictly a Jewish show. It was Jew against Jew. It wasn't the Christians hanging the Jews."

Another theory, advanced more recently by historian Daniel Yergin, was that Kaufman was in thrall to his hero worship of J. Edgar Hoover. Yergin has pointed out that prior to his appointment to the federal bench, Kaufman served briefly as a special assistant to the attorney general, during which time he had personal contact with Hoover and became a great admirer of both Hoover and the FBI. Yergin even quotes an unnamed "former senior FBI official" as recalling that "Kaufman was historically pro-Hoover. . . . Why, Hoover was like Jesus Christ to him."

But these theories offer, at best, partial explanations for Kaufman's decision. After all, Hoover had not wanted Ethel Rosenberg sentenced to death, as Kaufman knew from his conversation with Saypol on April 4. Nor can amateur psychoanalyzing about Kaufman's "Jewish complex" account for certain unusual features of the sentencing procedure—from the alleged *ex parte* communications described in FBI files to Kaufman's decision not to hear a formal sentencing recommendation on April 5.

To understand Kaufman's decision it is necessary, first of all, to place it in the context of the atom-spy hysteria. Kaufman had every reason to believe that public opinion favored death for both the Rosenbergs. Moreover, the actions of the judges in previous atom-spy cases—notably the trials of Alfred Dean Slack and Harry Gold—had set a precedent for sentences that exceeded the prosecutors' recommendations. And, finally, the official interest of the AEC and the Joint Committee on Atomic Energy in the presentation of the technical evidence offered impressive support for the assumption that the Rosenbergs' activities had dealt a severe blow to national security.

The extent to which these influences were reinforced by behind-the-scenes pressure remains a matter of speculation. The evidence of the FBI files, combined with the hints found in Gordon Dean's diary, while not conclusive proof of impropriety, certainly suggest that *ex parte* discussions of the case took place. And the suspicions aroused by these documents are only reinforced by Kaufman's insistence during the sentencing hearing that he was acting completely on his own. The irony is that, for whatever reasons, Kaufman—a New Yorker, a Jew, a Democrat, and a man of otherwise libertarian instincts—felt compelled to impose punishments harsher than even J. Edgar Hoover thought called for.

The double death sentence becomes an enigma only when viewed retrospectively, in the light of Kaufman's subsequent career. Irving Kaufman went on to compile a distinguished record on the federal bench and ten years after the Rosenberg trial he was elevated to a seat on the Second Circuit Court of Appeals, which he now holds. He is known for his scholarly opinions and special sensitivity to civil libertarian issues. As one lawyer who has practiced before the Second Circuit told us, "If you have a case that involves a free-speech issue, Kaufman is the judge you hope for." And the distinguished Harvard law professor Alan M. Dershowitz concluded after studying Kaufman's Court of Appeals opinions that "he was not a government man: he often chastised the United States Attorney's office" and that he even was sometimes prepared "to free obviously guilty criminals in order to enforce the principles of the Constitution."

Yet at the same time, Kaufman has never been able to emerge from the shadow of the Rosenberg case, either personally or professionally. His continuing obsession, as revealed in FBI documents released under the Freedom of Information Act, would extend (as we shall see) to extraordinary efforts to expedite the execution of the Rosenbergs' sentences and to frustrate the appeals of the third defendant, Morton Sobell, as well as to efforts to goad the FBI into action against those who criticized his conduct of the case.

20

An Informant of Unknown Reliability

Manny Bloch had suspected immediately that something more than dumb luck lay behind the FBI's last-minute discovery of the passport photographer, Ben Schneider. A jailhouse informer or a hidden microphone in Julius Rosenberg's cell were two obvious possibilities, and Bloch warned his client to be extremely careful in the future about what he said and to whom.

Rosenberg heeded the warning only in part. He could not imagine that the very few politically reliable prisoners he had befriended in jail were betraying him and, in any case, his contacts with other prisoners were now practically nonexistent since, immediately after his sentencing, he had been restricted to a single cell, open to constant observation by the corridor guards. He was no longer even permitted to join the other men for exercise period on the House of Detention's screened-in roof. The suggestion that his cell might be bugged did bother him for a time, so that he restrained himself from discussing sensitive subjects with the one inmate who had been given special permission to visit his cell for daily chess games.

But Julius's discretion went only so far. He could not resist explaining the reason for his newfound reserve to his chess partner, who soon came up with a suggestion. Perhaps the warden would grant permission for him to join Rosenberg during the latter's spe-cially scheduled twice-weekly exercise hours. There they would be able to talk without fear of eavesdropping guards.

The warden was only too happy to grant this request. Julius's chess partner, Jerome Eugene Tartakow, was in fact the informer whose existence Manny Bloch had suspected, and he had been deliv-ering regular and frequent reports to the FBI ever since December of the previous year. Tartakow, a young inmate serving a two-year sen-tence for interstate auto theft, had managed to become Rosenberg's closest companion inside the House of Detention. His information had already led the FBI to Ben Schneider and now, thanks to Rosen-berg's continued trust in the face of his attorney's warning, Tartakow would be able to remain close to Rosenberg right up to the day of the latter's transfer to the Sing Sing death house.

Tartakow's role as a prison informer was one of the most shock-ing disclosures contained in the FBI files that were made available in 1975. Defenders of the Rosenbergs' innocence dismissed Tartakow's secret reports as worthless, and author John Wexley, in a new edition of his book, referred to them as "police suck."

Skepticism about Tartakow's bona fides is certainly in order. It does seem surprising that Julius Rosenberg would have been incau-tious enough to make damaging revelations, particularly to a fellow inmate who was serving time on his third conviction and had a con-siderable record as a petty criminal. Tartakow, on the other hand, had everything to gain from convincing the FBI that he was getting inside information from Rosenberg. From the start, he made it clear that he hoped for special consideration in exchange for getting close to Rosenberg, even asking at one point for a ten-day furlough from jail.

It is easy to assail Tartakow's character and motives but more difficult to dismiss the content of the reports he supplied to the FBI. A full examination of Tartakow's extensive file shows that, while he may well have embroidered the facts at times, he was able to give the FBI much new and significant information—information the Bureau was later able to verify through its own independent efforts.

Perhaps it is not really that difficult to understand why Julius Rosenberg might have given way to the temptation to confide in Jer-ry Tartakow. Tartakow, now a California businessman, explained the genesis of the friendship very neatly in a letter he wrote to *Washing-ton Post* reporter William Chapman:

Julie and I had common interests, including but not limited to the working class backgrounds of our families and our militant political inclinations as youths. . . . We talked together for hours at a time; we provided each other with comissary [sic]; we played chess in the special exposed cell in which he was confined for the entire period of his post-trial detention. . . . Julie had only Emanuel Bloch, and, for all too brief moments, Ethyl [sic] to talk with during this terribly trying time. . . . When the day was over, only I remained on hand upon whom to vent his emotions, absorb his frustrations, his anger; and with whom to share his confidences.

There was another reason Julius trusted him. According to Tartakow, he came with the very highest personal references: he was introduced to Rosenberg by the general secretary of the Communist Party, Eugene Dennis, who was also a prisoner in the House of Detention, serving a sentence for contempt of Congress. As Tartakow recently said, "Dennis and I had become close friends," before he ever met Rosenberg. "Gene Dennis didn't want the three of us [Rosenberg, Dennis, and Tartakow] to be seen together at the time," he added, recalling the Communist Party's policy of ignoring the Rosenbergs. Therefore, it was understood that Tartakow would act as a liaison between the other two. And Julius, apparently wanting to bolster his image in the eyes of Dennis, not only talked to Tartakow, he boasted about his exploits.

FBI files show that, far from "planting" Tartakow in Julius's presence, the Bureau at first wanted nothing to do with this volunteer stool pigeon. When Tartakow first made contact with the FBI on December 12, 1950, he immediately began angling for an FBI recommendation of early parole, promising, in the words of the FBI memo, that "his friendship with Rosenberg had prompted Rosenberg to extend him an offer of employment with his lawyers." Skeptical of Tartakow's ability to deliver on his implied promise to become a spy within the Rosenberg defense camp, the FBI refused to make any promises.

On January 3, Tartakow was again in touch with the FBI, this time promising to "tell everything he knew . . . whether or not he received parole." As Tartakow told us recently, he was by then acting as a sympathetic friend concerned to rescue Rosenberg from the consequences of his own silence. If Julius were unwilling to provide the information that could save his own life, then Tartakow would do so for him. A more cynical view might be that Tartakow knew it would be necessary to win the confidence of the FBI by tantalizing them with bits and pieces of gossip—no strings attached.

Throughout December, Tartakow had been speaking with Special Agent Armand Cammarota, the same man who had arrested him in 1949, but for this early January interview he was brought down to the Foley Square courthouse to speak with Special Agents Norton and Harrington, who were conducting the Rosenberg investigation. Tartakow talked nonstop, saying among other things that Rosenberg was philosophical about his own situation, since he "had played the game and lost" but worried how his conviction would affect his wife, Ethel; that Rosenberg did not believe that Ethel or Sobell would be convicted; that he felt that even if he, Julius, received a thirty-year sentence, "he will not have to serve more than five years because by that time we will have a 'Sovietized America' "; that at the time the FBI first came to the Rosenberg apartment in June 1950 he had refused permission for a search because he was concealing a Leica camera and $7,000, both of which Ethel later gave to a neighbor for safekeeping; that some of this money was going to be sent to Emanuel Bloch, disguised as a contribution from an anonymous sympathizer; that given another week of freedom, he would have been able to escape to Mexico by small boat; and that he was now planning an underground newsletter to be titled *Retort*, which would have articles defending himself and other atom-spy suspects and which he hoped to print and distribute with help from his lawyer, Manny Bloch, and Abraham Brothman, who was also a prisoner in the Federal House of Detention at the moment.

Many of these items could not possibly be verified; how many of them, if any, were accurate is anyone's guess. Even at that early date, however, Tartakow gave the FBI a few facts that established that he really did have Rosenberg's confidence. Thus Tartakow reported there were actually two spy rings operating in Manhattan, and that Rosenberg had told him he had headed one group and "that the other group was headed by two men, one of whom was in Europe."

Tartakow also volunteered that the FBI had recently interviewed the aged mother of this man and that she had given them the names of some of her son's friends, who were subsequently called before the grand jury. This was obviously a reference to the FBI's interview with Joel Barr's mother. Curious to learn how Tartakow might have found out about its interest in Mrs. Barr, the FBI checked and discovered that members of the Barr family had had dinner with Vivian Glassman, Barr's former fiancée, and warned her about the FBI's investigation of Barr's past. Glassman in turn had passed the word along to Emanuel Bloch, who must have told Julius. Thus Tartakow, who was nothing if not shrewd, began to earn the trust of the FBI by giving them a report on their own activities.

Although tantalized by the prospect of the inside information Tartakow was promising, the FBI was still wary, especially since Tartakow had made clear to Agent Cammarota that he would refuse to back up any of his reports by testifying in court. Tartakow had spent enough time in jails to know that life could be very unpleasant for anyone known to the prison population as a squealer.

Then, in a March 23 typewritten letter sent to the FBI via a contact in the prison warden's office, Tartakow revealed something so important that the FBI's resistance to his demands began to melt away. Julius, Tartakow said, was extremely worried lest the FBI locate a certain photographer who had taken passport photos of the entire Rosenberg family shortly before David Greenglass's arrest. Until they received this letter, agents Norton and Harrington had never considered the possibility that the Rosenbergs had visited a commercial studio for passport shots. Now, however, a last-minute canvass of the Lower East Side led investigators to Ben Schneider's studio at 99 Park Row.

In light of the origins of the Schneider information, Bloch's characterization of the photographer's testimony as "the vulgar and tawdry part of this trial" takes on a new dimension. And it was after this incident that Bloch began warning Julius about the need for discretion and Tartakow, in turn, began to express fears that Julius's suspicions would sooner or later center on him. The practice of removing Tartakow to the Federal Building for interviews was abruptly dropped after the informer complained that Julius had questioned him closely about the reasons for his trips downtown. From this time on, Tartakow either delivered written reports to the warden's office or met briefly with Cammarota there.

FBI headquarters in Washington was still adamantly opposed to offering Tartakow any special favors, warning that he was "definitely a confidence man" who might be trying to "capitalize on his knowledge of information which may have been available to the press, prison sources, etc. to present a convincing story." But Edward Scheidt, special agent in charge of the New York office, was by now convinced that Tartakow had proved his reliability.

Throughout April and into May 1951, the Washington and New York offices of the Bureau argued back and forth about their plans for Tartakow. In the meantime, he was continuing to pass reports to Cammarota that encouraged the New York office to believe Ethel Rosenberg was on the point of confessing. Ethel had been removed to Sing Sing prison in upstate New York a week after her sentencing, ostensibly because the Women's House of Detention lacked the facilities to segregate her from its other inmates, as was required in the case of prisoners facing execution. Manny Bloch had immediately charged that the government's haste to place Ethel on death row, separating her from frequent contacts with her lawyer and the possibility of visits with her husband, was a cruel attempt to break her. And Tartakow's reports confirmed that Bloch was sincerely distressed. According to Tartakow, Bloch had reported to Julius that Ethel was in a state of "slight shock" over the verdict and both men were very worried about her ability to hold up under pressure. "Yesterday was the first time in our association that he [Julius] had tears in his eyes as he spoke of the urgency of this need to leave here and join her," Tartakow wrote of Rosenberg's reaction to Bloch's news.

On April 23, Tartakow again wrote to the FBI, saying:

> As I have estimated previously, I believe that he [Rosenberg] is at the lowest ebb since the beginning of our relationship. I judge this from the manner in which his mind flits disjointedly from one subject to another, from the lack of consistent concentration he gives to any one problem, and from the many unrealistic hopes (for the future) he expressed. Physically he is in poor condition. . . . There is hardly a day goes by that he does not send for medication and were it not for the fact that he has so many sympathizers his lot would be completely miserable.

Julius's problems, Tartakow emphasized, stemmed not so much from fear of his own death as from anguish at his physical separation from Ethel. "This separation," he concluded, "has been something they had not anticipated. . . . A continuation—with subsequent problems such as they face now—would, it seems, produce interesting results."

It soon became apparent that Ethel, at any rate, was adjusting to her new environment better than either the government or Bloch had expected. And on May 15, shortly after the courts denied Bloch's *habeas corpus* petition for Ethel's return to New York City, the government decided to transfer Julius to be near his wife on Sing Sing's death row.

The move put an end to Tartakow's immediate usefulness, but Edward Scheidt did not want to break his contact with Tartakow completely. He still hoped to be able to arrange for a full interrogation to pursue some of the leads provided in Tartakow's written reports. Unfortunately for the Bureau, Tartakow's requests for early parole had now become a moot point. He was due to be released in a matter of days.

On May 25, Edward Scheidt wrote to Hoover, suggesting that he authorize regular payments to Tartakow as a means of insuring the informant's continued cooperation. Washington reluctantly approved Scheidt's request, still cautioning that Tartakow be kept on a tight rein "in view of his propensity toward being a confidence man." But Washington's letter of authorization shows that, despite its apparently standoffish attitude toward Tartakow, it hoped to receive more than cooperation in additional interrogation for its money. The understanding expressed in the letter was that Tartakow would use his freedom "for the purpose of attempting to penetrate further into the Rosenberg espionage network."

One of the things the Bureau wanted most from Jerry Tartakow was a lead that might help them to build an espionage case against William Perl. The idea that Tartakow could provide the key to Perl's arrest was planted on March 22, when he had reported to Cammarota that Julius had told him that "contact with Vivian Glassman asking her to take two thousand dollars to Perl in Cleveland had been made directly by Russian agents." Tartakow also quoted Rosenberg as saying that Glassman was "a trusted courier of the Russians" and that Perl "is also a Russian agent and had been set up to furnish info with reference to aerodynamics should he have been successful in obtaining a position with the AEC."

Asked to pursue the subject further with Rosenberg, Tartakow came back to Cammarota fourteen days later with an amended version of his report. Julius had explained, he said, that just before his own arrest he had somehow "furnished his Russian contact with the name of Perl among others as a person to be helped to flee the U.S. and that his contact had selected Vivian Glassman for the job."

Complaining to Tartakow about his control's poor judgment, Rosenberg had allegedly lamented that the control had made a very unwise choice, "since Glassman was too well known as a Communist to be used in this capacity."

The FBI, which had already begun to gear itself up to arrest Glassman on the basis of Tartakow's first report, interpreted this new information to mean that Glassman was *not* a regular courier after all and might know little more than she had already told. Ironically, then, the very first result of Tartakow's reports was the dampening of the Bureau's enthusiasm for moving against Glassman. Although Glassman would still be closely watched, the FBI from this point on tended to regard her as a potential witness rather than a primary target for prosecution.

Tartakow also noted in this report that Rosenberg had apparently managed to exchange a few words with Perl himself, who was briefly incarcerated in the House of Detention in connection with his arraignment on perjury charges. Reflecting on this meeting back in his cell, Julius confided over the chessboard to Tartakow that Perl's loss of nerve in telling the FBI about Glassman had been "a serious blunder . . . and was the cause of 'blowing up the works.' " He blamed Perl for caving in under pressure, Rosenberg said, but he still felt that he owed him a debt of gratitude; though "not a revolutionist" Perl had furnished him with "much valuable info including the plans for the use of nuclear fission to propel airplane engines." Rosenberg had supposedly also described Perl as a mercurial but "brilliant" man who had furnished him with some "terrific" material.

So far, Tartakow had whetted the Bureau's appetite without giving them anything that could lead to the development of independent evidence against Perl. Then, on May 22, Tartakow came through by telling his interviewers of a specific incident that had occurred "on a holiday weekend, which he [Rosenberg] thinks was July 4 of last year."*

Tartakow claimed that William Perl had used a holiday leave from NACA in Cleveland to return to Columbia University. There he removed some secret files from his old physics laboratory and took them to one of Rosenberg's apartments for a marathon photog-

---

*Tartakow was uncertain of the year. Later he suggested that Julius might have meant 1949, since he had been in jail as of "last" year.

raphy session. Four men had been present at the session: Rosenberg, Perl, "a man called in from out of town," whom Tartakow believed to be Michael Sidorovich, and an unnamed "fourth man." Julius had told Tartakow that copying the documents kept the men busy with two cameras for seventeen hours, working against the clock so that Perl could return the documents before they would be missed.

Tartakow also said that the "fourth man" was a member of the spy ring whose name Julius refused to reveal even to him because he had so far been overlooked by the FBI. Julius had told him, however, that this individual was the same man who had acted as a go-between in carrying instructions from his control to Vivian Glassman.

As soon as the FBI received Tartakow's information, they moved to check it out. Rather to their amazement, since they still had serious doubts about Tartakow's reliability, the story fit the facts. Checking the personnel files of NACA in Cleveland, the Bureau discovered that Perl had taken a leave from his job from June 26 to July 9, 1948 (not 1949 or 1950), during which time he had visited the offices of Dr. Theodore von Karman, his old mentor at the Pupin Lab at Columbia University. They also learned that Michael Sidorovich had been on vacation from his job at Tucker Industries in Cleveland on July 5 of the same year. Moreover, Sidorovich, who had admitted to owning a Leica camera since 1945, had purchased a used Studebaker in Cleveland on July 21 for $750—without withdrawing any money from his bank account. William Perl had also received an unexplained financial windfall that July, depositing $505 in a newly opened New York bank account on July 6.

During his visit to Columbia, the FBI learned, Perl had checked out and signed for a huge amount of classified material—a total of thirty-five test reports on such aerodynamics problems as "a comparison of hovering performance of helicopters powered by jet-propulsion and reciprocating engines; high speed wind tunnel tests of a $\frac{1}{16}$ scale model of the D-558 research airplane; and preliminary tests of the NACA 66-006 airfoil." In addition, the FBI was told by several associates of von Karman that Perl had the combination of von Karman's personal safe, which contained classified material connected with Von Karman's role as chairman of the U.S. Air Force Scientific Advisory Board. In von Karman's absence, the safe was technically under the custody of Dr. Carl Kayman, head of the mechanical engineering department, but since Kayman knew Perl as von Karman's trusted aide, his entrance into the safe would never have been questioned. Von Karman himself told the FBI that he thought it likely that Perl could have removed documents from the safe "without the specific knowledge of Dr. Kayman."

Checking back through the Pupin laboratory records, the FBI learned that Perl had also checked out substantial numbers of reports in May and June of that same year (1948). This led them to consider the possibility that Perl had used his position as aide to von Karman, which he had held from 1947 through the early part of 1948, to funnel classified data to the Soviets on a regular basis.

Over at the U.S. Attorney's office, hopes of building an espionage case against Perl were revived, and Myles Lane in particular favored delaying the perjury prosecution long enough to see whether it might not be possible to charge him with the more serious crime. The problem was that no jury could be expected to convict on the basis of the circumstantial case the FBI had compiled so far, and Tartakow's testimony was worthless since it was both secondhand and from a highly questionable source at that. As late as February 1952, Lane, now U.S. attorney in his own right, still hoped that laboratory examination of the returned documents would turn up latent fingerprints or other physical evidence that could clinch the case. But when the final lab report arrived, it was disappointing.

This lab report, dated January 23, 1952, and given to Lane sometime in February, concluded "that four skilled or semi-skilled photographers using two Leica cameras would be able to photograph the pages included with the reports receipted for by Perl on July 3, 1948 and also the reports receipted for by Perl during April and May of 1948 [a total of 1,885 pages in all] without difficulty within a period of 17 hours." Unfortunately for Lane's hopes, however, the lab was unable to produce fingerprint evidence or even proof that the documents had been taken apart and reassembled, although the report concluded that "it would have been possible to photograph the contents of the items without taking them apart."

Given this report, it now seemed unlikely that the government could ever prove the July 4 photographing session had taken place— at least, not without direct testimony from one of the men involved. The FBI then turned to Tartakow's statement that Perl had given Rosenberg data on plans for an airplane "fueled by nuclear fission." To those agents who were familiar with the early stages of the

Greenglass-Rosenberg investigation, this item sounded familiar. David Greenglass, they remembered, had mentioned something similar back in his first complete signed statement on July 17, 1950—though he had been unable to name the person who had given the information to Julius.

The AEC advised the FBI that the information mentioned by both Greenglass and Tartakow most probably would have been related to the Lexington Report, a detailed study of the feasibility of nuclear-powered aircraft, which was produced in late 1948. Several former colleagues at NACA in Cleveland told the FBI that the Lexington Report was strictly confidential and would not have been read even by NACA scientists cleared to deal with classified data without specific authorization. However, Ben Pinkel, chief of thermodynamics at NACA, had speculated that copies of the report "could have been left around for some time and Perl might have gained access to them in an illegal manner." It was also established that Perl's NACA supervisor, who also happened to be one of the few colleagues who was a personal friend of his, had charged out a copy of the report from the NACA library.

Investigators never were able to prove that Perl had actually been in possession of a copy of the Lexington Report. But they did find out that, in connection with his own analytical studies concerning compressible flows at supersonic speed, Perl had traveled to Oak Ridge, Tennessee, in December 1949 to gain information on a certain chemical extraction process—"one of the more highly secret projects being conducted at the Oak Ridge National Laboratory [which] deals with the shielding of aircraft powered with atomic energy."

One other loose end from Greenglass's July 17 statement that became relevant at this time was his claim that during the latter half of 1948 Rosenberg had spoken of an espionage contact who had been a "$200 a day consultant on the Aswan Dam project."

This particular allegation would later draw fire from Miriam and Walter Schneir, whose book on the Rosenberg case singles it out as *proof* that Greenglass improvised his entire story about Rosenberg's espionage contacts. The Schneirs, who did not have access to Greenglass's original signed confessions, erroneously maintained that Greenglass never brought up this particular incident until 1957, when he was summoned from his prison cell to make an appearance before the Senate Internal Security Committee. In 1956 and after, say the Schneirs, "the proposed high dam at Aswan was very much in the news. . . . But *there had been no Aswan Dam Project at all in 1948*" (emphasis in the original).

But the Schneirs were wrong. There was an Aswan dam project in 1948—not the famous high dam of today but the so-called lower dam project that was built during the middle and late 1940s with Westinghouse International as one of the chief investors. The FBI knew this very well. On July 21, 1950, four days after Greenglass first mentioned Aswan to them, they began working through the State Department to obtain lists of Americans who had served as consultants on various aspects of the project. Inquiries to Westinghouse, Republic Steel, and other major U.S. companies involved with the project had led nowhere. But in 1952, the FBI finally established that the Hugh L. Cooper firm of New York had hired a certain young scientist to do calculations on aerodynamics principles relevant to the design of the dam. His name was William Perl.

This was one piece of information that was easy to confirm. Perl had listed the Aswan consulting project on his own résumé.

Reviewing all the evidence in early 1953, the U.S. Attorney's office was forced to conclude that there was still no possibility of an espionage prosecution against Perl unless Rosenberg gave in and confessed—something Tartakow had led them to believe he would do once the appeals route was exhausted. The U.S. Attorney's office, which had been delaying the Perl perjury case in spite of constant appeals from Hoover, decided to go ahead. Ironically, once the perjury trial had actually been scheduled, Assistant U.S. Attorneys Robert Martin and Lloyd MacMahon received a visit from Perl's lawyer, who confided that he planned to advise his client to plead guilty and cooperate with the government in giving information relating to espionage.

Perl, who learned of his lawyer's plan shortly after returning from a vacation in Florida, wanted no part of it, preferring to stick by his original story. When his trial on four counts of perjury opened in May, his counsel was unable to challenge the prosecution's proof that Perl actually knew the individuals he had denied knowing under oath. Perl fell back on the defense that he had interpreted the word "know" subjectively—in other words, though he admitted being acquainted with Rosenberg, Sobell, and the others, he had not felt in 1950 that he was well acquainted enough to say he "knew" them.

Though sympathetic enough to Perl's situation to recommend clemency, the jury found him guilty of perjury in denying his association with Rosenberg and Sobell under oath. On two other counts on which the prosecution's evidence had been less compelling—Perl's denials that he had known the Elitchers and the Sidoroviches—the jury found him innocent. This was exactly the outcome the U.S. Attorney's office had feared: it would now be impossible to turn around and prosecute the Sidoroviches for denying that they knew Perl.

J. Edgar Hoover, meanwhile, would continue to hope right up to the day of Julius Rosenberg's execution that he would change his mind and give evidence incriminating Perl. A memo to Hoover from D. M. Ladd, written on June 10, 1953, the day the courts denied one of several stay-of-execution requests, shows that the FBI's strategy was still intact at this late date. Said Ladd, "If Rosenberg talks, we can probably prosecute for espionage William Perl."

When Julius did not talk, Hoover never forgave Perl for slipping out of his grasp. While Perl was incarcerated in the New York Federal House of Detention serving his concurrent five-year sentences, Hoover continued to receive reports on his situation—reports showing that prison life was being made as difficult as possible for Perl. One note, dated July 2, 1953, from a New York FBI man, informs Hoover that Perl "is assigned to duties cleaning latrines." The note goes on to say that the prisoner, in view of his educational background, had requested "technical assignments or instructor's work." However, "he was told to do a good job on the toilets and he would then be considered for a promotion to sweeping floors."

Whether or not William Perl actually did supply data to the Soviets through Julius was never definitively established. Investigation of the subject continued fitfully for some years, particularly after a defecting Soviet scientist reported that copies of original NACA data sheets were being circulated inside Soviet research facilities. The suspicions of NACA engineers about Perl's possible role were reflected in a story published in the *New York World-Telegram* on July 9, 1953. The article quoted high Air Force and NACA officials as saying that they had reason to believe data stolen by Perl might have been used in the design of the Russian high-tailed MIG fighter used in Korea. According to an unnamed source described as a "top Air Force expert on aerodynamics, ... the unusual tail of the MIG was specifically a NACA development as was another antiturbulence design feature which showed up on the MIG a surprisingly short time after the Air Force, with NACA help, had perfected it." And NACA director Hugh Dryden was quoted as saying that "Perl was in a position to supply information which could fill out a bigger picture of a whole field of information."

It is difficult to understand why such a brilliant and dedicated young scientist would have risked his future to become involved with Julius Rosenberg's spy project—especially in light of Rosenberg's alleged comment to Tartakow that Perl was "not a revolutionist." Perl, now deceased, maintained at the time of his imprisonment in 1953 that he was innocent of any wrongdoing. He never discussed the subject publicly again.

In the summer of 1951, Special Agents Norton and Harrington set out to explore a second thread of the allegations leading from Tartakow's secret reports. This had to do with the identity of Rosenberg's so-called last recruit—a man they believed to be identical with the anonymous "fourth man" who had taken part in the July 4 photography session in 1948. Further information provided by Tartakow suggested that this same "recruit" may have also been a link between Rosenberg's activities in New York and Al Sarant in Ithaca.

The possibility of a connection between this "last recruit" and Sarant was revealed on June 20, when John Harrington and William Norton first had the opportunity to quiz Jerry Tartakow at length for any fragmentary information he might have picked up that could help them track down this elusive individual. According to a Bureau teletype reporting the outcome of this conference with Tartakow, the informant told Harrington and Norton that this unknown man (whom the FBI called "X") lived with another unnamed individual ("Y"), who was the son of a wealthy man, a former law student not actively practicing his profession, and a "personal friend" of O. John Rogge. This Y, said Tartakow, had split with his family over his political ideology. He also owned a 1949 or 1950 model Buick convertible that was black with a white top.

Now there were two unidentified men instead of one, but Tartakow still had not said all he had to say about X and Y. In a follow-up interview in July, he began to describe Rosenberg's travels to pick up information from contacts in Cleveland and Ithaca. On one such trip to meet Sarant in Ithaca, Tartakow said, Rosenberg had been driven by X in Y's two-tone Buick. Since Julius could not drive, X apparently borrowed his roommate's car on a number of occasions to take him on such trips. This drive in particular, however, had remained vivid in Rosenberg's memory, said Tartakow, because for some reason on the return trip X "drove like mad," at speeds of 65 or 70 miles per hour all the way back to New York despite the fact it was raining the whole time. As to precisely what Rosenberg might have gone to Ithaca to pick up from Sarant, Tartakow was vague. All he could recall was that Julius had mentioned to him that Sarant had two contacts at Cornell, one a man named "Bedda (pronounced phonetically) and the other a man named Morris or Morrison."

Had Tartakow produced a live hand grenade and flourished it under the noses of Norton and Harrington, they could not have been more surprised. The man Tartakow called "Bedda" could be none other than Hans Bethe, who had been chief of the theoretical division at Los Alamos from 1943 to 1946; "Morris or Morrison" looked to be a reference to Philip Morrison, at the time also a member of the Cornell physics department and, like Bethe, a consultant with the AEC. If Tartakow's information had proved to be correct, the scandal would have exceeded even that wrought by the confession of Klaus Fuchs. As it was, two innocent men promptly became targets of a full-scale FBI investigation—one their associates assumed to be in retaliation for both men's well-known support of civilian control of atomic energy.

In the beginning, the FBI had some grounds for thinking that Tartakow's allegations might be on the mark. Robert Lamphere, the Bureau's Fuchs expert, pointed out that the British scientist had been in direct contact with both men as late as 1947 when he attended an important declassification conference held at Cornell. What's more, Bethe's name had been prominent on the list of potential espionage recruits that David Greenglass had given to Julius in January 1945.

On closer examination, however, there was less to the Bethe/Morrison connection than met the eye. Asked to explain why he had considered Bethe a likely prospect for spying, Greenglass admitted that he had never even met the man personally but had relied entirely on gossip about Bethe's political views. Nor did intensive FBI probing into the private lives and professional conduct of both men ever turn up the slightest evidence that either had done anything improper.

Both physicists had known Al Sarant personally, but under the circumstances that hardly suggested espionage. Bethe, as he himself pointed out to the FBI, had been approached by Sarant through Louise Sarant's father, Victor Ross, to sponsor his son-in-law's application for graduate study in nuclear physics. He had refused to recommend him on the grounds that Sarant lacked the necessary academic background. In Bethe's estimation, Sarant was "a frustrated type," the sort of man who had a grudge against the world because he felt that his abilities—average, at best, in Bethe's view—were never fully appreciated. Philip Morrison, on the other hand, had been a good friend of Sarant's, largely because the latter had chosen to build his new house in Ithaca next door to the Morrisons. Far from considering the proximity of the two houses incriminating, the FBI thought it unlikely Sarant would choose to live so close to someone who was actively supplying him with scientific data.

So in the end the FBI concluded that Bethe and Morrison, themselves totally innocent, had most likely been assigned to Sarant as targets for espionage penetration. This explanation, which still seems the most credible one today in light of the information the Bureau gathered, accounts for all the initiatives Sarant made that seemed designed to bring him in close contact with members of the Cornell physics department. After his initial application for graduate study had been rejected, for example, Sarant managed to receive permission to use the physics department library, supposedly to do reading in preparation for a second attempt to gain admission as a student. Sarant never did reapply, though for some time he was a familiar figure around the library, which was located approximately seventy-five feet from the door to Bethe's office. Later, presumably through his friendship with Weldon Bruce Dayton, Sarant managed to secure a position as engineer on the Cornell synchrotron project. The synchrotron was not in itself a secret project; still, it is possible that Sarant was able to use his job to collect useful information about details of the synchrotron design or about the particular experiments in particle physics then being performed at Cornell.

The FBI's remaining hope of indicting more members of the Rosenberg spy ring now lay in finding and building a case against the man Tartakow had referred to as Julius's valuable "last recruit."

As it turned out, identifying Mr. X was easy. Proving that he had been an active espionage agent was something else again. To learn X's name, the Bureau had only to look in its own files: he was Maxwell Finestone, whose name had popped up in their investigation as early as July 1950, when it was among those listed in the address finder seized during the search of Alfred Sarant's home.

At that time, Louise Sarant had told the FBI that Finestone was a former Ithaca classmate of hers who had worked as a house painter for her husband in the summer of 1949 when the Sarants were building their own home. Suspicions were aroused when investigators learned that Finestone, formerly an active member of the Ithaca Communist Party, was already mentioned in their files of political activists. On a hunch, FBI agents showed Finestone's picture to the Morton Street building superintendent, Floyd Elwyn. He promptly identified Finestone, along with William Perl and Weldon Bruce Dayton, as having been three of the four men whom he had seen moving furniture out of the Morton Street apartment at the end of January 1950. Elwyn's memory was by no means entirely reliable—his identification of Dayton, in particular, may have been in error—but where Finestone was concerned, he turned out to be 100 percent correct. Further investigation showed that Finestone had indeed been the last to sublease the Morton Street apartment from Sarant, living there from the fall of 1949 until it was vacated at the end of January 1950. After leaving Morton Street, Finestone had moved to his friend James Weinstein's apartment on East Ninth Street.

The FBI did not attempt to talk to Finestone directly until August 21, 1950, a few days after Morton Sobell's well-publicized arrest. Finestone did not appear to be at all surprised by the FBI's appearance on his doorstep and he brushed aside agents Royal and Littlejohn's questions about Sarant, saying, "You know why you're here, and I know why you're here, so let's not kid each other." Before showing his visitors the door, Finestone assured them that he would consult his lawyer and would be in touch if there were anything further for him to contribute.

Finestone was eventually called to testify before the grand jury, where he took the Fifth Amendment, but in the meantime the FBI's interest in him lagged. Both David Greenglass and Harry Gold failed to identify his photograph and agent Royal concluded that although Finestone may have known some answers to the Bureau's questions about the Morton Street apartment, it was equally likely that he would continue to remain silent to avoid implicating Alfred Sarant.

The FBI became curious about Finestone again after the surveil-

lance team that was still busily tailing Vivian Glassman identified
him from a photograph as the "unknown subject" who had been seen
with Glassman on April 5—the evening of the day that the Rosenbergs were sentenced to death. Finestone, or at least a man the FBI
believed to be Finestone, had arrived at Glassman's apartment in a
car borrowed from the brother of her lawyer; the two had gone out
together, with Glassman not returning home until the "late hours."
The implication, as far as the FBI was concerned, was that anyone
who had been with Glassman on that particular evening, when she
must have been upset over the fate of her friend Ethel Rosenberg,
most likely knew her quite well.

As a result of this episode, the FBI finally got around to talking
to Gary Pickard, an Ithaca friend of Finestone's who had shared the
Morton Street apartment briefly at the end of 1949. Under the threat
of a grand jury subpoena, Pickard agreed to return from Utah, where
he was then living, to be interviewed by agents of the FBI's New
York office. Pickard denied that the Morton Street apartment had
been anything but a casual bachelor's residence, which he had moved
into on the invitation of Finestone, a former Cornell classmate he
had run across by chance in New York. He did recall, however, that
Finestone had been "very mysterious" about the identity of the Sarants, whose name was still on the doorbell and who apparently continued to pay the rent every month.

Gary Pickard also confirmed Floyd Elwyn's memory that four
men had been present on the day he and Finestone moved out. As he
remembered it, he had been busy packing his clothes when two
strangers showed up at the door asking for Max. He had told them
they could find his friend in the basement storage room, where Finestone was seeing to the storage of some furniture left behind by previous tenants. Later, when Pickard had finished gathering his things,
he went downstairs; there, Finestone introduced the two men to him
as "Bill" and "Bruce." Then they all got into Finestone's car, a late-
model Buick convertible borrowed from his new roommate, and
dropped the two men at the nearest subway stop. Shown "numerous"
photographs, Gary Pickard identified William Perl and Weldon
Bruce Dayton as being the strangers he had seen that day.

Was Pickard's story accurate? Weldon Bruce Dayton swore that
he had never been anywhere near 65 Morton Street, and the FBI half
believed him, especially since there were contradictions between the

statements of Floyd Elwyn and Pickard. Elwyn insisted that he had once seen Dayton in the kitchen of the Sarant apartment having breakfast in his pajamas. Pickard, on the other hand, was sure Dayton had never stayed at the apartment overnight and thought that it was he whom Elwyn had seen in pajamas.

The New York office of the FBI was still puzzling over the significance, if any, of the Pickard story when Tartakow began talking about "X" and "Y" on June 20, 1951. Now it was Pickard's mention of Finestone driving a borrowed Buick that stood out as the most intriguing part of the tale, and Special Agent Robert Royal, one of the pair of agents who had investigated Finestone a year earlier, was assigned to look into the matter.

Royal quickly concluded that Finestone's East Ninth Street roommate, James Weinstein, had to be the individual Tartakow called "Y": Weinstein was the "son of a wealthy man" (clothing manufacturer Joseph Weinstein), a law school dropout, and had owned not one but two Buick convertibles: a 1940 and a 1949 model. This conclusion was further confirmed when Special Agent John Harrington consulted with O. John Rogge the next day, June 22, and learned that Joseph Weinstein was indeed a former client of Rogge's. Rogge also agreed that the elder Weinstein had frequently quarreled with his son because he considered the young man's friends too "radical."

The FBI was now sure that Max Finestone was "X," but it was quite another thing to prove that he had played an active role in Rosenberg's spy ring. As agent Royal's summary report on the matter concedes, the Bureau could not even establish that Finestone had ever borrowed his roommate's car to drive Julius Rosenberg to Ithaca, much less that he was the courier who gave Vivian Glassman $2,000 for William Perl or one of the four photographers who had taken part in the alleged photography session on the July 4 weekend of 1948.

In an effort to shake loose more information, the government subpoenaed James Weinstein to appear before the federal grand jury. Weinstein's family begged him to talk, even calling on O. John Rogge, who also urged cooperation. But Weinstein, who had refused to speak with the FBI in 1950, also elected to remain silent before the grand jury.

Interestingly enough, FBI reports on its investigation of Weinstein and Finestone continue to refer to Jerome Tartakow as an informant of "unknown reliability" as late as the end of 1952. Nor is there any indication that the Bureau ever considered pressuring Tartakow to go public with his accusations. Even they did not see him as a potential witness. The skepticism of the FBI is, in the last analysis, the best proof that Tartakow was getting his information from Julius Rosenberg himself and not merely regurgitating information planted by the Bureau's own agents. What point would there be to fabricating an entire set of communications from an ersatz source if the FBI never intended to use the documents publicly? And if it did intend to set Tartakow up as a public accuser, why continue to fill the documentary record with negative comments on his reliability?

A final possibility, that Tartakow pieced together information gleaned from one or more third parties, is equally unlikely. It has been suggested, for example, that Tartakow might have talked with William Perl, who passed through the House of Detention briefly that spring. He might also have learned something of interest from Abraham Brothman, another inmate who was close to Rosenberg for a time until they had a falling out (presumably because Brothman grew frightened that associating with Rosenberg would complicate his own situation). There was no reason, however, for Perl to have placed any faith in Tartakow during the four-day period they were under the same prison roof. As for Brothman, he had little or no direct contact with Rosenberg during the posttrial period when Tartakow was producing his most valuable reports. It is theoretically possible that Rosenberg had earlier talked to Brothman, who much later relayed the stories to Tartakow. But even if Tartakow did gain his information in this circuitous way—which is difficult to believe—this does not change the fact that the original source must have been Rosenberg.

On the other hand, it would be as unwise now as then to take Tartakow's statements about X as having the weight of fact. Tartakow had named others as members of the spy ring who were not, in fact, involved, and his identification of X with the Glassman incident and the photographing of the Perl documents could have been guesswork. In this light, it is worthwhile to note that, on the subject of Rosenberg's trip to Ithaca, Tartakow remembered Julius saying he had asked both Louise Sarant and X to leave the room before speaking to Sarant about the purpose of his visit. Thus, even Tartakow's account leaves room for doubt about whether Julius's driver had been fully aware of the purpose of the journey.

But in spite of the hearsay nature of its information, the FBI did not give up easily in its effort to make an espionage case against Finestone. In an attempt to pressure James Weinstein into changing his mind about giving information against his former roommate, the FBI made periodic visits to his employer to "check" on his working hours and paid visits to his relatives during which it was suggested, none too subtly, that Weinstein himself could become a target of prosecution unless he chose to be more helpful.

Finestone, meanwhile, having already refused twice to answer questions put to him before a grand jury, was summoned for yet another grand jury appearance in 1953 in connection with the impending perjury prosecution of William Perl. This time the prosecutors took the highly unusual step of issuing an additional subpoena to Finestone's lawyer, Victor Rabinowitz. When Rabinowitz refused to testify, Assistant U.S. Attorney Robert Martin tried to have him cited for contempt, claiming that a joint conference Rabinowitz was known to have held with four of his clients—Finestone, Arthur and Muriel Boudin, owners of the car Finestone used to visit Glassman, and another woman—was not protected by attorney-client privilege. Martin's argument that the presence of more than one client vitiated the privilege of confidentiality did not impress federal judge Gregory Noonan, however, who refused to allow such a blatant abuse of the grand jury to intimidate a member of the bar. Victor Rabinowitz was excused from testifying.

Finestone's silence before the grand jury in 1953 marked the end, for all practical purposes, of the government's desperate bid to crack the Rosenberg spy ring from a new angle. Continually frustrated by their inability to find a new witness, the FBI and the prosecutors never seemed to comprehend that their failure was at least in part due to their own overzealousness. O. John Rogge had warned at the time David Greenglass received his fifteen-year sentence that the court's decision would effectively deter others from talking—provided, of course, that the awful prospect of becoming the instrument of a friend's death or incarceration for thirty years was not already enough of a deterrent. The draconian sentences meted out to the various principals in the atom-spy cases, confessed and unconfessed alike, ensured that others who had knowledge, however fleeting, of

Julius Rosenberg's espionage activities would retreat behind a wall of silence.

This wall of silence remained unbreached for nearly three decades while defenders of the Rosenbergs denigrated the government's hints about the existence of a wider spy ring as a paranoid fantasy born of the FBI's vendetta against the Left. But a uniquely placed source, speaking for publication for the first time, has now agreed to give independent confirmation of the existence of a postwar spy network. The new witness is James Weinstein, currently editor-in-chief of *In These Times*, a socialist newspaper published in Chicago, and the author of several books on the American Left. In the belief that the time had now come to set the record straight, Weinstein agreed to tell the story he refused to reveal to the FBI or to the grand jury in 1951.

During the academic year of 1948–49, Weinstein and his friend Max Finestone were both seniors at Cornell University and both members of the Communist Party. Sometime in the middle of the school year, Weinstein says, Finestone told him that he was quitting the Party to do "secret work." Weinstein had no idea what Max was up to and he knew enough not to ask for details. About this time, Finestone went to work for Alfred Sarant's small contracting business in Ithaca.

Many times during the school year, Max asked to borrow Weinstein's car, a 1940 Buick convertible. Weinstein assumed Max was using the car to visit his parents at their nearby farm. Later he came to believe that Max was using it for trips connected with his "secret work."

In June 1949, Weinstein graduated, moved back to New York City, and prepared to enter Columbia Law School. That fall, he paid a weekend visit to Cornell, staying at the Finestone farm. At the end of the weekend, Weinstein says, Max asked him to give someone a lift back to New York. The "someone" who shortly showed up at the farm—a plain-looking man with spectacles and a mustache—was introduced only as "Julius." During the long trip back to New York City, Weinstein reports, "Julius" sat in the back of the car and never said a word. (Another former Cornell student sat in front. Interviewed about the ride, this man said he could not, thirty years later, remember anything of it.) When they arrived at the George Washington Bridge, "Julius" asked to be let off.

In the fall of 1949, Max Finestone moved to New York. At first he stayed at the apartment at 65 Morton Street, which Al Sarant had made available to him. But at the end of December, he phoned Weinstein to say that he had to get out of the apartment and to suggest that they become roommates. Weinstein agreed to share his apartment with his old friend, and Finestone moved from the Morton Street address within a few days of their conversation. Finestone continued to borrow Weinstein's car on occasions (and it must have been sometime in May or June that he used it for the trip to Ithaca described by Tartakow).

One evening in early July 1950, there was a knock on the door of the East Ninth Street apartment that the two men now shared. Weinstein opened the door to find that the person standing there was the "Julius" he had driven back from Ithaca. Julius asked if Max was in. When Jim answered no, he responded, "Tell him Julius was here," turned on his heel, and left. Max came home later that evening and Weinstein mentioned that "Julius" had been around looking for him. According to Weinstein, Max asked nervously whether he was sure it was Julius. Weinstein replied that it was the same person he had driven back from Ithaca. At this, recalled Weinstein, "Max turned white as a sheet" and blurted out: "He knows he's not supposed to come here."

All these incidents didn't fall into place for Weinstein until two weeks later, when, recognizing Julius's picture on the front page of the newspaper, he read of his arrest for spying. Weinstein became enraged at Finestone, not so much for his clandestine activities as for moving in with him when the heat was on. Weinstein says Finestone never tried to explain, but merely said, "I thought it would look better."

Max Finestone is now in his late fifties. For most of the time since the Rosenberg trial, he and his wife have owned and operated a small summer resort. Interviewed at his upstate New York home, Finestone said that Weinstein was mistaken on several points in his account. On Weinstein's driving Rosenberg back from Ithaca, Finestone said: "I remember Julius being in Ithaca but I don't remember that incident." On Rosenberg appearing at their shared apartment in July 1950 and asking for him, Finestone denied that the incident ever occurred. "I think Jim is fantasizing. I never said to Jim, 'I told him never to come here.' That is pure fantasy." Weinstein, he added, was simply "remembering things I just don't remember."

Finestone did confirm that he dropped out of the Communist

Party at Cornell in the middle of his senior year, but claims it was because of schoolwork. He denies that he told Weinstein it was to engage in "secret work." Finestone said he moved out of the Morton Street apartment because sharing an apartment with Weinstein was simply "a better deal."

Concerning his relationship with Julius Rosenberg, Finestone said: "We were acquainted briefly in the 1940s." When pressed for more details, he replied, "You're asking me to tell you things about his movements and activities. I don't know where this is leading to. I'm disturbed by this line of questioning." Saying that for all he knew we might be FBI or CIA agents, Finestone stressed that he did not want to say anything that "could be used for purposes contrary to what I want them to be used for."

Later in the conversation, Finestone responded to our suggestion that lower-level espionage might have been going on after the war, saying: "If you get me and Joel Barr to say sure, we were engaged in espionage but it was only innocent industrial espionage for principled reasons—then the government gets hold of this and they say, at least they admit they were engaged in espionage." That, Finestone said, would help the government improve its case, and he was not about to do that. "Even if I knew anything that you don't know," he concluded, "I certainly wouldn't say anything." Then Finestone firmly denied knowing about any form of espionage involving himself, Barr, Sarant, or Rosenberg.

Jerry Tartakow's secret reports may not have led to any further espionage convictions, but when it came to keeping his promise that he would be able to infiltrate the Rosenberg camp, he proved as good as his word. In early July 1951, not long after his release from the House of Detention, Tartakow showed up at Manny Bloch's office armed with a letter of reference from Eugene Dennis and promising to do anything he possibly could to help his friend Julie.

Bloch apparently took the reference from Dennis at face value, but was somewhat at a loss at what to do with the services of a glib and perhaps overeager ex-convict. According to the report Tartakow later gave agent Cammarota, Bloch was extremely nervous about the possibility that his apartment and office were being bugged by the FBI and suggested they go outside to talk in the street, where they could be sure their conversation would be confidential. There, in the words of the FBI's summary of Tartakow's report, "Bloch stated that he believed in [Julius] Rosenberg's innocence but admitted that as a practical matter he realized that Rosenberg was involved in some manner of espionage."

This guarded admission can hardly have been very pleasing to the FBI since it was a major retreat from Tartakow's earlier assurances that Bloch knew all about Rosenberg's espionage activities and had been relaying messages from William Perl, Vivian Glassman, and others to Rosenberg in prison. Equally disappointing from the FBI's point of view, Tartakow said that Bloch had made a point of assuring him that he would never ask him to do anything illegal.

Bloch's statements during this conversation, even assuming that Tartakow was reporting them accurately, hardly sounded like the words of a man who was about to recruit anyone into an espionage network. Nevertheless, Tartakow, with full approval from his FBI contact, persisted in trying to win Bloch's confidence. Shortly after this meeting with Bloch, Tartakow wrote a personal letter to Julius Rosenberg, stressing his continued friendship and admiration and promising to do anything that might be of service to Julius and Ethel. Bloch hand-delivered the letter when he visited Sing Sing in August, but according to the secret report of the prison guard who eavesdropped on visits between the Rosenbergs and their lawyer, Julius was preoccupied with other matters, chiefly worries about his children and his anger over the news that prosecutor Irving Saypol was a candidate for a state supreme court judgeship. Like Bloch, Rosenberg was happy to have an expression of support from a friend but "did not appear to be enthused" at the offer of help.

While waiting for the appeals courts to act on their cases, Julius and Ethel's restricted visiting time with Manny Bloch was almost wholly taken up with the subject of their children. Bloch had managed by now to have the Rosenberg sons, Robby and Michael, removed from the Hebrew Children's Home in the Bronx and placed in the custody of their paternal grandmother, Sophie Rosenberg. But the new arrangement, far from relieving Manny Bloch of the responsibility for the children's interests, created problems of its own. Mrs. Rosenberg, frail and suffering from high blood pressure, was in no condition to cope with two troubled boys. It was soon necessary for Bloch to move a registered nurse into the household. But the nurse's attempts at discipline were resented by Sophie, who felt that she was losing her authority.

Julius and Ethel had always been affectionate, even overindulgent parents. Ethel, in particular, had difficulty refusing her sons anything. The courses in child psychology Ethel had taken, instead of building her confidence, seem only to have armed her with a host of theories and reinforced her anxiety that setting limits on the children's behavior would inhibit their natural spontaneity. Now, from jail, Ethel poured her anxieties into long letters to Manny Bloch, filled with detailed instructions for resolving the quarrel between Sophie and the nurse, for getting the boys to play quietly in the early morning hours so that Sophie's sleep would not be disturbed, for getting Sophie to the doctor more often, and so on.

Bloch accepted these new responsibilities without complaint, and when prison officials agreed to allow the children to come to Sing Sing for monthly visits with their parents, it was taken for granted that this, too, was a matter for Bloch to handle. Like many New Yorkers, Bloch was not at home behind the wheel of a car, and the problem of getting two nervous and overexcited children to the Hudson Valley hamlet of Ossining, where the prison was located, suddenly created a job for a willing volunteer. And so it happened that, beginning in October, Jerry Tartakow took over the task of chauffeuring Manny Bloch and the children on their trips to Ossining.

It must have been obvious by now that the suggestion that Julius Rosenberg would continue to direct an espionage network from his death-row cell was a fantasy—though whether it was entirely Tartakow's or had been partly Julius's own is anyone's guess. Tartakow had already informed the Bureau in advance that Bloch was in touch with the left-wing weekly the *National Guardian*, which had agreed to run a series of articles on the case. Once the *Guardian*'s articles began, Tartakow also reported that plans for the underground newsletter *Retort*, whose mailing list the FBI would dearly have loved to see, had been abandoned. Justification for planting an informant in the employ of a defense lawyer still actively working on his clients' appeals must have seemed shaky indeed, even to the FBI, and Bureau files reflect that Tartakow received a stern warning against interfering in or even discussing the appeals process with Bloch—a precaution that would undoubtedly have failed to impress the courts had Tartakow's role become known.

Tartakow himself, meanwhile, was growing increasingly uncomfortable with his role. Apparently genuinely admiring of Julius Rosenberg, he somehow had nonetheless convinced himself that informing would do his friend no harm. He stayed in Bloch's employ until mid-1952, when he decided to leave the small photo shop that had been set up with the help of the FBI and move on to upstate New York and a new business venture. His last contact with Bloch appears to have been in January 1953 when he wrote reiterating his admiration for Julius, "the epitome of the brave working class soldier," and expressing his willingness to do anything that might save the Rosenbergs from death.

Tartakow seems to have believed that he had done nothing to injure Julius Rosenberg. He had not testified to anything in court and the tidbits he offered the Bureau might even produce leads that would relieve some of the pressure on the Rosenbergs to confess or die. What neither he nor anyone outside the government realized was that Tartakow's confidences to the FBI would become the major basis for a secret Justice Department memorandum setting forth evidence for the existence of a Rosenberg spy network that had not been produced in court. Although several points in the memorandum were supported by other evidence, the most damaging segments—including Julius's evaluation of William Perl and his alleged admission that Al Sarant was "one of my boys"—came straight from Tartakow's reports to agents Cammarota and Harrington.

This memorandum, stamped "Top Secret," was prepared in the U.S. Attorney's office in New York. It would be read by Judge Kaufman before he passed on a motion by the Rosenbergs' attorney for a reduction of sentence. Later, it became a key document in the file of secret evidence that was used to justify the denial of executive clemency to the Rosenbergs.

Though the bulk of allegations in this document may well have been substantially correct, Ethel Rosenberg's name is mentioned only once, in the context of a minor item noting that Julius had expressed concern that a woman "who was on intimate terms with his wife" (presumably Vivian Glassman) might have given information to the government. And at least one item in the document, prominently listed as point 1, was surely misleading. It read:

> 1. A confidential informant of the New York office of the Federal Bureau of Investigation asked the defendant Julius Rosenberg why he did not cooperate with the authorities and admit his participation in espionage activities. To this query Rosenberg

stated that he would not consider cooperation until all avenues of appeal had been exhausted and all of his [Rosenberg's] espionage contacts had been given an opportunity to flee the United States.

The suggestion that Rosenberg intended to consider confession when and if it became clear that his case was otherwise hopeless was not at all an accurate summary of what Tartakow had told the FBI. This item was, at best, a reflection of wishful thinking on the part of the document's compiler, yet it served to keep alive the waning hope that the lever strategy would eventually work if only the executive branch stood firm in refusing clemency.

21

"Nobody Was Doing Anything"

Quite apart from the question of the Rosenbergs' guilt or innocence, there was good reason to doubt that anyone accused of spying for the Soviet Union could have received a completely fair trial in March 1951.

If any institution in the land could be expected to be immune from the pressures of the time, however, it was the United States Court of Appeals, Second Circuit. The three-judge panel that would hear Bloch's appeal consisted of Thomas Swan, Harrie B. Chase, and Jerome N. Frank, all highly respected for their scholarship and independence of mind. The Rosenbergs and their counsel held especially high hopes of receiving a sympathetic hearing from liberal jurist Jerome N. Frank. An outspoken civil libertarian, Frank had written extensively on the dangers of legislative and judicial tyranny. Frank also happened to be the nation's leading scholarly expert on the law of evidence, and thus could be expected to scrutinize with special care a case so dependent on accomplice testimony. The lengthy appeals brief prepared by Emanuel Bloch and his associate, Gloria Agrin, raised any number of points that Judge Frank might recognize as having merit: the failure of the government to prove that the defendants had acted with intent to do harm to the vital interests of the United States; the credibility of a case built on the testimony of accomplices with an obvious vested interest in receiving leniency for their own offenses; and the behavior of Judge Kaufman, who, the defense argued, had hopelessly prejudiced the jury by his frequent interjections and adverse rulings.

The appeal was argued on January 10, 1952, and for six weeks Emanuel Bloch lived in hope that the scrupulous conscience of Jerome Frank would rescue his clients from the death house. When the court's decision was handed down on February 25, it turned out that Frank had indeed been the judge assigned to write the court's opinion. But his meticulously worded reasoning went against the defendants on nearly every point. From being the Rosenbergs' best hope, Frank had suddenly become their nemesis: his conclusion that the trial had been substantially fair was bound to exercise a powerful influence on any member of the judiciary who might be faced with reviewing the case in the future.

On the question of Judge Kaufman's pronouncements from the bench, for example, Frank ruled that they fell well within accepted standards of behavior for a federal judge, who is permitted to exercise considerable latitude in commenting on evidence, even to the point of examining witnesses himself if such intervention will clarify points that might otherwise remain obscure. Quoting from a previous appeals court decision, Frank emphasized that "the function of a federal trial judge is not that of an umpire or of a moderator at a town meeting. . . . He should not hesitate to ask questions for the purpose of developing the facts . . . and it is no ground of complaint that the facts so developed may hurt or help one side or the other." Further, the decision noted, Kaufman's ruling that evidence of the Rosenbergs' allegiance to communism would be allowed for the purpose of establishing their motives was in line with a decision in an earlier case involving a pro-Nazi German spy.

Of course, Judge Frank was commenting only on the trial record, and indeed only on those aspects that had been cited by the defense. His decision had nothing to do with the allegations of *ex parte* communications that have arisen more recently. Frank was saying, in effect, that whatever Kaufman's private feelings may have been, he had not allowed them to become the basis of blatant judicial errors. He could not agree that the judge had given the jurors what Bloch termed "a green light to convict on emotions." On the contrary, Kaufman had explicitly warned the jury against allowing their judgment to be clouded by the use of the loaded word "Communist."

"It may be that such warnings are no more than empty ritual," Frank conceded. On the other hand, it was not enough for the defense to charge that the conditions for unfairness existed. They had to show specifically how the judge had used his position to steer the jury toward a guilty verdict, and in Frank's view, the instances cited in Bloch's appeal did not make a compelling case, particularly when weighed against Kaufman's scrupulously correct charge to the jury.

While Frank's opinion left no doubt that he believed the Rosenbergs had had their day in court and been justly convicted, it also revealed his profound distaste for the sentence that had been imposed. Under a rule that had been followed since the end of the nineteenth century, the federal appeals courts had no power to shorten legally imposed sentences. Nevertheless, Frank's comments revealed that he had been sorely tempted to violate this long-standing prohibition and recommend mitigation. This segment of Frank's opinion, all but inviting the Supreme Court to take up the question of sentence reduction and setting forth the steps the Rosenbergs' counsel might take to pursue the question, was the only crumb of hope in an otherwise resounding defeat.

For the Rosenbergs, dismay over the circuit court's decision was mixed with a feeling of vindication that events seemed to be confirming their conviction that American justice was a sham. Frank, who had been referred to most respectfully in letters by the Rosenbergs previously published by the *National Guardian*, was now dismissed by Julius as a "so-called 'liberal.'" As for Ethel, her first letter after hearing the "shocking news" made the point that "certainly it proves that all our analyses regarding the political nature of the case have been amazingly correct."

Ethel could allow herself the self-congratulatory feelings expressed in this letter because she and Julius had already begun to transfer their hopes from the court to the power of public protest. At almost the same time that they learned of Frank's negative opinion, the Rosenbergs received the news that the first mass meeting of their supporters had been scheduled for March 12, at the Pythian Temple in New York City. As Julius wrote on March 2:

> Dearest Wife,
> Yes, any illusions we may have had that the judges of the higher courts are above hysteria and politics are completely destroyed.

We must soberly realize that our only hope rests with the people. . . .

Since the interpretation of the law as set forth by Judge Frank puts in grave danger all progressives and non-conformists—and others as well—I am positive that our fellow citizens will rally to nullify this action.

I expect that at this late hour the campaign to bring our case before the public will gather momentum and after the meeting we'll begin to make headway. . . .

Julius's hope that the meeting coming up later that month would mark the launching of a mass movement on his and Ethel's behalf appeared to be as unrealistic as his notion that "the people" in general opposed the executions, or would if only they knew the true facts of the case. The tiny committee that had been organized to demand a new trial for the Rosenbergs had so far not managed to attract the support of any organized group or segment of the public at large and had received practically no attention from the press. And it seemed most unlikely that it ever would.

Like so many others who were to become activists in the National Committee to Secure Justice in the Rosenberg Case, the group's founder, Emily Alman, had followed the trial itself with no more than casual interest. Although Alman and her husband lived in Knickerbocker Village, the same housing complex inhabited by the Rosenbergs, the two couples did not know each other. There had been one casual meeting with Ethel Rosenberg, which, three decades later, Alman remembered as notable for its very banality: She had been walking with some neighbors on the street in front of the project, Alman recalled, when two of her friends stopped to chat with a short, anxious-looking woman who passed them on her way home from a shopping expedition. The conversation, which centered on a relative of the woman's who was ill with Hodgkin's disease, had not been particularly memorable. It was only after the stranger had gone on her way that Alman's companions hurriedly informed her that she had just met Ethel Rosenberg, the one whose husband had recently been arrested as a spy.

Ethel's arrest, coming little more than a week later, was greeted by Alman's social set with curiosity and no little skepticism. A member of Alman's own family knew the Greenglasses through her work as a volunteer at the Lower East Side's Henry Street Settlement House and had expressed astonishment that a young man as ordinary as David Greenglass—a kid who had not even had the drive to get through a few semesters at college—could be anything so exotic as an "atom spy."

Still, Alman had not read or heard anything that caused her seriously to question the Rosenbergs' guilt. Even the *Daily Worker*, which ran a brief article on April 6, 1951, protesting the death sentence and asserting that the Rosenbergs were being made America's scapegoats for the Korean War, did not go so far as to charge that the Rosenbergs had been framed. Alman's conviction that the Rosenbergs were innocent victims of a rising antiprogressive tide did not take shape until August 1951, a full year after her chance meeting with Ethel Rosenberg, when she began to follow a series of articles in the *National Guardian*.

The *National Guardian*'s focus on the plight of the Rosenbergs was to light the spark that turned the case into a movement and elevated the suspicion that the Rosenbergs were "the first victims of American fascism" into a commonplace among the American Left. *Guardian* editor James Aronson remembers that he first became interested in investigating the case sometime after the end of the trial when a friend who worked for the *New York Mirror* set up an appointment for him to meet Manny Bloch. Aronson and Bloch sat in a cafeteria across the street from the *Guardian*'s offices for two hours, "as Bloch poured out the story of the Rosenbergs' ordeal and his own Ancient Mariner's odyssey seeking help to keep Ethel and Julius alive. There were few lawyers to whom he could turn for guidance; scientists who could testify with authority about the delicate atomic evidence fled at his approach; the media had shut their doors and their conscience."

Aronson's instincts as a journalist and a crusader were immediately aroused. "It looks as if this has been a political case from the start," he told Bloch.

Back at the paper's office, Aronson consulted with his coeditor, Cedric Belfrage. Belfrage, too, was impressed with Bloch's tale and particularly concerned that the Rosenbergs' situation had received virtually no attention from the "progressive" press or the organized Left. "The CP, to which Ethel and Julius and Morton were routinely alleged to belong," writes Belfrage in his memoirs, "seemed too pre-occupied and threatened by its own leaders' [Smith Act] trials to come to the defense of these obscure people."

Once they had made their decision, Belfrage and Aronson phoned their top reporter, William A. Reuben, who had previously done investigative reporting on the celebrated Trenton Six case. The editors took up the case in full awareness, as Belfrage noted, "that if the Rosenbergs were innocent as Bloch was convinced and we sus-pected, we would be exposing no less than calculated murder by the U.S. government," the motive for which was "to silence, once and for all, through two typical rank-and-file members of the movement, the opposition to the government's imperialist war policy." Progressives now knew, Belfrage adds, that opposition to U.S. foreign policy "could land them in the electric chair."

Thus the line on the case was drawn from the start. The *Guard-ian*'s editors seemed as oblivious to the possibility that espionage may have actually been going on as the mainstream press was to the possi-bility of a miscarriage of justice. On August 15, the *Guardian* broke the story with a page-one headline: "THE ROSENBERG CONVIC-TION—IS THIS THE DREYFUS CASE OF COLD WAR AMERICA?" "We are convinced," the editorial announced, "of the overwhelming prob-ability that the Rosenbergs are completely innocent." Pledging to lead a campaign that would bring about the Rosenbergs' vindication, the paper announced it would run a seven-part investigative series from the pen of William A. Reuben proving that the Rosenbergs should have been acquitted and that "there are strong grounds for suspecting the Rosenbergs are victims of an out-and-out political frame-up."

In retrospect, the series of articles by William Reuben that fol-lowed is memorable for the very paucity of evidence brought forward to support these sweeping assumptions. The major investigative "rev-elation" of the series, presented in the context of an attempt to de-molish Elizabeth Bentley's testimony, was that Klaus Fuchs's full name was Emil *Julius* Klaus Fuchs, and that the physicist was "known to his friends . . . in London as Julius." The implication that Elizabeth Bentley's "Julius" had been Fuchs and not Rosenberg struck many *Guardian* readers as devastating. And Reuben later reit-erated this contention in a privately published book entitled *The Atom Spy Hoax*, notwithstanding the fact that he had been reminded in a private letter from the anti-Communist journalist Oliver Pilat that Klaus Fuchs did not even arrive in the United States until December 1943, after the last phone call described in Bentley's testimony.

In fairness, Reuben did not have access to the sources that would have made it possible for him to expose some of the prosecution's more questionable behind-the-scenes maneuvers. But he made up for this disadvantage by attacking the very premise that some American nationals might have been involved in spying for the Soviets. His articles pointed out, quite correctly, that wartime Soviet atomic research was more advanced than Americans had credited. But he then went on to conclude that the Russians had no need or use for stolen data; indeed, he suggested that they might have had the capability to explode a nuclear weapon long before 1949, but had refrained from doing so for humanitarian reasons.

Notwithstanding their shortcomings, the *Guardian* articles made a tremendous impact. In the context of the anti-Communist hysteria of the summer of 1951, many *Guardian* readers did not need hard facts to accept Reuben's contention that the Rosenbergs were innocent victims of a witch-hunt. It was all too plausible. Emily Alman in particular took them to heart. Reuben's articles suggested the formation of a defense committee to work toward saving Julius and Ethel Rosenberg, but when Alman looked into the matter she discovered that no one seemed to be actively involved in getting such an organization started. "Nobody was doing anything," she recalls.

With the help of her husband, David Alman, a novelist and playwright who was a staff member of both the Civil Rights Congress and the American Peace Crusade, two major pro-Communist organizations, Emily Alman was able to arrange through another attorney to meet Emanuel Bloch and volunteer her services. To her surprise, she got a cool reception. Bloch suggested that there was really not much that could be done at this late stage; if Alman were interested, she might try to collect some clothing for the Rosenberg children. As for the theory that the prosecution was an FBI frame-up, Bloch said he was not at liberty to discuss this, adding only that "my clients say they are innocent." Alman put down Bloch's unenthusiastic response to the skepticism of the veteran campaigner unable to suppress his "Where were you when I needed you?" response.

Undismayed, Alman and her husband managed on their own to

assemble a small group that was to become the active nucleus of the National Committee to Secure Justice in the Rosenberg Case. According to Alman, among those present at the founding meeting on November 8, 1951, were the writer Yuri Suhl; Joseph Brainin, a writer described by Alman as having "good connections with the Jewish community"; Columbia University anthropologist Gene Weltfish; and Zionist B. Z. Goldberg. *Guardian* reporter William Reuben was also present and, as Alman recalls, it was he who had the idea of inviting Mrs. Sobell. Up to that time, says Alman, she had given virtually no thought to the Rosenbergs' codefendant. ("We had never heard of him. We didn't know who he was.") Helen Sobell, however, was soon to become one of the mainstays of the group and its most effective public speaker.

Two months passed before the Committee made its first public appeal, in the form of a major ad in the *National Guardian*'s issue of January 16, 1952. By this time they had attracted a notable list of sponsors and advisers, including Robert Morss Lovett, Waldo Frank, W. E. B. Du Bois, Herbert Aptheker, and Nelson Algren. Louis Harap, editor of the Communist magazine *Jewish Life* (later *Jewish Currents*), was listed as chief officer, although the bulk of the organizational work was actually taken on by David Alman.

An intelligent and energetic woman, Emily Alman cheerfully describes herself in those days as "a maverick" who had joined many left-wing organizations at one time or another and been "tossed out" of all of them. And, in the beginning, the Committee attracted mostly other "mavericks" like herself. The sentiment among its founding nucleus was overwhelmingly that the Rosenbergs were victims of a frame-up, and the group's energies were focused on winning a new trial that would give the defendants a chance to prove their innocence. But, recalls Alman, the group was only too eager to accept support from all shades of the political spectrum: civil libertarians, opponents of the death penalty, Jewish organizations, and so on. Potential supporters were not necessarily expected to be convinced of the Rosenbergs' innocence as long as they were willing to join in the call for a retrial.

At first the Committee had little success in attracting supporters of any stripe. As late as April 1952, a rally in Far Rockaway, within the New York City metropolitan area where interest in the case might be expected to be greatest, drew only about eighty-five supporters. Rabbi S. Andhill Fineberg, an American Jewish Committee staff member who was following the Rosenberg Committee closely and later wrote a book attacking the Committee as a Communist front, found the atmosphere at the rally to be that of a revivalist meeting, with the already convinced urging each other on to greater and greater heights of rhetoric. According to Fineberg, Helen Sobell, the principal speaker, told the audience that "the sentence of death given to Ethel and Julie, and the sentence of thirty years given to Morty, is a warning to each of you. . . . If we die at Sing Sing, you move that much closer to Sing Sing." When the obviously unsympathetic Fineberg sought to ask questions (such as why Sobell, if innocent, had decided not to take the stand), Mrs. Sobell, he says, "dropped to the floor in a faint" while others present closed ranks to avoid having to debate with a hostile intruder.

Rabbi Fineberg concluded from this experience that the Committee was a Communist front. Quite the contrary, if the Committee had enjoyed the support of the Communist Party, it would not, after more than five months of effort, still have been struggling to attract national attention. Officially, the CP's policy was to ignore the existence of the Committee altogether. Moreover, the Party's attitude in private was even more chilling.

Emily Alman told us of one particularly disturbing incident which occurred during the early days of her organizing efforts: late one evening she answered a ring of her doorbell to find a "mysterious stranger" standing in the hallway. Without identifying himself, the man tersely informed her that "she was not to do the Rosenberg thing." Alman assumed that the message came from the Communist Party hierarchy. She ignored it.

Far less enigmatic was the result of her husband's visit to the CP headquarters to solicit support for the Committee's efforts. "I'll tell you the answer," Alman recalled. "The answer was 'They're expendable.' That finished David for all time with some human experiences."

Oddly enough, it never seems to have occurred to the Almans that the Party's attitude might have been determined by an awareness that the Rosenbergs were guilty. Who is more "expendable" than an exposed spy, particularly one whose method of operations has become obsolete, who is an embarrassment and a threat to the very future of the American Communist Party? Even in their disillusionment, the Almans did not suspect that the Central Committee would be guilty of such a Machiavellian outlook. They assumed that the Party's indifference was rooted in a reluctance to take up a dangerously provocative if just cause. The Rosenbergs were to become martyrs to expediency.

The Almans' impression that the Party was hostile to their Committee was no figment of their imaginations. Two former Party members who were working at the Party's New York headquarters at the time both recalled in recent interviews that the Rosenberg case was unofficially untouchable.

Max Gordon, then a senior editor of the *Daily Worker*, remembers vividly that Emanuel Bloch came to him on a number of occasions, begging him to take up the case in the *Worker*'s columns. Each time Bloch pressed the issue, Gordon had no choice but to come back with the same answer: "Until the ninth floor [the offices of the Party's Central Committee] gives the signal, there's nothing else for us to do."

In spite of their public silence, the CP leaders were hardly indifferent to the Rosenbergs. John Gates, a former member of the Party's Central Committee, told us of an encounter with the Party's cultural commissar, V. J. Jerome, that occurred on the ninth floor just after the Rosenbergs' sentencing. Jerome, Gates said, called him aside and "He whispered to me, 'They're heroes. They're going to their death and not saying a word.' " Gates had no doubt that Jerome meant the Rosenbergs were heroes not because they were innocent, but because they were going to their deaths rather than betray the Party.

Gates also recalled the reaction of Party General Secretary Eugene Dennis, who served a sentence for contempt of court in the Federal House of Detention at the same time that Julius Rosenberg was incarcerated there. Dennis, said Gates, "spoke with stars in his eyes" about seeing Rosenberg and passing him knowing glances while in the food line or on the exercise roof. Dennis's confinement coincided with the period during the trial when the Party was officially ignoring the case, and he himself avoided any direct contact with Rosenberg, yet he could not conceal his exultation at having been so near to the accused atom spy.

"If these people had no connection and weren't doing anything for the Party," Gates mused, "then why this attitude toward them?" Gates went on: "There was this admiration . . . for them because we knew they were indeed spies and it was considered an act of heroism not to reveal that they were working for the Soviet Union. And, in so doing, they were also protecting the American Communist Party." Gates also remembers thinking at the time that Manny Bloch had been "assigned to the case because he was not one of the very competent Party lawyers and the whole idea was that they should not win their case." Summing up, Gates searched for words to explain how he and other Party leaders were later able to defend the Rosenbergs' innocence publicly while privately believing quite the opposite: "It was taken for granted among us that they were guilty. We had this kind of double thinking. While they were guilty, of course they were innocent. They were framed. Because anyone who was indicted by the capitalists was *ipso facto* framed."

Throughout the summer of 1952, the Committee struggled on. Then, quite suddenly, the Committee's efforts seemed to take off. Emily Alman recalls that some time in November 1952, almost overnight it seemed, the Committee was flooded with eager volunteers and the donations began pouring in. A rally in the New York theater district sponsored by Paul Robeson, Ruby Dee, and Rockwell Kent raised thousands of dollars. By Christmas, the New York City branch of the Committee alone was able to charter an eight-car train to carry demonstrators to Ossining, New York, for a show of moral support for Julius and Ethel.

The Committee leadership welcomed the influx of new blood, at least at first. They soon found, however, that their original conception of an open, pluralistic organization was being shunted aside. The goal of working toward a new trial was almost forgotten amid a rising clamor for clemency. The Rosenbergs' salvation lay not in the judicial system but in vindication by the court of public opinion.

Now, too, the issue of anti-Semitism came increasingly to the forefront, though in a manner that seemed ill-calculated to win support from the Jewish community at large. In speeches and broadsheets, the fascist motivations of the public officials involved, including the judge and the prosecutor—both Jews—were taken for granted. Anyone who demanded evidence to support this assertion was either a fool or an obstructionist. Thus on October 23, 1952, Elaine Ross, an official of the Civil Rights Congress, told a rally audience: "Every Jew knows in his heart that the Rosenbergs have been convicted because of anti-Semitism." Her statement, noted the *Daily*

Worker in its account of the speech, "elicited gasps of 'yes, yes' from all sides of the hall."

The Communists saw no further leadership role on the Committee for those who supported a campaign for humanitarian or civil libertarian reasons. From now on, there would be increasing pressure to present the Rosenbergs' case in the "proper" political context—i.e., the assertion that the Rosenbergs were the victims of America's Cold War foreign and domestic policies. Thus William L. Patterson, a leading black Communist who was chairman of the Civil Rights Congress, wrote to Emily Alman chiding her for her efforts to forge a broad-based movement composed of supporters from across the political spectrum. The Right could not save the Rosenbergs, he argued. Its ranks only became involved to offset what he saw as "genuine" action by the people.

Politicization of the campaign meant a change of emphasis in its goals. No longer would the Committee stress its demand for a new trial—a demand that many had supported in spite of doubts about the Rosenbergs' guilt. From now on, there would be increasing insistence on the Rosenbergs' complete innocence.

On October 13, 1952, the Supreme Court announced that it had voted against granting *certiorari* on the Rosenberg-Sobell appeal—meaning that it had found insufficient cause to hear arguments on the issues. Judge Frank's comments on the severity of the Rosenbergs' sentences had not fallen on entirely deaf ears. At the judicial conference prior to the summer recess where the appeal was discussed, three justices—Hugo Black, Harold Burton and Felix Frankfurter—had expressed sympathy with various points made in the appeals brief, and Frankfurter, in particular, had argued vehemently that the Rosenbergs had been, in effect, tried for conspiracy and sentenced for treason. Since Frankfurter had a principle against making public his dissents on denials of *certiorari*, his position was not revealed when the court's decision was announced in October, however. The only dissent on record was that of Hugo Black, and it appeared that the Rosenbergs' legal position was grim indeed.

While Manny Bloch hastened to file a petition for a rehearing before district court judge Sylvester Ryan, the third defendant, Morton Sobell, was apparently plunged into the deepest despair. In the weeks just prior to the Supreme Court's announcement, FBI communiques between New York and Washington had been kept buzzing with rumors that Sobell was about to break down and throw himself on the mercy of the court. The Bureau had an inmate informant inside the Federal House of Detention, where Sobell was then incarcerated pending the appeals decision, and this inmate had been taunting Sobell with the "fact" (totally false) that if the Rosenbergs were granted a new trial, Julius intended to testify against Sobell in exchange for his and Ethel's lives.

In early October, the informant told his FBI control, agent Cammarota, that if Sobell's appeal were denied Sobell intended to write a letter to Judge Kaufman and would offer to testify at William Perl's forthcoming perjury trial in exchange for a reduction of sentence. Allegedly, Sobell had told the informant: "If I blow *certiorari*, I will abandon all hope of help from my lawyers."

Morton Sobell had always believed that his best hope lay in the separation of his own case from that of the Greenglass-Rosenberg atomic conspiracy. His lawyers' appeal, based on these grounds, had found favor only with Judge Frank, who concluded that the question should have been presented to the jury to consider. As the moment for the Supreme Court to announce its own opinion on this same point approached, Sobell had begun to come to terms with the fact that his chances for a victory were slim. Facing a thirty-year jail term, Sobell found it difficult to accept that everyone, the government and his allies alike, seemed content to regard his fate as a mere footnote to the Rosenberg case.

Worst of all, even his wife Helen seemed to feel that way. Since the early part of the year, Helen Sobell had become increasingly caught up in her work for the Committee to Secure Justice. Speaking at as many as four meetings and rallies every week, Helen was so preoccupied with the Committee that she could barely find time to write her husband letters, and the precious minutes of their limited visits together were increasingly consumed by Helen's accounts of her activities. Sobell, at this stage, felt a marked lack of enthusiasm for the Committee's efforts, despite his wife's reminders that the Committee was paying his legal bills. As Sobell has written of this period, "I never even considered the possibility that the Committee might also help cut my thirty years." And perhaps this opinion was motivated by more than personal pique, since Sobell also says that his wife actually suggested to him that the court's denial of *certiorari* was not entirely a bad thing, since "it was now easier to gather support for Julius and Ethel."

Whether Sobell in fact intended to appeal to Judge Kaufman is impossible to know. Sobell has certainly never admitted to having formulated such a plan. But the government believed their informant's story, and their reactions go far to explain the strategy that eventually led to Sobell's incarceration at Alcatraz, the maximum-security fortress in San Francisco Bay that was usually reserved for the most hardened and dangerous federal lawbreakers.

On October 17, 1952, just four days after the first denial of *certiorari*, supervisor T. Scott Miller of the FBI's New York office passed on the word that the informant had reported Sobell was already drafting his appeal to Kaufman and planned to mail it within the week. Miller's report goes on to say that Roy Cohn had informed the judge of Sobell's forthcoming communication and prepared a writ authorizing Sobell's appearance before Kaufman, which he was prepared to serve as soon as word came down that the letter had been delivered. Miller also added that, at the request of Judge Kaufman, two FBI agents would be waiting in the courtroom to take custody of Sobell immediately, should he agree to cooperate with the government. The purpose of this arrangement was to insure that Sobell did not fall into the hands of Cohn before the FBI had its opportunity to interrogate him directly.

This plan, apparently arranged without Cohn's knowledge by Miller and Kaufman, was still not enough to satisfy Hoover and his lieutenants in Washington. Bureau headquarters had never forgiven Cohn for botching their plan to make a surprise arrest of William Perl. Their reports consistently portray Cohn as pushy and inexperienced, though no doubt there was an element of professional rivalry behind this characterization. Hoover demanded that his minions keep a low public profile and maintain strict discipline within the chain of command. It must have rankled to see the young eager beaver in the U.S. Attorney's office operating with a much freer hand.

At any rate, FBI Security Chief A. H. Belmont warned New York that if Sobell were interviewed by the FBI, Cohn should not even be allowed to be present. "Further," he ordered, "in the event such an interview is conducted . . . no information concerning the result of the interview should be furnished to the United States Attorney's office or Roy Cohn without specific Bureau approval."

A surprising sidelight to these arrangements was the strict security precautions that were to be taken in the event of Sobell's being brought into Kaufman's presence. Sobell, who had no history of violent actions and whose previous attempts to flee justice bordered on the pathetic, was now regarded as an extremely dangerous man, at least by Judge Kaufman. Thus supervisor Scott Miller in New York advised his superiors: "The Judge has instructed that if Sobell appears before him, the United States Marshall is to thoroughly search Sobell for weapons and is to guard him closely while he is in court." Kaufman was later to complain that his role in the Rosenberg sentencing had made him the target of a barrage of vituperative and threatening letters. His fear of physical reprisals from some fanatical supporter of the Rosenbergs may not have been entirely illogical, but the notion that Sobell himself might ask for an audience in order to attack Kaufman certainly smacks of the ludicrous. The consequences were anything but humorous for Sobell, however, since this view no doubt made it easier for the prison authorities to rationalize their eventual decision to send him to Alcatraz.

When the month of October drew to a close and Sobell had still not mailed the letter that was supposedly already drafted, the FBI and its informant put the blame on Helen Sobell. She had always been adamantly opposed to any suggestion that her husband might cooperate with the government. Hoover himself, in a letter to the attorney general, noted that the warden at the House of Detention had refused Sobell's request for permission to write more than the allotted quota of letters to his wife, on the theory that the less opportunity he had to consult with her, the better the chances of his breaking. When Sobell still failed to mail his letter, the government began to look for a new way of applying pressure. Although mentions of the possibility of a Sobell confession suddenly disappear from the FBI papers, Sobell's prison memoir states that it was at just this time that "the Alcatraz rumors suddenly started again. I began to hear them from all sides; inmates, hacks, and lieutenants."

Sobell considered undertaking a hunger strike to protest his transfer to "the Rock," but Edward Kuntz, supposedly the most political of his lawyers, personally dissuaded him. Sobell acceded to Kuntz's advice, though he later concluded that Kuntz had been acting under the influence of Manny Bloch, who must have felt "that any action I took might de-focus attention from Julius and Ethel." In the meantime, the Supreme Court had issued a second opinion, denying the Rosenberg-Sobell lawyers' request for a rehearing on their *certiorari* petition. The newest member of the Sobell defense team, young Howard Meyer, went to court to ask for an order delaying his client's removal from New York on the grounds that his presence was needed to aid in the preparation of new motions for a reduction of sentence. At the hearing, the prosecutor suggested mysteriously that the government had important reasons for wanting to transfer Sobell immediately and alluded to elaborate security plans being made for the move. Judge Edward A. Weinfeld finally decided to continue the stay only until the following Wednesday, the day before Thanksgiving.

When Wednesday came, the government wasted no time in carrying out its plan. According to Sobell, he was subjected to a body search immediately after breakfast, given a suit of street clothes, and sent to a private conference with the warden, who pleaded with him in a "fatherly tone" to cooperate.

When Sobell refused to give in to the prison authorities' wheedling, he was flown to the West Coast the same afternoon in the company of two U.S. marshals. Sobell claims that he was not handcuffed and that supervision of him was so lax he felt he was almost being invited to attempt an escape, a prospect that became less tempting when he became aware of the presence at the airport and on the plane of several pairs of conservatively dressed men who seemed to be regarding his group with more than casual interest. Sobell assumed they were FBI agents.

Sobell's theory that there was a plot to bait him into escaping and then shoot him cannot be confirmed though it is not beyond the realm of possibility. Another possibility, which may be inferred from the FBI's files, is that the government had come to believe that Sobell really might be capable of attempting violence, or that he might be the focus of an escape attempt orchestrated by his supporters. Either way, the response to Sobell's rumored confession was certainly counterproductive. Threats and isolation may break down a prisoner's resolve, but for a highly politicized individual like Sobell, who had never thought of himself as a criminal, the government's tactics served only to reinforce the conviction that he was a political prisoner, thus strengthening his resolve to resist.

Morton Sobell remained on Alcatraz until February 1958, when he was transferred to the medium-security federal detention facility at Atlanta.

22

We Are Innocent

The Supreme Court's refusal to grant *certiorari* also intensified the pressure on Julius and Ethel Rosenberg and their counsel. In late November, Judge Kaufman rescheduled the Rosenbergs' executions for the week of January 12, 1953, and for the first time, the couple faced a date that might well hold firm.

But despite their deteriorating legal situation, Julius and Ethel appeared to be growing more confident and defiant by the day. They continued to express complete faith in Manny Bloch's handling of their case and to take an active interest in plotting strategy with Bloch during his visits to Sing Sing. Moreover, the emergence of the Rosenberg defense campaign had been a tremendously heartening development. And the Committee's sudden growth in the autumn of 1952 mitigated to some extent their disappointment over the Supreme Court's refusal to review their case. Indeed, Julius even echoed the sentiment of some Committee members that the Court's action was a good thing, since it would provide support for the claim that there was a government conspiracy against him and his wife. As he put it, "the latest action of the highest court in our country will make it easier to get the facts before the public."

The existence of a public campaign on their behalf also gave the Rosenbergs an opportunity to play an active role in their defense by permitting their correspondence to be published and disseminated by Committee supporters.

Ethel Rosenberg had been the first to break silence. Several of her letters were published in the *National Guardian* in October 1951, and Ethel and Julius both wrote messages to be distributed by their supporters in fact sheets and broadsides. "We are an ordinary man and wife," the couple wrote, ". . . Like others we spoke for peace, because we did not want our two little sons to live in the shadow of war and death. . . . That is why we are in the death house today, as warning to all ordinary men and women."

Such statements were hardly a defense attorney's dream. Where and when had the Rosenbergs spoken for peace? They had not been politically active for years. Where was the struggling businessman Julius claimed to be? Where in this statement was the average housewife who had told reporters that she was bewildered by her husband's arrest?

Manny Bloch probably could not have prevented Ethel and Julius from writing such potentially compromising statements even if he had wanted to. And in fact, he did not want to. Like Julius, who had planned the aborted newsletter *Retort* from his cell in the House of Detention, Bloch had believed all along that an organized publicity campaign might generate enough public pressure to bring about a mitigation of the sentences. When the Committee's efforts began to bear fruit, he approved of its plan to publish letters written by the Rosenbergs to each other and to himself. Bloch oversaw the Committee's editing of the correspondence and eventually set up a publishing firm that, operating out of his law office at 401 Broadway, issued two book-length editions of the letters.

The Rosenbergs' "death house letters," some of which originally appeared in the form of Committee broadsides and pamphlets or in the *Guardian*, offered their supporters a personal glimpse of Julius and Ethel's lives on death row. Julius, they learned, had adjusted to his situation by adopting many of the typical habits of the long-term inmate. He had become a chain smoker and an avid stalker of the cockroaches that invaded his cell each night. He wrote long letters to Manny Bloch, suggesting new legal angles that might make good material for further appeals. He played endless games of "remote control" chess, calling out his moves to a fellow inmate who kept a duplicate board in his adjoining cell. And he read indiscriminately, everything from *Cheaper by the Dozen* and *Look Homeward, Angel* to Telford Taylor's *Doctors of Infamy*. Although Taylor's book (which detailed the crimes of Nazi concentration camp doctors) seems depressing reading for a man facing the electric chair, Julius professed to see a hopeful moral in the fact that many of these same doctors' death sentences had eventually been commuted. How was it possible that he and Ethel would be asked to pay a penalty not even demanded of these notorious war criminals?

From the fall of 1952 on, Julius was by far the more prolific letter writer and, perhaps precisely because he had fewer literary pretensions than his wife, the more effective. In between bursts of rhetoric about "our sacred duty to expose the police state methods that are being practiced," there are glimpses of an often sympathetic individual who adored his wife, worried about getting fat on starchy prison food, took pleasure in watching a lone seagull as it soared past his cell window, and was tickled by an Italian magazine headline that referred to his sons as "I piccoli Rosenberghi."

Ethel's correspondence presents a grimmer picture. She, too, relied on books to pass the time: volumes of American history selected for her by Manny Bloch and *Gentleman's Agreement*, the bestselling novel on the theme of anti-Semitism. There were also regular handball games in her private exercise yard and the hours spent perusing songbooks, from which she practiced with the aid of a plastic pitch pipe (obtained by Manny Bloch, after a frantic search, when prison authorities refused to allow her to keep her metal one).

But Ethel, as the only woman awaiting execution, suffered through her ordeal in an isolation that her husband was spared. Even during religious services, when the inmates of the men's wing were allowed to mingle briefly, Ethel was forced to follow the proceedings from a chair placed out of sight in the corridor. Torn from a way of life that had revolved around taking care of her family, Ethel found it difficult to concentrate on anything except her own misery. She suffered from migraine headaches and back spasms and wrote that she cried herself to sleep every night. Increasingly, Ethel's mood swings revolved around what she termed "Wondrous Wednesdays," the days on which she and Julius were permitted their weekly visit together—even then separated by the wire mesh screen of the visiting room cubicle. Perhaps the surest measure of Ethel's depression is that in the latter months of 1952 she wrote fewer and fewer letters for publication, as she struggled with what the editors of one edition of the letters were to describe as "the exquisite emotions of the momentous experience."

Of course, Ethel's depression was exacerbated by the rejection of her by her own family. Unlike the Rosenberg relatives, who gradually began making regular visits to Sing Sing, no member of the Greenglass family appeared at the penitentiary until January 1953, when Ethel's mother, Tessie, paid her first and only visit. And when it finally came, Tessie's interview with her daughter was a disaster. Describing the conversation in an indignant letter to Manny Bloch, Ethel complained that Tessie had upbraided her for failing to confirm David's version of events:

"So what would have been so terrible if you had backed up his story?" Tessie had reportedly asked.

"I protested, shocked as I could be, 'But, Ma, would you have had me willingly commit perjury?'

"She shrugged her shoulders indifferently and maintained doggedly, 'You wouldn't be here!' "

It is hardly surprising that Tessie's plea threw Ethel into a "state of stupefaction." Here Ethel was on death row as the result of David's testimony against her, and Tessie's concern still seemed to revolve around her favored son. That Tessie was also pleading with Ethel to save her own life was something that Ethel could barely bring herself to acknowledge, since that course inevitably would mean betraying Julius.

No reader of the Rosenbergs' prison letters could fail to be moved by their anguish at their physical separation from each other or the sheer horror each obviously felt at the fact that the approaching execution date meant not just each one's own death but the death of a beloved spouse. On the other hand, it is impossible to ignore another aspect of the correspondence, namely, that the personalities that emerge from the printed page bear little resemblance to the Rosenbergs as they were portrayed by their more ardent defenders— gentle, family-oriented people, ordinary Americans whose only crime was their adherence to an unpopular political cause.

To begin with, numerous passages in the letters are gratingly shrill and strident. Ethel, in particular, fell all too easily into the rhetoric of a practiced hater, as when she wrote:

> The fact that no degree of pressure will ever cause us to repudiate those principles of democracy that sit beleaguered with us behind these repugnant bars does not in any way mitigate the heartbreak we suffer nor render less culpable the refusal to alle-

viate it in some more comparable degree. Wait, wait and trem-
ble, ye mad masters, this barbarism, this infamy you practice
upon us, and with which you regale yourselves presently, will
not go unanswered, unavenged, forever! The whirlwind gathers,
before which you must fly like the chaff!

Such bristling calls for vengeance no doubt contributed to the
prevalent rumor that Ethel was cold and emotionless, the real brains
behind the spy ring all along and the more fanatical member of the
couple, still enforcing on her weaker husband the decision to die unrepentant. In reality, there is no evidence for such an interpretation.
More likely, Ethel needed the release she found in writing such
broadsides to bolster her own courage. Nevertheless, even the Committee stalwarts appear to have found these shows of defiance embarrassing and counterproductive. Editors of the letters at times tried to
excise the more rhetorical portions and the particular passage cited
above was dropped when the letter in which it appeared was reprinted in the second edition of the correspondence.

No amount of editing, however, could have disguised the fact
that the Rosenbergs were thoroughgoing ideologues. As the critic
Leslie Fiedler pointed out in a retrospective essay on the letters, for
Julius and Ethel *everything* was grist for the dialectical struggle—
sports, religion, Americanism, and even their love for each other.
Thus, Ethel, listening in her prison cell to a radio broadcast of a
game between the Brooklyn Dodgers and the Phillies, meditates on
the Dodgers' "important contribution to the rooting out of racial
prejudice." For Julius, the Passover holiday is a reminder that "we
are imprisoned . . . by the modern Pharaohs" and George Washington's Birthday is the occasion for a letter extolling the virtue of truthfulness and chiding columnist Leonard Lyons for printing an item
that claimed Julius had rejected the visits of the prison rabbi. Even a
letter addressing Ethel as "Sweetheart Darling," which begins, "Here
it is still two more days before a young man's fancy turns to love,"
jarringly shifts in the very next sentence into a paean to the burgeon-
ing power of "the people, the most effective force we have."

Furthermore, while the Rosenbergs' letters repeatedly and insistently proclaim their innocence, it is difficult to discern exactly what
they are claiming to be innocent of. The correspondence contains few
references to the specific charges against them—and certainly no ma-

terial that would tend to refute the charges. Beginning in their earliest letters, Julius and Ethel insisted on redefining their crime and presenting themselves as political prisoners incarcerated because they had been advocates of peace—or, in Ethel's words, of "American democracy, justice and brotherhood . . . peace and bread and roses, and children's laughter." When Willie McGee was executed in Mississippi in May 1951, Julius wrote that the "medieval practice of lynching of Negroes" was now about to be extended "as in our case . . . to political prisoners." Julius's sense of himself as a patriotic dissenter was so strong, in fact, that on the following Fourth of July he removed a reproduction of the Declaration of Independence from his newspaper, added his signature to those of the Founding Fathers, and hung the document in his cell.

Regardless of their rhetorical excesses, the Rosenbergs' published letters had a tremendous impact, both in America and abroad. Julius and Ethel's repeated insistence on their innocence, made in the face of broad hints that they could save their lives by confessing, was difficult to dismiss as self-serving. The Rosenbergs were clearly sincere in their belief that they were victims of a grievous wrong. How could this be, if in fact they were spies? The best explanation, suggested in separate essays by Leslie Fiedler and Robert Warshow, is that the Rosenbergs could call themselves "innocent" with a clear conscience because of their special definition of the word: From their ideological perspective, the crimes of which they had been convicted were crimes only in the eyes of Cold War America: they were capitalist crimes. Considered from an objective Marxist viewpoint, there had been no crime at all. Therefore, there was no question of guilt. Therefore, they were innocent. This definition was hardly unique to the Rosenbergs. Readers in the know would realize that "helping" the Soviet Union had been justified as a contribution to the defeat of fascism and the cause of peace. Thus, even if the Rosenbergs had been involved in a form of espionage, they still felt perfectly justified in characterizing themselves as political prisoners.

Given this degree of ideological commitment, it was only a small step from the letters to a decision to allow the Committee to use the plight of their sons to generate sympathy. Pictures of the Rosenberg children, looking appropriately vulnerable, were featured prominently in Committee literature, and in January 1953, when the first pro-Rosenberg picket line appeared in front of the White House, Michael and Robert were permitted to make an appearance. The effectiveness of this kind of public exposure can be judged by the government's response: Thus when Michael Rosenberg delivered to the White House a letter begging President Eisenhower to "Please let my mommy and daddy go," the FBI actually engaged a handwriting expert to investigate whether the boy had written the letter himself. (In fact, the letter *was* in Michael's own hand, although he has acknowledged that the text had been dictated by an adult.)

The Rosenbergs have been harshly criticized for allowing the Committee to exploit their children. But such criticisms miss the point. The numerous references to the sons in Julius and Ethel's letters, extending to a concern for the smallest day-to-day details of their upbringing, leaves no doubt that they were devoted parents. They loved their sons inordinately. And like all parents, they wanted to leave them something of value, something that would become a source of solace and pride. But the Rosenbergs had nothing to pass on except this faith in their own innocence, and in their cause. Julius made this explicit in a letter he wrote in April 1953, vowing: "We stand together in unity of heart and mind, firmly defending our principles and our sacred honor. This legacy we can and will give to Michael and Robert no matter what the outcome of this case."

And, of course, there was always the possibility that the Committee's campaign would succeed and the family would eventually be reunited. The Rosenbergs could hardly have failed to be overoptimistic about the chances of this. The flood of articles, letters, and telegrams, the reports of Rosenberg defense committees springing up in foreign countries, the arrival of busloads of demonstrators who traveled all the way to Ossining for a Christmas carol service that the Rosenbergs could not even hear—all this must have raised their hopes and reinforced their belief that they were right to defy the government. After the long lonely months when the Party had refused to so much as acknowledge their existence, they had now become the focus of a major international effort, more famous and certainly better loved than Tom Mooney had ever been. And like Mooney, they were sure to be vindicated, by posterity if not in their own lifetimes.

Such heady thoughts did not make Manny Bloch's legal efforts irrelevant, but they were cause for a change in emphasis. The letters indicate that, from the autumn of 1952 on, the Rosenbergs began to pin their hopes on the pressure of public opinion. Bloch did not necessarily have to win a decisive victory on their behalf; if only he could drag out the legal process long enough, the government would back down and offer either executive clemency or mitigation of sentence through some other channel. This hope cushioned to some extent the disappointment when Ethel and Julius learned, on New Year's Day 1953, that Manny Bloch's second appeal had been dismissed by the Circuit Court of Appeals.

Bloch's second appeals brief had raised two major new issues. First, it charged that Irving Saypol's comments to the press at the time of William Perl's arrest had prejudiced the Rosenbergs' case. Second, it asserted that Ben Schneider, the passport photographer, had committed perjury when he said that he had not seen the Rosenbergs since the day they came into his shop for photos. (Actually, as had been revealed in Oliver Pilat's book on the trial, Schneider had been brought into the courtroom surreptitiously the day before his testimony to see whether he could identify Julius and Ethel.)

District Judge Sylvester Ryan made short work of the Schneider charge, ruling that the photographer had simply misspoken himself with no motive for falsehood. On the matter of Saypol's conduct, Ryan also found against the appellants, noting that Bloch had raised no objection at the time of the Perl arrest. Furthermore, the defense had still offered no evidence that any member of the jury was aware of Saypol's inflammatory remarks to the press.

Technically, Judge Ryan was on firm ground. Judicial procedures would degenerate into chaos if lawyers could wait until after the jury's verdict before deciding whether to protest on this or that legal point. The Court of Appeals therefore upheld Ryan's judgment. However, its opinion, prepared by Judge Thomas Swan, revealed that Swan was deeply troubled by Saypol's conduct. Characterizing Saypol's behavior as "totally reprehensible," Swan also criticized Manny Bloch for his failure to take prompt exception to such a flagrant abuse of the prosecutorial power.

The Rosenbergs' response to the Swan decision was an interesting one. Ethel immediately rushed into print with a letter which characterized Swan's rebuke as "perfidy" and almost made it seem that Bloch and not she and her husband was the party who had suffered most from the decision. "All legal considerations aside," Ethel wrote, "I am sick for the unconscionably sneering attitude, the snide insinuations you have had to suffer on our behalf."

Despite this vote of confidence, it is difficult to understand why Bloch waited so long to protest Saypol's conduct. His own explanation—that he had believed Saypol's assurances that the timing of the arrest was unconnected to his clients' case—is really no explanation at all, particularly coming from a lawyer who had vigorously protested supposedly prejudicial actions by Saypol throughout the trial. More likely, Bloch feared that, in one way or another, it would be dangerous to call attention to Perl's connection to the Rosenbergs—dangerous to them and to Perl, and fatal to the contention that there had been no espionage.

Certainly, the whole pattern of Bloch's defense made no sense to the original defense-committee stalwarts who believed the Rosenbergs innocent. Publicly, the Committee lionized Bloch; privately, the founding "mavericks" had their doubts. As Emily Alman said recently, Bloch's strategy could be summed up as "a defense of the Party and nothing of Ethel."

Yet Bloch had been bitterly angry at the Communist Party for its failure to come out in support of his clients. Gloria Agrin, Bloch's associate at the time, recalls his frustration and disappointment at the Party's press blackout of the trial, a memory confirmed by Max Gordon's recollection.

Any notion that the Rosenbergs were unwitting hostages of a defensive Party strategy as carried out by Bloch overlooks that fact that it was they who insisted from the beginning in disassociating themselves from the Party. Bloch may have agreed all too readily to this approach, but if he had not admired the Rosenbergs for taking the stand they did and wanted to aid them in carrying out their resolve, he probably would not have remained their lawyer for long. Once the defense committee had attracted worldwide attention to their case, the Rosenbergs surely could have attracted new legal counsel if they had wanted it, yet they continued to affirm their confidence in Bloch and to attack his detractors. This was partly out of gratitude: Bloch had not just defended Julius and Ethel Rosenberg; he had defended their innocence. Besides, now that the Party was behind an international pro-Rosenberg movement, Julius and Ethel firmly expected that their salvation would come from "the people"; they no longer expected Bloch to win them a new trial—always a risky proposition since the government might then be tempted to broaden the indictment by naming members of the larger spy ring.

Bloch's job was to keep the legal wheels turning until certain "political factors" changed and the voice of the people could triumph.

The hope that the government might eventually lose its will to follow through with the executions was by no means irrational. As historian Michael Parrish points out in his study "Cold War Justice," Julius and Ethel would probably have been spared if their case had somehow remained before the courts until 1954. By then, the Korean War was over, McCarthy had been censured by the Senate, and Earl Warren had replaced Fred Vinson as chief justice of the Supreme Court—not, perhaps, the revolutionary developments in the world struggle that Julius Rosenberg was looking for, but ones that would certainly have worked to his and Ethel's advantage.

Just as surely, however, in early 1953 the rising clamor of the defense committee made certain government officials all the more determined to press for a hasty resolution. On December 30, 1952, just one day before Judge Swan's decision for the court of appeals was announced, Judge Irving Kaufman rejected a motion for a reduction of the Rosenbergs' sentence and agreed to stay the execution, now just two weeks away, only long enough for Bloch to submit a formal clemency appeal to President Truman.

Privately, Kaufman was even more frightened than he had been in October, when he contemplated the possibility of a face-to-face conference with Morton Sobell. And this fear was shared by at least one key figure on the prosecution team—Roy Cohn. Cohn, convinced that his telephones had been tapped and his office bugged with hidden microphones, asked the FBI to inspect them. Kaufman was receiving special protection in the form of a team of plainclothes detectives from the New York City police force as well as a uniformed officer who stood guard outside the entrance to his Park Avenue apartment building.

The mounting tide of protest only made Kaufman more determined that the executions should be swiftly carried out. After President Eisenhower, who had inherited the issue from Truman, denied clemency in February 1953, Kaufman rescheduled the executions for the week of March 9—too little time for Bloch to appeal the Swan opinion to the Supreme Court. In February, Kaufman's action was undone by Learned Hand, Chief Judge of the Second Circuit Court of Appeals. When a government attorney objected to Hand's decision to grant a further stay of execution, he was sharply chastised. "People don't dispose of lives just because an attorney did not make a point," Hand said, adding that the duty of the prosecutor was "to seek justice, not to act as a timekeeper." Hand went on to suggest that the Supreme Court might be disposed to make its own evaluation of Saypol's conduct.

Learned Hand's warning against undue haste seems to have made no impression on Kaufman, who called the FBI's New York office two days later to discuss the ramifications of the new delay. According to the FBI's memorandum on the call, Kaufman was particularly alarmed that the Supreme Court might not get around to a final disposition that spring. "Consequently," the FBI memo says in summarizing Kaufman's remarks, "unless this matter is pushed vigorously by the government, this whole case may hang over until Fall. Judge Kaufman was of the opinion that the Department should push the matter vigorously now to get it before the Supreme Court." The Bureau, however, did not care to get involved, and Kaufman was told to take up his concerns directly with the Justice Department.

But Hand was quite correct in thinking that the Supreme Court might yet become involved. Justice Felix Frankfurter, for one, found the implications of Judge Swan's ruling deeply troubling. Should defendants be allowed to die because their attorney had failed to make a point? Should the ideal of justice be sacrificed to legal niceties? Announcement of the Supreme Court's determination against reviewing the case was held up for more than a month while Frankfurter wrestled with his conscience. He longed to write a dissenting opinion, but was paralyzed by the fear that once his doubts became known, they would become just so much more fodder for the propagandists. No matter how carefully worded a dissent might be, it would inevitably be interpreted, both in America and abroad, as an affirmation of the Rosenbergs' innocence. At the same time, Frankfurter feared that by drawing attention to Saypol's conduct, he might inadvertently "help to make a hero of him," just as Judge Harold Medina had been lionized in some circles for his methods in the Dennis case. Against these considerations was Frankfurter's conviction that only a full review by the Supreme Court could quiet the whirlwind of controversy that was sure to wreak havoc on the political scene long after the Rosenbergs were executed.

At the moment, it appeared that Frankfurter's moral dilemma was strictly a private matter. Only Justice Hugo Black, dissenting on principle in cases involving civil liberties or the death penalty, was prepared to overturn Swan's ruling; one other justice, Robert Jackson, was so disturbed by Saypol's actions that he might have gone along. What bothered Frankfurter the most was that his likely ally on the court, William O. Douglas, had so far shown not the slightest interest in the case. At the judicial conference on April 11, 1953, Douglas had voted once again against *certiorari*, entering his vote without discussion in an uncharacteristically gruff tone of voice that left Frankfurter both perplexed and dismayed.

If even Felix Frankfurter felt constrained from speaking out in a way that might be interpreted as playing into the defense committee's hands, how much more courage would be required for an elected official to grant clemency?

23

The Propaganda War: The Defense Committee

The sudden upswing in the fortunes of the National Committee to Secure Justice in the Rosenberg Case that had occurred in November 1952 was part of an international phenomenon. Seemingly overnight, the whole world rose in protest against the death sentences that had been imposed on Julius and Ethel Rosenberg. The founding of a British branch of the Committee to Secure Justice was announced in London on November 27, and the French kicked off their campaign just six days later, on December 3. By the end of the year, there were pro-Rosenberg committees in Austria, Belgium, Denmark, Italy, Sweden, Switzerland, Germany, Ireland, Israel and—of course—Eastern Europe.

The founders of the American defense committee could not take credit for their amazing success in the international arena. On the contrary, their affiliates abroad had sprung up at a time when the founders of the parent group were still all but overwhelmed by the influx of new members at home. And within a matter of weeks, the Rosenberg case had become a bigger issue in Europe than it was ever to be in the United States. In France, in particular, it was practically impossible to pick up a newspaper or a magazine without finding an article sympathetic to the Rosenbergs. The faces of Julius and

Ethel, and those of their young sons, stared out from scores of magazine covers. And from the kiosks of Paris to the public squares of the smallest provincial towns, France was blanketed with posters depicting a malevolently grinning Eisenhower with tiny electric chairs instead of teeth.

There could be no question that the rise in pro-Rosenberg sentiment, both in the United States and overseas, was the result of a tremendous outpouring of support from Communist intellectuals, publications, and trained organizers. What *Daily Worker* editor-in-chief John Gates has described as the long deferred "signal from the international movement" had finally come.

But why had the Communists suddenly decided to end their long silence? And why, after ignoring the Rosenbergs for more than two years, did the Party suddenly make their case the focus of a major international propaganda campaign?

One obvious consideration was that the Rosenbergs were continuing to maintain their innocence, even in the wake of their rebuff from the court of appeals. It was now abundantly obvious that Julius and Ethel were prepared to die if necessary. Moreover, the prospects for a new trial, which would give the public another chance to scrutinize the evidence against them, were greatly diminished.

But the precise timing of the Party's entry into the campaign to save the Rosenbergs can only be understood as a reaction to another event that was taking place simultaneously half the world away from the scene of the Rosenbergs' trial and imprisonment: on December 3, 1952—the same day as the founding of the Rosenberg defense committee in France—Rudolf Slansky and ten other former leaders of the Czechoslovakian Communist Party were executed in Prague.

The trial of Slansky and his top aides, which opened in Prague on November 20, had threatened to tear apart the Communist parties of Western Europe. The fourteen defendants, veterans of the Spanish Civil War with many friends and supporters in international Party circles, were tried en masse, and reports of the trial make it clear that the ritualized accusations by scores of hostile witnesses and the even more ritualized "confessions" of the defendants were designed to serve a political end. The full story of the Slansky trials was not to emerge until the 1970s, when the surviving defendants were allowed to defect to the West. But even without firsthand reports from the victims, the outline of what was going on in Prague was clear. Many

Party stalwarts, including some who had managed to close their eyes to the realities of the Stalin purges, found themselves hard put to join in the attack on Slansky.

The most indefensible aspect of the Czech purge was its rampant anti-Semitism. Eleven of the defendants, including eight who were eventually executed, were Jews. And among the purported "crimes" was Zionism. It had been an article of faith among Western Communists that anti-Semitism was not just illegal but obsolete under Communist regimes. But the Slansky trial, which was in part a move to purge the Czech Communist Party of its Jewish leadership, proved otherwise.

What the Western European Party leaders desperately needed at the moment was an issue that could deflect attention from the Slansky purge trial, and the Rosenberg case fit the bill perfectly. The role of spokesman for the shift in Party line fell, as it so often did, to Jacques Duclos, the staunchly pro-Stalinist chairman of the French Communist Party. Speaking in early December 1952, Duclos laid out the "correct" view of the relationship between the Rosenberg and Slansky trials. "The conviction of U.S. atom spies Julius and Ethel Rosenberg was an example of anti-Semitism," Duclos announced, "but the execution of eight Jews in Czechoslovakia last week was not."

Duclos's pronouncement was quickly taken up by Communist intellectuals both in Europe and in the United States. Replying to an "Open Letter" sent by philosopher and anti-Communist author Sidney Hook, the American Communist historian Herbert Aptheker flatly affirmed that while the Slansky trial carried "no anti-Jewish aspect," anti-Semitism "played and plays a part" in the Rosenberg case. Fuming at Hook's charge that a Marxist historian was incapable of objectivity, Aptheker chastised him for asserting that Slansky was framed while the Rosenbergs were guilty of a "heinous crime." Aptheker then explained the difference between the two trials, as he saw it:

> In one trial defendants charged with specific acts of treason, sabotage and murder . . . confess their guilt—but you are sure they were "framed"; in the other case the defendants, though offered their lives if they confess, refuse the offer and persist in maintaining their innocence, but you are sure they are guilty.

But Aptheker's reasoning in declaring the Rosenbergs innocent and Slansky and his associates guilty did much to prove Hook's point: Tom Mooney, Sacco and Vanzetti, and the Scottsboro boys had all been innocent, Aptheker said; by analogy, the Rosenbergs were innocent too. " 'Frame-up,' " wrote Aptheker, "is an American word."

The use of the Rosenberg case to counter criticism of the Slansky purge trials emerged as a common theme in the Rosenberg defense committees that sprang up in many nations. Beyond this, certain national variations rapidly emerged. In Belgium, plans were initiated for a mock tribunal with the debaters representing the Rosenbergs appearing as the accusers, the U.S. government as defendant. In Italy, stories about the plight of the Rosenberg children stressed the tragedy of a double execution that would destroy a family; as the campaign gathered momentum, there would also be strikes by public-service employees and dock workers. In Great Britain, Rosenberg defense-committee organizers used the slogan: "That Roosevelt's Ideals May Live the Rosenbergs Must Not Die."

But it was in France that the Party's claim that the Rosenberg case exposed the rottenness of American democracy was most eagerly seized on. The French were introduced to the Rosenbergs in November 1952 via an article by Howard Fast in L'Humanité. At the time, Fast was a member of the American Communist Party as well as one of its most internationally celebrated novelists. Fast had been approached by Manny Bloch as much as a year earlier with a request that he take up the cause of the Rosenbergs. He had expressed sympathy at the time, but it was not until the case had officially become a Party cause that he took up his pen on Julius and Ethel's behalf. Fast denounced "the stale smell of fascism" which "the Jewish masses of our country . . . detected around Eisenhower," perhaps playing to the very real fear in Europe that the anti-Red hysteria in America was but the first step toward a right-wing dictatorship. The Rosenbergs were no less than "hostages of the American peace movement," their condemnation "a threat to all those . . . who want to put an end to American imperialist aggression in Korea."

One might presume that Fast's readership would have felt sympathy for the Rosenbergs even if they had known that the couple were Communist sympathizers. L'Humanité was, after all, a Communist newspaper. Nevertheless, Fast insisted that Julius and Ethel were "Jews with the opinions of Progressives, but they were not Communists to the best of anyone's knowledge." David Greenglass was described by Fast as a confessed spy with "no connections to the Progressive movement"—this, though Greenglass's former membership in the Young Communist League had already been revealed in *The New York Times*.

Beyond this coyness about the political background of the accused, Fast also became the first to raise the ante on the anti-Semitism issue. In America, even Herbert Aptheker was careful to say that anti-Semitism had been only "an element" in determining the Rosenbergs' fate. Fast, however, suggested that the handling of their case by a Jewish judge and prosecuting attorney was the result of some undefined but sinister conspiracy. Jews "have been judged by Jews" and "sent to death by other Jews," Fast charged. "Exactly the old technique of the Jewish Tribunal employed by Hitler."

Fast's version of the facts in the Rosenberg case was tailor-made to confirm the worst fears of the French Left about the nature of postwar America. And it was embraced with enthusiasm. Thus in a June 1953 article in *Libération* (reprinted in the United States in the *Daily Worker* and the *National Guardian*), Jean-Paul Sartre called the impending execution of the Rosenbergs "a legal lynching which smears with blood a whole nation." The Rosenberg case, he warned his American audience, proves "the bankruptcy of the Atlantic Pact and your inability to lead the Western World." "Be careful," Europeans were saying, "the United States has rabies. Let us sever our ties— or we may in turn be bitten and catch the disease."

Sartre's anti-American screed was just one extreme French reaction to the Rosenberg case. As in the United States, the organizers of the official French Committee to Secure Justice in the Rosenberg Case made some attempt to keep their distance from the Party's uses of the case and to appeal to a broader spectrum of public opinion. Committee secretary Paul Villard has emphasized that he and the other Commit e organizers "never wanted to make the Rosenberg affair into an an . American war machine." But as Villard has also acknowledged, the Committee would have been nothing without Communist support and it gratefully and without the slightest skepticism incorporated the Party's version of the case into its own leaflets.

Fear of war, resentment of America's dominant role on the world scene, and a certain fuzziness about the facts of the case itself—all contributed to making *l'affaire Rosenberg* an overnight sensation. But it was the apparent parallel with France's own Dreyfus case that touched the deepest chords in the national psyche. Europeans in general were all too aware that Klaus Fuchs, a confessed high-level spy, had received only a fourteen-year sentence. Viewed from the other side of the Atlantic, America's insistence on executing two nonentities for the same crime was all too clearly motivated by the need for scapegoats. And the French, harking back to the example of Dreyfus—not to mention the more recent crimes of Nazi collaborators—awaited the approaching double execution in America with a horror not unmixed with satisfaction. The shame of the Dreyfus affair had, for the moment at least, become America's shame.

The charge that the Rosenbergs were victims of anti-Semitism, so widely believed abroad, was far from the majority view in the United States. Julius and Ethel Rosenberg were receiving no support whatsoever from mainstream Jewish organizations, and the American Civil Liberties Union had refused to acknowledge that the case raised any civil-liberties issues at all. The position of the ACLU and the American Jewish Committee (AJC) has long been a matter of public record and is frequently cited as support for the view that the Rosenbergs' trial and sentencing met the highest standards of fairness and legality. Certainly, the refusal of these organizations to jump aboard the propaganda bandwagon of the Committee to Secure Justice is admirable in its way; however, it does not necessarily follow that their reactions were entirely objective. Leaders of both the AJC and the ACLU not only withheld support from the Rosenbergs; they displayed an unseemly eagerness to use the case to curry favor with the government and dissociate themselves from any taint of Red.

In America as abroad, the fact the Rosenbergs were Jews was on everyone's mind. It was entirely possible to support the Rosenbergs' conviction and still question whether they would have received the extreme penalty if they had been Gentiles. Even if this question was ultimately unanswerable, it deserved some consideration, particularly in light of the crude anti-Semitic letters and poems that exulted in the impending executions. (Many newspaper editors and officials of Jewish organizations had been on the receiving end of at least one specimen of this genre; the Committee to Secure Justice in the Rosenberg Case kept a file of its anti-Semitic hate mail.)

Nevertheless, no less an authority than the noted Jewish scholar

Lucy Dawidowicz argued that conscientious Jews must not support the clemency campaign, even for purely humanitarian reasons. Writing in the December 22 issue of *The New Leader,* Dawidowicz rightly deplored the Communist Party's cynical comparisons between the Rosenberg sentencing and Nazi atrocities. The Party, she noted, was now attempting to use Jews as it had long used blacks as part of its "war against America." There could be no defensible reason for an anti-Communist to support clemency, Dawidowicz concluded. Even the "thousand to one" chance that Julius or Ethel might eventually confess could not be sufficient reason for sparing their lives—since to back down from the death sentence would carry with it the appearance of caving in to the Communists' "moral blackmail."

So, too, the American Jewish Committee not only declined to join in the call for clemency but became an open advocate of the death penalty. The AJC's position on the Rosenberg case was hardly surprising in view of its history of refusing to speak out on behalf of Jews whose civil liberties were threatened by HUAC investigations or Smith Act prosecutions. Privately, the AJC leadership did not doubt that there was an anti-Jewish current underlying much of the red-baiting that was going on. But their public reaction was to disavow the victims as in no way typical of the patriotic and anti-Communist American Jewish community.

When the "atom spy" scandal reached its peak with the arrest of Julius Rosenberg in July 1950, the AJC had begun frantic planning for a multifaceted propaganda campaign. As Victor Navasky has argued in his discussion of the AJC's policies during this period, fear that the Jewishness of so many of the atom-spy suspects would provoke an anti-Semitic reaction led to a defensive attempt to prove the patriotism of America's Jewish community and "scare off" Jews who might be attracted to the Left.

These concerns are reflected in a lengthy but highly revealing interoffice memo prepared by an AJC staff member for Executive Director John B. Slawson on July 31, 1950, just weeks after Julius Rosenberg's arrest. Entitled "Public Relations Effects of Jewish Atom Spies," it read:

> Considerable concern has been expressed over public disclosures
> of spy activities by Jews and people with Jewish-sounding names
> [obviously a reference to Klaus Fuchs, whom many mistakenly

believed to be a Jew]. The present situation is regarded as being potentially more dangerous than the situation which obtained during World War II; for now the enemy is seen as Communist Russia rather than Nazi Germany.

The main reason for concern is the belief that the non-Jewish public may generalize from these activities and impute to the Jews as a group treasonable motives and activities. . . .

We miss yet another bet in the use of our investigative staff. During recent years we infiltrated into rightist organizations to explore them, etc. Why can't we do this with Communist organizations, also using our knowledge to scare off Jews?

Because it seems likely that the AJC will undertake some propaganda campaign in connection with these problems I should like to make some constructive suggestions along propaganda lines. The principle underlying these suggestions is that the propaganda of the deed or propaganda of facts may have greater positive value than propaganda of exhortation. . . .

Instead of arguing exhortatively that Jews are not Communists, that they hate Russia, that Russia hates Jews, more positive approaches based on propaganda of fact can be used. One of the difficulties of propaganda of exhortation is not only that links may be established where none now exist, but also that there will always be instances to prove the exception of the propaganda claim; that is, there may be more Jewish atomic spies or Jewish Communist leaders who will be arrested and found guilty.

The following propaganda of fact ideas may be tried out:

1. Stories about how Russia stifles and oppresses its various minorities, including Jews, despite its claims to the contrary.

2. Stories about how Russia recruits spies and controls Communist Party members in this country. (Such an expose would be most useful in Yiddish and Anglo-Jewish newspapers.)

3. Stories of American party systems and voting, showing how party ties cut across all religious and ethnic lines. Possibly attention could be paid even to third party groups and parties left of center.

4. Exposes on how Communists work in this country, infiltrating into various institutions such as labor unions, etc., and

5. Stories of how Communists are fought in this country through constitutional means such as labor unions (Dubinsky kicks them out) and through government, featuring the work of such U.S. attorneys as Irving Saypol. (In this connection it may

be pointed out that Saypol and other Jews on the "right side" may have as much or little chance of recognition as do Jews on the "wrong side.")

6. Stories and reprints of stories on Russian attacks against Israel, against Zionists, against the use of the Hebrew language.

7. Reprints and stories of Israel siding with the United States against Korean aggression.

8. Stories of how the present government in Israel keeps down Communists. . . .

The subsequent efforts of AJC staff member Rabbi S. Andhill Fineberg to expose Communist infiltration of the Committee to Secure Justice sound very much like the "propaganda of fact" outlined in this memo. Beginning in 1952, Fineberg closely followed the activities of the Committee, compiling research for a book-length exposé. This work, *The Rosenberg Case: Fact and Fiction*, was eventually published in late 1953 and had the imprimatur of a semiofficial government document. Prepublication copies of the manuscript were submitted to James B. Kilsheimer of the U.S. Attorney's office in New York as well as to several individuals in the State Department.

Not surprisingly, Fineberg's book turned out to be a slavish endorsement of every aspect of the government's handling of the case. Fineberg had done his homework; much of his critique of the trial and the distortions spread about it by pro-Rosenberg propagandists was deadly accurate. However, the rabbi's shocking insensitivity to the humanitarian arguments in favor of clemency—coupled with an eagerness to brand anyone who questioned the death sentences as a Communist dupe or worse—can hardly have made a favorable impression on the liberal readership that he wanted to impress.

Rabbi Fineberg's willingness to produce what in the end amounted to no more than a counterpropaganda tract was matched, and in some ways even exceeded, by the efforts of the leadership of the American Civil Liberties Union to lend themselves to the government's campaign to get Julius and Ethel to recant.

The ACLU, as historian Mary Sperling McAuliffe has shown, had long ago embarked on a campaign to strengthen itself against attacks from the Right by placing itself on the record as staunchly anti-Communist. The organization had opposed the Smith Act in 1940 (though in the same year Communist Elizabeth Gurley Flynn was ejected from its board of directors), but by 1948 it refused to come out in support of Communists arrested under that law, finding no free-speech issue involved in the conviction of the defendants for teaching and advocating communism. Reconciling the organization's goal of defending the rights of individuals with its reluctance to defend individual Communists involved a delicate balancing act, and the leadership was often hard pressed to defend its policies to its own members. Behind the scenes, ACLU staffers sometimes resorted to tactics of exactly the sort that their group had been formed to combat. As was revealed in 1977, several ACLU leaders, including its long-time cocounsel Morris Ernst, maintained contact with the FBI for the purpose of informing the Bureau of the names of pro-Communist members in local affiliates and even passing on reports of ACLU meetings.

Under the circumstances, it was inevitable that the ACLU's board would resist pressure to get involved in the Rosenberg case. In fact, the organization went to the opposite extreme. Officially, the organization took no position at all on the Rosenbergs until the spring of 1952 when pressure from the membership could no longer be ignored. By this time, ACLU board member Osmond Fraenkel had studied the transcript of the trial and become concerned that the Rosenbergs had, in effect, been tried for treason without the benefit of any of the constitutional safeguards guaranteed to individuals accused of that crime. But Fraenkel's view was not destined to prevail within the board. It voted 18 to 4 in favor of a resolution that denied the case raised any civil-liberties issues.

The ACLU's decision, announced by its co-counsel Herbert Monte Levy at a May 2 press conference, dealt a serious blow to the still struggling Rosenberg defense committee. Not only did the ACLU go on record as affirming the fairness of the trial, but it found that the death sentence could not be termed "cruel and unusual punishment," since there were instances on record of capital sentences for other defendants convicted of peacetime espionage—even though none of these executions had ever been carried out. The statement read by Levy even hinted that the ACLU would not oppose new legislation mandating the death sentence for passing atomic data to allied nations in peacetime.

Except for the pro-Rosenberg *National Guardian*, the American press saw nothing unseemly in a leading civil-liberties organization's giving a green light to what amounted to an unprecedented expansion of the government's power of capital punishment. Overseas, however, the reaction was quite different: the more civil-libertarian and religious groups in America rushed to defend the government, the more the mainstream press abroad began to feel that America must have something to be defensive about.

Such suspicions were quite justified in view of the secret behind-the-scenes efforts of ACLU co-counsel Morris Ernst, who hoped to use his reputation as a champion of civil rights in order to gain a foothold in the Rosenberg defense camp, where he could then covertly serve the interest of the FBI. Ernst's interest in playing a role in the atom-spy cases was established even before Julius Rosenberg's arrest. On June 1, 1950, Ernst phoned his FBI contact L. B. Nichols to advise that some of his friends had suggested he volunteer to act as Harry Gold's defense counsel. If Nichols's report of the phone conversation can be believed, Ernst made clear from the beginning that he would undertake the chore only "if this was something he should do wherein he could render a service. . . ." Gold was by this time already fully willing to act as a government witness and Nichols dismissed Ernst's offer.

In December 1952 Ernst was back in touch with the Bureau again, this time to inform Nichols that Julius Rosenberg's sister and brother had visited him, asking him "to intersede [*sic*] in the Rosenberg case." The Rosenberg relatives had told Ernst—or so he claimed—that Manny Bloch "was not only agreeable" to his intervention but was ready to step aside. Ernst's own intentions in the matter, as summarized by Nichols, were somewhat less than disinterested:

> Ernst stated he would be interested on only one ground, namely, that he could make some contribution; that he knows that the . . . [Russians'] whole propaganda approach, not only in Russia, but in this country as well, is going to save the Rosenbergs; that he is convinced if Rosenberg breaks and tells all he knows this would be a terrific story and probably would be most helpful to the Bureau; that he is considering seeing Bloch and agreeing to get in on the case on one condition; that he see Rosenberg with Bloch once, and then talk to Rosenberg privately, at which time he will give his final decision . . . that he realizes it is a 100 to one shot; that he is interested from a psychological standpoint.

> For example, all the members of the family say that Rosenberg insists he is innocent, that his sentence was the result of a frame-up and he is hysterical, but never once does he mention Communism; that he, Ernst, is convinced that if Rosenberg made a complete confession this would save their lives, but that he did not want to contact Rosenberg or get into this case unless this was agreeable and he also wanted to have as much information as possible on the Rosenbergs to aid him in talking to them.

Nichols's memo paints a shocking picture of a lawyer offering to represent prospective clients only with the FBI's permission and then, in effect, only to act as the Bureau's servant. The Bureau, however, was not very warm to the plan. Nichols told Ernst that the case was now "out of our hands" though he did relay the message to Hoover, who agreed with Nichols's assessment that the FBI "simply could not under any circumstances become involved."

Ernst did not give up. On January 9, 1953, he dropped in at the FBI's headquarters to reiterate to Nichols that he was still willing to go to work for the Rosenberg defense "solely for the purpose of being able to talk to the Rosenbergs and possibly getting them to talk." Now, however, Ernst conceded that Bloch was no longer interested in stepping aside—assuming that he ever had been, in reality—and that in his view, "Bloch wants the Rosenbergs to be executed."

On this visit, Ernst also volunteered his own observations on the dynamics of the relationship between Julius and Ethel. In Nichols's words: "He [Ernst] has conducted quite a psychological study of the Rosenbergs and has come to the conclusion that Julius is the slave and his wife, Ethel, the master." Ernst had never even spoken with the Rosenbergs, so it is difficult to see how his amateur psychologizing could be given any serious consideration. Regardless, the theory was eagerly seized upon because it gave some semblance of justification for going ahead with the execution of Ethel. Echoes of the Ernst "psychological study" would later appear in official reports, statements by the attorney general, and eventually in Eisenhower's personal correspondence.

Ernst, meanwhile, continued to meet with members of the Rosenberg family and to pass on his reports to the FBI, even after it had become clear that he was unlikely ever to secure permission from Bloch for an interview with Julius and Ethel. As late as a week before the execution, Ernst reported to Nichols his latest theory that "the first break" in the Rosenbergs' wall of silence would come if and when authorities could find a way to get them to admit their Communist beliefs—something they had not conceded even to Julius's brother and sisters.

Although no direct link can be established, Ernst's plan for getting close to the Rosenbergs sounds curiously like a part of the program for a "psychological warfare project" involving the Rosenbergs hatched by the CIA sometime in late 1952 or early 1953. According to a January 22, 1953, memorandum passed along by Allen Dulles to an FBI liaison, the program called for using supposedly neutral third parties such as "rabbis, representatives of Jewish organizations . . . [or] former Communists" who might win the Rosenbergs' confidence in prison and then try to persuade them that the Soviet Union was really an anti-Semitic power bent on exterminating Jews within its borders. Once their illusions about the Soviet Union had been shattered, the Rosenbergs would receive clemency in exchange for their agreeing to "appeal to Jews in all countries to get out of the communist movement and seek to destroy it." The author of the memo, perhaps significantly, felt that the best possible choice for such a mission would be "intelligent rabbis, representing reformed Judaism, with a radical background . . . and with psychiatric knowledge."

The CIA proposal amounted to nothing more nor less than a proposal to convert the Rosenbergs to anticommunism. The memo goes on to explain the propaganda benefits that would ensue:

> The Communist Parties throughout the world have built up the Rosenbergs as heroes and martyrs to "American anti-Semitism." Their recantation would entail backfiring of this entire Soviet propaganda effort. It would virtually be impossible for world communism to ignore or successfully discredit the Rosenbergs.

The anonymous CIA strategist who conceived this plan at least deserves credit for being a better psychologist than his FBI counterparts. He (or she) recognized that whatever else one might think of the Rosenbergs, they had displayed tremendous courage. It was pointless to expect such people to "trade their principles for their lives," and an offer of mercy in exchange for naming accomplices would inevitably be rejected by them as an "appeal to cowardice."

Otherwise, the notion that the Rosenbergs might be induced to recant their allegiance to communism at this late date was unrealistic, to say the least. The author of the CIA memo seems to have been under the impression that the Rosenbergs had never heard any hint of the existence of Russian slave-labor camps or the Stalinist purges. If Julius and Ethel were informed of such horrors now "from an unimpeachable source," the memo speculates, the news might "come as a great shock to them." What this overlooks is that the Rosenbergs had undoubtedly heard of such charges and rejected them as so much capitalist propaganda; indeed, we can be sure that the Rosenbergs even knew about the Slansky trials since they continued to receive the *National Guardian* while incarcerated at Sing Sing.

In any case, it is most unlikely that anyone could have won the Rosenbergs' confidence for the purpose of putting the CIA's plan into action, as is demonstrated by the failure of Morris Ernst to so much as get an interview with Julius and Ethel. Manny Bloch had consistently rejected any overtures that would have led to personal contact between the Rosenbergs and third parties, whether would-be defense attorneys or Committee activists. Nor did the Rosenbergs ever give the slightest indication that they desired any such contacts. They had placed their complete trust in their beloved friend and counselor, Manny Bloch.

24

"New Evidence"

In mid-April 1953, the National Committee to Secure Justice in the Rosenberg Case announced that the missing console table had been found. The table, it seems, had been sitting in plain view in the Washington Heights apartment of Julius Rosenberg's mother, Sophie, for more than a year. Being illiterate and thus unable to follow press accounts of her son's trial, the elder Mrs. Rosenberg never dreamed that she was harboring a crucial piece of evidence. Nor had it ever occurred to Emanuel Bloch, who visited the Rosenberg children at the apartment on numerous occasions, to look for the elusive table in such an obvious place.

According to the Committee, the table had finally been identified by *National Guardian* reporter Leon Summit acting on an assignment from his editor. Armed with photos of the table and an affidavit from a Macy's employee supporting their contention that the table had indeed come from that store, the Committee called for the reopening of the Rosenbergs' case.

With this turn of events, the issue of the console table took on a new importance. The production of the table convinced a number of skeptics that the government's case had been built on a tissue of circumstantial evidence and perjured testimony. Prominent among the converts was Malcolm Sharp, a University of Chicago law professor who had previously been critical of the conduct of the Rosenberg-

Sobell trial but convinced of the defendants' guilt. Now Sharp agreed to join with Manny Bloch in preparing a motion for a new trial based in part on the discovery of the table.

In the same article that announced the table's discovery, the *National Guardian* reconstructed the course of events that had led to its disappearance. After the Rosenbergs' arrests, they had continued to pay rent on their Knickerbocker Village apartment until October 1950, when they ran out of funds. Realizing that they would never raise bail and could expect to be in prison for some time, no matter what the outcome of their trial, the couple authorized Manny Bloch to dispose of their household goods and vacate the apartment. Bloch inspected the apartment in the company of Julius's brother, David, and the latter agreed to see to the disposal of the furniture. Some time later, Bloch was informed that the entire lot had been sold by Sophie Rosenberg to a Lower East Side dealer in secondhand furniture.

What Bloch did not know was that Julius's sisters, Ethel and Lena, had visited the apartment before the furniture was sold and decided between them to salvage some of the household goods, so that Julius and Ethel would not have to begin from scratch when and if they set up housekeeping again. Lena had taken home some kitchen utensils and pots, and Ethel collected the children's toys and bureaus as well as the console table.

The table was stored in the basement of Ethel's home until the summer of 1951, when Bloch arranged for the Rosenberg sons to be removed from the Hebrew Children's Home, where they had remained during the trial, to the custody of Sophie Rosenberg. At that time, Sophie's daughter Ethel moved the children's things and the table was moved with them.

In an affidavit that Ethel Rosenberg Goldberg later made available to Manny Bloch, she said that neither she nor the other Rosenberg relatives had been aware of the trial testimony concerning a console table. Although members of the family had visited Julius and Ethel in prison, none had attended the trial. Ethel Goldberg also said that she had been too upset to read newspaper accounts of the proceedings. "Prior to the trial and for some time after," she explained, "I was in a state of semi-hysteria because of the impact of the arrests and the implications of the charges."

Manny Bloch, for his part, had believed the console table irretrievably lost, along with the rest of the Rosenbergs' furniture. When it became an issue at the trial, he simply assumed it had gone to one of the hundreds of pushcart dealers who operated on the Lower East Side and thought any effort at tracing its whereabouts would be futile. No one asked members of the Rosenberg family about the console table until the *National Guardian* took up the search in March 1953.

Having produced the table, the Rosenbergs' supporters' next step was to establish its authenticity. The *National Guardian* reporter visited the home of the elderly black maid, Evelyn Cox. Mrs. Cox reportedly recognized the console table, but she refused to sign any affidavit whatsoever, saying she was "sick and tired" of the whole subject and did not want to become involved in another controversy.

Photos of the table were also shown to Joseph Fontana, a Macy's furniture buyer for many years, who provided an affidavit identifying some chalk or grease-pencil markings still visible on the table's underside as being similar to those used in Macy's warehouses during 1944 and the years immediately following.

In a reflex response, the government would attempt to dispute the provenance of the table, sight unseen. James B. Kilsheimer, who had succeeded Saypol and Lane in the office of U.S. attorney, solicited a second affidavit from Fontana, in which he expressed some reservations about the table's markings: The ones he had seen in the photos appeared to be in white chalk but, as far as he knew, colored grease pencil had been used exclusively by Macy's. Another affidavit was provided by a Macy's warehouse foreman, Joseph Fitzgerald. Fitzgerald disputed the defense's contention that the number "1997" marked on the table could represent its price, since Macy's used a pricing code that involved the addition of certain apparently meaningless numbers. Possibly hundreds of tables were sold at $19.97; but the prices on such tables would have been indicated in code as 192972.

The government's affidavits sounded impressive but were really no more conclusive than the Committee's claims. Neither Fontana nor Fitzgerald had examined the table itself, and it is difficult to see how anyone could distingush white chalk from colored grease pencil by looking at black-and-white photographs.

In any case, even if the table could be proven genuine, it was of doubtful value as legal evidence. Malcolm Sharp, who was convinced enough about the relevance of the console table as an issue to devote three weeks to helping Manny Bloch prepare a motion for a new trial, realized that the chances of persuading the courts to grant a new trial on the basis of the table were slim. The rule of thumb regarding new evidence is that it must be so compelling that it would likely have resulted in the defendants' acquittal if presented at the time of the trial. The console table did not fit this requirement—unless, of course, it could be shown that the prosecutors had willfully misrepresented its significance, which was another matter.

But legal questions aside, what was the true story of the table's history? On the face of it, there would seem to be two possibilities. Either the *Guardian*'s story was a fraud and another table had been substituted for the original one, or the story was true, in which case the production of the real table would tend to confirm the Rosenbergs' innocence. Strangely enough, references to the table in the FBI files support neither of these alternatives.

Once again, it is the reports of the informer Tartakow that provide a lead to a startlingly different interpretation of the table's history. When Jerry Tartakow first mentioned the table in late March 1951, shortly after the subject had come up in the courtroom, it was only to report Julius Rosenberg's disappointment that Bloch had been unable to obtain a copy of the sales slip from Macy's records. Tartakow wrote then that as a result of this conversation he was "convinced that Rosenberg purchased the table as claimed."

A day later, however, we find agent Cammarota reporting the results of a second conversation between Tartakow and Rosenberg on the subject of the table. Tartakow now said that "Rosenberg stated that the console table which has three holes in it was left at his sister's house and was the one he used for photography work. Claims he photographed a one thousand page booklet on radar onto a small roll of microfilm, using this table."

The second part of this statement may be dismissed as worthless since Tartakow could easily have made it up to impress the FBI. But the remark, attributed to Julius, that the console table was "left at his sister's house" is curious indeed. How could Tartakow possibly have known this? And if he had heard it from Julius himself, which seems the only logical possibility, then why hadn't Julius instructed Bloch to go to Ethel Goldberg's house and secure the table—*unless* he felt that there might be something incriminating to him about the table's physical appearance.

The failure of the government to follow up on this lead is not at all mysterious. Cammarota's report was not filed until the last day of the trial, and by the time the information reached the U.S. Attorney's office it would have been too late to go looking for new evidence—evidence that was hardly necessary to support an already solid case.

What did strike us as mysterious about Tartakow's report is his description of the table as having "three holes in it." Just how these "three holes" might have constituted an adaptation for microfilming is unclear—as unclear, in fact, as Ruth Greenglass's testimony that the table had a "hollowed out" portion on its underside that was somehow used for mounting a lamp. But while we were not sure what the function of the three holes would have been, something about Tartakow's mention of them seemed very familiar. Checking back through FBI documents and the trial testimony about the table we could find nothing similar. Then, in a footnote to Malcolm Sharp's 1956 book on the Rosenberg case, we came upon this description, based on his firsthand examination of the table produced by the *National Guardian*:

> The appearance of the table seems to me to establish its identity beyond doubt. On the other hand, its physical condition would have introduced one new problem . . . and the Rosenbergs are not alive to give the testimony which they were prepared to give about this problem. The problem results, according to a statement made by Julius Rosenberg for Mr. Bloch, from Julius Rosenberg's amateur attempts to repair the table or tinker with it. The most interesting feature of the resulting condition is the presence of holes on one side of the table. The turning mechanism [which allowed one leaf of the console table to swing outward] was broken and the holes were evidently for a support, never completed. No one would describe the holes or anything that could ever have been connected with them as "a portion . . . hollowed out."

It would seem that the table seen by Malcolm Sharp was the same one Julius described to Tartakow at the time of the trial. If so, then the Rosenbergs were telling the truth when they testified that the table was an inexpensive model purchased from Macy's—though this does not necessarily prove that it was paid for by them and was not in some sense a gift from a Russian agent. On the other hand, Sharp's confidence that Julius Rosenberg would have been able to explain away peculiarities in the table's appearance seems touchingly naïve. Had Rosenberg been equally confident that the table would help his case he could have told Bloch where it was stored back in 1951, and the *Guardian* reporter's last-minute detective work would have been unnecessary.

One final piece of evidence that turned up in the FBI files supports the conclusion that the Rosenbergs knew the table's whereabouts all along and were not at all pleased by the efforts to produce it. In a February 1953 report on the results of surreptitious surveillance of the Rosenbergs' prison visits, there is a description of a conversation between Ethel Rosenberg and her sister-in-law Ethel Goldberg that had taken place several days earlier. According to this report, Ethel Goldberg asked something about the table, whereupon "Ethel Rosenberg flew into a rage and told Goldberg: 'Don't you mention that table in here. It doesn't concern you and you shouldn't mention it.'" Later, during their regular Wednesday visit together, the FBI report goes on, Julius mentioned to Ethel that his sister had also asked him about the table and he had told her "that she should not mention the table or the high chair, that it was none of their business." Julius's comment about a "high chair" mystified the author of the FBI report, who pointed out he could find no previous reference to it in any of the Bureau's investigative files on the case.

A second batch of "new evidence" in the Rosenberg case surfaced, quite surprisingly, in Paris, where the April 18, 1953, issue of the French paper *Le Combat* carried the texts of certain confidential memoranda that had been stolen from the files of David Greenglass's lawyer O. John Rogge. In the most sensational of these documents, Ruth Greenglass was quoted as saying that her husband had a "tendency to hysteria," that "once when he had the grippe he ran nude through the hallway screaming of 'elephants' and 'lead pants,'" and that "she had known him since he was ten years old . . . [and that] he would say things were so even if they were not."

There was also a very sketchy handwritten statement made by David Greenglass to his attorneys on the morning after his arrest, which included a comment that Greenglass feared that the technical data he had given Gold "may not be at all" what he had described to the Bureau the previous night and which mentioned only in passing Rosenberg's involvement. Still other papers revealed that there had been communications between the Greenglasses' lawyers and Myles Lane of the U.S. Attorney's office over the question of whether Greenglass would stand trial in New Mexico or New York.

As propaganda, the Rogge memos were pure gold. But on close examination they are far less compelling than the summaries of them in Committee leaflets and broadsides would have one believe. Ruth's statement about her husband's erratic behavior certainly inspires curiosity. On the other hand, it was made during a confidential conversation with her attorney at a time when it seemed that David might still wish to repudiate his confession. Ruth may well have been probing for an indication that a defense of mental instability could extricate her husband from a desperate situation.

As for the Committee's charge that certain memos showed evidence of a deal between Rogge's firm and the prosecutors, exchanging perjured testimony for the lenient treatment of David and Ruth, the documents themselves tell quite a different story. There were indeed conversations between Robert Gordon and Herbert Fabricant, on Rogge's behalf, and Myles Lane, but this in itself is hardly surprising given that Rogge's client was facing indictment in two states and had decided to plead guilty. Far from engaging in hard bargaining, however, the memos show that Rogge and his partners approached Lane gingerly. As late as August 23, 1950, more than a month after both Greenglasses had agreed to cooperate and given lengthy statements to the FBI, Rogge still did not know whether Ruth would be indicted. Thus Robert Gordon, reporting to Rogge after a discussion with Lane, wrote, "There is no indication that Ruth is to be indicted and neither Herb nor I wanted to raise the point. . . . I didn't even want to ask the question though you may desire to do so."

Another memo, of which the Committee made much, records Herbert Fabricant's first conversation with David Greenglass on the morning after the latter's confession. The version of this memo published by the Rosenbergs' defenders in France and in the United States contains only a cryptically worded reference to Rosenberg, noting that he "is very close to this situation" and that Greenglass had told the FBI that Julius once introduced him to "a man in a car" who had "apparently" made a request for secret data. This, according to the Committee, indicates that David was in the process of inventing a tale that would shift the blame for his crime onto

Rosenberg, and that the "man in a car" story was the only accusation against Rosenberg he had made to the FBI up to that point.

It would indeed have been odd if Greenglass had said nothing more about Rosenberg at this conference. But when the published Rogge memos are placed side by side with copies of the same documents obtained from O. John Rogge's own files it becomes clear that the Committee released only the first and third pages of a three-page memorandum. And on the second page, which clearly reads as a continuation of the first, one finds Greenglass's statement that Julius Rosenberg had given him "$4,000, nearly $5,000, and that Louis Abel has it." This page also records Greenglass's answer when asked by Fabricant if he planned to cooperate with the government. Greenglass exclaimed, "Hell, no," and added that he had tried as much as possible "to keep Julius Rosenberg out of the picture." Finally, Fabricant noted: "The client wants to see his brother-in-law Louis Abel and wants us to get in touch with Julius Rosenberg." This picture of Greenglass trying, however ineptly, to shield Rosenberg and send a warning to him via his lawyers would hardly have served the Committee's purposes.

One document among the batch of stolen memos did contain information that had potential value for the Rosenbergs' legal defense. This was Greenglass's handwritten statement that contained an admission that he was not sure that the data he gave Gold was as he had described it to the FBI. Here, however, it is clear that Greenglass is referring only to the technical content of the information. And it is true that when he was interrogated later on this subject his memory of certain details proved to be shaky, though his testimony remained the same in substance. In this same statement, too, Greenglass said that he had not recalled that Gold had visited his Albuquerque home twice in one day but had "allowed" this detail to be incorporated in his statement. This, while hardly proof of perjury, might have led a curious appeals judge to wonder whether Greenglass was equally open to suggestion on other topics.

While the "new evidence" revealed in the Rogge documents was actually less sensational than Committee descriptions of it led many to believe, the mystery of how material from Rogge's private files happened to find its way into the pages of a French newspaper was fascinating in itself. Rogge's firm, as it happened, did not even suspect that its files had been rifled until April 29, 1953, when an agent from the New York office of the FBI called to confirm the authenticity of the material that had by then appeared in France.

This was the first anyone in the Rogge firm had heard about *Le Combat's* scoop. Robert Gordon immediately ordered law secretary Helen Pagano to bring him the Greenglass file, which at the moment happened to be stored in a knee-level cubbyhole in the desk of Herbert Fabricant. Fabricant was out of the office on that particular day but both Gordon and Pagano knew he had taken the file to his office the previous week, intending to prepare for an interview with a journalist and that he had reported nothing amiss. Now, incredulous, they checked and rechecked the contents of the file folder, searching in vain for the originals of the memos that had appeared in *Le Combat*. Just as the FBI had intimated, all of the documents were missing.

The next morning, John Harrington, the New York FBI's chief investigator on the Rosenberg case, showed up at the Rogge offices to interview Herbert Fabricant, who in addition to being the last individual to see the memos in question was also the author of several of them. While explaining to Harrington that whoever took the memos appeared to have chosen selectively from a larger file, Fabricant removed the Greenglass folder from the desk cubbyhole where Helen Pagano had replaced it the afternoon before and began thumbing through the documents. And there, to his embarrassment, were the formerly missing memos!

Although the unnoticed disappearance of the memos, combined with their sudden overnight return, might at first suggest that the theft was an inside operation, Harrington soon concluded that this was by no means the only, or even a very likely, possibility, given that the Rogge firm was a small one with only a handful of trusted employees. Harrington's prime theory at first was that the burglary of the Rogge offices must have been the work of a paid professional—a theory supported by a tip from an anonymous FBI informer within the Committee who claimed that the organization had paid $25,000 for the memoranda. This tip (which was in fact never verified) began to look less compelling when Harrington learned that the Greenglass folder had been routinely kept in file cabinets in the stenographic pool, down the hall from the Rogge offices proper and adjacent to a law library used by several other law firms in the building, including that of Emanuel Bloch.

Suspicion that someone connected with the Rosenberg defense

effort might have used access to the law library as an opportunity to steal the Greenglass file did nothing to thaw the already embittered relationship between the two lawyers who were formerly close colleagues, and the argument was only exacerbated when Manny Bloch showed up several days later in the company of a secretary to discuss the matter. The existence of the memoranda had been reported that same morning in both *The New York Times* and the *Daily Worker*, which had picked up the story from French publications, but Bloch admitted in a tense meeting that he had been informed about the memos earlier through a cable from French defense-committee organizer Paul Villard.

According to Fabricant's account of the conversation, Bloch professed to be "outraged by the activities of all sorts of political figures and his committee." But now he was in a jam. Personally, he did not consider the stolen memoranda significant enough to turn the tide in the case; in his opinion, he felt that he had done more to undermine Greenglass's story in his cross-examination than the handwritten statement did. Nevertheless, if he failed to pursue the issue through legal channels he would be "castigated by his committee."

None of this lessened the anger of Rogge and Fabricant, who demanded that Bloch turn over the photostats of the documents, which had been sent to him by Paul Villard. Fabricant then asked "pointedly" how Villard had obtained the copies.

"I assume that he got them from *Combat*," Bloch replied.

"But how did *Combat* get them?" Fabricant pressed on.

"That," replied Bloch, "is a very good question and I am going to try to find the answer."

Although no one ever did come up with a definitive answer to the question of who took the documents, it seems clear in retrospect that Emanuel Bloch had nothing to do with the theft. Bloch had known about the existence of the memoranda for more than two weeks and, to the dismay of the Committee, had made no effort to use them as the basis for a new appeal. And even after May 4, 1953, the day the existence of the memos was revealed in the American press, Bloch insisted on submitting the question of his right to use them to the ethics committee of the New York City Bar Association. Bloch's further correspondence with O. John Rogge and with the Bar Association committee reveal his deep distress and embarrassment over the whole issue. If anything, Bloch appeared to be going out of his way to see even fewer legal possibilities in the use of the documents than they actually presented.

While Bloch kept official silence about the existence of the memos pending an answer from the Bar Association, the leaders of the National Committee to Secure Justice fumed. Those who truly believed that the Rosenbergs were victims of a government frame-up were convinced that the memos were just the tip of the iceberg and that a court-ordered review of the Greenglasses' pretrial statements would vindicate Julius and Ethel. Since these convinced disciples never seriously considered the possibility that a full disclosure might prove just the opposite—destroying the Rosenbergs' dearly held moral and political position even if by some slim chance it might provide the technical grounds for a new trial—they could not begin to fathom that this might be one of the reasons for Bloch's delays. As far as the Committee was concerned, the situation was in its eleventh hour and the time for worrying about the legal niceties had passed.

On May 11, the Committee, pressing Bloch, informed its branch correspondents that "a nation-wide campaign has been launched to bring the newly discovered evidence of perjury in the Rosenberg case to the American people." Copies of the documents themselves, along with pamphlets offering a "detailed analysis" of their significance, were in the mail and volunteers were needed to get the message into the streets. On June 4, keeping up the pressure, it announced the release of four new documents: actually, three memos from the original batch taken from the Rogge files along with an affidavit from Ethel and David's brother Bernard Greenglass concerning David's admission that he had stolen samples of uranium from Los Alamos, an incident already alluded to at the trial, but crucial to the Committee's contention that the FBI had already been "out to get" Greenglass before May 1950. Committee spokesman Joseph Brainin (who, coincidentally or not, had made a two-week trip in April to confer with leaders of the French committee) made no attempt to explain how the memoranda had managed to surface in France. Legally, however, the chain of circumstances was a fortunate one for the national leadership of the Committee, since they could hardly be prosecuted for their use of material they had only picked up from published sources abroad.

Manny Bloch, meanwhile, could no longer resist the pressure to use the "new evidence" as the basis for an appeal for a new trial.

With the assistance of Malcolm Sharp and another late addition to the defense team, the elderly but still combative veteran civil-rights lawyer John Finerty, Bloch drew up a motion, citing the revelations of the Rogge memos as well as the discovery of the controversial missing console table. The motions were served on Saturday, June 6, 1953, and on Monday afternoon Judge Kaufman heard several hours of oral arguments on the motion.

Judge Kaufman appeared impatient with the whole proceedings and spent only fifteen minutes in his chambers before emerging to deliver a negative decision, which took thirty-two minutes to read. Kaufman explained his ability to produce a thirty-two-minute statement in fifteen minutes by noting that he had been in possession of the Rosenberg lawyers' brief since Saturday and had had ample time to study it over the weekend and prepare notes.

Although Kaufman may well have been legally correct in his ruling that the new evidence did not merit a new trial, his obvious haste to dispose of the motion in a manner that would not delay the Rosenbergs' execution, now scheduled for June 18, their fourteenth wedding anniversary, certainly did nothing to quell the suspicions of those all over the world who suspected that the government case was a frame-up. But Judge Kaufman was not alone in wanting to avoid complications that would set the execution date back. On Wednesday, June 10, the court of appeals announced that it would affirm Kaufman's decision without hearing arguments on the motion itself or on the defense's application for a stay of execution. And that weekend, Supreme Court Justice Robert Jackson tried unsuccessfully to persuade his colleague William O. Douglas to provide the crucial vote that would enable the Rosenberg defense team to argue the same motions before the full Supreme Court.

25

Eisenhower and Clemency

The impact of the Rosenberg case on Franco-American relations had by now become a major headache for the newly installed Eisenhower administration. Virtually the entire spectrum of the French press—including the pro-NATO *Franc-Tireur*, the anti-neutralist *Le Figaro*, and the right-wing *L'Aurore*—had come out against the executions, if only in the name of mercy, and the normally staid *Le Monde* criticized the American courts' refusal to grant a new trial as "barbaric," editorializing that the situation had degenerated into "a test of nerves, not of truth."

As early as December 1952, before Eisenhower took office, the chief of the CIA's station in Paris had been concerned enough by the success of the Communists' propaganda effort to assign the embassy's young press attaché the task of preparing a white paper rebutting the charge that the Rosenberg-Sobell trial had been a frame-up. The press attaché, who happened to be Ben Bradlee, now executive editor of the *Washington Post*, was dispatched on a quick trip back to the United States to do research. When Bradlee arrived in New York, however, he missed meeting his CIA contact and had to call a Mr. Maran in the Attorney General's office to explain his mission personally. To Bradlee's dismay, Maran was not impressed. Told Bradlee was on an "urgent" mission, "sent here by Robert Thayer who is head of the CIA in Paris," and that he needed access to the Justice Department's confidential files on the Rosenberg case, Maran refused to show him anything without official clearance from the Department. And so Bradlee ended up spending his precious time in the Foley Square Courthouse, studying the transcript of the trial itself.

Although based on publicly available records, Bradlee's seven-thousand-word, thirty-three-page summary, entitled "Le Cas Rosenberg," had considerable success in countering the more blatantly inaccurate charges of the propagandists. More than five hundred copies were distributed to representatives of the press, to USIS branch offices, and to individuals who requested them; as one observer of the French scene noted, "the effect was salutary." In the month of January 1953, numerous French commentators, with the exception of Henri Pierre in *Le Monde* and the Socialist *Le Populaire*, acknowledged the guilt of the Rosenbergs, at least indirectly, though continuing to advocate clemency.

Le Combat's publication of the stolen Rogge files in April undid some of the effects of Bradlee's white paper, and by late April, the press attaché was in contact with James Kilsheimer, asking for more facts to rebut the French Committee's contention that the missing console table had been found and the perjury of the Greenglasses exposed. But the problem of French public opinion ran deeper than the lack of up-to-the-minute information rebutting Communist charges. As Bradlee himself said recently, commenting on his futile effort to stem the growing anti-American tide that spring, "the real issue in France was clemency," not the Rosenbergs' guilt or innocence.

Bradlee's analysis is confirmed by the contents of a May 15, 1953, Eyes-Only dispatch sent by our then ambassador to France, Douglas Dillon, to Secretary of State John Foster Dulles. Dillon warned that ill feeling in France over the Rosenbergs had reached crisis proportions and was likely to have serious long-term consequences for American foreign policy. In Dillon's view the State Department had done a creditable job of rebutting Communist propaganda, accomplishing all it could reasonably expect to do in persuading the French that the Rosenbergs were guilty as charged. Yet, the ambassador complained, "the fact of the matter is that even those who accept the guilt of the Rosenbergs are overwhelmingly of the opinion that the death sentence is unjustifiable punishment for offenses as revealed by the trial, particularly when compared with prison terms meted out to British scientists Alan Nunn May and Klaus Fuchs." Sentiment in favor of clemency was strengthened by sympathy for the Rosenbergs' situation as parents of young children, by doubts about the role of the Greenglasses, and by the fact that "a substantial segment of French opinion also makes a distinction between the degree of guilt of Rosenberg as a principal, and his wife as an accessory."

Dillon urged Dulles to bring these facts to the attention of Eisenhower in the hope that the U.S. government could find a way to accommodate French feelings:

> We should not (repeat not) deceive ourselves by thinking that this sentiment is due principally to Communist propaganda or that people who take this position are unconscious dupes of Communists. [The] fact is that the great majority of French people of all political leanings feel that [the] death sentence is completely unjustified from a moral standpoint and is due only to political climate peculiar to the United States now (repeat now) and at the time the trial took place.

Nor, Dillon complained, had they been helped by the recent whirlwind tour through France by Roy Cohn. Cohn's efforts to reassure the European press of his maturity and seriousness of purpose by bragging that, though young, he had been the prosecutor of the Rosenbergs did nothing to calm public opinion about the case. As Ambassador Dillon noted wryly, "nothing could be better calculated than this claim to convince waverers that the Rosenbergs, if executed, will be victims of what the European press freely terms McCarthyism."

John Foster Dulles passed Ambassador Dillon's cable on to the White House, where it received short shrift. Rather than show the cable to Eisenhower, the president's friend and adviser C. D. Jackson turned it over to General Walter B. Smith. Smith's reply to Dillon noted tersely that whereas the ambassador's comments were "appreciated," the issue was closed and "I do not feel there is any further recommendation at this time, which I can make to the President."

Dillon's telegram also aroused the ire of J. Edgar Hoover, who learned of it through a copy sent to Attorney General Herbert Brownell. Hoover was particularly incensed at Dillon's remark that the French considered the death sentence unduly harsh in comparison to the treatment of the British spies Fuchs and May. Why, he fumed, should the French expect the United States to emulate the "weaknesses" in the British security system?

Even more upsetting to Hoover was the argument that the French felt sympathy for Ethel as the mother of two sons and as a mere accomplice in a conspiracy masterminded by her husband. Forgetting that he had once advocated sparing Ethel's life on precisely the same grounds, Hoover now defended the death penalty on the excuse that Ethel was a callous woman bereft of normal human feelings. Ethel, Hoover noted, had refused to see her own mother for nearly two years and when she finally did, he claimed, she had brushed off her mother's pleas to confess for the children's sakes, saying, "Don't mention the children. Children are born every day of the week." Hoover's source for this story is unknown, but there can be little question that he preferred to believe it because he was groping for some justification for remaining firm. It simply would not do, Hoover thought, for the government to take any action that might be interpreted as a sign of weakness. As he explained to Brownell, "If the sentence is reduced, we may well be charged with knuckling under to Communist pressure, not only abroad but in this country."

Although the White House and Hoover considered the clemency issue settled once and for all, the campaign was still far from its peak.

In early June, the Archbishop of France joined those asking for mercy. And following him, the official publication of the synod of French Protestants, Edouard Herriot, president of the National Assembly, and four former prime ministers, including then Finance Minister Edgar Faure, joined in the appeal. Even Vincent Auriol, president of France, asked the American ambassador to support commutation—joining some eight thousand other French men and women whose telegrams poured into the American embassy during the first half of the month.

The Italian press, too, had by now joined in a single voice to call for a reduction of the sentence. Pope Pius XII had been besieged by appeals from Catholics the world over demanding to know why he had not made an attempt to intervene; in February, the Vatican press had announced that the Pope had transmitted an oral appeal using the Apostolic Delegate the Archbishop of Laodicea as an intermediary. The Pope's message, which asked for mercy "out of motives of charity proper . . . without entering into the merits of the case" had been received by Truman's Attorney General J. Howard McGrath, who did not see fit to inform the President, much less the press, of the Pope's intercession.

Britain, where interest in the case had so far not reached anything approaching the French passion for *le cas Rosenberg*, rallied belatedly behind the banner of clemency. One Labour member of Parliament who took to the floor to demand the closing of the American embassy was soundly reprimanded by his own party, but street demonstrations could not be so easily dismissed, and the vociferous marchers threatened to wreak havoc with the preparations for the coronation of Queen Elizabeth II, just days away.

And, grasping a propaganda advantage, the Polish government offered through official diplomatic channels to grant asylum to the Rosenbergs if the United States saw fit to release them.

Telegrams and letters were pouring into the White House—an estimated 21,500 in a single week. The signers included 2,300 American clergymen of all denominations as well as atomic scientists Harold Urey and Albert Einstein.

Even David Greenglass, not repentant but appalled that his testimony against his sister had come to this, wrote from his cell in Lewisburg Prison urging the President to mitigate her sentence.

President Eisenhower was, of course, the target of all these appeals. Shortly after his inauguration, the subject of Bloch's pending clemency appeal had come up at a cabinet meeting. The new President had shown then that he was disinclined to grant leniency. "He emphasized the unanimity of opinion on the part of officials concerned with the case," the cabinet minutes indicate. Eisenhower also cited "the unfavorable psychological effect of an Executive reversal of Justice in a case that seemed so clean-cut [*sic*]." But as the clemency movement really began to gain momentum, it transformed what had been a relatively safe and popular decision into one that now threatened to have the most serious ramifications, both at home and abroad. Reportedly, by late spring even Eisenhower's cabinet and personal staff were sharply divided over the clemency issue.

Eisenhower's friends knew him as a basically generous, fair-minded individual, and as such, a longtime acquaintance and former

Columbia University colleague, Professor Clyde Miller, wrote to him on June 8, appealing to his "humanity and fairness." Miller recalled a private conversation in which Eisenhower had said it was inconceivable to him "as one who had to pass on many sentences handed down in courts martial, that a person should be condemned without a full hearing and review of the case."

Miller also enclosed a copy of a pamphlet published by the Committee to Secure Justice that featured a photograph of the Rosenberg boys and the headline "PARENTS TO DIE ON WEDDING ANNIVERSARY—ROSENBERG CHILDREN PLEAD WITH PRESIDENT." (This referred to the then scheduled execution date of June 18.) The professor wrote that he had no idea whether the pamphlet's claims about the significance of stolen Rogge files had merit, though he suspected that they did. But he felt strongly that carrying out the death sentences would do great harm to America's image abroad. Moreover, Miller claimed to know one of the Rosenberg defense attorneys and, he confided, he had "grave doubts about the man's mental fitness if not his integrity."

Eisenhower was not impressed by any of these arguments. In a lengthy personal reply to Miller, the President insisted that the case had already been "reviewed and re-reviewed by every appropriate court in the land" (not quite true since the Supreme Court had dealt with the Rosenberg appeals by declining to review them) and went on to reveal his real reason for deciding against clemency: the executions were necessary to refute "the known convictions of Communist leaders all over the world that free governments . . . are notoriously weak and fearful and that consequently subversive and other kinds of activity can be conducted against them with no real fear of dire punishment. . . ." Further, Eisenhower was convinced that the Rosenbergs' espionage had "exposed to greater danger of death literally millions of our citizens" and he could not justify commutation, which would open up the possibility that these "arch criminals" could be paroled in as few as fifteen years.

Eisenhower also refused to consider Miller's suggestion that the execution of a young mother would look especially vengeful to America's critics abroad. Ethel, added the President, did not deserve leniency since she was "the more strong-minded and the apparent leader of the two." And he asked, rather ingenuously, "would we be justified in encouraging the Communists to use only women in their spying process?"

The striking thing about Eisenhower's letter, supposedly a personal and private response to an old friend, was that it followed point by point the argument raised by a so-called Psychological Strategy Board letter that had been prepared for President Truman's consideration before he left office. The letter, forwarded to the Eisenhower White House staff by the attorney general on January 30, had been used in the preparation of the denial of clemency in February and the President was still using it as his source for his letter to Miller in June, sometimes lifting whole phrases from the report (though "the many, many thousands of citizens" said to have been endangered by the Rosenbergs in the PSB draft had now become "literally millions"). The estimate of Ethel's importance to the spy ring had also increased in seriousness over the months, until now she was cited by the President himself as being the true power behind the conspiracy, an interpretation that owed more to Morris Ernst's pop psychologizing and the unofficial (and completely unverifiable) rumors being spread by J. Edgar Hoover than to anything in the investigative record.

Eisenhower's heavy reliance on the Psychological Strategy Board's view of the case, as well as his willingness to accept the view of Ethel's role now espoused by those who claimed to be in the know, strongly suggests that he was fudging when he assured his old friend Clyde Miller that he had thoroughly reviewed the evidence in the Rosenberg case. If the President had actually been thoroughly and candidly briefed on the case, he would have been aware that even Hoover, in communications with the Justice Department, was on record as opposing the death sentence for Ethel, citing the limited evidence of her involvement in the conspiracy. Had Eisenhower realized the true extent of the evidence against Ethel, it seems unlikely that he would have written as he did to Miller, and even less likely that he would have passed his interpretation of Ethel's guilt on to his own son, John, to whom he confided by letter that "in this instance it is the woman who is the strong and recalcitrant character, the man who is the weak one. She has obviously been the leader in everything they did in the spy ring."

Nevertheless, it would not do to assume that Eisenhower was somehow duped by C. D. Jackson and Attorney General Herbert Brownell, on whom he was relying for background and advice on the Rosenberg case. Eisenhower knew from his own wartime experience the important role played by intelligence in cracking the German military codes. He was a firm supporter of the fledgling CIA and the future sponsor of the Doolittle Report, which would conclude vis-à-vis the Soviet-American intelligence rivalry that "there are no rules in such a game. Hitherto acceptable norms of human conduct do not apply. If the United States is to survive long-standing American concepts of 'fair play' must be reconsidered." Given his view of the overriding importance of a strong intelligence service and his visceral anticommunism, Eisenhower considered the existence of possibly mitigating factors, in the case of both the Rosenbergs or of Ethel in particular, to be of minimal importance. The primary consideration was that going through with the executions would send a message to the Communists that from now on American nationals recruited into Soviet espionage networks would be treated with the utmost severity.

26

The Built-in Verdict

The more the National Committee to Secure Justice gained in follow-ers and international attention, the more its spokespeople seemed to be overcome by fatalism. Speakers at Committee rallies increasingly voiced the opinion that the group's efforts were doomed to failure since "they" were determined to murder the Rosenbergs. The verdict of death had been sealed from the first by a conspiracy of the fascist, anti-Semitic forces that now controlled America.

This theory of the "built-in" verdict infuriated many of the first wave of Committee activists, some of whom were veterans of the Mooney-Billings defense campaign. If "they" were omnipotent, then what was the point of organizing defense committees at all? What, indeed, was the point of any form of political activism? No one could doubt that the chances of saving the Rosenbergs from execution were slim at best, but now with world opinion aroused on Julius and Eth-el's behalf, surely it was the wrong time for despair. Some Committee supporters felt an uncomfortable suspicion that they were being invit-ed to give up the fight prematurely—while the Communist Party stood by ready to preside at the wake of two martyred heroes.

The fatalistic mood of the Committee particularly bothered Ir-win Edelman, a self-styled pamphleteer and soapbox orator who had been a member of the Los Angeles branch of the Committee since the dark days of the spring of 1952, when its meetings had attracted fewer than a dozen committed supporters. Edelman had suggested back then that one of the goals of the Committee ought to be recruiting and financing first-class legal talent to assist Manny Bloch in his defense effort. No one had seemed very interested in following up on this idea. Edelman was told that Bloch had considered several offers from other lawyers but was interested in help only from attorneys who had "the right orientation."

Edelman was not sure exactly what that meant, but he could guess. A former Communist, Edelman had been expelled from the Party in 1947 for criticizing the campaign against Browderite "deviationists." Later, he had gone on to play an active role in the California Progressive Party, only to part on bad terms with that group's leadership as well. From there, Edelman went on to found a one-man movement, only to be arrested on a charge of "dissolute vagrancy" while making a speech in a Los Angeles City park that, according to two witnesses, advocated violent revolution and "insulted the Pope." With the help of the ACLU, Edelman fought the conviction up through the courts and was eventually vindicated by a 1953 California appellate court decision.

As this history suggests, Irwin Edelman was the apotheosis of the breed of political mavericks who had been attracted to the fledgling National Committee. He was a loudmouth and an eccentric, and like many of his type he had an annoying habit of fastening on obvious truths that others found it more convenient to ignore. This was exactly what happened in September 1952 when Edelman read the newly published transcript of the Rosenberg-Sobell trial. The discovery that the Rosenbergs' own lawyer had called for the impounding of the evidence of what they were supposed to have stolen struck Edelman with the force of an epiphany.

Edelman had previously been asked by the L.A. chapter of the Committee to write a pamphlet bringing recent developments in the case up to date. When he showed up with the first draft in October, it included a strong, albeit circuitously worded, criticism of Manny Bloch's decision to impound the technical testimony. The steering committee was not at all pleased. According to Edelman, several of those present admitted that Bloch had probably made a serious error but objected to any public criticism of the defense, on the grounds that such talk could only sow confusion and disunity within the ranks of the Committee. Edelman argued that the point of the Committee was to save the Rosenbergs from the electric chair, not to keep all its supporters happy. He was willing to rephrase his argument in more tactful terms but not to forgo mentioning the point altogether.

At this stage, says Edelman, he was told by steering-committee member George Bell that the leadership would need more time to review the legal and tactical implications of his pamphlet. A week later, Edelman received the results of their review in the form of a note from chapter chairperson Sophie Davidson informing him that "by the action of the full committee at its regular meeting you have been expelled." This was the first Edelman had heard of any meeting, "regular" or otherwise.

The Committee had miscalculated, however, since its eagerness to dump Edelman served only to convince him that he had stumbled onto something really important. Thus he proceeded to have his pamphlet printed at his own expense complete with a new introduction which argued pointedly that unity was less important than the need to shed "the utmost light on every aspect of the case." The old saying, "God defend me from my friends, from mine enemies I will defend myself" seemed to apply aptly to the Rosenbergs, the author added. That November, just days after the Supreme Court had declined for the second time to review Jerome Frank's appeals-court decision, Edelman attempted to purchase a paid advertisement for his pamphlet in the *National Guardian*. The ad was rejected, on the grounds that "to pick flaws in the conduct of the defense is now an academic matter."

Unable to advertise in the *Guardian*, Edelman began distributing the pamphlet on his own. Through a mutual friend, a copy of the pamphlet happened to come to the attention of a Nashville, Tennessee, lawyer named Fyke Farmer. Farmer, with his wire-rimmed spectacles and slicked-down hair severely parted in the middle, looked the stereotype of the country lawyer but his ideas were international in scope. A zealous campaigner for world government with good contacts in the peace movement and among civil-liberties groups, he had attracted no little attention in those circles by becoming an income-tax resister on the grounds that lending financial support to U.S. war preparations would place him in violation of the Nuremberg law.

Farmer was impressed by Edelman's argument that impounding the Greenglass testimony and sketches was a serious error and ought to be reversed on appeal. But he was also inspired to do some research on his own and came up with a point that struck him as even more compelling: The Rosenbergs had been tried under the wrong law! In Farmer's view, the Espionage Act of 1917 was no longer applicable to atomic secrets since it had been superseded by the Atomic Energy Act of 1946. And under this statute, a death penalty could be imposed only if the prosecution proved specifically that the defendants had intended to injure the national defense of the United States and only on the recommendation of the jury. Although accounts of the Rosenberg case frequently imply that Farmer had latched onto some questionable and highly obscure technicality, his argument had real merit. The 1917 law, the product of an earlier Red-scare era, was so vaguely worded that scientific organizations had complained it confused legitimate exchanges of technical data with military espionage. One of the purposes of the 1946 act had been to establish clearer guidelines, at least with respect to atomic secrets.

Farmer had closely followed the debate over the control of the "atomic secret" and welcomed an opportunity to mount an attack on what he believed to be a misuse of the 1917 statute. He offered to join forces with Irwin Edelman but made clear at the outset that he wanted to work with Manny Bloch, not against him. As a fellow member of the bar, Farmer was inclined to empathize with the enormity of Bloch's problems. As he wrote to Edelman on December 17, 1952, Bloch "took the case when no one else would touch it. I would be the last to knock an attorney under such circumstances. If Mr. Bloch stepped aside, where is the attorney who would take his place?"

Nevertheless, Farmer agreed with Edelman that the National Committee had shown a peculiar lack of interest in exploring new legal avenues that might save the Rosenbergs. In the same December 17 letter, Farmer reported to Edelman on the results of his first contact with the Committee, when he stopped by their New York headquarters during a business trip to New York:

> A funny thing about these people is that they do not seem to want any outside comment or help. I went to the office of the committee when I first came here, Mrs. Sobell met me and talked to me—gave me literature and loaned me a copy of the record. But when I began to make suggestions in the form of questions, I learned that she was not interested.

Warning Edelman against offending Bloch with any more public criticism, Farmer did his best to interest the Rosenberg defense team in his arguments. On March 6, 1953, having drafted a legal memorandum supporting his and Edelman's major points, Farmer made a special trip from Nashville to New York to try to convince Bloch to use the new material in a petition for *habeas corpus*. Bloch spent just half an hour with Farmer before excusing himself to attend a press conference, and Gloria Agrin then discussed the issues for another half hour, seeming no more impressed than her senior associate. Farmer returned to Nashville, and four days later he received a letter from Bloch saying that he had not yet had time to study the memorandum and would be in touch later. Farmer knew that several other lawyers had been shown copies of the memorandum and had discussed its merits with Bloch, yet on April 9, he was still waiting for his answer.

Irwin Edelman, meanwhile, still chafing with impatience under Farmer's restriction against publishing any more broadsides, had managed to attract a few sympathizers from the ranks of the Committee's L.A. chapter. Among them was Daniel Marshall, a civil-rights lawyer and locally prominent Catholic layman who had been serving as the chapter's legal adviser. Perhaps it was word of Edelman's growing support that motivated Manny Bloch to invite Farmer to New York for a second conference.

Fyke Farmer was receiving no compensation for his efforts, and he excused himself on the grounds that he could not afford another trip to New York at the moment. However, he sent along to Bloch a draft of another *habeas corpus* petition, narrowly focused on a claim that the indictment against the Rosenbergs and Sobell was incorrectly worded. Farmer himself did not think this claim was as important as his major arguments; however, he chose to focus on it now as a peace gesture—precisely because he had heard that it was the one point in his original memorandum that Bloch and his associates had deemed impressive. Bloch replied to this overture with a letter saying that he agreed with the petition in substance, but thought it inadvisable to take any action on it until after the Supreme Court had announced whether or not it would review Judge Swan's ruling on the Saypol-Schneider incidents.

Farmer was now pretty well convinced that he was being given the runaround. Moreover, he felt that to put off introducing the motion any longer would only give the courts reason to suspect that the petition was a mere delaying tactic, and not introduced in good faith. Over the next two weeks, Farmer and Daniel Marshall exchanged a series of letters debating whether or not they would be justified in acting independently. This could only be done by filing a petition on behalf of some third party such as Edelman—an unusual though by no means unprecedented legal device known as a "next friend" petition. As attorneys, both men felt hesitant to take an action that was bound to be interpreted as an attempt to interfere with a colleague's case. But they were also deeply troubled by the possibility that their silence might cost the Rosenbergs their only opportunity for life and leave unexplored some important issues in a case of historic importance.

In a letter of May 8 to Marshall, Fyke Farmer at last gave vent to his true feelings about what he called Bloch's "thumb and screw" tactics, and he vowed that he would still walk away from the case if only he could be sure that the Rosenbergs knew of and rejected his intervention. "It is their necks that are involved," Farmer wrote, "but so far as we know they have not been asked."

Farmer and Marshall finally decided to file the second *habeas corpus* petition on their own. In the meantime, an L.A. Committee activist sympathetic to Edelman's ideas had written to the New York office of the Committee urging them to make one last effort to bring Bloch and Farmer together, and on May 13 Farmer received an urgent invitation from Committee chairman Joseph Brainin to come to New York for another conference with Bloch. Farmer agreed to come this time, but when he arrived he found that the mood was anything but conciliatory. Bloch, backed up by Brainin, capped the meeting by announcing that he had already written to the chief justice of the Supreme Court demanding that the court refuse to hear the Farmer-Marshall petition.

After the conference, Brainin offered to give Farmer a lift back to his hotel. In the car, Brainin seemed troubled. Finally he mused, "Suppose you win on these points? What is going to happen to our Committee?"

"Well," replied Farmer, "your goddamn Committee can just fold up. It will have achieved its purpose."

Two days later, after he had returned to Nashville, Farmer received a letter from Bloch reiterating his opposition. "Counsel of record," it said, "objects as sharply as words can convey thought to your filing this petition on behalf of Irwin Edelman [as "next friend"]. We consider that any such filing would constitute an unwelcome and unwarranted intrusion into the case and a breach of legal ethics."

This, as far as Farmer was concerned, was the end of the road. Then, much to his surprise, he learned from chance newspaper reference that Bloch himself was planning to submit the petition before Judge Kaufman. Farmer phoned Joseph Brainin, telling him that he was pleased that Bloch had decided to use his petition after all and would very much appreciate it if the Committee could pay his expenses so he could be in New York to hear Bloch's presentation. Brainin agreed, and on June 1 Farmer and his daughter, who lived in the city, were in the spectators' section of Kaufman's courtroom, filled with high expectations.

Fyke Farmer had heard Bloch argue another motion connected with the case before the appeals court just that morning and been considerably impressed. Now Bloch appeared to be another man entirely: ambivalent, indifferent, even hostile to the point he was supposedly asking the judge to support. At the outset of the presentation, Farmer recalls, Bloch turned his back on Judge Kaufman so that he appeared to be addressing Farmer in the spectators' section. Said Bloch:

> You see, Judge Kaufman, oddly enough this point or at least the kernel of this point, was conveyed to me by a Tennessee lawyer. I have a lot of well wishers throughout the country and when I first looked at it I thought that it was a highly sophisticated point, but the more I delved into it the more I was convinced that it was a point that was unassailable and unanswerable, and that is the reason I raise it before you where I had to screen a hundred suggestions and eliminate them because I thought the points invalid. It may well be, Judge, that this lawyer from Tennessee may well turn out to be a genius, and he may be right and we may all be wrong.

Farmer was dismayed. It was clear to him, and no doubt to Judge Kaufman, that Bloch's heart wasn't in his argument. "He presented in an indifferent, half-hearted way," recalls Farmer, "as if he didn't want to leave a stone unturned."

Kaufman then questioned Bloch about his "peculiar" timing of the motion:

Apparently you had this point some time back and, as you say, suddenly you come to the realization that perhaps you ought to urge it on the court. I daresay that if this is finally disposed of, you will have some other application ... but this timing has been your doing. ...

But he had not known of Farmer's petition for "very long," Bloch countered; besides "I am of the opinion—and maybe I am wrong here—that as long as I had an appeal going up to the Supreme Court, it would have only confused that Court if I bombarded the lower courts with other motions while the appeal was proceeding."

"I think you're giving the Supreme Court very little credit for intelligence," Kaufman replied acerbically. "I don't think you need to worry about them being confused."

Fyke Farmer could no more understand Bloch's reasoning than Judge Kaufman could. When the hearing ended—unsuccessfully— and Bloch departed without showing any interest in further consultations, the "Tennessee lawyer" decided that the time had come to act on his own. That same afternoon Farmer hired a typist from a stenographic service and set about preparing a formal petition based on his original theory about the Atomic Energy Act.

He had also talked privately to some of the Committee officers about his plans. That evening he wrote Edelman: "Arrived here last evening and discussed things with the Almans and Joseph Brainin. Apparently they will not defend Bloch any longer. They have no hope that the Rosenbergs can be saved."

The Almans and Brainin, however, "hit the ceiling" when they learned that Farmer planned to present his petition in the name of Irwin Edelman as "next friend." Edelman, contacted in Los Angeles, declared himself willing to end the impasse by stepping aside if Joseph Brainin could convince Julius's mother, Sophie Rosenberg, to sponsor the petition. But Brainin refused, saying that Mrs. Rosenberg was "too disturbed" to be able even to consider such a proposal. Brainin's countersuggestion was that Farmer file in the name of Professor Ephraim Cross, a lawyer and currently honorary chairman of the National Committee, but when Farmer discussed the matter with

Cross himself the latter had so many reservations about the petition that Farmer decided he could not be counted on to remain firm. In the end, he decided to leave Edelman's name on the petition.

Irwin Edelman and Fyke Farmer interpreted Joseph Brainin's failure to enlist Sophie Rosenberg as a sponsor of their petition as just another instance of stonewalling. Neither man realized how hard the Almans and Brainin had been working to mediate between Farmer and Bloch—and, for that matter, to patch up the growing differences between Communists and non-Communists within the Committee's ranks. At this point, the original Committee leadership was in a tricky position. Even if they had wanted to challenge the increasing dominance of the Communist cadres, they could hardly afford to do so. Open dissension would have destroyed their organization and discredited the cause of the Rosenbergs' defense in the bargain. On the other hand, the few independent celebrities who had been willing to lend their reputations to the cause of clemency, such as physicists Harold Urey and Albert Einstein, were increasingly restive at being associated with a cause that had attracted, in Urey's words, "so many avowed Communists."

In a March 1953 report summarizing the Committee's accomplishments up to that time, David Alman did his best to smooth over these differences. Alman noted with pride that the Committee's work had "stiffened the backbones of millions of our fellow citizens" against "McCarthyism and thought control generally." The clemency campaign had made so much progress that Western Union had recently asked the Committee to authorize a form telegram "like they have for birthdays." In Alman's view, Arthur Miller's current Broadway play *The Crucible*—which, indeed, had been interpreted by many critics as a parable on McCarthyism—was "really about the Rosenbergs"; and even a recently televised play about Joan of Arc had carried a subliminal message: "The death sentence faced by Ethel Rosenberg was surely not lost on the audience." After adding up all these reasons for hopefulness—presumably the list seemed more substantial then than it does in hindsight—Alman could not resist chiding certain unnamed individuals on the Left who had warned him two years earlier that the Rosenbergs should be "permitted to die" because Americans would never "fight for the lives of persons convicted on an espionage charge." This lack of faith in the American people had now been discredited, Alman insisted.

Having indirectly reminded the Communists just who was responsible for the Committee's existence in the first place, Alman went on to plead for unity. Personally, he welcomed any and all who fought for clemency—even those who reasoned that the Rosenbergs should be kept alive because they might later repent and talk. No matter what their motives, all advocates of clemency were "part of the same movement . . . objectively working towards the same ends."

This semipublic dissension within the Committee was nothing as compared to the private internecine warfare being conducted by its founders and Manny Bloch. It was now more than a year since the Committee's modest beginning at a meeting in the Almans' apartment; during this time, Bloch's attitude had ranged from guarded cooperation to outright hostility. What the Almans and Brainin resented most bitterly was that despite all their dedicated work they had never been permitted to meet or even communicate directly with the Rosenbergs themselves. Bloch, who might have been able to arrange for visiting rights and could certainly have gotten permission for the Rosenbergs to correspond with their defense-committee organizers, refused to let them get anywhere near his clients. Once, according to Emily Alman, Committee organizers had even tried to smuggle a message to the Rosenbergs in Sing Sing with Julius's sister, but she had become suspicious and given the note to Bloch instead. And that, of course, had led to another round of accusations and counteraccusations.

Manny Bloch may well have had good reasons for keeping the Committee organizers away from Sing Sing. For one thing, there was the risk that Julius and Ethel would not live up to the image of injured innocence that their defenders believed in implicitly. But to the Committee, Bloch's attitude was just another example of his pathological need to control "his" case. "It was interesting," Emily Alman recalls. "Nobody saw them [Julius and Ethel]. Nobody could get to them. . . . Manny fought [David] right down the line on that."

Work on readying the Rosenbergs' letters for publication had been another source of contention. What had been planned as congenial dinnertime editing sessions erupted into nasty quarrels. Bloch thought the professional writers from the Committee were too eager to make unnecessary improvements in his clients' prose. The Committee leaders protested that they only wanted to cut down on some of the more bludgeonlike rhetoric, to make Julius and Ethel seem more sympathetic. "We wanted them not as people trying to lead the Left into the future," says Emily Alman. "But they began to take this on."

Bloch's reluctance to use the "new evidence" of the console table and the stolen Rogge files had opened yet another chapter in the deteriorating relations between him and the Committee. The activists who were responsible for uncovering the console table and the Rogge files had acted with the best of motives, believing that the venture into private detective work and international intrigue was necessary to expose the dimensions of the government frame-up. But Bloch had reacted with disdain and anger. The incident led the Almans and Brainin to suspect that there was more merit than they had previously thought in the charges of the abrasive Mr. Edelman. Perhaps Edelman was right about the impounding issue after all.

In desperation, Committee leaders even approached Albert Einstein, who had agreed to examine David Greenglass's sketches and provide an affidavit assessing their importance (or lack of importance) when and if Bloch got the court to release the impounded material. But Bloch wanted nothing to do with the idea. "We were humiliated before Einstein on this," recalls Emily Alman. "What could we say to him—'We're pleading with the attorney'?"

Einstein's growing doubts about the motives of the Rosenberg defense are confirmed by a letter to the Committee from a colleague of his at the Institute for Advanced Study at Princeton. The Nobel prize–winning physicist had previously written to *The New York Times* to advocate clemency for the Rosenbergs, and he was constantly mentioned in Committee literature as chief among the luminaries who supported their cause. But when asked to sign an *amicus* petition to the Supreme Court that was being circulated by Committee activists, Einstein had balked. According to the report of his shocked colleague, Einstein expressed a reluctance to become more deeply involved in a cause he now felt was "Communist inspired." Further, Einstein confided, the objection of the Rosenbergs' attorney to the publication of the Greenglass technical testimony had led him to conclude that the Communists did not want the Rosenbergs to be saved. Einstein, who was normally generous in lending his name to good causes, told the colleague that he still favored clemency but no longer wished to be associated with the organized campaign.

Even after their attempt to enlist Einstein in an examination of the scientific evidence had failed, the Committee leaders continued to plead with Bloch to admit that he had "flubbed" on the impounding issue. When Fyke Farmer came to New York in June, the Almans met with Bloch and begged him to step aside to let Farmer try a new approach. Bloch adamantly refused.

"How can you do this, Manny?" the Almans pleaded tearfully.

Bloch, unmoved, insisted that he had no reason to be apologetic. He would not abase himself by publicly admitting to an error that in his mind he had never committed. "I knew that man planned to sentence them to death," he told the Almans defensively, "and I did the best I could."

No matter how disillusioned with Bloch they may have been, the Committee leaders would not go so far as to associate themselves with Irwin Edelman's public criticism of the Rosenberg defense. Looking back on Bloch's actions recently, Emily Alman hinted that, yes, Manny Bloch may have shown more enthusiasm for defending the Communist Party than for the interests of his own clients. But even from the perspective of several decades she could not subscribe to Edelman's view of Bloch as a Machiavellian operator, consciously sabotaging the Rosenbergs' cause. Bloch was a prisoner of his own limitations, exhausted and beleaguered, and all but immobilized by the fear—not at all unrealistic—that he would be dogged for the rest of his life by FBI harassment and even by trumped-up criminal charges in retaliation for his work on behalf of the Rosenbergs. "Bloch did all that he was capable of doing," Emily Alman concluded, "which is sad. Because he was not capable of doing anything."

Finally, any public admission that the Committee to Secure Justice was anything but 100 percent behind the Rosenberg defense team would have been an unthinkable breach of solidarity and an inexcusable diversion from the real focus of the struggle. After all, as Mrs. Alman insisted, it was the government that was out to kill the Rosenbergs, not Manny Bloch.

By the final weeks before the Rosenbergs' scheduled execution, their staunchest defenders were hopelessly divided. The international campaign for clemency was still gathering momentum. Enormous demonstrations were being planned in France and Italy; and American supporters were converging on Washington for a week of concerted picketing and protests. But the Committee leadership no longer had much faith in Bloch's ability to work a last-minute miracle. And Bloch, on his part, was committed to one last try to get the Supreme Court to consider his claim that David Greenglass had committed perjury—a claim based in large part on the "new evidence" he had once scorned.

In the meantime, Fyke Farmer was holed up in his Manhattan hotel room with a stenographer, putting the final touches on his new petition—a document that he was convinced might yet save the Rosenbergs, if only he could find a judge who was willing to act. It was 7:00 P.M. on Friday evening, June 12, 1953, before the final draft of the petition was complete, but Farmer decided that he could not afford to wait until the next week to begin his fight to win a hearing. The executions were set for the following Thursday, and every day that the petition went unread represented a precious opportunity lost.

Upon discovering that Judge Kaufman's home telephone number was unlisted, Farmer decided to drop in to see federal judge Edward Dimock, whom he knew slightly from meetings of the American Bar Association. When the judge learned that Farmer wanted him to consider a petition on behalf of the Rosenbergs, he was not pleased. Dimock "just turned pale and quivered almost," Farmer recalls with amusement. The judge did agree to call Kaufman at home, however. But Kaufman merely suggested that Farmer should first give a copy of his petition to Assistant U.S. Attorney Kilsheimer; if Kilsheimer thought the document had merit, he would pass it on. This unorthodox procedure did not appeal to Farmer; he told Dimock that he would prefer to take the petition back to his hotel and try to present it to Kaufman personally on Monday.

But Farmer did not have to wait. On Sunday morning, when he sat down to peruse the New York papers, Farmer found a brief news story reporting that Judge Kaufman had been the target of a bomb threat—by no means the first to come the judge's way since the clemency campaign had been attracting media attention. What interested Farmer was that the paper had obligingly printed Kaufman's home address.

Within minutes, Farmer had hailed a taxi and was on his way to the judge's upper Park Avenue apartment building. But there he met one more obstacle in the form of a skeptical and none too friendly uniformed doorman. Farmer insisted that he did not need to see the judge personally; he only wanted to drop off some documents for

Kaufman's perusal. Suspiciously, the doorman looked at the manila envelope containing the petition and read the attached note, which described the contents as "a proposed order for a writ of *habeas corpus* commanding that the Rosenbergs be brought into court Monday morning." The doorman studied the note for some minutes, his eyes fastening on the word "commanding." Finally he ordered Farmer to leave and take the offending envelope with him. He would not, under any circumstances, deliver a message "commanding" the judge to do anything!

Farmer, one of those rare individuals to combine dedication to defending unpopular causes with a wry sense of humor, returned to his hotel once again, more bemused than angry. The doorman's reaction had, after all, not been substantially different from that of Judge Dimock. If his manila envelope had contained a bomb, it would not have been any less welcome than it already was.

Later that day Farmer finally did manage to deliver his petition into the hands of Judge Kaufman's law clerk. But it did not take him long to discover that his frantic efforts had gone for nothing. Kaufman not only turned down the petition without hearing oral arguments, he denounced both Farmer and the petition's sponsor as "interlopers" whose intrusion into the case was not just unwarranted but an insult to the integrity of the judicial process. Farmer was not surprised to learn that Kaufman's opinion was shared by Assistant U.S. Attorney Kilsheimer, who had read the petition and pronounced its arguments "wholly frivolous." He was bitterly disappointed, however, to learn that Emanuel Bloch, along with Malcolm Sharp and John Finerty, had sent a telegram to Judge Kaufman, denouncing the petition and begging him not to give any consideration to the unwelcome intruders, Farmer and Edelman.

Kaufman's decision was not a total defeat for Farmer, however. At least the judge had disposed of the petition quickly, giving Farmer a few days to seek out a higher court judge who might be more sympathetic to his arguments. But that Bloch would actually go so far as to beg Kaufman to reject the petition left Farmer flabbergasted. He could understand why Bloch would have been unenthusiastic about the efforts of two outsiders whose view of the case was implicitly critical of the defense's actions during the trial. What he could not fathom was the overall pattern of Bloch's action: procrastination, misrepresentation of Farmer and Edelman to others, indifference, and finally a hostility that was so intense as to be destructive to the Rosenbergs' chances for avoiding execution. Even now, almost thirty years after the event, Farmer refuses to hazard an interpretation of Bloch's motives. "Bloch just gave me the complete cold shoulder," he recalls. "I just never have understood it."

Perhaps one cause of Manny Bloch's utter rejection lay in the nature of Farmer's new petition. After months of compromise, the Tennessee lawyer had finally decided to revert to his original argument that the Rosenbergs had been tried under the wrong law. Personally, Farmer was not even convinced that Julius and Ethel were totally innocent. All he was sure of was that they had not stolen the "secret of the atom bomb"—because, in his view, there was no such thing. Farmer was convinced that the AEC's insistence on the critical importance of the data stolen by Greenglass was no more than a cynical attempt to justify ever tightened atomic secrecy laws and build public support for the nuclear arms race. A new trial under the Atomic Energy Act would force the court to reassess the significance of the impounded testimony. The thrust of the new petition was, in Farmer's own words, to "attack the whole basis of the prosecution" and "raise the trial above the level of a family quarrel between Rosenberg and Greenglass."

For reasons Fyke Farmer could never quite grasp, this was the last thing that either the Rosenbergs or Bloch wanted. Julius and Ethel had by now come to see themselves as actors in a true-life morality play, with David and Ruth cast in the roles of the heinous informers. Aside from recognizing the practical dangers inherent in a new trial, which might well place in jeopardy accomplices who had so far escaped prosecution, the Rosenbergs' definition of their "innocence" was such that it could not matter *what* law they were tried under. Their position was that they were victims of a government frame-up; the verdict against them was a foregone conclusion. And in a sense, this was not entirely illogical. The Rosenbergs had to recognize that they were legally guilty even if, by their lights, morally innocent. Having no faith in capitalist American justice, they could hardly believe that they would be allowed to escape the electric chair on a technicality.

Manny Bloch appears to have shared this philosophy. This conclusion at least explains what Farmer characterized as Bloch's "thumb and screw" legal tactics—the use of one motion after another in an effort to gain time while keeping additional legal ammunition in reserve for a later day.

It was true enough that there were political pressures building up that would be felt even within the Supreme Court itself. But Bloch and the Rosenbergs were seriously mistaken if they believed that their best hope lay in the success of the clemency campaign. While President Eisenhower had never seriously considered giving in to the demands of clemency advocates, there were still those on the Supreme Court who were concerned to see that the Rosenbergs received a full measure of justice.

27

The Supreme Court

On Monday, June 15, 1953, the final day before they were scheduled to disperse for the summer, the nine justices of the Supreme Court listened to a powerful last-minute appeal on behalf of the Rosenbergs from that battle-scarred lion of the Left, John H. Finerty. Then in his mid-seventies, Finerty had led an unsuccessful attempt to have the convictions of Sacco and Vanzetti overturned by the Supreme Court and had been the strategist behind the appeal leading to the landmark *Mooney v. Holohan* decision in 1935.

The Supreme Court had so far declined to hear any substantive argument on the merits of the Rosenbergs' appeals, but Finerty's surprise application for a writ of *habeas corpus* had the effect of maneuvering the justices into hearing at least some discussion of the perjury issue raised by the stolen Rogge papers. The factual merits of Finerty's application may have been doubtful, but the historical significance of his appearance was surely not lost on anyone present: the Mooney case, too, had involved charges of perjury by key government witnesses; and Finerty's arguments drew heavily on the same reasoning that had led to Tom Mooney's release after years on death row.

No one was more impressed by the significance of Finerty's appearance than Justice Felix Frankfurter. As a younger man, Frankfurter had himself been involved in both of Finerty's most celebrated cases—first as the author of a report on the Mooney case prepared at the request of President Woodrow Wilson and later as the author of a book critical of the case against Sacco and Vanzetti. Frankfurter did not find any of the so-called "new evidence" highly persuasive, but he saw Finerty's action as one last chance to win the Rosenbergs the Supreme Court review he felt they deserved.

Oddly enough, the chief obstacle so far in Frankfurter's campaign to win review of the Rosenbergs' appeals had been Justice William O. Douglas, soon to become known to the public as the Rosenbergs' lonely champion. Douglas had been an outspoken critic of the loyalty-board program and one of two justices, along with Hugo Black, to vote to overturn the conviction of the *Dennis* defendants for the teaching of Communist doctrine. But Douglas had originally seen no constitutional merit in the Rosenberg appeals. On three separate occasions he had cast his vote against *certiorari*.

On May 22, 1953, however, Douglas had surprised his colleagues by circulating a memorandum announcing that he had given the Rosenberg case "more study" and changed his mind. Douglas now proposed to change his last *certiorari* vote, made in conference on April 11 but not yet publicly announced. Significantly, he also planned to register a formal dissent which would express his belief that Saypol's comments on the William Perl arrest had "probably prejudiced the defendants seriously." Frankfurter, who loathed Douglas as a political opportunist, felt that the May 22 memo was evidence of his colleague's total cynicism. If Douglas had undergone his change of heart after one of the earlier *certiorari* votes he would have provided the fourth and decisive ballot in favor of reviewing the case. By the April vote, however, only Frankfurter and Black had remained firm in favor of *certiorari*, so that Douglas's reversal would have no practical impact.

Justice Douglas was notoriously erratic in his work habits and it is possible that the issues raised by the Perl arrest had not dawned on him until some weeks after the April conference. Frankfurter, however, was convinced that Douglas had merely sniffed the rising tide of popular opinion against the Rosenbergs' executions and wanted to go on record at the last moment with a ringing but futile dissent. Nevertheless, Frankfurter seized the opportunity to remind Justice Robert Jackson that it would be wise for the Court to avoid the appearance of being closely split on such a sensitive issue. At a conference called during the last week in May to discuss Douglas's memorandum, Jackson offered to join the minority in favor of *certiorari* so that the case could be heard after all.

Douglas's reaction to this offer was exactly what Frankfurter and Jackson had anticipated: He preferred to withdraw his memorandum rather than force the issue. Just why Douglas backed down is another mystery. Perhaps he misunderstood the significance of Jackson's proposal. Or perhaps he genuinely dreaded the prospect of a review of the case which might end with him having to cast a vote in favor of upholding the Rosenbergs' conviction. Jackson at least had no doubt that he had foiled another Douglas play for press attention. On leaving the conference he told Frankfurter, "That S.O.B.'s bluff was called."

Douglas now appeared to have sided firmly with the majority, and on June 13, he was one of five justices to vote against a stay of execution that would have given the defense time to prepare formal arguments on the "new evidence" issue.

Notwithstanding Douglas's June 13 vote, Frankfurter still hoped to win him over to his way of thinking. Frankfurter had been tremendously disturbed by Saypol's conduct in the matter of William Perl's arrest—the same issue that Douglas had cited in his May 22 memorandum—and, in spite of their personal differences, he knew Douglas shared his concern that the Rosenbergs not be denied a full review because of the political passions aroused by their case. In the judicial conference that followed Finerty's *habeas corpus* application on June 15, Frankfurter, supported by Hugo Black, argued that the claim that Saypol had used perjured testimony by the Greenglasses to obtain a conviction was serious enough to at least warrant a full hearing. But Douglas remained intransigent, infuriating Frankfurter with a comment that seemed to him to be a purposely obtuse misconstruction of the significance of the *Mooney* decision. According to Frankfurter's notes on the meeting Douglas had commented, "[The prosecution has] got to do more than use perjured testimony. [It's] got to manufacture it." Frankfurter scribbled down this remark on the back of an envelope along with his own rejoinder: "Oh! No! Knowing use of perjured testimony is enough. I know a good deal about Mooney!"

For whatever reasons, Douglas had played a key role in destroying the Rosenbergs' chances of having their appeal heard by the Supreme Court. But his behind-the-scenes role was of course totally unknown outside the precincts of the Court conference room. Both the Bloch and Farmer teams, still desperately searching for a jurist who might be willing to issue a last-minute stay of execution order, continued to view Douglas, along with Hugo Black, as their best prospects.

On the same morning that John Finerty was arguing his *habeas corpus* application in Washington, Judge Kaufman in New York had formally rejected Irwin Edelman's "next friend" petition for a stay of execution, dismissing Edelman and his attorney Farmer as "intruders" and "interlopers" with no standing in the case. Kaufman's decision launched Farmer and Daniel Marshall on a hurried search for a higher court judge who might take a different view of their effort. After trying and failing to reach appeals court Judge Swan at his Connecticut home, the pair hurried to Washington in the hope of catching the ear of a member of the Supreme Court before the justices left on their summer vacations. Early on Tuesday morning they knocked on the door of the Alexandria, Virginia, home of Hugo Black. There was no answer. Their final hope was now Justice Douglas, who, they learned quite by chance, was going to be in his chambers that day, accepting yet another petition from the Rosenbergs' defense team.

When Farmer and Marshall arrived at the office of the clerk of the Supreme Court, they found Finerty and Sharp waiting with a new petition of their own and none too pleased to see them. Douglas, however, agreed to give the newcomers a half-hour appointment at 11:00 A.M. Farmer and Marshall reached the justice's chambers on schedule and found that Assistant U.S. Attorney Kilsheimer and two representatives of the Solicitor General's office were also to be present at the interview. Douglas listened attentively as Farmer argued that the Rosenbergs had been tried under the wrong law; Douglas appeared impressed that this point had never been raised in previous appeals. Then Farmer switched to the subject of the impounded Greenglass testimony. Had this material been included in the record that was sent to the Supreme Court for review? And if not, how could the Court be sure that the Rosenbergs had received a fair trial? Douglas, it seems, did not realize that there were omissions in the transcript he had seen. He looked to Kilsheimer for clarification, and the government attorney conceded that the impounded testimony was not in the transcript. Douglas looked distressed, and at that moment Farmer began to feel that the whole quixotic effort just might work.

There is no reason to suppose that Douglas was not genuinely impressed by the content of Farmer's presentation. In addition, Douglas no doubt felt disposed to listen sympathetically to an attorney who shared his own libertarian orientation. Despite his reputation for radicalism, Douglas was a staunch anti-Communist who profoundly disliked the prospect of becoming the instrument of a Party propaganda victory. Farmer's petition offered a more congenial intellectual platform.

But how was Douglas to proceed? There was still one last opportunity to bring up the new arguments in a forthcoming judicial conference; however, given his earlier vacillations, Douglas had good reason to suppose he would not find much support for his latest change of heart. Instead, Douglas consulted by phone with as many of his colleagues as he could reach. Chief Justice Vinson, in particular, was negative in the extreme. He felt that Farmer and Marshall had no standing before the court and, in any case, that their point about the Atomic Energy statute had been disposed of the previous November, when the Court had dismissed the more narrowly framed challenge to the indictment brought by Bloch on the basis of Farmer's brief. Hugo Black, on the other hand, was supportive, agreeing that Douglas's summation of the new arguments was an "enduring document." Felix Frankfurter, still leery of siding with a colleague whose steadfastness he no longer believed in, refused to second Black's enthusiasm. Though agreeing that the argument about the Atomic Energy Act was a point that "should be looked into," he avoided giving a wholehearted endorsement over the phone. Of course, it was Frankfurter's advice Douglas most wanted, since Frankfurter was likely to have the most influence over Jackson and Harold Burton, the potential swing votes. Early Wednesday morning, Douglas called Frankfurter a second time seeking advice. Should he try to present his newly written opinion at a judicial conference? Should he consult Jackson and Burton personally? Or should he go ahead and issue a stay on his own?

Exasperated, Frankfurter told Douglas, "Do what your conscience tells you, not what the Chief Justice tells you."

Later that same morning, June 17, Douglas stayed the Rosenberg executions. His order was accompanied by an opinion stressing that he had come to no definite conclusion about the propriety of the death sentence; however, "If we are not sure, there will be lingering doubts to plague the conscience after the event." Satisfied that he would have another chance to grapple with his conscience when court resumed in the fall, Douglas left Washington immediately on a cross-country automobile trip in the company of his wife-to-be, Mercedes Davidson.

Fyke Farmer and Daniel Marshall, meanwhile, had spent all day Tuesday waiting nervously in a visitors' lounge in the Supreme Court building for word of Douglas's decision. According to Farmer, Manny Bloch (who had just returned from visiting his clients in Sing Sing) arrived late that afternoon with Gloria Agrin, but walked right past Farmer, taking a seat without acknowledging his presence. The standoff resumed the next morning when both teams of lawyers returned to the lounge to take up their vigil. "I didn't feel it would serve any purpose to get down on bended knees and speak and beg Mr. Bloch and his associates to join us," Farmer wrote of the incident. "Justice Douglas had not seen fit to have Mr. Finerty and Mr. Sharp present when we argued in his chambers, and neither they nor Bloch were subsequently received by him. I felt that the petition would be granted or denied—on its merits."

At midmorning, some press photographers, tipped off that Justice Douglas was about to release an important announcement affecting the Rosenberg case, arrived in the lounge and began to set up their cameras for pictures of the mysterious newcomers who had precipitated the last-minute drama. Just as the photographers were preparing to snap a picture of Marshall and Farmer together, Supreme Court clerk Harold Willey emerged from Justice Douglas's chambers with the terse announcement: "Stay granted." In the joyful tumult that followed, Manny Bloch rushed up to Fyke Farmer and pumped his hand enthusiastically. This was the picture that the photographers came away with: a picture of an amity that had never existed between the two men—and never would.

Within minutes, news of the Douglas stay spread to the crowds gathered outside the Supreme Court building and in front of the White House. At Sing Sing, Warden Wilfred L. Denno broadcast radio stories about the stay over the loudspeaker system in an effort to ease the tension that had built up throughout the prison on the eve of the double execution. Julius and Ethel Rosenberg were given the news privately while they were in the midst of separate "last visits" with members of Julius's family. At word of the reprieve, the atmosphere of grief that had pervaded their separate visiting rooms suddenly dissolved into laughter and tears of relief.

Later, when both groups of lawyers had a chance to read Douglas's opinion in full, their spirits rose even higher. Douglas had done more than order a simple stay; he had called for the issue to go back to the district court. This meant that the case might well have to go all the way through the legal system a second time, with all the attendant opportunities for new appeals and motions, a process that would take at least a year and, more likely, several. The prospect of the executions ever taking place now seemed more remote than at any time since Judge Kaufman had handed down his verdict.

Julius and Ethel went to sleep Wednesday night believing their lives had been spared, at least for the foreseeable future. Back in Washington, however, the victory celebration turned sour as word spread that Chief Justice Vinson was planning to summon the court into special session the next day in order to dispose immediately of the issues raised by Douglas's stay.

William O. Douglas knew nothing about the special session until he heard it mentioned over his car radio while he was driving through Uniontown, Pennsylvania. Furious at what was apparently an attempt to overturn his action in his absence, Douglas turned his car around and hurried back to the capital.

Chief Justice Vinson would later tell columnist Marquis Childs that he *had* made an attempt to have Pennsylvania troopers locate Douglas in Pennsylvania—a move made at the risk of an unpleasant scandal since Douglas was traveling with his "mistress." Vinson's explanation makes a good story but it is certainly less than the full truth. FBI documents reveal that Vinson had met with Justice Jackson and Attorney General Herbert Brownell on Tuesday night and agreed ahead of time to call the special session should Douglas announce a stay. Vinson had ample time to inform Douglas of his decision before the latter left town, but he did not bother to do so. Douglas would believe to the end of his life that Vinson's action was not just procedurally improper but an outright set-up—that the chief justice had secured promises from five justices who agreed to vote to overturn the stay regardless of the merits of the arguments presented during the special session.

Fyke Farmer and Daniel Marshall also had to race back to Washington to attend the special session. On Wednesday evening, the two lawyers had gone to New York to prepare their petition to a district judge, as directed by the Douglas opinion. It was after 9:00 P.M. when they learned that the court session had been scheduled for noon the next day. Having neither cash nor plane reservations for the return trip, Marshall made an emergency call to Emily Alman, who met them in a downtown restaurant with expense money for the trip. Alman was cordial and obviously moved by Farmer's unexpected success, and Farmer hoped that the long-standing rift between himself and the Committee was finally mended.

But the next morning in Washington, when Farmer and Marshall met with Bloch, Finerty, and Agrin to try to devise a strategy for the afternoon's session, it soon became clear that the group would not be able to settle on a unified strategy for the critical court appearance. Manny Bloch, extremely agitated—"wound up," in Farmer's words—argued vehemently that it would be a fatal mistake to insist upon the applicability of the Atomic Energy Act. They were not prepared and, in any event, the point had no merit.

"Justice Douglas thought it had merit," Farmer retorted angrily. But to his dismay, Finerty and Agrin heartily agreed with Bloch, and even Marshall, always reluctant to oppose the wishes of the counsel of record, seemed inclined to go along. The session ended without reaching an agreement on which lawyers would speak and on what topics. Farmer alone continued to insist they come to agreement lest they seem to be stalling for time, which would be fatal.

When the attorneys arrived, separately, at the court, they learned from clerk Willey that they would have an hour and a half for their arguments, the time to be divided among Bloch, Finerty, and Farmer. Just as Farmer had anticipated, defense counsel were instructed to address themselves to two issues only: the standing of Edelman to petition as "next friend" and the merits of the argument that the Rosenbergs should have been tried under the Atomic Energy Act.

The government's arguments in favor of vacating the Douglas stay were presented first by Acting Solicitor General Robert L. Stern. The central legal question was whether the Atomic Energy Act, passed in 1946, could be legally applied to a crime committed in 1944 and 1945. Farmer's position was that it could, since the conspiracy described in the indictment had continued into the postwar years. Stern countered that to do so would be a clear example of applying a law *ex post facto*, and was thus unconstitutional.

Stern, arguing that the Rosenbergs had had "their day in court," attacked the new issue under discussion as no more than a frivolous delaying tactic. When, however, Justice Jackson later speculated from the bench that "the probabilities are that if the Atomic Energy Act covers this case, the whole case is out," Stern agreed that the government would most likely never obtain a conviction under the stricter provisions of the new law, a point that seemed to make a profound impression on Jackson.

Fyke Farmer and Daniel Marshall listened to Stern's presentation from seats in the second row of the spectators' stands. Manny Bloch had not invited them to sit at the defense table. When the time came for the defense to begin its presentation, Bloch motioned for Finerty to speak first. The old campaigner immediately launched into a tirade, which bore little resemblance to his impressively reasoned arguments of a few days earlier. Calling the special session an "insult" to Justice Douglas, Finerty went on to denounce Judge Kaufman and Irving Saypol, saying of the latter that "there never was a more crooked District Attorney in New York." These sentiments, while no doubt sincere, were hardly calculated to win any votes for his cause; yet Finerty persisted, ignoring a pointed remonstrance from Justice Tom Clark that a discussion of the merits would be more "helpful to the Court."

Next, Bloch gave the nod to Daniel Marshall, though he had not been scheduled to speak at all. Marshall continued in the vein Finerty had begun, protesting the hastiness of the scheduled session and even complaining at one point that not even "the meanest pimp" would be called to defend himself on such short notice. At this, Farmer, still seated in the spectators' section, could take no more. "I'm not maintaining we're not ready," he blurted out. "I'm anxious to get up before the bar and argue."

But Farmer's chance had still not come. Manny Bloch himself followed Marshall, pleading more calmly but even more lengthily for additional time to study the issue raised by the Douglas stay. Farmer, still squirming in his seat, was convinced that Bloch was damning with faint praise the very point he had supposedly risen to defend. As Farmer recalls it, "Bloch argued that the point at issue was an extremely fine and abstruse one. I felt that such an argument should have come from the Solicitor General rather than from the defense."

Farmer was not the only one present to conclude that Bloch was pleading for clemency while simultaneously undercutting the business at hand. At one point, Justice Black leaned forward in his chair and interrupted the presentation to engage Bloch in a colloquy:

"Mr. Bloch, you represent the Rosenbergs, do you not? And it's your duty to try to save them from the electric chair if possible, is that right?"

Bloch agreed that it was.

"Then, Mr. Bloch, at this late hour, whether these points that have been brought to your attention are big points or little ones, don't you think you ought to espouse them rather than denigrate them?"

When Bloch finally resumed his seat, just seventeen minutes remained for Farmer. Convinced someone had better address the issue at hand, Farmer used his time to summarize his original contention that the Atomic Energy Act must apply, since by the government's own contention the conspiracy had extended into the period covered by the new statute. Farmer had originally hoped to be able to bring up the impounding of the technical evidence. In his view, the fact that the Rosenbergs had received capital sentences on the basis of evidence that was never included in the trial transcript seen by the appeals judges was the real bombshell in the case, and the argument that had originally piqued Douglas's interest.

But with so little time available, Farmer feared that an attempt to work a new angle into his presentation would be dismissed as just another out-of-order digression. He stuck to his main argument. The decision seemed correct at the time. In later years, it would rest heavily on Farmer's conscience. For a few brief moments he had been given the chance to plead for the Rosenbergs' lives before the highest court in the land—and he had purposely withheld what he felt to be the strongest argument in their favor, all in the name of decorum.

But if Fyke Farmer felt a degree of guilt over his failure to bring the impounding issue into open court, he never forgave Manny Bloch for what he now believes was a consciously orchestrated campaign to obstruct a legal effort that might have saved the Rosenbergs' lives. Although Bloch, Finerty, and Marshall certainly had a point in protesting the court's unseemly haste, a dignified plea for more time would almost surely have been more effective than an hour and thirteen minutes of temper tantrums and stalling. The course the defense team had chosen could have only two purposes: to further inflame public opinion against the government and to prevent Farmer from arguing the impounding issue.

Farmer's conclusion that Bloch did not really want to see the stay upheld was shared by William O. Douglas. Douglas wrote in his memoir *The Court Years*:

> Bloch filed a brief against vacating my stay though even then he did not rest on the key point made by Fyke Farmer. My own impression was that Bloch never raised the point because the Communist consensus of that day was that it was best for the cause that the Rosenbergs pay the extreme price. That is a harsh thought, but it must be remembered that Stalin was still in power.

Douglas, the critic of loyalty boards and of McCarthyism, would have been the last to frivolously accuse anyone of being a dupe of Stalin. This opinion goes far to explain why Douglas resisted taking a firm stand on the case until Farmer and Marshall came on the scene. These opinions aside, the entire record of Bloch's dealings with Fyke Farmer and Irwin Edelman, including his confidential telegram begging Judge Kaufman not to consider the Farmer petition, lends credence to the belief that Emanuel Bloch preferred to see his clients dead rather than have them saved by the likes of these two men.

Yet there are other possible explanations for Bloch's behavior. Among them, there is ego. Bloch knew that Fyke Farmer wanted to raise the question of his call for the impounding of the technical evidence, a point that reflected badly on his conduct of the case no matter how tactfully it might have been phrased. No attorney could have relished the prospect of hearing his errors paraded before a special session of the Supreme Court. It is hardly surprising that Bloch would have been distraught to the point of irrationality to see Farmer succeed so easily in gaining the hearing he had failed to get in nearly two years of writing and arguing appeals briefs.

Yet injured pride alone cannot explain Bloch's reaction to Farmer. Unlike Finerty, Bloch had never indulged in courtroom tantrums. Throughout a long and grueling battle, he had shown remarkable self-control, never hesitating to swallow his own pride and heap compliments on the judge—and, in some cases, even on the government lawyers—as long as he felt that such self-abasement might win some leniency for his clients.

Indeed, Bloch's courtroom demeanor had frequently bordered on outright groveling. His shows of humility went so far that they mystified a number of Committee activists who believed strongly in the Rosenbergs' innocence. They led to still another set of theories by which these supporters sought to explain some of the defense counsel's apparently self-defeating tactics. At the extreme, Irwin Edelman eventually concluded that Bloch was a covert tool of the FBI, which he thought might explain why the judges who were on record as favoring the executions, including Kaufman and Justice Jackson, went out of their way to compliment Bloch's courtroom performance. Edelman's theory belongs to the realm of paranoid fantasy, but a contrary interpretation suggested by other former Committee activists is more persuasive. In this view, Bloch was increasingly paralyzed by fear of FBI retribution. Emily Alman, for example, told us that Bloch had expressed anxiety that the government would find some pretext to bring criminal charges against him.

Bloch, in fact, had good reason to fear the FBI, which had been compiling a dossier on him and fully intended to make him the subject of a Security Index investigation after the Rosenberg case was disposed of. Bloch knew the fate of the Dennis case lawyers, who had received substantial jail sentences for contempt and, in some cases, been subject to disbarment proceedings. He had every reason to believe that the FBI would persecute him for his role as the Rosenbergs' defender, all the more so if he were somehow successful in saving them from the chair.

But neither fear nor egotism can explain Bloch's bitter resistance to Farmer. Bloch had a long history of defending politically controversial cases. He was no stranger to political pressures and no coward. And if he had been that frightened, what could have been easier than to step aside and let Farmer take over the spotlight?

In the last analysis, one cannot deny that the pressures generated by the Committee to Secure Justice were at least as irresistible as any threat from the government—if not more so. Bloch had to know that the Communist element, which by now dominated the Committee, could only be satisfied by the Rosenbergs' martyrdom. And he also must have known that the well-meaning efforts of the Committee mavericks to dig up new evidence of his clients' innocence were bound to backfire in time. Finally, Bloch was all too painfully aware that, behind their outward defiance, Julius and Ethel Rosenberg were on the brink of despair, buoyed up only by the tide of worldwide support for their continued silence.

If the Douglas stay were upheld, particularly under circumstances clearly the result of Farmer's efforts, then the wave of public hysteria would surely subside and it would be all but impossible to deny Farmer personal access to the Rosenbergs. But Farmer, and many of the church-related liberals who lent financial support to his work, had never been entirely convinced of the Rosenbergs' innocence; rather, they had based their campaign on the grounds that the trial and sentencing were unfair. In Farmer and his ex-Communist supporter Edelman, Bloch could not help but see the shadow of another onetime ally, O. John Rogge, who had encouraged his clients to play the hated role of informer.

For Bloch, any influence that might lead the Rosenbergs to consider confessing was unthinkable, and for reasons that went deeper than any abstract demands of the Party line. Confession would have meant naming others—most likely many others, individuals who would then provide the fodder for a new round of atom-spy trials—and, perhaps, provide also the excuse for the wholesale roundup of leftists that so many in Bloch's circle believed was imminent. From this point of view, cooperation with the government could not possibly "save" Julius and Ethel Rosenberg. Rather, it would destroy them and everything they had suffered for, in a sense that not even the electric chair could.

Whatever may have motivated Bloch to keep Farmer and his argument from getting its hearing before the Supreme Court, there can be little question that he was by now a deeply troubled man. Bloch did not want the Rosenbergs dead, at least not consciously, as some outsiders had come to believe. He had long ago come to love Julius and Ethel, and in his love he paid them the compliment of seeing them as they saw themselves: as heroes willing to sacrifice their lives to frustrate a government witch-hunt. Bloch's emotional identification with the Rosenbergs had become his own prison, one from which there was no logical means of escape.

It was three o'clock in the afternoon when the lawyers for both sides finally wrapped up their arguments, and the nine justices then retired to their conference room. There the mood was hardly less acrimonious than that of the public session. Justice Hugo Black had come to the court that day directly from the hospital, where he had been preparing to undergo elective surgery. Black was livid with rage at Chief Justice Vinson's attempt to overturn a stay granted by a fellow justice and, moreover, he believed that the argument concerning the Atomic Energy Act had real merit. Felix Frankfurter agreed on both points. And Justice Harold Burton, though not convinced on the substance of the Atomic Energy Act question, was so disturbed by the precedent Vinson's actions had set that he voted in favor of prolonging the stay for at least three weeks so that the court could hear additional arguments on the subject. Along with the vote of Justice Douglas, this made four votes in favor of further debate.

On the other side, five justices, and particularly Jackson and Tom Clark, were vehement in their insistence that the Atomic Energy Act was inapplicable and that to attempt to apply it would be an obvious violation of the constitutional provision against *ex post facto* prosecutions. Whether a more substantial and reasoned presentation on the part of defense counsel could have changed even one member of the majority's mind is an academic question. Legal scholars have, however, pointed out that the justices' point about *ex post facto* was less compelling than it may have sounded since it could be argued that the Atomic Energy Act was intended to *narrow* the scope of the old Espionage Act and *modify* its sentencing provisions—whereas an *ex post facto* law, by definition, creates a new offense or imposes *additional* sentences.

According to William O. Douglas, among those impressed by the validity of the Atomic Energy Act argument was none other than Judge Jerome Frank. Douglas writes in *The Court Years* that Frank later told him "the 'key' point as far as the death penalty was concerned . . . had never been raised prior to the 'next friend' application to me and that if my stay had not been vacated and my ruling had reached the Court of Appeals, as it would have, there was no doubt that the Court of Appeals would have held that the imposition of the death sentence was improper."

To dwell on all the "ifs" in the appeals process that led to the Supreme Court's final disposition of the Rosenberg case would be futile. In retrospect, it seems that the government's handling of the case—particularly the choice not to indict under the Atomic Energy Act and Saypol's statements to the press at the time of the William Perl arrest—raised legal issues that might have resulted in overturning the death sentences, if only those had been pursued in a more timely and energetic manner. On the other hand, historian Michael Parrish may well be correct when he concludes his study of the Supreme Court and the Rosenbergs by saying that, given the Vinson court's previous record on cases involving Communists or Communist "sympathizers," "it seems very doubtful that the . . . Court would have saved the Rosenbergs even had the case been fully argued on four occasions."

One thing is certain. In the wake of the Douglas stay, the Supreme Court succumbed to the illusion that the Rosenberg issue could and would be resolved only by their speedy execution. Over varying degrees of objection from Frankfurter, Black, Douglas, and Burton, the majority of the justices were so averse to even a few weeks' delay that they dreaded the very possibility that Justice Douglas's opinion might have merit. As Felix Frankfurter wrote on the cover of his copy of Justice Vinson's opinion vacating the Douglas stay:

> The fact is that all minds were made up as soon as we left the Bench—indeed, I have no doubt . . . before we met on it! . . . Most of the time [in conference] was consumed by consideration whether [the] result should be announced that afternoon . . . or delayed until the next day noon! . . . No discussion of [the] merits.

The individual that Frankfurter held most responsible for the courts' less than dispassionate handling of the Rosenberg case was Judge Irving Kaufman. Writing to Judge Learned Hand in 1958, Frankfurter said of Kaufman, "I despise a Judge who feels God told him to impose a death sentence," and he vowed "I am mean enough to try to stay here [on the Supreme Court] long enough so that K will be too old to succeed me."

Frankfurter did more to frustrate Kaufman's ambitions than by obstinately staying alive. In 1957 Judge Kaufman's appointment to the Second Circuit Court of Appeals seemed almost inevitable, having won the backing of such influential figures as Senator Estes Kefauver and Representative Emanuel Celler. Incensed at what he condemned privately as Kaufman's "greedy ambition" and "scheming"—and sensitive to the fact that Kaufman's elevation was supported by some who considered it a vindication of the government's handling of the Rosenberg case—Frankfurter resorted to some discreet if not strictly proper scheming of his own. At one point, Frankfurter even managed to get Judge Charles Wyzanski and Learned Hand, then retired, to influence Senator Jacob Javits against Kaufman and in favor of a rival candidate for the post. And later, armed with what he called a "nifty" letter from Hand, Frankfurter took his case directly to Senator Lyndon Johnson. Largely as the result of these machinations, Kaufman did not win a place on the court of appeals until 1961.

28

The Execution

On the next-to-the-last day of the Rosenbergs' lives, their defenders and federal judge Irving Kaufman finally found a subject that they could agree upon. Neither thought it right that the condemned should die on the Jewish Sabbath.

Rhoda Laks, a lawyer representing the Rosenberg defense team, first raised the point with Judge Kaufman on Thursday morning. To the attorney's surprise, Kaufman readily agreed that to carry out the execution at 11:00 P.M. on Friday, June 19, as then scheduled, would be totally unacceptable. He had already discussed the matter with Attorney General Brownell, who was of the same opinion. Nothing could be done at the moment, pending the Supreme Court's final decision, but Kaufman assured Laks that if the stay were overturned, Brownell planned to announce a change in the timetable.

Laks left Judge Kaufman's chambers greatly relieved. Julius and Ethel would have an additional twenty-four hours at minimum. Moreover, if the executions were not carried out within a week of June 12, the time limit specified by Kaufman, the court would have to set a new date, perhaps weeks in the future. But on Friday morning, the Supreme Court revealed its decision to vacate Douglas's stay. Then in midafternoon the problem of the Sabbath was solved—by moving the executions *forward* to eight o'clock that evening, minutes before sundown.

Brownell's unexpected announcement created chaos among the Rosenbergs' defenders and their jailers alike. At Sing Sing, Warden Denno quickly alerted the state police, who had promised to surround the penitentiary with 170 officers, including some stationed in patrol boats on the Hudson River, in an attempt to forestall any last-minute demonstrations. U.S. Marshal William Carroll, meanwhile, tried frantically to get in touch with the executioner, a Cairo, New York, electrician who was not scheduled to leave his home until some time after 6:00 P.M., too late to reach Ossining and complete the execution before sundown. Finally two FBI agents were dispatched to Cairo with orders to find the missing executioner and bring him to Sing Sing with all possible speed.

There was not even time for Julius and Ethel Rosenberg to dine on the traditional last meal of the condemned. Upon learning that the time of their deaths had been moved forward, the couple elected to pass up dinner and spend the few remaining hours talking together in the visitors' cubicle.

In Washington, meanwhile, Emanuel Bloch hurriedly began to play out the remaining cards in his hand. Although he had done his best to keep Fyke Farmer from saying his piece before the Supreme Court, Bloch had clung to the irrational belief that the court would not go against precedent and humiliate Douglas by voiding the stay. Just two days earlier he had expressed his confidence to John Wexley, who had come to him with what he considered proof that Harry Gold's Hilton registration card was a forgery. There would be plenty of time to follow this trail later, Bloch had assured Wexley. The stay would be upheld.

After the court's decision was announced on Friday morning, Bloch, face to face with reality at last, retired to the sweltering basement cafeteria of the court and, with Gloria Agrin, drafted one final clemency appeal. In it, he begged Eisenhower to read carefully Justice Jackson's latest ruling, which included a phrase saying that the denial of the stay in no way constituted an approval of the death sentence. At the same time, Daniel Marshall was dispatched to New York by Bloch to seek a last-minute audience with Judge Kaufman, who had agreed to see him at 7:00 P.M. and hear yet another appeal for a delay of the executions.

At about 6:00 P.M. Bloch phoned U.S. Marshal Carroll and asked him to deliver one last message to Julius and Ethel. "Tell them

I did the best I could for them," the message read. "Tell them I love them. And so does the whole world." Then Bloch and Miss Agrin left for the White House. Pushing their way through crowds of pro- and anti-Rosenberg demonstrators, they begged in vain to be allowed to deliver the clemency plea to Eisenhower's aide Sherman Adams or press secretary James Hagerty. Along with the clemency appeal, Bloch carried a letter to Eisenhower written by Ethel Rosenberg that Tuesday. In striking contrast to Ethel's previous writings, in which she had referred to Eisenhower as a "Gauleiter," the letter obsequiously addressed the President as "one whose name is one with glory" and asked him not to countenance the destruction of a "small unoffending Jewish family." Curiously, perhaps, considering Ethel's firm insistence that she and her husband had done nothing wrong, she compared their situation to that of William Oatis, a confessed American spy who had recently been released from a Czechoslovak jail.

Fyke Farmer, too, had undertaken a final mission of mercy on behalf of the Rosenbergs. Along with an officer of the Women's International League for Peace and Freedom, he was in a car threading its way through the tangle of the capital's evening rush-hour traffic on the way to the Alexandria, Virginia, home of Justice Hugo Black. Black was the one Supreme Court member who had opposed the death sentence all along and Farmer reasoned that the justice might be angry enough now to accede to a final appeal for more time. As Farmer drove, he listened on the car radio to a blow-by-blow description of the advancing preparations at Sing Sing. The Rosenbergs had wrapped all their personal possessions and delivered them to their jailers to be passed on to relatives; the three wire-service reporters who were to be the only outside witnesses to the execution had taken their place in the death chamber; the prison barber had shaved a patch on Julius's leg to make attachment of the electrodes easier (Julius was to go first to the chair, so that Ethel would not have to walk past his holding cell on the way to her own death).

Sometime after seven o'clock, Farmer and his companion reached the Black home in Alexandria and pounded on the front door, hoping for a miracle. But there wasn't even to be a last chance to plead. Justice Black had returned to the hospital. No one answered the door at his home.

The only agency whose preparations seemed firmly in place was the FBI. Confident that the executions would go ahead on Friday as planned and that there was still a chance the Rosenbergs might break down in their final hours, J. Edgar Hoover had kept his plans moving forward while the rest of the world waited for the Supreme Court to decide on the Douglas stay.

In the predawn hours of the previous day, Thursday, a car filled with FBI agents had slipped through the gates of Sing Sing and headed straight for the warden's garage. There the FBI set up a secret command post whose existence was known only to Warden Denno and U.S. Marshal Carroll. In addition to John Harrington, the chief FBI field officer in the Rosenberg investigation, and two male stenographers, the Bureau's team included Maurice W. Corcoran, who had handled the FBI's case against William Perl; Richard A. Minahan, familiar with the investigation of Michael and Ann Sidorovich; and a fourth agent who was chief of the New York office's espionage division. Two direct phone lines had been installed to the FBI's New York office—one from the garage command post itself and one from "special quarters" on the second floor of the death house, which had been prepared for the interrogation of Julius and/or Ethel, should either of them show signs of wanting to confess.

Procedures for stopping the executions at any moment had been carefully rehearsed with Warden Denno. There had even been an exchange of memos on what to do "if the Rosenbergs desire to talk after they go into the execution chamber and even after they are strapped into the chair." And in the event the Rosenbergs did break, the FBI agents were ordered to stay on for marathon sessions within the death-house walls, as one FBI memo put it, "as long as they [FBI agents] desire, extending into months if necessary."

FBI field offices in New York and Cleveland, meanwhile, had been personally ordered by Hoover to place under "discreet surveillance" Maxwell Finestone, Michael and Ann Sidorovich, and other suspected members of the Rosenberg ring, in case they should attempt to flee the country in the event Julius and Ethel confessed. William Perl, already incarcerated in the wake of his recent perjury conviction, was being watched carefully.

Although the FBI reports speak about the possible breakdown of either member of the pair, there is no question that it was Julius Rosenberg on whom they had pinned their hopes.

But not Ethel. One of the most shocking documents in the FBI files is a thirteen-page memorandum, dated June 17, 1953, listing the questions the FBI agents at the death house were to put to Julius Rosenberg if he was ready to talk. There is one question in the entire memorandum concerning Ethel. It reads: "Was your wife cognizant of your activities?"

That single question stands out in the memorandum like a red flag. When it was composed by a top Bureau official, Ethel Rosenberg was about to be executed as a "full-fledged partner" in her husband's crimes, to use the words spoken by Judge Irving Kaufman. And yet the U.S. government seemed willing to let her die when the FBI was not even sure she was aware of Julius's espionage activities.

A second FBI memorandum neatly summarized what the Bureau still hoped to gain if Julius made a last-minute confession. "If Rosenberg talks," the memo said, meaning Julius and not Ethel, "we can probably prosecute for espionage, William Perl, an aeronautical engineer; . . . and Michael Sidorovich, a craftsman; . . . we can also possibly secure wartime espionage indictments against Alfred Sarant and Joel Barr, both engineers . . . whereabouts unknown; . . . we can possibly prosecute Ann Sidorovich at least for conspiracy to commit espionage." The memo also mentioned possible prosecutions of Maxwell Finestone and Vivian Glassman, though not in connection with any particular charge.

Minutes before 8:00 P.M., the focus of J. Edgar Hoover's extraordinary gamble stepped into the execution chamber accompanied by Sing Sing's Jewish chaplain, Rabbi Irving Koslowe. Earlier that day, Julius had made out a last testament, leaving guardianship of his children to Emanuel Bloch and imposing on his friend and attorney one final burden: "Be strong for us, beloved friend," the letter said, "and we wish you long life to continue your fruitful work in health and happiness. . . . NEVER LET THEM CHANGE THE TRUTH OF OUR INNOCENCE." From that moment on, through the gruesome ritual of being dressed and shaved for the electrocution, Rosenberg had expressed not the slightest inclination to make a statement, to the rabbi or to anyone else.

As he entered the brightly lit, white-walled execution chamber, Julius winced involuntarily. Then, as he approached the oak-paneled electric chair, his knees seemed to buckle. But there were no last words, and no sign of a changed heart to cause Warden Denno to pick up the open line to the command post nearby where the six-man

FBI team was waiting for a last-minute summons. Unwilling to prolong the agony longer, Warden Denno gave the signal for the guards to fasten into place the leather helmet that covers the condemned's face, sparing witnesses the sight of the involuntary contortions and ruptured eyes induced by the first seconds of electric shock.

Julius Rosenberg was pronounced dead at 8:06 P.M. Even as his limp body was being carted away, a guard stepped forward to mop up the urine that had collected on the seat and underneath the electric chair, using a strong ammonia solution that also mercifully masked the stench of burnt flesh. Immediately after the guard finished his task, Ethel was brought into the room by two matrons. She looked astonishingly composed despite a last-minute appeal from the rabbi that she reconsider her silence and confess for her children's sake. Planting a good-bye kiss on the cheek of one matron who had been especially kind to her and shaking the other's hand as if she were departing on a routine journey, Ethel walked to the chair unaided and, ignoring the efforts of the guards to strap her hands and secure the electrodes to her head and leg, fixed her gaze firmly on the three press-corps witnesses. At her side, Rabbi Koslowe intoned the words of the Thirty-first Psalm:

> In Thee, O Lord, have I taken refuge;
>   let me never be ashamed;
> Deliver me in Thy righteousness.
>   . . . .
> Because of all mine adversaries I am become a reproach,
> Yea, unto my neighbors exceedingly,
>   and a dread to mine acquaintance;
> They that see me without flee from me.
> I am forgotten as a dead man out of mind;
> I am like a useless vessel.
> For I have heard the whisperings of many,
> Terror on every side;
> While they took counsel together against me,
> They devised to take away my life.

Ethel's serene expression, which discomfited the watching reporters even more than had the sight of her husband's ashen-faced pallor, seemed to promise that she had one more surprise in store for them. And she did. After the standard three shocks, one short and two long, the waiting doctor stepped forward to check for a heartbeat and announced that the prisoner was still alive. Two more shocks, and a total of four minutes and fifty seconds in all, were required before Ethel finally expired.

News of the execution did not touch off the violent actions that the government had convinced itself might be in the offing, but it did evoke violent extremes of emotion.

Near New York's Union Square a crowd estimated at between five and seven thousand—some carrying signs proclaiming "WE ARE INNOCENT"—listened to news of the deaths in anguished silence, then dispersed quietly after nervous police disconnected the public address system.

In Europe, where it was already past midnight, it was relatively quiet, but mass demonstrations in Paris earlier that day had included a march on the American embassy that ended with one man dead and hundreds jailed. In Italy, placards and graffiti calling for "DEATH TO THE KILLERS OF THE ROSENBERGS" appeared overnight, and by Sunday morning crowds surged through the streets of Rome marching on the American embassy there in a mood that Leslie Fiedler, who happened to witness the demonstrations, claimed was less that of a wake than of a victory celebration.

In some American cities, elation over the executions was undisguised. Outside the White House, the anti-Rosenberg pickets, some carrying signs that urged "DEATH TO THE COMMUNIST RATS," eventually outnumbered the couple's supporters, and when the radios flashed news that the death sentences had been carried out, hundreds of motorists honked their horns in approval and celebration. In Los Angeles, too, cheering counterdemonstrators outshouted the mourners. Irwin Edelman, still persona non grata as far as the Los Angeles branch of the Committee was concerned, took it upon himself to mount a stairway in Pershing Square and remonstrate with the celebrating crowds. "If you are happy about the Rosenbergs, then you are rotten to the core!" he screamed, but the counterdemonstrators, in no mood to feel guilty, simply turned their fury on him. Edelman fled just steps ahead of the advancing mob and took shelter in the lobby of the Biltmore Hotel.

29

The Aftermath

An estimated eight thousand mourners gathered for Julius and Ethel's funeral on Sunday morning, June 21. The emotionally charged crowd packed Brooklyn's Church Avenue near the I. J. Morris funeral home, waiting for a glimpse of the Rosenbergs' coffins. Many wept openly as inside, before an audience that included several hundred Committee activists as well as members of the Rosenberg family, Emanuel Hirsch Bloch delivered a eulogy that denounced President Eisenhower, Attorney General Brownell, and J. Edgar Hoover for the murder of his clients and beloved friends. "America today is living under the heels of a military dictatorship dressed in civilian garb," said the anguished Bloch. "These people have no hearts. They have stones for hearts."

Later, a cortege of three chartered buses and hundreds of private cars followed the caskets on their journey to a Long Island cemetery while members of the crowd that was left behind scuffled with police. It was the martyrs' funeral that the Rosenbergs would have wanted.

To say that the Rosenbergs had become secular martyrs of the American Communist Party is no rhetorical exaggeration. The *Daily Worker*, which had so pointedly ignored Julius and Ethel while their case was before the courts, pulled out all the stops to eulogize them in death. A front-page statement by the Party's Central Committee characterized their execution as "a brutal act of fascist violence" planned by our "desperate rulers" and abetted by a "terrorized" jury. "The world speaks its admiration for this humble and obscure couple whose souls were as pure as their executioners were vile," the statement went on, concluding with the prophetic promise that the fight to establish their innocence "is just beginning." Nor was this merely the excess of the moment. As late as 1979, the Party's top leader, Gus Hall, was still writing of the martyrdom of the Rosenbergs and excoriating any suggestion that they may not have been total innocents as a desecration of their "sacred memory."

The National Committee to Secure Justice in the Rosenberg Case also vowed to continue the fight. Even before the funeral, the Committee had announced its intentions to remain active. In the absence of a practical short-term goal, however, the group was soon reduced to a remnant of stalwarts. By the fall of 1953, it had reorganized around the cause of Morton Sobell, the hitherto forgotten third defendant.

The Committee also organized a speaking tour for Emanuel Bloch with the goal of raising $50,000 for a trust fund for the Rosenbergs' sons. Benefit audiences throughout the country heard Bloch hailed as a hero, the man who had dedicated his life to saving the first martyrs of the new fascism. But it did not take long for the simmering conflict between Bloch and the Committee to erupt into the open. Bloch had been named the sole legal guardian of the children and he was soon fighting for complete control of the trust fund as well. As the argument heated up, Bloch charged the Committee with misappropriating funds from earlier campaigns that had been raised in the children's names. It was true that surprisingly little was left of the many thousands of dollars raised by the Committee in its heyday. Much had gone to further the group's own campaign, and little had been set aside for the Rosenberg family. There is, however, no evidence to support a charge of outright malfeasance. Even HUAC, when it investigated the Rosenberg-Sobell Committee (as it was by then called) in 1956, could find no evidence of financial irregularities.

As guardian of the Rosenberg sons, Manny Bloch also had to deal with the pressing problem of custody arrangements. Since the fall of 1951, when Sophie Rosenberg had finally decided that the task of caring for the boys was beyond her capabilities, the children had been living in Toms River, New Jersey, with Mr. and Mrs. Bernard Bach, friends of the Rosenbergs. The Bachs had been good foster parents. However, the arrangement had never been intended to be permanent. Beyond that, the children's identities and whereabouts had received wide publicity as the result of their appearance on Committee picket lines, and the Toms River school board had challenged their right to attend public schools since their legal guardian, Bloch, was not a local taxpayer.

Bloch decided that the children needed a new and permanent home, one where they could live quietly outside the public eye. From numerous offers of adoption, he chose that of Abel and Anne Meeropol, he a songwriter who could encourage the musical talent that Michael Rosenberg had inherited from his mother and she a nursery school teacher with experience in dealing with troubled children. Whatever his limitations as a lawyer, Bloch had certainly gone beyond professional duty in carrying out his responsibilities to the children. His choice of the Meeropols was a wise one, and it seemed, for the moment at least, that the problem of the children's future was settled.

Aside from the successful solution of this problem, not much was going right for Manny Bloch. It can have been little satisfaction to him that he was now lionized by the Party as the chief apostle and advocate of the martyred Rosenbergs. His personal life was in ruins—he was separated from his wife. And his law practice had dwindled to the vanishing point. The retribution that he had feared—and indeed almost courted by his statements at the funeral—had already begun. A bar association committee was investigating disbarment charges, based not only on Bloch's funeral oration but on a statement made just after the Supreme Court's voiding of the Douglas stay: "I am ashamed to be an American."

One day in January 1954, Manny Bloch failed to show up for an appointment with Gloria Agrin, who had volunteered to help research his fight against disbarment. That afternoon, when Bloch had still failed to check in with his office, Agrin went to his tiny apartment and opened the front door with a spare key. The door was chain-locked from the inside, but it opened just wide enough for her to glimpse Bloch's pajama-clad body in the bathroom, slumped over a tub full of water. Only fifty-two years old, Bloch had survived the Rosenbergs by little more than seven months.

A squad of agents from the New York office of the FBI was on the scene minutes after the arrival of the police. They searched the apartment thoroughly in an effort, according to FBI documents, to investigate the possibility that the attorney had been murdered on orders from the Communist Party because he "knew too much." These suspicions proved baseless. The door to Bloch's apartment had been chained from the inside and the medical examiner found the cause of death to be a heart attack. The Bureau did note, however, that the New York police officers present had derived considerable merriment from the fact that Bloch died clad in red pajamas.

Bloch's death stilled but did not quite put an end to the need of a small group of vocal anti-Communist crusaders to exact a final revenge from the Rosenbergs for their success in turning their own deaths into a propaganda victory. The Rosenberg sons were out of the public eye for the first time in years and had already begun using the names of their foster parents. They hardly seemed in need of saving. Nevertheless, S. Andhill Fineberg, the National Committee's most vocal critic, charged that the latest fund-raising campaign constituted a continued attempt to exploit the children's names. Fineberg's accusations were featured in Walter Winchell's column along with the suggestion that the boys would be raised to become Communist "dupes." Several weeks after Bloch's death, a social worker for a private child-protection agency filed a neglect complaint, and a family court judge issued an order for the Meeropols to produce the children in his courtroom. The order was executed that very evening by a team of police officers and city welfare workers, who showed up at the Meeropols' Riverside Drive apartment intending to take the boys into custody that very night, an action that would surely have stirred cruel and traumatic memories of their father's own arrest. The Meeropols, however, managed to forestall it by phoning the judge, who agreed to leave the boys where they were until the court proceedings the next day.

Legal wrangling over custody opened all the old wounds. The children's attempt to fit in quietly in their new school and neighborhood was destroyed by newspaper stories branding them as the "spies' orphans" and the judge in their case received thousands of letters and telegrams from partisans on both sides. It seemed, as he noted at one point, that every worker in France was taking a personal interest in the resolution of the custody fight.

Finally, a New York Supreme Court judge came up with a solution worthy of Solomon himself. Coguardianship of the children was awarded jointly to the grandmother, Sophie Rosenberg, and Kenneth Johnson, dean of the New York School of Social Work, a Columbia University affiliate. Johnson was a personal friend of Eisenhower and had impeccable establishment credentials; fortunately, he also placed the interest of the children above the demands of Rabbi Fineberg and others who had argued that placing the children with a welfare agency would better assure their being reared as "normal" Americans. Johnson waited until the publicity had died down and then, armed with a battery of psychological tests and expert recommendations, announced that he and Mrs. Rosenberg had agreed that the boys should be returned to the Meeropols.

While the battle over control of the Rosenbergs' children dragged on in the New York courts, Senator Joe McCarthy had already announced that he would succeed where the government had failed—in ferreting out still undiscovered remnants of the Rosenberg ring through an investigation of wartime espionage. The focus of the new spy hunt was to be Fort Monmouth, the New Jersey Signal Corps Laboratory where Joel Barr, Vivian Glassman, and other Rosenberg contacts had once worked. The source of McCarthy's information on Fort Monmouth was none other than Roy Cohn, who had by now left the U.S. Attorney's office to become the senator's chief aide. In October 1953, McCarthy, Cohn, and a sizable entourage descended on Lewisburg Penitentiary to interview David Greenglass about his knowledge of spying at Fort Monmouth.

FBI documents show that the McCarthy-Cohn investigation evoked both ridicule and alarm from Hoover and his top assistants. Indeed, their internal memos denouncing the "lurid" and "sensational" aspects of the probe read like an ACLU press release. The possibility that Barr, Sarant, and Glassman had already been involved in espionage while they worked at Fort Monmouth had not been overlooked by the FBI. A thorough investigation, however, had turned up no proof to support this suspicion. "Cohn is smart enough to know that it is not necessary for him to produce factual evidence to establish an espionage connection," complained D. M. Ladd in a report to Hoover; the impending congressional investigation would only provide an excuse for "the Communists to propagandize the issue as showing the Rosenbergs were the victims of a McCarthy smear."

Hoover and Ladd were correct in maintaining that David

Greenglass had already been exhaustively interviewed and would have nothing new to tell the McCarthy committee. In 1956, when HUAC went so far as to have Greenglass subpoenaed from prison to testify before them, the witness's own nervousness combined with the uninformed, scattershot questioning of the Committee staff elicited nothing but a garbled version of what he had told the Bureau years earlier. In fact, the only "revelations" that either group of congressional investigators succeeded in getting from Greenglass concerned his by now fuzzy memory of the incident of the stolen proximity fuse and the "thinking machine"—actually, a computer for tracking guided missiles. The FBI had heard about these stories years earlier and had already determined that both thefts belonged to a period after Joel Barr had left Fort Monmouth.

A more substantial as well as more intriguing postscript to the Rosenberg case came to light in 1957, following the arrest of the Soviet spy chief Colonel Rudolph Abel. At Abel's trial that October, prosecution witness Reino Hayhanen testified that in 1955 he had been given $5,000 by a Soviet contact with instructions to turn the money over to the wife of a certain agent code-named "Stone." In preparation for the assignment, which he had been instructed to arrange at New York's Bear Mountain State Park, Hayhanen took the money to the park and buried it. He never carried through with the rest of his assignment, however, because he had discovered that Stone's wife, whose real name was Helen Sobell, was still being closely watched by agents of the FBI.

Hayhanen's story was decried by the Rosenberg-Sobell Committee as just one more clumsy attempt by the government to implicate innocent parties through perjured testimony. It may well have been just that. But another aspect of the Abel case revealed the possibility of a new and mysterious tie-in with the Rosenbergs. Among Abel's personal effects at the time of his arrest, the FBI had found photographs of a couple identified as Morris and Lona Cohen. The Cohens, who were supposedly acquaintances of the Rosenbergs, had vanished from their New York apartment some time after the Rosenbergs were arrested in June 1950, certainly—as Louise Bernikow writes in her book on Colonel Abel—a matter of "suspicious timing."

The Cohens were still missing at the time of Abel's trial in 1957, but in 1961 they turned up in London, where they had been living as Peter and Helen Kroger, antiquarian book dealers who specialized in, among other subjects, volumes on torture and sadomasochism. And in March 1961, the Cohens/Krogers were convicted by a British court as having been part of the "Naval Secrets" spy ring; its central figure was Gordon Lonsdale, a Soviet national who had masqueraded for many years as a Canadian businessman. The FBI's files on the Cohens/Krogers have never been released, and whatever substance this may or may not have with regard to the Rosenberg case remains an unexplored chapter in the annals of FBI counterespionage.

From time to time, also, there was speculation in the press about possible connections between the Rosenberg spy ring and certain new developments in Soviet technology. These rumors reached a new peak in October 1957, when the Soviets launched Sputnik, the first orbiting space satellite. A front-page story in the *Chicago Tribune* quoted former U.S. Attorney Myles Lane as confirming that Sputnik was no less than the fruit of the "sky platform" data that had been given to the Russians by Rosenberg. In response to Lane's charges, the Senate Internal Security Committee announced it planned to hold a full hearing on the matter and its counsel, Robert Morris, was dispatched to Lewisburg Penitentiary to take yet another deposition from David Greenglass. It turned out that Greenglass knew no more about the sky platform than he had told the FBI and the U.S. Attorney's office seven years earlier, and plans for the hearings were ultimately abandoned in the wake of skeptical newspaper editorials suggesting that the whole issue was an attempt to divert the public's attention from the shortcomings of the American space program.

The indifference and even ridicule that greeted Lane's charges in 1957 was a measure of how far the mood of the country had moved away from the atom-spy hysteria of 1950. The public was tired of seeing ex-Communists trotted out for congressional investigations that never lived up to their sensational advance billing. Nor could anyone find much solace in blaming "the enemy within" for the Soviets' success with Sputnik. The possibility that the space satellite concept might have been stolen from us originally only made it more difficult to explain why the Russians had surpassed us since.

This new skepticism about the importance of espionage in the larger scheme of things was a healthy development. However, the connection drawn by Lane between the sky platform and Sputnik was by no means as baseless as many assumed. When David Greenglass talked to the FBI in July 1950, he had been able to describe the sky platform in only the vaguest of terms. The project, he said then, was "in the stage where the mathematics were being worked out" and its goal was the establishment "of a platform at a point in space where gravity ceases to exist." It was also Greenglass's impression that work on the platform idea was being done somewhere in upstate New York. FBI investigators had forwarded this sketchy description to Air Force intelligence, which readily identified the sky platform as Project Rand, a pioneering proposal for an artificial earth satellite that had been developed by the Rand Corporation in California shortly after the war. Edward Scheidt of the New York Bureau office duly reported to Hoover that a comprehensive report on the platform had indeed been in circulation sometime during 1946 or 1947 and might have come to Rosenberg's attention; however, the project was now a dead letter, having been abandoned by the Air Force because, in Scheidt's words, "the cost estimates were so huge."

What bothered Scheidt at the time, since he was primarily concerned with checking the authenticity of Greenglass's story, was that Project Rand had been developed in California and not in upper New York State. Scheidt told Hoover that he had discovered something which might possibly account for Greenglass's belief that the information had come from New York: it happened that copies of the Rand report—whose correct title was "Preliminary Design on an Experimental World-Circling Spaceship"—had been distributed to several aeronautical laboratories in various parts of the United States, among them the Aeronautics and Ordnance System Division of General Electric's Schenectady, New York, research facility, the same lab in which Morton Sobell had been employed as a project engineer until mid-1947. The FBI was never able to develop any hard evidence that Sobell had actually given the Rand report or segments of it to Julius Rosenberg, so the subject was never mentioned in court.

Myles Lane may well have been disappointed to see his attempt to reopen the sky-platform issue come to nothing. However, like most of the principals on the government side of the case, he had no reason to be anything but pleased by the effects on his career of his work as one of the Rosenberg-Sobell prosecutors. Irving Saypol had been nominated for a seat on the New York State Supreme Court just months after the Rosenberg-Sobell trial ended; Lane, after a brief time as U.S. attorney, soon followed his mentor to the state supreme court bench. Cohn, of course, had used his experience as one of the Rosenberg prosecutors to catch the eye of Senator McCarthy. And J.

Edgar Hoover continued to cite the Rosenberg case as one of the FBI's major triumphs, particularly when it came time to send his budget requests to Capitol Hill.

The one public official who had occasion to regret his role in the trial was Judge Irving Kaufman. Kaufman had courted public attention with his statement at the sentencing arrogating to himself the moral responsibility for the Rosenbergs' fates. When the clemency campaign later gained worldwide publicity, he had to live with the consequences. Hate mail and even threats were just part of the judge's problem. Questions about the wisdom of the sentences had been raised by international figures of some standing, creating a lingering controversy that did nothing to advance Kaufman's career on the federal bench.

Kaufman had good reason to be bitter over the wild accusations that he had knowingly allowed his courtroom to be used for the frame-up of two innocent individuals. However, his reaction to criticism went well beyond the bounds of justifiable indignation, to say nothing of judicial propriety. Kaufman's obsessive need for vindication is revealed in his continuing communications with the FBI over a period of more than twenty years.

Harvard Law School professor Vern Countryman, who was at one time associated with the Morton Sobell defense effort, sums up the case against Kaufman when he writes that during the trial itself:

> Kaufman seems to have been in regular contact with the Justice Department prosecution staff, who were in turn passing information to the FBI. In the middle of the trial, before the defense had put on any witnesses, a Justice Department official had told an FBI agent he knew the judge would impose the death penalty if the Rosenbergs were convicted, "if he doesn't change his mind." After the jury returned its guilty verdict and two days before sentencing, assistant prosecutor Roy Cohn told an FBI agent that Judge Kaufman "personally favored" the death penalty for the Rosenbergs and would give a prison term to Sobell. Needless to say, this kind of *ex parte* communication ... with the prosecution—discussing the sentence before the trial is over—is highly improper.

Kaufman also interfered in the Rosenberg case after it left his jurisdiction. In February 1953, while the petition for *certiorari* was before the Supreme Court, he phoned the Bureau and expressed his fear that the court might not get to the case before the scheduled spring adjournment, and he urged that the FBI encourage the Justice Department to "push the matter vigorously." And after Justice Douglas received an application for stay of execution—on June 16— Kaufman the very next day phoned the Bureau to report that the Attorney General and Chief Justice Vinson had met and decided that if Douglas did grant a stay, the court would be reconvened.

The Rosenbergs' executions did not end Kaufman's interference. He continued to use the FBI as a private complaint bureau, registering his distress over ongoing legal efforts to free Morton Sobell and encouraging efforts to discredit and even stifle the appearance of books, plays, and records favorable to the Rosenbergs.

In 1957, to cite just one example, Kaufman is described in an FBI memo as "very much upset" over an appeal brought by Sobell's lawyers that charged him with committing a prejudicial error in allowing the prosecutor to question Ethel Rosenberg about her use of the Fifth Amendment before the grand jury. According to an FBI memo forwarded to Clyde Tolson by FBI public relations chief L. B. Nichols: "Irving is afraid that the [Supreme] court might upset the case unless the Department vigorously defends it. . . . I wonder if it wouldn't be a good idea to send a memorandum to the Attorney General pointing out Judge Kaufman's concern."

Kaufman had good reason for worry since the Supreme Court's decision in the *Grunewald* case, also in 1957, had disallowed the use of grand jury testimony under very similar circumstances. This was brought to public attention five years later when Sobell's attorneys put forward another appeal, heard by a circuit court of appeals panel that included Thurgood Marshall, the future Supreme Court justice. Referring to the *Grunewald* precedent, Marshall had asked an assistant U.S. attorney: "If Sobell had been tried last Spring and we had him before us today, wouldn't it have been necessary for the court to reverse the decision?" The government attorney conceded that Marshall was probably right.

Forgetting his own concern over the implications of the *Grunewald* decision back in 1957, Kaufman called C. D. ("Deke") De-Loach, Hoover's right-hand man and protégé, to complain about Marshall's remarks. Fuming that *Grunewald* was not good law and certainly did not apply to Sobell's case, Kaufman went on to characterize Marshall (who is pointedly identified in the FBI memos as "formerly attorney for the NAACP") as "naïve" and "inexperienced." What's more, Kaufman predicted, the "stupid" answer of the assistant U.S. attorney would soon become the subject of articles in *The Nation*, *The New Republic*, and the *National Guardian*. In this, at least, he was correct.

Another theme that runs through the FBI documents dealing with Kaufman is the judge's obsessive concern with print and media accounts of the case. In 1957, for example, the judge wrote to Attorney General Brownell praising a *Look* magazine article that had been written by a journalist working in close cooperation with the FBI. "As you know," wrote Kaufman, "I have never uttered a word—as indeed I should not—in answer to these horribly concocted Communist charges concerning my conduct in the trial, although I must confess on occasion that it was rather difficult to remain silent."

But while Kaufman appreciated the virtue of public silence, he does not seem to have had any qualms about interfering behind the scenes. Not one month after the above letter was written, Kaufman called Hoover to discuss reporter Jim Bishop's plans for a forthcoming book on the Rosenberg-Sobell trial. The judge had heard that Bishop planned to interview Helen Sobell, a concession to objectivity that he thought "unwise." Perhaps, suggested Kaufman, FBI agent Nease, who was already working with Bishop, could advise against such an interview. This request seems to have tried Hoover's patience, though for all one knows he had been agreeing with Kaufman all through their phone conversation. At any rate, at the bottom of his memo on the phone call, Hoover added the peevish note, "I see no reason to do this unless Bishop raises it with Nease."

Again, in 1969, when a play sympathetic to the Rosenbergs had a short run in a Cleveland, Ohio, theater, Kaufman contacted the Bureau to express his "alarm" over the fact that the play had received not one but two reviews in different sections of *The New York Times*. The FBI was concerned too; in fact, its agents had already done a "background" investigation of the play's author. A summary of the investigation's results was sent along to the judge, who replied with the news that his former colleague on the bench, Simon Rifkind, was planning to write a letter to the *Times* protesting the play's favorable treatment in their pages.

Rifkind's name comes up again in 1974 after two documentaries advancing the theory that the Rosenbergs were victims of a frame-up had been aired on national television. According to the FBI's W. A. Branigan, during a visit to Bureau headquarters Judge Kaufman mentioned that Simon Rifkind was preparing a rebuttal article for *TV Guide* and that "they" (Rifkind and Kaufman) were also hoping to place the article in the *Times.*

When the FBI's files on the Rosenberg case were first made available to public scrutiny, Harvard law professor Vern Countryman called on the House and Senate judiciary committees to investigate the entire pattern of Judge Kaufman's actions—beginning with allegations that Kaufman had participated in *ex parte* discussions with Justice Department officials while the Rosenberg-Sobell trial was still in progress. Countryman's letter was cosigned by one hundred law professors and in 1977 it was supported by a resolution passed by the American Civil Liberties Union.

The New York Times promptly rushed to the defense of Judge Kaufman's reputation in an editorial hinting that the ACLU resolution was a cunningly engineered ploy organized by die-hard defenders of the Rosenbergs to gain publicity for their discredited cause. The investigation that ensued, however, was undertaken by a special subcommittee of the American Bar Association in 1976. The language of the ABA's charge to the subcommittee suggests that the group was set up, not so much to investigate the Kaufman allegations, as to refute what were assumed to be "unwarranted charges" and "unfounded criticism" of him. The subcommittee's chairman was Simon Rifkind, a partner in the prestigious law firm of Paul, Weiss, Rifkind, Wharton & Garrison—and the Kaufman colleague mentioned in several of the FBI memoranda. Rifkind's report has never been released to the public, and despite numerous attempts to gain access to it, the Bar Association remains adamant in refusing anyone the chance to examine its contents.

30

The Scientific
Evidence

Thirty years have passed since the execution of Julius and Ethel Rosenberg. And yet the case continues to be the focus of major controversy. The prosecution claimed at the time that the Rosenbergs had in effect stolen *the secret* of the atomic bomb, as prosecutor Saypol put it in his opening remarks to the jury, the "one weapon, that might well hold the key to the survival of this nation." And when he presented his charge to the jury, Judge Irving Kaufman stated that "the government claims that the venture was successful as to the atom bomb secret." Kaufman elaborated upon this charge as he sentenced the couple to death, condemning them for "putting into the hands of the Russians the A-bomb years before our best scientists predicted Russia would perfect the bomb."

As we have seen, the government relied heavily in its case against the Rosenbergs on the testimony of David Greenglass, who by his own word, had engaged in the passing of atomic-related information. In recent years critics have mounted an impressive challenge to the concept that the Rosenbergs' espionage was of real significance. It is impossible, they argue, for an army mechanic with a high school education and a second-class security clearance to have had the capability of producing anything that could have been of real value to the Russians, not to speak of sketches and data that comprised the "secret" of the atomic bomb. A mere mechanic, the critics say, would never have had access to the complex technical data that would have been of practical value to Soviet atomic scientists, much less the educational background to understand and transmit such data accurately. As Nobel prize–winning physicist Harold C. Urey contended in a telegram to President Eisenhower just days before the Rosenbergs' execution, "A man of Greenglass's capacity is wholly incapable of transmitting the physics, chemistry and mathematics of the bomb to anyone."

Harold Urey was certainly a better scientist than either Saypol or Kaufman, and it would seem that his view of David Greenglass's capabilities ought to prevail. Urey's opinion has also been supported by an apparently impressive body of expert testimony: In 1966 Morton Sobell's lawyer Marshall Perlin succeeded in winning the court-ordered release of technical testimony that had been impounded during the Rosenberg-Sobell trial. Perlin then asked several former Los Alamos scientists to examine the material and evaluate its scientific importance.

One of the affidavits Perlin secured came from Philip Morrison of Cornell University, coholder of the patent on the Nagasaki implosion-type bomb and a major Los Alamos physicist. Of the Greenglass sketch showing a cross section of this bomb, Morrison said, it is "barren of any meaningful or correct *quantitative* information" (emphasis in the original), while the accompanying description "demonstrates a lack of comprehension."

An even more strongly worded affidavit was submitted by Dr. Henry Linschitz, a physical chemist who had headed a team in the explosives division at Los Alamos and been intimately involved with the experiments leading to the development of the bomb's implosion-type lens. Linschitz's statement characterized Greenglass's data as "garbled" and "naïve." And it went on to challenge the very notion that "the results of a two-billion-dollar development effort [could be condensed] into a diagram, drawn by a high-school graduate machinist on a single sheet of paper." In summary, Linschitz concluded, "The information in question purporting to describe the construction of a plutonium bomb was too incomplete, ambiguous, and even incorrect to be of any service or value to the Russians in shortening the time required to develop their nuclear bombs."

Linschitz's affidavit received the general endorsement of both Harold Urey and J. Robert Oppenheimer, and his conclusions were widely quoted. At first glance, they offered the final damning proof that David Greenglass's atomic "secrets" were worthless—and, moreover, that this must have been obvious to the AEC's expert witnesses.

This interpretation leaves a number of crucial questions unanswered. Why would the Soviets have risked the cover of Klaus Fuchs's own espionage courier, Harry Gold, in order to make contact with an informant who was educationally and professionally "incapable" of giving them any valuable data? And why, after having months to examine Greenglass's June 1945 report and presumably discover its worthlessness, would they solicit further information in September? Finally, why would the Russians have continued dealing with Julius Rosenberg on up through 1949 if the information and contacts he supplied them with were not merely unproductive but laughably inaccurate and "naïve"?

One way to dispose of such questions is to conclude that Greenglass's entire story was a fabrication and that the Rosenberg spy network never existed. This is the argument of Miriam and Walter Schneir, who suggest in their book on the case that Greenglass's description of the Nagasaki bomb was improvised long after 1945 from a combination of half-remembered Los Alamos gossip, speculation, published newspaper reports, and perhaps information gleaned from the data of the Smyth report, which was released in 1945.

However, Atomic Energy Commission documents now declassified and available to the public show that the AEC staff went to considerable trouble to evaluate the content of Greenglass's statement and verify that the technical data was learned by him firsthand at Los Alamos. Concerning the Nagasaki bomb, for example, David Greenglass had given the FBI this description: .

> The A bomb is made up of 36 pentagonal shaped molds. When all set together the molds formed a sphere made of high explosives with balls of plutonium in the center. Inside the plutonium is a sphere of beryllium. A plastic shield is in between the plutonium and the high explosives. The high explosive has two detonators for each high explosive segment. The detonators were connected to a number of condensers possibly about 36 or 72. The condensers are also called capacitators. The number of detonators was twice the number of molds and the number of condensers were equal in number to the number of detonators. The

beryllium had a hollow center. The beryllium had a number of cone shaped holes in it, the apex of each cone being toward the periphery of the beryllium. The beryllium was gold plated which prevented it from emitting neutrons. The detonation of the high explosives causes the plutonium to be crushed or imploded and, therefore, increases the number of plutonium neutrons which are free. The beryllium also becomes crushed and the beryllium neutrons are jetted out through the cones into the mass of the plutonium which sets off the chain reaction of the plutonium which results in the atomic explosion.

Shortly after David Greenglass made this statement on July 19, 1950, the FBI gave it to the AEC's security division, just as it had passed along earlier information—including a version of the lens mold sketch that Greenglass drew shortly after his arrest, his descriptions of the Los Alamos complex, and the names of scientists whom he had identified to the Russians. The AEC was also provided with a Lucite disk found in the Greenglass apartment. (This disk was identified by the AEC as "part of an experimental model of a detonator"; it was not introduced as evidence during the trial.) In early August, the AEC reported back to the Bureau that the Greenglass material was inaccurate in several respects: the description of the beryllium sphere was misleading and did not include the information that the sphere contained polonium. Also, Greenglass was mistaken about the number of condensers and detonators used in the assembly. Nevertheless, the AEC's division of security concluded that the material was substantially accurate and still sensitive enough that it might pose security problems if revealed at the trial.

No final decision was made on just how much of the data the AEC would consider declassifying for trial purposes until February 1951. At that time, Dr. James Beckerley, head of the AEC's division of classification, set out to discover just how an ordinary machinist, whose access to classified data was supposedly on a strict "need to know" basis, could have put together such a comprehensive, albeit imprecise, picture of the bomb's design. On February 2, Beckerley guided Myles Lane through a six-hour interrogation of Greenglass, dissecting his description of the bomb phrase by phrase in order to learn the source of each item of information. Under intensive questioning, Greenglass altered several details given in his original statement. However, his explanation of the sources of his knowledge was sufficient to convince Beckerley that the description could have indeed been gleaned surreptitiously by a Los Alamos enlisted man. The thoroughness of Beckerley's investigation on this matter is revealed in this excerpt from his report:

ITEM	SOURCE
"36 pentagonal molds"	Worked on individual experimental molds. Assumed they were used in weapon. Number derived from detonator information (see below).
"molds form a sphere made of HE with ball of plutonium in center."	Was asked to section imploded natural uranium spheres. Found out in conversation that plutonium would be used and that the uranium was intended to simulate plutonium.
"inside . . . a sphere of beryllium"	Was asked for assistance by someone who was machining the beryllium. From shape and size (about 2 inches) he assumed it to be the center of the weapon. Saw that sphere was hollow.
"a barium plastic shield"	Saw one in Sigma building.
" . . . two detonators"	Heard that there was an extra one for safety. Assumed use in weapon.
"number of condensors . . . 36 or 72"	Saw Trinity unit (didn't know the name of it) during visit to C building. Counted condensors [sic]. Was told in conversation of intended use. Noted that condensors [sic] were mounted on a metal plate.
"number of detonators is twice"	Assumed from knowledge of total number of condensers.
"The beryllium. . . emitting neutrons"	Saw the unit including conical projections. (Proud of his knowledge of "Munroe Effect.") Was told about shaped charges in conventional ordnance when previously at Aberdeen.
"neutrons are jetted out"	Deduced.

As Yogi Berra once said in another context, "You observe a lot just by watching." Six hours of interrogation convinced Beckerley that Greenglass had been able to pick up an amazing fund of information, all without ever stealing a document or entering a restricted area. Greenglass's knowledge was broad—including knowledge of the still (in 1982) classified levitation experiments as well as of work on the Nagasaki implosion bomb—but it was also extremely shallow. Since he did not understand the underlying principles at work, he was prone to make nonsensical errors and become rattled under questioning. Beckerley had no way of knowing how many of the errors in Greenglass's statement had been incorporated in the material passed to Gold and how many were the result of the five-year lapse since the information was originally delivered. Comparison of statements given by Greenglass over time, however, suggested that the more he tried to remember details, the more confused he became. It was during the interview witnessed by Beckerley, for example, that Greenglass added the information that the plastic shield used in the bomb was made of barium; this was wrong—the shield was of boron.

Far from coaching Greenglass to improve his testimony, Beckerley took care not to tip off the witness that parts of his statement were wrong. Greenglass gave essentially the same description of the Nagasaki bomb in his trial testimony, except that he rose to the occasion of his public appearance by adding a few more vivid and quite erroneous details. These included the explanation that "the beryllium shield protects the high explosives from the radiation of the plutonium" as well as the information that the bomb was dropped "on a parachute." Strikingly enough, these were two aspects of the Greenglass testimony that Philip Morrison would criticize most harshly in the affidavit he gave Marshall Perlin. The mention of the bomb being dropped by parachute was especially suspect since Greenglass almost certainly picked it up from newspaper accounts printed after the attack on Nagasaki. (Witnesses to the bombing had seen instrument packs dropped by parachute and assumed in the confusion that the chutes were used in the delivery of the bomb itself.)

It is quite true, then, as charged in a 1980 article by Gerald Markowitz and Michael Meeropol, that the AEC's expert witnesses knew there were "gross errors" in the Greenglass testimony and did nothing to point this out to the judge and jury. But it might be argued that, as the law then stood, it was not the business of the government's witnesses to point out the flaws in the Greenglass testimony. AEC documents show that the Commission fully expected Bloch to mount a vigorous attack on the technical evidence, just as they believed that all the technical testimony would go into the permanent record of the case. It was Bloch's request for impoundment that prevented the exposure of Greenglass's errors. And in any case, as pointed out in a 1966 letter to *The New York Times* by James Beckerley himself, it was not the accuracy of Greenglass's data that was on trial. If Greenglass had not managed to give the Soviets a complete picture of the plutonium bomb, it was not for lack of trying.

According to Philip Morrison, Emanuel Bloch told him long after the trial that the impounding had been a grievous error which came about because he was ignorant of the testimony's import and lacked the resources to challenge it effectively. Markowitz and Meeropol, in their article on this same subject, say that Bloch was "intimidated into believing that Greenglass' testimony would contain vital secrets" and thus wanted to impress the judge and jury with his concern for national security. A more extreme view is that Bloch believed the Greenglass testimony supported the government's case and felt his clients' interest would be best served in the long run by keeping the evidence away from public scrutiny.

Whatever his precise motives may have been, Bloch did make a belated effort to attack the government's scientific evidence. In October 1952, after the Rosenbergs had lost their first round with the court of appeals, Bloch wrote letters to a number of prominent scientists, soliciting their opinion on such questions as:

> Could a person of Greenglass' background and experience have produced in 1945 the sketch of a cross section of the Nagasaki type of atom bomb, together with twelve pages of matter explaining the functions and workings of such a bomb, drawing solely from memory and without the aid or assistance of any person or written matter or technical or scientific source or coaching?

Several prominent French and British scientists gave Bloch exactly the answers he was looking for. The most strongly worded support came in the form of an affidavit from the British physical chemist J. D. Bernal. Bernal noted, quite accurately, that the general principle of implosion had been known since 1792 and was thus hardly a secret. Implosion would be "the first [solution] to occur to any explosives expert" faced with designing a fission bomb. Nor, Bernal went on, could Greenglass's description have been of "real use" to anyone since it failed to supply the absolute dimensions of the bomb. As it happened, implosion had not been the first solution studied at Los Alamos, and the definition of "real use" is highly subjective. Bernal's affidavit was primarily effective as counterpropaganda to the notion that the Rosenbergs had made off with *the* secret of the atom bomb. It was widely circulated by the Rosenberg defense committee; however, its value was somewhat undercut by Bernal's reputation as a supporter of the British Communist Party and a generous contributor of his name to any and all Party causes.

If the basis of the government's case had been an obvious fraud, as Bernal claimed, then surely Bloch would have been able to persuade at least one prominent American scientist to come out and say so. But not one came forward in response to Bloch's letter. Was the scientific community bullied into silence by the belief that anyone who spoke in the Rosenbergs' defense would be persecuted as a Red? No one can deny that there was good reason for potentially sympathetic scientists to feel intimidated. But some of the recipients of Bloch's questionnaire did send in responses—responses that were never used because they did nothing to help the Rosenbergs' case.

Philip Morrison, for example, informed Bloch that he had "quite mixed feelings" about the Bernal affidavit. Morrison noted that Bernal was an expert in high explosives, which might explain his judgment that "critical volume" was the "main secret" of the bomb. As a nuclear physicist, Morrison felt compelled to take issue with this. He explained to Bloch that from his point of view "the implosion and all that lies behind it" was crucial.

Perhaps the most discouraging reply to Bloch's query came from none other than Hans Bethe. Dr. Bethe answered Bloch's question quoted above with a resounding yes.

"In order to make such a drawing," Bethe went on to explain, "a person must have a good memory, preferably a visual one, and must have had close contact with the making of the lens mold. Apparently Mr. Greenglass worked on these molds for a considerable period of time and must therefore have been familiar with their charge."

In answer to the question of whether Greenglass could have given an accurate written description of the bomb, Bethe once again replied in the affirmative: "Yes. . . . It is not certain of course that his description was accurate but, if this description came into the hands of a trained Russian scientist, it is likely that it could have been deciphered even if it were not accurate."

Another set of definite yes answers came from Dr. Samuel K. Allison of the University of Chicago's Institute for Nuclear Studies. Allison explained his reply to the question about the potential accuracy of the lens mold sketch as follows:

> These sketches may not have permitted the reproduction of a lens exactly of the dimensions of those used in our bomb, but this is not important. They would have revealed the idea of the lenses, and with this idea, a trained physicist could have easily designed them accurately.

Allison ended his letter by giving his unsolicited opinion that, while he deplored the death penalty, he believed the Rosenbergs guilty as charged.

Not even Dr. Harold Urey, aside from Einstein the only senior American physicist to associate himself with the Rosenberg defense, was willing to endorse Bernal's position. Urey's support for the Rosenbergs was based less on his estimate of the value of the scientific evidence than on his gut reaction to the fact that the Rosenbergs had been convicted on an informer's testimony. Malcolm Sharp learned this to his dismay in the mid-1950s when he attempted to solicit a statement from Urey on behalf of Morton Sobell. As Sharp noted in a 1958 memo to the Sobell defense committee:

> [In 1953] Mr. Finerty had understood that Dr. Urey was prepared to go farther than he went in the affidavit in speaking about the limitations of Greenglass. I believe that Dr. Urey chose his words very carefully. . . . Though the record indicates clearly the rough character of the lens mold sketches, I judge that Mr. Urey thinks they could have had some value for the Russians in indicating the lines along which our scientists thought it worthwhile to work.

When we asked Philip Morrison for his reaction to the Malcolm Sharp memo, he conceded that the Greenglass data, including the lens mold sketch and the impounded material, might have had some value to the Soviets "solely . . . because they tended to show that Fuchs did not make the whole thing up." Morrison then went on to admit, very reluctantly, what we had already guessed from perusing a letter he had exchanged on the subject with Helen Sobell—that he had always believed the Rosenbergs were "technically guilty."

Pressed to reconcile these private reservations with his public statements on behalf of the defense, Morrison said that he had always felt that the government must have some secret evidence linking the Rosenbergs to espionage, evidence never revealed during the trial. "My guess is, they didn't pick them at random," Morrison said. And later, he added: "I think they [the FBI and the CIA] had some evidence of some people who were approached by a leaky Soviet network. And I think [they were approached] for the primary intelligence goal of corroborating the detailed story of Fuchs. . . . Here was this network of a machine shop foreman who presumably never saw Fuchs [that] was very good corroboration. I think there's little doubt there's a real connection there." After speculating in this vein for a minute or two, Morrison went on to say that the Rosenbergs would have been a poor channel of information at best and that he believed the case presented against them in court was largely "fabricated."

In Morrison's view, the injustice done by the government to the Rosenbergs was so great that, by comparison, the question of their actual guilt pales into a mere technicality—one that he could bring himself to discuss at all with only the greatest hesitation. Rereading his 1966 affidavit with this in mind, one cannot help noticing that it is carefully worded to avoid endorsing the position there could have been no espionage at all. On the contrary, Morrison limits himself to a conscientious discussion of the errors in the Greenglass material, coupled with an attack on the myth there was such a thing as a single atomic "secret" that could have meant the difference between success and failure to a foreign power's A-bomb program.

In fact, even Henry Linschitz's strongly worded affidavit can be read primarily as an exposé of this myth. As Linschitz says in his conclusion: "The statement made by Judge Kaufman, when passing sentence on the Rosenbergs, regarding the technical importance of the information conveyed by Greenglass has no foundation in fact. Rather, it expressed a misunderstanding of the nature of modern technology." But not even Linschitz was willing to dismiss entirely the possibility that the Soviets might have benefited to a degree from stolen data. Linschitz's flat denial that the Greenglass material could have been of "any service or value" to the Russians was followed by a qualifying statement, which Markowitz and Meeropol, in their article on this subject, do not quote. "This conclusion," Linschitz adds, "is even more firmly established *in view of the information presumably given by Klaus Fuchs*" (emphasis added).

As this remark suggests, the most pertinent question about David Greenglass's role in atomic espionage is not whether he was capable of giving Soviet intelligence any useful information, but what he could possibly have offered that had not already been provided in much greater detail by Klaus Fuchs.

The precise content of the information that Klaus Fuchs gave the Soviets through Harry Gold is in fact that real "atomic secret" which was never revealed at his trial or during the course of the related Rosenberg-Sobell prosecution. The portion of Fuchs's confession dealing with the technical data he stole from Los Alamos was classified as secret by the British government, and as far as they are concerned it is still secret even today. In 1979, when Ronald Radosh appealed for release of this document through the U.S. Department of Energy, he was informed that the position of the United Kingdom was that "their version of the Fuchs confession was classified and cannot be downgraded or released."

However, the FBI has released a document summarizing the interrogation of Fuchs conducted in prison by Hugh Clegg and Robert Lamphere in May 1950. This report, which was prepared for distribution to the staff of the Atomic Energy Commission in July of that same year, says that in June 1945 Klaus Fuchs provided "Raymond" with a detailed description of the plutonium (or Nagasaki) bomb, including "a sketch of the bomb and its components with important dimensions indicated; the type of the core; a description of the initiator; details as to the tamper; the principle of the [illegible] calculations; and the method of calculating efficiency."

Attached to one of the copies of this report was the sketch that Fuchs had drawn for Clegg and Lamphere—one he said was similar to that he had given Raymond. This sketch, never before seen by any independent investigator of the case, confirmed with devastating finality that the Soviets had received a detailed description of the Nagasaki-type bomb from Fuchs in June 1945—three months before

Greenglass drew his comparatively babyish version for Julius Rosenberg. Fuchs's diagram shows the array of spherical components of the bomb, and reveals how its high-explosive outer layers are arranged to generate a spherically symmetric, inwardly converging detonation wave, which in turn causes rapid compression of the uranium tamper and the plutonium within it. It contains specific calculations—deleted by the Bureau—which show the progressively decreasing radius of the core. It came as no surprise, when one of us showed a copy of this sketch to Philip Morrison, that he told us: "It's the real thing."

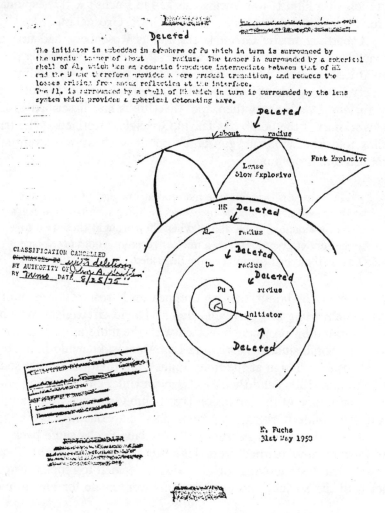

Why then did the Soviets need David Greenglass?

The mystery is not so great when one considers the timing of David Greenglass's recruitment. Klaus Fuchs was transferred from New York to Los Alamos in August 1944. By his own testimony, he did not warn Raymond of his impending departure, and for some months after arriving in New Mexico he was undecided about whether he wanted to reopen his communications with the Soviets. He did not make contact with Raymond again until the week of February 13, 1945, when he went back east to vacation at the home of his sister Kristel Heineman and learned that Raymond had been trying to get in touch with him. It was during this gap in Fuchs's active espionage career that Julius Rosenberg recruited David Greenglass.

According to the Greenglasses, Julius Rosenberg had first approached Ruth before her trip to New Mexico in November 1944. David delivered the first installment of his material—including the first crude lens-mold sketches—when he returned home for his January furlough, and it was then, too, that Julius first described to him the workings of the bomb. As David Greenglass testified at the trial, Julius told him about a "gun-type" bomb, such as was eventually dropped on Hiroshima:

> He said there was fissionable material at one end of a cube and at the other end of a cube there was a sliding member that was also of fissionable material and when they brought these two together under great pressure, a nuclear reaction would take place. That is the type of bomb that he described.

Only one A-bomb, the one dropped on Hiroshima, was built at Los Alamos using this particular design. David Greenglass, who had been working on projects connected with the more advanced implosion-type bomb since his arrival at Los Alamos, knew nothing about the Hiroshima design at the time. Julius's information did not sound right to him. Julius and the Soviets, meanwhile, knew nothing about the construction of the implosion-type bomb Greenglass was familiar with. No wonder Greenglass promised to be a valuable recruit.

A month later, in February 1945, Klaus Fuchs came back east on vacation and learned from his sister that Harry Gold ("Raymond") had been looking for him. Fuchs decided to reopen his contact with the Soviets, and arrangements were made for him to meet

Gold the following June. With Fuchs back in line, the interest in David Greenglass must have cooled considerably. Nevertheless, it would not do to put too much confidence in the British physicist. Anything might have happened in the long hiatus since he had dropped from sight—even the possibility that he had been turned into a double agent had to be considered. David Greenglass's data would be valuable, if for no other reason than to serve as a check on the accuracy of what Fuchs was prepared to divulge.

The sketches David Greenglass gave Gold in June showing experimental setups for testing an implosion lens may not have been extremely helpful in themselves. But in the very least, they confirmed that Fuchs was telling the truth when he claimed the United States had now settled on the plutonium, implosion-type bomb, abandoning the uranium model as a dead end. This information was not a magic formula for A-bomb production, but it could well have enabled the Russians to avoid the highly expensive and elaborate duplicate efforts undertaken by the United States, which had included building enormous fuel-processing plants in two locations—one for plutonium in Washington State and two for different methods of uranium processing in Tennessee.

Once the reliability of Fuchs's information was verified, David Greenglass was no longer of great interest to the Russians. This explains why Greenglass was henceforth handled directly by Julius Rosenberg. And it also accounts for the apparent mystery behind the two contradictory evaluations of Greenglass's material that Gold claimed to have been given by his control, Anatoli Yakovlev. Gold's statements to the FBI reflect that, several weeks after his June meeting with Greenglass, he was told by Yakovlev that the Greenglass material had been "extremely valuable." Months later, when Gold asked about contacting his new source again, he was told that the material had not been very useful after all. Only the first evaluation, which of course emphasized the damage done by the Rosenbergs' crime, was ever mentioned by Gold in his testimony at the trial.

More important, perhaps, than what the Klaus Fuchs sketch reveals about David Greenglass is what it reveals about Hoover's FBI and the Rosenberg prosecution. J. Edgar Hoover personally followed unfolding developments in the Fuchs case and had to have realized that the material David Greenglass had passed to the Soviets was a mere footnote to the information they were receiving from Fuchs.

Yet Hoover made every effort—legal and, it seems, illegal—to assure that the prosecution, the judge, and the public would believe that the Rosenberg-Sobel conspirators were responsible for nothing less than the theft of the atom-bomb secret.

Hoover's motives are not difficult to fathom. Never burdened with much perspective when it came to evaluating the threat posed by subversives, Hoover was genuinely shocked and alarmed by the revelations of Harry Gold and David Greenglass. The fact that the information passed to the Russians by Greenglass and other members of the Rosenberg ring may have been of limited strategic value did not strike him as a mitigating factor. And of course the Rosenbergs' refusal to confess and name others, stopping the FBI's great spy roundup dead in its tracks, was unforgivable in Hoover's eyes.

Although it was Hoover who defined the Rosenberg case as "the crime of the century," what is really striking about the trial and its aftermath is that the Atomic Energy Commission, the Justice Department, the judge, and eventually the President himself, all eventually went even beyond what Hoover originally demanded in their zeal to punish the convicted atom spies. To this extent, the Rosenbergs were indeed scapegoats, forced to pay with their lives for America's shock and dismay at its loss of the nuclear weapons monopoly.

Though in retrospect it seemed shockingly lax that a soldier with David Greenglass's background had been cleared for work at Los Alamos, there was really nothing unusual about his receiving the assignment. Individuals who had been close to the Communist Party in the years before the war were found at all levels of the Los Alamos operation; even J. Robert Oppenheimer's brother, himself a Manhattan Project physicist, had been a Party member at one time, as had Oppenheimer's own wife.

No one, moreover, was seriously worried about the possibility of Los Alamos being infiltrated by Soviet agents because it was taken for granted that the Russians had no access to high-grade uranium ore and could not possibly make a serious effort to develop an atomic weapon, no matter how much information they might have. The individual responsible for this reassuring but totally mistaken theory was none other than General Leslie Groves, military chief of the Manhattan Project. Groves had concluded, on the basis of old geological survey maps, that the Soviet Union had no deposits of high-grade uranium or thorium ore within its own borders; as early as 1943 he had begun a secret project code-named the Murray Hill Area (because it was an offshoot of the Manhattan District, the project's formal name), which was aimed at cornering the world supply of uranium and thorium.

As late as 1945, General Groves reported to a joint U.S.-British atomic advisory committee that only an unforeseen "revolution" in processing technology could make it possible for the Soviets to begin to build an atomic bomb. He estimated that this revolution was at least ten years away, and probably longer. This optimistic prediction was so confidently expressed that signs which ought to have alerted policymakers to the existence of a Soviet atomic research effort were all too often ignored.

One very troubling indication of the Soviets' position surfaced at the Truman-Stalin summit meeting at Potsdam, held on July 24, 1945, just eight days after the first American bomb was tested at Alamogordo. Truman had wrestled with his conscience for days before the conference opened, trying to decide whether or not to reveal the existence of the new weapon to our then ally Stalin. Finally Truman approached Stalin in private as they were leaving the conference table and delivered an enigmatic warning that the United States was now in possession of a "new weapon of unusual destructive force." Whatever reaction Truman was expecting, it was not the one he got. Stalin showed not the slightest flicker of interest, and Truman, nonplussed, did not pursue the subject further. Later Secretary of State James Byrnes ascribed Stalin's lack of curiosity to his failure to "grasp the importance" of what Truman was telling him.

Not until 1955, when Truman wrote of this incident in his published memoirs, did it occur to anyone that Stalin had failed to take the bait because he already knew about the bomb. And no doubt he did—Soviet intelligence having received Fuchs's description of the plutonium bomb the previous June. (Greenglass, however, did not give Julius his description of this bomb until the following September.)

The glow of false confidence in American nuclear monopoly persisted after the war, despite warnings from civilian scientists, the CIA, and army intelligence that the Russians could be expected to test an A-bomb by mid-1951 or even earlier. As late as 1948, when Atomic Energy Commission member Lewis Strauss suggested setting up a system to monitor for evidence of a Soviet test blast, he encountered opposition on the grounds that the system would not be needed for years to come. The system went ahead nevertheless, and was needed all too soon. Yet even after learning that evidence of the first test had been picked up in September 1949, President Truman continued to suspect that it was all a mistake and there was no Russian bomb.

In the meantime, of course, the political climate had changed drastically. Left-wing backgrounds that were once taken for granted had become the basis for suspicion of disloyalty, and the continuing sniping between the armed forces and the civilian AEC made the latter the target of frequent charges of laxity in screening out security risks. But it was one thing for the press and Congress to probe the backgrounds of left-wing scientists and quite another to uncover actual spies. The FBI had inherited Army intelligence's ongoing investigation of J. Robert Oppenheimer, for example, but not even Hoover seriously believed that Oppenheimer was involved in espionage. Nor was the Bureau very successful in following up any of numerous leads—from the Canadian spy case, from the Gold-Brothman grand-jury investigation, or from Bentley—that might have led them to Fuchs or Rosenberg or both.

Harry Gold's confession in May 1950 was not just a stroke of luck for Hoover's FBI and for the advocates of military control of atomic energy, it was an opportunity—for the Atomic Energy Commission, for a New York Jewish judge with ambitions to rise to the Supreme Court, even for the ACLU and American Jewish Committee leadership—for anyone, in fact, who needed a chance to prove that he or she was not soft on communism when it really counted and national security interests were at stake. Julius Rosenberg was not innocent. He was guilty of spying; and Ethel, though convicted on tainted evidence, was almost certainly his accomplice. Yet their defenders are also correct in saying that they were scapegoats, condemned to death less because of the nature and seriousness of their crime than because at a particular moment in time their deaths served a cathartic function—for Communists and anti-Communists alike.

That moment passed quickly, though it left permanent scars. In 1954 Congress passed the so-called "Rosenberg Law" making espionage a capital crime in peacetime, yet the extreme penalty has never been invoked; nor was it even asked for by the prosecution when the KGB spy Colonel Rudolph Abel was tried under the law in 1957. And just one year after the executions, General Leslie Groves, the man who had done the most to promote the myth of an "atomic secret" after his own confident prediction of nuclear monopoly was shattered, told a closed meeting of the AEC:

> I think that the data that went out in the case of the Rosenbergs was of minor value. I would never say that publicly. Again, that is something while it is not secret, I should think it should be kept very quiet, because irrespective of the value of that in the overall picture, the Rosenbergs deserved to hang, and I would not like to see anything that would make people say General Groves thinks they didn't do much damage after all.

Epilogue

For three decades now, discussions about the Rosenberg case have tended to be dominated by two extreme and mutually contradictory points of view. The first, propounded by the government and given wide credence at the time of the trial, was that Julius and Ethel Rosenberg were traitors whose theft of "the secret" of the atomic bomb played a significant role in bringing America's nuclear weapons monopoly to an untimely end. The second viewpoint, which has come to seem more plausible over time, is that the Rosenbergs could not possibly have been of any importance as spies since they lacked both the sophistication and the access to highly specialized scientific knowledge necessary to qualify them for such a role. In the final analysis, however, both of these views are wrongheaded, since they fail to place the Rosenbergs' activities in their proper context.

The evidence is compelling that Julius Rosenberg, amateur though he may have been, managed over a period of years to become the coordinator of an extensive espionage operation whose contacts were well placed to pass on information on top-secret military projects in the fields of radar and aeronautics. Ethel Rosenberg probably knew of and supported her husband's endeavors, and it seems almost certain that she acted as an accessory, at least in the activation of her own brother, David Greenglass. It is not our contention that Ethel was uninvolved; nevertheless, it is striking that the FBI investigative files contain no hard information to show that Ethel's active participation in the spy ring extended beyond the Greenglass incident. The legal case against her, moreover, was based in large part on a last-minute change of testimony by the key witnesses against her and was relatively weak, even so.

The Rosenberg spy ring was surprisingly productive, given its origins, but it was never the primary conduit of U.S. atomic secrets to the Soviets. The data stolen by David Greenglass, while not without significance, was less important than that provided by Klaus Fuchs. For all its rhetoric about the uniqueness of the Rosenbergs' crimes, the government was well aware of this. J. Edgar Hoover admitted as much in his private March 1952 memo (previously cited), which informed agents in the field that the Russians had not gained atomic data "solely through the operations of the Rosenberg network" and that Soviet scientists conducting independent research had "undoubtedly developed certain phases" of nuclear bomb design on their own.

The real reasons the federal prosecutors, the FBI, and the AEC wanted the Rosenberg case pursued to the limits of the law had little to do with the precise nature of the crime at hand. There was the expectation, first of all, that Julius Rosenberg could provide the names of other amateur spies in important positions—though not necessarily connected to atomic research. And, secondly, there was the very real desire to frighten other individuals who might potentially lend themselves to such activities in the future.

The government's zeal to promote these ends led to questionable tactics and, eventually, to a grave miscarriage of justice. There is no question, to cite just one example, that the precipitous arrest of Ethel Rosenberg was made for one reason and one reason only: so that she could be held hostage in order to pressure her husband into breaking his silence. The cynical treatment of Ethel as an adjunct to her husband's case continued right up to the moments before her death, when a team of agents stood at the ready with an interrogation plan that included asking Julius the belated question, "Was your wife cognizant of your activities?"

Of course, the gravest injustice of all—and the one J. Edgar Hoover correctly prophesied would cause a "psychological reaction" by the public—was the double death sentence. The law under which the Rosenbergs were tried permitted capital punishment for wartime espionage. In the opinion of many legal scholars, however, the intent of the law was never to allow the execution of individuals, however misguided, who spied for our nation's wartime *allies*. As the noted lawyer and civil libertarian Zechariah Chafee wrote to Judge Jerome Frank, it was a "matter of justice" that the extreme penalty apply only to those who aided our country's enemies. "It is absurd to punish the betrayal of [sic] Russia in 1944 or 1945 with death," Chafee wrote on November 14, 1952, "when a similar betrayal today, which would be far more injurious to the United States, would be punished only with life imprisonment." It is noteworthy that, despite the passage of the so-called "Rosenberg Law," a 1954 amendment to the espionage statutes, which allowed the death sentence for peacetime espionage, no individuals convicted of the same crime as the Rosenbergs have suffered execution.

Although well aware that they could make a deal for their lives, Julius and Ethel Rosenberg chose to face death rather than betray their ideals and implicate their associates in espionage. In many respects, the Rosenbergs were not admirable people: the portrait that emerges from their letters and other sources is one of rigid, self-righteous ideologues motivated by contempt for their countrymen and, at times, reveling in the knowledge that they were earning for themselves a place in history. Nevertheless, by anyone's standards, they showed tremendous courage and loyalty, virtues that were hardly reciprocated by the Party they died to defend.

The Communist Party at first ignored the Rosenbergs. Then, long after the trial, when it saw an opening to use their plight for propaganda purposes, it launched a campaign that exploited their suffering and their family's suffering as a mechanism for deflecting international attention away from the anti-Semitic Slansky purge trial in Czechoslovakia.

So, while the Rosenbergs were not the victims of a frame-up, they were indeed hapless scapegoats of a propaganda war—a war in which their deaths would be counted as a victory for both sides. One of the very few observers at the time who saw clearly the case's political uses by both the U.S. government and international communism was journalist I. F. Stone. Stone's comments, written on July 2, 1956, on the basis of what was known at the time from press reports and the trial transcript, still hold up well today.

"By American standards," Stone wrote, "the Rosenberg case is unsatisfactory. . . .The Supreme Court never reviewed the case; the way the Douglas stay was steamrollered was scandalous; the death sentence—even if they were guilty—was a crime."

Yet as Stone went on to note,

> the Communists also have cause for shame. The false cry of anti-semitism, the eagerness abroad to use the Rosenbergs to equate the U.S.A. of Truman with the Germany of Hitler, the wild cries of frame-up, sacrificed calm consideration of the Rosenberg case to the needs of world Communist propaganda. After all, no picket lines circled the Kremlin to protest the executions of Jewish writers and artists; they did not even have a day in court; they just disappeared. Slansky was executed overnight without appeal in Prague. How the same people could excuse Slansky and the "doctor's plot" and at the same time carry on the Rosenberg campaign as they did calls for political psychiatry.

One can only agree with Stone's conclusion that on the whole "the Rosenbergs were treated a good deal more fairly here than Slansky and other Jewish victims of Stalinist injustice." Yet the conduct of the case hardly fulfilled the high standards of American justice and fair play. The fate of the Rosenbergs remains a blot on America's conscience.

At the time we began work on this book, many well-meaning individuals warned us that dredging up the truth about the Rosenbergs' espionage activities could only obscure their case's value as a symbol of the tragic excesses of Cold War red-baiting. But if the Rosenberg case has an ultimate moral, it is precisely to point up the dangers of adhering to an unexamined political myth. Julius and Ethel Rosenberg and their accomplices were so captive to their blind adulation of Stalinist Russia that they failed to perceive the true implications of their espionage, much less to comprehend how their actions would discredit the Left in the eyes of their fellow Americans. The Rosenbergs' accusers, on the other hand, were oblivious to the fact that the danger to national security from ideologically motivated amateur spies—already a vanishing breed by the time of the trial— was far less than the damage that would be done by allowing American justice to appear to serve as a handmaiden to Cold War politics. Partisans on both sides were convinced that they held a monopoly on truth and that the end justified the means. The result was the grisly tandem electrocution of a husband and wife—a sentence that seemed justified by the passions of the moment but that had begun to inspire public revulsion even before it was carried out. The execution of the Rosenbergs stands as an ominous footnote to the first decade of post-nuclear history.

APPENDIX

Harry Gold and the Hilton Hotel Card Conspiracy

The ideological fires lit by the Rosenberg case continue to burn brightly in the numerous books, articles, plays, and film documentaries it has inspired. Nearly all literature on the Rosenbergs is highly partisan. Either Julius and Ethel were the victims of a sinister government conspiracy or the case against them was flawless, an inspiring example of American justice in action. On the whole, the Rosenbergs' advocates have had the better of the propaganda war. Pro-Rosenberg authors—John Wexley and Miriam and Walter Schneir, in particular—have presented a far more convincing case for the existence of a government frame-up than was ever set forth during the Rosenbergs' lifetime. And on another level, belief in the Rosenbergs' innocence has become part and parcel of an entire value system. Along with Joe Hill and Sacco and Vanzetti, Julius and Ethel Rosenberg have been securely installed in the pantheon of the Left. To suggest that they may not have been quite so innocent after all, is to take sides with Hoover and the red-baiters.

It would be impossible to refute in detail all the theories that have been set forth at one time or another in defense of the Rosenbergs' innocence. Conspiracy theories thrive on debate; as soon as one is struck down, two more spring up in its place. However, there is one line of argument that gained such widespread attention—and which, on initial inspection, seems so plausible, that it cannot be dismissed out of hand. This is the theory of the forged Hilton Hotel registration card—evidence, it is claimed, that the story of Harry Gold's June 1945 visit to Albuquerque was an FBI-sponsored fabrication.

Manny Bloch never tried to refute Harry Gold's testimony during the Rosenbergs' trial. Instead Bloch chose to hope that the jury would decide Gold's testimony did not connect his clients to a conspiracy. But no author who set out to analyze and attack the prosecution's case after the fact could allow Gold's story to go unchallenged. To admit that Gold's account was true even in part, that he and the Greenglasses had actually been involved in some form of espionage in June 1945, was to raise questions that were at best politically awkward. For example, who had brought the two men together, if not Julius Rosenberg? And if not Julius, did this mean there were one or more atom spies who had escaped exposure as the result of the framing of the Rosenbergs? In which case, wouldn't a championing of the Rosenbergs' cause lead to a reopening of the atom-spy hunt?

It was far easier to start from the premise that Gold's entire testimony was a fabrication. And one promising way to attack Gold's credibility was through attacking the authenticity of the hotel registration card, the only physical evidence that actually placed him in Albuquerque at a time when the Greenglasses were also there.

The origins of the forged-hotel-card theory go back to early 1953, when author John Wexley was researching his book on the Rosenberg case. Wexley found it hard to believe that Harry Gold would have checked into a hotel for just a few hours on the afternoon of his meeting with the Greenglasses. On a trip to Albuquerque, he discovered that there was another Hilton registration card from Gold's stay at the hotel the following September. Its existence had never been revealed in court.

Wexley had no hard evidence that there had been any tampering with the photostatic copies of the registration card produced by the FBI. All he had were lots of suspicions. He found it incredible that Gold, in his words "a trained spy," would have registered under his real name—and just as incredible that he would have given a false address and incorrect information about his employment at the time of the September visit. There was no reason for Gold to have been in Albuquerque at all in September, since the city is not on the direct route from Chicago to Santa Fe. (Gold had stated that he was told to follow a "devious" route.) And above all, what must the hotel clerk have thought when Gold, with his "Eastern accents" and without luggage, registered at the hotel that Sunday in June? Continues Wexley: "Let us visualize the result of the chambermaid's report on the next morning that the stranger did not even sleep over."

Wexley, it must be admitted, has a talent for making the most ordinary occurrences reek with improbability. Even in Albuquerque, hotel clerks must be used to encountering guests with "Eastern accents." Nor would Gold have been the first weary business traveler, faced with a few hours to kill in an unfamiliar city, to check into a comfortable hotel for a nap. Hotel chambermaids see stranger things than this.

It was left to Miriam and Walter Schneir to flesh out the broad outlines of Wexley's suspicions. In the course of preparing their book, the Schneirs examined the photostatic copies of the September and June registration cards, both of which were in the archives of the Foley Square courthouse in New York. Studying the June card—the one that had actually been introduced at the trial—the Schneirs noticed something very odd indeed: The front of the card bore the date June 3, 1945, exactly as stated in the trial transcript. But the reverse side of the card carried an official hotel stamp that read, "RECEIVED jun 4 12 36 PM '45." Why the discrepancy in the dates?

The Schneirs then interviewed an employee of the hotel, Linda Hughes, and the former manager, Fletcher Brumit. Both agreed that as a matter of policy the stamped date on the back of the card would normally be accepted as the correct date of registration. Neither could explain why the two dates were not identical, as they should have been.

It was not difficult to think of an explanation. The card was a clumsy FBI forgery! The Schneirs had learned from another Hilton employee that after Gold's arrest, FBI agents had spent several days checking through outdated records stored in the hotel's attic. They hypothesized that the agents had been looking for the ingredients they needed to concoct a fraudulent card: old registration forms, information about 1945 rates, the number of the rooms that had been vacant on the day in question, et cetera. In the end, the FBI men had slipped up. Someone had stamped the wrong date on the back of the card.

Next, the Schneirs spoke with Anna Kindernecht Hockinson, the hotel clerk whose initials appeared on both the June and the September cards. Mrs. Hockinson obligingly provided samples of her handwriting, which were submitted, along with the photostatic copies of both cards, to a noted handwriting expert, Elizabeth Mc-Carthy. Mrs. McCarthy concluded that there were "some real doubts" as to whether the initials on the June card were authentic. She pointed out that the stationery used in the June card was slightly different from that of the September card.

By now the Schneirs were not only convinced that the June card was fraudulent; they felt sure that they had found the smoking gun of the case: documented proof that the story of Gold's June 1945 visit to Albuquerque was an FBI lie. Gold had never met David Greenglass prior to his arrest. What's more, he had never even been a spy. His whole career was a pathetic psychopathic fantasy. The FBI must have urged the suggestible Harry Gold to make a false accusation against David Greenglass. And Greenglass, in turn, realizing that he was in deep trouble, had taken the easy way out and confessed—but only after deciding to make things easier on himself by giving the FBI two more victims, Julius and Ethel Rosenberg.

The Schneirs' theory has all the elements of intricately plotted detective fiction. In fact, the story of the Hilton Hotel registration card as revealed in the FBI files, while far less exciting, is a good deal more plausible.

To begin with, the Schneirs stress that the two registration cards were not handled by the FBI in the same manner. The September card bore the initials of three FBI agents and the date May 23, 1950. The June card had no such markings; instead, there were only the initials of the hotel manager, Fletcher L. Brumit. Why? The answer, quite simply, is that the cards did not come into the FBI's possession at the same time.

Harry Gold first confessed to being Fuchs's courier on the morning of May 22, 1950. In his very first statement to the FBI, Gold described his meeting with Fuchs in September 1945 and mentioned staying at the Albuquerque Hilton while he was in New Mexico. At this point, Gold was still hoping that he would be able to avoid revealing the existence of his other espionage contacts, so he did not describe his visit to the Greenglasses in June. Nor, naturally, did he reveal that he had also stayed at the Hilton on June 3. On the day after Gold's confession, agents from the Albuquerque office of the FBI went to the Hilton and secured Gold's registration card from the hotel files. They had no reason to look for any additional cards at that time.

It was not until June 2, 1950, that Gold began talking about his contact with a certain GI who lived on High Street in Albuquerque. Now the Bureau learned for the first time that Gold had also registered at the Hilton during this journey. And sure enough, FBI files reveal that by June 6, agents had returned to the hotel and found the second registration card. A routine Bureau memorandum of that date describes the card as follows:

> Registration card of the Hilton Hotel, #65841, dated June 3, 1945, in pencil on the front side, signed "HARRY GOLD" and stamp dated June 4, 1945, on the reverse side.

A second document, dated June 7, 1950, and addressed to the attention of J. Edgar Hoover in Washington, gives an identical description of the card and adds the information that Gold's signature had been examined by an FBI handwriting expert, who pronounced it authentic. This memo also notes that the face of the card "carries a pencilled notation that this man arrived on June 3, 1945, and occupied Room 1001 at the rate of $1.50 with the notation day rate until 8:00 P.M." (Wexley may be forgiven for being unaware that commercial hotels not uncommonly offer day rates—or dressing room charges—but it does rather spoil his theory about the shocked chambermaid discovering that Gold had not even stayed the night.)

There remains the discrepancy between the stamped date on the back of the June card and the written date on the front. The FBI files show that this inconsistency bothered the bureau's agents in Albuquerque almost as much as it did the Schneirs. In an effort to figure out the significance of the two dates, the agents returned to the Hilton and spoke with its executive assistant manager, Coby Briehn, who produced carbon copies of Gold's records from his "folio"—a file of duplicate registration cards and hotel bills that was kept alphabetically by guest's names. The carbon copies—showing both sides—

were identical to the originals, and Briehn could offer no explanation for the confusion.

Interestingly enough, it was Briehn who much later told the Schneirs that the FBI agents had spent several days rummaging through old records stored in the hotel's attic. The search for additional evidence that could pin down exactly what day Gold had stayed at the hotel—June 3 or June 4—may be one reason the FBI spent so much time over their task. At any rate, the primary purpose of the investigation, according to the FBI's files, was that the agents were looking for records of any long-distance telephone calls Gold might have made while a guest at the hotel. Also, the Bureau wanted to check to see whether Gold might have stayed at the hotel on other occasions, perhaps using one of his aliases.

In a further effort to explain the dates on the June registration card, FBI agents interviewed Fletcher Brumit, the hotel manager. FBI records of this conversation show that Brumit provided a very simple explanation for the confusion:

> [Brumit] explained that all registration cards received on June 3, 1945, were stamped "June 4." He could only offer the opinion that through mechanical error the time and date stamp machine had erroneously set the date as June 4, rather than the correct date of June 3.

The Bureau was not satisfied with Brumit's first hunch as to what had occurred. Agent Henry McConnell asked him to check the hotel records again. This time Brumit reported back that examination of all the other registration cards for guests who stayed at the Hilton on June 3 showed that all the date stamps carried the date of June 4, or, as McConnell explained, "on June 3 the automatic date and time stamp used by the hotel had set itself for June 4 instead of the correct date of June 3."

Simple mechanical error—an incorrect setting on an automatic date stamp—is a rather dull solution to so tantalizing a mystery. However, it is also such an obvious and likely explanation that it is surprising that it never seems to have occurred to the Schneirs. It seems that Brumit had also forgotten this item of information by the time he was interviewed by the Schneirs. But Brumit, who admitted that he could no longer recall the details of the incident, did ascribe the discrepancy in dates to "clerical error," not to forgery.

Of course evidence from the FBI files is unlikely to change the minds of firm adherents of the forged-hotel-card theory. If the Bureau could forge the registration cards, it could, at least in theory, have fabricated the entire series of Bureau memoranda that trace the card's passage through the Albuquerque office and on to the FBI laboratory in Washington. But if one sets aside for a moment the Schneirs' guesswork about the FBI's activities in the Hilton attic, what evidence of forgery is left? Nothing but the opinion of the hand-writing expert Elizabeth McCarthy.

In her report to the Schneirs, Mrs. McCarthy had concluded that the date, room number, room rate, and initials on the September 1945 registration card were all written by the hotel clerk Anna Kindernecht Hockinson, since they showed "all of her important, underlying unconscious writing characteristics." But McCarthy had doubts about the June card. In this instance, the writing showed "hesitation, irregularity and slowing down in the writing line of these figures and words, and her handwriting samples [provided in 1961] display no such irregularities and hesitations." In particular, in discussing the clerk's initials as they appeared on the June card, Mrs. McCarthy noted: "there are stops with the a and the k in numerous places, heavy and light pressure and a lack of coordination which is absent from her standard writing."

How conclusive were these findings? Interviewed during the research for this book, Mrs. McCarthy seemed far less certain than the Schneirs' book would have one believe. Despite her evident desire to serve the cause of the Rosenbergs' exoneration as best she could, Mrs. McCarthy admitted that "she couldn't be sure" that forgery was involved since the photostatic copies she had worked with were not well focused. There had been, she recalled, some differences between Anna Kindernecht Hockinson's initials on the two cards, but these differences might have been due to the "ineptness of the copy" rather than to forgery. "I wish I could have been more definitive," Mrs. McCarthy said. "It's just a shame I didn't have the original."

At the time the Schneirs wrote their book, they had every reason to assume that the originals of the cards were still in the FBI files and they called for the government to release them. Unfortunately, when Morton Sobell's lawyers tried to obtain the same originals in the course of one of their appeals, it was discovered that the original cards were no longer in existence. Some years after the trial, they had been returned to the Hilton, where they were routinely destroyed in

1957 along with other outdated records. This method of handling evidence from a historically significant investigation may be deplorable, but it hardly constituted proof of a continuing FBI frame-up, as the Schneirs were to suggest in a revised edition of their book. After all, there was a good reason why the FBI had never placed any particular importance on the originals of the cards: the photostatic copy of the June card, which was placed in evidence at the trial, was accepted as genuine by the defense. And Harry Gold's testimony that he had stayed at the Hilton had never been questioned.

Even in the absence of the original cards, the Sobell appeal did provide an occasion for a thorough review of the forgery theory by federal judge Edward Weinfeld. Reexamining Mrs. McCarthy's report on handwriting discrepancies, Weinfeld ruled that, although he too could see differences between the initials on the two cards, this observation did not "warrant the inference that the June 3 card was not a record kept in the regular course of the Hotel Hilton's business."

Even if he accepted as correct Mrs. McCarthy's conclusion that the body of the two cards were in different handwriting, Judge Weinfeld stressed that there still would not be a presumption of forgery.

> The circumstances that at a public and busy hotel the same initials appear on the two cards . . . [while] the data as to rate, stay, departure and room number are in different handwriting, does not, in one fell swoop, permit the inference that it was "forged; that the government knew it was forged . . . [and] that Gold did not register at the Hotel Hilton on June 3."

In other words, one hotel employee may have filled in the information before another one initialed it.

It also struck Judge Weinfeld as significant that the Sobell brief did not include an affidavit from the clerk, Anna Kindernecht Hockinson, even though Sobell's counsel knew her whereabouts and had been in contact with her. The implication was that testimony from the clerk would not have supported the brief's argument.

Unknown to Judge Weinfeld, however, Sobell's legal representatives had engaged a second handwriting expert in an attempt to buttress their case for appeal. Buried in the files of the Sobell defense committee is correspondence showing that, in January 1966, one of

Sobell's lawyers, William Kunstler, had provided Hanna F. Sulner—a handwriting analyst—with photostats of the two hotel cards, a sample of Harry Gold's handwriting, and samples of Mrs. Hockinson's handwriting.

Mrs. Sulner's report was discouraging. For one thing, she dismissed out of hand the suggestion that the difference in the stationery of the June and September cards was evidence of forgery. Elizabeth McCarthy had taken special note of a defect in the printing of the word "No." (abbreviation for "number") that appeared on the June card—an observation that might support the hypothesis that the June stationery was a clumsy printing job ordered by the FBI long after the fact. Mrs. Sulner had another suggestion. In her opinion, the defect had to be disregarded "because it is possible that some stain got to that portion of the paper . . . and stains are not visible on photostats."

When it came to examining the hotel employee's writing on the two cards, Mrs. Sulner echoed Mrs. McCarthy's more recent statement, noting that it is "very difficult" to make comparisons based on photostats. She did agree that portions of the information at the bottom of the two cards had not been filled in by the same hand, and she saw differences in the number "5" and the initials "a.k." as well as some hesitant writing on the June 3 card.

At this point, however, Mrs. Sulner raised a serious objection, one obviously not to the liking of Sobell's counsel:

> As to the identity or difference between certain words on the Hilton Hotel cards and Anna Kindernecht Hockinson's handwriting; there is no basis for comparison because of the 14 years of date difference. A 1947 [*sic*] handwriting sample certainly cannot be compared with writings obtained in 1961.

But comparison of handwriting samples made years apart (actually in 1945 and 1961) was precisely the basis of the analysis done by Mrs. McCarthy for the Schneirs. It is little wonder that Sobell's lawyers, William Kunstler and Arthur Kinoy, decided not to cite Mrs. Sulner's findings in their appeal.

Setting aside the question of the Hilton registration card, what remains is the broader and more devastating charge that Harry Gold was a pathological liar, a man who simply imagined that he had been acting as a Soviet spy courier.

This interpretation holds together only if one is willing to throw out the bulk of the evidence relating to Gold's activities (including everything he and David Greenglass ever said about their relationship) and concentrate on a highly selective and one-sided interpretation of what remains. In light of the evidence available today, the interpretation is completely untenable. Gold's version of his activities has been substantiated in any number of ways: The statements of Thomas Black to the FBI; the fact that Klaus Fuchs, who had no incentive to lie, did eventually identify Gold's picture; the cache of technical reports, addresses, and even fragments of old identification signals found in Gold's Philadelphia house; the fact that Gold gave detailed descriptions of many people and locales that he would not have known of otherwise, including descriptions of the names and physical appearances of several high-level Soviet intelligence agents; and, not least of all, by the fact that his testimony was twice accepted by juries.

Even the evidence the Schneirs cite in support of their charge that Gold was a liar turns out to be less than compelling. Much of their case is based on the 1955 perjury trial of Benjamin Smilg.

Harry Gold, then a prisoner at Lewisburg Penitentiary, was taken to Dayton, Ohio, to appear as the chief prosecution witness against Smilg. There he was exposed to a blistering cross-examination by Smilg's attorney, William F. Hopkins. Forcing Gold to recapitulate his earlier testimony at the Brothman-Moskowitz trial, Hopkins had Gold admit that he had created a complex cover story for himself involving a nonexistent wife and twin children. Gold also admitted that, to maintain his double life as chemist and spy courier, he had been forced to lie repeatedly to his family and his employers. And he conceded that he had lied under oath in 1947 when he told a federal grand jury the story that he and Brothman had made up to explain Brothman's connection with Jacob Golos.

> HOPKINS: Did you make this statement [at the Brothman-Moskowitz trial]: "It is a wonder that steam didn't come out of my ears at times"?
> GOLD: It really is remarkable that it didn't occur.
> HOPKINS: Because of all the lies you told?

GOLD: I had gotten into one of the doggondest tangles.
HOPKINS: You lied for a period of six years?
GOLD: I lied for a period of sixteen years, not alone six.

In trying to explain the psychological strain of living a double life, Gold told the Smilg jury: "When I went on a mission for the Russians, I immediately turned a switch in my mind. . . . Just set my mind, just as if it were an automaton set to do a particular job." And not surprisingly, Hopkins countered by asking Gold whether he had ever "suffered from schizophrenia."

Hopkins's mention of schizophrenia in the presence of the jury was a clever ploy, but it should hardly be interpreted as a definitive diagnosis of Gold's mental state. Gold had admitted to conscious lies, not delusions. Neither during the Smilg trial nor anywhere else did Harry Gold say anything to indicate that he had ever believed that his imaginary family was real, or that he had ever been confused about the distinctions between truth and falsehood.

But the jury acquitted Smilg. And, according to the critics, this is proof that the jury held no credence in the chief prosecution witness.

A closer examination of the Smilg trial suggests that this is not quite what happened. On the contrary, it seems that the jury acquitted Smilg because it believed Gold was telling the truth.

Harry Gold had first talked about Benjamin Smilg in June 1950. Gold recalled then that in 1938, when he was studying at Xavier University in Ohio, his Soviet superior, "Fred," had ordered him to contact a young aeronautical engineer who worked nearby at the Wright-Patterson Air Force base. This engineer turned out to be Benjamin Smilg. Gold made several attempts to sound out Smilg, but the young man was not at all sympathetic. When he reported this to Fred, the Soviet agent insisted that he try again, taking a harder line. Still Smilg refused to cooperate.

Although Gold's statement did not implicate Smilg in any illegal activities, the engineer was called in for questioning by the FBI, and he confirmed Gold's story. Smilg told the Bureau that Gold had first come to see him in 1938, using the not very convincing pretext that he was a student, new in town, who wanted to make friends. During his fourth visit, in late 1938, Smilg said, Gold had tried to solicit information about aircraft design. When Smilg angrily told Gold that he "had no business receiving such information," Gold argued back, saying that "the Russians were fighting our war" (referring to antifascism as "our" cause) and "it was the duty of everyone to help Russia in its efforts." At this point, said Smilg, he still dismissed Gold as "an overzealous, enthusiastic, 'pink' student."

Soon, however, Gold's tactics changed from persuasion to attempted blackmail. It seemed that when Smilg was a student at MIT during the years 1931 to 1935, he had earned pocket money by tutoring a Russian exchange student. The Russian had asked Smilg to sign receipts, which he said he needed in order to account to the Soviet government for his educational expenses. Now, years later, Harry Gold suddenly produced one of those receipts and threatened that, unless Smilg agreed to cooperate, it would be used as proof that the young engineer was already accepting money from the Soviets.

Smilg told the FBI that Gold's ability to produce the receipt had left him "petrified." At that moment, he said, he concluded that Gold "apparently had definite connections with the Russians, and was working as a Russian spy." Nevertheless, he did not think a single piece of paper that he had innocently signed during his student days could incriminate him, and he continued to refuse to give data to Gold.

The FBI concluded that Smilg was innocent of any wrongdoing. His troubles appeared to be over. Unfortunately, during a grand jury investigation, Smilg was questioned under oath about his dealings with Gold and he denied that he had ever known Gold to be a Soviet agent. This was in contradiction to his earlier statement to the FBI, and an ambitious prosecuting attorney decided that he had a perjury case against Smilg.

Gold's testimony at the Smilg trial was essentially a repetition of what he had told the FBI five years earlier. As *The New York Times* reported on June 19, 1955, Gold "testified that he had visited Mr. Smilg on several occasions, but did not obtain information." The prosecutor, in his summation, told the jurors that if they believed Gold was telling the truth about his visits to Smilg, then they would have to find Smilg guilty of perjury. Technically, this was true, but the jury apparently chose to take a more sympathetic view. Smilg may have suspected and feared that Gold was a Soviet agent, but even Gold agreed that Smilg had never participated in espionage. So maybe Smilg didn't "know" Gold was a spy. The jury gave Smilg the benefit of the doubt and found him innocent. Their verdict was not so much a repudiation of Gold as a rebuke to the prosecutor for attempting to convict an innocent man on a technicality.

If Harry Gold were really a compulsive liar, a man with a distorted sense of reality and a quiescent conscience, as his critics claimed, then Smilg would never have gone free. The prosecutor would no doubt have been delighted if Gold had suddenly "remembered" that Smilg had been involved in espionage. But Gold stuck to the straight story. As Gold later wrote to his lawyers,

> All I had to do in 1950—ten years after I last saw Smilg—was to aver that he had given me data for the Soviet Union. Who could gainsay me? Yet I stated over and over again, and insisted on it at the trial, that Smilg not only never gave me information but in fact had actively resisted my efforts to make him do so.

When *Invitation to an Inquest* was published in 1965, Harry Gold was still very much alive and still a prisoner in Lewisburg Penitentiary, where he had become, by his own account, a happy man. The need to follow orders had always been an important part of Gold's personality. The desire to serve a larger cause and to accept discipline without question had led Gold ever deeper into his role as a Soviet courier, deeper indeed than his natural abilities warranted. And once in prison, Gold happily adapted to the curtailment of his freedom. He worked hard in the pentitentiary's medical research lab, studied mathematics on his own time, and maintained his weight at a normal 140 pounds—a goal he had never been able to achieve before his arrest. Gold's psychological need to serve had also made him a garrulous and cooperative prosecution witness on those occasions when he was called upon. However, there is no reason to believe that Gold had ever played the role of government stooge. With the possible exception of his use of the phrase "greetings from Julius," Gold had never said anything on the witness stand that contradicted the original series of statements he had given the FBI after his arrest in 1950, and on that one exception he had resisted until the very day before the trial.

Gold read the Schneirs' book in his prison cell and was outraged at their charge that he had connived in the murder of two innocent people by committing perjury. Hoping to lay to rest this slur on his reputation once and for all, Gold prepared for his lawyers an eighty-four-page statement, answering point by point each of the arguments made by the Schneirs. Gold's statement is a very convincing document, filled with vivid and accurate details that leave no doubt he actually was in Albuquerque on that weekend in June 1945.

Gold argues that checking into a hotel, even at midday, was standard operating procedure for a courier who found himself in a strange city with secret documents in his possession. (He even lists several other occasions when he resorted to the same expedient, along with the names of the hotels and their locations.) On that particular Sunday in Albuquerque, Gold recalls, he had an especially good reason to seek out a hotel for the afternoon. He was exhausted. When he had arrived in Albuquerque the previous evening Gold sought out the Greenglasses, only to discover they were not at home. There was no choice but to stay the night; however, all the hotels he checked were fully booked—a common situation in New Mexico during the war. Eventually, Gold had to settle for sleeping on the floor of a cheap, overcrowded rooming house. Not surprisingly, the night was traumatic. In addition to the discomfort, Gold was nervous about the lack of privacy, since he was already carrying an envelope of documents given to him by Fuchs. He could not allow himself to fall into a deep sleep, for fear that a thief looking for money among his belongings would stumble over his secret. And all night long he kept hearing the sirens of the MPs' cars, prowling the streets on the lookout for disorderly servicemen. The fear that one of those sirens might turn out to be the police coming for him preyed on his mind.

Of his movements the next day, Gold says:

> I clearly remember that on leaving the rooming house the next morning I was anxious to get to High Street before the Greenglasses might go out again. So, likely, I checked my bags at the station, as it was right in the direction I was going, i.e., about halfway along from the rooming house. (I don't even know if this ever came up in FBI questioning, since it was not a significant detail.) And then, finding out from Dave that I would have to stay over till that afternoon, I do remember inquiring at the Santa Fe [railroad] station about reservations eastward. Then I likely went on to the hotel. With a stay in between for breakfast? That puts the morning's events right up to the 12:36 registration time.

Still carrying the Fuchs documents, which he had been afraid to check with his luggage, Gold needed a safe place to rest for a few hours, and the Hilton—busy, anonymous, and with good security—seemed ideal.

Inside the hotel, Gold found the lobby crowded as overburdened clerks tried to deal with a rush of weekend guests waiting to check out and pay their bills. There was much "confusion and bustling," Gold recalls, with impatient departing guests "crowding around the registration desk and possibly behind it." Perhaps the uncharacteristically jerky handwriting of the hotel clerk was simply the result of her writing hurriedly, in a cramped position, and, "maybe in all this turmoil, that's how the wrong date got stamped."

Gold knew very well that not even his ability to describe the Greenglasses' neighborhood or their second-floor apartment on High Street would ever convince his detractors. (At the trial, Gold had described the staircase leading to the Greenglasses' door as "steep." Wexley pounced on this error in his book; he had climbed the staircase himself and it was not particularly steep at all. Now, Gold allowed that perhaps Wexley may have been right; nevertheless, for him—overweight, out of shape, and suffering from a sleepless night—they had seemed formidable.)

Searching his memory for a detail that could confirm beyond doubt that he had been in Albuquerque on that particular day in June, Gold remembered something that had occurred that morning when he was on his way to the railroad station to check on outgoing trains:

> I was rather anxious to get across the main street of Albuquerque and over to the Santa Fe railroad station . . . [but] I was delayed by a lengthy (as it seemed to me) religious parade, a Roman Catholic one. So I leaned on a low stone wall watching it, till I finally could get across. . . . this religious parade is a vital item. Five years later [when Gold recalled it in his statement to the FBI] I could hardly have known of such an event.
>
> Since it was a long parade, and seemed to be such an important affair, some record of it may still exist. . . .

And, indeed, a record does exist.

Unknown to Gold, who was under the impression that the FBI had never bothered to verify this particular detail of his story, the Albuquerque office of the Bureau had prepared a rather thorough report on the incident. In addition to a newspaper clipping announcing the parade—headlined "CATHOLICS OF CITY HONOR EUCHARIST IN PUBLIC RITES"—the agents had secured an affidavit from the city manager substantiating that the parade route had indeed run along Central Avenue past the Santa Fe railroad station just as Gold claimed. And there was even a file of photographs taken by a local amateur photographer, along with a release noting that the owner of the pictures had agreed to provide negatives "for use in any judicial proceedings." The file was compiled in February 1951, more than six months after Gold originally described this episode in his statements to the FBI and after he had already been sentenced. Its purpose was to aid the prosecutors in proving Gold's presence in Albuquerque if the defense chose to attack his story during the trial.

If the defense had chosen to cross-examine Harry Gold when it had the opportunity, it is safe to say that the Hilton Hotel card controversy could never have arisen.

BIBLIOGRAPHICAL NOTE

A NOTE ON THE FBI FILES

One of the major sources for this book, indeed standing at the heart of the study, is the more than 250,000 pages of material released under a Freedom of Information Act suit to Michael and Robert Meeropol in 1975 and subsequent years. This material is available for public use and inspection at the FBI Building in Washington, D.C.

These documents are a rich source, providing much information previously unavailable about the Rosenberg case. But one must approach use of these FBI files with utmost caution. Some have argued that these files can hardly be relied on at all. This view was expressed by historian Athan Theoharis, editor of *Beyond the Hiss Case* (Philadelphia: Temple University Press, 1982). In that book, Theoharis writes that J. Edgar Hoover held a personal "not-to-be-filed file" that was destroyed immediately after his death. "The possibility," he goes on, "remains that the most sensitive FBI . . . documents either have been destroyed or, if extant, are not retrievable through a name search of the agency's 'central indices.' For this reason, the most troubling questions about these cases may never be resolved."

Other scholars working in the FBI files have pointed to other pitfalls. In a series of articles in *The Nation* magazine, historian John Rosenberg pointed out that the Bureau has sought to destroy field-office files and that the FBI uses catches in the Freedom of Information Act to withhold important data. See John Rosenberg, "Catch in the Information Act," *The Nation*, Feb. 4, 1978, pp. 108–11; "The FBI Would Shred the Past," *The*

Nation, June 3, 1978, pp. 653–55; and "The FBI's Field Files," *The Nation*, March 3, 1979, pp. 231–32.

Under the terms of the Freedom of Information Act, deletions in material released can be made legally if done to prevent the release of classified information that would damage the national defense or U.S. foreign policy or to protect the identity of "confidential sources." Hence the FBI can omit any material that might lead a reader to identify the name of a previously anonymous FBI informant.

Although the FBI has in other cases of interest acted to shred local field-office files, this is not the case with the Rosenberg material. FBI files include both the headquarters and local field-office files. The files do, as a matter of course, contain deletions as described above. In addition, the FBI has refused to release a great deal of material on security grounds. Final judgment, then, must be suspended until future generations are able to look at the complete record.

Yet enough material has been released that some judgment is in order. The files that have been released provide such a substantial record that students of the case have sufficient material to subject the official record to a critical examination.

Indeed the released FBI files often provide a wealth of information that reflects poorly on the FBI, on the practices of J. Edgar Hoover, and on official prosecution claims at the trial and during its aftermath. Much of this material has already been selectively cited by critics of the case as final proof of their long held conspiracy thesis.

It is also clear that the Bureau violated its own promise of confidentiality to a key informant when it released the name of Jerome Eugene Tartakow as the major informant against Julius Rosenberg. The Bureau did this by failing to delete his name from a document reporting to FBI agents on his conversations. Although a Bureau spokesman claimed this was inadvertent, most observers believe it was done because the Bureau thought Tartakow's revelations would show the public that Julius Rosenberg was involved in espionage and that the FBI was engaging in an espionage investigation rather than a witch-hunt. The appearance in the FBI files of Tartakow's name was not an accident.

Critics are correct when they plead that all such revelations be taken with a grain of salt. Frank Donner has written wisely, in *The Age of Surveillance* (New York: Knopf, 1980), pp. 23–24:

> all intelligence practice balances the value of the information against the risk of obtaining it. When the risks are minimized by secrecy, intelligence tactics become bolder. Although we generally view with suspicion activities conducted in secret, the clan-

destine character of [the] intelligence process tends, ironically, to legitimate it. Information derived from clandestine sources is assumed to be intrinsically valuable . . . the fact that the information is obtained secretly invites the inference that it is accurate—in the nature of an admission because obtained without the subject's knowledge.

We agree with Donner's warning, and with the sharp observation of historian David J. Garrow, who writes in *The FBI and Martin Luther King, Jr.* (New York: Norton, 1981), p. 13, "simply because the Bureau holds certain data tightly does not mean that that information is accurate, and one must constantly guard against accepting as fact every statement contained in a once highly classified document." We have been more than aware of this concern. Hence we have tried to demonstrate that the FBI files are simply tools to be used along with other corroborative evidence.

A preliminary challenge to our use of the FBI files has already occurred. On June 23, 1979, *The New Republic* published an article by Sol Stern and Ronald Radosh, "The Hidden Rosenberg Case: How the FBI Framed Ethel to Break Julius." After the appearance of this article, Rosenberg case critics jumped on our use of the informant Tartakow's revelations. They responded that one cannot simply accept any of them as valid evidence. They have pointed out (in letters published in *The New Republic*'s issue of August 4–11, 1979) that even the FBI files refer to him as presumably "unreliable," and they have chastised us for going on to repeat his tales.

Such critics ignore the fact that Bureau reports referring to Tartakow in this way were later amended to indicate that information furnished by him had proven accurate. Among the verifiable information was Tartakow's revelation that Julius Rosenberg was worried the Bureau would discover he and his family had had passport photos taken. That tip led the FBI to find the passport photographer who appeared the very last day of the trial as a surprise witness.

Other critics maintain that the FBI files show that the Bureau was supplying Tartakow with information, rather than the other way around. That suggestion is simply preposterous. Having first said that Tartakow was unreliable even to the Bureau, they then propose that FBI agents spent hundreds of hours feeding him information which he then spilled right back to the FBI, and which the Bureau then stuffed into its own secret files. What would be the purpose of such an exercise? It could not have been to manufacture a corroborating witness, since the FBI promised Tartakow he would not have to be a witness, and his connection to the case was undisclosed until 1975.

We have tried to demonstrate throughout that any suppositions we make as to the nature of espionage and the involvement of various parties is borne out by corroborative evidence. The FBI files are used in the context of other sources. Thus we have shown how James Weinstein's independent recollections—years after the event—are mirrored in the information offered the FBI by Tartakow. And the one thing the FBI agents could never have fed Tartakow was the fact that Julius Rosenberg had an association of any kind with James Weinstein's roommate, Max Finestone, because they didn't know anything about it. They had no reason to believe that Weinstein or Finestone had ever met Rosenberg. The Tartakow memo we discuss in the book thus is completely and independently confirmed by our interview with James Weinstein. We too originally took Tartakow's fantastic stories with a grain of salt, until we realized that the memos paralleled the story James Weinstein told us independently. No critic of the case has presented any convincing argument to support the conclusion of author John Wexley that Tartakow's memos are simply a "police suck."

When the FBI files indicate omissions, we have noted this in the text. We cite the strange absence of any interrogation of Ruth Greenglass that might indicate what she actually said—as distinct from a summary of her conversation by an agent—at the critical time when she supposedly told the FBI of Ethel Rosenberg's typing of atomic data for the Russians.

Despite our care in use of the FBI files, we realize that critics who believe the Rosenbergs were executed as part of a giant Cold War conspiracy orchestrated by the FBI may not be satisfied. They may continue to maintain that the complete files will prove a frame-up took place. They may also argue—as some people have already suggested to us—that the released files have been tampered with, that documents such as the reports of Tartakow's conversations, or the text of Elizabeth Bentley's 1945 confession, were all written in 1975—the year the files were released—to provide phony documentation to bolster the government's discredited case.

We find this conspiracy theory too mind boggling to take seriously. All the FBI files have serial numbers composed at the time of origin. We have seen scores of FBI files from different field offices that contain cross-references to or excerpts from other FBI files—reports or statements by Tartakow, for example. To forge all these would have been a gargantuan and overwhelming task—consuming the time of legions of FBI agents, working day and night for years on end. It is simply an impossibility.

But there is a more basic flaw in the critics' stance. They have themselves made liberal use of these very same FBI files, selectively calling attention to certain documents that exemplify government skullduggery. The National Committee to Re-Open the Rosenberg Case has already published two pamphlets making use of information from the FBI files. And historian Athan Theoharis, who told one of us that the files can hardly be relied on at all, ignored his own advice to author an article, "A Break in the Rosenberg Case" (*The Nation*, July 1, 1978, pp. 5–6), in which he argues that the "files recently released . . . suggest that the FBI engineered a key point in the testimony of the two main prosecution witnesses," Harry Gold and David Greenglass. Theoharis made that judgment after examining only the particular documents and FBI reports in question—and not after examination of even a tiny fraction of the entire FBI file. Yet he did not hesitate to reach a definite judgement.

We argue that the evidence does indicate that some of the arguments of the Rosenberg case critics have been well taken. We also argue that, on other points, they have been proven wrong. Our critics—the unabashed defenders of the Rosenbergs' total innocence—cannot have it both ways. They cannot cry foul when they go on making selective use of the same FBI documents we use, challenging their use only when the documents do not validate their own arguments.

PRIMARY SOURCES

FBI files on the Rosenberg Case, J. Edgar Hoover Building, FBI Reading Room, Washington, D.C.

The FBI files examined by the authors include those on the following individuals:

Julius and Ethel Rosenberg
David and Ruth Greenglass
Harry Gold
Klaus Fuchs
Max and Helene Elitcher
Ann and Michael Sidorovich
Morton and Helen Sobell
William Perl, AKA William Mutterperl
Vivian Glassman
Joel Barr
Alfred Sarant
James Weinstein
Maxwell Finestone
O. John Rogge
Abraham Brothman
Anatoli Yakovlev
William and Sylvia Danziger
Elizabeth Bentley

Oscar Vago
Kristel and Robert Heineman
Thomas Lessing Black
Weldon Bruce Dayton
Herbert Fabricant
Stanley Robert Rich
Louise Sarant
Harold Urey
George Kistiakowski
J. Robert Oppenheimer
Fletcher Brumit
Emanuel H. Bloch
Gloria Agrin
Irving R. Kaufman
Roy M. Cohn
James Kilsheimer
Rosenberg/Sobell Committees

The FBI files include both headquarters and field-office files for each subject. Each file has its own document and serial number. We have chosen not to cite these, and have included them only when other internal forms of identification, such as date and name, are absent from a cited document. When a citation is identified as Julius Rosenberg file, or Joel Barr file, it refers to the FBI file for that particular individual.

The FBI files also include documents from other governmental agencies, and are called "referral" files. Some of them have only been released as late as 1980. Agencies whose documents are included in the material deposited with the FBI files include those from the Central Intelligence Agency, Internal Revenue Service, Department of Naval Affairs, U.S. Post Office, U.S. Air Force, NASA, Department of Energy and U.S. Army Intelligence.

Other Government Documents

Other government documents examined by the authors include the following:

Records of U.S. Army Intelligence, Newark Signal Corps Inspection Zone, National Archives, Washington, D.C.

Files of the Atomic Energy Commission; AEC file No. 403 and the Diary of Gordon Dean. Department of Energy, Washington, D.C.

Files of the Department of Justice, prosecution file on the Rosenberg Case. U.S. Attorney's office, Foley Square, New York.

Dwight D. Eisenhower Library, Abilene, Kansas. Administration and Cabinet Series of Presidential Papers (Ann Whitman File); the Official and

General Files of Eisenhower's Records as President (White House Central Files); the C.D. Jackson Papers, including Minutes of Cabinet meetings.

Harry S. Truman Library, Independence, Missouri. Papers of J. Howard McGrath; Files of Philleo Nash; Papers of Harry S. Truman, Official File; Papers of Harry S. Truman, General File.

Nongovernmental Manuscript Collections

Nongovernmental manuscript collections the authors examined include:

Papers of O. John Rogge, including Rogge's file on the Rosenberg case, with memoranda relating to conferences. The law offices of the Rogge firm, New York City.

Papers of the Committee to Secure Justice for Morton Sobell, including the Papers of the National Committee to Secure Justice in the Rosenberg Case, State Historical Society, Madison, Wisconsin. This collection includes all legal records, financial records, publications, newspaper clippings, and correspondence, including copies of the original Rosenberg death-house letters and the prison correspondence of Morton and Helen Sobell.

Papers of David and Emily Alman, Boston University, Boston, Mass.

Papers of Fyke Farmer, including Farmer's files on the Rosenberg case and correspondence. The personal possession of Fyke Farmer, Nashville, Tennessee.

Papers of Augustus S. Ballard and John D. M. Hamilton, including the Harry Gold file. Held at the firm of Pepper, Hamilton, and Scheetz, Philadelphia. The collection includes memos, articles, and writings of Harry Gold.

Papers of J. Robert Oppenheimer. Library of Congress, Washington, D.C.

Papers of Allen Dulles and papers of John Foster Dulles. Princeton University Library, Princeton, New Jersey.

Papers of Gloria Agrin, including papers of Emanuel Bloch pertaining to the Rosenberg case. The personal possession of Ms. Agrin, New York City.

Correspondence of Irwin Edelman. Mr. Edelman's correspondence is printed verbatim in his unpublished autobiographical memoir, "Religion, the Left and the Rosenberg Case," New York, n.d. [final edition prepared 1970s].

Interviews

The interviews were conducted between 1978 and 1982, on the telephone or in person, by Sol Stern and/or Ronald Radosh. Exact citations as to date and interviewer are listed in the appropriate notes. Some of those interviewed (whose names appear below) provided only general background information and readers will not find them cited in the text. Those of whom interviews were requested but who refused to be interviewed include Judge Irving Kaufman, Myles Lane, John Harrington, Vivian Glassman, and Michael and Robert Meeropol. We would like to thank all those who consented to be interviewed. They are:

O. John Rogge
Herbert Fabricant
David and Ruth Greenglass
Roy Cohn
James B. Kilsheimer
Gloria Agrin
Fyke Farmer
Henry Linschitz
Philip Morrison
Bernard Connors
Robert Lamphere
Emily Alman
Gladys Meyer
Junius Scales
Max Gordon
Maxwell Finestone
James Weinstein
Electra Sarant Jayson
Jeremy Sarant
Jerome Eugene Tartakow
Marshall Perlin
Bonnie Brower
Victor Rabinowitz
Sam Neuberger
William A. Reuben
Morton Sobell
Peggy Dennis
Herman Starobin
Elizabeth McCarthy
Samuel Perl
Bernard Barr
Weldon Bruce Dayton
John Gates
Lillian Gates

Dorothy Healy
David Kennedy
Howard Meyer
Hans Bethe
Walter and Miriam Schneir
Benjamin Bradlee

Some correspondence pertaining to points raised by the authors was carried out with Peggy Dennis and with Karel Kaplan of Prague, Czechoslovakia, now living in Munich. The authors also spoke with Judge Simon Rifkind, who tried but was unable to help us in our effort to obtain the secret American Bar Association report on the Rosenberg case.

BOOKS

The authors will not succumb to the temptation to list all the important books on McCarthyism and post–World War II America. Those seeking a general bibliography on these subjects should turn to David Caute, *The Great Fear* (New York: Simon and Schuster, 1978) or to Allen Weinstein, *Perjury: The Hiss-Chambers Case* (New York: Knopf, 1978). General books of specific use are cited in the appropriate notes. The listing that follows is limited to printed material pertaining directly to the Rosenberg case.

Books on the Rosenbergs fall into two contrasting categories: those that argue their guilt and those that assert their innocence. Many of them contain information about the Rosenbergs' personal life, and many on both sides manage to offer insights, to provide significant data, and to come up with thought-provoking interpretations.

The earliest books arguing the government's side of the case, even generally supporting the official contention that the couple had stolen the "secret" of the A-bomb, include *New York Post* reporter Oliver Pilat's *The Atom Spies* (New York: Putnam's, 1952). Pilat's book was based on contacts with both the prosecution and the FBI. Nevertheless, the newly released FBI files indicate that the Bureau was severely dissatisfied with Pilat's book because information he revealed did not display the FBI in its best light.

A thorough critique of the Rosenberg defense campaign may be found in S. Andhill Fineberg, *The Rosenberg Case: Fact and Fiction* (New York: Oceana, 1952). Fineberg, a rabbi on the staff of the American Jewish Committee, mirrored the need of the Jewish establishment to distance itself from the Rosenberg case. The book is marred by its dogmatic defense of the death penalty, and its quasi-official sponsorship by the Eisenhower administration is hidden from the reader's knowledge.

A conservative journalist's case for the prosecution is offered by Ralph DeToledano, *The Greatest Plot in History* (New York: Duell, Sloan and Pearce, 1963). DeToledano accepts the prosecution witnesses' trial testimony by itself as proof that their presentation of events was entirely accurate; he conducted no independent research. He is, however, the first author to make use of Harry Gold's unpublished autobiographical memoir. A book appearing in the same year with a better balance is Jonathan Root, *The Betrayers* (New York: Coward McCann, 1963). A solid narrative with many sound insights, Root's book suffers from its dependence on the trial transcript, newspaper articles, and secondary sources. The author concludes that while "there is no reasonable doubt now surviving about the guilt of the Rosenbergs, . . . time has not substantiated" the sentence of death.

A book following the interpretive line developed by Root is that by Louis Nizer, *The Implosion Conspiracy* (New York: Doubleday, 1973). Nizer's book is undoubtedly the one volume that most Americans have read to learn about the Rosenberg case. As a shrewd, knowledgeable master trial lawyer, Nizer comes up with interesting comments pertaining to legal strategy during the trial. But his book is essentially based only on the trial transcript and a reworking of previously published books on the case. Moreover, Nizer edits and changes courtroom testimony for literary style without indicating he has done this; more important, he has even invented an entire scene that never took place.

The most recent book on the case that argues guilt and claims to be based on the newly released FBI files is by the British author H. Montgomery Hyde, *The Atom Bomb Spies* (New York: Atheneum, 1980). It is a volume noteworthy for its total lack of research. In particular, Hyde's estimate of the Rosenberg case is taken almost completely from the article by Sol Stern and Ronald Radosh that appeared in *The New Republic* on June 23, 1979. Although he cites this article, he goes on to present its analysis and pattern of evidence as his own.

Numerous books on the Rosenberg case have been written by writers who argue that the Rosenbergs were victims of a government frame-up. The argument was first put forth by left-wing journalist William A. Reuben, in the series of articles he wrote for the *National Guardian*. Reuben's findings were incorporated in his book *The Atom Spy Hoax* (New York: Action Books, 1955). Reuben argues that all atomic espionage, including that purported to have been carried out by Klaus Fuchs, was a hoax drummed up by the American and British governments to gather support for the Cold War. Outside of his own "progressive" community, Reuben's book had little influence. More influential because of the background information it provided on the Rosenbergs' early personal life, information on which all subsequent authors on the case have depended, is the book by Virginia Gardner, *The Rosenberg Story* (New York: Masses and Mainstream, 1954).

The first book attempting to prove the Rosenbergs' complete innocence that made an impact on the public was playwright John Wexley's *The Judgment of Julius and Ethel Rosenberg* (New York: Cameron and Kahn, 1955). He has recently revised the book and it has been published in a new paperback edition, with the same title (New York: Ballantine Books, 1977). The revised edition contains a new long introduction and new author's appendixes commenting on Wexley's response to FBI material released in 1975, as well as substantive changes in the text of different chapters. It has been necessary for us to cite and use both versions, since some material used in the first 1955 edition does not appear in the 1977 edition, and vice versa.

The response to Wexley's work is exemplified by that of two historians of the Hollywood blacklist, who have written that Wexley's book "carefully and thoroughly destroyed the government's case" (Larry Ceplair and Steven Englund, *The Inquisition in Hollywood* [New York: Anchor Press/Doubleday, 1980], p. 416). Despite such grandiose claims, Wexley's methodology is to draw a picture of a typical espionage agent, and then show that Julius Rosenberg and Harry Gold did not fit that picture. Wexley was the first author to offer the argument that the Hilton Hotel registration card, introduced as evidence to prove that Harry Gold was in Albuquerque on June 3, 1945, was an FBI forgery.

Undoubtedly the most influential and widely quoted book seeking to prove the frame-up thesis is Walter and Miriam Schneir, *Invitation to an Inquest* (New York: Doubleday, 1965), republished, with a new chapter written in 1967, by Delta Books in 1968 and by Penguin Books in 1973. The Schneirs' book appears as a cautious and calm investigation into prosecution charges. The book is undoubtedly the brief for the defense that Emanuel Bloch was never able to prepare adequately for the Rosenbergs. The Schneirs devote an entire chapter to the theory that a spy ring set up by Julius Rosenberg existed. But they write only to denigrate that possibility as pure fiction, and they ignore any evidence—even what they themselves offer—that might indicate such a ring was actually in existence. Following Wexley's lead, they present a seemingly incontrovertible argument that the Hilton Hotel card was indeed an FBI forgery. With the appearance of the Schneirs' volume, that claim has become part of the mythology surrounding the Rosenberg case.

Perhaps the most honest and serious book written by a critic of the government's case was law professor Malcolm P. Sharp, *Was Justice Done? The Rosenberg-Sobell Case* (New York: Monthly Review Press, 1956). Unlike the investigations by Reuben, Wexley, or the Schneirs, Sharp confines himself to a careful examination of the legal strategy in the prosecution's case. He is not always right, and much of his hypothesizing is outdated. But his book includes its own scathing critique of both Wexley and Reuben. Sharp shows that these authors both ignored or distorted evidence that tended to contradict their arguments. Sharp's book is calm, judicious, and carefully constructed. And many of his judgments on the legal issues involved in the case still hold up.

The most recent book by a critic of the case, based on interviews with FBI agents and defense-team members, is the text of a TV documentary, Alvin H. Goldstein, *The Unquiet Death of Julius and Ethel Rosenberg* (New York and Westport: Lawrence Hill, 1975). The book includes an introductory essay by journalist Nat Hentoff, who argues that the Rosenberg case may be seen as the key to the "criminal continuum" that extended from the 1950s through Watergate.

In 1974, partially as a result of their hostile response to the Nizer book, the Rosenbergs' two sons surfaced to lead a new public campaign to exonerate their parents. One result of going public was their book, Robert and Michael Meeropol, *We Are Your Sons* (Boston: Houghton Mifflin, 1975). The Meeropols' book is a moving and powerful memoir about growing up as children of convicted "atom spies" who had been executed in Cold War America. They are, truly, the real victims of the government's death sentence. Their book is less satisfactory when it deals with the issues of the case. Michael Meeropol's appendix, "A Dialogue of Generations," is a tortured attempt to reconcile the politics of his generation's New Left with those of his parents' Old Left. The path to unity, he seems to think, is through uniting around the campaign to vindicate the Rosenbergs.

The book is important because they present for the first time the text of many of the unexpurgated and complete death-house letters of the Rosenbergs. These complete versions complement and correct the edited and partial versions published as *Death House Letters of Ethel and Julius Rosenberg* (New York: Jero, 1953) and as *The Testament of Ethel and Julius Rosenberg* (New York: Cameron and Kahn, 1954).

Codefendant Morton Sobell offers his own version of the story in *On Doing Time* (New York: Scribner's, 1974). Sobell's book is skimpy in its discussion of the case, and most of it concentrates on his experience during his imprisonment.

ARTICLES

To list all the articles that have appeared concerning the Rosenberg case would be to create an undue burden upon the reader. It is our intention here to cite only some of the most important recent contributions to the literature.

New evaluations of the scientific evidence in the Rosenberg case appear in three articles. Roger M. Anders, historian at the Department of Energy, argues the case for Greenglass's credibility in "The Rosenberg Case Revisited: The Greenglass Testimony and the Protection of Atomic Secrets," *The American Historical Review,* vol. 83, no. 2 (April 1978), pp. 388–400. A contrasting view is offered in Gerald E. Markowitz and Michael Meeropol, "The 'Crime of the Century' Revisited: David Greenglass's Scientific Evidence in the Rosenberg Case," *Science and Society,* vol. 44, no. 1 (Spring 1980), pp. 1–26. These authors argue that Greenglass's information was inaccurate, insignificant, and worthless. A more balanced assessment, featuring an interview with scientist George Kistiakowsky, who evaluates the Greenglass sketch, is Daniel Yergin, "Victims of a Desperate Age," *New Times,* May 16, 1975.

Judicial and legal questions concentrating on the role played by Justices Frankfurter and Douglas may be found in Michael E. Parrish, "Cold War Justice: The Supreme Court and the Rosenbergs," *The American Historical Review,* vol. 82, no. 4 (Oct. 1977), pp. 805–42.

One outstanding article written during the 1950s, perhaps the only one to offer an independent and probing look at the case, is Nathan Glazer, "A New Look at the Rosenberg-Sobell Case," a Tamiment Institute Public Service Pamphlet, included as a special insert in *The New Leader,* July 2, 1956. Glazer attempts a dissection of the so-called new evidence brought to light by the defense committee, and he alone of all commentators discussed the possibilities of espionage conducted by Joel Barr, Alfred Sarant, and others usually not discussed at the time.

Readers seeking a synopsis and evaluation of the case should consult Allen Weinstein's brief article in Supplement Five to the *Dictionary of American Biography, 1951–1955,* pp. 588–90. Weinstein argues that a "convergence of opinion" exists that in a "less frantic and less fear-ridden political atmosphere, the couple would almost certainly have been granted either executive clemency or some form of judicial relief from execution." He sees the Rosenbergs' death as a monument "of the degree to which anti-Communist hysteria at the height of the Cold War prevented Americans from tempering the demands of justice with an equally full measure of mercy."

The role of Judge Irving Kaufman in handing out that death sentence is examined in the publication of FBI documents issued by the National Committee to Re-Open the Rosenberg Case, "The Kaufman Papers" (New York: n.d. [c. 1975]). The issue of *ex parte* communication and Judge Kaufman is discussed as well in Vern Countryman, "Out, Damned Spot: Judge Kaufman and the Rosenberg Case," *The New Republic,* Oct. 8, 1977, pp. 15–17.

OTHER DOCUMENTS

The transcript of the trial is available as Transcript of Record, *United States of America v. Julius Rosenberg, Ethel Rosenberg, Anatoli A. Yakovlev,*

David Greenglass and Morton Sobell, U.S. District Court, Southern District of New York, C.134–245, March 6–April 6, 1951. The transcript was reprinted by the National Committee to Secure Justice in the Rosenberg Case to accompany the petition for writ of *certiorari* in 1952. These eight volumes of the transcript, with new pagination, were widely distributed by the Committee, and this is the version held by most libraries. We have used these volumes and their pagination, and refer to this version in the text and notes as Trial Transcript.

NEWSPAPERS

Most helpful for coverage of the case were the various New York City papers, including *The New York Times*, the *New York Herald Tribune*, the *New York Daily News*, the *New York World-Telegram*, the *New York Daily Compass*, the *Daily Worker*, the *National Guardian*, and, after the collapse of the *Compass*, *I.F. Stone's Weekly*.

NOTES

PROLOGUE

Page

1 In 1933, when Rosenberg was a senior: Julius Rosenberg to Emanuel Bloch, Dec. 22, 1952, in *The Testament of Ethel and Julius Rosenberg* (New York: Cameron and Kahn, 1954), pp. 113–15. Also printed in Robert and Michael Meeropol, *We Are Your Sons* (Boston: Houghton Mifflin, 1975), pp. 167–71.

1: KLAUS FUCHS CONFESSES

Page

5 Americans had power: Godfrey Hodgson, *America in Our Time* (New York: Doubleday, 1976), pp. 16, 34–37.

6 "The reason why we find ourselves . . .": U.S. Congress, *Congressional Record*, 81st Congress, 2d Sess., 1950; pp. 96, 1954–1957. During a Senate speech delivered on Feb. 20, 1950, McCarthy entered into the record a copy of what he said was his Wheeling speech of Feb. 9, 1950. Historians generally agree that this speech was not his Wheeling speech, since it made no mention of the 205 security risks still employed in the State Department. L. Brent Bozell and William Buckley, in *McCarthy and His Enemies* (Chicago: Regnery, 1954), claim McCarthy had offered a speech he

actually delivered in Reno a few days later. Whatever the truth, this statement is a typical example of McCarthy's outlook.

7 The first clue to the existence: The NKGB was renamed the MGB in 1946 and eventually was reorganized as the KGB in 1953. For simplicity's sake, all references in the text use "KGB" as the name of this organization, regardless of the year. Essentially a branch of the Soviet civilian secret police, the NKGB/KGB was one of the two arms of Soviet intelligence operating in the United States during the period covered by this book—the other being military (Red Army) intelligence, or the GRU. Since the internal organization of the Soviet espionage system is not our primary focus, we have referred on various occasions to "Soviet agents" and "Soviet intelligence" without specifying the agency involved. However, it is generally accepted that Jacob Golos was an agent of the NKGB/MGB.

Golos, a Russian-born American Communist, was head of a Communist firm (World Tourists), a member of the Communist Party's Central Control Commission, head of the Party's secret work, and its liaison with the KGB. In this role, he became Elizabeth Bentley's espionage superior and eventually her lover. According to Harry Rositzke, a former Soviet specialist with the CIA, Anatoli Yakovlev was also an NKGB agent, and the Rosenberg spy ring operated throughout its history under the control of this agency. See Harry Rositzke, *The KGB: The Eyes of Russia* (New York: Doubleday, 1981). Some earlier sources dispute this, naming Yakovlev as a GRU agent and the Rosenberg ring as a GRU operation (see David Dallin, *Soviet Espionage*, New Haven: Yale University Press, 1955).

Others have claimed that Julius Rosenberg was an agent of Czech intelligence. Karel Kaplan, a former Czech Communist who supported Alexander Dubcek during the Prague Spring of 1968, reported in the May 3, 1977, issue of the Italian magazine *Panorama* that Czech intelligence files he had seen indicated that Julius Rosenberg was referred to in a file as "our agent." See *Time*, May 9, 1977, p. 38.

Kaplan was interviewed in Munich on March 27, 1977, by historians David Kennedy of Stanford University and Allen Weinstein of Smith College. Kaplan did not show them any documents, and Kennedy stresses that he does not feel Kaplan is a particularly trustworthy source. Nevertheless, Kennedy notes that Kaplan claimed to have seen a file in the archives of the Central Committee of the Czech Communist Party that referred to Julius

Rosenberg as "our agent." Kaplan told them that these documents indicated that Rosenberg was not innocent, and that the Czechs played a role in providing money that was sent to Rosenberg. He also asserted that material passed to the Russians by Rosenberg went first through France, where its worthiness was evaluated by pro-Communist scientist Frédéric Joliot-Curie. Kaplan also said that material was passed on to the Czechs and Russians through the World Peace Council in Paris. This organization, however, did not exist in 1945—when the atomic material given to Julius Rosenberg by David Greenglass was supposedly transmitted. Interview with David Kennedy by Ronald Radosh, June 14, 1978.

Karel Kaplan himself now denies that he had any information whatsoever to offer pertaining to the Rosenbergs, and he says that *Time* "misinterpreted" his remarks. Karel Kaplan to Ronald Radosh, July 7, 1978.

7 one of the first significant messages: Interview with Robert Lamphere by Ronald Radosh, June 23, 1980. Also see *Newsweek*, May 19, 1980, p. 32, where journalists David C. Martin and Allan J. Mayer report on the deciphered codes. They argue that the information found in the codes offers support to Max Elitcher's testimony at the Rosenberg trial, since the codes placed "a Soviet spy at [Elitcher's] house at the same time Rosenberg admitted being there." The codes were never introduced as evidence at the trial, Mayer and Martin write, because the government didn't want the Soviets to know that they had been deciphered. Also see David C. Martin, *Wilderness of Mirrors* (New York: Harper and Row, 1980), pp. 41–44.

8 Lamphere turned Barr's case over: Memo from Alan R. McCracken, acting assistant director, CIA Group, to J. Edgar Hoover, March 8, 1949, CIA Referrals, Rosenberg file.

8 "speed [must be] sacrificed for the sake of discretion": Ibid.

8 Momentarily stymied, Lamphere continued to hope: Lamphere interview, June 23, 1980.

9 Soviet operative sought out Klaus Fuchs's American courier: Statement of Harry Gold to U.S. Attorney Myles J. Lane, Aug. 1, 1950, in the presence of FBI Special Agents William F. Norton and John A. Harrington, Gold file.

10–11 Discussion of Klaus Fuchs's life, references to and quotations from his courtroom confession, and references to his interrogations by British intelligence, are taken from Alan Moorehead, *The Traitors* (New York: Harper and Row, 1963), pp. 49–172, and

from the Joint Committee on Atomic Energy, U.S. Senate, 82nd
Congress, 1st Session, *Soviet Atomic Espionage*, April 1951, pp.
13–38.

12 "At first I thought . . .": Fuchs confession, Jan. 27, 1950, cited in
Moorehead, *Traitors*, p. 147.

14 Before he left England: Signed statement of Emil Julius Klaus
Fuchs, Wormwood Scrubbs Prison, London, May 26, 1950, to
FBI Assistant Director Hugh H. Clegg and agent Robert J. Lam-
phere, witnessed by William James Skardon, Fuchs file.

Fuchs's recollections of his contact with "Raymond," his
American courier, were independently corroborated by Harry
Gold, who told FBI agents in Philadelphia about his contacts
with Fuchs. See signed statement of Harry Gold, May 23, 1950,
Gold file. Discrepancies in testimony were inconsequential—e.g.,
Fuchs spoke later in his statement of holding a "tennis ball" in
one hand as a form of identification; Gold remembered that
"Fuchs was to carry a handball in one hand." Also see A. H. Bel-
mont to C. E. Hennrich, May 23, 1950, Gold file. Also see J. Edgar Hoover to Communications Section, May 28, 1950, Gold file.

14–15 Fuchs failed to keep an appointment: See supplemental signed
statement of Harry Gold, concerning his meetings with Fuchs, to
SA's T. Scott Miller, Jr., and Richard E. Brennan, July 10, 1950,
Gold file.

Also see report of interview with Kristel and Robert Heineman. Mrs. Heineman confirmed that "three weeks before her
brother, DR. FUCHS, arrived in Cambridge in February 1945, an
unidentified chemist called at her home and inquired as to whether or not FUCHS had arrived." Report of SA Joseph C. Walsh,
Jr., May 29, 1950, Gold file. See also Moorehead, *Traitors*, pp.
98–107.

16 rumor circulated among Manhattan Project scientists: Robert
Jungk, *Brighter Than a Thousand Suns* (New York: Harcourt
Brace Jovanovich, 1958), p. 156.

16 an advance American intelligence unit: Ibid., pp. 163–66. Also see
pp. 156–90 for discussion of scientists' reactions to the discovery.

17 "In 1945, we ceased worrying . . .": Szilard quoted in ibid., p. 178.

18 "We were very friendly together . . .": Bethe quoted in Joint Committee on Atomic Energy, *Atomic Espionage*, p. 14.

18 Fuchs himself had a different explanation: Fuchs confession, cited
in Moorehead, *Traitors*, p. 154.

18 "unique . . . a new precedent . . .": Christmas Humphreys before
the Chief Magistrate of Britain at Bow Street, Feb. 10, 1950,
quoted in ibid., p. 154.

2: THE SEARCH FOR RAYMOND

Page

21 Hoover was under pressure: Walter and Miriam Schneir, *Invitation to an Inquest* (Baltimore, Penguin, 1973), p. 68.

21 The FBI did have descriptions: Summary report on interview of Kristel and Robert Heineman by agents of Boston office, in Report of Special Agent Joseph C. Walsh, Jr., May 29, 1950, Gold file.

21 more than a few million men: This point was made in a widely discussed article published under J. Edgar Hoover's name, "The Crime of the Century," *Reader's Digest*, May 1951, p. 154. Describing the manhunt for Raymond, Hoover dwelt almost lovingly on the sketchy nature of Fuchs's information—"A description which might have fit millions of men!" Hoover claimed that his agents had sifted through data on more than 1,200 suspects before zeroing in on their final target. Hoover's article was a masterpiece of public relations. However, its florid account of FBI exploits served only to confuse the issue of how Raymond was actually found.

21 Research into the Bureau's own files: Special agent in charge, New York, to J. Edgar Hoover, March 13, 1950; D. M. Ladd to A. H. Belmont, March 9, 1950; FBI to Communications Section, n.d. [1950]; Gold file.

22 Both men had been named: Signed statement of Elizabeth Terrill Bentley, Nov. 30, 1945, pp. 13–14 (of a 107-page statement).

The Bentley statement is filed under a report prepared by SA Thomas G. Spencer, dated Dec. 5, 1945, and is part of the Nathan Gregory Silvermaster file. It is filed under FBI serial number 65-56402-220.

The cover page of the report indicates that Bentley was interviewed in New York City numerous times between November 9 and 29, 1945, by SA's Joseph M. Kelly and Harold V. Kennedy, and that she signed her statement in the presence of both of these agents. Preceding the actual report, on the title page, is the notation "Report of Special Agent Harold V. Kennedy, New York, 12-3-45."

All future references to this Bentley report shall simply be Signed statement of Elizabeth Bentley, Nov. 30, 1945.

Also see interview with Bentley by SA Robert M. Kane, June 15, 1950; and special agent in charge, New York, to director, July 26, 1950, Rosenberg file.

22 all-out effort to locate Harry Gold: Report of SA John R. Mur-

phy, Jr., June 30, 1950, containing interviews with Brothman of May 15, May 16, May 20, and June 16, 1950. Brothman file. Also, summary report of D. M. Ladd to Hoover, May 25, 1950, containing summary of facts relating to the investigation of Harry Gold, Gold file, and report of Ladd to Hoover, May 18, 1950, Gold file, concerning possible identification of Gold as "Unknown Subject," and containing summaries of the interviews by agents with Gold and Brothman. By this date Ladd had concluded: "While it cannot be conclusively stated, it would appear from the information obtained in these interviews, together with the previously known information concerning Gold, that Gold may be identical with Unknown Subject." Ladd cited Bentley's claim that "in 1941 Brothman was furnishing blueprints via Gold to Jacob Golos, known Soviet agent," and he writes that "the origin of the association between Brothman and Gold was an espionage matter, though they did not admit that it was such when interviewed in 1947."

22 Gold was still living with his father: Report of SA Edward Scheidt to A. H. Belmont, May 16, 1950, Gold file. Scheidt quotes Miller and Brennan's interview in his report to Washington. He quotes from the notes taken by these agents during their interview with Gold.

22 "It was advisable . . .": Miller and Brennan quoted in ibid.

23 He had been expecting: Harry Gold, "The Circumstances Surrounding My Work as a Soviet Agent—A Report," Oct. 11, 1950, delivered by Gold to his lawyers, Augustus S. Ballard and John D. M. Hamilton, Oct. 19, 1950, pp. 70–80.

A typed and rewritten version of this report is to be found in the FBI's Harry Gold file. We have chosen to use and to cite the original 110-page, handwritten report prepared by Gold, located in the files of Augustus Ballard.

23 "Curiously enough when Special Agents Miller and Brennan . . .": Ibid.

23 "The beginning was a relatively innocent one": Statement delivered by Harry Gold to his lawyer John Hamilton, July 20, 1950, p. 1. This statement is also in the files of Augustus Ballard.

24ff The entire biographical account of Gold's life is taken from Gold's memoir, "The Circumstances Surrounding My Work as a Soviet Agent," pp. 2–5.

All quotations through p. 33—including those not specifically cited below as well as those that are—are from Gold's memoir.

25 "Beginning about 1926, my father . . .": Ibid., pp. 5–6.

26–27 "There I met . . .": Ibid., pp. 14–15.

30 "The planning of a meeting . . .": Ibid., pp. 38–39.
30 "When on a mission . . .": Ibid., pp. 40–41.
33 Elizabeth Bentley had described ten meetings: Signed statement of Elizabeth Bentley, Nov. 30, 1945, Silvermaster file. Also see interview with Elizabeth Bentley by SA Thomas G. Spencer, May 22, 1950, cited in report of SA Joseph C. Walsh, Jr., May 29, 1950, Gold file.
34 Brothman freely admitted turning over blueprints: Report of interview with Abraham Brothman by agents Donald E. Shannon and Francisco D. O'Brien, May 29, 1947; signed statement by Abraham Brothman, May 29, 1947, Gold file.
34 Brothman called in his then employee Harry Gold: Reports of interview conducted with Harry Gold on June 16, 1950, by agents Miller and Brennan, contained in a report filed by agent Robert G. Jensen, along with signed statement of Harry Gold to Miller and Brennan, July 11, 1950, Gold file, pp. 40–54 of Jensen report. Gold's reconstruction of what transpired between Brothman and himself is taken from his lengthy statement to agents Miller and Brennan.
37 "The FBI is looking for . . .": Gold's statement that he had told Black he was Fuchs's American courier was corroborated by Thomas Black. See Memo, special agent in charge, June 17, 1950, including signed statement of Thomas L. Black, June 15, 1950, Black file. Also see A. H. Belmont to D. M. Ladd, June 15, 1950, reporting on interviews by Philadelphia Bureau agent Cornelius with Black. Cornelius noted that Black argued that his own activities "were not of an espionage nature," with the notation that a portion of an enclosed memorandum "deals with the admission of Black that he had knowledge that Harry Gold was the American contact of Fuchs but failed to inform authorities of this knowledge." A handwritten note by Hoover asked that Black's case be "*promptly* considered by Dept. if approved Black is *immediately* arraigned. We cannot afford to hold him." Black was never indicted; indeed, the FBI sought to make him available at the trial, should Gold's credibility on the witness stand be challenged. Also see signed statement of Thomas Black, June 15, 1950, in report of SA William B. Welte, Jr., July 26, 1950, Black file, pp. 48–49. Black wrote:

> During this walk HARRY told me that he had been FUCHS' American contact and that if anything should happen to him he wanted me to look after his father and brother. As nearly as I can recall his exact words were "The FBI is

looking for FUCHS' American contact and I am that man."
He said that if he should be caught he was going to take an
overdose of sleeping tablets. . . . I tried to persuade him [*sic*]
from committing suicide.

Black added that he trusted Gold's word and knew that he had
been to Albuquerque before the A-bomb tests, "because he telephoned me from a hotel in Albuquerque and asked me to telegraph him some funds." Black said he did not inform the
authorities of Gold's confession because "I was frankly very
scared at the time and I did not want to become involved if it
could be avoided."

37 But on May 16, 1950, two FBI agents: D. M. Ladd to the director, May 18, 1950, Gold file. Ladd summarizes the interview held
by agents with Miriam Moskowitz on May 16. He wrote to Hoover: "Moskowitz related that when Gold came with the firm in
1946, he frequently spoke of his wife . . . and his twin children. He
also claimed his brother, a paratrooper, had been killed in the Pacific."

37 "redheaded wife and two children": Ladd to director, May 18,
1950, Gold file; Notes in FBI report on "Interviews with Harry
Gold Preceding Arrest," citing interviews of Gold by T. Scott
Miller, Jr., and Richard E. Brennan on May 15, 1950, and May
19, 1950. Gold's account is taken from his memoir, "The Circumstances Surrounding my Work as a Soviet Agent," pp. 80–83.

37–38 "Yes, I was almost in the clear . . .": Gold, "Circumstances Surrounding My Work," pp. 85–86.

38 "First a copy . . .": Ibid., pp. 86–87.

38–39 "Then came the stunning blow . . .": Ibid., p. 87.

39 On May 20, FBI agents . . . interrogating Fuchs: Report by SA
Joseph C. Walsh, Jr., May 29, 1950, containing report on Fuchs's
description of Gold made on Feb. 17, 1950, Gold file; for Fuchs's
comments to Clegg and Lamphere, see J. Edgar Hoover, report to
Communications Section, May 28, 1950, based on London cables
of May 20 and 22, 1950, Gold file.

39–40 On May 22, Clegg and Lamphere: Hoover report to Communication Section, May 28, 1950.

40 "PHILADELPHIAN SEIZED AS SPY . . .": *The New York Times*, May
24, 1950.

40 In a widely publicized article: J. Edgar Hoover, "The Crime of the
Century," *Reader's Digest*, May 1951, p. 167. Robert Lamphere
states that the article was actually written by Fern Stukenbroeker,
who also ghostwrote Hoover's book *Masters of Deceit*. Lamphere

says he personally passed on the article, and carefully looked over various drafts. "For it to have a factual inaccuracy," Lamphere says, "surprises me." He also says Hoover passed on the article as well. Interview with Robert Lamphere by Ronald Radosh, Jan. 23, 1982.

40–41 FBI investigations chief A. H. Belmont: Memo of A. H. Belmont to D. M. Ladd, May 22 and 23, 1950, Gold file.

41 In the meantime, Clegg and Lamphere: Ibid.

41 Fortunately for the FBI, which was already committed: Addendum to signed confession of Klaus Fuchs, May 26, 1950, noting Fuchs's statement to Robert Lamphere. Also see FBI summary report, Gold file. This report notes that, on May 20, Fuchs was shown new still photos of Gold "and he did not identify them, though he stated he could not reject them." On May 22, Fuchs saw repeat showings of motion pictures of Gold and said it was "very likely" Gold was his contact. It was this *abrupt and inconclusive* identification that the FBI received at 11:08 A.M. on May 22, a time that corresponded with Gold's confession of 10:45 A.M. on May 22, Philadelphia time. The report goes on to state that on May 25, the Bureau got word that photos taken in Philadelphia on May 21, "and which were flown to London by a commercial pilot on May 23, 1950, had been viewed by Fuchs and he had made a positive identification of Gold as being his American contact." But this final positive identification took place *after* Gold had already signed a full confession.

41 repeating the Hoover version: Lamphere interview, Jan. 23, 1982.

42 charges of some Rosenberg-case critics: See, for example, the comments of FOIA, Inc., lawyer Marshall Perlin, who represents Michael and Robert Meeropol, in Alvin H. Goldstein, *The Unquiet Death of Julius and Ethel Rosenberg* (New York and Westport: Lawrence Hill, 1975), no page number. Goldstein writes: "Gold's believability as a key government witness rested on the assumption that Klaus Fuchs had indeed identified him." After quoting Lamphere's recollection that Fuchs had identified Gold from the film he was watching, Goldstein quotes Marshall Perlin, who visited Fuchs "some years later" in his British prison quarters. According to Perlin, "the clear and unequivocal evidence that came out of Fuchs's mouth was, 'No, he never identified Gold as the courier, either to the FBI, British intelligence, or to his attorney.'" Lamphere then supposedly retorted to Goldstein: "[that] is absolutely not what happened. It [*sic*] was a representative of MI 5 there, there was an assistant director of the FBI, and I was there." Perlin then is quoted as saying: "He told us how they kept

importuning him to identify him [Gold], saying, 'For God sakes, say he's the man—Gold insists he is.' British intelligence said the same thing. And in substance Fuchs said, if he insists he's the guy, he's the guy, let him be the person, but I never—Fuchs said to us that he never identified Gold."

We cannot dispute that Fuchs said this to Marshall Perlin, although we have only Perlin's word that this conversation took place. It may indeed be true—as we have suggested—that the Bureau informed Fuchs that Gold had confessed, and that, having learned of this, Fuchs felt free to corroborate that Gold was his courier. But the evidence clearly establishes that, contrary to what Fuchs told Perlin, Fuchs had definitely identified Gold after viewing the film shown to him on May 23, 1950.

42 he had not wanted to "turn 'rat' . . .": Gold, "Circumstances Surrounding My Work," p. 90.

43 "exhaustively interviewed for all information . . .": A. H. Belmont to D. M. Ladd, May 22, 1950, Gold file. Belmont dictates the advice he had given to the SA in charge in Philadelphia, Mr. Cornelius.

43 The seven-page statement: Signed statement of Harry Gold, May 22, 1950, Gold file.

43 "I travelled to Albuquerque . . .": Ibid.

43–44 on that day, Gold announced: C. E. Hennrich to A. H. Belmont, June 1, 1950, Gold file.

44 " . . . A soldier, non-commissioned . . .": Ibid.

44–46 These are recorded in two documents: Gold signed statement to SA's Richard E. Brennan and T. Scott Miller, Jr., June 2, 1950, Gold file; and D. M. Ladd to Hoover, June 2, 1950, Gold file.

46 Harry Gold was shown two photographs: Teletype report to Washington and New York from SA Cornelius, June 3 and 4, 1950, Gold file.

46 " . . . Gold had no knowledge of unsub . . .": Unsigned teletype report summing up observations of agents Brennan and Miller, June 9, 1950, Gold file.

47 "Even considering the most profitable outcome . . .": Ibid.

47 Gold had found the house unrecognizable: Report of SA Robert G. Jensen, Philadelphia, June 10, 1950, for period of June 1–10, 1950, on subject: "Unknown American no. 5, Albuquerque, New Mexico"; Gold file.

47 Gold was shown some photos of Greenglass: Report of SA Robert G. Jensen, June 27, 1950, reporting on the period June 15–26, 1950, including report on session of agents T. Scott Miller, Jr.,

and Richard E. Brennan with Harry Gold held on June 15, 1950; Gold file.

47 Greenglass admitted that, as a machinist: Signed handwritten statement of David Greenglass, June 16, 1950; witnessed by agents John W. Lewis and Leo H. Frutkin, and typed statement of Greenglass dated June 15, 1950.

Greenglass began confessing on June 15 at 10:45 P.M. and he finished his statement at 2:00 A.M., June 16. The person who typed his statement typed the date of June 15 on the typewritten statement, while the handwritten signed version has the accurate date of June 16, reflecting the time of completion.

3: "EITHER CONVERT OUR FRIENDS OR DROP THEM"

Page

48 "If I go, I'll never read . . .": Interview with David and Ruth Greenglass, by Ronald Radosh and Sol Stern, June 12, 1979, conducted at the law office of O. John Rogge.

49 "I was young, stupid, and immature . . .": Interview with David and Ruth Greenglass and O. John Rogge, by Ronald Radosh, March 21, 1979, conducted at Smith and Wollensky's restaurant.

49–51 Ethel Greenglass, born in 1915: The story of the Rosenbergs' life as young adults is based on Virginia Gardner, *The Rosenberg Story* (New York: Masses and Mainstream, 1954). Although the tone of Gardner's book approaches hagiography, her account of the Rosenbergs' early years is an invaluable source, since it is based on scores of interviews with family, teachers, and friends.

51 a major much favored: FAECT is described by Irving Howe and Lewis Coser as one of the unions that was "minor on the scale of CIO power," yet "not without some strength," which "the Communists quickly took control of." They write that at first FAECT was made up of "mainly the technical staffs of the WPA." It functioned as a means for the Communists to approach "various occupational group and middle-class neighborhoods." See Irving Howe and Lewis Coser, *The American Communist Party: A Critical History* (New York: Praeger, 1962), p. 374.

53 full membership in the Communist Party: At the time of the Rosenberg trial and the subsequent appeals battle, the assertion that Julius and Ethel were CP members was controversial. The couple invoked the Fifth Amendment on this question at the trial, and defense-committee members charged that calling the Rosenbergs

Communists was red-baiting, since the couple were only "progressives" who had been singled out as a lesson to all opponents of the Cold War.

In the 1970s, controversy over whether or not the Rosenbergs were Party members dissipated. Their sons, Robert and Michael Meeropol, now acknowledge that "recent investigations have permitted us to conclude that our parents probably were members of the American Communist Party." See Robert and Michael Meeropol, *We Are Your Sons* (Boston: Houghton Mifflin, 1975), p. 352.

Government files released under the Freedom of Information Act confirm the accuracy of their judgment. A photostatic copy of Julius Rosenberg's Communist Party membership card, showing an induction date of Dec. 12, 1939, and membership number 6603, is part of the file on Rosenberg in the U.S. Army Intelligence file gathered pertaining to his Signal Corps employment. The file contains another photostat indicating that the couple had moved, and that their Party membership had been shifted from Branch 16B to a neighborhood East Side Party club. See Army Service Forces, Headquarters, Second Service Command, "Summary Report re: Julius Rosenberg," Army Intelligence files; cited in report of Maj. E. M. Scherer, March 26, 1945, citing FBI memo of March 13, 1945; U.S. Army Intelligence files.

Also see E. E. Conroy, special agent in charge, to Col. S. V. Constant, Oct. 6, 1944, Rosenberg (FBI) file.

In addition to the above, various FBI informants corroborated the Rosenberg's Party membership. An interview conducted on March 17, 1951, with Nathan and Gertrude Sussman, by Special Agents Bert S. Taylor and Robert F. Royal, indicated that Sussman was asked to join the CP in the latter half of 1942 by either Rosenberg or Joel Barr. Included in Branch 16B, Sussman told the agents, were the Rosenbergs, Joel Barr, Alfred Sarant, and the Sussmans. Sussman told the agents that Julius Rosenberg was the chairman of the group, and that he, Sussman, was the secretary-treasurer. Sussman also told the Bureau that in February 1944 the Industrial Division headquarters of the Party issued transfer cards to neighborhood units, and that Branch 16B held a farewell party at a New York restaurant, at which "ETHEL ROSENBERG sang as part of their entertainment." Report of interview with Nathan and Gertrude Sussman, in Report of SA Robert F. Royal, April 14, 1951, pp. 17–23 of report, Sarant file.

In addition, interviews conducted by the authors with well-known Communist Party leaders—including Central Committee member and *Daily Worker* editor-in-chief John Gates; Junius Scales, chairman of the Party in North Carolina; and Max Gordon, editor and reporter for *The Daily Worker*—all confirmed the awareness on the part of leading CP cadre that the Rosenbergs had been active Party members during the 1940s.

53 Party members were being urged: For solid accounts of the Communist Party and its policies, see Joseph Starobin, *American Communism in Crisis, 1943–1957* (Cambridge: Harvard University Press, 1972); and Maurice Isserman, *Which Side Were You On? The American Communist Party During the Second World War* (Middletown, Conn.: Wesleyan University Press, 1982). The dissolving of industrial Party clubs and their reorganization into neighborhood units was part of Earl Browder's attempt to Americanize the Party and to make its main units similar to regular American political party organizations. Neighborhood units demanded less intense participation than the rigidly structured industrial branches, and Party members no longer had to regularly attend branch meetings. Isserman discusses the significance of the new Party structure on pp. 150–51 of his book.

54 he and Ethel quietly dropped out: The Party restructuring afforded the perfect opportunity for active members to drop out of formal participation without calling attention to themselves.

54 Ruth Greenglass would later charge: Signed statement of Ruth Greenglass, July 17, 1950, to agents John A. Harrington and William F. Norton, Jr., Greenglass file.

54 Rosenberg . . . made a spirited defense: Statement of Julius Rosenberg at special hearing on March 4, 1941, quoted in report of agent Thomas V. Kingham, U.S. Army Signal Corps; included in Summary Report, Army Service Forces, Headquarters, Second Service Command, Governor's Island; New York, for Newark Signal Corps Inspection Zone, File 2s-318821, completed Feb. 1945.

55 Rosenberg admitted that his wife: Statement of Julius Rosenberg on March 8, 1941, in ibid.

56 something of a cause célèbre: See Memo for File, report of Maj. E. M. Scherer, March 26, 1945, citing a March 13, 1945, FBI memo from a confidential source. See also file memorandum of March 23, 1945, by Capt. John W. Henderson; supplemental memo for file, April 25, 1945, by Maj. E. M. Scherer; Army Signal Corps Intelligence files.

In the April 25 memo, Major Scherer wrote that Captain Henderson's "action was entirely unauthorized, irregular, contrary to specific instructions given him and in violation of War

Department policy," and that all "inquiries into union activities of individuals and the programs and policies of the unions will be avoided to the greatest extent consistent with development of information concerning subversive activities." To dismiss an individual on the basis of membership in FAECT, Scherer noted, would "cause serious embarrassment to the War Department since that organization is a member of the CIO" and such dismissal could be interpreted as "anti-union bias on the part of the War Department." See also Julius Rosenberg to Capt. Henderson, April 3, 1945, in which Rosenberg writes: "I am not now, and never have been a Communist. . . . I know nothing about Communist branches, divisions, clubs, or transfers." See also Lewis Allen Bern, president of FAECT, to War Department, March 30, 1945, in ibid.

The Signal Corps investigation was opened in 1944 after the FBI passed on to Army Intelligence information from an anonymous source—almost certainly an FBI informer within the Party—that Rosenberg had been until quite recently a member of Branch 16B of the Industrial Division of the Party. Rosenberg fought the charge by arguing he was being persecuted because of FAECT membership. He was fired nevertheless, since the Army based its decision on his CP membership. Yet Rosenberg was never told about the existence of the photocopy of his Party card nor how it had come into the hands of the Signal Corps. Hence he denied, in his letter to Captain Henderson, that he had ever belonged to the CP—a denial he had been careful not to make under oath in 1941. But his protest was of no avail.

56 "By and large, anyone who became a spy . . .": Interview with Max Gordon by Ronald Radosh, July 10, 1978.

57 "Julius Rosenberg was very active . . .": Interview with John Gates by Ronald Radosh, June 14, 1978.

57 "one of the surefire things . . .": Interview with Junius Scales by Ronald Radosh, July 25, 1978.

57 The Greenglass correspondence is to be found in "Report made by Agent John W. Lewis, June 26, 1950, for period June 5–20, 1950," Greenglass file.

This file folder contains the transcribed text of the letters found by the agents during the search of the Greenglasses' apartment conducted on June 15, 1950. On p. 17 of his report, agent Lewis writes that "a foot locker or hand trunk was found . . . in the room adjacent to the kitchen" and that it was "almost full of letters." Greenglass allowed the FBI to take the letters.

The originals were photographed in negative photocopies, and the file includes these poor-quality copies of the original letters, as well as excerpts from them in a transcribed typed report. The file also contained the comments and analysis of the letters made by FBI agents, as well as answers from both Ruth and David Greenglass to queries about them. The copies of the originals are of a poor quality, barely readable, but it has been possible for us to compare the handwritten texts with the excerpts typed out in agent Lewis's report. The FBI returned the originals to the Greenglasses.

We found the photocopies of each letter cited and excerpted in the agent's typed report—except for one letter found only in the original photocopy that *was not excerpted*, which will be discussed later.

57–58 Julius Rosenberg's later assertion under oath: Trial Transcript, p. 1252.

58 "Although I'd love to have you . . .": David Greenglass to Ruth Greenglass, April 28, 1943.

58 "While at Fort Dix I met . . .": David to Ruth, May 1, 1943.

59 "Well darling here it is Sunday . . .": Ruth to David, May 2, 1943.

59 "Dearest, remember what Julie told you . . .": Ruth to David, May 26, 1943.

59 "Although we are materialists . . .": David to Ruth, June 3, 1943.

60 "I saw Ida tonight . . .": Ruth to David, July 14, 1943.

60 "Darling, during lunch I had . . .": David to Ruth, Aug. 24, 1943.

61 "Phyllis finished dressing first . . .": Ruth to David, Sept. 19, 1943.

61 "Darling, you are right . . .": David to Ruth, Dec. 27, 1943.

61–62 "I am reading another book . . .": David to Ruth, Jan. 2, 1944.

62 "Sweetheart, that comrade . . .": Ibid.

62 "Still I hope . . .": Ruth to David, Jan. 2, 1944.

62–63 "I went to the meeting . . .": Ruth to David, Jan. 10, 1944.

63 "Dearest, I felt terribly let down . . .": David to Ruth, Jan. 17, 1944.

64 "I wanted to answer . . .": David to Ruth, Jan. 18, 1944.

64 "Of late I have been having . . .": David to Ruth, Jan. 25, 1944.

64 "It seems that the Party . . .": Ruth to David, Feb. 13, 1944.

65 "Darling, I have been reading . . .": David to Ruth, June 29, 1944.

65 "Dear, don't worry . . .": David to Ruth, July 6, 1944.

65 "Julie was in the house . . .": David to Ruth, July 31, 1944.

66 "Dear, I have been very reticent . . .": David to Ruth, Aug. 4, 1944.

66 "I want to speak to that person . . .": David to Ruth, Oct. 23, 1944.

66 "I am worried about whether . . .": David to Ruth, Nov. 9, 1944.
This is the one letter that was not transcribed and typed for excerpt in the report prepared by FBI agent John W. Lewis. We found it in the photocopies of the original letters. We showed the poor-quality copy to David Greenglass, and he confirmed that it was his handwriting and that he had written the letter.

It is possible, of course, that David Greenglass may have been alluding to an innocent family gathering that Julius was planning for the future. But if this were the case, then how does one account for the cryptic message sent in October or for the opening of this letter, which refers to a telegram (of which no copy exists) that was evidently meant to be worded in a form unintelligible to the Western Union operator?

We consider it significant, moreover, that this letter and this letter alone was omitted from the typed transcript of the correspondence prepared by the FBI. Someone inside the Bureau may well have realized that this letter could be used to show that Ruth had not been caught wholly off guard when Julius Rosenberg raised the subject of espionage with her later the same month. Since Ruth was not under arrest, and was needed as a friendly witness, it was not to the FBI's advantage to draw attention to evidence that showed that she was anything less than a malleable young woman acting under the influence of trusted older relatives. As it happened, the omission of this letter from the FBI's report was irrelevant, since the prosecutors did not use any of the Greenglass correspondence during the trial.

66–67 When we showed this letter: David and Ruth Greenglass interview, June 12, 1979.

67 Julius was tremendously excited: Trial Transcript, pp. 677–80.

68 Julius Rosenberg came alone to her Stanton Street apartment: Ibid., pp. 684–85.

68 The next stage of the conspiracy: Ibid., pp. 685–88.

68 David and Ruth went to the Rosenbergs' apartment: Ibid., pp. 686–89.

69 Julius asked Ruth to step into the kitchen: Ibid., pp. 689–90.

69 David would later testify: Ibid., p. 447.

69 in August 1950 Ann Sidorovich conceded: Report of SA John B. O'Donoghue, Aug. 9, 1950, Michael and Ann Sidorovich file.

69 one final incident occurred: Trial Transcript, pp. 394–406.

70 Ruth suffered a miscarriage in April: Ibid., p. 697.

70 David Greenglass told his visitor: Ibid., p. 456–60.

70 David . . . gave Julius Rosenberg the last installment: Ibid., pp. 489–500.

71 David Greenglass was due to be discharged: Signed statement of David Greenglass, July 17, 1950, witnessed by agents Leo H. Frutkin and John W. Lewis, Greenglass file.

71 Julius . . . was keeping two apartments: Ibid.; also J. Edgar Hoover to the attorney general, July 17, 1950, Greenglass file.

73 "We've got to be like soldiers . . .": David and Ruth Greenglass interview, June 12, 1979.

74 But the chief cause of the strain: David Greenglass's signed statements to the FBI and his testimony in court placed the first warning from Julius in February 1950, *after* Fuchs's arrest. In talking to the authors, however, Greenglass insisted that the subject had come up the previous October. When we reminded him that Fuchs was not arrested until early 1950, he was surprised and insisted that something about Fuchs's impending capture must have been published the previous October, since Julius had been aware of it. But an interview with David by FBI agent John W. Lewis in July 1951, cited in report of SA John A. Harrington, July 27, 1951, confirms that Greenglass placed Julius's initial warning in late 1949. The mystery of how Julius could have known that Fuchs would be exposed was resolved when we surmised that Soviet intelligence must have had advance warning from Kim Philby.

74–75 By Christmas, David was broke: Interview of David Greenglass by John W. Lewis, cited in report of SA John A. Harrington, July 27, 1951, Greenglass file. The next few paragraphs are based on the material presented in this interview by David Greenglass.

75–76 During the last weekend in January: Previous mentions of this incident have placed it in February, based on David's recollection, but FBI documents show it happened at the very end of January. Hoover to Assistant Attorney General Warren Olney III, March 31, 1953, Greenglass file.

76 Although one of the uranium hemispheres: Ibid. Hoover notes that the FBI commenced an investigation in 1949—referred to as the case of "Dr. Ralph Eugene Lapp, et al., Atomic Energy Act, Theft of Government Property"—for the purpose of recovering stolen uranium hemispheres taken as souvenirs by Los Alamos workers, since the material had been "classified as restricted data by the Atomic Energy Commission." He notes that "individuals who had access to these hemispheres, including Greenglass, were interviewed by Bureau agents" who sought their return. He also notes that "prosecutive action was not warranted" because of the "number of instances involving the possession of such material by

former employees," which in 1953 led the AEC to remove urani-um hemispheres from the restricted data classification. See affida-vit of Bernard Greenglass to Gloria Agrin, May 31, 1953, in which David's older brother, Bernard, swore that in 1946 David had told him he had "taken a sample of uranium from Los Ala-mos without permission of the authorities," and that before his ar-rest, "David told me that he had thrown this uranium into the East River." Critics like John Wexley have called this theft the "nucleus of Greenglass's fear"—the fact that accounted for his desire to cooperate with the government and concoct fraudulent stories of espionage concerning his sister and brother-in-law. See John Wexley, *The Judgment of Julius and Ethel Rosenberg* (New York: Ballantine, 1977), pp. 110–12, 124, 135.

The evidence indicates that the uranium theft was a com-monplace occurrence, and that Greenglass and Rosenberg's reac-tion to FBI awareness of the stolen uranium was a sense of relief. Henry Linschitz, who worked in the explosives-chemistry section at Los Alamos and who prepared an affidavit for the Sobell de-fense in 1966, stressed to us in an interview that the taking of ura-nium hemispheres was as common as picking up mica in a park, and that he has always disagreed with the attempt of the Rosen-berg-Sobell defenders to make a great deal out of the Greenglass uranium theft. Interview with Henry Linschitz by Ronald Ra-dosh, June 13, 1978.

76 Julius came down to Rivington Street: Signed statement of David Greenglass, July 17, 1950.

78 David was to go to the Plaza: Ibid.

79 Ruth and David discussed for the first time: Ibid. See also inter-view with Ruth Greenglass by SA Edward Scheidt, n.d.; FBI tele-type; and Scheidt to J. Edgar Hoover, July 17, 1950, Greenglass file.

79 ". . . reading too much science fiction": David and Ruth Green-glass interview, June 12, 1979.

80 Julius was by now so nervous: Interrogation of David Greenglass by Myles J. Lane, Aug. 4, 1950, and statement of David Green-glass to U.S. Attorney Myles J. Lane, in the presence of SA Wil-liam F. Norton, Aug. 4, 1950. Greenglass first told this story of his encounter with the Einsohns on this date. He later repeated it during his testimony in court. The Einsohns were listed as prose-cution witnesses by the government in the trial—a tactic meant to impress the defense with the likelihood that, if called, they would confirm Greenglass's account of the brief encounter.

That is possibly why, in court, Julius Rosenberg admitted to his argument with his brother-in-law, although Rosenberg claimed that David was demanding money of him. Julius most likely feared that, had he denied the meeting, the Einsohns would be brought forth as rebuttal witnesses.

80 Ruth was ordered into the hospital: David and Ruth Greenglass interview, June 12, 1979.

80–81 Then, on the afternoon of June 15: John W. Lewis, Leo H. Frutkin, John A. Harrington, and William F. Norton were the agents sent to apprehend Greenglass.

81 about two dozen snapshots: A. H. Belmont to D. M. Ladd, June 15, 1950, folder marked, "Unknown American #5," Greenglass file.

82 "attorney and mentioned the name . . .": Ibid.

82 The statement that Greenglass signed: Signed statement of David Greenglass, dictated on June 15, 1950, to agents John W. Lewis and Leo H. Frutkin, Greenglass file.

83 Rogge charged that the Department was planning: Rogge is quoted in Starobin, *American Communism in Crisis*, pp. 172–73.

83 he became one of three CRC lawyers: Rogge's role working with the Civil Rights Congress forms the basis for the wild conspiracy thesis developed by Irwin Edelman—the man responsible for the last-minute stay of execution granted the Rosenbergs by Supreme Court Justice William O. Douglas.

Because one of Rogge's co-counsels on the Trenton Six case was none other than Emanuel Bloch—later to be squared against Rogge as the Rosenbergs' counsel—Edelman deduces that both Rogge and Bloch were FBI plants in the Communist movement, and he argues that it was the Bureau that picked Rogge to be the Greenglasses' lawyer. Edelman offers no evidence or proof for his theory. See his privately circulated book, "Religion, the Left and the Rosenberg Case," New York, n.d. [1970s], pp. 66–70.

83 For example, he had joined: The Peace Information Center, which closely followed the Party line, concentrated on the threats to world peace that it saw as emanating from the American war machine; Soviet policy was never criticized. Du Bois subsequently wrote about his efforts as head of this body in a short book, *In Battle for Peace* (New York: Masses and Mainstream, 1952).

83 the famous Stockholm Peace Petition: The petition carefully avoided condemning the testing of nuclear weapons, since the Soviet Union still planned to conduct numerous aboveground tests.

84 Rogge used his position: Rogge's role and his estrangement from

the American Communist movement is discussed in David A. Shannon, *The Decline of American Communism* (New York: Harcourt, Brace, 1959), pp. 204–05. See also the *Daily Worker*, Nov. 21, 1950; Nov. 14–15, 1951; *The Worker*, Sept. 11, 1949. Harsh condemnations of Rogge appear in the official Cominform (Communist Information Bureau) newspaper set up by Stalin, *For a Lasting Peace, For a People's Democracy!*, Sept. 22, 1950.

Rogge's untrustworthiness, as far as pro-Communists were concerned, became evident when he dared to criticize both American *and* Soviet imperialism at a speech before a Communist peace conference held in Mexico City in 1949. Such evenhanded condemnations were not normally heard at World Peace Congress deliberations. The Communists accused Rogge of being a slanderer for his speech at that meeting.

84 government sought . . . to prosecute Du Bois: The United States indicted Du Bois and two of his associates in the Peace Information Center in 1951 as "agents of a foreign power," accusing them of failing to register under the terms of the Foreign Agents Registration Act. A key government witness against Du Bois was O. John Rogge, who testified only that the defendants held markedly pro-Soviet foreign policy views. The judge threw the case out of court, and Du Bois castigated Rogge in a chapter of *In Battle for Peace* called "Oh! John Rogge." When Rogge was asked at the trial to describe the aims and purposes of the Peace Information Center, he answered: "Its stated objective was to work for world peace . . . actually it was an agency of Soviet foreign policy." But he admitted under cross-examination by defense counsel Vito Marcantonio that he did not regard "these organizations as a foreign government, political party or principal." That admission caused journalist I. F. Stone to comment: "O. John Rogge betrayed himself and the cause of peace when he testified for the government . . . if this is his opinion; he should have been a witness for the defense, not for the prosecution" (*National Guardian*, Nov. 21, 1951).

84 Greenglass . . . had thought of Rogge: David and Ruth Greenglass/Rogge interview, March 21, 1979.

84 Greenglass, whose own political loyalties were drifting: Ibid.

85 His confused state of mind: Memo from Herbert Fabricant to O. John Rogge, June 16, 1950, O. John Rogge papers, law offices of O. John Rogge, New York City.

The above was one of several memos stolen from the Rogge-Fabricant office in 1953 by anonymous Rosenberg defense-committee partisans and subsequently printed (in abbreviated form) in

Paris newspapers. The memos were then reprinted by the National Committee to Secure Justice in the Rosenberg Case and were widely circulated in the United States. We are quoting from the complete memos as they appear in the files of O. John Rogge—not from the versions published by the defense committee.

85 Ruth Greenglass, meanwhile: J. Edgar Hoover to Assistant Attorney General James M. McInerney, June 25, 1950, Greenglass file. Hoover's letter relates the contents of an interview held by agents with Ruth on June 16.

85 That same afternoon, Ruth heard: Fabricant memo, June 16, 1950.

85 Rogge and his other law partner: Memo initialed by Robert H. Gordon, June 19, 1950, Rogge papers.

85–86 Rogge recalled his shock and dismay: Interview with O. John Rogge by Ronald Radosh and Sol Stern, June 10, 1978. Also see Gordon memo, June 19, 1950.

86 Rogge laid out for the group: Memo from Herbert Fabricant to files, n.d. [the memo reflects the details of the visit of June 19, 1950], Rogge papers. Also see Gordon memo, June 19, 1950.

86–87 Rogge met with ... Saypol: Memo by Raymond F. Whearty, reporting on Irving Saypol's interview with Rogge on June 21, 1950, Rogge file.

87 Rogge called the Washington office: D. M. Ladd to J. Edgar Hoover, June 21, 1950, Rogge file.

88 Hoover penned a warning: Hoover's handwritten comments are added on to Ladd to Hoover, June 26, 1950, Rogge file.

88 "It was all in my mind . . .": David and Ruth Greenglass interview, June 12, 1979.

88 Rogge informed the FBI: FBI teletype, June 28, 1950; Hoover to Assistant Attorney General McInerney, June 30, 1950, Greenglass file.

4: "YOUR GUY AND MY GUY ARE RELATIVES"

Page

89 a penciled note from Hoover: A. H. Belmont to D. M. Ladd, June 15, 1950, folder titled, "Unknown American #5," Rosenberg file.

89–90 told Rosenberg . . . Greenglass had been picked up: Julius Rosenberg's account of his FBI interrogation may be found in the Trial Transcript, pp. 1137–41. See also "Urgent" teletype to Washington, Newark, and Philadelphia from New York, June 17, 1950, Rosenberg file.

90 Harrington abruptly changed course: The conversation here is from the Trial Transcript, pp. 1137–41.

90 From Foley Square, Julius Rosenberg went: Interview with Victor Rabinowitz by Ronald Radosh, Oct. 28, 1978. Years earlier, in 1945, Rabinowitz had served Rosenberg as a FAECT lawyer. See FBI report of Special Agent Edward E. Kachelhoffer, July 3, 1950, reviewing personnel files of the U.S. Army Signal Corps, St. Louis, Missouri. The agent's report cites a letter by Rabinowitz to the secretary of war, Feb. 16, 1945, protesting the Corps's dismissal of Rosenberg.

91 Bloch apparently had no premonition: Bloch is quoted in an interview conducted by critic John Wexley in his book *The Judgment of Julius and Ethel Rosenberg* (New York: Cameron and Kahn, 1955), pp. 113–14. Wexley cites this interview in the original 1955 hardcover edition of his book; he has deleted the reference to it in the 1977 paperback edition.

91–92 Nelson, a former close friend: Nelson's own account of this episode is in Steve Nelson, James R. Barrett, and Rob Ruck, *Steve Nelson: American Radical* (Pittsburgh: University of Pittsburgh Press, 1981), pp. 294–95. Nelson asserts sharply, "I never had any links with Soviet espionage in the United States" and argues that the charges against him were "backed up only with the false testimony of FBI agents and informers." He considers that the government might have been seeking to "build up an atomic spy conspiracy linking me to Oppenheimer," since he and Oppenheimer would have been "bigger and probably more plausible targets than the Rosenbergs." Nelson also says he simply could not have been engaged in espionage, since it "would have been political suicide for the district leader to risk implication in any illegal activities."

Other accounts differ from Nelson's. See, for example, Anthony Cave Brown and Charles B. MacDonald, *On a Field of Red: The Communist International and the Coming of World War II* (New York: Putnam's, 1981), pp. 620–22. The authors of this book charge that FBI files show that Joseph W. Weinberg, a former Oppenheimer student, had passed to Nelson what Major General Leslie Groves described as "the object and progress of the project, materials and means used, and the location of other installations engaged." Nelson purportedly passed this data to a Soviet vice-consul in San Francisco, and FBI phone taps proved that the vice-consul in turn passed it on to the KGB chief in North America. They also state that Oppenheimer had admitted to U.S. Army counterintelligence that an unnamed American CP leader had tried to get him to provide information about the atomic bomb.

92 his normal day-to-day routine: Teletype, Washington from New York, from SA A. J. Tuohy, June 14, 1950, Rosenberg file.

92–93 a surveillance man's nightmare: Ibid.

93 In spite of Tuohy's reluctance: Trial Transcript, pp. 1203–04.

94 This speculation was capped: The *Journal-American*'s dispatch is cited in Tuohy teletype, June 14, 1950.

94 Ruth later claimed in court: Trial Transcript, p. 714.

94 Ruth . . . was actually afraid that Ethel: Interview with David and Ruth Greenglass by Ronald Radosh and Sol Stern, June 12, 1979, conducted at the law office of O. John Rogge.

95 Bernard would dismiss the family-feud theory: Memo of Herbert J. Fabricant to O. John Rogge, reporting on an interview of Bernard Greenglass by Emanuel Bloch, October 27, 1950, held in the presence of Fabricant; O. John Rogge papers.

95–96 At his wit's end, Tuohy teletyped: Teletype to Washington from New York, from SA A. J. Tuohy, June 14, 1950, Rosenberg file.

96 David had agreed to submit to another interrogation: Teletype to Washington and Philadelphia from New York, by SA Edward Scheidt, July 14, 1950, Greenglass file.

96 David's Monday statement: Signed statement of David Greenglass, July 17, 1950, Greenglass file.

97 "the solicitude of the Dept. . . .": A. H. Belmont, memorandum for D. M. Ladd, June 17, 1950, with Hoover's handwritten note on the bottom, Rosenberg file.

97 Ethel . . . had the presence of mind: A. H. Belmont to D. M. Ladd, July 17, 1950, Rosenberg file.

97–98 "Your guy and my guy . . .": Interview with O. John Rogge by Ronald Radosh and Sol Stern, July 10, 1978; interview with Herbert J. Fabricant by Ronald Radosh, July 11, 1978. Fabricant independently offered his recollection of this event, and stressed that this plea by Bloch is what convinced him of the Rosenbergs' guilt.

98 "Neither my husband nor I . . .": *Journal-American*, July 18, 1950, p. 1.

98–99 "The indications are definite . . .": Belmont to Ladd, July 17, 1950.

99 "There is no question . . .": J. Edgar Hoover confidential to attorney general, July 19, 1950, Rosenberg file.

99 Saypol's eagerness shocked Richard Whelan: A. H. Belmont to D. M. Ladd, Aug. 1, 1950, Rosenberg file.

99 Belmont fired off a private memo: Ibid.

100 Irving Saypol may have foreseen: A. H. Belmont to D. M. Ladd, August 10, 1950, Rosenberg file.

102 Arrest left Ethel devastated: The account of Ethel's reaction to her arrest is based on Virginia Gardner, *The Rosenberg Story* (New York: Masses and Mainstream, 1954), pp. 72–84.

5: THE OTHER SPY RING

Page

104 Joel Barr disappeared: FBI file, July 30, 1950, at Paris, France, received via State Department, Sarant file. See also New York to J. Edgar Hoover, Aug. 9, 1950, Barr file.

104 That same day, in New York: All material and notes pertaining to Sobell and his activities are to be found in chapter 16.

104–05 For Sarant and Dayton disappearance, see FBI teletype, Albany to director and special agent in charge, New York, July 26, 1950, Sarant file.

105 William Perl, a noted aeronautical engineer: Letter of Special Agent R. J. Abbaticchio to J. Edgar Hoover, July 27, 1950, Perl file.

105 David Greenglass had been able: Signed statement of David Greenglass, July 17, 1950, Rosenberg file.

105 Joel Barr was also: Barr's 1948 file opens with a memo, headed "Strictly Confidential," referring to Barr's suspected 1944 activities, noting he "is believed to have acted as an intermediary between person or persons who were working on wartime nuclear fission research and for MGB agents." "Report on Unknown Subject" by SA T. Scott Miller, Jr., Oct. 18, 1948, Barr file. (As explained earlier, the MGB is one of the earlier incarnations of the KGB.)

106 the FBI had somehow learned: FBI teletype, Office of the Director to Communications Section, July 25, 1950, Barr file. See also New York to Hoover, Aug. 9, 1950, Barr file. This latter memo notes that "Legal Attache in Paris was instructed on July 25, to locate and interview Barr concerning his knowledge of and participation in the espionage activities of the Rosenberg network," and that "Barr has not yet been located in France, although it was known that he was in Paris on June 2, 1950."

106 The landlady of the Villa Régine: FBI file, July 30, 1950, at Paris, France.

106 FBI agents interrogating Greenglass found: Signed statement of David Greenglass, July 17, 1950. Greenglass stated that Rosen-

berg "said that more important persons than I have left the country already and that Joel Barr had left the U.S. before Fuchs was arrested and is doing work for the Russians overseas." Also see FBI report of interview with Ruth Greenglass, teletype to Washington, to Hoover and Special Agent in Charge, July [date not decipherable, but most likely July 17] 1950, Rosenberg file. The report states: "Ruth said that Joel Barr used to visit Julius and Ethel Rosenberg years ago and that Barr went to Europe under the pretext of studying music. She believes that he travels extensively. She thought Barr went to Finland about a year or two ago."

107 The development of airborne radar systems: James F. Baxter III, *Scientists Against Time* (Cambridge: M.I.T. Press, 1968), p. 96; see also all of chapter 6, "Air Warfare," pp. 83–99.

107 The mathematical theory for such "computers": Steven J. Heims, *John von Neumann and Norbert Wiener: From Mathematics to the Technologies of Life and Death* (Cambridge: M.I.T. Press, 1980). According to Heims, from 1943 to 1945 von Neumann was serving as a consultant to the Navy Bureau of Ordnance.

108 As Ted Taylor . . . told the FBI: Report on Joel Barr by SA Frederick C. Bauckham, Oct. 20, 1951, Barr file.

108 Eric J. Isbister: Ibid.

108 In a written statement submitted: "Report on Unknown Subject" by Miller, Oct. 18, 1948.

108–09 when Barr first began talking: Report on Joel Barr by SA Frederick C. Bauckham, Sept. 11, 1950, Barr file.

109 The text of this message: "Report on Unknown Subject" by Miller, Oct. 18, 1948.

109 In the course of trying: Ibid.

109–10 "[A] confidential source further advised . . .": Report on Joel Barr, June 1951 [no exact date], Barr file.

110 One of the first people: Summary of interview with A. Sarant, July 20, 1950, Sarant file. See also memo to agent Kelley re: Security Index Listing, n.d. [1950], Sarant file.

110 a "highly confidential" informant: This information and the FBI's attempts to verify it are discussed in C. E. Hennrich to A. H. Belmont on Morton Sobell, Nov. 20, 1950, Sobell file.

110 On the afternoon of July 19, 1950: FBI teletype, Albany to Washington, July 20, 1950, Sarant file.

111 They did not believe: For Wall's comments see memo from A. H. Belmont to D. M. Ladd, July 19, 1950, Sarant file.

111 Sarant continued to "stand for it": For a summary of interviews with Sarant for period from July 19 to July 25, 1950, see report by SA John D. Mahoney, Albany Division, Oct. 17, 1950, Glassman

file; see also report by Peter Maxson on Julius and Ethel Rosenberg, Aug. 7, 1950, Rosenberg file.

112 the picture that emerges of the Morton Street apartment: See, for example, the summary of an account of a party at Sarant's apartment offered the FBI by Helene Elitcher. She recounted an evening in 1946 when she and her husband, Max, William Perl, Julius Rosenberg, Joel Barr, and Morton Sobell went to 65 Morton Street. "They found the apartment darkened, and people inside the apartment sitting around listening to music from a record player." At yet another visit, she, Julius Rosenberg, and Joel Barr went to Sarant's apartment, "they found that he was asleep in bed, but he got up, admitted them to his apartment, and played some recordings for them." Interview of Helene Elitcher, Sept. 7, 1950, by SA Charles F. Silverthorn and Vincent J. Cahill, in report of Vincent J. Cahill, Oct. 2, 1950, Elitcher file.

112–13 When the romance broke up: See FBI interviews with Nathan and Gertrude Sussman, in report of SA Robert F. Royal, April 14, 1951, interview conducted March 17, 1951, pp. 17–23 of file.

113 At least partial confirmation: Interview with Gladys Meyer by Ronald Radosh, July 25, 1978.

113 A confidential source, presumably inside: Report of Mahoney, Oct. 17, 1950.

114 FBI investigators in New York sought out: Edward Scheidt teletype to J. Edgar Hoover and SAC, July 1950 (date illegible but from content obviously after July 19), Sarant file.

114 Confronted with this description, Sarant denied: Report of Maxson, Aug. 7, 1950.

114 he and Joel Barr had rented a storefront: See summary of a July 25, 1950, interview regarding this storefront in report on Joel Barr by SA Frederick C. Bauckham, Oct. 11, 1950, Barr file.

114 But when Sarant was first asked: Report of Maxson, Aug. 7, 1950.

115 the letter was Sarant's reply: Alfred Sarant to Navy Bureau of Ships, June 27, 1945, addendum to report of Mahoney, Oct. 17, 1950.

115 Sarant is described in an FBI report: Report of Mahoney, Oct. 17, 1950.

116 Under the circumstances, the FBI office: FBI teletype, Albany to director and SAC, New York, July 26, 1950.

116 Mrs. Electra Jayson, the only member: Interview with Electra Jayson by Sol Stern, April 16, 1979.

117 U.S. consular officials in Spain finally managed: Report on Barr by Bauckham, Oct. 11, 1950.

117 A supporting report in the FBI files: "Re: Joel Barr," Confidential FBI report-File 65-15392-668, date of report unreadable, Barr file.

117–18 In a recent interview, Samuel Perl confirmed: Interview with Samuel Perl by Sol Stern, July 8, 1978.

118 This is exactly the theory: Walter and Miriam Schneir, *Invitation to an Inquest* (Baltimore: Penguin, 1973), pp. 304–05.

118 During the stressful days following: Ibid. The Schneirs base their account on testimony given by Weldon Bruce Dayton during a court appearance relating to the State Department's refusal to grant him a passport so that he could accept a teaching position abroad (*Dayton v. Dulles*, 357 U.S. 144 [1958]).

118–19 A letter written by Carol Dayton: Carol Dayton to Judith Bregman, Aug. 8, 1950, in report of SA Frederick M. Connors on Alfred Sarant, Sept. 7, 1950, Sarant file.

120 The suggestion . . . that Sarant and Dayton: Interviews with Philip Morrison by Ronald Radosh, Sept. 19 and Nov. 13, 1978.

120 Joel Barr's disappearance: Not even Walter and Miriam Schneir had been able to come up with a plausible explanation. In later editions of their book *Invitation to an Inquest* (issued in 1968 and 1973 respectively), the Schneirs cite a leaked report given to *Look* magazine in 1957 (see issue of Oct. 29) that said that Barr and Sarant have "disappeared behind the Iron Curtain," only to quote an article in *The Nation* magazine that criticized this report as "biased." The Schneirs note that the two men were "previously reported to be in Western Europe and Mexico, respectively" but fail to add that neither has been heard from since the summer of 1951. The Schneirs' lack of curiosity about this particular aspect of the Rosenberg case is striking. (See pp. 296–98 in the 1973 Penguin edition.)

120 a *Look* magazine reporter: Bill Davidson, "Exclusive: The Atomic Bomb and Those Who Stole It," *Look*, Oct. 29, 1957.

121 As for the relatives: Interview with Louise Sarant by Ronald Radosh, May 22, 1978; interview with Bernard Barr by Sol Stern, July 31, 1978; interview with Weldon Bruce Dayton by Sol Stern, May 15, 1978.

121 Perl gave a rather vague account: FBI teletype from SA R. J. Abbaticchio in Cleveland office to J. Edgar Hoover and SAC, July 20, 1950, Perl file.

121 Then, on July 24, Perl phoned: Letter of Abbaticchio to Hoover, July 27, 1950.

121–22 "she had been instructed . . .": Signed statement of William Perl,

July 26, 1950, contained in a report by SA John B. O'Donoghue on Vivian Glassman, Aug. 8, 1950, Glassman file.

123–24 The living room was furnished: Memo on William Perl, summarizing interview of SA's Edward Cahill and Harold F. Good with Mr. and Mrs. Joseph Blum, July 27, 1950, Perl file. Mrs. Blum was a relative who had had occasion to visit Perl at Morton Street.

124 the NACA loyalty board found out: In an April 22, 1950, letter to James J. Kelley, Jr., chairman of the NACA loyalty board, Perl responded to questions about Barr and Sarant by saying that he knew Barr only slightly from CCNY and had been introduced to Sarant by Barr. He insisted that his true residence in New York had been with his parents and that he had used the Morton Street apartment only occasionally, as a solitary place to study. NACA followed up this letter with a seven-item questionnaire. One of the questions asked Perl to explain Henrietta Savidge's claim that Joel Barr had once been a guest in their home. Perl denied that Barr had ever visited them. It is understandable that Perl, even if completely innocent, would have sought to minimize his past contacts with Barr in order to avoid being tainted by association. Nevertheless, the number of obvious lies in Perl's replies to this questionnaire are striking. Perl says, for example, that he lived at Morton Street intermittently between the fall of 1946 and the spring of 1948, calling first to make sure that "he [Sarant] and his family were away." But, of course, the Sarants were living in Ithaca at this time, as Perl must have known. It may well be asked whether NACA's interest in Joel Barr and the Morton Street apartment as of May 1950 did not indicate that the FBI was already focusing its attention in this direction, for reasons that had nothing to do with Julius Rosenberg. Apparently, however, there was an element of coincidence at work. It seems that the loyalty board had first raised questions about the past political associations of Perl's ex-wife. She, in turn, was interviewed and mentioned, perhaps in all innocence, that Perl knew Barr (who had been the subject of FBI and CIA espionage investigations in 1948) and that he had once lived at the Morton Street address. NACA was curious about Morton Street, first because Perl had failed to list it as a residence in his original questionnaire, and second because the lease was in the name of Sarant, a suspected Communist and associate of Barr's. The questionnaire asks nothing about the presence of photographic equipment in the apartment, or of other circumstances that might be related to espionage; however, it does inquire about the presence of "Communist literature."

Copies of Perl's NACA file that came into FBI hands at a later date included numerous letters of reference submitted on Perl's behalf in late April and early May 1950, attesting to his patriotism and good character. William Perl file.

125–26 two more "suspicious" incidents: Signed statement of William Perl, July 28, 1950, Perl file.

126 The chief result of Perl's attempts: The interview with Glassman is included in FBI teletype on Vivian Glassman, Aug. 4, 1950, Glassman file.

127 In spite of the fact that she had no idea: Ibid.

128 Summoned to appear before the grand jury: J. Edgar Hoover to SAC, New York, Sept. 7, 1950, Glassman file.

128 She still refuses to comment: Interview with Vivian Glassman by Ronald Radosh, June 13, 1978.

6: MAX ELITCHER: THE RIDE TO CATHERINE SLIP

Page

130 One name that stood out: FBI memorandum on Max and Helene Elitcher, prepared by Special Agent Vincent J. Cahill, Aug. 5, 1950, Elitcher file.

130–31 Elitcher had first come to the attention: Investigative report on Morton Sobell and Max Elitcher, U.S. Naval Intelligence, prepared by Lt. W. C. Shipman, USNR, Jan. 3, 1941, Sobell file; also report of Corrado J. Agliette to inspector general, headquarters, U.S. Air Force, Nov. 18, 1948, Sobell file.

For a summary of the 1948 surveillance, see also J. Edgar Hoover to Edward Scheidt, Jan. 17, 1950, Sobell file; and authorization for technical surveillance in "Memorandum for the Attorney General," signed by Hoover, June 18, 1948, and memo by SA T. Scott Miller, Jr., Oct. 15, 1948, both in Elitcher file.

131 His friend Morton Sobell had not appeared: Signed statement of Max Elitcher, July 20, 1950, witnessed by SA's Vincent J. Cahill and James T. O'Brien. On Sobell's absence from work, see also memo on Morton Sobell by SA Rex I. Shroder, Aug. 5, 1950, p. 16 of file, Sobell file.

132 That afternoon, Max Elitcher sat down: Statement of Max Elitcher, July 20, 1950.

132 "the great role Russia was playing . . .": Ibid.

132 During this meeting, Elitcher later recalled: Cahill, memo on Max and Helene Elitcher, Aug. 5, 1950, p. 6 of file under heading, "Additional Information re: Julius Rosenberg."

133 Questioned repeatedly about this, Elitcher: Ibid., p. 32 of file, based on interviews with Elitcher on July 20, 21, 22, 24, 25, 26, and 27, 1950.

133 Elitcher learned that Helene: Interview of Helene Elitcher by SA's Robert F. Royal and Edward F. McCarthy on July 20, 1950, included in Cahill memo on Max and Helene Elitcher, Aug. 5, 1950, pp. 34–38. Also see Helene Elitcher's handwritten statement to her lawyer, O. John Rogge, describing the events of that day, Rogge papers.

134 In retrospect, the thick files: See report on Sobell and Elitcher by Lt. Shipman, USNR, Jan. 3, 1941; "Report re: Morton Sobell, Suspected Communist," prepared by Ensign C. T. Wilson, Jr., USNR, for U.S. Naval Intelligence Service, Third Naval District, New York, for period Nov. 19–25, 1941, Sobell file.

135 At first the FBI's efforts: Cahill memo on Max and Helene Elitcher, Aug. 5, 1950.

135 Then, on July 24, the Washington office: Memo on Sobell by Shroder, Aug. 5, 1950, p. 22.

135 a check of airline records: Ibid., p. 23.

136 His quite accurate assessment: Memo on internal security by SA Vincent J. Cahill, March 31, 1952, Elitcher file.

136 This lack of progress: Memo of Myles Lane to files, Aug. 3, 1950, Department of Justice files.

136 McInerney sympathetically suggested: Ibid.

136–37 Two days later, Edward Scheidt: Special Agent in Charge Edward Scheidt to J. Edgar Hoover, Aug. 5, 1950; Scheidt to Hoover, Sept. 21, 1950, reiterating the New York bureau chief's reluctance to waste time interviewing Elitcher about his political past; both in Elitcher file.

137 By mid-August 1950: For Sobell's own account of his kidnapping see "Joinder by Sobell in Motion and Denial Thereof," Trial Transcript, pp. 1586–93.

138 In a brief statement announcing Sobell's arraignment: Saypol quoted in William A. Reuben, *The Atom Spy Hoax* (New York: Action Books, 1955), p. 458.

138 The next morning, the New York *Daily News*: New York *Daily News*, Aug. 19, 1950; New York *Herald Tribune*, Aug. 19, 1950.

138 Helen Sobell, who had made her own way: See John Wexley, *The Judgment of Julius and Ethel Rosenberg* (New York: Cameron and Kahn, 1955), pp. 170–71. Wexley bases his account on his interview with Helen Sobell and on an article by Mrs. Sobell in the *National Guardian*, Nov. 30, 1953. This discussion, however, is deleted from the 1977 paperback edition of Wexley's book. See

also a somewhat different account presented by Sobell himself, in his memoir, *On Doing Time* (New York: Scribner's, 1974).

138–39 Elitcher's story involved a house-hunting trip: Signed statement of Max Elitcher, Oct. 23, 1950, witnessed by agents Vincent J. Cahill and Rex I. Shroder, quoted verbatim in Shroder memo on Morton Sobell, Nov. 13, 1950, Sobell file.

140 As one critic notes: Author John Wexley calls this portion of Elitcher's story "cloak and dagger material" with the aura of "a B picture scene on a water front." Why, he asks, would Sobell have gone to Catherine Slip that night "*with the same detectives* [who had followed Elitcher] *hot on his heels?*" (emphasis in the original). Wexley ignores Elitcher's statement that he believed he had left his tail behind in Manhattan. Wexley, *The Judgment of Julius and Ethel Rosenberg* (New York: Cameron and Kahn, 1955), p. 307.

140 "On July 30, 1948, the physical surveillance . . .": Memo on Max and Helene Elitcher, by Miller, Oct. 15, 1948.

141 "It should be stated . . .": Ibid.

141 In telling this story: On the discrepancy of dates, see memo on Max and Helene Elitcher by SA Vincent J. Cahill, Oct. 2, 1950, Elitcher file.

7: GORDON DEAN OF THE AEC

Page

142–43 As the prosecutors worked to prepare: The discussion is based on Roger M. Anders, "The Rosenberg Case Revisited: The Greenglass Testimony and the Protection of Atomic Secrets," *The American Historical Review*, vol. 83, no. 2 (April 1978), pp. 388–400.

143–44 Waters, who agreed, suggested: Waters to AEC, Feb. 1, 1951, file no. 403, AEC files.

144–45 In an appearance before the five: Waters to AEC, Feb. 7, 1951, file no. 403/1, AEC files.

145 In a memorandum he prepared for Saypol: Myles Lane to Irving Saypol, Feb. 14, 1951; Lane's report on "Conference at Washington, D.C. with the Atomic Energy Commission and appearance before the Joint Senate and House Committee on Atomic Energy, on February 8, 1951," Justice Department files.

145 "Greenglass has been talking . . .": Gordon Dean Diary, Feb. 6, 1951, AEC files.

145 Sure enough, when Myles Lane met: Ibid., Feb. 8, 1951.

145 Finally, Lane left the conference room: Lane to Saypol, Feb. 14, 1951.

146–48 Immediately after this conference ended: U.S. Congress, Proceedings of Joint Committee on Atomic Energy, Feb. 8, 1951, pp. 3, 6, 8–9, 14, 27. All the quotes from this meeting are from this document, and from the above cited pages; AEC files.

148 "It might be difficult . . .": Lane to Saypol, Feb. 14, 1951.

148 This concern is reflected in a letter: Irving Saypol to Peyton Ford, Feb. 13, 1951, AEC files.

148–49 Down in Washington, Gordon Dean did not: Gordon Dean Diary, March 7, 1951.

149 "We are quite disturbed . . .": Ibid.

149 he received a phone call from Hickenlooper: Ibid., March 8, 1951.

150 Dean wrote again to Peyton Ford: Gordon Dean to Peyton Ford, March 8, 1951, AEC files.

150 Picking up the telephone, he managed: Gordon Dean Diary, March 9 and 10, 1951.

150–51 After a March 2 meeting between Saypol: A. H. Belmont to D. M. Ladd, March 2, 1951, Rosenberg file.

152 first victim of the "atom spy" syndrome: Signed statement of Alfred Dean Slack, June 15, 1950, in FBI Albany, New York, report, Aug. 18, 1950, by Special Agent Paul R. Bibler, Slack file.

152 Confronted with blueprints and notes: Report of an interview with Slack on Aug. 4, 1950, and of material pertaining to Slack found in Harry Gold's residence, prepared at Knoxville, Tennessee, FBI office on Aug. 28, 1950, by SA Robert E. Marigison.

153 Brothman, known as "The Penguin": Signed statement of Elizabeth Bentley, Nov. 30, 1945.

153 "In an espionage case against Brothman . . .": J. Edgar Hoover to James M. McInerney, July 31, 1950, Gold file.

153 And indeed, when Brothman was finally: The citations for Brothman and Gold may be found in chapter 3. See, especially, D. M. Ladd to J. Edgar Hoover, May 25, 1950, Gold file.

154 these activities had gone unchecked despite: See David Dallin, *Soviet Espionage* (New Haven: Yale University Press, 1955), pp. 473–74 and chapter 9 *passim*.

154 In a tough cross-examination: Transcript of trial, *U.S. v. Brothman and Moskowitz*, U.S. District Court, Southern District of New York, Cr. No. 133–166.

155–56 The most important of these potential witnesses: Signed statement of Thomas L. Black, June 15, 1950, Black file.

The FBI was ready to bring forth witnesses who would testify to the credibility of Black's testimony. One such witness was an old friend of his named Jacob Fass. Fass told the Bureau that before the date of Gold's arrest, Black had told him about Gold's relationship with Fuchs—immediately after Gold had told Black. Fass knew as well about Black's early involvement with Soviet industrial espionage, and he told the Bureau why he never saw fit to tell them about Black's work for the Soviet Union.

> First of all, no government documents were involved. . . . Secondly, at the time he had helped them, Russia was a struggling backward country, and not considered a menace to this country. Only dedicated socialists and Trotskyites considered her a menace then. Finally, it happened in the past.

Signed statement of Jacob I. Fass, July 17, 1950; in FBI Newark Bureau Report by SA Louis G. Turner, Aug. 23, 1950, pp. 5–6; Black file.

157 Reporting the change to Hoover: A. H. Belmont to D. M. Ladd, July 19, 1950, Rosenberg file.

157 "What possible reason was there . . . ?": John Wexley, *The Judgment of Julius and Ethel Rosenberg* (New York: Cameron and Kahn, 1955), p. 205.

157 the relationship between Gold and Greenglass: Memo to Hoover, no author cited, Feb. 21, 1951, Greenglass file.

157–58 The versions of their June 1945 meeting: Signed statement of David Greenglass, June 15, 1950, Greenglass file; signed statement of Harry Gold, June 1 and July 10, 1950, Gold file. Interestingly enough, neither Gold nor David Greenglass had originally remembered that the recognition signals they had shown each other had consisted of portions of a Jell-O box label. In his first statements to the FBI, David had recalled only that the signal was a cut or torn piece of card. And Gold, in his July 10 interrogation, had spoken of "two torn pieces of paper of an irregular shape, but which matched when put together." It was Ruth Greenglass, in her first signed statement of July 17, who identified the signal as the halves of a Jell-O box panel. This was not surprising, perhaps, since it was Ruth who had allegedly watched Julius Rosenberg cut up the Jell-O package and who had kept her half of the signal in her purse for five months. The first statement in which Gold spoke of the "paper" as a Jell-O box side came on August 2, suggesting that perhaps someone had said something to refresh his memory on this point.

158–59 "During a conversation I had . . .": Signed statement of Harry

Gold, July 10, 1950, to SA's T. Scott Miller, Jr., and Richard E. Brennan, in Philadelphia, file prepared by SA Robert G. Jensen, July 24, 1950, Gold file, p. 2.

159 The record of an August 1 interrogation: Harry Gold statement, Aug. 1, 1950, questioned by Myles J. Lane, with SA's William Norton and John Harrington present, Greenglass file. The other quoted statements from the Aug. 1 interview are from this same file.

159 "I said I brought greetings . . .": Ibid.

160-61 A simultaneous interview of the two men: Memo of SA Joseph C. Walsh, Dec. 28, 1950, Philadelphia FBI, Gold file.

160 "GREENGLASS stated that GOLD introduced himself . . .": Ibid.

160-61 "Concerning the reported salutation . . .": Ibid.

161 In the words of one writer: John Anthony Scott, " 'Greetings from Julius,' The FBI Makes a Lie," pamphlet printed by the Fund for Open Information and Accountability, Inc., New York, May 1978. Scott uses these words in his analysis of the Walsh memo.

161 Historian Athan Theoharis, for example: Athan Theoharis, "A Break in the Rosenberg Case," *The Nation*, July 1, 1978, pp. 5–6.

161 Harry Gold, in a 1965 communication: Statement of Harry Gold to Augustus Ballard, Sept. 24, 1965, p. 37. This handwritten statement, refuting charges made by Walter and Miriam Schneir, that Gold was a poseur, was prepared by Gold in prison.

161 "Granted that this is about . . .": Ibid.

161-62 interview with filmmaker Alvin Goldstein: Quoted in Alvin H. Goldstein, *The Unquiet Death of Julius and Ethel Rosenberg* (New York and Westport: Lawrence Hill, 1975). The book is the text of the made-for-TV documentary produced and directed by Alvin H. Goldstein for the National Public Affairs Center for Television.

162 finally, agent Walsh was able to report: Report of SA Joseph C. Walsh, March 5, 1951, Gold file.

162 Ruth claimed that Ethel had been present: Signed statement of Ruth Greenglass, July 17, 1950, in report of SA Joseph C. Walsh, July 28, 1950, Greenglass file.

163 nearly six months since Ethel's arrest: It is significant that separate investigative reports pertaining to Ethel Rosenberg are conspicuously absent from the FBI files. Instead, one finds only scattered references to Ethel in Julius Rosenberg's file.

163 The FBI files released so far: Edward Scheidt teletype on Ruth

Greenglass, from New York to Washington, Feb. 1951 [exact date illegible]. This is Scheidt's six-page summary of his interrogation of Ruth.

163 Two days later, David Greenglass was also: Edward Scheidt teletype on David Greenglass, from New York to Washington, Feb. 1951 [exact date illegible]. In this document, Scheidt summarizes his reinterview with David.

164 "Julius took the info...": Scheidt teletype on Ruth Greenglass, Feb. 1951.

164 the explanation given by James B. Kilsheimer: Interview with James B. Kilsheimer by Sol Stern and Ronald Radosh, July 11, 1978.

164 "Almost as soon as I got...": Signed statement of David Greenglass, July 17, 1950, Greenglass file.

165 Shortly before Ethel's arrest: Statement of David Greenglass to Myles Lane, in the presence of SA William F. Norton; in Report on David Greenglass by SA John W. Lewis, Sept. 26, 1950.

165–68 during the two-and-a-half-hour interview: Interview with David and Ruth Greenglass by Sol Stein and Ronald Radosh, June 12, 1979, conducted at the law office of O. John Rogge.

167 Lane attempted to maneuver Ruth: Transcript of interrogation of Ruth Greenglass by Myles Lane, Aug. 2, 1950, Greenglass file.

169 According to this informant: Edward Scheidt to Washington, July 1951 [no exact date], FBI doc. 1125, Rosenberg file. This cites information from the FBI's major informant, Jerome Eugene Tartakow.

8: THE TRIAL BEGINS

Page

170 already familiar in outline to readers: See the following articles in the *Jewish Daily Forward* by Louis Schaeffer: "At the Home of David Greenglass—A Talk with His Wife," Aug. 20, 1950, p. 4; "Mrs. Greenglass Tells How Her Husband Was Misled by His Brother-in-law," Aug. 30, 1950, p. 4; "My Husband Was Misled, But He Is Not a Traitor, Says Ruth Greenglass," Sept. 2, 1950, p. 6. English translations of the articles appear in an FBI report by Special Agent William F. Norton, March 16, 1951, Greenglass file.

171 "...another Milton Berle": Trial Transcript, p. 1437.

171 "the nation's Number One legal hunter...": *Time*, July 23, 1951.

171 no secret to the opposing counsel: Ted Morgan, "The Rosenberg

Jury," *Esquire*, May 1975, pp. 126–27. Morgan received this information from an interview with Bloch's associate, Gloria Agrin.

172 "an indefinable tenseness...": *The New York Times*, March 7, 1951.

173 "The evidence will show," Saypol promised: Trial Transcript, p. 180. Saypol's opening statement is to be found on pp. 177–84.

175–77 Virtually the entire case: The following discussion of Elitcher's testimony is based on Trial Transcript, pp. 197–394.

176 "In the course of this conversation...": Ibid., p. 258.

176–77 Helen Sobell was particularly outraged: Mrs. Sobell told this story to numerous interviewers, including the Schneirs, who report it in *Invitation to an Inquest* (New York: Penguin, 1973), p. 326.

178 March 9 telephone conversation with Ray Whearty: Transcript of telephone conversation between Irving Saypol and Ray Whearty, March 9, 1951, 4:50 P.M., Justice Department files.

178–79 As Irving Saypol informed the judge: Trial Transcript, p. 435. All discussion pertaining to the "threat" against Elitcher and to the ruling on his pretrial statements to the FBI are based on Trial Transcript, pp. 430–38.

180 for all practical purposes unemployable: Memo from Herbert J. Fabricant to O. John Rogge, March 19, 1951, Rogge papers.

9: DAVID GREENGLASS

Page

181 David Greenglass, who followed Max Elitcher: Greenglass's testimony may be found in the Trial Transcript, pp. 394–430, 438–66, 489–500, and 510–76.

181 The heavyset, wavy-haired, twenty-nine-year-old: For accounts of David Greenglass's appearance and demeanor on the witness stand see *The New York Times*, March 10, 13, and 14, 1951.

182 The AEC hoped that certain categories: Transcript of conference between AEC liaisons and prosecutors, March 9, 1951, Justice Department files.

182 David Greenglass received stern instructions: Ibid.

182–83 Cohn backtracked, looking: Trial Transcript, p. 428.

183–84 Shortly after five o'clock: Transcript of AEC/prosecutors conference, March 9, 1951.

183 "DENSON: We proceded...": Ibid.

185 "SAYPOL: Well, once again, so that...": Trial Transcript, p. 470.

Koski's complete testimony appears on pp. 466–86. Koski was not a nuclear physicist, as he is frequently identified, but a physical chemist, employed by Brookhaven Laboratories at the time of the trial.

185 "SAYPOL: And up to that point . . .": Ibid., pp. 478–79.
186 "THE COURT: Counsel . . . doesn't take issue . . .": Ibid., p. 479.
186–87 "SAYPOL: Would I be exaggerating if . . .": Ibid., p. 484.
187 ". . . there was fissionable material at one end . . .": Ibid., p. 493.
188 "BLOCH: Not a strange request . . .": Ibid., p. 499.
189 "BLOCH: . . . I was not at all sure . . .": Ibid., p. 500.
189 "I would like to stipulate . . .": Ibid., p. 502.
190 the Greenglass description combined: Howard Blakeslee, in the *Albuquerque Tribune*, March 13, 1951.
191 Gloria Agrin, the young lawyer: Ted Morgan, "The Rosenberg Jury," *Esquire*, May 1975. Agrin made the same points to Ronald Radosh and Sol Stern in their December 14, 1978, interview.
191 Bloch later said that his call: This was the explanation that Bloch later gave to Irwin Edelman, an activist in the Rosenberg clemency campaign who had been publicly critical of Bloch's performance during the trial. Edelman's conversation with Bloch, which took place in Los Angeles on December 4, 1953, is described in his unpublished manuscript, "Religion, the Left and the Rosenberg Case," New York, n.d. [1970s], p. 266.
191 a "grandstand play": Agrin interview, Dec. 14, 1978. Again, Ted Morgan's article, "The Rosenberg Jury," mentions Agrin as having given an identical explanation for Bloch's action.
192 "Hollis . . . called to say . . .": Gordon Dean Diary, March 12, 1951, AEC files.
192–93 agreed that Bloch's ploy: Ibid.
193 "I was quite young . . .": Trial Transcript, p. 611.
195 "I had a kind of hero worship . . .": Ibid., p. 553.

10: RUTH GREENGLASS

Page
196 The appearance of Ruth Greenglass: The discussion of Ruth's testimony is based on the Trial Transcript, pp. 677–787.
197–98 ". . . and I asked her what . . .": Ibid., p. 691.
200 "BLOCH: . . . Did you tell Julius . . .": Ibid., p. 775.
200 "SAYPOL: I think Mr. Bloch . . .": Ibid.
200–201 "RUTH: . . . This was not . . .": Ibid., p. 786.

11: THE ARREST OF WILLIAM PERL

Page

202–03 Morton Sobell . . . first learned of Perl's arrest: Morton Sobell, *On Doing Time* (New York: Scribner's, 1974), pp. 189–92.

203 The Rosenberg-Sobell jury was never sequestered: One juror told journalist Ted Morgan: "You can shut yourself off to a certain extent, but I'd be riding on the subway, and I'm a guy that likes to read sports, you're bound to see a newspaper. . . ."

203 In discussing this incident in his book: Ted Morgan, "The Rosenberg Jury," *Esquire*, May 1975. John Wexley, *The Judgment of Julius and Ethel Rosenberg* (New York: Cameron and Kahn, 1955), pp. 488–92.

204 The U.S. Attorney's office had at least: Judith Coplon was arrested on March 4, 1949, by the FBI, in the act of passing reports to a Russian, Valentin Gubichev. Coplon had prepared the reports on the basis of information she had gathered from FBI documents available to her as a result of her job with the Department of Justice. Coplon was tried in 1949 for stealing government documents from Justice and was tried in 1950 for conspiracy to commit espionage. She was found guilty in each trial. In December 1950, Coplon's convictions were overturned on the grounds that she had been arrested without a warrant and that the government had used illegal wiretapping to gain their indictment. See David A. Shannon, *The Decline of American Communism* (New York: Harcourt Brace, 1959), pp. 78–79. Also see Allen Weinstein, *Perjury: The Hiss-Chambers Case* (New York: Knopf, 1978), pp. 402–04.

204 Hoover had been eager: Irving Saypol to James McInerney, March 9, 1951, Rosenberg file.

204 But the FBI was hard to resist: Teletype report from Edward Scheidt to J. Edgar Hoover, March 6, 1951, Perl file.

204–05 Cohn called Perl into his office: A. H. Belmont to D. M. Ladd, March 13, 1951, Perl file.

205 When the news of what Cohn had done: Ibid.

205 Saypol had informed McInerney: Saypol to McInerney, March 9, 1951.

205 Saypol went to the grand jury: L. B. Nichols addendum of March 13, 1951, to report of Belmont to Ladd, March 13, 1951. A note from Hoover is at the end of the addendum, simply stating, "I agree."

205–06 feisty Edward Kuntz: Kuntz's objections appear in the Trial Transcript, pp. 756–57.

206 Kuntz and Saypol, who were bitter enemies: Years earlier, in

1936, Kuntz and Saypol had had a political fight over Kuntz's candidacy for the Court of General Sessions on the left-wing American Labor Party ticket. During the summation at the Rosenberg trial, Kuntz almost brought up this incident to the jury, thereby risking a judicial declaration of mistrial. See note for p. 268 in chapter 18, "The Summation and the Jury's Verdict."

12: HARRY GOLD

Page

208 he recognized Julius Rosenberg from newspaper photos: Transcript of interrogation of Harry Gold by Myles J. Lane, with Special Agents William Norton and John Harrington in attendance, Aug. 1, 1950, Rosenberg file.

209 Gold badgered junior Assistant U.S. Attorney: Memo by John M. Foley, Dec. 15, 1950, Justice Dept. files. Gold, however, had visions of a melodramatic courtroom confrontation that would occur when he took the witness box, pipe in hand. Surely, he thought, Rosenberg would betray himself by giving some sign of recognition.

210 Gold began his testimony by acknowledging: Gold's testimony appears in Trial Transcript, pp. 798–848.

211 "Yakovlev then gave me . . .": Ibid., p. 822.

212 He returned to the Greenglass apartment: When Gold told Yakovlev about receiving the brother-in-law's phone number from Ruth Greenglass, the Soviet spymaster must have been appalled by the casual manner in which the Greenglasses gave out information to a courier they had never seen before.

213 "He said that a very important person . . .": Trial Transcript, p. 839.

214 ". . . Yakovlev almost went through the roof . . .": Ibid., p. 844.

215 "I didn't ask him one question . . .": Ibid., pp. 1479–80.

215 As Louis Nizer has pointed out: Nizer's discussion of Bloch's handling of Harry Gold is found in Louis Nizer, *The Implosion Conspiracy* (New York: Doubleday, 1973), pp. 172–95.

13: THE PROSECUTION WRAPS UP ITS CASE

Page

217 Dr. Bernhardt opened the proceedings: Dr. Bernhardt's testimony may be found on pp. 848–57 of the Trial Transcript.

217 The doctor then told Rosenberg: Walter and Miriam Schneir (*Invitation to an Inquest* [Baltimore: Penguin, 1973], p. 165) have pointed out that no such inoculations were legally required of tourists entering Mexico. But this does not prove that the conversation Bernhardt testified to never took place. Either Bernhardt was misinformed about the legal requirements or was discussing the inoculations he considered desirable.

218 The Rosenbergs were simply unable to believe: Emily Alman, the founder of the National Committee to Secure Justice in the Rosenberg Case, recalled to us that she had gone to a party at which Communist Party leader Gus Hall was present, and where she had said something nasty about Dr. Bernhardt. Much to her surprise, she said, Hall and the other CPers "all defended him," arguing that Bernhardt was scared that his own children and other left-wing sympathizers would be taken to the [detention] camps, and that he simply "had to do it." Interview with Emily Alman, by Sol Stern, Aug. 3, 1978.

218–20 William Danziger, the friend who had forwarded mail: Danziger's testimony is to be found in the Trial Transcript, pp. 857–67. For Danziger's story as told to the FBI, see report of Special Agent Rex I. Shroder, Sept. 21, 1950, Sobell file. Danziger's interview with SA's Charles P. Silverthorn and James T. O'Brien on Aug. 28, 1950, is summarized in this report, pp. 9–13.

219 A report, admittedly unverifiable, that the FBI: FBI teletype from Edward Scheidt to J. Edgar Hoover, April 11, 1951, reporting on information provided by informant J. E. Tartakow, Rosenberg file.

220 Giner de Los Rios . . . recalled: Trial Transcript, p. 922. His testimony appears on pp. 919–27 of the Trial Transcript.

222 "I don't think it was offered . . .": Ibid., p. 915.

223 Moreover, Bloch and his father: Ibid., pp. 919–27; the quotation on "fatal" testimony is on p. 922.

223 Bloch countered, "The reason I put it . . .": Ibid., p. 951.

14: ELIZABETH BENTLEY: THE NORFOLK CONNECTION

Page

224–26 By the time she appeared: The information pertaining to Bentley's background is summarized from her autobiography. Elizabeth Bentley, *Out of Bondage* (New York: Devin-Adair, 1951), pp. 78–139 and passim.

224 For the next several years, Bentley was: For Bentley testimony, see Trial Transcript, pp. 964–1023.

225 But Bentley's personal devotion to Golos: Bentley originally told the FBI that, between 1938 and 1945, at least two dozen Washington officials had delivered secret documents to her. The group included, according to Bentley, Lauchlin Currie, former aide to President Roosevelt; Harry Dexter White, once a director of the International Monetary Fund; and Nathan Gregory Silvermaster, who had been with the Department of Agriculture, the Board of Economic Welfare, and, after 1944, with the U.S. Treasury Department. Bentley claimed that Silvermaster had put together the group that gathered documents from government offices.

Bentley originally told her story to the FBI in 1945. She repeated it in 1948 to the federal grand jury that indicted twelve leaders of the Communist Party for violation of the Smith Act, and she also repeated portions of it to a public meeting of the Senate Investigating Committee headed by Senator Homer Ferguson on July 30, 1948, where Bentley first implicated Commerce Department official William Remington.

Bentley was then called to appear before HUAC, where she first made her entire story public. Appearing before them on July 31, Bentley made headlines with her dramatic charges that her contact with government officials resulted in her receipt of secret documents meant to be transmitted to Moscow. President Truman dismissed her accusations as false and politically motivated, and Bentley had produced no corroboration to back up her charges. Walter Goodman comments:

> That Elizabeth Bentley was associated with a Communist underground in the early nineteen-forties is certain. Much less certain from her testimony was the extent of the involvement of the officials she named. . . . She was not clear in many instances whether an official knew that he was involved with the Russians or believed that he was merely doing a good turn for the American Party. Her judgment of the quality and importance of the information that passed through her hands was extremely faulty.

Walter Goodman, *The Committee* (New York: Penguin, 1969), pp. 244–49, quote on p. 245. Also see Allen Weinstein, *Perjury: The Hiss-Chambers Case* (New York: Knopf, 1978), p. 4.

226 When Bentley decided to publish an autobiography: For a discus-

sion of the roles played by Bentley and the grand-jury foreman, John Brunini, in Remington's case see Herbert L. Packer, *Ex-Communist Witnesses: Four Studies in Fact-Finding* (Stanford, Ca.: Stanford University Press, 1962), pp. 84–90. Remington's conviction on this indictment was eventually overturned on appeal. However, Remington was tried again on technically different charges and eventually died in prison, stabbed by a fellow inmate.

226–27 Even Louis Nizer, who believed: Louis Nizer, *The Implosion Conspiracy* (New York: Doubleday, 1973), p. 178.

227 Herbert L. Packer, whose study: Packer, *Ex-Communist Witnesses,* p. 84.

227–28 Never one to minimize her own importance: Interestingly, the general description of espionage methods that Bentley gave on the witness stand had little to do with the operation of the Rosenberg ring. It was, however, an accurate description of the secret Communist underground that had flourished for a time in Washington, D.C. Bentley said, for example, that the great majority of her contacts had continued as Party members, paying dues and receiving Party literature regularly. As Bentley put it, "We kept them good Communists." An alert defense counsel might have pointed out that this method of operation directly contradicted the Greenglasses' statement that Julius and Ethel had given up open political activities when they became involved in spying.

There was another apparent contradiction between the meeting arrangements described by Harry Gold and those described by Bentley. Gold had spoken of elaborate procedures, including meetings scheduled at randomly chosen locations; by comparison, the assignation referred to by Bentley appears to have been much more casual. But these differences are an accurate reflection of the differences in operation between Golos's relatively loose operation and the more professional methods followed by Soviet controllers concerned with military espionage. The FBI obviously recognized the distinction when it guessed that Golos had met his contact in the vicinity of the latter's home.

For a discussion of the Communist underground in Washington, D.C., written by one of its former members, see Hope Hale Davis, "A Memoir: Looking Back at My Years in the Party," *The New Leader,* Feb. 11, 1980, pp. 10–18.

228 "the use of the word 'Julius' . . .": Malcolm Sharp, *Was Justice Done? The Rosenberg-Sobell Case* (New York: Monthly Review Press, 1956), p. 87.

229–30 "Another group of whose existence . . .": Signed statement of Elizabeth Bentley, Nov. 30, 1945.

231 As early as August 1950, the FBI suspected: Edward Scheidt to J. Edgar Hoover and Special Agent in Charge, Aug. 11, 1950, Bentley file.

231–32 Bentley . . . continued to stand firm: Scheidt to Hoover, Feb. 17, 1951, Bentley file.

232 "the bulk of the information . . .": Ibid.

233 Its prime suspect Julius Korchein: L. B. Nichols to Clyde Tolson, Dec. 14, 1951, Rosenberg file.

234 ". . . a survey of all the tenants . . .": Ibid.

15: JULIUS ROSENBERG FOR THE DEFENSE

Page

236 Julius's ideas of how his defense: For a discussion of the disagreement between Emanuel and Alexander Bloch, see the discussion in the original edition of John Wexley, *The Judgment of Julius and Ethel Rosenberg* (New York: Cameron and Kahn, 1955), p. 243.

237 Although Alger Hiss had been convicted: The most thorough account of the Hiss case is Allen Weinstein, *Perjury: The Hiss-Chambers Case* (New York: Knopf, 1978).

237 When the moment finally arrived: The Julius Rosenberg story and his response to cross-examination may be found in the Trial Transcript, pp. 1051–1199, 1282–86, 1307–10.

239 "KAUFMAN: Did you ever discuss . . .": Ibid., pp. 1078–79.

239–40 "BLOCH: Do you owe allegiance . . .": Ibid., p. 1079.

240 "ROSENBERG: No, I did not . . .": Ibid.

241 "Well, your Honor, are you referring . . .": Ibid., p. 1080.

241 "ROSENBERG: Ruthie told me something . . .": Ibid., p. 1089.

242 ". . . I don't remember the specific incident . . .": Ibid., p. 1108.

242 " 'Julie, you got to get me $2000 . . .' ": Ibid., p. 1119.

243 " 'Well, Julie, I just got to have the money . . . ' ": Ibid., p. 1130.

243 "everybody was very cool . . .": Ibid., p. 1131.

244–45 "Your Honor, I read in the newspapers about . . .": Ibid., pp. 1159–60.

245 "Now, in the posture of the case . . .": Ibid., p. 1160.

246 Naturally, Manny Block objected: Ibid., pp. 1164–65.

246 "Isn't it a fact . . . that you gave . . .": Ibid., pp. 1192–96.

247 "Well, I saw the name of his wife . . .": Ibid., p. 1199.

247 ". . . you couldn't buy a console table . . .": Ibid., pp. 1204–14.

248 "It didn't enter my mind . . .": Ibid., p. 1204.

249 "ROSENBERG: Well, Mr. Saypol, David Greenglass talked . . .":
Ibid., p. 1224.

250 "KAUFMAN: Blackmail you? . . .": Ibid., p. 1269.

251 "Did you go to a photographer's shop . . .": Ibid., p. 1278.

251 "I don't recall telling . . .": Ibid.

16: MORTON SOBELL'S SILENCE

Page

253–54 Morton Sobell writes in his autobiography: Morton Sobell, *On Doing Time* (New York: Scribner's, 1974), p. 92.

255 Comparing Sobell's own account: Memorandum entitled "Martin [*sic*] Sobell—Cross examination," Justice Department files. There are no initials indicating which member of the prosecution team drew up these tentative questions, to be asked of Sobell if he underwent cross-examination. Other documents in the series indicate most questions of this sort were composed by either Myles Lane or Roy Cohn.

255–56 "In addition to . . .": Sobell, *On Doing Time*, p. 60.

256 "The evening headlines on Friday, June 16 . . .": Ibid.

257 "One peculiarity of my character . . .": Ibid., p. 58.

257–58 With just this turn of events: Interview with Edward J. Garrett, in FBI investigative report of Jan. 2, 1951, pp. 122–23, FBI Document 646, Rosenberg file.

258 In addition to a long list: Justice Department memo on cross-examination of Morton Sobell.

258 the prosecutors wanted to ask Sobell: FBI memo by Special Agent Rex I. Shroder, Aug. 5, 1950, Sobell file.

17: ETHEL ROSENBERG IN COURT

Page

259–63 Ethel's examination by Alexander Bloch: Ethel Rosenberg's testimony is found in the Trial Transcript, pp. 1293–1306, 1310–77, 1378–97, and 1398–1402.

263 *Grunewald v. United States*: The Grunewald case involved a prosecution for conspiracy to evade taxes. One of the accused conspirators (not Grunewald) had taken the Fifth Amendment before a federal grand jury. In a 1957 decision the Supreme Court ruled, five to four, that this grand-jury testimony should not have been allowable at the trial for purposes of demonstrating inconsistency. The court's decision noted that there could be numerous reasons

for taking the Fifth Amendment before the grand jury, not all of them necessarily inconsistent with a subsequent decision to testify.

263 "I didn't believe I was guilty . . .": Trial Transcript, p. 1396.

263–64 Saypol informed the court: Evelyn Cox's testimony is in ibid., pp. 1406–12.

264 Mrs. Cox was followed: Helen Pagano's testimony is in ibid., pp. 1420–22.

264 Saypol's third rebuttal witness: Ben Schneider's testimony is in ibid., pp. 1424–40.

265 These suspicions quickened in 1952: Oliver Pilat, *The Atom Spies* (New York: Putnam's, 1952), p. 287.

266 "Now there are some Saturdays . . .": Trial Transcript, pp. 1436–37.

18: THE SUMMATION AND THE JURY'S VERDICT

Page

267–68 Manny Bloch, as the chief defense lawyer: Bloch's summation may be found in the Trial Transcript, pp. 1452–92.

268 Edward Kuntz . . . displayed no such hesitation: Kuntz's summation may be found in ibid., pp. 1493–1507.

When it came Saypol's turn to make his summation, he tried to retort personally, by implying that when Kuntz had argued it was no crime to travel to Mexico, he was acting out of an attempt to settle an old score—a fight he had had with Saypol years earlier over Kuntz's political life in the left-wing American Labor Party. Thus Saypol interrupted by stating to the jury that Kuntz had run for the court of general sessions in 1936 on the American Labor Party ticket. Judge Kaufman immediately remonstrated: "No, let us not get into that," and Emanuel Bloch objected that "any discussion about Edward Kuntz in any of his political ideas or candidacy might prejudice my client." Saypol answered that he had mentioned Kuntz's 1936 candidacy only to illustrate to the jury what motive Kuntz might have had "to get even with me." Ibid., pp. 1510–12.

In an interview, Roy Cohn claimed that Kaufman called the lawyers to the bench after noticing that Saypol had brought with him an old 1930s issue of the *New York Law Journal* with material on their old fight in that era. Realizing that Saypol was planning to read the material to the jury, Kaufman told Saypol that he would take such an action to mean that Saypol was calling Kuntz a Communist, and that he would then declare a mistrial. Cohn has told others that it was he who had spotted Saypol's copy of the journal, and having anticipated Saypol's plan, had informed Kaufman. If that version is true, it amounts to an unprecedented *ex parte* communication. Cohn also says that it was he, not Saypol, who traveled to Mexico to gather evidence pertaining to Sobell's flight. Interview with Roy Cohn by Ronald Radosh and Sol Stern, June 15, 1978. Cohn's version of his role in stopping Saypol from elaborating on his old fight with Kuntz comes from conversations with an anonymous source who is close to Cohn.

268–69 The privilege of speaking last: Saypol's summation may be found in the Trial Transcript, pp. 1508–36.

269 "These defendants before you . . .": Ibid., p. 1535.

270 There was not a single Jew: After the trial, the charge would frequently be made that anti-Semitism played a part in the case; that the absence of Jews on the jury indicated a strong bias on the part of the jurors against the defendants. Ironically, as the panel proceeded into the courtroom to announce its verdict, a small bit of evidence was uncovered that indicated the possibility that indeed at least one of the jurors—the foreman—might have had an anti-Semitic bias.

As the jury walked to the courtroom, Associated Press reporter Jimmy Parlatore and several other newsmen decided to take a look at the room used by the jurors during their deliberations. "There," FBI official A. H. Belmont noted, "they found two pieces of paper, one of which appeared to be merely doodling on the part of a juror; the other, a sheet of paper near the head of the table where the Foreman of the jury would sit. This sheet of paper carried the word 'Jude.' "

Reporter Parlatore was quite disturbed—not at the implications of what was on the paper, but at his realization that "should the [left of center] *Compass* or the *Daily Worker* get wind of this, they might charge the jury with anti-Semitism." Parlatore handed the paper with the word "Jude" to the FBI rather than to the U.S. attorney or to Judge Kaufman. As for the FBI, agent Edward Scheidt called this to the attention of prosecutor Saypol, so that the FBI "would not be holding it in the event [one of the other reporters] printed an article concerning it." A. H. Belmont to D. M. Ladd, March 29, 1951, Rosenberg file.

270 ff As Charles Duda, youngest of the jurors: Ted Morgan, "The Rosenberg Jury," *Esquire*, May 1975. Unless otherwise noted, all other citations from the views of jurors are from Ted Morgan's article.

271 "The desire to avoid the performance . . .": Trial Transcript, pp. 1574–75.

19: THE SENTENCING

Page

275 One of the first and most chilling: New York *Journal-American*, April 3, 1951. Leonard Lyons columns appeared in the New York *Post*, April 6 and 9, 1951; Hy Gardner's column appeared in the New York *Herald Tribune*, April 12, 1951.

276 Roy Cohn has told us: Interview with Roy Cohn by Ronald Radosh and Sol Stern, June 15, 1978.

276 "Whether or not the death penalty . . .": "Memorandum re: Sentence Recommendation for Julius and Ethel Rosenberg et al."; James B. Kilsheimer to Irving Saypol, April 5, 1951, Justice Department files.

276 Julius and Ethel Rosenberg stood before him: Trial Transcript, p. 1612.

277 The first indication that Judge Kaufman: Gordon Dean Diary, Feb. 7, 1951, AEC files.

277 Dean himself, as a member of the bar: A further entry in Dean's diary supports the conclusion that Gordon Dean believed Judge Kaufman could be approached. On March 8, two days after the trial opened, Dean had a lengthy phone conversation with Republican Senator Bourke Hickenlooper, who was highly agitated about the possibility that prosecutor Saypol might mishandle the presentation of the technical evidence in the case. Attempting to calm Hickenlooper's fears, Dean assured the senator that "as a matter of fact, he would tell the judge we are concerned about the scope of this thing. There is a national interest in this and if it comes to that, GD [Dean] thinks he will do that [tell the judge we are concerned]."

Did Dean ever carry out his intention of taking his concern over the national-security implications of the case directly to Kaufman? His diary does not answer this question one way or the other. Ibid., March 8, 1951.

277 "While talking to Whearty . . .": A. H. Belmont to D. M. Ladd, March 16, 1951. This memo, along with some others cited in this chapter, has been distributed by the National Committee to Re-Open the Rosenberg Case, in a booklet entitled: "The Kaufman Papers" (New York, n.d. [c. 1975]).

278 Thus, according to information: D. M. Ladd to J. Edgar Hoover, April 3, 1951, Rosenberg file.

278 Roy Cohn not only has denied: Letter of Roy Cohn, *The New Republic*, Aug. 4–11, 1979, pp. 25–26.

278–79 a 1975 letter from Irving Saypol: Irving Saypol to Clarence Kelley, March 13, 1975, Rosenberg file. Also printed in "The Kaufman Papers."

279 The first indication of uneasiness: J. Edgar Hoover to Tolson, Ladd, Belmont, and Nichols, April 2, 1951, Rosenberg file.

280 When Ladd complied, Hoover personally annotated: D. M. Ladd to J. Edgar Hoover, April 2, 1951. See also a supplemental memo by Ladd dated April 3 and "Memorandum for the Director" signed by W. M. Whelan, April 3, 1951, for additional insights into the FBI's views on the possible sentences. For Hoover's formal recommendation, see Memorandum for the Attorney General, April 2, 1951, Rosenberg file.

281 "although the evidence was not as great . . .": Ibid.

281 "It was at a public function . . .": Saypol to Kelley, March 13, 1975.

282 Irving Saypol chimed in his agreement: Trial Transcript, p. 1599.

282 Attacking Saypol for his attempt: Ibid., p. 1608–12.

283 Reacting to Bloch's argument: Ibid., pp. 1612–16.

283 "The issue of punishment . . .": Ibid., pp. 1613–14.

285 Kaufman . . . visited his synagogue: *The New York Times*, April 6, 1951.

285 "the FBI did a fabulous job . . .": A. H. Belmont to D. M. Ladd, April 5, 1951, Rosenberg file. The next day Hoover wrote a reply to Kaufman, expressing his "heartfelt appreciation" of the judge's compliments and noting that "the Communist underground ranks . . . have been stunned by your forthright action." Hoover to Kaufman, April 6, 1951.

285 Only one coconspirator remained: For the text of the Greenglass sentencing hearing, see Trial Transcript, pp. 1621–38.

286 aware of the talk of capital sentences: Rogge's quoted remarks in filmmaker Alvin H. Goldstein's 1975 television documentary, *The Unquiet Death of Julius and Ethel Rosenberg*, leaves no doubt that he blamed David's relatively lengthy sentence on Kaufman's grandstanding. "When the time came for the sentencing," Rogge told Goldstein, "the judge wrapped himself in the flag." Also quoted in the printed version of the filmscript, *The Unquiet Death of Julius and Ethel Rosenberg* (New York: Lawrence Hill, 1975).

286–87 Rogge delivered an impassioned plea: Trial Transcript, pp. 1624–36.

287 While praising Rogge: Ibid., pp. 1637–38.
287 an effusively fawning profile: Oliver Pilat, "Rosenberg Case: Judge Kaufman's Two Terrible Years," *Saturday Evening Post*, Aug. 8, 1953.
288 The first hint that it might not: *Jewish Day*, April 16, 1951, cited in John Wexley, *The Judgment of Julius and Ethel Rosenberg* (New York: Cameron and Kahn, 1955), pp. 604–06.
288 A remark made by Vincent Lebonitte: Quoted in Ted Morgan, "The Rosenberg Jury," *Esquire*, May 1975.
Ironically, if the FBI memo referred to in the note for p. 270 can be believed—indicating that the jury foreman had scribbled the word "Jude" on a piece of paper—Lebonitte might have harbored anti-Semitic feelings himself.
288 Another theory, advanced more recently: Daniel Yergin, "Victims of a Desperate Age," *New Times*, May 16, 1975, pp. 21–28.
289 As one lawyer who has practiced: Interview with source who has requested anonymity.
289–90 "he was not a government man . . .": Alan M. Dershowitz, *The Best Defense* (New York: Random House, 1982), p. 74.

20: AN INFORMANT OF UNKNOWN RELIABILITY

Page
291 A jailhouse informer: FBI teletype, Edward Scheidt to J. Edgar Hoover, April 13, 1951, Rosenberg file; New York to Hoover, April 16, 1951, Rosenberg file. These reports reflect the facts that Rosenberg told Tartakow of Bloch's warning and that Tartakow expressed fear to the FBI that Rosenberg would sooner or later figure out that Tartakow was an informer. The reports also state that Bloch raised his suspicions directly with prison authorities, who reported Bloch's conversation to the FBI.
291–92 Perhaps the warden would grant permission: FBI teletype, New York to Hoover, n.d. [1951], Document #1036, Rosenberg file.
292 Defenders of the Rosenbergs' innocence: John Wexley, *The Judgment of Julius and Ethel Rosenberg* (New York: Ballantine, 1977), pp. 231–32. Wexley denies that Tartakow could have been a confidant of Rosenberg's at all. Asks Wexley: "What motives would Julius have, as a veteran spymaster, for confiding in a stranger at the risk of putting his neck in the noose? Indeed, as an *experienced* spy, he would be especially suspicious about an inmate attempting to win his confidence." Wexley, as usual, builds his argument by putting forth his own definition of what an "experi-

enced spy" would do and then "proving" Rosenberg innocent since he does not fit the description. Following this same method of reasoning, one might suggest that placing confidence in Tartakow would not be surprising for an incautious and unprofessional sort of spy who had courted his own discovery by trusting unreliable recruits such as the Greenglasses and Elitcher.

Further challenges to Tartakow's credibility have been made by Walter and Miriam Schneir in a rebuttal to the article by Sol Stern and Ronald Radosh, "The Hidden Rosenberg Case," which ran in *The New Republic*, June 23, 1979. See their letter to the editor, *The New Republic*, Aug. 4–11, 1979, p. 26. The Schneirs' methodology is to attempt to discredit Tartakow's reliability by stressing his prior convictions "for white slavery (pimping) and for armed robberies," as well as by citing his acquittal on "the accusation in 1955 that he had kidnapped and sexually molested an 11-year-old girl." They also argue that details offered by Tartakow to the FBI came from the FBI itself, who fed the information mouthed by Tartakow to Tartakow: "The Bureau's method of working with Tartakow was to provide him with information about people and activities in which they were interested."

The Schneirs are correct about Tartakow's awful criminal record. But they fail to ask why such a man would later drive Manny Bloch and the Rosenberg children to Sing Sing to visit the condemned couple. Citing FBI files that describe him as "unreliable," they ignore those that go on to point out that the information he provided checked out. Their suggestion that the FBI was supplying Tartakow with information, rather than the other way around, makes no sense. First they argue that Tartakow was so disreputable that even the FBI didn't trust him. Then they propose that top FBI agents spent hundreds of hours feeding this unreliable, disreputable, and untrustworthy inmate information that he then spilled right back to the Bureau, which in turn stuffed this material into its own secret internal files. What would have been the purpose of such an exercise? It could not have been to manufacture a corroborating witness, since the FBI promised Tartakow he would not have to be a witness, and in fact his connection to the case was undisclosed until 1975. Not one shred of evidence exists to suggest the FBI was feeding information to him.

292–93 Tartakow . . . explained the genesis of the friendship: Jerome E. Tartakow to William Chapman, n.d. [1975]. Tartakow's letter was never published by the *Washington Post*. Tartakow wrote it to journalist Chapman, who was not sure whether or not it was genuine; interview with Chapman by Ronald Radosh, June 2, 1982.

The authors testify to the authenticity of Tartakow's letter: in conversation with us, Tartakow assured us of his authorship; also, his letter bears similarity to the letter he sent to *Seven Days* magazine.

293 There was another reason Julius trusted him: Interviews with Jerome Tartakow by Sol Stern, Aug. 21, 1978, Dec. 5, 1978, and Oct. 5, 1979. Before Tartakow told us this, a source close to the Rosenberg defense effort over the years confirmed to us that Dennis had been friendly with Tartakow. After Tartakow's release from prison, this source said, Dennis had recommended to Bloch that he hire Tartakow.

John Gates confirmed that it was the official policy of the Communist Party to keep its hands off the Rosenberg case. He notes that when he spoke with Dennis after his release from prison, Dennis told him he had been most careful never to be seen talking to Rosenberg, and that he had kept his contact to "knowing and furtive glances" when he passed Rosenberg in places like the cafeteria or roof recreation area. Interview with John Gates by Ronald Radosh, June 14, 1978.

Gates's recollection has been refuted by Peggy Dennis, Eugene Dennis's widow. She writes that "upon his release from prison in May, 1951, Gene had told me he had met Julius often and talked with him as frequently as possible, especially during the prison's recreation-time in the barbed-wire roof area. . . . Obviously Gene did not 'need' a liaison to Rosenberg." Peggy Dennis statement, *Morning Freiheit*, July 29, 1979.

We have carefully considered Peggy Dennis's argument and concluded that the weight of the evidence indicates she is incorrect. A well-known and influential left-wing journalist, whose confidentiality we are respecting, told us that during the period of the case, he had interviewed Abraham Brothman—who also was held at the Tombs during the same period as Dennis and Rosenberg. Brothman, who *was* openly friendly with Julius Rosenberg in prison, told this journalist that Rosenberg was angry and upset that Dennis consistently refused to talk with him, although Rosenberg was most anxious to.

Gloria Agrin, then working as part of Bloch's legal staff on the case, stressed in an interview with us that the Communist Party played a "cowardly" role in the case, that all of its leaders refused to help the Rosenbergs, and that even CP leaders in prison avoided them. She mentioned that while women prisoners in the House of Detention purposely befriended Ethel Rosenberg, CP leader Elizabeth Gurley Flynn studiously avoided her. Interview with Gloria Agrin by Ronald Radosh and Sol Stern, Dec. 14, 1978.

Peggy Dennis is undoubtedly correct when she writes in *Morning Freiheit* that her late husband was "reticent" and "alert to the use of informers in prison," and that he had an "excessive emphasis on security-consciousness." Gates agrees with this assessment of Dennis's character.

Eugene Dennis was indeed security-conscious. As the top American Communist, he assumed that his every move in prison was being monitored. Dennis was serving his term in the Tombs precisely at the time that his organization had adopted its hands-off-the-Rosenberg-case policy. By openly befriending and talking to Julius Rosenberg, Dennis would have jeopardized the Party's policy—perhaps even providing ammunition to the government to be used to prove a Communist Party–Soviet espionage link. Eugene Dennis, more than anyone, would have acted to avoid at all costs opening the Communist Party to such a charge. That, indeed, is why Peggy Dennis's claim makes little sense.

293   When Tartakow first made contact: FBI teletype, New York to J. Edgar Hoover, Dec. 12, 1950, Rosenberg file.

293–94   On January 3, Tartakow was again in touch: Special Agent in Charge, New York, to J. Edgar Hoover, Jan. 3, 1951, Rosenberg file.

295   March 23 typewritten letter: Summarized in FBI teletype, Edward Scheidt to J. Edgar Hoover, March 24, 1951, Rosenberg file.

295   FBI headquarters in Washington was still adamantly: A. H. Belmont to D. M. Ladd, April 17, 1951, Rosenberg file.

295–96   But Edward Scheidt ... was by now convinced: Confidential memo, SAC, New York, to J. Edgar Hoover, May 31, 1951, Rosenberg file.

296   "As I have estimated previously . . .": FBI teletype, New York to Washington, April 23, 1951, Rosenberg file.

297   On May 25, Edward Scheidt wrote: Edward Scheidt to J. Edgar Hoover, May 25, 1951, Rosenberg file.

297   Washington reluctantly approved: A. H. Belmont to D. M. Ladd, May 31, 1951, Rosenberg file. Also see SAC, New York, to Hoover, May 31, 1951.

297   on March 22, when he had reported: Teletype, New York to Washington, from Edward Scheidt, March 24, 1951, Rosenberg file.

297–98   Asked to pursue the subject: Teletype, New York to Washington, from Edward Scheidt, April 5, 1951, Rosenberg file.

298   Reflecting on this meeting: Ibid.

298–99 on May 22, Tartakow came through: Teletype, Scheidt to Washington, May 23, 1951, Rosenberg file. Tartakow was not certain that Rosenberg meant the year 1950. He suggested to the FBI that Rosenberg might have actually meant the year 1949, since he had been in jail as of the "last" year.

299 As soon as the FBI received: Summary report on William Perl by Special Agent J. B. O'Donoghue, July 2, 1951, Perl file, pp. 16–19.

299–300 Perl had checked out and signed for: Ibid., pp. 31–42 of summary report.

300 As late as February 1952, Lane: Teletype, Scheidt to Washington, Feb. 13, 1952, Perl file.

300 This lab report, dated January 23, 1952: Summary report on Perl by O'Donoghue, July 2, 1951, pp. 42–44. Also see report of the FBI Laboratory to SAC, New York, Jan. 23, 1952.

301 The AEC advised the FBI: The possibility of a nuclear-powered airplane that could stay aloft for months at a time was first mentioned in newspaper accounts in 1945, and a secret Air Force project to build such a plane was begun a year later despite opposition from atomic scientists J. Robert Oppenheimer and Edward Teller, who warned that the crash of an atomic-powered aircraft could do as much damage as a hydrogen warhead.

The scientist-authors of the Lexington Report also expressed serious doubts about the plane's feasibility. However, Pentagon and political support for the project was strengthened by later reports, beginning in 1953, that the Soviets were developing atomic-powered aircraft of their own. It is now considered likely that the Soviets never had such a project but used stories planted in technical journals to spread the suspicion that they did. The American effort was finally abandoned in 1961 as a white elephant that had cost more than a billion dollars over a fifteen-year period. For additional history of the project, see John Tierney, "Take the A-Plane: The $1,000,000,000 Nuclear Bird that Never Flew," *Science 82*, Jan.–Feb. 1982 (vol. 3, no. 1), pp. 46–55.

301 However, Ben Pinkel, chief of thermodynamics: Summary report on Perl by O'Donoghue, July 2, 1951, p. 2.

301 Perl had travelled to Oak Ridge: Summary report on William Perl by SA J. B. O'Donoghue, March 27, 1951, Perl file. (This is a different summary report from the one previously cited.) This report concludes:

> Informants stressed that possession of the mathematical compilations would not indicate that they were received from

anyone at NACA since any competent physicist could advance such compilations accurately. Information concerning the line of research regarding the shielding [of the on-board reactor] would be of value since it could avert unnecessary research and experimentation.

301–02 This particular allegation: Walter and Miriam Schneir, *Invitation to an Inquest* (Baltimore: Penguin, 1973), pp. 348–49.

302 On July 21, 1950, four days: A. H. Belmont to D. M. Ladd, July 21, 1950, Perl file. Also see "Investigation to Identy [*sic*] of Consultant Contact of Julius Rosenberg," Rosenberg file, pp. 36–39. The reason the FBI took such a long time to sort this matter out was that they originally assumed that the "consultant" had actually worked in Egypt. Their search was successful only when they began checking the names of experts who had done their work in the United States.

302 Ironically, once the perjury trial: Teletype, New York to Washington, from SA Leland V. Boardman, April 30, 1953, Perl file.

302 When his trial on four counts: U.S. Court of Appeals, Second Circuit, brief for the United States in *United States v. William Perl*.

303 A memo to Hoover from D. M. Ladd: Ladd to J. Edgar Hoover, June 10, 1953, Rosenberg file.

303 "... duties cleaning latrines": Leland V. Boardman to J. Edgar Hoover, July 2, 1953, Perl file.

303–04 The suspicions of NACA engineers: New York *World-Telegram and Sun*, July 9, 1953. These suspicions had been reported to the FBI as early as April 1951. A letter dated April 16, 1951, from Hoover to the special agent in charge of the San Francisco office refers to a statement by an NACA official in California to the effect that "it was the opinion of some engineers who have seen photos of the Russian MIGs that these planes looked too much like certain jet planes which have been tested as prototypes or models in NACA laboratories," and that the design so closely resembled the design on contemplated U.S. planes that it appeared to be more than a coincidence. And another FBI memorandum, from W. A. Branigan to A. H. Belmont, dated Jan. 24, 1952, reports that Engineer Lieutenant Colonel Grigorii A. Tokaev, a Soviet defector in British hands, had reported seeing in the Soviet Union "original NACA data sheets, diagrams, and descriptive data" relative to a certain wind-tunnel design for testing jet engines.

304 The possibility of a connection: Teletype, New York to Washington, from Edward Scheidt, June 21, 1951, Rosenberg file.

304–05 he began to describe Rosenberg's travels: Teletype, New York to Washington, from Edward Scheidt, July 11, 1951, Rosenberg file.

306 Bethe, as he himself pointed out: Report from Seattle, Washington, by SA William C. Tower, Aug. 7, 1950, for period of July 28, 1950, Sarant file. Interview by Tower with Bethe is summarized.

306 the FBI concluded that Bethe and Morrison: Hoover to SAC, San Francisco, March 24, 1952, Sarant file. Answering a query, Hoover stressed that "Fuchs freely discussed the extent of his contacts with Bethe," and had denied that "Bethe had anything to do with his espionage activities."

One scientist, Dr. Robert L. Thornton of the University of California Radiation Laboratory, had argued in a June 12, 1950, letter to the FBI that "in order for the Russians to have desired the answers to some of the questions put to FUCHS they must have received information from persons other than FUCHS," since the patterns "of questions asked and information supplied by FUCHS is somewhat analogous to the development of a chain," and that there were "missing links needed to complete it." Bureau agents commented that perhaps Bethe and Morrison were furnishing information to Rosenberg through Gold, and that Fuchs had recruited them as well. They also suggested that perhaps Bethe himself was "acting as an agent" and the Russians were only using Fuchs "as a check on BETHE." If that was so, Sarant might have moved to Ithaca to be in touch with Bethe. "It is not clear," the agents wrote to Hoover, "whether SARANT moved there to recruit BETHE or to serve as intermediary in obtaining BETHE's information for ROSENBERG." SAC, San Francisco, marked confidential, to Hoover, Feb. 26, 1952, Sarant file.

In the unusual and important communication cited at the beginning of this note (Hoover to SAC, San Francisco, March 24, 1952), Hoover quickly scotched the fantasizing of his San Francisco agents. First, he pointed out that Fuchs thoroughly denied having worked with Bethe in espionage activities. Second, he argued that Dr. Thornton's theories were wrong; there was not "sufficient basis for considering that such additional information would materially assist in connecting him . . . with Soviet espionage." Moreover, the "missing link" argument of Thornton "fails

to account for the known factors that the Soviet scientists themselves were working on atomic energy projects during this period
and had undoubtedly developed certain phases thereof independent of any data received from outside sources."

Noting that the Soviets did not gain atomic information
"solely through the operations of the Rosenberg espionage network in this country," Hoover argued that the information they
solicited from Fuchs referred to areas in which "their own scientists were in doubt or having particular difficulty." He concluded
that evidence showed Fuchs was not "aware of any espionage activities on the part of Bethe or Phillip Morrison," and that it
could not be concluded Gold had picked up material from them
just because he had been a courier for Greenglass and Fuchs. "It
would be more logical," the FBI director wrote, "to assume that
Rosenberg would have utilized the services of Alfred Sarant."
That is why they surmised Sarant had moved to Ithaca—"for the
purpose of his either recruiting Bethe or obtaining information
from Bethe for Rosenberg."

Hoover also pointed out that Bethe had a Q clearance with
the AEC and had a legitimate right to possess material relating to
nuclear propulsion of airplanes and other AEC top-secret data.
Morrison had a Q clearance prior to 1949, and was in the same
position "with respect to the AEC information." Thus, Hoover
wrote: "In view thereof and in the absence of specific information
indicating that Bethe or Morrison actually engaged in espionage
activities . . . it would not appear that a check of all secret documents furnished to Bethe and Morrison would be warranted."
Moreover, even showing utilization by the Soviets of information
that was accessible to the two scientists "would serve no purpose
in establishing espionage on their part."

307 Louise Sarant had told the FBI: Summary report by SA Robert F.
Royal, Aug. 7, 1951, pp. 17–18, Finestone file.

307 The FBI did not attempt: Ibid, pp. 4–5.

307–08 The FBI became curious about Finestone again: Ibid., pp. 15–16.

308 As a result of this episode: Ibid., pp. 39–51.

308–09 Weldon Bruce Dayton swore: Ibid., pp. 74–77.

309 James Weinstein, had to be . . ."Y": Ibid., pp. 5–9.

309 This conclusion was further confirmed: Ibid., p. 7.

309 the Bureau could not even establish: Ibid.

311 the FBI did not give up easily: W. A. Branigan to A. H. Belmont,
Dec. 5, 1952, Weinstein file.

312–13 Weinstein agreed to tell the story: Interviews with James Weinstein by Ronald Radosh, April 16 and June 19, 1978.

313–14 Finestone said that Weinstein was mistaken: Interview with Max Finestone by Ronald Radosh and Sol Stern, May 23, 1978.

314 Tartakow showed up at Manny Bloch's office: A source close to the Rosenberg defense over the years confirmed to Sol Stern and Ronald Radosh that Tartakow had been recommended to Bloch by Eugene Dennis. This anonymous source also gave Stern and Radosh a Xerox copy of a previously unavailable letter written by Tartakow to Bloch in 1953.

314–15 Bloch was extremely nervous: Teletype, New York to Washington, from Edward Scheidt, July 6, 1951, Rosenberg file.

315 Tartakow wrote a personal letter: Teletype, New York to Washington, from Edward Scheidt, Aug. 8, 1951, Rosenberg file. A prison guard at Sing Sing assigned to guard Julius Rosenberg during his conferences with Bloch was passing regular reports to the FBI. For a summary of his account of Julius's response to Tartakow's letter, see this FBI teletype.

316 Tartakow had already informed the Bureau: Teletype, Edward Scheidt to J. Edgar Hoover, Aug. 28, 1951, Rosenberg file. The decision to use Tartakow for spying on Bloch created a precedent for future FBI infiltration of the Rosenberg defense committees, though the specific information he produced would hardly seem to have been worth the risk; it amounted to little more than the names of alleged contributors to the Rosenbergs' legal defense, some of them previously named in earlier "atom spy" cases; and others were respected businessmen who would no doubt have been highly distressed at the knowledge that their interest in helping the Rosenbergs was known to the FBI.

317 His last contact with Bloch: Tartakow to Bloch, Jan. 24, 1953. An anonymous source close to the Rosenberg defense showed us the original of this handwritten letter and allowed us to make Xerox copies of it. Sol Stern showed the copy to Tartakow when he interviewed him in California, and Tartakow confirmed he had written that letter, requesting a copy for his own files.

The text of Tartakow's letter reads as follows:

Dear Manny:
  You will no doubt be surprised to hear from me. Pleasantly surprised. I hope! However, since I'm quite certain that you are now in the very midst of the most strenuous mental and physical struggle of your career I desire not to waste your precious time with unnecesary [sic] words.
  Leaving the city as hurridly [sic] as was necessary for me made it impossible to say goodbye even to you. The business

I now have was a proposition which required my immediate presence and few people knew of my departure. Nevertheless, during the past four months I have thought constantly of you and the tragic plight of our friends. It has constantly been difficult for me to ignore a consistent feeling of guilt—the shameful guilt a man feels when he turns away—intentionally or otherwise—from a dear friend. And believe me, Manny: *no* one feels closer to Julie than I. Among his friends, that is. Thus, I feel now that I must once again appeal to you to permit me to do something—*anything*—that might in some way alleviate the distressing circumstances in which our friends are now found. It may be important for you to know also that I am no longer bound by certain rules and regulations as in the past. I am free to come and go as I please—even insofar as my business is concerned.

And there is something else I would like for you to know. Something you should have known many months ago—and a fact you can easily corroborate. Manny, for almost a year no one—and I include you in this seemingly broad statement—*no one* was closer to our friend than I! I repeat again: *no one!* We ate, drank, played, walked and slept together. We laughed when laughing was possible—and we were silent when silence was eloquent. We shared each other's aspirations—personally and politically—we shared even the past—and for my friend, this was the greatest fight—the highest token he could bestow upon me. All this may be difficult for you to understand and accept, but it is true. Fate threw together two men: one with an overwhelming love for his fellow-men, and the other with an almost equally overwhelming feeling of contempt. From Julie I learned what *true* greatness is; from him I learned humility and patience. I lived at that time with another great man—a man whom I considered a mental giant, one who was accepted by freedom loving people throughout this nation as a leader. And this man also accepted me as a friend. But of the two men I very easily consider Julie my *dearest* friend, because in simple, peace loving, far-sighted Julie, I found the epitome of the brave working class soldier.

Unfortunately, there is too much of the realist within me to be able to accept the very likely death of my friend. I feel it is very wrong for him to die in the manner of a "Nathan Hale"; wrong and far too melodramatic to fit congruously in the scheme of a working class world. Wrong *and totally un-just.*

And so now you may understand why I have decided to write. I want you to know—and more important I want Julie to know—that I am prepared to do anything humanely possible to aid him and Ethel. I have no ties at present, nothing to prevent me from coming to the city, or going wherever else it is possible for me to assist.

In closing I wish to add one personal bit of opinion, perhaps a little presumptuously, but by all means an opinion born of *personal experience*: It is no longer the time of editorials and press statements. If there is any possible, decent, honorable way to save our friends [*sic*] lives it must be chosen immediately. And if there is another way that excludes these aforementioned virtues—choose that way for *me*.

Most sincerely,
Jerry

How is one to read this amazing letter? First, it clearly seeks to build upon the friendly terms existing between Bloch and the informer, Tartakow. Second, Tartakow seems to be trying to hint to Bloch (when he says that he and Julie shared the past between themselves) that he, Tartakow, knew more than Bloch might have thought about Rosenberg's past. Tartakow's reference to knowing another individual while in prison—"another great man . . . accepted by freedom loving people . . . as a leader"—seems to be a veiled reference to Eugene Dennis, whose name Tartakow shrewdly saw fit not to mention in a letter that might be seen by others aside from Bloch. Finally, Tartakow ends by asking Bloch to allow the Rosenbergs to choose a dishonorable way to save their lives, if that remained the only course open. The entire letter, we think, can be read as a not-so-veiled plea by Tartakow to ask Julius Rosenberg to cooperate and to tell the FBI what he had already conveyed to Tartakow. One might speculate that Tartakow tried this tactic as a last-ditch attempt to pay off the FBI for the favors he had received from them.

317 This memorandum, stamped "Top Secret": "Top Secret" memo, Jan. 14, 1953, with cover letter from U.S. Attorney Myles Lane to Daniel M. Lyons, Esq., Pardons Attorney, the President's Office, Rosenberg file. Despite the letter from Lane, the memo was actually written by James B. Kilsheimer.

317–18 ". . . A confidential informant . . .": Ibid.

21: "NOBODY WAS DOING ANYTHING"

Page

320 When the court's decision was handed down: Justice Frank's decision is *U.S. v. Rosenberg*, 195 F. 2nd 583 (1952).

The opinion of the U.S. Court of Appeals for the Second Circuit, Oct. Term, 1951, decided February 25, 1952, is appended to the Trial Transcript, pp. 1640–1700.

321 Frank ... was now dismissed by Julius as: Julius Rosenberg to Ethel Rosenberg, Feb. 28, 1952; Ethel to Julius, Feb. 26, 1952; cited in Robert and Michael Meeropol, *We Are Your Sons* (Boston: Houghton Mifflin, 1975), pp. 128–29.

321–22 " ... Yes, any illusions . . .": *Death House Letters of Ethel and Julius Rosenberg* (New York: Jero, 1953), p. 89.

322 Like so many others: All material pertaining to Emily Alman's views and recollections, unless otherwise noted, comes from interview with Emily Alman by Sol Stern, Aug. 3, 1978.

323 James Aronson remembers: Cedric Belfrage and James Aronson, *Something to Guard: The Stormy Life of the National Guardian: 1948–1967* (New York: Columbia University Press, 1979), pp. 169–71. The *National Guardian* was founded in 1948 as a newspaper to support the Progressive Party candidacy of Henry Wallace. Its editors considered themselves part of the "Socialist camp" led by the Soviet Union. Although privately socialist in conviction, they described themselves as "progressives," and above all else supported a third-party electoral effort as the main way to create an alternative to the Cold War consensus. For a critical discussion of the paper's politics, see the review essay by Ronald Radosh in *The New Republic*, Feb. 17, 1979, pp. 34–37.

323–24 Aronson consulted with his coeditor, Cedric Belfrage: Belfrage and Aronson, *Something to Guard*, p. 165.

324 On August 15, the *Guardian* broke the story: *National Guardian*, Aug. 15, 1952.

324 the series of articles by William Reuben: Reuben's articles appeared in the *National Guardian* in seven parts beginning with the issue of Aug. 22, 1952, and ending with that of Oct. 30, 1952. His assertion about Fuchs's name appeared in the issue of Aug. 29.

324–25 he had been reminded in a private letter: Oliver Pilat to William A. Reuben, Dec. 8, 1951, papers of the Committee to Secure Justice for Morton Sobell. This collection, in repository at the State Historical Society, Madison, Wisconsin, incorporates the papers of the original National Committee to Secure Justice in the Rosenberg Case, in which files the Reuben-Pilat correspondence may be found.

327 Fineberg . . . was following the Rosenberg Committee: S. Andhill Fineberg, *The Rosenberg Case: Fact and Fiction* (New York: Oceana, 1952), pp. 42–45.

328 Max Gordon, then a senior editor: Interview with Max Gordon by Ronald Radosh, July 10, 1978.

328–29 John Gates, a former member: Interview with John Gates by Ronald Radosh, June 14, 1978.

329–30 Elaine Ross . . . told a rally audience: *Daily Worker*, Oct. 25, 1952.

330 William L. Patterson, a leading black Communist: William Patterson to Emily Alman, Dec. 31, 1952, Papers of David and Emily Alman.

330 there would be increasing insistence: Thus Shirley Graham, wife of W. E. B. Du Bois and an influential "progressive" leader in her own right, argued with a defense-committee leader about the orientation she felt the committee should take. Informing Aaron Schneider on how she had spoken frequently about the case before diversified groups on the West Coast, Graham wrote: "From here on out, I think it is important that we stress the innocence of the Rosenbergs. . . ." Shirley Graham to Aaron Schneider, March 8, 1953, papers of the Committee to Secure Justice for Morton Sobell.

330 On October 13, 1952, the Supreme Court announced: Michael E. Parrish, "Cold War Justice: The Supreme Court and the Rosenbergs," *The American Historical Review*, Vol. 82, No. 4 (October 1977), pp. 816–18.

331 The Bureau had an inmate informant: Special Agent in Charge, New York, to J. Edgar Hoover, Oct. 5, 1952; SAC to Hoover, July 1, 1952 and April 21, 1952, Sobell file.

331 Speaking at as many as four meetings: Morton Sobell, *On Doing Time* (New York: Scribner's, 1974), pp. 338–41.

332 just four days after the first denial of *certiorari*: Cited in A. H. Belmont to D. M. Ladd, Oct. 17, 1952, Sobell file.

332 A. H. Belmont warned New York: Ibid.

333 Hoover himself, in a letter: J. Edgar Hoover to the attorney general, Oct. 27, 1952, Sobell file. The letter is marked "Security-information-confidential."

333 Sobell's prison memoir states: Sobell, *On Doing Time*, p. 342.

333 Sobell acceded to Kuntz's advice: Ibid., pp. 343–53.

22: WE ARE INNOCENT

Page

335 "the latest action of the highest court . . .": Julius to Ethel, Oct. 16, 1952, in Robert and Michael Meeropol, *We Are Your Sons* (Boston: Houghton Mifflin, 1975), pp. 152–53. This letter was not published in the original editions of the Rosenbergs' correspondence. However, a letter by Julius dated October 13, reprinted on p. 111 of *The Testament of Ethel and Julius Rosenberg* (New York: Jero Publishing Co., 1954) voices a similar sentiment: "I believe this latest action by the highest court in our land will galvanize many people in positive action on our behalf." (*The Testament* was the second book-length edition of the Rosenbergs' letters and includes correspondence from the last months before the executions.)

336 "We are an ordinary man and wife . . .": Papers of the Committee to Secure Justice for Morton Sobell.

336–37 Although Taylor's book . . . seems depressing reading: Julius Rosenberg to Emanuel Bloch, Nov. 28, 1952, reprinted in Meeropol, *We Are Your Sons*, pp. 157–60.

337 "our sacred duty . . .": Julius to Ethel, June 4, 1953, in *The Testament of Ethel and Julius Rosenberg*, p. 169.

337 the surest measure of Ethel's depression: Ibid, p. 141.

338 Tessie's interview with her daughter: Ethel Rosenberg to Bloch, Jan. 21, 1953, in *Death House Letters of Ethel and Julius Rosenberg* (New York: Jero, 1953), pp. 127–28.

338–39 "The fact that no degree of pressure . . .": Ethel to Julius, Sept. 15, 1952, in Meeropol, *We Are Your Sons*, pp. 149–50. This passage was apparently too rhetorical for the editors of the original edition of the Rosenbergs' letters, and was thus excised; see *Death House Letters of Ethel and Julius Rosenberg*, p. 106.

339 As the critic Leslie Fiedler: Ethel to Julius, Oct. 1, 1951; Julius to Bloch, Feb. 23, 1953; Julius to Ethel, March 9, 1953, in *Death House Letters of Ethel and Julius Rosenberg*, pp. 31, 67, 139–40, 147–48.

Leslie Fiedler cites two of these same examples in his scathing analysis of the dogmatic mentality revealed in the Rosenbergs' correspondence. See Leslie Fiedler, "Afterthoughts on the Rosenbergs," in Fiedler, *An End to Innocence* (Boston: Beacon Press, 1955), pp. 22–45. Also see Robert Warshow, "The 'Idealism' of Julius and Ethel Rosenberg," in Warshow, *The Immediate Experience* (New York: Doubleday, 1962), p. 43.

Inevitably it has been suggested that the Rosenbergs did not write these letters. Yet there is nothing in the quality of the letters to make one believe they could not have written them; they were people of no eloquence and little imagination, and their letters display none.... The letters, if they were not written by the Rosenbergs, are what the Rosenbergs would have written. In their crudity and emptiness, in their absolute and dedicated alienation from truth and experience, these letters adequately express the Communism of 1953.

340 Julius and Ethel insisted on redefining their crime: Ethel to Julius, May 27, 1951; Julius to Ethel, May 9, 1951; in *Death House Letters of Ethel and Julius Rosenberg*, pp. 39, 35.

340 How could this be: Writing in 1953, literary critic Leslie Fiedler addressed himself to just this question. Fiedler noted two complementary attitudes held by the Rosenbergs' defenders: "the *wish* that the Rosenbergs might actually be innocent; and the conviction that they were *symbolically* guiltless whatever action they may have committed." Even if they had committed the crime of which they had been accused, Fiedler wrote,

treason was not what they had meant; they had been acting for a better world, for all Humanity (i.e., for the Soviet Union, whose interests all the more enlightened had once known were identical with those of mankind;) and, anyhow, Russia had been our ally when the Rosenbergs gave them a helping hand, standing with us side by side against the Nazis ... so that sharing the atomic secret in this somewhat unorthodox fashion was really a blow for world peace; just look at the present detente, etc., etc. In light of all which, isn't it better simply to declare that the Rosenbergs are 'innocent,' as a kind of shorthand for an analysis too complicated to explain to the uninitiated without re-educating them completely.

Fiedler concludes his essay with this argument:

the Rosenbergs were quite incapable of saying in their last letters just what it was for which they thought they were dying. ... They could not even tell the world for what beliefs they were being framed. Beyond the cry of frame-up, they could only speak in hints and evasions, so that they finished by seeming martyrs only to their own double talk, to a handful of banalities: "democracy and human dignity," "liberty and peace," . . . "bread and roses and the laughter of children." But one must look deeper, realize that a code is involved, a substitution of equivalents whose true meaning can be read off immediately by the insider. "Peace, democracy and liberty," like "roses and the laughter of children," are only conventional ciphers for the barely whispered word "Communism," and Communism itself only a secondary encoding of the completely unmentioned "Defense of the Soviet Union." . . . And to this principle the Rosenbergs felt that they had been true; in this sense, they genuinely believed themselves innocent, more innocent than if they had never committed espionage.

See Fiedler, "Afterthoughts on the Rosenbergs," pp. 25–45, quotes on pp. 30–31; 44–45. Fiedler's essay appeared originally in *Encounter*, Oct. 1953.

Commenting on the fact the Rosenbergs kept on saying "we are innocent" and that Julius Rosenberg told Bloch that "I could never commit the crime I stand convicted of," critic Robert Warshow asks "whether the literal truth had not in some way ceased to exist for these people." What Rosenberg really meant by his statement to Bloch, Warshow argues, is "something like this: If it were a crime, I could not have done it. Since in the language of the unenlightened what I did is called a crime, and I am forced to speak in that language, the only truthful thing to say is that I did not do it." As Warshow concludes, in a brilliant exegesis on the question of truth and the Rosenbergs:

Or, finally, consider that most mystical element in the Communist propaganda about the Rosenberg case: the claim that Julius and Ethel Rosenberg are being "persecuted" because they have "fought for peace." Since the Rosenbergs had abstained entirely from all political activity of any sort for a number of years before their arrest, it follows that the only thing they could have been doing which a Communist might interpret as "fighting for peace" must have been spying for the Soviet Union; but their being persecuted rests precisely on the claim that they are innocent of spying. The main element here, of course, is deliberate falsification. But it must be understood that for most partisans of the Rosenbergs such a falsification raises no problem; all lies and inconsistencies disappear in the enveloping cloud of the unspoken "essential" truth: the Rosenbergs are innocent because they are accused; they are innocent, one might say, by definition.

Warshow's arguments appear in Warshow, "The 'Idealism' of Julius and Ethel Rosenberg," pp. 33–43, quotes on pp. 36–37. The block quotation is from Robert Warshow, "The Liberal Conscience in *The Crucible*," also in *The Immediate Experience*, p. 146. Warshow's essays appeared originally in *Commentary* magazine in 1953.

For a critique of Fiedler and Warshow, see the contemporary criticism by Morris Dickstein, "Cold War Blues: Politics and Culture in the Fifties," in his book *Gates of Eden: American Culture in the Sixties* (New York: Basic Books, 1977), pp. 25–50. Dickstein sees the era as one of a "low ebb of American civil liberties," and he comments that "Robert Warshow and Leslie Fiedler wrote essays attacking the Rosenbergs and their sympathizers rather than the men who had just executed them." Dickstein argues that both Fiedler and Warshow "completely dehumanize the Rosenbergs and turn their execution into an impersonal act, almost a merciful one. . . . In line with the strategy of blaming the victim, they accuse the Rosenbergs of having destroyed themselves—by adhering to ideology, by becoming a 'case.' . . . The implicit moral is that they were so empty, so crude, so bereft of style that there was nothing left for the electric-chair to kill." It is Dickstein's contention that the Fiedler and Warshow essays "show an eerie displacement of politics into aesthetics: issues of power and justice . . . are argued in terms of taste and style." To these 1950s critics, he comments, the Rosenberg death-house letters "provide an ideal foil for the myopic fifties highbrow with an axe to grind, for the literary mentality with a tendentious cult of style." He sees their real goal as using the Rosenbergs to achieve a cultural purge of the real Jewish radical, so that the "quaint Popular Front 'progressive,' will be sacrificed so that the children of immigrants, the despised intellectuals with their foreign ideas, can become full-fledged Americans." Dickstein's discussion of Fiedler and Warshow appears on p. 29 and pp. 41–45 of *Gates of Eden*.

Dickstein, we think, is unfair to Warshow and Fiedler. Rather than viewing their execution as merciful, as Dickstein claims, Fiedler cites with sympathy and approval the statement supposedly made by Irwin Edelman at the time of the execution: "If you are happy about the execution of the Rosenbergs, you are rotten to the core!" And Fiedler notes that "in trying to dehumanize our opponents we may end by dehumanizing ourselves." Moreover,

Fiedler praises Irwin Edelman's effort to gain a stay of execution for the Rosenbergs, and he refers to Edelman as a "survival of the old-fashioned American radical, refreshingly honest." In a "presumably hysterical America," he comments, "it was the real radical who was free to come to their aid." Of course, Fiedler ignores that Edelman was not successful in his effort. But Dickstein's comments do not speak to the critique offered by both Fiedler and Warshow. Fiedler, "Afterthoughts on the Rosenbergs," p. 35.

341 Thus when Michael Rosenberg delivered: Meeropol, *We Are Your Sons*, pp. 222–23.

341 "We stand together . . .": Julius to Ethel, April 12, 1953, *The Testament of Ethel and Julius Rosenberg*, pp. 153–54.

342 District Judge Sylvester Ryan: *United States v. Rosenberg*, 108 F. Supp 798 (1952).

342 "All legal considerations aside . . .": Ethel Rosenberg to Emanuel Bloch, Jan. 5, 1953, cited in Meeropol, *We Are Your Sons*, p. 176.

343 "a defense of the Party and nothing of Ethel": Interview with Emily Alman by Sol Stern, Aug. 3, 1978.

343 Gloria Agrin, Bloch's associate: Interview with Gloria Agrin by Ronald Radosh and Sol Stern, July 11, 1978; interview with Max Gordon by Ronald Radosh, July 10, 1978.

344 As historian Michael Parrish points out: Michael E. Parrish, "Cold War Justice: The Supreme Court and the Rosenbergs," *The American Historical Review*, vol. 82, no. 4 (Oct. 1977), p. 840.

344 Cohn, convinced that his telephones: L. B. Nichols to Clyde Tolson, Nov. 28, 1952, Rosenberg file. This document is reprinted in "The Kaufman Papers" (New York: National Committee to Re-Open the Rosenberg Case, n.d. [c. 1975]). Hoover took no immediate action on Cohn's complaint, noting only that "if Cohn follows it up again NY can make a general check."

344–45 Kaufman's action was undone by Learned Hand: Judge Hand's comment is cited in John Wexley, *The Judgment of Julius and Ethel Rosenberg* (New York: Cameron and Kahn, 1955), p. 494.

345 According to the FBI's memorandum: A. H. Belmont to J. Edgar Hoover, Feb. 19, 1953, Rosenberg file, printed in "The Kaufman Papers."

345 Justice Felix Frankfurter, for one: Parrish, "Cold War Justice," pp. 840–42. Parrish writes:

> Frankfurter would probably have granted the Rosenbergs a new trial on the basis of Saypol's behavior during the Perl indictment. "Saypol's conduct as set forth in Swan's opinion," Frankfurter told [Charles C.] Burlingham, "could not but

leave me with disquietude and the Government never contested the allegations against Saypol which Swan condemned. I could say much more—but the rest is silence."

The Frankfurter quote is dated June 24, 1953, and can be found in the Felix Frankfurter Papers, Library of Congress.

345 At the same time, Frankfurter feared: Parrish, "Cold War Justice," p. 823. Frankfurter, "Memorandum for the Conference," May 20, 1953, Box 65, File 7, Frankfurter Papers, Harvard Law School Library. Frankfurter commented that Judge Medina had "been made a hero of for conduct in which no English judge would dare to indulge, no matter what his passion or his egotism."

23: THE PROPAGANDA WAR: THE DEFENSE COMMITTEE

Page

347 In France . . . it was practically impossible: Unless otherwise noted, material pertaining to the activities of the French Rosenberg defense committee is based on: Robert B. Glynn, "L'Affaire Rosenberg in France," *Political Science Quarterly*, vol. 70, no. 4 (Dec. 1955), pp. 498–521.

348 What . . . Gates has described: Interview with John Gates by Ronald Radosh, June 14, 1978.

348 The full story of the Slansky trials: For accounts from two of the purge trial's victims, see Arthur London, *The Confession* (New York: Morrow, 1980) and Eugene Loebl, *My Mind on Trial* (New York: Harcourt Brace Jovanovich, 1976).

349 Replying to an "Open Letter": Hook's "Open Letter" of Dec. 12, 1952, was published in the New York University student newspaper, and Herbert Aptheker excerpts from it and responds to various passages in his book *History and Reality* (New York: Cameron Associates, 1955), pp. 100–102.

The same arguments made by Aptheker were offered by the editors of the *National Guardian*. (Editorial, *National Guardian*, "Moscow, Prague, Anti-Semitism," Jan. 22, 1953; and James Aronson, "The Facts on the Prague Treason Trials," *National Guardian*, Dec. 18, 1952.) Calling the charge of anti-Semitism in the Slansky prosecution "nonsensical," the *Guardian*'s editors set forth their own analysis of the differences between the two cases: "In Prague the defendants have confessed in open court while the

Rosenbergs still proclaim their innocence." Reporting on the trials, Aronson wrote: "The prosecutor presented photostats and documents to support the accusations." Noting that eleven of the defendants were Jewish, he pointed out that they had "confessed" to espionage for Zionist organizations, and he explained that this did not disturb him, since in Czechoslovakia "anti-Semitism is a crime punished with severe sentences." Evidently, the mere fact of prosecution by state authorities in Eastern Europe was satisfactory to convince the *Guardian* editors of the defendants' guilt.

In their memoir, *Something to Guard*, Aronson and Belfrage explain that although privately they knew that "we could no longer delude ourselves that socialism and frameups were a contradiction in terms," publicly, they had to write the opposite. Belfrage explained that "the essence of our position was that the great hope of mankind was still in the womb of the Soviets"; and that if Western foreigners attacked the Soviets for their wrongs, they would be joining the "hue-and-cry led by the West's vilest people." If Moscow's enemies attacked them, then Moscow would turn these attacks into a justification for their actions; if their friends attacked them, "they promptly became enemies in Soviet eyes." Always welcoming Soviet-bloc protest against capitalist injustice as principled acts of solidarity, Belfrage and Aronson obviously agreed with Stalin that any criticism of the USSR made one automatically into an enemy of socialism. Their "logic" revealed the mind set of American "fellow travelers" in the 1950s. Indeed, Belfrage even explained in his book that "the [Slansky] trial was on the eve of America's execution of the Rosenbergs," as if that was sufficient reason for not condemning Eastern-bloc suppressions of political freedom. Ironically, Belfrage's rationale shows that he failed to grasp how Stalin used the Rosenberg case to deflect criticism of the events in Eastern Europe. Belfrage and his paper played the exact role they were meant to play. See Cedric Belfrage and James Aronson, *Something to Guard: The Stormy Life of the National Guardian: 1948–1967* (New York: Columbia University Press, 1978), pp. 90–95.

For another contemporary comment on this, see Marie Syrkin, "Slow Learners on the Left," *Midstream*, May 1982, pp. 39–41. Syrkin writes, speaking of the Slansky trial:

These outrageous proceedings were accepted as *bona fide* by an amazing proportion of the committed Left. . . . An interesting sidelight on the double standard applied by the Left to all happenings was provided by the fact that the Prague trials coincided roughly with the case of Ethel and Julius Rosenberg. In the furor surrounding the Rosenbergs the questions of anti-Semitism constantly surfaced, certainly a possibility not to be discounted. However, whatever one's views of the Rosenbergs' guilt, the evidence against them could not be brushed aside. Nevertheless, the individuals most exercised by the hypothetical anti-Semitism of the American government in judging a complex case of evidence and counter-evidence never so much as noticed the monstrous charade in Prague going on at the same time and the execution of unquestionably innocent Jews for "treason."

350 The French were introduced to the Rosenbergs: Howard Fast, "The Rosenberg Case," *L'Humanité*, Nov. 14, 1952; translated and attached to: Légat, Paris, to J. Edgar Hoover, Nov. 20, 1952, marked "Secret–Air Courier," Rosenberg file.

351 Sartre called the impending execution: Sartre's article, "I Accuse!," which appeared in the June 20, 1953, *Libération*, appeared in the *Daily Worker* on July 12, 1953, and the *National Guardian* on July 6, 1953.

352–53 Lucy Dawidowicz argued: Lucy S. Dawidowicz, "The Rosenberg Case: 'Hate-America' Weapon," *The New Leader*, Dec. 22, 1952. The article was distributed by the United States Information Service. Dawidowicz argued that the Rosenberg defense committee "was used only as an operational base for the international anti-American campaign," the purpose of which was "to blackmail America, rather than to defend the Rosenbergs."

353 As Victor Navasky has argued: Victor S. Navasky, *Naming Names* (New York: Viking, 1980), pp. 112–27.

353–55 "Considerable concern has been expressed . . .": Slawson memo cited in ibid., pp. 115–16. The original copy of the memo is located in the library and records of the American Jewish Committee, Institute of Human Relations, New York City.

355 Prepublication copies of the manuscript: Interestingly, Kilsheimer agreed to review the manuscript only after he had consulted the FBI and learned that there was "nothing derogatory about the Rabbi in the Bureau's files." James B. Kilsheimer to Mr. Lumbard, cc. to Mr. Bauman, Aug. 20, 1953; Rosenberg file.

On July 10, 1953, the President's cabinet met, and set up a meeting with C. D. Jackson, William Rogers, Jesse McNight, Murray Snyder, and others, to discuss the Rosenberg case. The group agreed, in C. D. Jackson's words, to "promote Fineberg's book." C. D. Jackson file, Eisenhower Library Presidential Papers.

355–56 The ACLU, as historian Mary Sperling McAuliffe: Mary Sperling McAuliffe, *Crisis on the Left: Cold War Politics and American Liberals, 1947–1954* (Amherst, Mass.: University of Massachusetts Press, 1978), pp. 89–107.

356 ACLU leaders . . . maintained contact with the FBI: The story of the ACLU's cooperation with the FBI in the 1950s is dealt with in Frank J. Donner, *The Age of Surveillance* (New York: Knopf, 1980), pp. 146–47. Donner writes:

> A network of collaborative arrangements between ACLU leaders in field affiliates and the FBI flourished from the mid-forties on. During a seven year perod in the fifties national ACLU officials and staff members fed the FBI on a continuing basis internal reports, memoranda, files, minutes, and other materials and documents dealing with the ACLU's policies, plans and activities. They provided the FBI with information on the politics and private lives of individuals, informing it of pending actions, divulged internal conversations and discussions. In return, they sought Bureau assistance in identifying or clearing suspected Communists and solicited the agency's help both to influence ACLU policy and to implement its ban on Communist board members.

> Donner stresses that this unique relationship between some ACLU leaders and the FBI was the result of "ideological considerations," revealed in documents dealing with Irving Ferman, Director of the Washington, D.C., ACLU office (1952–1954), and Morris Ernst, who was ACLU general counsel and national board member. "Both Ferman and Ernst," Donner writes, "in implementation of a militant anti-Communism, cultivated Bureau bigwigs and took an insider's pleasure in this special relationship. . . . Ernst shared internal communications with Bureau officials and became in effect its agent in ACLU councils." Donner cites many "My Dear Edgar . . . for your eyes alone" letters written to Hoover by Ernst, concerning internal ACLU matters. He also refers to Ernst's well-known December 1950 *Reader's Digest* article, "Why I No Longer Fear the FBI." Ernst, he notes, "gloated over his intimacy with the powerful Director," only to find that in 1964, Clyde Tolson had him dropped from the

"personal correspondence list" established by Hoover, because Ernst had the indiscretion to refer to Hoover as his "treasured friend" before a Senate subcommittee. From that point on, Ernst received replies to his letters only from an impersonal aide of the director.

356 Under the circumstances, it was inevitable: McAuliffe, *Crisis on the Left*, p. 103.

356 The ACLU's decision: "To: Whom It May Concern; From: Herbert Monte Levy, Staff Counsel, American Civil Liberties Union; May 2, 1952; Subject Rosenberg, Atomic Espionage Case" Files of the Committee to Secure Justice for Morton Sobell.

356 Except for the pro-Rosenberg *National Guardian*: *National Guardian*, editorial, "An Open Letter to the Officers of the American Civil Liberties Union," May 29, 1952. The editors observed, correctly, that the "effect of the 'memo' by Staff Counsel Levy is to give positive support to a death-sentence conviction."

357 Ernst's interest in playing a role: L. B. Nichols to Clyde Tolson, June 1, 1950, Gold file.

357 In December 1952 Ernst was back in touch: L. B. Nichols to Clyde Tolson, Dec. 20, 1952, Rosenberg file.

357–58 "Ernst stated he would be interested . . .": Ibid.

358 Ernst did not give up: L. B. Nichols to Clyde Tolson, Jan. 9, 1953, Rosenberg file.

358 Echoes of the Ernst "psychological study": Various individuals who came into contact with the Rosenbergs gained the impression that Ethel was the stronger personality, and the more ambitious and disciplined member of the pair. See, for example, the comments by friends reported in Virginia Gardner's *The Rosenberg Story* (New York: Masses and Mainstream, 1954). It is a long way from this, however, to Ernst's theories of a master/slave relationship—and still a longer distance to Eisenhower's conclusion that Ethel was the "apparent leader" of the spy ring (see our chapter 25).

358–59 As late as a week before the execution: L. B. Nichols to Clyde Tolson, June 10, 1953, Rosenberg file.

359 January 22, 1953, memorandum: "Memorandum: Subject: The Rosenberg Case," Jan. 22, 1953, attached to B. P. Keay to A. H. Belmont, Feb. 2, 1953, made available to Liaison Agent Keay by Allen Dulles. Dulles passed on the memorandum "solely for the Bureau's information," and he emphasized that "no psychological warfare projects concerning the Rosenbergs should be promoted without first consulting with the FBI." He confirmed, however,

that "various individuals handling political and psychological warfare matters in the CIA have given attention to the Rosenberg case."

See Blanche W. Cook, *The Declassified Eisenhower: A Divided Legacy* (New York: Doubleday, 1981), pp. 162–63. Cook discusses this memo in her book, but she incorrectly claims that the memo spells out a "deal to reunite the Rosenbergs with their children" that was actually "offered to the Rosenbergs." Moreover, she attributes the memo to Allen Dulles, although the cited file makes it clear that Dulles had only passed on a memo written by an anonymous agent in the psychological warfare division of the CIA.

360 If Julius and Ethel were informed: While it is true that the Rosenbergs heard many of these charges and had rejected them as capitalist propaganda, the issue of Soviet anti-Semitism, could it have been proved accurate to them, would have been particularly sensitive. What might have been their reaction had the CIA been able to acquaint them with the fate suffered by the Soviet Jewish leaders?

Stalin in 1952 ordered the murder of Itzik Feffer and Solomon Mikhoels, two Soviet writers who had headed the wartime Soviet Jewish Anti-Fascist Committee. Both men had toured the United States in the 1940s, raising funds from Jewish audiences for Russian war relief. They were both heroes to American Jewish Communists, who always referred to their work and their role as proof that the USSR had eliminated the old Russian anti-Semitism.

Indeed, it was not until 1981 that Paul Robeson, Jr., in a speech to a Memorial Meeting to the Martyred Soviet Yiddish Writers (Aug. 12, 1981), revealed that his father had met Feffer in Moscow in 1949, and that the Soviet poet, already imprisoned, had indicated to Robeson that he was doomed. Robeson hid this news from Western audiences, since, as his son explained in 1981, he had "compelling reasons for covering up his meeting with Feffer," these reasons being the usual concern of fellow-travelers not to give "U.S. imperialism" more ammunition for its anti-Soviet propaganda.

It is interesting to look at the reaction to Robeson, Jr.'s revelations by one of the editors of a small Jewish left-wing monthly, *Jewish Currents*. During the 1950s, this magazine, then named *Jewish Life*, was close to the Communist Party, and its editors became major activists in the Rosenberg defense campaign. Its chief editor, Morris U. Schappes, wrote in 1982 that "it was not until the Khrushchev report became available early in 1956 that we on this magazine finally had to admit to ourselves . . . that there had been a frame-up of the Soviet Yiddish writers. Until then, our will to disbelieve reduced the evidence of innumerable reports to mere 'anti-Soviet fabrications.' " Schappes adds that it was the assurances of Paul Robeson in 1949 "that anti-Semitism in the Soviet Union was unthinkable that fed our blind faith. Robeson, like us, was a 'true believer' and believed that the Soviet system . . . would be able to correct itself. . . . He was wrong."

Would the Rosenbergs have accepted the truth about Stalin's murder of the heralded Yiddish writers if it had been presented to them by sources they viewed as tainted? We doubt it. They most likely would have rationalized the truth in the manner described by Morris Schappes. Whether they would have adopted a different stance after 1956—or as late as 1981—is but a matter for speculation. And even if they had, it might not have led them to decide to reveal all the truth about their own wartime activity.

Paul Robeson, Jr.'s, speech, "How My Father Last Met Itzik Feffer, 1949," appears in *Jewish Currents*, Nov. 1981, and Schappes's comments on it appear in *Jewish Currents*, Feb. 1982.

24: "NEW EVIDENCE"

Page

361 That the missing console table had been found: "The Missing Table: The Proof that Key Rosenberg Case Witnesses Lied," *National Guardian*, April 13, 1953, pp. 4–5.

361–62 among the converts was Malcolm Sharp: Malcolm Sharp, *Was Justice Done? The Rosenberg-Sobell Case* (New York: Monthly Review Press, 1956), p. 11.

362 In an affidavit that Ethel Rosenberg Goldberg: Ethel Goldberg's affidavit was among the supporting documents filed with a Section 2255 Petition by the defense in June 1953. C.134–245, Justice Department Files.

363 The *National Guardian* reporter visited: The *National Guardian* claimed that Mrs. Cox was terrified of FBI harassment. The FBI version of Mrs. Cox's reasons for not signing an affidavit for the defense are contained in Bureau teletype dated April 16, 1953, in which Special Agent L. V. Boardman wrote that SA's John Harrington and Richard Menahan had gone in April to the Cox home in Queens, where they learned that Mrs. Cox had been visited several times since the trial: The first visit was by a black minister

who told Mrs. Cox that he had a "humanitarian" interest in the case. Shortly thereafter, in March 1953, this minister returned with another unidentified man who brought along the console table. Subsequently, there was a third visit from an unidentified white man, presumably *Guardian* reporter Leon Summit, who asked her to sign an affidavit. According to the FBI, Mrs. Cox refused to sign because she had some doubts about the authenticity of the table—the one she remembered was new and shiny whereas the table she had been shown recently was "badly nicked and the finish was dull and dirty." By the time Harrington and Menahan finished with Mrs. Cox, she expressed still more doubts. It does seem, from reading between the lines of the FBI report, that the opposition of her daughter and son-in-law had played a decisive role in Mrs. Cox's refusal to sign any affidavit whatsoever for the Rosenberg defense.

363 Photos of the table were also shown: Section 2255 Petition, June 1953. Fontana's affidavit was also reprinted in *National Guardian*, April 13, 1953.

363 James B. Kilsheimer, who had succeeded Saypol: Second affidavit of Joseph Fontana, submitted to the U.S. Court of Appeals on June 8, 1953.

363 Another affidavit was provided: Affidavit of Joseph Fitzgerald, manager of Macy's Long Island warehouse, submitted to U.S. Court of Appeals on June 8, 1953.

364 The rule of thumb regarding new evidence: See Sharp, *Was Justice Done?*, pp. 152–53. Sharp cites *Hensley v. Commonwealth*, 241 Ky., 367 (1931) and *Coates v. United States*, 174 F.2d 959 (1949). The FBI teletype of April 16, 1953, by Boardman, cites *United States v. On Lee*, U.S. Court of Appeals, 2nd Circuit, decision of Feb. 15, 1953.

364 When Jerry Tartakow first mentioned the table: SA Edward Scheidt teletype, New York to Washington, March 26, 1951, Rosenberg file.

364 "Rosenberg stated that the console table . . .": SA Edward Scheidt to Washington, Urgent teletype, March 27, 1951, Rosenberg file.

365 "The appearance of the table . . .": Sharp, *Was Justice Done?*, pp. 12–13. Sharp's description of the table offers striking confirmation of Tartakow's report.

366 In a February 1953 report: See FBI teletype by SA L. V. Boardman, Feb. 5, 1953, reporting on conversations overheard on Jan. 31 and Feb. 3, 1953. Ethel Goldberg's mention of the table in January seems to indicate that she was not telling the truth when she claimed to have been unaware of its existence before being con-

tacted by the *Guardian* reporter. On the other hand, the FBI reporter does not specify what Goldberg asked about the table, so it was possible that she was merely telling the Rosenbergs about inquiries made by a reporter or some other third party.

366 A second batch of "new evidence": *Le Combat*, April 18, 1953.

366 In the most sensational of these documents: Copies of the stolen memos (in the original English) were widely circulated in the United States by the National Commitee to Secure Justice in the Rosenberg Case, and the bulk of these memos are also found reprinted in an appendix to John Wexley, *The Judgment of Julius and Ethel Rosenberg* (New York: Ballantine Books, 1977), pp. 537–46.

368 But when the published Rogge memos: Herbert J. Fabricant memo, "Re: David Greenglass," to file, June 16, 1950, 11:45 A.M., Rogge papers.

368–69 Rogge's firm, as it happened: Helen Pagano, memo to herself, n.d., Rogge papers.

369 The next morning, John Harrington: Herbert Fabricant to file, May 1, 1953; Rogge papers. Also FBI teletype by SA L.V. Boardman to Washington, April 30, 1953, Rosenberg file.

369 Harrington's prime theory at first: The FBI's tip came from one David Brown, chairman of the Los Angeles branch of the Rosenberg defense committee, who was also a paid FBI informant. The informant later recanted his role, and confessed to David Alman and the Committee leaders that he had been in the pay of the Bureau.

369–70 Suspicion that someone connected: Herbert J. Fabricant to file, May 4, 1953, Rogge papers. This memo, as well as Fabricant's memo of May 1 and Helen Pagano's undated memo, both cited above, confirm the version of events given by the FBI. Apparently, then, the Greenglass file had to have been removed from the Rogge office on two occasions—once to steal the memos and again, after May 29, for the purpose of returning the originals, which had by then been photocopied and published. Although Fabricant had taken the entire file to his office in the interim, he had never examined it or at least had not looked closely enough to realize that anything was missing. Fabricant admitted that he often left his office door unlocked overnight, and if he left a marker in the file cabinet indicating that he had signed out the file (a detail not specified in his memo), then a thief looking for the folder in the steno-pool file room would have known that it was probably in his desk.

370 According to Fabricant's account of the conversation: Transcript

of conference on Monday, May 4, 1953, 11 A.M., at office of O. John Rogge, with Rogge, Fabricant, and Bloch, Rogge papers.

370 Personally, he did not consider: For a forgotten but amazingly insightful article dealing with the issue of the stolen Rogge files, see Nathan Glazer, "A New Look at the Rosenberg-Sobell Case," *The New Leader*, July 2, 1956. Glazer's report was published separately as a pamphlet by the Tamiment Institute and was included as an insert in this issue of *The New Leader*.

Referring to a Rogge affidavit of June 8, 1953, Glazer argued that the stolen files "only showed what Mr. Bloch had known at the trial—that David Greenglass had told the same story from the beginning." Bloch had tried to claim that the stolen files proved Greenglass had perjured himself. But in his June 8 affidavit, Rogge related his account of a May 4, 1953, conference among himself, Fabricant, and Bloch. At that meeting, according to Rogge, Bloch had "stated that the handwritten memorandum of David Greenglass contained less material than he himself had brought out on cross-examination . . . but that if he did not use the statement he would be accused by the National Committee to Secure Justice in the Rosenberg Case of throwing the case." Bloch also admitted, Rogge stated in his affidavit, "that this memo undermined one of his basic positions, in that it showed that in the original statement that David Greenglass had made to the FBI he brought in Julius Rosenberg, whereas it had been his, Mr. Bloch's position that the FBI had induced David Greenglass at a later time to bring in the name of Julius Rosenberg."

Glazer comments that critic John Wexley, in his book on the case, chose not to inform his readers about the text of this Rogge affidavit. The missing page of the Fabricant memo—the page that those who stole the memos chose not to print—is further proof of the consistency shown by Greenglass in his testimony. It is possible that at the conference concerning the stolen files, held in Rogge's office, Bloch had a look at the complete file.

370 Bloch had known about the existence: Bloch made available to Rogge's law firm copies of his correspondence with Paul Villard in France. Villard to Bloch, April 18, 1953; Bloch to Villard, April 21, 1953; Rogge papers.

371 On May 11, the Committee, pressing Bloch: Leaflet issued by the National Committee to Secure Justice in the Rosenberg Case, May 11, 1953, papers of the Committee to Secure Justice for Morton Sobell.

372 Judge Kaufman appeared impatient: Sharp, *Was Justice Done?*, p. 156.

372 Justice Robert Jackson tried unsuccessfully: Michael E. Parrish, "Cold War Justice: The Supreme Court and the Rosenbergs," *The American Historical Review*, vol. 82, no. 4 (Oct. 1977), pp. 836–37.

25: EISENHOWER AND CLEMENCY

Page

373 The impact of the Rosenberg case: For the positions taken by the French press, see Robert B. Glynn, "L'Affaire Rosenberg in France," *Political Science Quarterly*, vol. 70, no. 4 (Dec. 1955), pp. 498–521.

373 CIA's station in Paris had been concerned: Maran to Myles Lane, Dec. 13, 1952, Justice Department Archives.

374 Summary entitled "Le Cas Rosenberg": See Glynn, "L'Affaire Rosenberg."

374 *Le Combat*'s publication: Benjamin C. Bradlee to James B. Kilsheimer, April 22, 1953, Justice Department Archives.

374 "the real issue in France was clemency": Interview with Benjamin Bradlee by Ronald Radosh, Jan. 1982.

374–75 Eyes-Only dispatch sent by . . . Douglas Dillon: Secret Security Information dispatch from Ambassador Douglas Dillon for the Secretary of State, "Eyes Only" category, May 15, 1953, Ann Whitman file, Eisenhower Library. Attached to memoranda from Mrs. Whitman of May 21, 1953, including Acting Secretary Walter B. Smith to the President, May 20, 1953, and Walter B. Smith to Douglas Dillon, May 20, 1953.

375 "We should not (repeat not) . . .": Ibid.

375 tour through France by Roy Cohn: Cohn, by this time, had left the Justice Department and had joined the staff of Senator Joseph McCarthy, as chief counsel to his Senate Government Operations Committee. McCarthy sent Cohn and G. David Schine to Europe in April 1953, to investigate "subversive" books found on the shelves of U.S. Information Center libraries. Their journey, filled as it was with publicity-seeking antics, was treated with scorn by the European press.

375 Smith's reply to Dillon: Smith to Dillon, May 20, 1953.

On June 12, Dulles heard personally from Paul Henri Spaak that the "R case most troublesome affecting US-Eur relations." Four days later, on June 16, Dulles forwarded further memos to the President on the subject of the European response to the scheduled executions.

It is probable that Eisenhower never read this material prior to the execution. On June 23, Eisenhower phoned Dulles to ask the Secretary if he had given the European ambassadors a summary of the Rosenberg case. Dulles's secretary's memo of the call reads: "Pres says he was amazed by Clare Luce's report that this case was allowed to achieve the import that it did in Europe. He did not have the info in advance that they were so interested. He said that the State dept reports to him indicated it would be better to go ahead, and not let the Commies brag that they had influenced our justice. Sec agreed that this had been his view." Memos of phone calls by John Foster Dulles for June 12, June 16, and June 23, 1953; John Foster Dulles papers.

375–76 Dillon's telegram also aroused the ire: J. Edgar Hoover to Herbert Brownell, May 22, 1953, Rosenberg file.

377 the subject of Bloch's pending clemency appeal: Minutes of cabinet meeting, Feb. 12, 1953, Eisenhower Library.

378 Professor Clyde Miller: Clyde Miller to Eisenhower, June 8, 1953, Eisenhower Library.

378 In a lengthy personal reply: Eisenhower to Clyde Miller, "Personal and Confidential," June 10, 1953, Eisenhower Library.

379 The striking thing about Eisenhower's letter: See "PSB Draft of Presidential Statement on Rosenberg Case," Dec. 30, 1952, enclosed in Tom Stephens to Herbert Brownell, Jan. 30, 1953, Eisenhower Library. Stephens notes that the statement was prepared by the Psychological Strategy Board, and had been "prepared for President Truman."

379 "in this instance it is the woman . . .": Dwight D. Eisenhower to John Eisenhower, quoted in Stephen E. Ambrose with Richard H. Immerman, *Ike's Spies* (New York: Doubleday, 1981), pp. 182–83. The original of this letter is in the Eisenhower Library.

26: THE BUILT-IN VERDICT

Page

382 Edelman was not sure exactly: Irwin Edelman, "Religion, the Left and the Rosenberg Case," New York, n.d. [c. 1970s], pp. 166–69.

382 Edelman fought the conviction: *Edelman v. California* 344 U.S. 357.

382 several of those present admitted: Edelman, "Religion, the Left and the Rosenberg Case," pp. 169–74.

383 A week later, Edelman received: Sophie Davidson to Edelman, n.d., in ibid., p. 172.

383 pamphlet . . . complete with a new introduction: Ibid., pp. 172–73, for citation of his introduction. The pamphlet, privately printed, was issued with the title of "Freedom's Electrocution" in November 1952. It may be found in the files of the Committee to Secure Justice for Morton Sobell.

384 As he wrote to Edelman: Fyke Farmer to Irwin Edelman, Dec. 17, 1952, Farmer papers. Fyke Farmer mailed to the authors a complete copy of his entire file, including correspondence, pertaining to the Rosenberg case. A copy of the complete Farmer-Edelman correspondence is also to be found in Edelman, "Religion, the Left and the Rosenberg Case."

384 "A funny thing about these people . . .": Farmer to Edelman, Dec. 17, 1952.

385 Farmer made a special trip: Fyke Farmer to Irwin Edelman, April 10, 1953, quoted in Edelman, "Religion, the Left and the Rosenberg Case," pp. 182–84. Farmer to Emanuel Bloch, April 10, 1953, papers of the Committee to Secure Justice for Morton Sobell.

385 he received a letter from Bloch: Emanuel Bloch to Fyke Farmer, March 10, 1953, Farmer papers.

385 another *habeas corpus* petition: Fyke Farmer to Emanuel Bloch, April 29, 1953, Farmer papers.

385 Bloch replied to this overture: Emanuel Bloch to Fyke Farmer, May 6, 1953, Farmer papers.

386 exchanged a series of letters debating: Fyke Farmer to Daniel Marshall, May 8, 1953; Farmer to Marshall, May 11, 1953; Irwin Edelman to Farmer, May 12, 1953; Farmer to Edelman, May 13, 1953. All quoted in Edelman, "Religion, the Left and the Rosenberg Case," pp. 193–99. Quote in text is from letter of May 8.

386 an L.A. Committee activist . . . had written: Warwick Tompkins to National Committee to Secure Justice in the Rosenberg Case, May 18, 1953; cited in Edelman, "Religion, the Left and the Rosenberg Case," p. 205.

386 After the conference, Brainin offered: Interview with Fyke Farmer by Sol Stern, June 14, 1978. Also see an account Farmer prepared describing his efforts in the twenty days preceding the Rosenbergs' execution, in Edelman, "Religion, the Left and the Rosenberg Case," pp. 215–17.

386–87 "Counsel of record . . .": Emanuel Bloch to Fyke Farmer, May 19, 1953, Farmer papers.

387 Bloch turned his back on Judge Kaufman: Edelman, "Religion, the Left and the Rosenberg Case," pp. 215–17, and excerpt from the record, quoted in ibid., pp. 217–19.

387 Farmer was dismayed: Farmer interview, June 14, 1978.

388 "Apparently you had this point . . .": Excerpt from the record, cited in Edelman, "Religion, the Left and the Rosenberg Case," p. 218.

388 But he had not known of Farmer's petition: Ibid., pp. 218–19.

388 "Arrived here last evening . . .": Fyke Farmer to Irwin Edelman, June 1, 1953, quoted in ibid., p. 220.

388 Edelman . . . declared himself willing: The account is based on ibid., pp. 219–39; Farmer interview, June 14, 1978; and the Farmer papers.

389 In a March 1953 report: David Alman, "Report by David Alman at Eastern Seaboard Conference," March 7, 1953, to the National Committee to Secure Justice in the Rosenberg Case, papers of the National Committee to Secure Justice for Morton Sobell.

390 Committee organizers had even tried: Interview with Emily Alman by Sol Stern, Aug. 3, 1978. All quotes from Alman through the end of the chapter are from this interview.

391 Einstein had balked: G. Kallianpur to Dear Friends, March 31, 1953, papers of the Committee to Secure Justice for Morton Sobell. Einstein also feared that a brief might do more harm by stiffening the attitude of the authorities.

392 "How can you do this, Manny?": Emily Alman interview, Aug. 3, 1978.

393–94 In the meantime, Fyke Farmer: See the account written by Farmer in Edelman, "Religion, the Left and the Rosenberg Case," pp. 228–34, 236–39; also Farmer interview, June 14, 1978.

394 He was bitterly disappointed: Telegram from Emanuel Bloch, John F. Finerty, and Malcolm Sharp to Judge Irving R. Kaufman, June 14, 1953, Farmer papers. Also see Farmer's recollections in Edelman, "Religion, the Left and the Rosenberg Case," p. 233.

395 Farmer refuses to hazard an interpretation: Farmer interview, June 14, 1978.

27: THE SUPREME COURT

Page

397 landmark *Mooney v. Holohan* decision: In the years following Tom Mooney's 1917 conviction new evidence came to light to show that several key witnesses against him had committed perjury. Mooney's death sentence was commuted, but he remained in

prison until 1935, when John H. Finerty, then a Washington attorney, petitioned the U.S. Supreme Court for a writ of *habeas corpus* on the grounds that Mooney had been denied his right to due process under the Fourteenth Amendment. The court, in a landmark decision, agreed. Tom Mooney did not win his freedom immediately since he was directed to seek remedy from California state courts, but *Mooney v. Holohan* had established the important principle that the knowing use of perjured testimony by the state constituted a violation of the defendant's due-process rights.

397–98 No one was more impressed: For Frankfurter's youthful involvement with the Mooney and Sacco and Vanzetti cases, see Harlan Phillips, *Frankfurter Reminisces* (New York: Reynal, 1960), pp. 130–44, 202–17.

398 Frankfurter did not find: For an authoritative account of the Supreme Court's handling of the Rosenberg case and the personal views of the nine justices, Frankfurter in particular, see: Michael E. Parrish, "Cold War Justice: The Supreme Court and the Rosenbergs," *The American Historical Review*, vol. 82, no. 4 (Oct. 1977), p. 833.

A parallel account focusing on the ambivalent role played by William O. Douglas may be found in James F. Simon, *Independent Journey: The Life of William O. Douglas* (New York: Harper and Row, 1981), pp. 291–313.

398 On May 22, 1953, however: Simon, *Independent Journey*, pp. 291–313, and Parrish, "Cold War Justice," pp. 823–25.

399 According to Frankfurter's notes: Felix Frankfurter, Rosenberg Memorandum—Addendum, June 19, 1953, quoted in Parrish, "Cold War Justice," p. 833.

400 Kaufman's decision launched Farmer: Fyke Farmer's verbatim account, in Irwin Edelman, "Religion, the Left and the Rosenberg Case," New York, n.d. [c. 1970s], pp. 236–39. Also Interview with Fyke Farmer by Sol Stern, June 14, 1978.

401 Hugo Black, on the other hand: Black's and Frankfurter's comments are quoted in Parrish, "Cold War Justice," p. 834.

401 "Do what your conscience . . .": Quoted in ibid., p. 834.

402 His order was accompanied by an opinion: *Rosenberg v. United States*, 346 U.S. 273 (1953), 321.

402 The standoff resumed the next morning: Verbatim account of Fyke Farmer, in Edelman, "Religion, the Left and the Rosenberg Case," p. 238.

403 the victory celebration turned sour: In his book on the case, Louis Nizer depicts a grateful Bloch, tearfully exchanging toasts with

Fyke Farmer at a victory party (*The Implosion Conspiracy* [New York: Doubleday, 1973], pp. 496–97). According to Nizer, Bloch said: "Now I want to drink to Fyke Farmer and Dan Marshall . . . I love them." Earlier, Nizer writes that when Farmer laid out his argument to Bloch, "he embraced Marshall and Farmer and their idea enthusiastically" (ibid., p. 481). None of this happened. Indeed, Fyke Farmer points out (interview of June 14, 1978) that he was not even invited to the victory celebration.

403 Vinson . . . *had* made an attempt: Childs quoted in Simon, *Independent Journey*, p. 308.

403 FBI documents reveal that Vinson: A. H. Belmont to D. M. Ladd, June 17, 1953, Rosenberg file. Further confirmation for Brownell's role in this matter is found in a memorandum of a telephone conversation between Attorney General Brownell and Secretary of State John Foster Dulles on June 17, 1953. Dulles's secretary noted that "AG amazed at Douglas decision and says they are asking Vinson to call court back." John Foster Dulles papers. The authors would like to thank Professor Richard Challener for calling this material to our attention.

404 Having neither cash nor plane reservations: Except for several isolated disbursements of expense money like this, Farmer received no reimbursement for his services from the National Committee to Secure Justice in the Rosenberg Case. He paid for his work from his own funds and by using money raised by Irwin Edelman and by the L.A. branch of the Unitarian Church, or donated by other sympathetic individuals.

404 Manny Bloch, extremely agitated: Farmer interview, June 14, 1978.

405–06 Fyke Farmer and Daniel Marshall listened: Verbatim account of Fyke Farmer, in Edelman, "Religion, the Left and the Rosenberg Case," pp. 247–48, and Farmer interview, June 14, 1978. Transcripts of hearings before the Supreme Court were not made until 1968. The text of remarks made must therefore be taken from sources such as Farmer's memoir or from press reports of covered hearings.

406 At one point, Justice Black . . . interrupted: Ibid.

407 "Black filed a brief . . .": William O. Douglas, *The Court Years* (New York: Random House, 1980), pp. 79–80.

408 subject of a Security Index investigation: See Frank J. Donner, *The Age of Surveillance* (New York: Knopf, 1980), pp. 162–65. The Security Index, Donner explains, was a rechristened wartime program meant to prepare a list of potential traitors subject to

forced detention should a war break out with a Communist enemy. The secret FBI program included detention of listed individuals, suspension of the writ of *habeas corpus,* and summary arrests without court review. "Those listed on the Security Index," Donner writes, "were subject to more penetrative investigation than run-of-the-mill subversives, including such areas as their private lives, financial resources and day-to-day activities."

410 Legal scholars have . . . pointed out: See the discussion in Parrish, "Cold War Justice," pp. 838–39. Parrish writes:

> The decisive issue—as Black, Frankfurter, and Douglas pointed out—was that the Rosenbergs had been charged with a conspiracy to commit espionage, including atomic and nonatomic subjects, from 1944 to 1950. No question would have arisen had they been charged only with nonatomic espionage or with a conspiracy lasting from 1944 to 1946, before the Atomic Energy Act came into force. But the Rosenbergs' conspiracy, Frankfurter wrote, "is one falling in part within the terms of the Atomic Energy Act," and he doubted that they could be executed for that conspiracy under the Espionage Act, especially in view of the sentencing provisions adopted by Congress in the "newer and specific" law. "Congress does not have to say in so many words that hereafter a judge cannot without jury recommendation impose a sentence of death on a charge of conspiracy that falls within the Atomic Energy Act," Frankfurter concluded. "It is enough if in fact Congress has provided that hereafter such a death sentence is to depend on the will of the jury."

Parrish cites *Rosenberg v. United States,* 346 U.S. 273 (1953), 304–07 and 313.

410 among those impressed by the validity: Douglas, *The Court Years,* pp. 79–80.

411 historian Michael Parrish may well be correct: Parrish, "Cold War Justice," pp. 839–42.

411 As Felix Frankfurter wrote: Frankfurter's comment, written on his copy of *Rosenberg v. United States* (346 U.S. 273 [1953], 309), is quoted in ibid., p. 837.

411 "I despise a Judge . . .": Felix Frankfurter to Learned Hand, Jan. 25, 1958, Learned Hand Papers, Harvard Law School Library, Box 105; cited in Bruce Allen Murphy, *The Brandeis/Frankfurter Connection* (New York: Oxford University Press, 1982), p. 331.

412 Incensed at what he condemned privately: Murphy, *The Brandeis/Frankfurter Connection,* pp. 334–36. Murphy's citations from previously unpublished correspondence make it clear that Frankfurter acted not just from a preference for his own candidate for the post, Henry Friendly, but from a deep-seated dislike for Kaufman. As Murphy points out, Frankfurter's objection to Kaufman appears to have been based on the same grounds as his resistance to the promotion of Judge Harold Medina, who had presided over the Smith Act conviction of Eugene Dennis and other Communist leaders. Of Medina, Frankfurter wrote: "This business of giving Judges rewards for presiding over trials that fit in with the passionate prejudices of the day is not very edifying." And, writing three weeks after the Rosenbergs were sentenced, Frankfurter quipped in a letter to Learned Hand: "let Medina b'ware! or he'll be outshone by a Kaufman with a glitter rare!" See Frankfurter to Charles Burlingham, April 25, 1951, Felix Frankfurter Papers, Library of Congress, Box 36, and Frankfurter to Learned Hand, April 22, 1951, Learned Hand Papers, Harvard Law School Library, Box 105, cited in Murphy, *The Brandeis/ Frankfurter Connection,* p. 331.

28: THE EXECUTION

Page

413 Rhoda Laks ... first raised the point: *The New York Times,* June 20, 1953.

414 Brownell's unexpected announcement created chaos: Last-minute confusion caused by the change in timing of the execution is reflected in five memoranda from J. Edgar Hoover to Tolson, Ladd, Belmont, and Nichols, June 19, 1953. On preparation for the execution in general, see D. M. Ladd to Hoover, June 18, 1953, Rosenberg file.

Another last-minute snag that almost kept the executions from proceeding as scheduled was Denno's insistence that official notification of the Supreme Court's action be formally served on him at Sing Sing. It was finally delivered by an FBI courier who flew from Washington to LaGuardia Airport in New York, arriving at Ossining just minutes before the Rosenbergs were moved to the preexecution holding cells.

414 Just two days earlier he had expressed: John Wexley, *The Judgment of Julius and Ethel Rosenberg* (New York: Ballantine Books,

1977) p. 535. Wexley writes: "Mr. Bloch, confident that the Supreme Court in its hearing the next morning, would uphold the Douglas stay, decided that these facts would have more impact with his next move. . . . As a lawyer, he felt it wiser to hold back our trump card."

414–15 At about 6:00 P.M. Bloch phoned: Quoted in Virginia Gardner, *The Rosenberg Story* (New York: Masses and Mainstream, 1954), p. 124.

415 the letter obsequiously addressed the President: For the text of Ethel's letter, see *The Testament of Ethel and Julius Rosenberg* (New York: Cameron and Kahn, 1954), pp. 181–83. Ethel Rosenberg to President Dwight D. Eisenhower, June 16, 1953. This letter·was in addition to a joint clemency plea signed by both Julius and Ethel and dated the same day, which Bloch had turned over to Justice Department Pardon Attorney Daniel Lyons.

415 Fyke Farmer, too, had undertaken: Interview with Fyke Farmer by Sol Stern, June 14, 1978.

416 In the predawn hours: A. H. Belmont to D. M. Ladd, June 10, 1953; Belmont to Ladd, June 15, 1953; Ladd to J. Edgar Hoover, June 15, 1953.

416 an exchange of memos on what to do: Ibid.; quotes are from Ladd to Hoover, June 15, 1953. Warden Denno had strenuously objected to the possibility of giving the Rosenbergs a chance to talk after they entered the execution chamber, noting that this was a violation of the prison's strict policy against allowing the condemned to deliver any "last words."

416–17 One of the most shocking documents: W. A. Branigan to A. H. Belmont, June 17, 1953, Rosenberg file. The memo makes it perfectly clear that the questions included were to be "asked [only] of Julius Rosenberg in the event he desires to cooperate." One of the questions is: "(1) Identify for us by name the persons in your network from whom you received information on behalf of the Russians."

The questionnaire goes on to summarize statements made about Rosenberg's activity by Greenglass and others, and asks him to elaborate on them. Question 2 asks: "What type of information was furnished to you by your sub-agents and identify these sub-agents?" Question 3 asks if he photographed the materials received, where the work was done, and who assisted him. Another question asks to whom Rosenberg paid money for espionage. Another asks if anyone ever indicated to him a desire to work for the Russians. He was to be asked whether he ever requested technical assistance from the KGB "in obtaining and handling the information [he] obtained." Julius Rosenberg was to be asked if he knew Harry Gold, and to elaborate on his relations with Jacob Golos and Elizabeth Bentley. In all there were eleven main points to be covered. The question regarding Ethel was number 9.

417 A second FBI memorandum neatly summarized: D. M. Ladd to J. Edgar Hoover, June 10, 1953, Rosenberg file.

417 Julius had made out a last testament: Julius Rosenberg to Emanuel Bloch, June 18, 1953, *The Testament of Ethel and Julius Rosenberg*, pp. 185–87.

417–19 As he entered the brightly lit . . . chamber: *The New York Times*, June 20, 1953.

419 News of the execution did not: *The New York Times*, June 19 and 20, 1953; for eyewitness accounts by Americans of European protest, see Leslie Fiedler, "Afterthoughts on the Rosenbergs," in Fiedler, *An End to Innocence* (Boston: Beacon Press, 1955), pp. 35–38; and a letter from Claire H. Bishop to *Commonweal* magazine, Sept. 11, 1953. Irwin Edelman's confrontation in Pershing Square is described by Jonathan Root, *The Betrayers* (New York: Coward-McCann, 1963), pp. 279–80.

29: THE AFTERMATH

Page

420–21 The *Daily Worker*, which had so pointedly ignored: *Daily Worker*, June 23, 1953.

421 As late as 1979: Gus Hall, statement for the Central Committee of the Communist Party of the United States, "The Rosenbergs and the Loathsome Duo," *Daily World*, July 26, 1979. Hall's statement was in response to "The Hidden Rosenberg Case" by Sol Stern and Ronald Radosh, which appeared in *The New Republic*, June 23, 1979, pp. 13–25.

421–22 Even before the funeral: The information herein is based on Virginia Gardner, *The Rosenberg Story* (New York: Masses and Mainstream, 1954), and Robert and Michael Meeropol, *We Are Your Sons* (Boston: Houghton Mifflin, 1975).

422 A squad of agents: Handwritten report of Special Agent Bernard D. Warren, Jan. 30, 1954, Bloch file.

424 the McCarthy-Cohn investigation: D. M. Ladd to J. Edgar Hoover, Oct. 6, 1953; Ladd to Hoover, Nov. 4, 1953; W. A. Branigan to A. H. Belmont, Nov. 27, 1953; Rosenberg file.

425 elicited nothing but a garbled version: A. H. Belmont to L. V. Boardman, May 8, 1956, Greenglass file.

425 postscript to the Rosenberg case: Louise Bernikow, *Abel* (New York: Ballantine, 1982), pp. 168–74.

425–26 the FBI had found photographs: Ibid., p. 170. Bernikow writes that a link between the Cohens and the Rosenbergs "is questionable. No one has ever proved that the Cohens were involved in espionage with the Rosenbergs at all. They did mysteriously disappear from their New York apartment just after the Rosenbergs were arrested in June 1950 and it was suspicious timing."

Also see Harry Rositzke, *The KGB: The Eyes of Russia* (New York: Doubleday, 1981), pp. 55–56. Rositzke, who worked in Soviet counterintelligence for the CIA, notes that the guilt of the Cohen/Krogers is beyond doubt. They were caught with a

> short-wave radio for listening to Moscow on high frequency bands, a high speed transmitter powerful enough to reach Moscow, a microdot reader in a box of face powder, microfilm ... cipher pads ... call signs and schedules for broadcasts to Moscow, cameras and chemicals, seven passports, and thousands of pounds, dollars and travelers checks. Tried and convicted, the Krogers were traded by the Russians for a British spy in 1965.

The authors tried to gain access to the Cohen/Kroger FBI file for this study, but were turned down, on the grounds that the couple are apparently still alive, and that only they can request their own file. If there is material pertaining to the alleged Rosenberg-Cohen link, it is undoubtedly among the Rosenberg-case FBI files that still have not been released.

426 A front-page story: Lane's charges are discussed in Walter and Miriam Schneir, *Invitation to an Inquest* (Baltimore: Penguin, 1973), pp. 279–81.

427 Scheidt ... duly reported to Hoover: Special Agent in Charge, New York, to director, Sept. 25, 1950, Rosenberg file.

428 "Kaufman seems to have been...": Vern Countryman, "Out, Damned Spot: Judge Kaufman and the Rosenberg Case," *The New Republic*, Oct. 8, 1977, pp. 15–17.

The information on the Justice Department official's communicating with an FBI agent about Kaufman's intentions is also available from A. H. Belmont to D. M. Ladd, March 16, 1951, Rosenberg file. This and the other documents discussed relating to Kaufman have been reprinted in facsimile form by the National Committee to Re-Open the Rosenberg Case as "The Kaufman Papers," New York, n.d. [c. 1975].

The information on Cohn is also available from Ladd to J. Edgar Hoover, April 3, 1951, Rosenberg file; and from Countryman, "Out, Damned Spot," p. 15.

428–29 In February 1953 . . . he phoned the Bureau: A. H. Belmont to J. Edgar Hoover, Feb. 19, 1953, Rosenberg file.

429 And after Justice Douglas received: A. H. Belmont to D. M. Ladd, June 17, 1953, Rosenberg file.

429 Kaufman is described in an FBI memo: L. B. Nichols to Clyde Tolson, Sept. 15, 1957, Rosenberg file.

429 Referring to the *Grunewald* precedent, Marshall had asked: C. D. DeLoach to W. M. Felt Mohr, Dec. 21, 1962; and W. A. Branigan to W. C. Sullivan, Dec. 26, 1962; Rosenberg file.

430 ". . . I have never uttered a word . . .": Irving Kaufman to Herbert Brownell, Oct. 15, 1957, Rosenberg file

430 Kaufman called Hoover to discuss: Memo for Clyde Tolson and Nease from J. Edgar Hoover, Nov. 12, 1957, Rosenberg file.

430 a play sympathetic to the Rosenbergs: W. A. Branigan to W. C. Sullivan, May 2, 1969; also Irving Kaufman to J. Edgar Hoover, May 7, 1969, and Branigan to Sullivan, May 19, 1969; Rosenberg file.

430–31 Rifkind's name comes up again: W. A. Branigan to W. R. Wannall, March 12, 1974; and Heim to Franck, April 10, 1974; Rosenberg file.

431 When the FBI's files: Countryman, "Out, Damned Spot," pp. 15–17.

431 The investigation that ensued: Ronald Radosh and Sol Stern tried unsuccessfully to obtain a copy of the ABA subcommittee's report on the Rosenberg case. They briefly looked through a copy at James J. Kilsheimer's law office, but were denied access by the ABA itself, which stated that the report was for the information of its own committee members only, and that it is considered a closed internal document.

30: THE SCIENTIFIC EVIDENCE

Page

432 "one weapon . . .": Trial Transcript, p. 183.

432 "the government claims . . .": Ibid., pp. 1551–52.

432 "... Russia would perfect the bomb": Ibid., pp. 1614–15.

433 "A man of Greenglass's capacity...": Harold Urey to Eisenhower, June 12, 1953; quoted in John Wexley, *The Judgment of Julius and Ethel Rosenberg* (New York: Ballantine, 1977), p. 369.

433 "barren of any meaningful...": Notarized affidavit of Philip Morrison, Aug. 9, 1966.

433 An even more strongly worded affidavit: Notarized affidavit of Henry Linschitz, Aug. 17, 1966.

433–34 Linschitz's affidavit received the general endorsement: See Elinor Langer, "The Case of Morton Sobell: New Queries from the Defense," *Science*, Sept. 1966, pp. 1501–05.

434 However, Atomic Energy Commission documents: Much of the following discussion parallels the argument offered by Roger M. Anders, "The Rosenberg Case Revisited: The Greenglass Testimony and the Protection of Atomic Secrets," *The American Historical Review*, vol. 83, no. 2 (April 1978), pp. 388–400. The authors would like to think Mr. Anders, archivist in the Historian's Office, U.S. Department of Energy, for sending us the entire Atomic Energy Commission file pertaining to the Rosenberg case. Mr. Anders concludes his study with the observation that AEC records "tell us that the technological details about the atomic bomb in [Greenglass's] courtroom testimony were fairly accurate."

434–35 "The A bomb is made up of ...": Signed statement of David Greenglass, July 19, 1950, Greenglass file.

435 the AEC reported back to the Bureau: Francis Hammack, acting director of security, AEC, to J. Edgar Hoover, Aug. 2, 1950, AEC files.

435–36 On February 2, Beckerley guided Myles Lane: Memorandum of James G. Beckerley and Arnold Kramish to files, Feb. 2, 1951, included as Appendix A in C. Arthur Rolander and J. A. Waters's report of Feb. 7, 1951, file no. 403/1, AEC files.

437 It is quite true, then, as charged: Gerald E. Markowitz and Michael Meeropol, "The 'Crime of the Century' Revisited: David Greenglass's Scientific Evidence in the Rosenberg Case," *Science and Society*, vol. 44, no. 1 (spring 1980), pp. 22–23.

438 as pointed out in a 1966 letter: James G. Beckerley to *The New York Times*, Aug. 5, 1966, AEC files.

438 Emanuel Bloch told him long after: Interview with Philip Morrison by Ronald Radosh, June 19, 1978.

438 Bloch was "intimidated into believing...": Markowitz and Meeropol, "The 'Crime of the Century' Revisited," p. 9.

438 "Could a person of Greenglass' background . . .": Questionnaire sent by Emanuel Bloch to numerous scientists, Oct. 19, 1952, Gloria Agrin files.

438-39 The most strongly worded support: Affidavit of J. D. Bernal, Nov. 10, 1952, Gloria Agrin files.

439 Philip Morrison, for example, informed Bloch: Morrison to Bloch, n.d. [1952], Papers of the Committee to Secure Justice for Morton Sobell. In his letter, Morrison wrote that he had enclosed "two different statements" written "from the point of view of a scientist." He added that he was not sure the longer statement "would be of value for our purposes," since "the new elements it tends to inject had best be left to the prosecution!" Unfortunately, neither statement written by Morrison was to be found among the defense committee's papers.

439-40 Perhaps the most discouraging reply: Emanuel Bloch to Hans Bethe, Oct. 21, 1952; Gloria Agrin files; Bethe to Bloch, Oct. 30, 1952, FBI Bloch file. Bethe cleared his answers with the AEC Security Division. See J. A. Waters to W. W. Boyer, Nov. 4, 1951, AEC files. According to another AEC memo (Arthur Rolander to Waters, Oct. 29, 1952), Bethe was told that whether or not he replied to Bloch's inquiry was his own business, provided he did not disclose any classified data in his answer.

440 "These sketches may not have permitted . . .": Samuel K. Allison to Emanuel H. Bloch, Oct. 24, 1952, Gloria Agrin files.

440 "Mr. Finerty had understood . . .": Memorandum of Malcolm Sharp, 1958, papers of the Committee to Secure Justice for Morton Sobell.

440-41 When we asked Philip Morrison: Morrison interview, June 19, 1978.

441 a letter he had exchanged: Philip Morrison to Helen Sobell, June 18, 1958, papers of the Committee to Secure Justice for Morton Sobell. Morrison was advising Mrs. Sobell to "separate the question of the Rosenbergs' innocence from" her husband's case.

441-42 "The statement made by Judge Kaufman . . .": Linschitz affidavit, Aug. 17, 1966.

442 "their version of the Fuchs confession . . .": E. L. Ellman, director, Division of Policy Operations and Support, Office of Classification, U.S. Department of Energy, to Ronald Radosh, July 10, 1979.

442 a document summarizing the interrogation of Fuchs: Statement of Klaus Fuchs to Hugh H. Clegg and Robert J. Lamphere, May 26, 1950, witnessed by W. J. Skardon, security officer of the United Kingdom; Fuchs file. Also excerpts of Fuchs's statement in memo

of C. L. Marshall, deputy director of classification, to Tyler, Mc-
Cormack, Colby, and Williams, July 18, 1950, Fuchs file.

443 when one of us showed a copy: Interview with Philip Morrison by
Ronald Radosh Nov. 14, 1978.

444 "He said there was fissionable material . . .": Trial Transcript, p.
493.

445–46 Yet Hoover made every effort: J. Edgar Hoover to Special Agent
in Charge, San Francisco, March 24, 1952, Sarant file.

By taking such a stance, Hoover was being thoroughly dis-
honest. He had told some of his own agents, in a letter of March
24, 1952, that the Soviets had not gained atomic information
"solely through the operations of the Rosenberg espionage network in this country." Indeed he stressed that the information the
Russians got from Fuchs was in areas in which "their own scientists were in doubt or having particular difficulty." He acknowledged at the beginning of the letter that Soviet scientists
themselves were "working on atomic energy projects during this
period and had undoubtedly developed certain phases . . . independent of any data received" through espionage.

446 No one . . . was seriously worried: Much of the following discussion is based on the excellent book by Gregg Herken, *The Winning Weapon: The Atomic Bomb in the Cold War, 1945–1950*
(New York: Knopf, 1980). See in particular chapter 6, " ' Atom
Spies' and Politics," pp. 114–36, and chapter 5, "Pax Atomica:
The Myth of the Atomic Secret," pp. 97–113. Herken is wrong,
however, when he writes that "Fuchs's efforts were probably of
little or no use to the Russians," because Fuchs's work was "primarily concerned" with "uranium enrichment, not the chemistry
of plutonium" (p. 322). Herken based this assessment on an ambiguous FBI document pertaining to another matter, *not* on the
Clegg and Lamphere reports.

447 indication of the Soviets' position: J. A. Waters to K. F. Fields,
"The Influence of Klaus Fuchs on Stalin's Reaction at Potsdam—
A Report by the Division of Security," Jan. 6, 1956, AEC files.

447 when Truman wrote of this incident: Harry S. Truman, *Memoirs,
Vol. 1: Year of Decisions* (New York: Doubleday, 1955), p. 416.

449 "I think that the data . . .": Groves is quoted in U.S. Atomic Energy Commission, *In the Matter of J. Robert Oppenheimer,* vol. 4,
testimony of April 10, 1954, p. 570. This citation was originally
deleted from the published transcript of the AEC Commission
hearings, and was released only under court suit by the Meeropols' lawyer. Quoted in Markowitz and Meeropol, "The 'Crime of
the Century' Revisited," p. 1.

APPENDIX: HARRY GOLD AND THE HILTON HOTEL CARD CONSPIRACY

Page

456 the forged-hotel-card theory: John Wexley, *The Judgment of Julius and Ethel Rosenberg* (New York: Ballantine, 1977), pp. 328–33.

457 It was left to Miriam and Walter Schneir: Walter and Miriam Schneir, *Invitation to an Inquest* (Baltimore: Penguin, 1973), pp. 378–91.

458 the hotel clerk whose initials: Mrs. Hockinson was not yet married in 1945. The initials she used (a.k.) are, of course, those of her maiden name.

459 "Registration card of the Hilton Hotel . . .": Albuquerque teletype to Bureau, Philadelphia and New York, June 6, 1950, Gold file.

459 A second document: Special Agent in Charge, Albuquerque, to director, June 7, 1950, Gold file; report of the FBI Lab, June 7, 1950.

459–60 In an effort to figure out: Albuquerque report of June 21, 1950, by Special Agent Finis I. Parrish, for June 16, 1950, Gold file.

460 At any rate, the primary purpose: An "administrative page" in the FBI's Gold file states that the Philadelphia division advised on June 16, 1950, that Gold's old friend Thomas L. Black had signed a statement admitting he knew Gold had been to Albuquerque before the atomic bomb was exploded in New Mexico, because Gold had telephoned him in Texas from a hotel in Albuquerque, asking him to telegraph $50. But an effort at the El Paso Bureau to determine whether the local phone company had any record of Gold's call proved unsuccessful. Moreover, the FBI interview with Coby Briehn showed that the "folio records did not reflect a long distance telephone call." The Bureau also found that Western Union records were routinely destroyed after six months, hence they would have no available records to show whether anyone had received money by telegraphic order in 1945.

Gold, of course, could have made his long-distance and local calls from a pay telephone.

460 " . . . all registration cards received on June 3, 1945 . . .": SAC Albuquerque to director, June 7, 1950. The report also states that Brumit "has placed his initials in pencil on the reverse side of this card for purposes of future identification." This accounts for the observation by the Schneirs (*Invitation to an Inquest*, p. 382): "we had seen a copy of Gold's registration card and had observed on

the back the initials FLB." When they asked Brumit (now deceased) about this, he told them "he had no specific memory of ever having seen or initialed the card."

Brumit either had a faulty memory or was not being honest with the Schneirs. The FBI files indicate that he met with them, initialed the card, and even asked that after FBI examination, the card be returned to the hotel, although he promised the FBI that "the card will be available for us [the FBI] in any proceedings desired but that the hotel would prefer to maintain the card in their possession until that time." Indeed an attached memo headed, "MR. FLETCHER BRUMIT, Resident Manager, Hilton Hotel" indicates that upon issuance of a subpoena, Mr. Brumit "can produce and testify concerning: A registration card of the Hilton Hotel, Albuquerque, New Mexico, for 'HARRY GOLD, *6923* Kindred Street, Philadelphia 24, Pennsylvania,' reflecting GOLD represented the firm of 'Terry and Seibert' and disclosing that the room was occupied by the registrant from 12:36 P.M. to 8:00 A.M [*sic*] June 3, 1945."

460 The Bureau was not satisfied: Report from Albuquerque by SA Henry L. McConnell, June 10, 1950, Greenglass file.

461 In her report to the Schneirs: Schneir, *Invitation to an Inquest* (Baltimore: Penguin, 1973) pp. 386–87.

461 Interviewed during the research for this book: Interview with Elizabeth McCarthy by Sol Stern, July 26, 1979.

462 the Sobell appeal did provide an occasion: *Sobell v. United States,* 264 F. Supp. 579 (SDNY 1967), aff'd 378 F2d 674 (2d Cir. 1967), Cert. denied 389 U.S. 1051 (1969).

462 "The circumstances that . . .": Ibid.

462–63 Buried in the files: Hanna F. Sulner to William M. Kunstler, Jan. 26, 1966, Papers of the Committee to Secure Justice for Morton Sobell.

Another challenge to the conspiracy theory of the Schneirs may be found in the review essay by Herbert Packer, "The Strange Trial of the Rosenbergs," *The New York Review of Books,* Feb. 3, 1966, pp. 5–7. On the forgery theory, Packer writes:

> They do not offer an explanation of why the forgers were so clumsy as to have one date on the front and another on the back of the fake card . . . nor do they tell us whether their expert examiner [Mrs. McCarthy] was forewarned as to which card was suspected to be a forgery, an omission which . . . renders the conclusion suspect.

463 "As to the identity . . .": Sulner to Kunstler, Jan. 26, 1966.

464–65 Forcing Gold to recapitulate: Smilg's trial for perjury was held at the U.S. District Court in Dayton, Ohio, on June 13–18, 1955. See Schneir, *Invitation to an Inquest* (Baltimore: Penguin, 1973), pp. 363–64 for their quotation from the trial transcript and their analysis; also see John F. Taylor, "The Rosenbergs—Our National Agony," *The Churchman*, Aug.–Sept. 1979, pp. 8–9. Taylor writes that "the Rosenberg jury, unfortunately, heard no evidence of [Gold's] lying," but that defense counsel Hopkins, armed with the information from Wexley's book, found out how Gold had been exposed as a liar at the Brothman-Moskowitz trial. This assumes that the testimony of that trial was unknown to Bloch. But that trial occurred before the Rosenberg case; it produced major headlines. Taylor does not explain how Bloch could not have known about it. Herbert Packer, on the other hand, notes: "We will never know why [Bloch] . . . chose not to cross-examine Harry Gold at all, even though he *must have know* that only a few months earlier Gold's credibility had been quite seriously shaken in the Brothman-Moskowitz trial." Packer argues that one could develop a "startling" conspiracy theory based on trying to explain Bloch's failures. Indeed, this is precisely what Irwin Edelman did. Packer, "The Strange Trial of the Rosenbergs," pp. 5–7.

465 Harry Gold had first talked: See the text of Gold's pretrial meetings with his counsel, John D. M. Hamilton and Augustus S. Ballard. Transcription from tape, reel 3, recorded on June 1, 1950, by Hamilton and Ballard; papers of Ballard and Hamilton. Gold stressed to his counsel that it was "very difficult for me to judge whether Smilg was actually a recruit [of the Russians] or not." Later, in March or April 1941, his Soviet control told Gold that they "had decided to drop the matter of Smilg entirely," and Gold no longer had to try to make approaches to him.

465–66 Gold had first come to see him: Report of SA Wade H. Alley, Cincinnati Bureau, Aug. 9, 1950, reporting on interview with Benjamin Smilg, Gold file.

467 "All I had to do in 1950 . . .": Gold memo on the Schneirs' book, addressed to Augustus Ballard, Sept. 24, 1965, pp. 58–59; papers of Ballard and Hamilton.

468 "I clearly remember that on leaving . . .": Ibid., pp. 42–43.

469 Gold found the lobby crowded: Ibid., pp. 33–35.

469 "I was rather anxious . . .": Ibid., p. 48.

469–70 Unknown to Gold, who was under: FBI report by SA Henry L. McConnell, Feb. 5, 1951, Rosenberg file.

ACKNOWLEDGMENTS

This book could not have been written without the cooperation, aid, and support of Sol Stern, coauthor with Ronald Radosh of "The Hidden Rosenberg Case: How the FBI Framed Ethel to Break Julius" (*The New Republic*, June 23, 1979). Stern was always available to discuss theories of the case and to offer suggestions and suggest paths of inquiry. In addition, he conducted many of the interviews that were used for this book. Our debt to him is extensive.

From the beginning of this enterprise, Martin Peretz of *The New Republic* has been a friend whose own understanding of the turbulent 1950s served as the basis of many a think session. At a very early stage, Peretz agreed to take on a portion of this project as a *TNR* article.

At *The Nation*, editor-in-chief Victor Navasky has served a somewhat different function—that of skeptical observer and sharp critic, yet also as a friend who has proved to be of help in ways too numerous to itemize.

Scholars who have been more than willing to spend time offering their insights and judgments include Allen Weinstein, John Rosenberg, Athan Theoharis, Morris Dickstein, Marshall Berman, and Harold Josephson. Critics of our work who have been willing to sit down with us, if only to give us the benefit of their doubts and objections, include Mark Naison, Maurice Isserman, and Aaron Katz of the National Committee to Re-Open the Rosenberg Case.

The authors owe a great debt to James Weinstein, an old and valued friend, now the copublisher and editor-in-chief of *In These Times*, the independent socialist newspaper published in Chicago. It was Weinstein who, almost ten years ago, told Ronald Radosh his story—now related in this book—and who urged him to consider that the whole truth about the Rosenberg case had not been told.

Steve Delibert gave valuable advice on matters of the law pertaining to the Rosenberg case. He did some legal research as well, answering numerous questions and providing data on court cases and decisions.

Fyke Farmer, Gloria Agrin, Augustus Ballard, and the late O. John Rogge were willing to allow us to use and freely examine their papers pertaining to the case. We are much obliged. In particular, O. John Rogge gave unstintingly of his time, consenting to many interviews and showing great interest in our work. Were it not for his efforts, we would have been unable to make contact with, and eventually interview, David and Ruth Greenglass. We regret that he will not be able to read the fruits of our labor.

At the FBI Reading Room, Frank Underwood and Larry Fann proved tireless and indefatigable guides to the Rosenberg case files. Fann in particular answered queries, looked up specific files, and led us through computer printouts. Without the help he and his entire staff gave us, it would have proved the most formidable of tasks to work through these masses of material.

Gerald Barrett, our typist, worked from the most impossible of rewritten drafts to put this into shape. We thank him.

At Holt, Rinehart and Winston, our editor, Marian Wood, performed wonders. Working through various drafts, she subjected the manuscript to rigorous criticism, catching contradictions in our argument and challenging our assessments. Also at Holt, her assistant, Jacqueline Cantor, performed an invaluable series of tasks. Trent Duffy, the production editor, supervised the copy editing, worked with the editor, and showed a careful attention to detail at all stages of the complex process of turning a manuscript into a book. Finally, we offer many thanks to our superb copy editor, Kathie Gordon; she did a remarkable and careful job on a most complicated manuscript and helped save us from many an error.

RONALD RADOSH AND JOYCE MILTON
New York City, 1982

PERSONAL ACKNOWLEDGMENTS

At a critical moment in the writing of this book, when I was subject to severe personal attacks of a most vitriolic nature, valued support and encouragement was given by Irving Howe, David Horowitz, Peter Clecak, William Appleman Williams, and Louis Menashe. They helped me weather the storm.

My literary agent, Betty Anne Clarke, has been there from the start. She has firmly supported my efforts and offered valued advice. I owe her endless thanks.

Finally, this book could not have been accomplished without the love and support of my family. My wife, Allis Wolfe, discussed the ramifications of my work on this case at length and often. As a fellow historian, she always encouraged me to hold firm in a commitment to the truth, whatever opposition it produced. Together we talked over the issues and materials, and she helped to clarify many points. And she did all this while completing a doctoral dissertation and a book and having a baby at the same time. She knows just how much I owe her.

My children Laura and Daniel Radosh have been a source of joy and strength. Laura's success at college and Daniel's enthusiasm and spirit have always given me a lift. And our new son, Michael Aaron Radosh, provided me with immense happiness and diversion during his first year of life while the book was being completed.

RONALD RADOSH

I would like to extend special thanks to Joel Agee, for his role in bringing me together with my coauthor, Ronald Radosh; Steven Delibert for acting as my legal representative; John Harvey, for advice, moral support, and patience during a year of takeout meals and neglected social life; and, finally, my parents, Kent and Elsie Milton, and all those friends who bore up without complaint during endless discussions of the progress of the book.

JOYCE MILTON

INDEX